Minority Rights, Freedom of Expression and of the Media:
Dynamics and Dilemmas

SCHOOL OF HUMAN RIGHTS RESEARCH SERIES, Volume 44.

The titles published in this series are listed at the end of this volume.

Minority Rights, Freedom of Expression and of the Media: Dynamics and Dilemmas

Tarlach McGonagle

intersentia
Cambridge – Antwerp – Portland

Intersentia Ltd
Trinity House | Cambridge Business Park | Cowley Road
Cambridge | CB4 0WZ | United Kingdom
mail@intersentia.co.uk

Tarlach McGonagle
Minority Rights, Freedom of Expression and of the Media:
Dynamics and Dilemmas

Intersentia
Cambridge – Antwerp – Portland
www.intersentia.com | www.intersentia.co.uk

GPRC
Guaranteed
Peer Reviewed
Content

ISBN 978-94-000-0215-9
D/2011/7849/107
NUR 828

British Library Cataloguing in Publication Data. A catalogue record for this book is available from the British Library.

Acknowledgements

This book is a revised and updated version of my doctoral thesis, *Minority Rights and Freedom of Expression: A Dynamic Interface*, which I successfully defended at the University of Amsterdam on 7 October 2008. As such, many of these acknowledgements concern the original thesis and the process leading to its completion.

I would like, first of all, to thank Professor Egbert Dommering and Professor Nico van Eijk for their input into my thesis in their capacities as promoter and supervisor, respectively. Professor Geoff Gilbert accepted the invitation to come on board as co-promoter at the outset and I am extremely grateful for the keen interest he has taken in the thesis and book projects from start to finish, as well as for the very helpful comments and encouragement he has given me throughout.

Secondly, I would like to thank the Committee members, Dr. Yvonne Donders, Dr. Aernout Nieuwenhuis, Professor Patrick Thornberry and Professor Dirk Voorhoof, for their insightful remarks which have helped to enhance the quality of the thesis.

My colleagues at IViR have shown me support in many ways over the past years, for which I am also very grateful. The support has come from all quarters and in many shapes and forms – far too many to itemise here – so I hope no one will feel in any way slighted if I simply thank all my colleagues, past and present, collectively for their individual support.

Support, encouragement and – the lifeblood of any thesis – information and insights, have been forthcoming from many sources unconnected with my thesis or IViR. The late Professor Kevin Boyle, Dr. Yvonne Donders, Dr. Tom Moring and Donncha O'Connell deserve special mention for generously dispensing wisdom and humour and for always leading by example. David Goldberg, Dr. Susanne Nikoltchev, Dr. Wilfred Steenbruggen and Professor Dirk Voorhoof have also been invaluable sources of advice, encouragement and information.

I have been helped enormously by very obliging staff in a number of libraries, in particular, Rosanne van der Waal, Henja Korsten, William McKinney and Elvira Caneda Cabrera, but also more generally the staff in various libraries at the University of Amsterdam, in particular the Law Faculty and Communications Science libraries.

I am also indebted to a large number of colleagues for generously sharing their knowledge and passing on references and elusive documents: Wouter Gekiere, Karol Jakubowicz, Ilze Brands Kehris, Toby Mendel, Mario Oetheimer, Andrei Richter, Helena Sousa, the Secretariat of the Council of Europe's Media & Information Society Division, the Press Office of the European Court of Human Rights.

Since I started my thesis, many individuals and organisations have provided me with valuable fora in which to develop and present my ideas, orally and in writing, including: Vincent de Graaf, Michael Hertz, Sally Holt, Antti Korkeakivi, Heike Klempa, Eva Konecna, Danilo Leonardi, Stéphanie Marsal, Christian Möller, Peter Molnar, John Packer, Milica Pesic, Monroe Price, Mary Ruddy, Damian Tambini, Krzysztof Zyman and the organisations to which they are/were affiliated, as well as the European Audiovisual Observatory and KATTI, Faculty of Law, University of Helsinki. I would like to acknowledge my gratitude to all of them.

I am very grateful to Intersentia and Editorial Board of the School of Human Rights Research for their faith in this manuscript and their willingness to publish it. My thanks are due, in particular, to Tom Scheirs and Isabelle Van Dongen at Intersentia for their efficiency and for taking the stress out of the publication process. My thanks are equally due to Anouschka Boswijk for designing such a striking and symbolic image for the cover of this book.

I would like to thank my parents and Conall and Ríona and the rest of my family for being there for me throughout the thesis-period, as they always are. Thanks also to those friends who never let tedious thesis-talk spoil our relationships and maintained a healthy interest in the project right to the end: Wouter Gekiere, Clíona Hartigan, Karen Lim, Laurence O'Brien and Seána Ryan. I would like to thank my in-laws for their support, especially Ingeborg van der Waal who has perfected the art of the timely text message and Peter Boswijk who has perfected the art of the knowing nod.

I cannot even begin to express my gratitude to Rosanne, who has been with me every step of the way on the Ph.D. and book odysseys. She has believed in me even after that belief had deserted myself. The roles played by Ciara and Megan must also be fully acknowledged. Without ever realising it, they ensured that the sails were trimmed and that the port was reached.

Ar deireadh, ba mhaith liom an tráchtas seo a thíolacadh do mo thuismitheoirí, ceannródaithe beirt, a shiúil an bóthar romham, a chas timpeall agus a shiúil an bóthar liom.

Contents

List of selected abbreviations

AC	Advisory Committee [on the FCNM]
ACHPR	African Charter on Human and Peoples' Rights
AMARC	*Association Mondiale des Radiodiffuseurs Communautaires*/World Association of Community Radio Broadcasters
CAHMIN	[CoE] *ad hoc* Committee of Experts for the Protection of National Minorities
CDDH	[CoE] Steering Committee on Human Rights
CDMC	[CoE] Steering Committee on the Media and New Communication Services
CDMM	[CoE] Steering Committee on the Mass Media
CERD	[UN] Committee on the Elimination of Racial Discrimination
CESCR	[UN] Committee on Economic, Social and Cultural Rights
CM	[CoE] Committee of Ministers
CoE	Council of Europe
CRC	Convention on the Rights of the Child
DH-MIN	[CoE] Committee of Experts on Issues Relating to the Protection of National Minorities
EBU	European Broadcasting Union
ECHR	European Convention on Human Rights
ECJ	Court of Justice of the European Communities
ECRI	European Commission against Racism and Intolerance
ECRML	European Charter for Regional or Minority Languages
ECTT	European Convention on Transfrontier Television
EU	European Union
EUMC	European Monitoring Centre on Racism and Xenophobia
FCNM	Framework Convention for the Protection of National Minorities
FRA	[EU] Fundamental Rights Agency
HCNM	[OSCE] High Commissioner on National Minorities
HRC	[UN] Human Rights Committee
ICC	International Criminal Court
ICCPR	International Covenant on Civil and Political Rights
ICESCR	International Covenant on Economic, Social and Cultural Rights
ICERD	International Convention on the Elimination of All Forms of Racial Discrimination
ICT	Information and communication technologies
ICTR	International Criminal Tribunal for Rwanda
ICTY	International Criminal Tribunal for the Former Yugoslavia
IGO	Intergovernmental organisation
ILO	International Labour Organisation

NGO	Non-governmental organisation
NWICO	New World Information and Communication Order
OAS	Organization of American States
OHCHR	Office of the [UN] High Commissioner for Human Rights
OJEC	Official Journal of the European Communities
OSCE	Organization for Security and Co-operation in Europe
PACE	Parliamentary Assembly of the Council of Europe
PCIJ	Permanent Court of International Justice
PSB	Public service broadcasting
PSM	Public service media
RFOM	[OSCE] Representative on Freedom of the Media
S&CR	Self- and Co-regulation
SAPG	[UN] Special Adviser on the Prevention of Genocide
UDHR	Universal Declaration of Human Rights
UN	United Nations
UNGA	United Nations General Assembly
UNESCO	United Nations Educational, Scientific and Cultural Organization
WSIS	World Summit on the Information Society

Introduction

Chaque génération, sans doute, se croit vouée à refaire le monde.
La mienne sait pourtant qu'elle ne le refera pas.
Mais sa tâche est peut-être plus grande.
Elle consiste à empêcher que le monde se défasse.[1]

Many journeys are born out of necessity or curiosity or, as in the case of this book, both. The necessity was to explore the underdocumented interface between freedom of expression and the rights of persons belonging to minority groups, as well as the impact thereupon of both familiar and new communications technologies. The curiosity was to determine the potential for synergic interaction between these traditionally distinct areas of international human rights law and international media regulation.

The concern at the heart of Camus' stark analysis, cited epigraphically, could perhaps be put more temperately in another way: "[w]e must re-imagine liberty in every generation, especially since a certain number of people are always afraid of it".[2] Any conception of rights and freedoms – individually or *en bloc* – is doomed to inevitable relativity; to the inescapable contingencies of context, time and place. Every wave of history throws up new navigational perils and priorities. The past century alone has experienced several dramatic changes of *Zeitgeist*: the imperial/colonial excesses at the dawn of the century; the attrition and grinding destruction of the First World War; the short-lived League of Nations which sought to champion the rights of smaller nations; the unprecedented nihilistic horrors of the Second World War; the defiant emergence of a new creed of universal, indivisible human rights; the ideological divisiveness of the Cold War; the thrusts towards (partial) European economic integration; the dismantling of the Soviet Bloc; the internecine mutilation in the Balkans under the watchful eye of the international community; the fits and starts of successive (so-called) generations of human rights…

Most recently, the sea-change in political and broader societal attitudes to human rights and security issues, for which the atrocities of 11 September 2001 were the ultimate catalyst, has been much-documented.[3] The resultant polarisation of

1 Albert Camus, Acceptance speech for the 1957 Nobel Prize for Literature, City Hall, Stockholm, 10 December 1957.

2 Arthur Miller, quoted in Salman Rushdie, 'Arthur Miller at Eighty' in *Step across this line: collected non-fiction 1992–2002* (London, Vintage, 2002), pp. 51–53, at 53.

3 See generally, Conor A. Gearty, "Reflections on Civil Liberties in an Age of Counter-Terrorism", 41 *Osgoode Hall Law Journal* (2003), pp. 185–211; Michael Ignatieff, *The Lesser Evil: Political*

perspectives has, and will continue to have, implications for the three main focuses of this study: freedom of expression, the rights of minorities and the influence of traditional media and new communications technologies on the interplay between them.

It is important to emphasise the very real danger that hard-won standards of human rights could be/are being sapped of their vitality by invidious practices of politicisation. This trend involves applying the politics of fear and exploiting individual and societal yearning for security. Conor Gearty makes the point both imaginatively and effectively when he describes a "super-virus" that has infected the international human rights movement.[4] The virus works like a standard computer virus – it has entered the system and is wreaking havoc from within. Like many computer viruses, it is known by its acronym: GWOT. This virus "causes the human rights idea to manifest itself in gross human rights violations and egregious human rights abuses which it presents not as incompatible with but as necessitated by human rights".[5] GWOT, of course, stands for Global War on Terror: the emotive reason routinely given by many States authorities for their dismantling of much human rights architecture in recent times.

An increasing number of human rights bodies and mechanisms are proving alert to the grave dangers posed by the GWOT virus. The general thrust of their warnings is that the events of 11 September 2001 and the subsequent (re-)actions of States – individually and collectively – have occasioned a veritable sea-change in international relations and protection of human rights. The revival and re-legitimisation of historical forms of discrimination unleashed by GWOT are identified as particularly troubling.[6] As noted in a joint report by the UN Special Rapporteur on freedom of religion or belief and the UN Special Rapporteur on contemporary forms of racism, racial discrimination, xenophobia and related intolerance:

Ethics in an Age of Terror (Princeton, New Jersey, Princeton University Press, 2004); J.L. Holzgrefe & Robert O. Keohane, Eds., *Humanitarian intervention: ethical, legal and political dilemmas* (Cambridge, Cambridge University Press, 2003).

4 Conor Gearty, "Is the idea of human rights now doing more harm than good?", Lecture at the Centre for the Study of Human Rights, London School of Economics, London, 12 October 2004. For further insights into Gearty's reflections on related themes, see: Conor Gearty, *Can Human Rights Survive?* (Cambridge, Cambridge University Press, 2006).

5 *Ibid.*, at p. 7 of the transcript of the lecture.

6 Implementation of General Assembly Resolution 60/251 of 15 March 2006 entitled "Human Rights Council", Report of the Special Rapporteur on freedom of religion or belief, Asma Jahangir, and the Special Rapporteur on contemporary forms of racism, racial discrimination, xenophobia and related intolerance, Doudou Diène, further to Human Rights Council decision 1/107 on incitement to racial and religious hatred and the promotion of tolerance, 20 September 2006, A/HRC/2/3, para. 7. See also, in this connection, paras. 5–8.

> Discrimination is practised based on the two main national issues that Governments consider to be threatened by terrorism: security and identity. In this regard, with the proclaimed motivation of preserving national security, Governments have adopted policies gradually curtailing or disregarding civil and political rights or selecting those rights more fitting to that goal. In the same spirit, on the grounds of protection of national identity, cultural, social and economic rights, particularly those guaranteeing the rights of national minorities, immigrants and foreigners, are deliberately violated or marginalized. Rights related to culture and religion are particularly targeted. [...][7]

In a similar vein, the UN Special Rapporteur on the promotion and protection of human rights and fundamental freedoms while countering terrorism has noted that:

> [...] the very old trend of States resorting to the notion of "terrorism" to stigmatize political, ethnic, regional or other movements they simply do not like, is also very much a new trend. What is new is that, since September 2001, the international community seems to have become rather indifferent to the abuse of the notion of terrorism. The result is that calls for and support for counter-terrorism measures by the international community may in fact legitimize oppressive regimes and their actions even if they are hostile to human rights [...].[8]

These considerations of the post-2001 political *Zeitgeist* have considerable bearing on contemporary interpretations of the provisions of international human rights law that are central to freedom of expression and the struggle against racist discrimination.[9] Such considerations also generally serve to harden societal attitudes towards (especially unfamiliar) minorities and to colour relevant controversies, as will be demonstrated below.

Problématique and methodology

This is a study of the right to freedom of expression of persons belonging to minorities, as vouchsafed by international human rights law. Its geographical focus is Europe, which necessarily involves engagement, not only with relevant European standards and approaches, but also with those which apply globally, including in Europe. Various international and European treaties contain provisions on the right to freedom of expression and provisions on the rights of persons belonging to minorities. Treaty provisions on the right to freedom of expression of persons belonging to minorities are, however, fewer in number.

---

7 *Ibid.*

8 "Promotion and protection of human rights", Report of the Special Rapporteur on the promotion and protection of human rights and fundamental freedoms while countering terrorism, Martin Scheinin, 28 December 2005, E/CN.4/2006/98, para. 56(a).

9 For an NGO perspective, see: "Global 'war on terror' has become a global war on minorities", Minority Rights Group International Press Release, 8 September 2006.

The main objectives of this study are therefore to: (i) identify and group; (ii) contextualise and describe, and (iii) critically evaluate prevailing international and European legal standards concerning the dynamic interface between the right to freedom of expression and the rights of persons belonging to minorities. The critical evaluation will be concerned, above all, with the effectiveness of the right to freedom of expression of persons belonging to minorities in practice. The central research question pursued could therefore be formulated as follows: are the conceptualisation and calibration of relevant international and European legal standards sufficiently nuanced and robust to ensure that persons belonging to minorities are able to exercise their right to freedom of expression in an effective manner?

The international and European legal systems for the protection of human rights are made up of many disparate provisions which are binding on States to varying degrees. The macro picture is forged out of mulitple micros. The study's aim to explore the actual content and potential reach of international and European law necessarily entails an examination of *de lege lata* (the law as it is) and *de lege ferenda* (the law as it ought to be or may in the future be).[10]

The approach taken is primarily that of international and European human rights law, but it is impossible to cordon off those branches of law from other branches of international and European law. Where relevant, the constraining interpretive impact of other areas of international and European law has been taken into consideration.[11]

What is the particularity of the right to freedom of expression of persons belonging to minorities? The ultimate purpose of international human rights law is to ensure that human rights are rendered real, meaningful and effective for everyone. Principles of freedom of expression, as enshrined in international treaties, have to undergo a double translation exercise before they can truly be considered real, meaningful and effective for persons belonging to minorities. First, the (often) lapidary textual provisions articulating relevant principles need to be translated into a vital body of standards. In turn, this vital body of standards needs to be translated into a vital body of standards that concord with the specific needs and interests of persons belonging to minorities. The double translation exercise can be regarded as a normative process to operationalise the first principles; to turn them into

10 *Oxford Dictionary of Law* (New Edition) (Oxford, Oxford University Press, 1997).

11 EU media regulation is a good example of supra-national regulation which, although partly grounded in human rights, is largely shaped by regulation targeting other concerns such as the free movement of services within the EU, the consolidation of the Internal Market, the prevention of unfair competition, etc.

something workable. In terms of the Council of Europe, this normative process can be schematised as follows:[12]

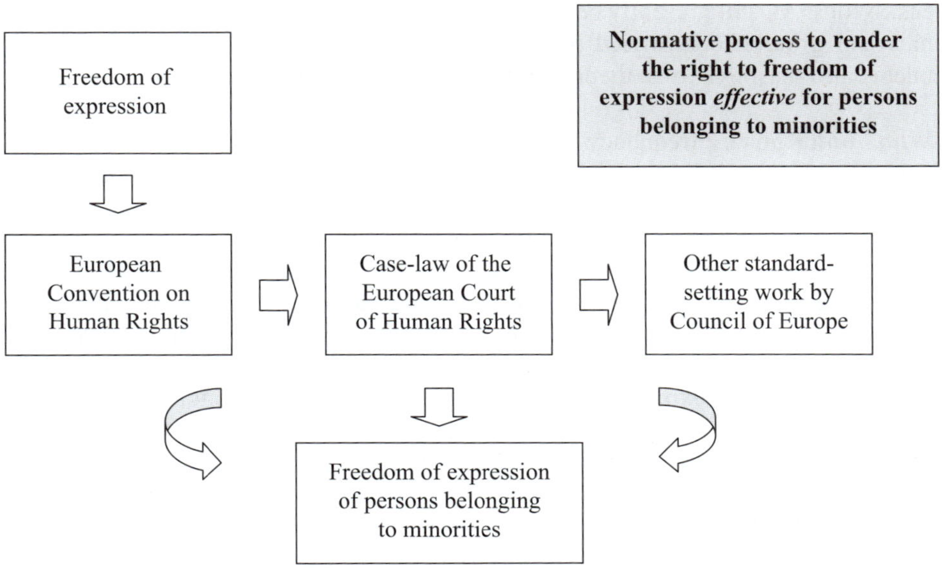

By way of further elucidation of this schematisation, it is important to mention that "other standard-setting work" includes relevant treaties (as well as their monitoring processes, which help to give expression to the "organic vitality"[13] of the treaties themselves) and political measures adopted by various organs of the Council of Europe. Whether relevant standard-setting takes place within treaty monitoring structures or whether, driven by other political impulses, it is pursued via processes that are extraneous to treaty law, it can certainly aid evaluations of the effectiveness of existing international law. For instance, standard-setting can facilitate the:

- elucidation of the content of treaty provisions when applied to concrete situations;
- provision of a level of detail that is generally lacking in treaty provisions;
- interpretation of treaty provisions in a way that is in tune with the times;
- identification of good or best practices;
- establishment of appropriate bench-marks.

12 A more complex schematisation would obviously apply to the normative process operationalising freedom of expression in the context of UN structures and standards, owing to the greater multiplicity of bodies, treaties and standard-setting texts implicated.

13 Italo Calvino, *Six Memos for the Next Millennium* (Cambridge, Massachusetts, Harvard University Press, 1988) (Trans. Patrick Creagh), p. 110.

Yet even bearing those extra considerations in mind, the schematisation remains incomplete. The entire process is also influenced (to varying degrees) by the application of academic theories and the negotiation of political priorities and sensitivities. As will presently become evident, this study is indebted to the valuable analytical groundwork carried out by other scholars and seeks to build on their endeavours. It aspires to be theoretically informed and politically aware.

"With unfortunate frequency", writes Frederick Schauer, "particular legal approaches to particular social concerns remain imprisoned in their particularism, ignoring the extent to which specific rules or principles may affect other rules and principles located some doctrinal distance away".[14] It would be ambitious, one would think, to seek to apply this remark to the right to freedom of expression, given its very firm anchorage at the heart of international human rights law, not to mention its polyvalent character and its importance in facilitating the realisation of numerous other human rights. However, the developing relationship between the right to freedom of expression and the rights of persons belonging to minority groups (i.e., rights which have much looser (and more recent) conceptual moorings) is perhaps the exception that proves the rule. The influence exerted by the traditional mass media and new communications technologies on this relationship cannot possibly be understated.

As a result of the evolution of international legal norms concerning freedom of expression, the mass media have come to benefit from a more robust right to freedom of expression than the ordinary individual. This can be explained by the crucial role of the media as a lynchpin of democracy. The ability of members of minority groups to enjoy unhindered and indeed sometimes even facilitated access to the media is crucial for the exercise of their right to freedom of expression. It is also inextricably linked to the practice of their religion or language, assertion of their cultural or linguistic identity and the safeguarding of their right to effective participation in public life.

The media's privileged legal standing and increased freedom are accompanied by the expectation-cum-obligation of heightened social responsibility. Thus, the danger that the media might be used as a mouthpiece for offensive or hateful expression must be vigilantly guarded against. This danger is compounded by the fact that disagreement tends to stymie attempts to fix the outer definitional demarcations of the right to freedom of expression (as opposed to the impregnable inner zone of inoffensive speech, the existence of which is undisputed). As members of minority groups are the most frequent victims of extremist, racist or so-called "hate speech", its examination is highly warranted. This invites an analysis of the most appropriate

---

14 Frederick Schauer, "Commercial Speech and the Architecture of the First Amendment", 56 *University of Cincinnati Law Review* (1988) pp. 1181–1203, at p. 1181.

balancing of the public's right to receive information and ideas of all kinds with the wishes of minorities not to be portrayed in a biased, stereotyped or prejudicial manner. Although issues are often treated with reasonable sensitivity by certain sections of the mainstream media, biased and unfair reporting and loaded agenda-setting nevertheless persist.

The protection of minority rights is one of the most burgeoning areas of international law and has yet to be fully consolidated, or indeed, explored. The very notion of minority rights is likely to undergo much development – in both conceptual and practical terms – in the near future. Only a small number of universally-applicable, generalist international treaties contain significant provisions on minority rights, most notably the International Covenant on Civil and Political Rights (ICCPR) and the Convention on the Rights of the Child (CRC).[15] Supplementing those treaties of a more generalist character, an increasing body of international instruments is now treating the issue in a specific manner (eg. the Council of Europe's Framework Convention for the Protection of National Minorities, the European Charter for Regional or Minority Languages, the United Nations General Assembly Declaration on the Rights of Persons Belonging to National or Ethnic, Religious or Linguistic Minorities, etc.). A consolidation and, indeed, acceleration of this trend can reasonably be expected.

As already hinted, freedom of expression is crucial to minorities; both as an individual right and as a collective or associative one. The facets of the right to freedom of expression that are of greatest concern to minorities are not necessarily those which preoccupy members of majority groups within any given society. For instance, linguistic and cultural issues are necessarily uppermost in the priorities of many minorities owing to the (often) precarious status of their languages and culture. In short, the enjoyment of freedom of expression is very often the guarantor of the whole panoply of rights (civil and political, economic, social, cultural, linguistic and others) to which members of minority groups lay claim – either individually or collectively.

While the proliferation of media outlets in contemporary society would suggest the existence of increased communicative opportunities for minorities, this implicit promise has not always materialised. Concerns for pluralism and diversity remain because the internationalisation and concentration of media ownership, as well as the commercialisation of content, have been very much in step with the aforementioned proliferation of media outlets. When viewed from such a perspective, it is clear that minority rights have yet to extend in a meaningful way to the structural regulation of the mass media. Trends of globalisation in the mass media, with particular emphasis on their implications for minority rights, identities

15 Article 27, ICCPR and Article 30, CRC.

and interests, demand careful scrutiny. Against the background of such trends, the importance of public service, regional/local and community, media is especially salient. This consideration will be pondered within a broader analysis of attempts to check the ongoing erosion of cultural and linguistic specificities.

The future development of international standards and jurisprudence concerning freedom of expression will not necessarily follow the same curves as in the past. Increased technological convergence in broadcasting and the first, occasionally tentative, steps of broadcasters and the traditional print media into the online world are likely to radically alter the familiar features of the mass media. The heightened levels of individualisation in the media and specialised, niche-interest broadcasting (for example) are engendering greater individualisation and fragmentation in society as a whole. It is inconceivable that the relationship between democracy and the media will remain untouched by the changing nature of the latter. It is therefore timely to examine how the technology-driven modifications of current media regulatory orders, structures and practices are likely to impact on minority rights, both directly and indirectly.

Overview of issues

I. Theoretical and normative approaches to minority rights

Chapter 1

The first Chapter of this book seeks to establish the conceptual parameters of "minority rights".[16] This entails an examination of past and projected evolutions of existing legal approaches to persons belonging to minorities and their rights, as well as an examination of the nature of relevant definitions and terminology and of alternatives proposed in other quarters. Among the notions explored here is the observation that minority rights – not least as shaped by current international legal and political standards – have individual and collective dimensions to them, thus rendering them clearly distinguishable from individual human rights *tout court.* A multi-layered argument is also advanced concerning the complementary relationship between the individual and collective dimensions.

There is a dearth of definitional provisions in the existing corpus of relevant international instruments and even where definitions do exist, they are not always coterminous with one another. In general, these attempts to define minorities tend

16 Although minority rights and the rights of indigenous peoples share certain similarities, they are not one and the same. The latter are subject to a specific regime of protection under international law, central pillars of which include the ILO Indigenous and Tribal Peoples Convention, 1989, and the UN Declaration on the Rights of Indigenous Peoples, 2007. It should be noted that an analysis of this regime of protection is beyond the scope of this book.

to pivot on the criterion of the national/ethnic, religious, linguistic and cultural distinctiveness of minority groups, or various permutations and combinations of the same. In any event, for definitional purposes, these attributes ought to be enduring and not merely transient and elective. Otherwise, it is often contended, the associative element that is key to group identity would be rendered ancillary or whimsical and the definitional sluice-gates would be thrown open. According to one of the most widely quoted definitions of a minority group, its members should, *inter alia*, "show, if only implicitly, a sense of solidarity, directed towards preserving their culture, traditions, religion or language".[17] A related – and fascinating – question concerns the extent to which these characteristics can be eclectically chosen by would-be beneficiaries of minority rights. How much scope is there for individual differentiation within any group and what are the absolute identity *sine qua nons* for membership?

Notions of numerical strength and degrees of dominance in society are frequently encountered in (attempted) definitions of minority groups. So, too, is the consideration of territorial concentration/geographical dispersity. As definitions are the bedrock of legal provisions, there is a need to create a more solid conceptual base for minority rights. The clarification of these kinds of notions can have crucial practical implications, such as for the distribution of States' allocative resources.

Chapter 2

Wrangling over definitional minutiae has not prevented the growth of substantive minority rights at the international level. This section will sift through existing international standards and jurisprudence with a view to enhancing the clarity of the panorama of minority rights at the present time. Considerable attention will be paid to the structures and processes giving shape to this area of international human rights law, as well as to the political context in which they are embedded.

Although minority rights are no longer, strictly speaking, *in statu nascendi* in international law, there is nevertheless a lengthy period of consolidation and growth ahead in this domain. This will assuredly entail a shift of focus from generalities to specifics; not least in respect of the specific issues under consideration here. Any new developments as regards international standards are likely to emanate from the relevant sections of the United Nations, the Council of Europe, the Office of the OSCE High Commissioner on National Minorities and the European Union, thus warranting an assessment of the *modi operandi* of each. The agendas of these hubs of norm-fixing activity have been scanned for indicators of future priorities, without, however, neglecting the importance of ideas and initiatives generated by regional and national bodies and NGOs.

---

17 Francesco Capotorti, *Study on the rights of persons belonging to ethnic, religious and linguistic minorities* (E/CN.4/Sub.2/384/Rev.1) (1979), p. 96, para. 568.

This chapter will conclude by examining whether some rights which are a fusion of individual and collective elements and generally considered to be "minority" rights proper could be extended to an even broader spectrum of potential beneficiaries (most notably so-called "new" minorities (i.e., immigrant populations), social minorities, etc.). The basis for such an enquiry is that these rights are often the inevitable outcrops of general democratic principles. More concretely, then: the realisation of the right to freedom of expression – as enjoyed by members of minority groups – depends on the existence of effective structural and other practical accommodations. Such facilitation of a particularised form of the right to freedom of expression need not, the argument runs, be contingent on the traditional definitional constrictions of minority rights. Insofar as a central rationale for following through on the derivative implications of the right to freedom of expression is to redress "historical inequities"[18] or contemporaneous social inequalities of particular groups, it could be argued that definitional attributes such as "national"/"ethnic", "cultural", "religious" or "linguistic" should not be considered exhaustive. When seeking to determine the enduring characteristics of potential beneficiary groups, some of the wider-embracing language of extant equality and non-discrimination provisions could usefully be borrowed instead. Such language typically includes references to sex, race, colour, national/social origin, etc.

II. Theoretical and normative approaches to freedom of expression and minority rights

Chapter 3

The third chapter opens with a brief distillation of the main theories of the right to freedom of opinion, expression and information (hereinafter 'freedom of expression'), with particular emphasis on their importance from the perspective of minorities. The analysis progresses from the more general rationales for freedom of expression to narrower, more specific justifications and purposes of the right.

With its empowering and facilitative qualities, freedom of expression allows for political, social, cultural, economic, legal and other forms of engagement by members of minority groups. Its importance as a cornerstone in the democratic edifice is magnified in the context of minority rights as full enjoyment of the right obviates – or at least diminishes – the risk of disenfranchisement of minority sections of any given society.

This focus leads logically to a careful consideration of the indispensable role played by freedom of expression in the assertion of minority rights: how the effective

18 *Bernard Ominayak and the Lubicon Lake Band v. Canada*, United Nations Human Rights Committee Communication No. 167/1984, adopted on 26 March 1990, para. 33.

enjoyment of freedom of expression can ensure the preservation and even promotion of minority cultures, languages, shared religious and political beliefs and other values. This section sifts through pertinent theories before analysing the protection provided for the potentially synergic coupling of freedom of expression and minority rights under international law.

It is also demonstrated that the media's right to freedom of expression is more vigorous than that of the ordinary individual, owing to the watchdog and corrective political roles played by the media in a democratic society. Such is the importance of these roles that some commentators refer to the media as "the Fourth Estate" – an additional pillar of State to complement the conventional tripartite division of State power (the so-called "separation of powers" doctrine holds that liberty is best safeguarded by the division of the legislative, executive and judicial functions of government between separate independent organs). Indeed, the media's role in safeguarding and enhancing democracy and equality constitute a *leitmotif* of this book.

It is important to note that the media cannot fulfil the democratic tasks ascribed to them unless they operate in a suitable "enabling environment". This notion is unpacked, demonstrating the importance of media regulation for safeguarding relevant expressive freedoms, but also the limitations of formal, legislative regulation for the achievement of the same.

References to "the media" deceptively suggest a unitary and unified entity. For analytical purposes, it is desirable to examine individual media separately: as they possess different characteristics, they are used for different purposes. Here, the notion of media functionality enters into play. The question of media functionality – the correspondence of media types and formats with the communicative needs and resultant media preferences of the public – is of acute importance for minorities as they are often only able to draw on a more restricted *relevant* range of media types and formats (due to linguistic or other obstacles). Media functionality is therefore also important to the extent that it provides minorities with a "context of choice"[19] in terms of cultural output.

When analysing the different categories of media (community, public service, commercial and transnational), the touchstone is the extent to which they: (i) carry out their informational and communicative missions in a manner that is sensitive to public interests; (ii) accommodate the needs, interests and perspectives of minorities in their various informational and communicative activities. As such, they are analysed along the axes of purpose, functionality and reach.

19 Will Kymlicka, *Multicultural Citizenship: A Liberal Theory of Minority Rights* (New York, Oxford University Press, 1995), eg. at pp. 82–84.

The transformative impact that the advent of new media and communications technologies has had and continues to have on paradigms of media operation and media regulation is then discussed. One of the net results of such technological developments is that the discursive and participatory capacities of the media have been significantly enhanced. On the other hand, the public sphere has become increasingly fragmented and individualised, thereby following changes in the nature of media technologies themselves. These developments have ambiguous consequences for minorities seeking both inter- and intra-group communication. The potential of co-regulatory structures for enhancing minority participation in the area of media policy and regulation is explored.

Chapter 4

The fourth chapter of this book posits that the right to freedom of expression and minority rights have not been coupled in an explicit and extensive way in international human rights treaties of generalist scope. It explains why various formal attempts to do so ultimately did not prevail. In that explanation, it draws on various rationales for the particular importance of freedom of expression for minorities, as detailed in Chapter 3. It points up the limitations of international treaty law generally, before examining the extent to which two thematically-specific regional European treaties have managed to offset the apparent neglect of generalist treaties at the international level. The treaties in question are the Council of Europe's Framework Convention for the Protection of National Minorities and its European Charter for Regional or Minority Languages. Operative articles of both treaties are introduced, with a view to facilitating a more probing analysis of specific focuses within those articles in subsequent chapters. A final focus is on the extent to which the interstices of international treaty law (general and specific) can filled by "soft law", a problematic and much-criticised term, but one which is not – as is shown – devoid of pratical usefulness for normative endeavours.

III. Regulation and restriction of expression to protect minority rights

Chapter 5

The fifth chapter begins with a critical examination of societal responses to the heterogeneous realities of its composition. It explores, in turn, notions of pluralism and tolerance, both in the sense of ideologies and of societal practices. Whereas pluralism is essentially value-neutral and descriptive, tolerance is value-laden and capable of holding any of several meanings (varying in affective intensity). Before embracing tolerance, however, its theoretical basis and outer limits must first be identified. Competing individual and societal interests are at stake here and their problematic interface is very fertile ground for analysis.

That exploration reveals an irresistible tendency of both notions to converge into pluralistic tolerance. That composite notion is then developed into comprehensive pluralistic tolerance: the idea that pluralistic tolerance should be comprehensive in its scope, both by its extension to everyone in society and by its application in all spheres of public life. The realisation of comprehensive pluralistic tolerance depends on a number of infrastructural prerequisistes at societal level. The operative public values of any society are best shaped in inclusive dialogical fora. The media are an important forum for such purposes to the extent that they constitute sites for the realisation of expressive opportunities and the mediation of narratives and ideologies. The potential of the media for fostering inter-group dialogue, understanding and tolerance is also dwelt upon.

Chapter 6

Chapters 6–11 examine the extent to which international human rights law provides for, or requires, the restriction and facilitation of expression affecting minorities. Chapter 6 deals *mainly* with negative State obligations concerning freedom of expression and minorities, whereas Chapters 9–11 deal *mainly* with positive State obligations concerning the same (pluralism and access respectively). This conceptual division follows the writings of Isaiah Berlin and others, but it uses the distinction between positive and negative State obligations as an organizing principle rather than as a distinction between two hermetic categories. In fact, positive and negative State obligations are positioned here on a continuum of State obligations. Moreover, additional conceptual refinements apply.

Chapter 6 provides a meticulous analysis of restrictions on the right to freedom of expression under international law. It does so from the perspective of restrictions that are most relevant to the rights and interests of minorities. It highlights individual inconsistencies which potentially and in practice tend to undermine the presumptive coherence of relevant provisions across treaties. Article 4(a), ICERD, seems to have a particularly frictional relationship with the right to freedom of expression, as enshrined in other international legal conventions. This friction should, however, be seen as less a conceptual challenge to the conceptualisation of human rights as interdependent and inter-related than a zealous normative approach to tackle a particular issue which suffers from crucial drafting deficiencies – conceptually and stylistically.

Chapter 7

The term "hate speech" is increasingly used to justify restrictions on freedom of expression. The term is neither included in nor defined in relevant international treaties. Although the approximate meaning of the term is reasonably clear, an authoritative legal definition at the international is required urgently. Law- and policy-makers and international adjudicative bodies rely on this term, without taking adequate account of how it has been explored and developed in critical race theory. Critical race theory is (to put it very summarily) an approach to racism where the victim and the victim's perspective are given pride of place.[20] It seeks to ensure that law and policy are adequately informed by circumstances and experiences of victims of racism. The ramifications of the term, "hate speech", are therefore potentially more expansive than is commonly realised. In itself, the broad meaning of the term is not problematic, but if it is to continue to be viably employed in any legal sense, it must be suitably defined. It may be that a more circumspect term or definitional approach would be better-suited to describing relevant permissible restrictions on freedom of expression, as recognised by international law.

A selection of current controversies – genocide-denial, "defamation" of religions and the protection of founders of religions (from severe criticism and insult) – are measured against international human rights standards. They are considered from the perspectives of freedom of expression, freedom of religion and freedom from discrimination. Each controversy involves a complex interplay of rights and concepts.

Chapter 8

Section III – Regulation and restriction of expression to protect minorities – rounds off with Chapter 8, which explores and critically analyses the potential of integrated approaches for effectively countering "hate speech". After laying the theoretical foundations for such an approach, it examines the Council of Europe's strategies for combating "hate speech" and racism as a case study. Those strategies reveal different emphases and they are not centrally coordinated in a formal way. Nevertheless, their approximate and at times serendipitous coherence is worthy of further contemplation. The approach taken under the Framework Convention for the Protection of National Minorities is particularly interesting: it focuses on the twin goals of facilitating and creating expressive opportunities for minorities and of promoting intercultural dialogue, understanding and tolerance. In doing so, it endorses the often sceptically-received argument that "more speech" or "counter-speech" can be an effective means of combating hate speech.[21] However, its

---

20 See generally: Mari J. Matsuda, Charles R. Lawrence III, Richard Delgado & Kimberlè Williams Crenshaw, Eds., *Words That Wound: Critical Race Theory, Assaultive Speech, and the First Amendment* (Boulder, etc., Westview Press, 1993); Richard Delgado & Jean Stefancic, Eds., *Critical Race Theory: the cutting edge* (2nd Edition) (Philadelphia, PA, Temple University Press, 2000); Richard Delgado & Jean Stefancic, *Understanding Words That Wound* (Boulder, CO, Westview Press, 2004).

21 See further: Katharine Gelber, *Speaking Back: The Free Speech Versus Hate Speech Debate* (Amsterdam/Philadelphia, John Benjamins Publishing Company, 2002).

endorsement of that argument rests on a re-conceptualisation of counter-speech as a pre-emptive – and not merely reactionary – force. Such thinking places considerable faith in the empowering and identity-sustaining properties of speech. It also implicitly recognises the importance of egalitarian public debate and dialogical interaction as prerequisites for pluralistic tolerance.

IV. Regulation and facilitation of expression to promote minority rights

Chapter 9

Section IV, with its focus on positive State obligations concerning freedom of expression and minority rights, draws extensively on a number of earlier chapters. It builds on the earlier theoretical discussion of State obligations and affirms that the main generic positive State obligations within this thematic interface involve upholding media- and information-related pluralism, cultural and linguistic diversity, and access to the media and other expressive opportunities.

Chapter 9 takes the general discussion of pluralism and tolerance in Chapter 5 to a new level of application: the starting point of Chapter 9 is that media- and information-related pluralism is a specific scion of the more generic notion of pluralism. The right to receive information is qualitatively affected by the existence of media pluralism and diversity. These two notions are unravelled and explained. Structural and substantive aspects of media-related pluralism are considered generally and also in terms of their specific relevance for qualitatively assessing states of media-related pluralism. Such an assessment necessarily focuses on State obligations and media responsibilities.

To what extent should the public's right to receive a diverse range of information and ideas (particularly from the media) be trammelled by the right of minorities – and of individual members of minority groups – not to be portrayed in a negative light? What are the limits of each of these rights? Considerations of individual and collective dignity are obviously highly relevant. So, too, is society's need for diversity of opinion; the starting-point for this very debate. As such, this chapter follows through on and advances the discussion of pluralistic tolerance in Chapter 5.

The chapter assesses the extent to which the various theories and concepts concerning media-related pluralism are actually taken up in international law instuments before assessing the extent to which those provisions are applied in practice.

Chapter 10

Chapter 10 provides an examination of international instruments promoting the goal of cultural and linguistic diversity. It begins with an overview of the main rationales for the promotion of cultural diversity as a policy goal and a public value. It grounds the concept, *inter alia*, in theories of pluralistic tolerance, as set out earlier in Chapter 5. The examination pays particular attention to the different roles played by the media towards the attainment of this objective, as well as the importance of this objective from the perspective of persons belonging to minorities. As such, it continues the analytical approach that disaggregates the media in terms of their functionality and objectives.

Chapter 11

Chapter 11 then shifts to the other generic component of positive State obligations: rights of access to the media and other expressive opportunities. As such, it draws on underlying theories of access introduced in Chapter 3 and examines the resonance they have achieved in international standards and their actual implementation in practice. This analysis connects in an important way with Chapter 5. This is because access rights are typically not only about freedom of expression, but also non-discrimination/equality and participation (in particular). The interaction with these additional rights strengthen the legal justification of access rights for minorities and the dynamism of relevant synergies is duly noted. As the object of access rights – the media – are undergoing fundamental technological changes, the nature of access rights is also changing. This introduces additional dynamism into rights-dimension of media access questions.

In practical terms, access can take a number of forms: to content (i.e., information and ideas), as well as the media, structures and processes which ensure the dissemination of content. A selection of the main mechanisms for access are enumerated and evaluated. They include the right of reply and public access channels. Chapter 3's emphasis on community, public service, commercial and transnational media is also relevant here.

Finally, the question of access – as guaranteed by minority-specific treaties – is addressed. This involves analysing a range of factors which affect the access of persons belonging to (national) minorities to the media. The primary vehicle for this analysis is the monitoring experience built up under the FCNM, but it also incorporates the monitoring experience accumulated under the ECRML, as well as relevant academic theories. The engagement of both treaties' monitoring bodies with real-life situations facilitates the task of evaluating whether provisions of international law guaranteeing the right to freedom of expression for persons belonging to minorities are adequate or effective in practice.

Summary & Conclusions

The conclusions to this study comprise a synopsis of the issues examined and the main points of evaluation.

Part I

Theoretical and normative approaches to minority rights

Chapter 1
General theories and definitional entrapment

World is crazier and more of it than we think,
Incorrigibly plural.[1]

Introduction

The primary function of this chapter is that of scene-setting. It introduces the main rationales for the recognition, protection and promotion of the rights of persons belonging to minorities in international law. It also explains the deep difficulties involved in defining the concept of a minority for the purposes of international law. It demonstrates how past and prevalent approaches to definitional questions tend to restrict the scope of minority rights in practice. Finally, it tentatively argues that a more expansive interpretation of minority rights could be assured by re-examining the key rationales for the protection of minority rights and moving beyond current definitional fixations.

1.1 Theoretical conundrums and definitional dilemmas

Truly homogenous societies are virtually non-existent in contemporary Europe; any pockets of homogeneity that have managed to survive at all tend to be small and scattered. Pluralism in modern society can therefore be taken as a given. It is also a *sine qua non* of democratic society (see further, *infra*).

The choice of epigraph to introduce this chapter serves to point up the tendency to view pluralism in negative terms, rather than celebrate its enriching properties. To regard pluralism as incorrigible is to liken it to an irreversible phenomenon, an irretrievable situation or an incurable ill. According to such a logic of negativity, unfamiliarity feeds distrust and suspicion, which in turn feed tension and animosity. It is a kind of logic that suggests a slippery slope, but it also testifies to ingrained societal wariness of deviations from dominant social or cultural norms.[2] Particularly

1 Louis MacNeice, 'Snow', in *Louis MacNeice Poems selected by Michael Longley* (London, Faber & Faber Ltd., 2001), p. 18.

2 In this connection, it is perhaps of anecdotal interest to note that in various languages, largely synonymous terms denote foreignness and strangeness. In French, *étranger* means foreign(er) and outside(r). In Dutch, *vreemdeling* means foreigner or literally, stranger. In the Irish language, *coimhthíoch* has a variety of meanings, including alien, foreign, unfamiliar, strange, outlandish… it is only rarely used in the more positive-sounding sense of "exotic". Indeed, an Irish proverb states that the outsider gets the blame for everything: *An mhaith is an t-olc i dtóin an choimhthígh*. This discussion is also ongoing in sociological circles. See, for example, William

during periods of heightened societal tension – such as the present and enduring post-9/11 climate, the otherness of minorities is projected as a threat: to human rights; to societal values; to political unity; to national security. The fear of clashes between co-habiting cultures looms large (we are told) and to honour rights of participation and autonomy would invite secession and further splintering of society (we are assured) – is it any wonder that such emotive issues tend to leave polities at sixes and sevens?

This logic is preoccupied with notions of otherness, and the essence of membership of a minority group is, by definition, all about otherness. One of the greatest preliminary challenges facing the international regime for minority rights protection is to counter this logic, and to counter it resoundingly. It is only by countering prevailing attitudes that an environment conducive to the assertion of the positive and inclusive goals of minority rights protection can be created.

While certain sections of the political and media communities would not think twice about lumping minorities and immigrants together into one and the same category (and then meting out the same disparaging treatment to both), the actual definitional picture is much more complex. There is a significant hiatus between prevailing sociological understandings of the term 'minority' and its generally accepted meaning in the context of international human rights law. The latter is considerably more restrictive than the former, which includes the ordinary, everyday sense of the term.[3] Some line-drawing and qualification are therefore necessary at the very outset.

No hard-and-fast definition of a minority group has yet achieved unanimous acceptance in international human rights law. Of the definitions that have enjoyed widest currency, there is a discernible tendency to stipulate certain objective characteristics pertaining to such groups (especially ethnicity or nationality, language and religion) which would qualify them as minorities. It is also widely accepted that these objective characteristics must co-exist with a subjective criterion, namely that members of the group should share a consciousness of their status as a group (on the basis of the aforementioned objective characteristics) and a desire to preserve/develop that cohesion. The application of such criteria when determining whether a group may have minority status obviously restricts how widely the net of recognition can be cast.

A looser, more open-ended approach to the definition of minorities in sociological circles means that a broader range of social groups could be considered to have

---

B. Gudykunst & Young Yun Kim, *Communicating with Strangers: An Approach to Intercultural Communication* (3rd Edition) (USA, McGraw-Hill Companies, Inc., 1997), esp. pp. 24–27.

3 See further: Manfred Nowak, *U.N. Covenant on Civil and Political Rights – CCPR Commentary* (2nd revised edition) (Kehl, N.P. Engel, 2005), p. 648.

minority status. When the distinctiveness of a group does not have to be aligned in terms of shared ethnic, national, linguistic or religious characteristics, there is no shortage of other shared characteristics that could be chosen to replace them. Sexual orientation, gender identity, age and (dis)ability instantly spring to mind.[4]

The range of characteristics deemed to be constitutive of identity for the purposes of international law will be examined in s. 1.2, while the important differences between social minorities and minorities as recognised under international human rights law will be explored in greater detail in s. 1.3.

Another crucial question meriting preliminary treatment is whether there is any need for specific minority rights, given the impressive panoply of individualistic human rights enshrined in international law in the aftermath of the Second World War and fortified ever since. In order to provide an adequate answer to this question, two considerations must be addressed: (i) the purpose of minority rights/protection;[5] (ii) the added value of minority rights.

Minority rights can, in theory, serve any number of purposes. As will be seen in Chapter 2, international law has tended to root minority rights provisions in objectives of existence/survival and non-discrimination/equality. The right to group or cultural identity is also frequently invoked. Central to the mandate of the OSCE High Commissioner on National Minorities is conflict prevention, another aim of minority rights protection.

Combinations of purposes are also possible, and indeed, all of the goals mentioned above have been braided together by some commentators. Athanasia Spiliopoulou Akermark, for instance,[6] focuses on peace and security (concepts which "entail not only the absence of war and conflict but also the absence of threat"[7]); human dignity (which she describes as "a right to self-preservation (existence), accompanied by a right to develop one's own personality according to an own plan of life (self-fulfilment)"[8]); cultural identity and diversity.

The essential reasons for seeking to protect the interests of minority groups can also be extrapolated from a pronouncement of the Permanent Court of International Justice:

---

4 See further: Iris Marion Young, *Justice and the Politics of Difference* (Princeton, Princeton University Press, 1990), p. 64.

5 Athanasia Spiliopoulou Akermark has postulated that there is a significant difference between minority rights and minority protection: the latter is preferred by her, on the grounds that it is more expansive, covering the recognition of rights and other methods of protecting minorities.

6 Athanasia Spiliopoulou Akermark, *Justifications of Minority Protection in International Law* (The Hague, Kluwer International Law, 1997), p. 68 *et seq.*

7 *Ibid.*, p. 71.

8 *Ibid.*, p. 78.

> [...] to secure for certain elements incorporated in a State, the population of which differs from them in race, language or religion, the possibility of living peaceably alongside that population and co-operating amicably with it, while at the same time preserving the characteristics which distinguish them from the majority, and satisfying the ensuing special needs.[9]

While the particulars and variables are open to change, depending on circumstances, the basic puzzle/conundrum remains the same: finding optimal ways to reconcile the State's legitimate interest in integration, on the one hand, with minorities' interests in "non-exclusion, non-assimilation and non-discrimination",[10] on the other. "Integration differs from assimilation in that while it develops and maintains a common domain where equal treatment and a common rule of law prevail, it also allows for pluralism" in areas such as culture, language and religion.[11] This is perhaps best qualified as equitable integration, based on the principles of parity of opportunity and parity of esteem for all sections of society.

It is important to frame the conundrum within political parameters such as these because secessionist claims and fears often distract from core minority rights. Misunderstandings of any (putative) secessionist consequences of minority rights and the true import of the right of peoples to self-determination often confound debates on minority rights: these topics (and recurrent misunderstandings of their meanings) will be treated in Chapter 2.

The added value offered by a regime of minority rights to broader human rights protection under international law will now be analysed, but only in conceptual terms. The added *substantive* value of specific minority rights will be scrutinised in Chapter 2. The very notion of minority rights was until recently considered a vexed one in international law circles. It is a close cousin of other equally vexed notions, in particular the so-called "three generations" of human rights (i.e., civil and political rights; social, economic and cultural rights, and so-called solidarity rights (eg. right to development, peace, environmental protection, etc.)[12]) and group rights as human rights.

---

9 *Minority Schools in Albania*, Permanent Court of International Justice, Advisory Opinion, 6 April 1935, Series A/B, No. 64, pp. 4–36, at 17.

10 Asbjorn Eide, "Cultural Rights and Minorities: Essay in Honour of Erica-Irene Daes", in Gudmundur Alfredsson & Maria Stavropoulou, Eds., *Justice Pending: Indigenous Peoples and Other Good Causes – Essays in Honour of Erica-Irene A. Daes* (The Hague, Marinus Nijhoff Publishers, 2002), pp. 83–97, at 96–97.

11 Commentary of the Working Group on Minorities to the United Nations Declaration on the Rights of Persons Belonging to National or Ethnic, Religious and Linguistic Minorities, Doc. No. E/CN.4/Sub.2/AC.5/2005.2, 4 April 2005, para. 22.

12 For a concise overview, see: Cees Flinterman, "Three Generations of Human Rights", in Jan Berting *et al.*, Eds., *Human Rights in a Pluralist World: Individuals and Collectivities* (USA, UNESCO/Roosevelt Study Center, 1990), pp. 75–81.

On one reading, human rights inhere in every individual by virtue of his/her humanity or morality.[13] As such, the argument runs, there can be something very contrived about trying to ascribe *human* rights to groups *qua* groups.[14] Such a thesis does not in any way deny the existence of group rights; it merely objects to their classification as human rights. The argument is not merely the academic rehearsal of dogmatic nicety. Given the moral and fundamental nature of human rights,[15] and their ability to "trump"[16] other (run-of-the-mill, legal) rights, it is (or at least can be) important to have a clear idea of whether rights are also human rights.

Further refinement can be added to the debate when one begins to examine various conceptions of group rights. If these are conceived of as collective rights (i.e., with all group members exercising certain rights jointly as opposed to severally), then a plausible case can be made for describing the group rights "as human rights or as closely akin to human rights".[17] On the other hand, if group rights are styled as corporate[18] rights (i.e., exercised by a corporate (possibly even representative) body on behalf of all members of the group), then they cannot legitimately be described as human rights *stricto sensu*. Peter Jones furnishes the additional argument that "they are also rights grounded in whatever gives those corporate entities their special moral status rather than rights grounded in the status of humanity or personhood".[19] This thesis has also been relied on by others.[20]

The foregoing has documented some theoretical tensions in the debate concerning the competing merits of individual and group rights for assuring minority rights in international law, and indeed concerning the legitimacy of group rights as human rights. Some commentators, however, have sought to play down the importance of theoretical discord, opting instead to formulate the *problématique* – as they see it – in the vocabulary of liberal democratic theory:

---

13 Jack Donnelly, "Human Rights, Individual Rights and Collective Rights" in *ibid.*, pp. 39–62, at 41.

14 *Ibid.*, p. 43.

15 Koo van der Wal, "Collective Human Rights: A Western View", in *ibid.*, pp. 83–98, at 88.

16 See generally: Ronald Dworkin, *Taking Rights Seriously* (Great Britain, Duckworth & Co. Ltd., 1977).

17 Peter Jones, "Human Rights, Group Rights, and Peoples' Rights", 21 *Human Rights Quarterly* (1999) pp. 81–107, at 88.

18 "Corporate" is used here in the non-commercial sense of the term.

19 *Ibid.*

20 For example, Jack Donnelly writes: "There is no necessary logical incompatibility between the idea of human rights and peoples' rights (or other group rights) – so long as we see peoples' rights as the rights of individuals acting as members of a collective group, and not rights of the group against the individual." – Jack Donnelly, "Human Rights, Individual Rights and Collective Rights", *op. cit.*, at 48.

> Focusing solely on whether the rights are exercised by individuals or groups misses what is really at issue in cases of ethnocultural conflict. The important question is whether the familiar system of common citizenship rights within liberal democracies – the standard set of civil, political and social rights which define citizenship in most democratic countries – is sufficient to accommodate the legitimate interests which people have in virtue of their ethnic identity. Are there legitimate interests which people have, emerging from their ethnocultural group membership, which are not adequately recognized or protected by the familiar set of liberal-democratic civil and political rights...[21]

From a purely purposive point of view, it becomes apparent by returning to Akermark's collation of justifications for the protection of minorities in international law, *supra*, that these tensions do not carry over into the practice of international law. Each of the three justifications mentioned have a different focus and necessitate different types of protection:

> 1. Such measures [i.e., "justifications"] may wish to ensure human dignity and the well-being of the individuals belonging to a minority. Rights which have as an underlying interest the good of human dignity, are individual human rights. This is *individual oriented minority protection.*
> 2. Such measures may wish to ensure the preservation of the minority group and the minority culture as such. Here the purpose of international law is to protect culture, cultural diversity and pluralism. In this case the method of protection may be that of collective processes, including collective rights; This purpose of minority protection is more *group or subject oriented.*
> 3. Finally, minority protection may aim at preventing inter-state and intra-state conflicts, at the preservation of peace and security, in which case the protection is mainly *state oriented.*[22]

Under the modern international human rights regime heralded by the adoption of the United Nations Charter, individuals are typically the beneficiaries, and therefore, the subjects of human rights. Consequently, some commentators would argue that the existing range of individual rights should suffice to cover all the rights to which minorities lay claim (with the possible exception of the right of peoples to self-determination), especially if these rights were to be enforced more effectively than is presently the case.[23] This would appear to be a thesis advanced by Sir Nigel Rodley, who favours the inclusion of such rights under existing legal safeguards for

---

21 Will Kymlicka & Ian Shapiro, "Introduction", in Ian Shapiro & Will Kymlicka, Eds., *Ethnicity and Group Rights* (New York, New York University Press, 1997), pp. 3–21, at 4.

22 Athanasia Spiliopoulou Akermark, *Justifications of Minority Protection in International Law*, *op. cit.*, pp. 83–84.

23 Jack Donnelly, "Human Rights, Individual Rights and Collective Rights", *op. cit.*, at 49.

non-discrimination and equality, suggesting that "the notion of minority rights [...] is and should be treated as a conceptual diversion".[24]

It is submitted here that there are two possible flaws in this line of argumentation. First, it appears to underappreciate the collective/group/communitarian/associative dimension to minority lifestyles and ensuing rights. This group element is an important qualitative difference between traditionally-recognised individual rights and the rights enjoyed by minorities. Indeed, all concepts of rights for minority groups are premised on the group dimension to relevant individual rights. The example of discrimination is illustrative of the importance of this group dimension as it "generally takes place because somebody belongs to a racial, political, social or linguistic community".[25] As a result, discrimination usually "presupposes the existence of a minority community and the victim's membership of that group".[26] Another pertinent example is freedom of association, which is rendered meaningless for members of minority groups if assembly for the purpose of promoting cultural issues is ruled beyond the purview of this freedom.

The importance and pervasiveness of cultural interests within concepts of minority rights tie in with the second criticism of Rodley's approach: it overestimates the potential of non-discrimination and equality provisions to guarantee all minority rights. To focus exclusively on non-discrimination and equality is to ignore the importance of cultural, educational, autonomy, identity (and other) rights for minorities. Gudmundur Alfredsson has argued that group rights are needed not only to ensure "equal enjoyment" of the aforementioned rights, but also "to otherwise approximate circumstances enjoyed by the majority, to allow individuals to draw on the strength of their groups, and to facilitate interaction of groups with the States in which they live and with international organizations".[27]

A shift of focus is therefore required in order to appreciate that one key specificity of minority rights is their dual nature: the collective dimension of a distinct spectrum of individual rights. While the need for a right may be individual (eg. the right to use one's mother tongue), the exercise of the right can conceivably be collective and therefore dependent on interaction with others (eg. the ability to *effectively* use one's mother tongue). This is what Gabor Kardos terms "the

24 Nigel S. Rodley, *Conceptual Problems in the Protection of Minorities: International Legal Developments*, 17 *Human Rights Quarterly* (1995), pp. 48–71, at 71.

25 Gabor Kardos, "Human Rights: A Matter of Individual or Collective Concern?", in Istvan Pogany, Ed., *Human Rights in Eastern Europe* (Aldershot, etc., Edward Elgar, 1995), pp. 169–183, at 172.

26 *Ibid.*

27 Gudmundur Alfredsson, "A Frame an Incomplete Painting: Comparison of the Framework Convention for the Protection of National Minorities with International Standards and Monitoring Procedures", 7 *International Journal on Minority and Group Rights* (2000), pp. 291–304, at 295.

interdependence of the individual and collective elements"[28] of minority rights. Further, Kardos has emphasised that the collective dimension of individual rights (i) "never removes the individual's right to have recourse to the courts in defence of the given right" and (ii) does not "divide the right into two parts, producing separate rights for the individual and for the collectivity".[29]

In light of the foregoing observations, it can be said that rights protected as minority rights are often a fusion, or symbiotic co-existence, of individual and collective rights. There is a steadily growing body of opinion that discounts the notion that there is a clear conceptual cleavage between individual and collective rights. It can therefore be concluded, as John Packer does, that no such dichotomy exists;[30] rather it is often a case of continuity and/or complementarity between them.

1.2 Historical and conventional approaches to minority rights

A precise and universally-acclaimed definition of a minority has eluded the drafters of international instruments to date. This state of affairs is the product of a combination of factors, most notably intractable conceptual differences and the adoption of intensely politicised and unyielding stand-points by State authorities/ representatives (see further Chapter 2).

Undoubtedly, agreement on and the adoption of a legal definition of a minority would greatly enhance legal certainty in this domain, but in the absence of such a definition (and no realistic prospects of achievement of the same), other techniques have been adopted in order to circumvent this potential obstacle to progress.

It has been asserted (in relation to the United Nations Declaration on the Rights of Persons belonging to National or Ethnic, Religious and Linguistic Minorities) that "a precise definition is not necessary, that the answer is known in 90 percent or more of the possible cases, and that governmental and intergovernmental practice, including the jurisprudence of judicial organs, will eventually bring clarity to any remaining problems".[31] The same confidence in an ability to identify minority groups underlies the now-famous quip by the first OSCE High Commissioner on

---

28 Gabor Kardos, "Human Rights: A Matter of Individual or Collective Concern?", *op.cit.*, at 173.

29 *Ibid.*, p. 174.

30 John Packer, "Problems in Defining Minorities", in Deirdre Fottrell and Bill Bowring, Eds., *Minority and Group Rights in the New Millennium* (The Netherlands, Kluwer Law International, 1999), pp. 223–273, at 241 *et seq.*

31 Gudmundur Alfredsson & Alfred de Zayas, "Minority Rights: Protection by the United Nations," 14 *Human Rights Law Journal* 1993, pp. 1–9, at 3.

National Minorities, Max van der Stoel, "I know a minority when I see one";[32] a remark which set the tone for his tenure of the position.

This prompts two observations. First, particularly in the early years of the Office's existence, the OSCE HCNM worked the current vagueness as regards definitions to great advantage in the discharge of his mandate. The flexibility of approach that the Office has enjoyed is a direct consequence of the definitional vacuum. It is submitted here that such flexibility is ideally suited to the particular mandate of the HCNM, *viz.* preventive diplomacy (see further, Chapter 2). Second, although greater definitional firmness could have helped to raise levels of certainty and predictability, it could also have resulted in a more rigid and therefore restrictive approach to minority issues. The correct definitional balance to be struck remains a significant challenge for international law.[33]

Meanwhile, the elusiveness of clear consensus among academics, activists and States explains why the definition designed for the application of Article 27, ICCPR, first proposed by Francesco Capotorti, then Special Rapporteur for the UN Sub-Commission on Prevention of Discrimination and Protection of Minorities, in 1979, is still very much *de rigueur* today. He defines a minority in the following terms:

> [A] group numerically inferior to the rest of the population of a State, in a non-dominant position, whose members – being nationals of the State – possess ethnic, religious or linguistic characteristics differing from those of the rest of the population and show, if only implicitly, a sense of solidarity, directed towards preserving their culture, traditions, religion or language.[34]

Notwithstanding the proven ability of this definition to perdure, it includes a number of features (some of which are potentially problematic) which require further elucidation:

- Numerical inferiority
- Non-dominance
- Nationality
- Range of distinctive, constitutive characteristics

32 (paraphrasing Potter Stewart J. (speaking of pornography), in *Jacobellis v. Ohio*, 378 US 184 (1964)). Cited in Walter A. Kemp, Ed., *Quiet Diplomacy in Action: The OSCE High Commissioner on National Minorities* (The Hague, etc., Kluwer Law International, 2001), pp. 29–30.

33 For further discussion of definitional and other relevant criteria, see: Stephen J. Roth, "Toward a Minority Convention: Its Need and Content", in Yoram Dinstein & Mala Tabory, Eds., *The Protection of Minorities and Human Rights* (Dordrecht, Martinus Nijhoff Publishers, 1992), pp. 83–116, and Richard Bilder, "Can Minorities Treaties Work?", in *ibid.*, pp. 59–82.

34 Francesco Capotorti, *Study on the rights of persons belonging to ethnic, religious and linguistic minorities* (E/CN.4/Sub.2/384/Rev.1) (1979), p. 96, para. 568.

- Sense of solidarity
- Combination of objective and subjective criteria for recognition

Each of these will be addressed in turn, after briefly dealing with a crucial preliminary consideration.

Despite its well-documented failings, the League of Nations can boast a jurisprudential legacy that is of certain (persuasive) value to the modern international human rights order. Some of the most fundamental principles concerning contemporary international protection for minorities can be traced to this period. Take, for instance, the seminal observation of the Advisory Opinion of the Permanent Court of International Justice (PCIJ) in the *Greco-Bulgarian "Communities"* case: "[t]he existence of communities[35] is a question of fact; it is not a question of law".[36] The importance of the principle articulated in the PCIJ's observation cannot be overstated.[37] In effect, it means that the existence of a minority group, and consequently, the international protection to which its members are entitled, are not contingent on the official recognition of such a group by State authorities. Rather the existence of a minority is determined by various criteria, which in practice tend to be both objective and subjective. The most frequently cited criteria crop up in the Capotorti definition and will now be examined.

1.2.1 Numerical inferiority

The requirement that the group be "numerically inferior to the rest of the population of a State" has given rise to what John Packer has dubbed the "problems of numbers".[38] Athanasia Spiliopoulou Akermark opines that it is necessary, in the interest of legal certainty, to determine the scope of the rights accorded to national minorities.[39] Geoff Gilbert strikes a similar chord when he writes that "one cannot accord rights to wholly nebulous concepts".[40] It is worth noting that the proposed

---

35 Author's footnote: the vogue term for 'minority' at the relevant time was 'community'.

36 PCIJ Advisory Opinion No. 17, July 31, 1930, Series B, No. 17, pp. 4 – 46, at 22. See also the corroborating statement at p. 27: "it is incorrect to regard the "community" as a legal fiction existing solely by the operation of the laws of the country".

37 Rosalyn Higgins has asserted that the UN Human Rights Committee regards the question of the existence of minorities (under Article 27, ICCPR) to be "an *objective and verifiable* fact" (emphasis added), thereby reinforcing the PCIJ formulation: Rosalyn Higgins, "Minority Rights: Discrepancies and Divergencies Between the International Covenant and the Council of Europe System" in Rick Lawson & Matthijs de Blois, Eds., *The Dynamics of the Protection of Human Rights in Europe: Essays in Honour of Henry G. Schermers* (Vol. III) (Dordrecht, Martinus Nijhoff Publishers, 1994), pp. 195–209, at 200.

38 John Packer, "Problems in Defining Minorities", *op. cit.*, at 260.

39 Athanasia Spiliopoulou Akermark, *Justifications of Minority Protection in International Law*, *op. cit.*, p. 87.

40 Geoff Gilbert, "The Council of Europe and Minority Rights", 18 *Human Rights Quarterly* 160 (1996), at 162.

wording for the article to deal with minorities considered at the first session of the Drafting Committee of the ICCPR included a reference to "a substantial number of persons of a race, language or religion other than those of the majority of the population…".[41]

The conceptual concretisation of the scope of minority rights is also crucial from an administrative point of view, in order to specify the extent of entitlements arising out of such rights. Gilbert, again, points out that: "while a minority must be numerically smaller than the majority population, it must also constitute a sufficient number for the State to recognise it as a distinct part of the society and to justify the State making an effort to protect and promote it. There must be a group, not simply a few individuals".[42] This observation is an important consideration in respect of the State's role in ensuring distributive justice throughout its jurisdiction. While it cannot be gainsaid that some sort of proportionality in this regard generally tends towards the achievement of substantive social equality (as opposed to equality which is purely formal), the needs and desires of a group cannot and should not be calculated merely in numerical or quantitative terms. It is widely held that cognizance should also be taken of the kind of "historical inequities" alluded to in the *Lubicon Lake Band* case,[43] for instance.[44]

1.2.2 Non-dominance

The allusion to "historical inequities" serves as a useful bridge between considerations of numerical strength and non-dominance, as in practice, both usually coincide. In addition, reference should also be made to what Patrick Thornberry has termed the "reverse minority" situation in South Africa that prevailed during the apartheid years.[45] That was a rare example of numerical

---

41 The proposal *E/CN.4/21*, annex A (Secretariat) art. 46 [27], as cited in Marc Bossuyt, *Guide to the "Travaux Préparatoires" of the International Covenant on Civil and Political Rights* (Dordrecht, etc., Martinus Nijhoff Publishers, 1987), p. 493.

42 Geoff Gilbert, "The Legal Protection Accorded to Minority Groups in Europe", XXIII *Netherlands Yearbook of International Law* 1992, pp. 67–104, at 72–73.

43 United Nations Human Rights Committee, Communication No. 167/1984, *Chief Bernard Ominayak and the Lubicon Lake Band v. Canada*, 10 May 1990, para. 33. Ted R. Gurr considers that discriminatory treatment directed at a minority grouping can be the result of widespread social practice and/or deliberate government policy, or "the residue of historical circumstances" – Ted R. Gurr, *Minorities at Risk: A Global View of Ethnopolitical Conflict* (Washington, United States Institute of Peace, 1993), p. 6. He has also referred to "the enduring heritage" of major historical processes in this connection, *ibid.*, p. 34.

44 It is interesting to note that some commentators prefer a *tabula rasa* approach to minorities and the discrimination that has defined their history.

45 Patrick Thornberry, *International Law and the Rights of Minorities* (Oxford, Clarendon Press, 1991), p. 9; a situation also alluded to by John Packer, "Problems in Defining Minorities", *op. cit.*, at 261.

inferiority not going hand in hand with a position of non-dominance, thus thwarting the applicability of standard definitions of a minority.

It is appropriate to stress the importance of the non-dominant feature of the Capotorti definition because a major current in the international protection of minority rights seeks to redress positions of societal non-dominance and to ensure effective participation and political empowerment. This feature is therefore inextricably bound up in considerations of non-discrimination and equality.

1.2.3 Nationality

The requirement that members of a minority group ought to also be nationals of a State has proved contentious, as it fails to provide for complicated exceptions (eg. the application of restrictive criteria for the acquisition of citizenship; foreign kinship; nomadic lifestyles; patterns of migration and immigration). While these particular circumstances may not always be compatible with accepted understandings of a minority under international human rights law, further reflection on the exclusionary potential of the nationality criterion would be welcome. The debate has often veered towards the desirability of the term "national minority" (which is included in many other legal texts – though without necessarily being defined). Attempts to determine the precise meaning of the term have proved particularly problematic. The various arguments that have animated the relevant debate are examined in detail in the context of the analysis of the Council of Europe's Framework Convention for the Protection of National Minorities in Chapter 2.2.3.

1.2.4 Range of distinctive, constitutive characteristics

It has been reasoned by one commentator, Ted R. Gurr, that: "[i]n essence, communal groups are psychological communities: groups whose core members share a distinctive and enduring collective identity based on cultural traits and lifeways that matter to them and to others with whom they interact".[46] He continues:

> People have many possible bases for communal identity: shared historical experiences or myths, religious beliefs, language, ethnicity, region of residence, and, in castelike systems, customary occupations. Communal groups – which also are referred to as ethnic groups, minorities and peoples – usually are distinguished by several reinforcing traits. The key to identifying communal groups is not the presence of a particular trait or combination of traits, but rather the shared perception that the defining traits, whatever they are, set the group apart.[47]

46 Ted R. Gurr, *Minorities at Risk: A Global View of Ethnopolitical Conflict*, *op. cit.*, p. 3.
47 *Ibid.*

In order to facilitate the task of identifying minorities that are entitled to specific protection under international law, there is a tendency to home in on certain characteristics that collectively give shape to group identity. These characteristics should distinguish group members from the rest of the population. This exercise has revealed a preference for markers such as ethnic, linguistic and religious criteria. The centrality of generic features such as ethnicity, language and religion to minority identity is explored extensively in Chapter 1.3. For the moment, it is sufficient to draw attention to the conviction that such characteristics are so deeply ingrained in minority identity, so immutable, that they provide permanent indicators of the distinctiveness of the group.

This kind of thinking prevailed for a long time, but more recently, it has been subjected to sustained challenges, most notably on the grounds that (group) identity cannot be regarded as a static, unchanging concept. Put simply, groups evolve and adapt and so do their identities. Another argument which has the wind in its sails at the moment is that group identity cannot be regarded as homogeneous. It is a composite concept, comprising an array of individual identities. Notwithstanding the important points of commonality among these individual identities, the collective identity must also reflect its inherent variegation and nuances. A third criticism of these constitutive characteristics is that they are too traditional and restrictive. In other words, they exclusively reflect traditional markers of identity and thereby fail to countenance the possibility that groups defined in terms of their sexual orientation (for example) might be considered as a minority under international law. The suitability of these constitutive characteristics for application in contemporary times is revisited in detail in s. 1.3, *infra*.

1.2.5 Sense of solidarity

Without wishing to invite any unnecessary semantic quibbling, the sense of solidarity referred to here can be read as being essentially a sense of cohesion. It refers to a consciousness among group members that they constitute a distinct group by virtue of sharing certain characteristics. Moreover, there must be a willingness to preserve the group. Marlies Galenkamp is highly critical of reliance (specifically by Will Kymlicka, but presumably also by others) on (as she puts it) "the wish to preserve one's own culture".[48] However, as a foil to her criticism, it could be argued (as has already been done *supra*) that culture is a defining element of minority identity, thus conferring extra legitimacy on its conception as a right to be honoured by States.

48 Marlies Galenkamp, "The Rationale of Minority Rights: Wishes Rather Than Needs?", in Juha Raikka, Ed., *Do We Need Minority Rights? Conceptual Issues* (The Hague, Martinus Nijhoff Publishers, 1996), pp. 41–57, at 47.

In addition to the symbolic importance of this sense of solidarity, there are very obvious practical considerations at play. In the absence of any internal feeling of cohesion within the group, any attempts to preserve the group as a group would have a presumably external or one-sided dynamic and would consequently be very contrived.

The Capotorti definition notes that the requisite sense of solidarity need not be express or formal. Rather, it can be implicit and even merely inferred from the behaviour of members of the minority group. The acceptance of implicit expressions of cohesive tendencies is to the advantage of groups that do not boast elaborate (or indeed any) internal organisational structures. Nevertheless, from a practical perspective, as has been posited by Michael Walzer, it remains a truism that "[t]he survival and flourishing of the groups depends largely upon the vitality of their centers".[49]

1.2.6 Combination of objective and subjective criteria for recognition

As already mentioned, State recognition is never a prerequisite for determining the existence of a minority. Indeed, the United Nations Human Rights Committee has stated as much in its General Comment 23: "[t]he existence of an ethnic, religious or linguistic minority in a given State party does not depend upon a decision by that State party but requires to be established by objective criteria".[50] If this were not the case, Patrick Thornberry has argued, "the protection afforded by Article 27 would be nullified by simple legislative inaction on the part of States".[51]

Flowing from the aforementioned requirement that there be some kind of *esprit de groupe* within the group, based on its shared distinctive characteristics, along with the desire to nurture such a sense of cohesion, the definitional criteria for minorities can be described as double-barrelled (i.e., objective and subjective):

> *Objectively*, the group at issue must constitute a non-dominant minority of the population (usually a relatively small percentage of the population, even if a substantial number of people), and its members must share distinctive characteristics such as race, religion or language. Some of those characteristics will be natural, immutable; others (subject to cultural constraints) may be open to change. *Subjectively*, (most) members of this group must hold or evidence a sense of belonging to the group, and evidence the desire to continue as a distinctive group.[52]

---

49 Michael Walzer, "Pluralism: A Political Perspective", in Will Kymlicka, Ed., *The Rights of Minority Cultures* (New York, Oxford University Press, 1995), pp. 139–154, at 152.

50 UN Human Rights Committee General Comment 23: The rights of minorities, CCPR/C/21/Rev.1/Add.5, 8 April 1994, para. 5.2.

51 Patrick Thornberry, *International Law and the Rights of Minorities*, *op. cit.*, p. 157.

52 Henry J. Steiner & Philip Alston, *International Human Rights in Context* (2nd Edition) (Oxford & New York, Oxford University Press, 2000), p. 988.

By way of conclusion to this section and in the interests of comprehensiveness, a couple of other significant definitions of a minority ought to be referenced. Among the earlier attempts at a legal distillation of a minority was the aforementioned Advisory Opinion of the PCIJ in the *Greco-Bulgarian "Communities"* case:

> By tradition, which plays so important a part in Eastern countries, the "community" is a group of persons living in a given country or locality, having a race, religion, language and traditions of their own and united by this identity of race, religion, language and traditions in a sentiment of solidarity, with a view to preserving their traditions, maintaining their form of worship, ensuring the instruction and upbringing of their children in accordance with the spirit and traditions of their race and rendering mutual assistance to each other.[53]

In 1985, Jules Deschênes submitted a new definition to the UN Sub-Commission on Prevention of Discrimination and Protection of Minorities for its consideration. The Deschênes proposal was essentially a refinement of the Capotorti definition, differing only slightly from its forerunner.[54] The main points of difference were that it would have excluded indigenous populations, non-citizens and majority groups in non-dominant positions. It reads:

> A group of citizens of a State, constituting a numerical minority in a non-dominant position in that State, endowed with ethnic, religious or linguistic characteristics which differs from those of the majority of the population, having a sense of solidarity with one another, motivated, if only implicitly, by a collective will to survive, and whose aim it is to achieve equality with the majority in fact and in law.[55]

This proposed definition failed to win "general approval" by the Sub-Commission, and the Sub-Commission itself stated as much when passing the study containing the proposed definition to the UN Commission on Human Rights.[56]

1.3 Troublesome taxonomies and the notion of fixed features

Traditionally, one of the greatest obstacles to the furtherance of minority rights protection has been the fear persistently held by States that according minority groups enhanced rights would – through the empowerment of their subjects – stimulate secession (or in the event of the minority group in question having links

53 PCIJ Advisory Opinion in the *Greco-Bulgarian "Communities"* case, *op. cit.*, p. 21.

54 For a meticulous comparison of the Capotorti and Deschênes definitions, see: Patrick Thornberry, *International Law and the Rights of Minorities*, *op. cit.*, p. 7.

55 UN document E/CN.4/Sub.2/1985/31.

56 Sub-Commission Resolution 1985/6, preambular para. 5. See further, Asbjorn Eide, "The Sub-Commission on Prevention of Discrimination and Protection of Minorities", in Philip Alston, Ed., *The United Nations and Human Rights: A Critical Appraisal* (Oxford, Clarendon Press, 1992), pp. 211–264, at 222.

with a so-called kin-state, irredentism). This fear is captured in the allusion to "the spiral 'cultural autonomy, administrative autonomy, secession'".[57] These fears have persisted in the face of the development of a corpus of international law[58] and a large volume of cogent academic legal writings that clearly distinguish between relevant aspects of minority rights and the right of peoples to self-determination. The refractory nature of these fears confirms their deep-rooted nature and the still all-too-frequent perception of minority rights as a bogeyman of international law and politics. Having at this stage examined relevant theories, it is timely to re-emphasise the importance of crafting a suitable definition of a minority group:

> It may be observed that international standard-setting has out-paced articulation of, and consensus on, basic concepts. In other words, the international community has established 'rights' and even procedures through which to pursue respect for these rights without fully or clearly delimiting either the subjects/beneficiaries of the rights or the specific content of the rights. This opens the door to possibly unfounded or 'unjust' invocations of the stipulated rights and raises the prospect of social conflicts concerning the legitimacy of claimants and the full content of their rights. The lack of clarity has also led to tremendous uncertainty, unfounded assumptions and fear on the part of several interested parties, especially governments who worry that according 'minority rights' may be a precursor to political disintegration threatening the territorial integrity of the State. It is, therefore, imperative to clarify the matter not only for theoretical cleanliness, but also for practical reasons of the general interest – to avoid conflicts (especially armed ones).[59]

The system of classification for different types of minorities (*viz.* in terms of specific characteristics, eg. ethnicity, language, religion, culture) routinely employed is broadbrush. While it may be useful for indicating more salient distinctions at the macro level, it fails to deliver on the necessary detail and precision at the micro level. This is largely a result of the blurring of definitional distinctions and the prevalence of intersectionality in practice. Identity is forged from a composition of numerous different characteristics and preferences, various permutations and combinations of which are possible. As Geoff Gilbert has argued:

> Classification, in the end, is irrelevant. Minorities often straddle these classes and need guarantees about linguistic rights, religious freedom, and the protection of their culture. To categorize them adds nothing to the fact that they are a minority and minority rights should attach in general. The adjectives go to the areas of protection

---

57 Heinrich Klebes, "The Council of Europe's Framework Convention for the Protection of National Minorities", 16 *Human Rights Law Journal* (No. 1–3, 1995) pp. 92–98, at 96.

58 For illustrative purposes, see paras. 2, 3.1 and 3.2 of General Comment No. 23 – The rights of minorities, and also by way of contrast, General Comment No. 12 – The right to self-determination of peoples.

59 (footnotes omitted) John Packer, "Problems in Defining Minorities", *op. cit.*, at 226.

and guarantees, rather than to the definition of those accorded that protection and those guarantees.[60]

This cluster of arguments has a number of corollaries. One preliminary remark is that categorisation should not be confused with definition. The purpose of categorisation is to identify the characteristics which distinguish categories – in their own right and in respect of adjacent categories; to enhance understanding of what each category entails. Definition, on the other hand, is the prior and more generic exercise of seeking to trace the full circumference of a notion, of all categories taken together.

In abstracto, the difference between definition and categorisation can appear very fine, but *in concreto*, in the particular example of minority rights, once one recognises that minority rights are at issue, the enquiry must turn to the particular type of minority rights that are involved. This is where categorisation comes into its own and its purpose is more clearly illustrated, not at the earlier definitional stage. As will be argued, *infra*, depending on the category of minority involved, the expectations and entitlements of the bearers of the rights, as well as the duties of the addressees of the rights, will be qualitatively different. Linguistic minorities do not necessarily share the same objectives and needs as religious minorities, for instance.

Another corollary also helps to scotch the argument that categorisation can play an effective definitional role in this context. It centres on the question of determining which characteristic(s) should be deemed the most salient and therefore the most appropriate for definitional purposes when more than one fundamental characteristic or set of characteristics distinguishes a minority from the remainder of the population. First, in individual cases, it can be very difficult to decide – for the purposes of categorisation – which set of characteristics should prevail, or how the necessary balancing exercise should be performed.

There may not even be unanimity among group members on the question of its distinctive characteristic(s). In the event of group consensus, however, there is no guarantee whatever that State authorities would agree with that consensual collective opinion.[61] Endless and ultimately futile debates on sensitive-*cum*-explosive divergences of opinion could result, such as: language/dialect, religion/(cultural) practice, freedom-fighter/terrorist. It is, as Gilbert correctly concludes, much more helpful to use categorisation as a tool to point towards the specific

60 Geoff Gilbert, "The Council of Europe and Minority Rights", *op. cit.*, at 169.

61 See further: Asbjorn Eide, *Possible ways and means of facilitating the peaceful and constructive solution of problems involving minorities*, Report submitted to the UN Commission on Human Rights – Sub-Commission on Prevention of Discrimination and Protection of Minorities, E/CN.4/Sub.2/1993/34/Add.4, 11 August 1993.

nature of "protection" and "guarantees" required in specific circumstances. Categorisation is thus a necessary component of a broader approach of "graduated differentiation" to minority rights protection advocated by Asbjorn Eide. An approach of "graduated differentiation"[62] should be able to respond to "different categories of groups which might be entitled to different sets of rights 'depending on objective criteria justifying reasonable distinctions'".[63]

The very idea of group identity comprising fixed, constitutive elements is itself flawed. It is not possible to reduce individual identity (let alone group identity) to any one of its many facets.[64] This is widely recognised in international human rights instruments. As stated in the Preamble to the UN Declaration on the Elimination of All Forms of Intolerance and of Discrimination Based on Religion or Belief: "[c]onsidering that religion or belief, for anyone who professes either, *is one of the fundamental elements in his conception of life* and that freedom of religion or belief should be fully respected and guaranteed".[65] Instances of such intersectionality are frequent: a religious minority can simultaneously be an ethnic or linguistic minority; with religious and cultural practices/rights being particularly seamless.[66]

Furthermore, the traditional range of perceived fixed features (ethnicity (or nationality), language and religion) is highly restricted. It fails to take account of other crucial dimensions to identity. In other words, the emphasis has tended to be placed on a certain number of innate or inherited characteristics, to the exclusion, or at least significant neglect of those that are voluntarily acquired. As stated in the Lund Recommendations on the Effective Participation of National Minorities in Public Life, "[i]ndividuals identify themselves in numerous ways in addition to their identity as members of a national minority".[67] The corresponding section of the Explanatory Report to the Lund Recommendations elaborates:

---

62 Asbjorn Eide, *Classification of minorities and differentiation in minority rights*, E/CN.4/Sub.2/AC.5/1996/WP.2, 6 March 1996, para. 4.

63 Citing *ibid.*, John Packer, "Problems in Defining Minorities", *op. cit.*, at 245.

64 Peter Leuprecht, "Minority Rights Revisited: New Glimpses of an Old Issue", in Philip Alston, Ed., *People's Rights* (Oxford, Oxford University Press, 2001), pp. 111–126, at 124.

65 (emphasis added) Fourth preambular paragraph, UN Declaration on the Elimination of All Forms of Intolerance and of Discrimination Based on Religion or Belief, proclaimed by UN General Assembly Resolution 36/55 of 25 November 1981.

66 See further, Yoram Dinstein, "Freedom of Religion and the Protection of Religious Minorities", in Yoram Dinstein and Mala Tabory, Eds., *The Protection of Minorities and Human Rights*, *op. cit.*, pp. 145–169, at 159; Clive Baldwin, "Do Vulnerable Groups within Ethnic, Religious or Linguistic Minorities Need Special Standards?", in Kristin Henrard, Ed., *Double Standards Pertaining to Minority Protection* (Leiden/Boston, Martinus Nijhoff Publishers, 2010), pp. 243–258.

67 Para. 4, Section I – General Principles, The Lund Recommendations on the Effective Participation of National Minorities in Public Life, OSCE HCNM, 1999.

> In open societies with increasing movements of persons and ideas, many individuals have multiple identities which are coinciding, coexisting or layered (in an hierarchical or non-hierarchical fashion), reflecting their various associations. Certainly, identities are not based solely on ethnicity, nor are they uniform within the same community; they may be held by different members in varying shades and degrees. Depending on the specific matters at issue, different identities may be more or less salient. As a consequence, the same person might identify herself or himself in different ways, depending upon the salience of the identification and arrangement for her or him.[68]

In the same vein, identity is anything but static or immutable; it is constructed, de-constructed and re-constructed constantly throughout the course of our lives; "[w]e constantly define and redefine our identity through contact, dialogue and exchange, and sometimes also through conflict with others".[69] There is a kind of Brownian motion of characteristics in each of us, and which particular characteristics are the most salient at any given time is determined – at least in part – by extraneous situational factors.

In sociological circles, the notion of the fluidity of individual and group identities has been developed rather extensively.[70] According to the theory of "liquid modernity" expounded by Zygmunt Bauman,[71] the "melting powers" of modernity[72] have caused previous "configurations, constellations, patterns of dependency and interaction" to be "recast and refashioned".[73] He continues:

> It is such patterns, codes and rules to which one could conform, which one could select as stable orientation points and by which one could subsequently let oneself be guided, that are nowadays in increasingly short supply. It does not mean that our contemporaries are guided solely by their own imagination and resolve and are free to construct their mode of life from scratch and at will, or that they are no longer dependent on society for the building materials and design blueprints. But it does mean that we are presently moving from the era of pre-allocated 'reference groups' into the epoch of 'universal comparison', in which the destination of individual self-constructing labours is endemically and incurably underdetermined, is not given in advance, and tends to undergo numerous and profound changes before such labours reach their only genuine end: that is, the end of the individual's life.[74]

---

68 Para. 4, Explanatory Note to the Lund Recommendations.

69 Peter Leuprecht, "Minority Rights Revisited: New Glimpses of an Old Issue", *op. cit.*, at 124.

70 See further: John Packer, "Problems in Defining Minorities", *op. cit.*, at 259–260.

71 See further: Zygmunt Bauman, *Liquid Modernity* (United Kingdom, Polity Press, 2000), pp. 7–8; 83–84.

72 For Bauman, the crucial attribute of modernity is "the changing relationship between space and time" – *ibid.*, p. 8.

73 *Ibid.*, p. 6.

74 *Ibid.*, p. 7.

This fluidity can even be identified in distinctive characteristics traditionally ascribed to minorities – grouped in somewhat generic terms as ethnicity/nationality, language, religion (and culture) – and traditionally also thought to be unchanging. It might, for instance, be expected that one's mother tongue would be one of the most stable and constant features of a person's life, but such an assumption is predicated on a somewhat restrictive definitional and analytical paradigm. Tove Skutnabb-Kangas and Sertac Bucak identify four different definitions of the "mother tongue" concept: origin (the language(s) one learned first); identification (internal and external); competence (the language(s) one knows best) and function (the language(s) one uses most).[75] From the perspective of linguistic human rights, they stress that "*mother tongue(s) is/are the language(s) one has learned first and identifies with*".[76] However, they submit that under any of these definitions, a person can have two or more mother tongues, and with the exception of the "origin" definition, all definitions allow for the possibility that a person's mother tongue might change – "even several times".[77] Needless to say, such switches would almost invariably constitute gradual, protracted responses to profound changes in one's personal circumstances or one's social environment. For present purposes, though, the essential point is that such changes are not *per se* precluded.

Similar argumentation can be developed as regards a person's religious affiliation. Changes of religion are a fact that has to be reckoned with, despite a marked reluctance within certain religions to recognise or accept religious conversion or apostasy. While the right to renounce one's religion, to adhere to an alternative religious faith, or to cease to profess any faith whatever are all encompassed by the right to freedom of thought, conscience and belief, as guaranteed by international law, such legal recognition has proved difficult to achieve on the international plane. Certain religious denominations consider apostasy to be a crime and vehemently dispute assertions that it is an integral element of the right to freedom of religion. Be that as it may, the European legal experience does entertain the possibility of changing one's religion. This mounts a further challenge to the assumption that minority groups are undifferentiated entities. They are not. They are composite entities that must necessarily admit freedom of individual choice. As such, generalist assumptions about shared or constitutive characteristics should be made with utmost caution.

At the group level, the subjective element of membership is also revealed to have a "fluid and changeable nature" as the "criteria by which ethnic groups choose to

---

75 Tove Skutnabb-Kangas & Sertac Bucak, "Killing a mother tongue – how the Kurds are deprived of linguistic human rights", in Tove Skutnabb-Kangas & Robert Phillipson (in collaboration with Mart Rannut), Eds., *Linguistic Human Rights: Overcoming Linguistic Discrimination* (Germany, Mouton de Gruyter, 1994), pp. 347–370, at 360.

76 (emphasis per original), *ibid.*, at 361.

77 *Ibid.*, at 361.

identify themselves, moreover, may vary not only from group to group, but also within one group over a period of time".[78] The apparent presumption of ossified group traits is challenged in societal terms by Jack Donnelly:

> Human nature is thus a social project as much as it is a given. Just as an individual's "nature" or character emerges out of a wide range of given possibilities through the interaction of natural endowment, individual action and social institutions, so the species (through the instrument of society) creates its essential nature out of itself.[79]

Individuals and groups can have several potential identities,[80] the strength of which are influenced by societal and situational factors. These identities can be real or strived after, thereby contributing to the concept of "imagined communities":[81] communities or nations that are imagined and created, or, to put a more negative spin on it, fabricated.[82] This concept is famously – and probably also customarily – applied by theorists to nations. However, Benedict Anderson, unravelling his own theories, has extrapolated that "all communities larger than primordial villages of face-to-face contact (and perhaps even these) are imagined".[83] This postulation is premised on the subjectivity of group cohesion, its tenuous and often ineffable nature, and its innate resistance to qualification and quantification. Finally, it should by no means be ruled out that the virtual dimension to group identity will gain in importance in the future, given the increasing role being played in contemporary society by communications technologies that rely on and promote interaction in virtual, online fora (see further, Chapter 3.3).

Marlies Galenkamp, while recognising that "people's preferences are ever shifting and endogenous to political processes rather than fixed and exogenous",[84] has nevertheless cautioned against any inclination to elevate mere desires to the level of rights. Her word of warning – on the grounds that it would be theoretically inconsistent to do so – merits attention.[85] Not every desire warrants protection by

---

78 Thomas D. Musgrave, *Self-Determination and National Minorities* (Oxford, Oxford University Press, 2000), p. 164.

79 Jack Donnelly, "Human Rights, Individual Rights and Collective Rights", *op. cit.*, p. 42.

80 Crispin Jones, "Educational Rights and the Definition of Minorities", in Deirdre Fottrell & Bill Bowring, Eds., *Minority and Group Rights in the New Millennium*, *op. cit.*, pp. 205–222, at 211.

81 Benedict Anderson, *Imagined Communities: Reflections on the Origin and Spread of Nationalism* (Revised Edition) (London, Verso Books, 1991).

82 *Ibid.*, p. 6.

83 *Ibid.*, p. 6.

84 Marlies Galenkamp, "The Rationale of Minority Rights: Wishes Rather Than Needs?", *op. cit.*, at 48.

85 An argument grounded in political pragmatism could also be advanced in this connection, *viz.* that minority groups themselves ought to be mindful of the tactical risks involved in overstating their demands. Obviously, there is a greater chance that reasonable or realistic demands would be granted by (mildly) sympathetic authorities. Minorities are counselled in the Explanatory Note to The Hague Recommendations Regarding the Education Rights of National Minorities,

the law, much less human rights law. It is worth recalling the propelling rationales of human – and minority – rights protection: peace and security; human dignity (premised on the right to existence and the right to non-discrimination and equality); cultural identity and diversity. Mere whims should not be mistakenly dressed up as interests or desires that exert a crucial influence on the formation of one's identity. Minority rights protection should not be stretched beyond its elastic limit to include interests of insufficient weight and substance. This is an important consideration when it comes to legitimising special access for minority groups to limited media resources and airtime, as discussed at length in Chapter 11.

Yet this last assertion does not fully lay the matter to rest. How should distinctions be drawn between features or interests that contribute to the formation of identity? Who should be vested with the responsibility for such an important evaluation exercise – and which criteria should apply? Or should the determination of identity-forming characteristics be a purely subjective exercise, left entirely to groups themselves? What implications would such a solution have for minorities within minority groups and for questions of adequate representation and agency in minority groups which lack organisational structures?

Once one dispenses with the "fixed features" approach, it becomes very difficult to replace it with an alternative set of criteria for identifying minorities. To stick with identity-formation as the central consideration (in light of earlier comments on the fluidity of identity), determining the appropriate threshold for relevance remains problematic. One of the classical arguments for seeking to limit the criteria for recognising minorities is that doing so helps to avoid an overabundance of claims for special status and enjoyment of accruing rights. To abandon the identity criterion could result in a move towards more open-ended associational rights and lose the specific minority dimension. If the middle-ground were to be taken, the identity criterion would have to be applied in conjunction with other criteria, but there would nevertheless still have to be some cut-off point between features and points of cohesion that are serious-minded and those that are frivolous. This would have to be determined in a non-discriminatory manner.

Conclusions

Under international human rights law, the concept of minority is at far remove from its straightforward signification in everyday language. The concept rests on a complex of quantitative, qualitative and political criteria. There is no authoritative,

OSCE HCNM, 1996, to: "give due consideration to such legitimate factors as their own numerical strength, their demographic density in any given region (or regions), as well as their capacity to contribute to the durability of these services and facilities over time" (section entitled "General Introduction").

legally-binding definition of minority in international law, but various definitional indicia can be gleaned from a number of non-binding sources, most notably the Capotorti report, and these are widely regarded as setting the conceptual parameters for relevant discussions.

According to those definitional elements, it is necessary but not sufficient for a group to be in a position of numerical inferiority *vis-à-vis* the rest of the population in order for it to be considered a minority. It must also be in a position of non-dominance. These definitional requirements are uncontentious, unlike the further requirement that members of the group must be nationals of the State in question. That requirement is highly politicised and it is at odds with the transversal obligation on States to ensure the effective exercise of human rights for everyone without discrimination. Insistence on a nationality criterion holds considerable exclusionary potential and is open to abuse by States which are reluctant to guarantee the full panoply of human rights for immigrants or so-called "new" minorities. This criterion is sometimes packaged as a group's traditional or historical presence in the State, which again is open to abuse by States authorities in the absence of clear criteria for determining when such a presence can be considered "traditional" or "historical" or "long-standing". The recognition of minorities and their rights should not be contingent on such criteria, although it is conceivable that they could legitimately influence the nature and extent of State obligations that are correlative to minority rights. However, they should not be used as definitional criteria for the recognition of minorities as such.

As already mentioned, some of the definitional criteria are qualitative in nature: minority groups must display a range of constitutive characteristics that distinguish them from majority sections of the population. In practice, these characteristics are primarily ethnic, religious or linguistic. A definitional focus on constitutive group characteristics can be explained by some of the main underlying rationales for recognising the specificity of minority rights over and above human rights *simplicter*. According to those rationales, minority rights go beyond mere guarantees of non-discrimination and equality (indeed, for those rights to be secured for persons belonging to minorities, additional (temporary) restitutive measures are often required by States) to embrace concerns for the preservation of specific, fundamental features of the collective identities of minorities. References to "fundamental" features should not be confused with "fixed" features: the fact that features are fundamental does not preclude their natural evolution or concerted development. Rather, the term points to their deep-seated character.

The focus on those particular characteristics is further explained by another definitional criterion, i.e., a sense of cohesiveness or associative purpose that is shared by group members and that is directed at the preservation of their constitutive characteristics. It could therefore be argued that other constitutive characteristics excluded from the present selection are not powerful enough in terms of their ability to sustain a distinct group identity to merit inclusion. The chosen characteristics must be seen as having unifying propensities, but without having homogenising effects. The sense of cohesiveness does not have to be explicit – it can also be implicit. This brings welcome flexibility to the definitional exercise as it cannot be assumed that groups are composed of formal, representative structures that would be mandated to issue explicit statements of cohesive purpose.

The definition outlined above manages to strike a complicated and precarious balance between a number of criteria that are difficult to reconcile. The combination of subjective and objective elements for definitional purposes represents an important safeguard against arbitrariness on the side of minorities and on the side of State authorities. Its insistence on objective criteria seeks to prevent subjective attempts by groups to inflate the concept of minority rights beyond its intended scope, while also seeking to prevent States from subjectively denying minority rights. Conversely, the inclusion of a subjective sense of belonging is designed to ensure that the existence of a minority group *qua* group is grounded in realism and not based on the subjective perceptions of some group members or of non-group members.

This Chapter – and book – recognises the conceptual complexities and overt politicisation involved in the definitional challenge. In most of its important respects, it follows the approximate definition outlined above, with the notable exception of the nationality criterion. The existence of minorities is a question of fact, not of law or politics. If a group satisfies all the other proposed definitional elements, then the length of time it has been present in a given State should not preclude its recognition as a minority or its ability to exercise minority rights. The question of classification of minorities (for the purpose of ascertaining their needs and the extent of State duties towards them) is a separate and subsequent question to the questions of definition and recognition. The question of the inclusion of "new" minorities under the protection of minority rights guarantees in international treaty law is very divisive. This Chapter and book favour their inclusion under relevant standards of protection. The highly politicised nature of the question should not detract from the imperative of securing human rights for everyone. The importance of an effective right to freedom of expression is very often most acute for "new" minorities, migrant workers, recent immigrants and non-citizens, who are otherwise politically disenfranchised and are generally excluded from expressive fora and participatory structures and processes in public life. On such a view, the ability of "new" minorities to exercise their right to freedom of expression in an effective manner is a litmus test for the vigour of the right generally.

Chapter 2

The shaping of theories through international legal and political frameworks

Introduction

This chapter provides an overview and critique of the main international and European treaty provisions dealing with the rights of persons belonging to minorities. The analysis also includes international and European standards that are not legally-binding on States, to the extent that they supplement standards that are legally-binding. Elements of historical and political contextualisation are integrated into the analysis. The conceptual complexities and definitional dilemmas set out in Chapter 1 feed into the present chapter: the normative standards under scrutiny here have either been informed by, or have contributed to, those complexities and dilemmas.

2.1 International instruments with focuses on minority rights

This chapter focuses on the post-World War II era; an era when concerted efforts were made to develop and systemise a modern conception of human rights law at the international and regional levels. Prefaced by a brief exploration of the *status quo ante*, the analysis will comprise the largely UN-dominated standard-setting and enforcement at the international level, as well as various comparable endeavours at the European level. Patrick Thornberry has observed that:

> [t]hroughout the history of international law there are examples of protective treaties concluded for the benefit of specific groups; the treaty is the paradigmatic instrument recognizing the right of minorities to fair treatment. The treaties produce a wilderness of single instances rather than any comprehensive scheme.[1]

This historical pattern was, however, interrupted by the establishment of the League of Nations.[2] While it is widely accepted that the protection afforded minorities under the League of Nations' constellation of treaties – despite its documented imperfections – represented a major development in international law, the continued direct relevance of the principles and practices it developed is disputed. The better

1 (footnotes omitted) Patrick Thornberry, *International Law and the Rights of Minorities*, (Oxford, Clarendon Press, 1991), p. 25.

2 For the history of the League of Nations, with a special emphasis on its efforts and achievements in the realm of minority rights protection, see: *ibid.*, pp. 38–54; John Eppstein, *Ten Years' Life of the League of Nations* (London, May Fair Press, 1929).

view would appear to be that the legal inheritance in question is merely of persuasive value. This view builds on the argument that the international legal and political order underwent such fundamental upheaval during World War II that the new post-war dispensation was a completely new departure, built on new conceptual foundations and comprising new political architecture. In light of this fundamental change of circumstances,[3] the principle of *rebus sic stantibus* is taken to apply,[4] thereby prompting commentators such as Thornberry to refer to the advent of the UN taking place in a *tabula rasa* situation.[5]

2.1.1 Genocide Convention

The absolute baseline for minority rights protection is a guarantee for minorities' existence and first and foremost their physical existence. On the basis of this thinking, "the protection of minorities through individual rights was backstopped by a convention designed to prevent the most egregious violation of minority rights: the Convention on the Prevention and Punishment of the Crime of Genocide".[6] The absolute nature of the prohibition of genocide is underlined by unanimous acceptance that it constitutes a crime under customary international law as well. Indeed, the Convention codifies customary international law in this respect.

In Article I of the Convention,[7] the Contracting Parties "confirm that genocide, whether committed in time of peace or in time of war, is a crime under international law which they undertake to prevent and to punish". Article II sets out the definition of "genocide":

> In the present Convention, genocide means any of the following acts committed with intent to destroy, in whole or in part, a national, ethnical, racial or religious group, as such:
> (a) Killing members of the group;
> (b) Causing serious bodily or mental harm to members of the group;
> (c) Deliberately inflicting on the group conditions of life calculated to bring about its physical destruction in whole or in part;

3 See further, Article 62 of the Vienna Convention on the Law of Treaties, which deals with the issue.

4 This was the contemporaneous approach adopted by the fledgling UN; for background details, see: John P. Humphrey, *Human Rights & the United Nations: a great adventure* (New York, Transnational Publishers, Inc., 1984), pp. 47–48.

5 Patrick Thornberry, *International Law and the Rights of Minorities*, *op. cit.*, p. 54.

6 Charles F. Furtado, Jr., "Guess Who's Coming to Dinner? Protection for National Minorities in Eastern and Central Europe under the Council of Europe" 34 Colum. Hum. Rts. L. Rev. 333 (2003), at 338–339.

7 Approved and proposed for signature and ratification or accession by General Assembly Resolution 260 A (III) of 9 December 1948; entry into force 12 January 1951.

(d) Imposing measures intended to prevent births within the group;
(e) Forcibly transferring children of the group to another group.

Article III lists the acts punishable under the Convention as: genocide, conspiracy to commit genocide, direct and public incitement to commit genocide, attempt to commit genocide, and complicity in genocide.

While the final text of the Genocide Convention focuses on the physical existence of groups, serious consideration was given in the drafting process to the notion of "cultural genocide", which was defined in one version of the draft Convention as follows:

> Destroying the specific characteristics of the group by (a) forced transfer of children to another human group; or (b) forced and systematic exile of individuals representing the culture of a group; or (c) prohibition of the use of the national language even in private intercourse; or (d) systematic destruction of books printed in the national language or of religious works or prohibition of new publications; or (e) systematic destruction of historical or religious monuments or their diversion to alien uses, destruction or dispersal of documents and objects of historical, artistic or religious value and of objects used in religious worship.[8]

In another draft text of the Convention, "cultural genocide" was taken to mean:

> [...] any deliberate act committed with the intent to destroy the language, religion or culture of a national, racial or religious group on grounds of the national or racial origin or religious belief of its members such as:
> 1 Prohibiting the use of the language of the group in daily intercourse or in schools or the printing and circulation of publications in the language of the group:
> 2 Destroying or preventing the use of libraries, museums, schools, historical institutions and objects of the group.[9]

Together, these proposed definitions illustrate the approximate scope of the notion. The vagueness of the notion and the interpretative difficulties to which it would have led in practice appear to have been the most persuasive arguments in the intense debates which eventually led to a decision to drop the notion of "cultural genocide" from the Convention at a late stage in the drafting process. Thornberry concludes that "the majority opinion [in the relevant debates] seems to have been that genocide is *sui generis*, and must be differentiated from questions of human and minority rights".[10]

8 Article I of the Secretariat's Draft Convention, as cited in Patrick Thornberry, *International Law and the Rights of Minorities*, *op. cit.*, p. 71.

9 Article III of the Ad Hoc Committee's Draft Convention, as cited in *ibid.*, p. 72.

10 *Ibid.*, p. 73.

Notwithstanding the narrow definitional focus ultimately prescribed for the Genocide Convention, the right to existence implies more than just physical existence. The right also includes the right to exist on a given territory, especially when a minority group has special (historical, cultural, religious, etc.) attachment to the same. It also includes the right of access of minorities to "the material resources required to continue their existence on those territories".[11] In addition to these physical, territorial and basic subsistence rights involved in the right to existence, its "cultural and spiritual dimensions" also merit recognition.[12] Indeed, a case could even conceivably be built for the inclusion of a right to "permanent sovereignty over natural resources",[13] at least insofar as it relates to the territorial-based cultural objectives of minority groups.

2.1.2 United Nations Charter

An acute awareness of the urgent and enduring nature of minority rights is reflected in the institutional structures of the United Nations. Article 68 of the UN Charter provides for the creation of a Commission on Human Rights under the auspices of the Economic and Social Committee (ECOSOC)[14] to develop and implement the provisions of the Charter relating to human rights and fundamental freedoms. The protection of minorities comes within the remit of the Commission. Under the specific authorisation of ECOSOC, the Commission established its Sub-Commission on Prevention of Discrimination and Protection of Minorities[15] (later renamed as

11 Para. 24, ECOSOC, Commission on Human Rights, Sub-Commission on the Promotion and Protection of Human Rights, *Commentary of the Working Group on Minorities to the United Nations Declaration on the Rights of Persons Belonging to National or Ethnic, Religious and Linguistic Minorities*, E/CN.4/Sub.2/AC.5/2005/2, 4 April 2005, p. 6.

12 Patrick Thornberry, "The UN Declaration on the Rights of Persons Belonging to National or Ethnic, Religious and Linguistic Minorities: Background, Analysis, Observations, and an Update", in Alan Phillips and Allan Rosas, Eds., *Universal Minority Rights* (Abo Akademi University Institute for Human Rights/Minority Rights Group, Turku/Abo and London, 1995), pp. 13–76, at 40.

13 See further, James Crawford, "The Rights of Peoples: 'Peoples' or 'Governments'?", in James Crawford, Ed., *The Rights of Peoples* (Oxford, Oxford University Press, 1988), pp. 55–67, at 63–65.

14 Article 7 of the UN Charter provides for the establishment of ECOSOC as one of the "principal organs" of the UN. Its functions and powers are set out in Articles 62 *et seq.* of the UN Charter. Of particular importance for present purposes is Article 62(2), which reads: "It may make recommendations for the purpose of promoting respect for, and observance of, human rights and fundamental freedoms for all". Article 62(3) is of similar importance: "It may prepare draft conventions for submission to the General Assembly, with respect to matters falling within its competence". Also worthy of mention is Article 64, which empowers ECOSOC to obtain reports from specialised UN agencies. Currently, it coordinates the activities of 14 of the UN specialised agencies, nine functional commissions and five regional commissions.

15 See further: Asbjorn Eide, "The Sub-Commission on Prevention of Discrimination and Protection of Minorities", in Philip Alston, Ed., *The United Nations and Human Rights* (Oxford, Clarendon Press, 1992), pp. 211–264.

the Sub-Commission on the Promotion and Protection of Human Rights). Over time, the mandate of the Sub-Commission expanded considerably beyond its dual eponymous objectives.[16] In 1995, the UN Working Group on Minorities was set up under the auspices of the Sub-Commission.[17] It acted primarily as a forum for dialogue, involving minorities, States representatives and other interested parties, until its functions were subsumed in those of the newly-created Human Rights Council, which replaced the UN Commission on Human Rights in 2006.[18]

2.1.3 Universal Declaration of Human Rights

However, this (institutional) consciousness has not always translated into action. To date, no United Nations *convention* specifically addresses minority rights in an exclusive manner. Moreover, neither the United Nations Charter nor the Universal Declaration of Human Rights (UDHR) – the two foundational documents of the post-World War II regime of international human rights law – contains any specific mention of minority rights (as distinct from association with a minority as one of the listed grounds of impermissible discrimination). The initial draft (the so-called "Secretariat Outline") of the UDHR did, however, include a provision dealing specifically with minority rights,[19] which read:

> In states inhabited by a substantial number of persons of a race, language or religion other than those of the majority of the population, persons belonging to such ethnic, linguistic or religious minorities shall have the right to establish and maintain, out of an equitable proportion of any public[20] funds available for the purpose, their schools and cultural and religious institutions, and to use their own language before the courts and other authorities and organs of the state and in the press and in public assembly.[21]

As will duly be shown, the definitional component of this provision includes some of the main elements of other leading definitions of minority rights. Its purposive component, however, is more far-reaching than similar provisions that were subsequently incorporated into various UN treaties. Its express provision for an

---

16 See further, *ibid.*, at 213; 222–226.

17 It was established pursuant to ECOSOC Resolution 1995/31 of 25 July 1995. See further: Asbjorn Eide, "Commentary: Global and regional approaches to situations involving minorities", in *Filling the frame: Five years of monitoring the Framework Convention for the Protection of National Minorities* (Strasbourg, Council of Europe Publishing, 2004), pp. 51–58, at 54–55.

18 UNGA Resolution 60/251, "Human Rights Council", adopted on 15 March 2006.

19 The draft text was prepared by the Division of Human Rights (i.e., John Humphrey and his staff): UN Yearbook on Human Rights for 1947 (Lake Success, United Nations, 1949), p. 484; also reproduced in Mary Ann Glendon, *A World Made New: Eleanor Roosevelt and the Universal Declaration of Human Rights* (New York, Random House, Inc., 2001), pp. 270–274.

20 Note: Humphrey omits the word "public" (p. 69), whereas Glendon includes it (p. 274).

21 Article 46, *ibid.*

equitable portion of available public funding to be ear-marked for minorities to allow them to pursue the text's stated provisions was particularly far-reaching and proved very controversial. When René Cassin revised the initial draft of the UDHR, he removed the reference to public funding because France did not allocate funds to private educational institutions.[22] Even without the reference to public funding, the proposed article remained so controversial that the Human Rights Commission dropped it, with the result that the draft text sent to the UN General Assembly did not include any provision focusing specifically on minority rights.

This omission is generally explained by the conceptual complexity and political sensitivity of the issue, as well as the high level of divergence in relevant State practice.[23] A number of States (including many Latin American States), either with assimilationist policies or particular understandings of the concept of "minorities", claimed that minorities did not exist on their territories and were therefore opposed to the very idea of an article guaranteeing special rights to minorities.[24] Also, in keeping with the prevailing legal thinking of the day, some of the drafters of UN Charter and the UDHR presumed that strong non-discrimination and equality provisions would assure adequate protection for the human rights of all and sundry, including minorities.[25] These two resasons go a long way towards explaining the omission of specific provisions for the protection of minority rights from the Charter and UDHR.

Nevertheless, the issue was not erased from the UN agenda, but continued (nominally and initially, at least) to command a high level of priority. On the same day as the UN General Assembly adopted a Resolution proclaiming the Universal Declaration of Human Rights,[26] it adopted another Resolution entitled "Fate of

22 This explanation was given subsequently by the French delegate, Mr. Samuel Spanien: Doc. E/CN.4/Sub.2/SR.11, p. 20. See also: Albert Verdoodt, *Naissance et signification de la Déclaration des droits de l'homme* (Louvain, E. Warny, 1964), p. 288; John P. Humphrey, *Human Rights & the United Nations: a great adventure*, *op. cit.*, p. 69.

23 See, for example, Francesco Capotorti, *Study on the rights of persons belonging to ethnic, religious and linguistic minorities* (E/CN.4/Sub.2/384/Rev.1) (1979), p. 27; Asbjorn Eide, "The Sub-Commission on Prevention of Discrimination and Protection of Minorities", *op. cit.*, at 220. The changes introduced by the so-called "Cassin draft" were, in the main, more stylistic than substantive: Mary Ann Glendon, *A World Made New: Eleanor Roosevelt and the Universal Declaration of Human Rights*, *op. cit.*, p. 64. The "Cassin draft" is reproduced in *ibid.*, pp. 274–280.

24 Albert Verdoodt, *Naissance et signification de la Déclaration des droits de l'homme*, *op. cit.*, pp. 289 *et seq.*; John P. Humphrey, *Human Rights & the United Nations: a great adventure*, *op. cit.*, p. 69.

25 Natan Lerner, "The Evolution of Minority Rights in International Law," in Catherine Brölmann, René Lefeber & Marjoleine Zieck, Eds., *Peoples and Minorities in International Law* (Dordrecht, Martinus Nijhoff, 1993), pp. 77–101, at 87; John P. Humphrey, *Human Rights & the United Nations: a great adventure*, *op. cit.*, pp. 20 and 69.

26 UN General Assembly Resolution 217 A (III) of 10 December 1948.

Minorities".[27] That Resolution stated that the United Nations could not remain indifferent to the fate of minorities, even if the issue was fraught with complications. It called on the Sub-Commission to "make a thorough study of the problem of minorities" with a view to enabling the UN to "take effective measures for the protection of racial, national, religious or linguistic minorities".[28] The Resolution was clearly intended as a sop for the non-inclusion of a specific article on minority rights in the Universal Declaration of Human Rights. Although the Sub-Commission on the Prevention of Discrimination and the Protection of Minorities went about its task diligently, it encountered considerable political resistance in the Human Rights Commission and ECOSOC.[29] In fact, it has been claimed that its commitment to the question of the "fate of minorities" was one of the reasons why ECOSOC sought, unsuccessfully, to abolish the Sub-Commission in 1951.[30]

2.1.4 International Covenant on Civil and Political Rights

The ICCPR marks a shift from the line of thinking that prevailed during the drafting of the UDHR, at least insofar as its text and *travaux préparatoires* reveal concerns that the envisaged provisions of non-discrimination and equality would prove insufficient for safeguarding the rights of individuals belonging to minorities. It was clearly felt that supplementary or complementary provisions would be required to redress the envisaged shortcomings of the draft text.[31] This viewpoint eventually won the day, leading to the drafting and inclusion of what would become Article 27, ICCPR.

Of the existing conventions that do contain (detailed) provisions treating minority rights, the ICCPR and the Convention on the Rights of the Child (CRC), are the two which lay the strongest claim to being universally applicable. However, in both cases, only one article deals specifically and exclusively with minorities. Article 27, ICCPR reads:

---

27 UN General Assembly Resolution 217 C (III) of 10 December 1948.

28 *Ibid.*, para. 5. For details of how the Sub-Commission went about carrying out this study, see Asbjorn Eide, "The Sub-Commission on Prevention of Discrimination and Protection of Minorities", *op. cit.*, at 220 *et seq.*

29 John P. Humphrey, *Human Rights & the United Nations: a great adventure*, *op. cit.*, pp. 56 and 69–70. See further, *ibid.*, p. 103.

30 *Ibid.*, p. 70.

31 "It was agreed that, while article 2, paragraph 1, and article 24 [26] of the draft Covenant on Civil and Political Rights contained a general prohibition of discrimination, differential treatment might be granted to minorities in order to ensure them real equality of status with the other elements of the population. It was felt that an article on this question should be included in the draft Covenant on Civil and Political Rights.": Commission on Human Rights, 5th Session (1949) – A/2929, Chapt. VI, Para. 183, as cited in Marc Bossuyt, *Guide to the "Travaux Préparatoires" of the International Covenant on Civil and Political Rights* (Dordrecht, etc., Martinus Nijhoff Publishers, 1987), p.

> In those States in which ethnic, religious or linguistic minorities exist, persons belonging to such minorities shall not be denied the right, in community with the other members of their group, to enjoy their own culture, to profess and practise their own religion, or to use their own language.

Striking textual similarities reveal the extent to which Article 30, CRC, was modelled on Article 27, ICCPR:

> In those States in which ethnic, religious or linguistic minorities or persons of indigenous origin exist, a child belonging to such a minority or who is indigenous, shall not be denied the right, in community with other members of his or her group, to enjoy his or her own culture, to profess and practise his or her own religion, or to use his or her own language.

While there is broad consensus that Article 27, ICCPR, is the "preeminent"[32] provision in positive international law vouchsafing minority rights, it is also widely recognised that the provision nevertheless only offers "fairly modest"[33] protection. The crucial phrase, "shall not be denied" *prima facie* sets the tone for the entire article. The choice of wording seems begrudging and parsimonious. Indeed, one leading commentator went so far as to claim that "[a] weaker statement than the one in Article 27 could, however, be hard to imagine".[34] The emergence of the final wording can be easily traced in the drafting history of the article.[35] An earlier proposal by the USSR for a more positive wording ("the State shall ensure to national minorities the right [...]") was rejected for fear that "under such a text which imposed a positive obligation on States, minority consciousness could be artificially awakened or stimulated".[36] It was generally felt among State delegations that the phrase, "shall not be denied the right [...]", "seemed to imply that the obligations of States would be limited to permitting the free exercise of the rights of minorities".[37]

However, in its General Comment 23, the UN Human Rights Committee has interpreted the phrase as allowing for a more positive reading than its apparent negativity would suggest. The operative paragraphs are phrased as follows:

---

32 Henry J. Steiner & Philip Alston, *International Human Rights in Context* (2nd Edition) (Oxford & New York, Oxford University Press, 2000), p. 992.

33 Manfred Nowak, "The Evolution of Minority Rights in International Law: Comments", in Catherine Brölmann *et al.*, Eds., *Peoples and Minorities in International Law*, *op. cit.*, pp. 103–118, at 104.

34 John P. Humphrey, *Human Rights & the United Nations: a great adventure*, *op. cit.*, p. 102.

35 See further, Marc Bossuyt, *Guide to the "Travaux Préparatoires" of the International Covenant on Civil and Political Rights*, *op. cit.*, p. 496.

36 *Ibid.*

37 *Ibid.*

> 6.1 Although article 27 is expressed in negative terms, that article, nevertheless, does recognize the existence of a "right" and requires that it shall not be denied. Consequently, a State party is under an obligation to ensure that the existence and the exercise of this right are protected against their denial or violation. Positive measures of protection are, therefore, required not only against the acts of the State party itself, whether through its legislative, judicial or administrative authorities, but also against the acts of other persons within the State party.
>
> 6.2 Although the rights protected under article 27 are individual rights, they depend in turn on the ability of the minority group to maintain its culture, language or religion. Accordingly, positive measures by States may also be necessary to protect the identity of a minority and the rights of its members to enjoy and develop their culture and language and to practise their religion, in community with the other members of the group. [...][38]

Thus, Article 27, ICCPR, not only sets out positive obligations for States, it even goes so far as to envisage the horizontal application of those obligations, as is clear from the final sentence in para. 6.1. This emphasis on the *specific* (positive) duties of States *vis-à-vis* minority rights is consistent with the *general* duties to which States Parties are bound by virtue of Article 2, ICCPR. It reads (in part):[39]

1. Each State Party to the present Covenant undertakes to respect and to ensure to all individuals within its territory and subject to its jurisdiction the rights recognized in the present Covenant, without distinction of any kind, such as race, colour, sex, language, religion, political or other opinion, national or social origin, property, birth or other status.
2. Where not already provided for by existing legislative or other measures, each State Party to the present Covenant undertakes to take the necessary steps, in accordance with its constitutional processes and with the provisions of the present Covenant, to adopt such laws or other measures as may be necessary to give effect to the rights recognized in the present Covenant.

In its General Comment No. 31, the UN Human Rights Committee stresses that the obligation under Article 2(1) to "respect and ensure" Covenant rights has "immediate effect" for all States Parties and that Article 2(2) provides the "overarching framework" within which those rights are to be "promoted and protected".[40] The legal obligation enshrined in Article 2(1) "is both negative and positive in nature", implying that as well as refraining from violating any Covenant rights, States must equally "adopt legislative, judicial, administrative, educative and

38 See also para. 9, *ibid.*, which refers, *inter alia*, to the "specific obligations" imposed on States by Article 27, and the duty of States "to ensure that the exercise of these rights is fully protected".

39 Article 2.3 concerns the availability of effective remedies and their enforceability by competent authorities.

40 General Comment No. 31 [80] – The Nature of the General Legal Obligation Imposed on States Parties to the Covenant, adopted on 29 March 2004, para. 5.

other appropriate measures in order to fulfil their legal obligations".[41] Furthermore, States' positive obligations under Article 2(1) "will only be fully discharged if individuals are protected by the State, not just against violations of Covenant rights by its agents, but also against acts committed by private persons or entities that would impair the enjoyment of Covenant rights in so far as they are amenable to application between private persons or entities".[42]

The foregoing analysis of relevant General Comments establishes that States are under clear and strong positive obligations in the field of minority rights protection. It can therefore be concluded that these positive obligations serve to offset the narrowness and negativity suggested by the actual wording of Article 27, ICCPR. However, such a reading asks profound questions about the importance of the doctrine of original intent, and of the competing merits of literal and teleological/ purposive approaches to the interpretation of treaties. It could also be taken as casting certain doubt on the role of *travaux préparatoires* for treaty interpretation generally.[43]

Article 27 offers little in the way of elucidation as to the individual/collective nature of the rights its negative formulation purports to safeguard.[44] As has already been demonstrated in Chapter 1, minority rights do not necessarily have to be individual rights. A shift of focus is required in order to appreciate the unique nature of minority rights, or, to employ its most frequently-used formulation, "the rights of persons belonging to minorities". Manfred Nowak points out that this formula was introduced at the drafting stage of the text of the ICCPR by the British delegation because according to the prevailing judicial thinking of the day, groups *qua* groups could not be the holders of rights.[45]

Whatever about its persuasive power, this conclusion was an inaccurate reading of international law at the time,[46] and even moreso when judged against the standards of today. The concept of right-holding groups was already well-established in the

41 *Ibid.*, paras. 6, 7.

42 *Ibid.*, para. 8. It continues: "There may be circumstances in which a failure to ensure Covenant rights permitting or failing to take appropriate measures or to exercise due diligence to prevent, punish, investigate or redress the harm caused by such acts by private persons or entities". See further: Article 2(3), ICCPR.

43 See in this connection: Jan Klabbers, "International Legal Histories: The Declining Importance of *Travaux Préparatoires* in Treaty Interpretation?", *Netherlands International Law Review* (2003), pp. 267–288.

44 For a synthesis of various viewpoints on the question of whether individuals or groups are the relevant right-holders for the purposes of Article 27, see Manfred Nowak, *U.N. Covenant on Civil and Political Rights – CCPR Commentary* (2nd revised edition) (Kehl, N.P. Engel, 2005), pp. 652–657.

45 *Ibid.*, p. 639.

46 See further in this connection, *ibid.*, pp. 652–653.

contemporary canon of international human rights law (eg. the Genocide Convention) and it was to be reaffirmed in the context, *inter alia*, of the right of peoples to self-determination in the ICCPR and ICESCR, which would imminently be concluded. It would have been more accurate and less disingenuous for the British delegation to have argued that there was limited precedent for the recognition of group rights in international law. In sum, although practice has proven the original assertion to be incorrect, the drafters of the ICCPR rejected an exclusively group-oriented formulation of the provision securing minority rights protection.

As stated in General Comment No. 23, what is at issue in Article 27 is "a right which is conferred on individuals belonging to minority groups" to enjoy their own culture, to profess and practise their own religion, and/or to use their own language.[47] Francesco Capotorti, however, is at pains to point out that the final choice of phraseology for Article 27 "limits, but certainly does not exclude, the existence of purely individual rights of persons belonging to minorities (e.g., the right to hold opinions without interference)".[48] This interpretation of Article 27 reverberates in General Comment No. 23, which describes the right in question as being "distinct from, and additional to, all the other rights which, as individuals in common with everyone else, they [i.e., individuals belonging to minority groups] are already entitled to enjoy under the Covenant".[49] This is also consistent with Capotorti's findings in his seminal report, where he wrote that:

> Article 27 does not refer to minority groups as the formal holders of the rights described in it, but rather stresses the need for a collective exercise of such rights. Therefore it seems justified to conclude that a correct construction of this norm must be based on the idea of its double effect – protection of the group and its individual members [...].[50]

It has succinctly been pointed out by Patrick Thornberry that the drafters of the ICCPR created "a hybrid between individual and collective rights because of the 'community' requirement", as such an approach "presupposes a community of individuals endowed with similar rights".[51] This prompts him to describe the rights in question as "benefiting individuals but requiring collective exercise".[52]

---

47 General Comment 23, para. 1.

48 Francesco Capotorti, "Are minorities entitled to collective international rights?", in Yoram Dinstein & Mala Tabory, Eds., *The Protection of Minorities and Human Rights* (Dordrecht, Martinus Nijhoff Publishers, 1992), pp. 505–511, at 511.

49 *Ibid.*

50 *Ibid.*, at 507–508.

51 Patrick Thornberry, *International Law and the Rights of Minorities*, *op. cit.*, p. 173.

52 *Ibid.*

The use of the verb "exist" in Article 27 has generated considerable discussion, particularly as regards whether it connotes a particular degree of permanence. Relevant discussions were fuelled by General Comment No. 23, which scotches such notions. The adoption of such an approach by the Human Rights Committee prompted Hurst Hannum to reason that: "[t]he Committee does not refer to the relevant legislative history to support its conclusions, and the General Comment is perhaps best interpreted as representing the personal views of Committee members than an authoritative interpretation of the text of the Covenant. At the same time, however, the expansive reading is generally consistent with the more detailed principles set forth in the 1992 General Assembly Declaration".[53]

The question of nationality as a criterion for determining an individual's membership of a minority grouping must be considered in distinct contexts: that of universally applicable legal standards and that of analogous European provisions. As regards UN-sponsored standards, individuals do not have to be nationals of a given State to enjoy the rights to which members of that State's own minorities can ordinarily lay claim. General Comment 23 is instructive in the matter of the scope of the applicability of Article 27's provisions: "the obligations deriving from article 2.1 are also relevant, since a State party is required under that article to ensure that the rights protected under the Covenant are available to all individuals within its territory and subject to its jurisdiction, except rights which are expressly made to apply to citizens, for example, political rights under article 25. A State party may not, therefore, restrict the rights under article 27 to its citizens alone".[54] Thus, by way of corollary, any consideration of (degrees of) permanence of residence in this connection is redundant.[55]

In practice, reservations and heavy-handed declarations have been entered in respect of Article 27. It is likely that refusals to enter into the spirit of the operative article were prompted by: (i) a fear that it would lead to obligations to take affirmative action (including the financial implications which such obligations would incur) in order to improve the lot of minorities, or (ii) a genuine belief that the cause of national unity would be best served by integrationist or assimilationist policies (with the assumption that similar treatment for all persons on a national territory, amounting to formal, legal equality, would be sufficient from a human rights perspective). Thornberry has commented that "some of the disclaimers on the existence of minorities in a State reveal rather tortuous and evasive reasoning".[56]

53 Hurst Hannum, "New Minority Rights for the Twenty-First Century", in Yael Danieli, Elsa Stamatopoulou & Clarence J. Dias, Eds., *The Universal Declaration of Human Rights: Fifty years and beyond* (New York, United Nations Publishing, 1999), pp. 163–173, at 169–170.

54 General Comment 23, para. 5.1.

55 *Ibid.*, para. 5.2.

56 Patrick Thornberry, *International Law and the Rights of Minorities*, *op. cit.*, p. 158.

France is the most eminent European country to have given formal expression to its objections to Article 27. The French Government, upon ratification of the ICCPR, declared, *inter alia*, that Article 27 of the Covenant was not applicable in France, in light of Article 2 of the 1958 French Constitution.[57] A similar declaration was made by the French authorities in respect of Article 30 of the CRC, upon ratification of that Convention. The United Nations Human Rights Committee has been critical of France's continued refusal to endorse the provisions of Article 27:

> The Committee has taken note of the avowed commitment of France to respect and ensure that all individuals enjoy equal rights, regardless of their origin. The Committee is, however, unable to agree that France is a country in which there are no ethnic, religious or linguistic minorities. The Committee wishes to recall in this respect that the mere fact that equal rights are granted to all individuals and that all individuals are equal before the law does not preclude the existence in fact of minorities in a country, and their entitlement to the enjoyment of their culture, the practice of their religion or the use of their language in community with other members of their group.[58]

The Committee has repeatedly held France's 'declaration' made in respect of Article 27 "to be tantamount to a reservation and [that it] therefore precludes the Committee from considering complaints against France alleging violations of article 27 of the Covenant".[59]

2.1.5 UN Declaration on the Rights of Persons Belonging to National or Ethnic, Religious and Linguistic Minorities

The 1992 UN Declaration on the Rights of Persons Belonging to National or Ethnic, Religious and Linguistic Minorities, has been hailed as "a document that is more assertive than previous UN instruments".[60] This is largely because of its pro-active overall tenor. Article 1 enjoins States to adopt appropriate legislative and other measures with a view towards promoting minority identities; an objective (and concomitant requirement) that reverberates in Article 4.2. The Declaration, although adopted by consensus, does not create any legal obligations on the governments of

---

57 Article 2 of the Constitution of the Fifth French Republic (1958) reads: "La langue de la République est le français. L'emblème national est le drapeau tricolore, bleu, blanc, rouge. L'hymne national est la Mareillaise. La devise de la République est Liberté, Egalité, Fraternité. Son principe est: gouvernement du peuple, par le peuple et pour le peuple."

58 Concluding observations of the Human Rights Committee: France. 04/08/97. CCPR/C/79/Add.80, para. 24.

59 *C.L.D. v. France*, Communication No. 439/1990, 8 November 1991, para. 4.3. See also, *T.K. v. France*, Communication No. 220/1987, 8 November 1989, para. 8.6.

60 P. Dunay, "Nationalism and Ethnic Conflicts in Eastern Europe: Imposed, Induced or (Simply) Reemerged," in Istvan Pogany, Ed., *Human Rights in Eastern Europe* (Aldershot, etc., Edward Elgar, 1995), pp. 17–45, at 34.

its States signatories. Nor does it define minority rights or provide an exhaustive enumeration thereof. The Declaration does, however, represent a pronounced shift in the UN's approach to minority rights, moving from a negatively formulated focus on non-discrimination in Article 27, ICCPR, to the more positive-sounding language of protection and promotion.[61] The importance of the 1992 Declaration was affirmed, *inter alia*, by references to it in the 1993 Vienna Declaration (para. 19) and Programme of Action (Section B2, paras. 25–27).[62]

2.1.6 UN institutional approaches to minority rights

The position of Independent Expert on Minority Issues was established by Resolution 2005/79 of the UN Human Rights Commission.[63] The mandate of the Independent Expert reads as follows:

> (*a*) To promote the implementation of the Declaration on the Rights of Persons Belonging to National or Ethnic, Religious and Linguistic Minorities, including through consultations with Governments, taking into account existing international standards and national legislation concerning minorities;
> (*b*) To identify best practices and possibilities for technical cooperation by the Office of the United Nations High Commissioner for Human Rights at the request of Governments;
> (*c*) To apply a gender perspective in his or her work;
> (*d*) To cooperate closely, while avoiding duplication, with existing relevant United Nations bodies, mandates, mechanisms as well as regional organizations;
> (*e*) To take into account the views of non-governmental organizations on matters pertaining to his or her mandate.

The position was initially created for a two-year period and its first incumbent was Ms. Gay McDougall. The Resolution establishing the position requests the office-holder to "submit annual reports on his/her activities to the Commission, including recommendations for effective strategies for the better implementation of the rights of persons belonging to minorities". In her first annual report, the Independent

61 See further: Patrick Thornberry, "The UN Declaration on the Rights of Persons Belonging to National or Ethnic, Religious and Linguistic Minorities: Background, Analysis, Observations and an Update", *op. cit.*; Asbjorn Eide, *Commentary to the Declaration on the Rights of Persons Belonging to National or Ethnic, Religious and Linguistic Minorities*, Working paper submitted to the Working Group on Minorities of the Sub-Commission on Promotion and Protection of Human Rights of the United Nations Commission on Human Rights, 27 April 2000.

62 Vienna Declaration and Programme of Action, adopted by the World Conference on Human Rights in Vienna on 25 June 1993.

63 Rights of persons belonging to national or ethnic, religious and linguistic minorities, Resolution 2005/79, Commission on Human Rights (61st session, 2005). For background information, see: Rianne Letschert, *The Impact of Minority Rights Mechanisms* (The Hague, T.M.C. Asser Press, 2005), pp. 122–127.

Expert identified "four broad areas of concern relating to minorities around the world, based on the Declaration on the Rights of Minorities and other relevant international standards relating to minority rights".[64] They were:

(a) Protecting a minority's existence, including through protection of their physical integrity and the prevention of genocide;
(b) Protecting and promoting cultural and social identity, including the right of individuals to choose which ethnic, linguistic or religious groups they wish to be identified with, and the right of those groups to affirm and protect their collective identity and to reject forced assimilation;
(c) Ensuring effective non-discrimination and equality, including ending structural or systemic discrimination; and
(d) Ensuring effective participation of members of minorities in public life, especially with regard to decisions that affect them.

Although the holder of the specialised mandate is called an Independent Expert, this official title does not necessarily reflect any distinction of status compared with other specialised UN mechanisms/mandates. The various titles employed to designate such experts (including special rapporteurs, independent experts, representatives of the Secretary-General or representatives of the Commission) "neither reflect a hierarchy, nor are they an indication of the powers entrusted to the expert".[65] Rather, the titles of the mandates are the product of political negotiations.[66] Part of the thinking behind the establishment of the mandate was the view that "some challenges facing minorities have not been appropriately covered by existing mandates, for structural or functional reasons. As minority issues do not constitute the main focus of the existing mandates, inevitably the mandates are unable to reflect the full range of concerns relevant to minorities".[67] In other words, the need was felt to create a mechanism that would strive to make the piecemeal nature of the system of protection of minorities more coherent and integrated.[68]

---

64 Specific Groups and Individuals: Minorities, Report of the independent expert on minority issues, Gay McDougall, Commission on Human Rights (62nd session, 6 January 2006), E/CN.4/2006/74, para. 22.

65 Seventeen frequently asked questions about the United Nations special rapporteurs, UN Human Rights Fact Sheets, No. 27, Geneva, 2001, p. 6.

66 *Ibid.*

67 Report of the High Commissioner for Human Rights on the rights of persons belonging to minorities, E/CN.4/2004/75, 24 February 2004, para. 35.

68 For an overview of the Independent Expert's activities, see: Gay McDougall, "Postscript: The United Nations Independent Expert on Minority Issues", in Kristin Henrard & Robert Dunbar, Eds., *Synergies in Minority Protection: European and International Law Perspectives* (Cambridge, Cambridge University Press, 2008), pp. 81–87; Anna Meijknecht, "Reducing the Risk of Differential Standards in Minority Protection: The Holistic Approach of the UN Independent Expert on Minority Issues", in Kristin Henrard, Ed., *Double Standards Pertaining to Minority Protection* (Leiden/Boston, Martinus Nijhoff Publishers, 2010), pp. 145–162.

2.2 European instruments with focuses on minority rights

Standard-setting activities in respect of minority rights at the international and European levels share many similarities. Although normative instruments at both levels largely reinforce or complement each other, they remain distinct from each other in some crucial respects, including their specific purpose, focus and ambition. The advantages of "the regional instrument" have been enumerated by Patrick Thornberry as the following:

- Grounding in a coherent political or cultural tradition;
- Greater possibilities of inter-state cooperation through proximity;
- Closer access for members of minority groups to centres of decision-making and enhanced possibilities of participation and redress of grievances.[69]

These observations can hardly be gainsaid, not least because they are the progeny of the sense of shared heritage and destiny that originally led to the drafting of the European Convention on Human Rights (ECHR). The final preambular paragraph in the ECHR, for instance, refers to (a collectivity of) "European countries which are like-minded and have a common heritage of political traditions, ideals, freedom and the rule of law". Nevertheless, with the continuing growth of the Council of Europe, the coherence of political and cultural traditions between Member States is increasingly being questioned.[70] The development of the principle and a culture of subsidiarity in decision-making is also of paramount importance, as will be demonstrated, *infra*. One should, however, additionally point to legal frameworks as another factor that attests to the strengths of regional resolutions of minority issues.

Firstly, geo-political and socio-economic considerations have given great thrust to European integration, through the efforts of various European IGOs. The overarching legal structures of these IGOs are therefore applicable to many – or in some cases, most – European States. While the majority of laws adopted and enforced or monitored by relevant IGOs do not directly concern minority rights issues, they undoubtedly play a formative role in shaping the legal environment in which specific laws are adopted and applied.

Secondly, the inevitable intertwining of destinies of neighbouring States results in broad parallelisms in the development of legal systems at the national level. Put

---

69 Patrick Thornberry, "The UN Declaration on the Rights of Persons Belonging to National or Ethnic, Religious and Linguistic Minorities: Background, Analysis, Observations and an Update", *op. cit.*, at 61.

70 Such questioning is, of course, much more pronounced in the case of the OSCE, which currently comprises 56 Participating States (as opposed to the Council of Europe's 47).

more plainly, geographical proximity often leads to shared or similar origins of legal systems; similar rates and triggers of development of those systems, and similar responses to issues with which they are confronted.

Taken together, these considerations are of great contextual importance.

2.2.1 European Convention on Human Rights

The (European) Convention on the Protection of Human Rights and Fundamental Freedoms (ECHR)[71] is the veritable bedrock of human rights protection in Europe. In keeping with other international human rights instruments elaborated contemporaneously with it, the ECHR takes a predominantly individualistic approach to human rights protection and contains no provision akin to Article 27, ICCPR. In other words, no *specific* rights are envisaged for minorities as such. This was stated emphatically by the (now-defunct[72]) European Commission of Human Rights in *G. & E. v. Norway*, although it did also concede that "disrespect of the particular life style of minorities may raise an issue under Article 8".[73]

Nevertheless, members of minority groups are not debarred from seeking redress for their grievances via the European Court of Human Rights. Procedurally, the Convention Article that is of most relevance in this regard is Article 34, which allows for groups of individuals to petition the Court:

> Article 34 – Individual applications
>
> The Court may receive applications from any person, non-governmental organisation or group of individuals claiming to be the victim of a violation by one of the High Contracting Parties of the rights set forth in the Convention or the protocols thereto. The High Contracting Parties undertake not to hinder in any way the effective exercise of this right.

71 Adopted on 4 November 1950, CETS No. 5.

72 The Commission was abolished pursuant to Protocol No. 11 to the Convention for the Protection of Human Rights and Fundamental Freedoms, restructuring the control machinery established thereby, CETS No. 155, 11 May 1994 (entry into force: 1 November 1998).

73 *G. & E. v. Norway*, Decision of inadmissibility by the European Commission of Human Rights of 3 October 1983, Appn. Nos. 9278/81 & 9415/81, paras. 1 and 7 at pp. 35 and 38, respectively.

In practice, cultural associations,[74] churches,[75] political parties,[76] media outlets,[77] NGOs[78] and villages/communities[79] have all been found to have *locus standi* before the Court.

From a more substantive perspective, it is also possible for individual members of minority groups to make applications to the European Court of Human Rights by virtue of Article 14, ECHR. Like Article 1 ('Obligation to respect human rights'), ECHR,[80] this Article is informed by the principle of equal enjoyment of rights by all. However, as stated by the former European Commission of Human Rights in *X. v. Austria*:

> The Convention does not provide for any rights of a ... minority as such, and the protection of individual members of such minority is limited to the right not to be discriminated in the enjoyment of the Convention rights on the grounds of their belonging to the minority (Article 14 of the Convention).[81]

Article 14, entitled 'Prohibition of discrimination',[82] reads as follows:

> The enjoyment of the rights and freedoms set forth in this Convention shall be secured without discrimination on any ground such as sex, race, colour, language, religion, political or other opinion, national or social origin, association with a national minority, property, birth or other status.

It can thus be seen that Article 14 enumerates a non-exhaustive list of impermissible grounds for discrimination. Among the enumerated grounds are, "national or social origin" and "association with a national minority". The ascertainment of the precise

---

74 *Stankov and the United Macedonian Organisation Ilinden v. Bulgaria*, Judgment of the European Court of Human Rights (First Section) of 2 October 2001.

75 *Canea Catholic Church v. Greece*, Judgment of the European Court of Human Rights of 16 December 1997, Reports 1997-VIII, paras. 30, 31.

76 *United Communist Party v. Turkey*, Judgment of the European Court of Human Rights (Grand Chamber) of 30 January 1998, Reports 1998-I.

77 *The Sunday Times (No. 1) v. United Kingdom*, Judgment of the European Court of Human Rights of 26 April 1979, Series A, No. 30.

78 *Liberty & Others v. United Kingdom*, Judgment of the European Court of Human Rights (Fourth Section) of 1 July 2008.

79 *Noack & others v. Germany*, Judgment of the European Court of Human Rights of 25 May 2000; *Konkama & 38 other Saami villages v. Sweden*, Decision of inadmissibility of the European Commission of Human Rights of 25 November 1996, Appn. No. 27033/95.

80 Article 1, ECHR, reads: "The High Contracting Parties shall secure to everyone within their jurisdiction the rights and freedoms defined in Section I of this Convention."

81 *X. v. Austria*, Application No. 8142/78, 18 DR 88 at 92–92 (1979).

82 For a general overview of the application of Article 14, see: Janneke Gerards, "The Application of Article 14 ECHR by the European Court of Human Rights", in Jan Niessen & Isabelle Chopin, Eds., *The Development of Legal Instruments to Combat Racism in a Diverse Europe* (Leiden/Boston, Martinus Nijhoff Publishers, 2004), pp. 3–60.

meaning of the latter term has proved highly troublesome, although not so much in the context of the ECHR as the Framework Convention for the Protection of National Minorities (discussed *infra*). The European Court of Human Rights noted, *obiter dictum*, in *Gorzelik and others v. Poland* (see further, *infra*), that the formulation of a definition of "national minority" "would have presented a most difficult task", given the absence of such a definition in any international treaty (even the FCNM).[83] The Court then balked at the opportunity to discuss what the essence of such a definition might entail (although it did provide a more reasoned explanation for its stance when the case was subsequently referred to the Grand Chamber).[84]

No free-standing right to non-discrimination was provided for in the original text of the European Convention. Article 14 prohibits discrimination merely in relation to "the rights and freedoms set forth" elsewhere in the Convention. Thus, whenever it is invoked, Article 14 must be pleaded in conjunction with other (substantive) rights guaranteed elsewhere in the ECHR. It can only be said to be autonomous to the extent that its application does not presuppose a breach of one or more of the other substantive provisions of the Convention or its Protocols.[85] However, it has been noted that "there seems to be a degree of uncertainty as to when and why the Court actually proceeds to an examination of Article 14 violations".[86] Protocol No. 12 to the Convention was therefore devised in order to address the fact that Article 14, ECHR, is essentially accessory in character.[87] The pith of the Protocol is 'Article 1 – General prohibition of discrimination', which reads:

> (1) The enjoyment of any right set forth by law shall be secured without discrimination on any ground such as sex, race, colour, language, religion,

83 *Gorzelik & others v. Poland*, Judgment of the European Court of Human Rights (Fourth Section) of 20 December 2001, Application No. 44158/98, para. 62.

84 *Gorzelik & others v. Poland*, Judgment of the European Court of Human Rights (Grand Chamber) of 17 February 2004.

85 *Thlimmenos v. Greece*, Judgment of the European Court of Human Rights of 6 April 2000, para. 40. See also, *ibid.*, para. 44, and *Cha'are Ve Tsedek v. France*, Judgment of the European Court of Human Rights of 27 June 2000, para. 86.

86 Sia Spiliopoulou Akermark, "The Limits of Pluralism – Recent Jurisprudence of the European Court of Human Rights with Regard to Minorities: Does the Prohibition of Discrimination Add Anything?", *Journal on Ethnopolitics and Minority Issues in Europe* (No. 3, 2002), p. 21 of article (note: *JEMIE* is an online journal and the page number cited here refers to the page in the article itself rather than a page number in the journal, as such), available at: www.ecmi.de/jemie/.

87 Protocol No. 12 to the Convention for the Protection of Human Rights and Fundamental Freedoms, ETS No. 177. For commentary, see: Jeroen Schokkenbroek, "A New European Standard against Discrimination: Negotiating Protocol No. 12 to the European Convention on Human Rights", in Jan Niessen & Isabelle Chopin, Eds., *The Development of Legal Instruments to Combat Racism in a Diverse Europe*, *op. cit.*, pp. 61–79.

political or other opinion, national or social origin, association with a national minority, property, birth or other status.

(2) No one shall be discriminated against by any public authority on any ground such as those mentioned in paragraph 1.

Having obtained the requisite 10 ratifications, Protocol No. 12 entered into force on 1 April 2005. It is still too early to tell what its exact impact will be at the European level and also in the domestic legal orders of Member States, but it is likely to eventually prove portentous.

A purely literal reading of Article 14 suggests that the provision is restrictive in scope. However, some commentators have argued that a more teleological reading of the provision belies its apparently limited character.[88] A key argument in this connection is that following the far-reaching precedent set in *Thlimmenos v. Greece*,[89] Article 14 can be activated when the grounds for acts of (direct or indirect) discrimination – and not merely the actual acts of discrimination – are considered to come "within the ambit"[90] of another ECHR right.[91]

In *Thlimmenos*, the applicant was refused membership of the Greek Institute of Chartered Accountants (thereby in effect barring him from entry into the accounting profession) because of a previous conviction for a serious crime. The serious crime in question was insubordination for having refused to wear the military uniform at a time of general mobilisation. As a Jehovah's Witness – and therefore a committed pacifist, the applicant had refused to wear the uniform because of his religious beliefs. He was nonetheless convicted and subsequently served a prison sentence. The European Court of Human Rights was of the view that the "set of facts" involved fell "within the ambit" of a Convention provision (Article 9 – Freedom of thought, conscience and religion), thereby rendering Article 14 applicable.[92] It found the imposition of a further sanction on the applicant as a result of his initial conviction to be disproportionate and that "there existed no objective and reasonable justification for not treating the applicant differently from other persons convicted of a serious crime".[93] The Court concluded that there had been a violation of the Article 14 *juncto* Article 9, because of the respondent State's failure to introduce

88 See, in particular: Robert Wintemute, "'Within the Ambit': How Big is the 'Gap' in Article 14 European Convention of Human Rights? Part 1", E.H.R.L.R. 2004, 4, 366–382; Robert Wintemute, "Filling the Article 14 'Gap': Government Ratification and Judicial Control of Protocol No. 12 ECHR: Part 2", E.H.R.L.R. 2004, 5, 484–499.

89 *Op. cit.*

90 *Inze v. Austria*, Judgment of the European Court of Human Rights of 28 October 1987, para. 36.

91 See further, Robert Wintemute, "'Within the Ambit': How Big is the 'Gap' in Article 14 European Convention of Human Rights? Part 1", *op. cit.*, at 372. Wintemute makes this point in terms of the denial of opportunity (as opposed to discrimination *tout court*, as above).

92 *Thlimmenos v. Greece*, *op. cit.*, para. 42.

93 *Ibid.*, para. 47.

legislation with suitable exceptions to the rule preventing persons convicted of serious crimes from entering the profession of chartered accountants.

Some recent trends in case-law from Strasbourg would appear to bear out such a positive evaluation of Article 14's potential scope. Article 14 is increasingly being relied upon by persons belonging to minority groups seeking "[judicial] adjudication and redress"[94] of their complaints, and the resultant case-law has been described as "burgeoning",[95] if "equivocal".[96] There is certainly scope for building on existing precedents of members of minority groups seeking redress for their grievances by invoking the non-discrimination provision(s) of the ECHR. For example, the Court has noted that "[W]here a general policy or measure has disproportionately prejudicial effects on a particular group, it is not excluded that this may be considered as discriminatory notwithstanding that it is not specifically aimed or directed at that group".[97]

Within this "burgeoning" jurisprudence, one can observe a growing tendency on the part of the Court to pay attention to the *particular* circumstances of *specific* minority groups, especially the Roma, Gypsies and Travellers. The disproportionately high incidence of discrimination suffered by those groups in most countries offers a plausible explanation as to why cases involving their members are featuring relatively prominently in the Court's minority-oriented case-law. It is noteworthy that "deep concern" at the "ongoing manifestations of racism, racial discrimination, xenophobia and related intolerance, including violence" against members of the aforementioned groups and the Sinti, has also been expressed in other contexts, such as the Durban Declaration.[98]

---

94 Gaetano Pentassuglia, "Monitoring Minority Rights in Europe: The Implementation Machinery of the Framework Convention for the Protection of National Minorities – With Special Reference to the Role of the Advisory Committee", 6 *International Journal on Minority and Group Rights* (1999), pp. 417–461, at 422.

95 Geoff Gilbert, "The Burgeoning Minority Rights Jurisprudence of the European Court of Human Rights" 24 *Human Rights Quarterly* (2002) 736–780.

96 Patrick Thornberry, "Treatment of Minority and Indigenous Issues in the European Convention on Human Rights" in Gudmundur Alfredsson & Maria Stavropoulou, Eds., *Justice Pending: Indigenous Peoples and Other Good Causes* (The Hague, Martinus Nijhoff Publishers, 2002), pp. 137–167, at 167.

97 *Hugh Jordan v. the United Kingdom*, Judgment of the European Court of Human Rights (Third Section) of 4 May 2001, para. 154.

98 World Conference against Racism, Racial Discrimination, Xenophobia and Related Intolerance: Declaration, Durban, 2001, para. 68. See also the corresponding Programme of Action, paras. 39–44. By way of aside, it should be noted that it is very important to distinguish between each of the groups mentioned as, first, they are not one and the same, and second, the principle of self-identification or choosing one's own designation, is crucial, not only for members of those groups, but also for persons belonging to minorities generally. Such distinctions and the principles on which they rest are consistent with best international practice; see further: CERD General Recommendation 27 ("Discrimination against Roma") (2000), para. 3; ECRI General

In its Chamber judgment in *Nachova v. Bulgaria*,[99] in particular, the Court showed its resolve to take a tough stance against racism. It found a violation of Article 14 *juncto* Article 2 (Right to life), ECHR,[100] in its substantive and procedural respects, for the failure of the State Party to adequately investigate inferences of discrimination and racism on the part of its officials: (i) in the death – at their hands – of a member of the Roma community, and (ii) in the subsequent inquiry into his death. The Court referred to "the need to reassert continuously society's condemnation of racism and ethnic hatred and to maintain the confidence of minorities in the ability of the authorities to protect them from the threat of racist violence".[101] It then continued by trenchantly declaring that to treat "racially induced violence and brutality on an equal footing with cases that have no racist overtones would be to turn a blind eye to the specific nature of acts that are particularly destructive of human rights".[102] The Chamber judgment in *Nachova* represented the culmination of a string of cases with similar facts, but which had less favourable results as regards the consideration of the ethnicity component.[103]

The Grand Chamber of the European Court of Human Rights – to which the case was subsequently referred by the Bulgarian Government – affirmed that "the authorities must use all available means to combat racism and racist violence, thereby reinforcing democracy's vision of a society in which diversity is not

---

Policy Recommendation No. 3 ("On Combating Racism and Intolerance against Roma/Gypsies") (1998), indent 2.

99 *Nachova and others v. Bulgaria*, Judgment of the European Court of Human Rights (First Section) of 26 February 2004.

100 "Article 2 – Right to life

1. Everyone's right to life shall be protected by law. No one shall be deprived of his life intentionally save in the execution of a sentence of a court following his conviction of a crime for which this penalty is provided by law.
2. Deprivation of life shall not be regarded as inflicted in contravention of this article when it results from the use of force which is no more than absolutely necessary:
   a. in defence of any person from unlawful violence;
   b. in order to effect a lawful arrest or to prevent the escape of a person lawfully detained;
   c. in action lawfully taken for the purpose of quelling a riot or insurrection."

101 *Ibid.*, para. 157.

102 *Ibid.*, para. 158.

103 In the earlier case of *Velikova v. Bulgaria*, the Court had also considered whether the ethnic origin of the victim's death, coupled with allegations of popular societal prejudice and the prevalence of racially-motivated violence against the Roma community (of which he had been a member), were relevant to the case. On that occasion, the Court held that on the basis of the evidence before it, it was unable "to conclude beyond reasonable doubt that Mr Tsonchev's death and the lack of a meaningful investigation into it were motivated by racial prejudice, as claimed by the applicant." – para. 94, *Velikova v. Bulgaria*, Judgment of the European Court of Human Rights (Fourth Section) of 18 May 2000. See also: *Anguelova v. Bulgaria*, Judgment of the European Court of Human Rights of 2002-IV. In *Nachova*, the Court again adduced the seriousness of the arguments of racial motivation in the killing of two Roma in police custody in the *Velikova* and *Anguelova* cases: see para. 173.

perceived as a threat but as a source of its enrichment".[104] However, unlike the Chamber, a majority of the Grand Chamber found no violation of Article 14 in conjunction with Article 2 in its substantive respect, i.e., in respect of allegations that the events leading to the fatal shootings under examination constituted an act of racial violence.[105] The Chamber had shifted the burden of proof – to establish "beyond reasonable doubt" whether racism was a causal factor in the shootings – to the respondent Government. The Grand Chamber dealt with this point at length:

> The Grand Chamber reiterates that in certain circumstances, where the events lie wholly, or in large part, within the exclusive knowledge of the authorities, as in the case of death of a person within their control in custody, the burden of proof may be regarded as resting on the authorities to provide a satisfactory and convincing explanation of, in particular, the causes of the detained person's death [...]. The Grand Chamber cannot exclude the possibility that in certain cases of alleged discrimination it may require the respondent Government to disprove an arguable allegation of discrimination and – if they fail to do so – find a violation of Article 14 of the Convention on that basis. However, where it is alleged – as here – that a violent act was motivated by racial prejudice, such an approach would amount to requiring the respondent Government to prove the absence of a particular subjective attitude on the part of the person concerned. While in the legal systems of many countries proof of the discriminatory effect of a policy or decision will dispense with the need to prove intent in respect of alleged discrimination in employment or the provision of services, that approach is difficult to transpose to a case where it is alleged that an act of violence was racially motivated. The Grand Chamber, departing from the Chamber's approach, does not consider that the alleged failure of the authorities to carry out an effective investigation into the alleged racist motive for the killing should shift the burden of proof to the respondent Government with regard to the alleged violation of Article 14 in conjunction with the substantive aspect of Article 2 of the Convention. [...][106]

Although it did not find a violation of Article 14 *juncto* Article 2 in its substantive effect, the Grand Chamber did find a violation of its procedural effect. It thus endorsed the Chamber's finding that the State authorities had failed in their duty to "take all possible steps to investigate whether or not discrimination may have played a role in the events".[107]

---

104 *Nachova and others v. Bulgaria*, Judgment of the European Court of Human Rights (Grand Chamber) of 6 July 2005, para. 145. See also: *Timishev v. Russia*, Judgment of the European Court of Human Rights (Second Section) of 13 December 2005, para. 56; *D.H. and Others v. the Czech Republic*, Judgment of the European Court of Human Rights (Grand Chamber) of 13 November 2007, para. 176.

105 See also in this connection the Joint partly dissenting opinion of Judges Casadevall, Hedigan, Mularoni, Fura-Sandström, Gyulumyan and Spielmann, annexed to *ibid.*

106 *Nachova and others v. Bulgaria*, *op.cit.*, para. 157.

107 *Ibid.*, para. 168.

The Court's classification of racism as "a particularly invidious kind of discrimination", which "in view of its perilous consequences, requires from the authorities special vigilance and a vigorous reaction"[108] was further developed in its judgment in the *Timishev* case. The case involved a restriction on the applicant's right to liberty of movement solely on the ground of his ethnic origin and thus constituted racial discrimination. The Court observed that:

> Ethnicity and race are related and overlapping concepts. Whereas the notion of race is rooted in the idea of biological classification of human beings into subspecies according to morphological features such as skin colour or facial characteristics, ethnicity has its origin in the idea of societal groups marked by common nationality, tribal affiliation, religious faith, shared language, or cultural and traditional origins and backgrounds.[109]

The Court's judgment in *Timishev* iron-plated its earlier findings by adding that "no difference in treatment which is based exclusively or to a decisive extent on a person's ethnic origin is capable of being objectively justified in a contemporary democratic society built on the principles of pluralism and respect for different cultures".[110]

In another string of cases, the Court has gradually become more sensitive to the plight of Gypsies in the UK. In *Buckley*, the Court held that "[T]he vulnerable position of gypsies as a minority means that some special consideration should be given to their needs and their different lifestyle both in the relevant regulatory framework and in reaching decisions in particular cases".[111] Building on this statement in *Chapman*, the Court ruled that there is consequently "a positive obligation imposed on the Contracting States by virtue of Article 8[112] to facilitate the gypsy way of life".[113] The Court also acknowledged "an emerging international

---

108 *Nachova & others v. Bulgaria, op. cit.*, para. 145. See also: *Timishev v. Russia, op. cit.*, para. 56 and *D.H. & others v. the Czech Republic, op. cit.*, para. 176.

109 *Timishev v. Russia, op. cit.*, para. 55.

110 *Ibid.*, para. 56. See also, *D.H. and others, op. cit.*, para. 176.

111 *Buckley v. United Kingdom*, Judgment of the European Court of Human Rights of 26 August 1996, para. 76, 80, 84. See also, *Chapman v. United Kingdom*, Judgment of the European Court of Human Rights of 18 January 2001, para. 96; *Connors v. United Kingdom*, Judgment of the European Court of Human Rights of 27 May 2004, para. 84.

112 [author's footnote] Article 8 (Right to respect for private and family life), ECHR, reads:
"1. Everyone has the right to respect for his private and family life, his home and his correspondence.
2. There shall be no interference by a public authority with the exercise of this right except such as is in accordance with the law and is necessary in a democratic society in the interests of national security, public safety or the economic well-being of the country, for the prevention of disorder or crime, for the protection of health or morals, or for the protection of the rights and freedoms of others."

113 *Chapman v. United Kingdom, op. cit.*, para. 96. See also, *Connors v. United Kingdom, op. cit.*, para. 84.

consensus amongst the Contracting States of the Council of Europe recognising the special needs of minorities and an obligation to protect their security, identity and lifestyle ([...] in particular the Framework Convention for the Protection of National Minorities), not only for the purpose of safeguarding the interests of the minorities themselves but to preserve a cultural diversity of value to the whole community".[114]

Nevertheless, neither *Buckley* nor *Chapman* led to the finding of a violation of the Convention.[115] In *Connors*, however, the Court went one step further and – in its application of the same principles to the facts of the case at hand – did find a violation of Article 8, ECHR. According to Kristin Henrard, "this gradual emergence of a sub-class of more specific minority standards for a certain type of minorities confirms that the field of minority rights is maturing and becoming more refined".[116] This statement has been borne out by subsequent case-law. In *D.H. and others v. Czech Republic*, a case involving procedures which led to disproportionately high numbers of Roma children being placed in segregated schools for children with mental disabilities, the Grand Chamber found a violation of Article 14 in conjunction with Article 2 of Protocol 1. The importance of the *D.H. and others* case derives both from the judgment itself and the manner in which it was reached. The Court set considerable store by relevant findings of the Advisory Committee on the FCNM, ECRI and the Council of Europe Commissioner for Human Rights, as well as sources extraneous to the Council of Europe, such as data or conclusions from the European Monitoring Centre on Racism and Xenophobia and CERD. Its reliance on such sources demonstrated its willingness to engage with a growing body of standard-setting and monitoring texts concerning minority rights. This development is further evidence of the importance of non-binding standard-setting and monitoring work beyond its immediate focus. This kind of cross-fertilisation, or better, cross-corroboration, is conducive to overall consistency across the approaches adopted by various international (and especially Council of Europe) organs to specific themes.

2.2.2 Standard-setting by the Parliamentary Assembly of the Council of Europe

Over the years, the Council of Europe has witnessed a number of abortive attempts to mainstream minority rights, either by grafting a special protocol onto the ECHR, or by elaborating a separate, multilateral convention. Many of these attempts to

---

114 *Chapman v. United Kingdom*, *op. cit.*, para. 93. As discussed, *infra*, this impact of this statement was weakened by the Court's refusal to accept that the "emerging international consensus" was concrete enough to offer jurisprudential guidance, *ibid.*, para. 94.

115 See, however, the joint dissenting opinion of Judges Pastor Ridruejo, Bonello, Tulkens, Straznicka, Lorenzen, Fischbach and Casadevall in *Chapman*.

116 Kristin Henrard, "Charting the gradual emergence of a more robust level of minority protection: minority specific instruments and the European Union", 22 *Netherlands Quarterly of Human Rights* (Issue No. 4, 2004), pp. 559–584, at 574.

push the minority rights agenda within the Council of Europe have originated in the Parliamentary Assembly of the Council of Europe (PACE). Table 1 provides an overview of PACE Recommendations dealing with minority rights *in general* and summarises their main proposals.[117] It should be noted in passing that most of these Recommendations also urged (the Committee of Ministers to press) Member States to sign and ratify various relevant Council of Europe instruments (eg. the European Charter for Regional or Minority Languages, the Framework Convention for the Protection of National Minorities, the European Charter of Local Self-Government, Protocol No. 12 to the ECHR).[118]

Table 1

Recommendation	**Title**	**Main points**
213 (1959)	Position of national minorities in Europe	– Encourages negotiations and peaceful settlements of disputes between States concerning the status of national minorities
285 (1961)	Rights of national minorities	– Recommends CM initiative for inclusion in 2nd Protocol to ECHR of article securing cultural, linguistic, educational and religious rights of persons belonging to national minorities
1134 (1990)	Rights of minorities	– Full implementation of relevant OSCE commitments – CM to draft new Protocol to ECHR on protection of minority rights
1177 (1992)	Rights of minorities	– Proposed convention on protection of minorities – deficient supervisory machinery; additional protocol to ECHR preferable – In addition, CM to adopt declaration on principles of minority rights protection – CM to set up new mediation body to: observe and record; advise and forestall; discuss and mediate
1201 (1993)	Additional protocol on the rights of minorities to the European Convention on Human Rights	– Text of proposed additional protocol to ECHR – Definition of "national minority"

117 For comprehensive treatment, see Patrick Thornberry and María Amor Martín Estébanez, *Minority Rights in Europe* (Strasbourg, Council of Europe, 2004), Chapter 8 – 'The evolution of the work of the Parliamentary Assembly in relation to minority protection', pp. 387–458.

118 Rec. 1201 (1993), para. 4; (1231 (1994), para. 8(i)); Rec. 1255 (1995), paras. 6, 12a; Rec. 1285 (1996), para. 16; (Rec 1300 (1996), paras. 7, 10, 11); Rec. 1345 (1997), paras. (4), 11; Rec. 1492 (2001), paras. (6, 9) 12; Rec. 1623 (2003), paras. 5, 11, 12; Rec. 1773 (2006), para. 13.1; Rec. 1904 (2010), paras. 1.1, 1.2.

Recommendation	Title	Main points
1231 (1994)	Follow-up to the Council of Europe Vienna Summit	– CM should revise decision on additional protocol to ECHR – Failing that, CSCE commitments should be reflected in draft framework convention and draft ECHR protocol on cultural rights
1255 (1995)	Protection of rights of national minorities	– Assessment of text of FCNM – Recommendations for strengthening AC – Provisions of Rec. 1201 for inclusion in additional protocol to ECHR on cultural rights
1285 (1996)	Rights of national minorities	– Recommendations for making AC more independent, effective and transparent – Resume and conclude drafting of additional protocol to ECHR on cultural matters
1300 (1996)	Protection of rights of minorities	– Completion and revision of Rec. 1285's proposals for the AC
1345 (1997)	Protection of national minorities	– Regret that PACE proposals for election of AC not followed – CM to resume work on draft protocol to ECHR on cultural matters – Increase cooperation with EU to ensure CoE monitoring relied on more systematically by EU
1492 (2001)	Rights of national minorities	– CM to draft additional protocol to FCNM empowering ECtHRs or other CoE general judicial authority to give advisory opinions on interpretation of FCNM – CM to draft additional protocol to ECHR on rights of national minorities, drawing on Rec. 1201 and incl. the definition therein – Attach to CoE Commissioner on Human Rights officer with special responsibility for minority rights
1623 (2003)	Rights of national minorities	– CM to draft additional protocol to FCNM empowering ECtHRs to give advisory opinions on interpretation of FCNM – Revision of certain monitoring procedures under FCNM – Encourage AC to adopt thematic approach to issues

Recommendation	Title	Main points
1773 (2006)	The 2003 guidelines on the use of minority languages in the broadcast media and the Council of Europe standards: need to enhance cooperation and synergy with the OSCE	– CM to increase signatures and ratifications (without reservations and restrictive declarations) of ECRML, FCNM and ECTT – CM invite States to ensure improved access to broadcast media in own languages, in accordance with leading CoE standards and 2003 Guidelines – CM to regularly take 2003 Guidelines into account in monitoring of implementation of ECRML and FCNM – CM to instruct that relevant concerns be considered in any revision of ECTT – Encourage further synergies between CoE and OSCE HCNM, also involving civil society
1904 (2010)	Minority protection in Europe: best practices and deficiencies in implementation of common standards	– CM to enhance efforts for speedy ratification of FCNM, ECRML and Protocol 12, ECHR – CM to promote intercultural dialogue and education in interests of diversity and social cohesion – CM to pursue international cooperation to ensure coherent interpretation and implementation of policies for protection of national minorities – CM to ensure dissemination of information about best practices on the implementation of the FCNM – CM to encourage AC to develop thematic reports on specific issues, in particular minority groups' participation in socio-economic and cultural life

The most noteworthy of the ultimately unsuccessful Council of Europe initiatives to ensure greater prominence and protection for minority rights were:

- Proposal for a European Convention for the Protection of Minorities by the European Commission for Democracy through Law;[119]
- PACE Recommendation 1201.

The Proposal for a European Convention for the Protection of Minorities by the European Commission for Democracy through Law (hereinafter "the Venice

119 Adopted by ECommDL on 8 February 1991. See further: Giorgio Malinverni, "The draft Convention for the Protection of Minorities – The Proposal of the European Commission for Democracy through Law", 12 *Human Rights Law Journal* (No. 6–7, 1991) pp. 265–273. It is interesting to note that this draft instrument was originally designed for application not only within CoE States, but also in States which had yet to join the CoE.

Commission") contains a number of noteworthy features. In substantive terms, it includes an explicit safeguard against "any activity capable of threatening their existence" (Article 3(1)). It also guards against attempts at forced assimilation of minorities on the part of State authorities (Article 6). The particular circumstances of internal minorities (or minorities within minorities, i.e., "any region where those who belong to a minority represent the majority of the population") is also countenanced (Article 16 *juncto* Article 15(2)). Concern for such minorities is often merely implied or derived rather than explicitly set forth in international instruments.

One cause for concern, however, was the inclusion of a so-called "loyalty clause" (Article 15). The operative provision read: "[a]ny person who belongs to a minority shall loyally fulfil the obligations deriving from his status as a national of his State".[120] At first glance, this provision may appear innocuous, or even a reasonable expectation of *quid-pro-quo* for those wishing to benefit from minority rights. Nevertheless, one must not overlook the failure of the reasonable theory behind such a provision to be matched with similar reasonableness in practice. Such clauses have frequently attracted criticism for providing States with a convenient excuse for denying minority rights to certain minority groups whose political objectives do not coincide with their own (see further, *infra*). More often than not, calls for the introduction of loyalty clauses for persons belonging to national minorities, or non-nationals generally, are inherently discriminatory and are coated in only the thinnest veneer of objectivity.

The observance of States' undertakings in respect of the Convention would have been entrusted to a new body, the European Committee for the Protection of Minorities (Article 18). The Committee would have comprised "a number of members equal to that of the Parties" (Article 19(1)), known for their "competence" (not expertise or experience!) in human rights and "in particular the fields covered by" the draft Convention (Article 19). Members would have been elected by the CoE Committee of Ministers (making the election procedure a highly political exercise); the Committee would have held its meetings in camera, gathering "as the circumstances require, at least once a year" (Articles 20–22). The highlighted provisions, if they had ever been implemented, would have amounted to serious procedural deficiencies and would have greatly hampered the efficiency of the Committee in carrying out its mandate. The proposition that it could devise its own Rules of Procedure (Article 22) would have been cold comfort in an already restricted zone of operational autonomy: (i) "[States] Parties shall provide the Committee with the facilities necessary to carry out its tasks" (Article 23); (ii) the Committee would forward States reports (see *infra*) to the CoE Committee of Ministers with its observations (Article 24(2)), and (iii) a majority of two-thirds of

120 Article 15(1).

all Committee members would have been required before the Committee could make "any necessary recommendations to a Party" (Article 24(3)).

The proposal envisaged a separate Convention[121] which would have relied on its own protection machinery (rather than relying upon the existing adjudicative organs of the European Convention on Human Rights). The draft Convention foresaw three means of control: obligatory periodic State reporting (Article 24); optional State petitions (Article 25) and optional individual petitions (Article 26). As signalled in the previous paragraph, a two-thirds majority of Committee members was required before the Committee could "make any necessary recommendations to a [State] Party", which appears quite a demanding minimum requirement for engaging with a State. The use of the term "necessary" also suggests that only very serious matters could be addressed in this context, and not matters that are not quite so extreme, yet nevertheless of considerable importance. No provision was made for sanctions arising out of the State reporting mechanism, nor was it set out what role the CoE Committee of Ministers should play subsequent to its receipt of State reports and the Committee's observations, apart from the vague formulation "may take any follow-up action it thinks fit in order to ensure respect of the Convention" (Article 29(3)).

The provision for inter-State complaints was styled as optional owing to the political sensitivities involved in minority issues: it was submitted that if this provision were to be compulsory, it would dissuade States from ratifying the Convention. In a confusing and self-contradictory logic, it was equally submitted that "contrary to the experience found in the framework of the ECHR, in such a politically sensitive area as minorities, a large number of State petitions would be brought".[122] Similarly, the right of individual petition was rendered contingent on the State targeted by a complaint having first accepted the competence of the Committee to receive such petitions; another factor likely to limit the effectiveness of the control machinery.

PACE Recommendation 1201 proved to be a very hot political potato, for two main reasons. First, by setting out a catalogue of rights for national minorities in the form of a proposed additional protocol to the ECHR, the clear intention was to *ipso facto* render those rights justiciable. The consequences of such an approach, had it been endorsed at the highest level, would have been very far-reaching. Second, the Recommendation strode boldly into territory where no other IGO-angels had ever

---

121 See further: Opinion of the European Commission for Democracy through Law on the proposal drawn up by the Committee on Legal Affairs and Human Rights for an additional protocol to the European Convention on Human Rights concerning the rights of minorities (AS/Jur (44) 23 and AS/Jur (44) 41) drawn up by Giorgio Malinverni, 7 January 1993. This document compares the PACE and Venice Commission approaches.

122 Giorgio Malinverni, "The draft Convention for the Protection of Minorities – The Proposal of the European Commission for Democracy through Law", *op. cit.*, p. 269.

dared to tread: it sought to bring the highly contested concept of "national minority" within firm definitional parameters. According to Article 1 of the proposed additional protocol:

> the expression "national minority" refers to a group of persons in a state who:
>
> a. reside on the territory of that state and are citizens thereof;
> b. maintain longstanding, firm and lasting ties with that state;
> c. display distinctive ethnic, cultural, religious or linguistic characteristics;
> d. are sufficiently representative, although smaller in number than the rest of the population of that state or of a region of that state;
> e. are motivated by a concern to preserve together that which constitutes their common identity, including their culture, their traditions, their religion or their language.

Any possible disputes about the substantive content of the proposed additional protocol were eclipsed by the controversy surrounding the aforementioned points of justiciability and definitional scope. As it happens, the substantive articles in the draft text were largely uncontroversial, with the possible exception of Article 11, which provided, *inter alia*, for "appropriate local or autonomous authorities" for minorities.[123] It did so in the following terms, which some considered to have the potential to lead to territorial destabilisation:

> In the regions where they are in a majority the persons belonging to a national minority shall have the right to have at their disposal appropriate local or autonomous authorities or to have a special status, matching the specific historical and territorial situation and in accordance with the domestic legislation of the state.

The draft additional Protocol put forward in PACE Recommendation 1201 was rejected by the heads of State and Government of the Member States of the Council of Europe at the Vienna Summit in 1993. Instead, the heads of States and Governments instructed the Committee of Ministers to: (i) "draft with minimum delay a framework convention specifying the principles which contracting states commit themselves to respect, in order to assure the protection of national minorities [...]"; (ii) begin drafting a protocol complementing the ECHR "in the cultural field by provisions guaranteeing individual rights, in particular for persons belonging to national minorities". The first instruction led to the adoption of the Framework Convention for the Protection of National Minorities in 1995, but the second led

---

123 It is worth noting in passing that although the draft additional Protocol provided for freedom of association for minorities, as well as certain autonomous measures, it lacked any express general provision for their effective participation in public life. See generally: Opinion on the interpretation of Article 11 of the draft Protocol to the European Convention on Human Rights appended to Recommendation 1201 of the Parliamentary Assembly, Venice Commission, 22 March 1996.

only to fitful periods of work, and the project is currently in abeyance, with little evidence of intentions to reactivate it.[124]

Nevertheless, despite the set-back at the Vienna Summit, PACE Recommendation 1201 continues to hold considerable relevance as a point of reference.[125] Since the Summit, the PACE has consistently argued – in the face of considerable political adversity – for the adoption of Recommendation 1201.[126] In its Recommendation 1231, the PACE expressed its deep regret[127] that the Summit had not followed its Recommendation 1201, and did not hesitate to call on the Committee of Ministers to revise that decision.[128] The PACE stuck to its guns in Recommendation 1255, reaffirming its commitment to the principles and definition contained in Recommendation 1201; pointing out shortcomings of the FCNM; insisting on the urgency of an additional protocol to the ECHR on cultural matters and specifying the principles from Rec. 1201 which could most usefully be incorporated into the same.

As noted by the PACE itself, "the political undertakings and standards" set out in the draft additional protocol contained in Rec. 1201 "have been raised to the status of legal obligations in friendship treaties drawn up between various member states of the Council of Europe".[129] It even went on to speculate that "[t]hese treaty obligations might eventually acquire customary status at regional level".[130]

Under PACE Order 484, the PACE's Legal Affairs Committee is required to have regard to the draft Protocol in its assessment of applicant States' suitability for admission to the CoE.[131] It has been pointed out that this requirement means that in practice, applicant States are expected to meet standards of minority rights

---

124 For an overview of the process, see: Patrick Thornberry & Maria Amor Martin Estebanez, *Minority Rights in Europe*, *op. cit.*, p. 205.

125 See, for example, European Parliament resolution on the protection of minorities and anti-discrimination policies in an enlarged Europe (2005/2008(INI)), 8 June 2005, OJ C 124 E/405 of 25 May 2006, para. 7.

126 See, for example, Rec. 1285 (1996), para. 15; Rec. 1300 (1996), para. 2; Rec. 1492 (2000), para. 7 and 12 (xi).

127 PACE Recommendation 1231 (1994) on the follow-up to the Council of Europe Vienna Summit, para. 5. See also, Rec. 1255, para. 4; Rec. 1285, para. 12;.

128 *Ibid.*, para. 8(ii).

129 Rec. 1492 (2000), para. 8.

130 *Ibid.*

131 More specifically, the PACE "instructs its Committee on Legal Affairs and Human Rights [...] to make scrupulously sure when examining requests for accession to the Council of Europe that the rights included in this protocol [set out in Recommendation 1201] are respected by the applicant countries": Point 2(ii) of Order No. 484 (1993) on an additional protocol on the rights of national minorities to the European Convention on Human Rights, adopted by the PACE on 1 February 1993.

protection that were deemed politically unpalatable (read: too far-reaching) by existing Member States.[132] In this context, it is difficult to refute accusations of double standards or a two-tiered approach, or perceptions of an "East-West divide".[133] Indeed, it should be noted that claims of differentiated approaches to minority rights protection that are geo-politically inspired are not limited to the Council of Europe context: they have also found resonance in a broader European context.[134]

Accusations of double standards within the Council of Europe as regards minority rights protection have been propagated in various quarters and at various stages. These accusations can be explained (but that is not to say excused) by the specific historical context in which the Council of Europe's interest in minority rights was re-ignited. The catalyst was certainly the drawing back of the Iron Curtain at the very beginning of the 1990s. The CSCE played a trail-blazing role in the recognition of acute minority-related issues in the former Soviet Bloc, and the Council of Europe found itself obliged to gear up to follow that trail. Despite the fact that its own house was not in order, the Council was beginning to square up to States in Central and Eastern Europe to confront them on their track record regarding minority rights protection.[135] The predicament arising from this state of affairs is described by André Liebich in the following manner:

> Looking eastward, the Council's mandate clearly encompassed norm setting, supervision and enforcement of minority rights. However, this mandate could only be defined in universal legal terms which, *nolens volens*, encompassed the Western States as well. There was little point in simply affirming that West Europe did not have a minority problem whereas East Europe did.[136]

---

132 See, for example, Geoff Gilbert, "Minority Rights Under the Council of Europe", in Peter Cumper & Steven Wheatley, Eds., *Minority Rights in the 'New' Europe* (Great Britain, Kluwer Law International, 1999), pp. 53–70, at 62–63.

133 See further, *ibid.*, and also, Heinrich Klebes, "The Council of Europe's Framework Convention for the Protection of National Minorities", 16 *Human Rights Law Journal* (No. 1–3, 1995) pp. 92–98, at 92.

134 See further, Kristin Henrard, "'The EU, Double Standards and Minority Protection': A Double Redefinition and Future Prospects", in Kristin Henrard, Ed., *Double Standards Pertaining to Minority Protection*, *op. cit.*, pp. 21–70, and generally, Annelies Verstichel *et al.*, Eds., *The Framework Convention for the Protection of National Minorities: A Useful Pan-European Instrument?* (Antwerp/Oxford/Portland, Intersentia, 2008).

135 There was a certain feeling of *déjà vu* in the recent accessions to the European Union as regards the attention paid to minority rights in the Copenhagen criteria (see further elsewhere in this chapter).

136 André Liebich, "Janus at Strasbourg: The Council of Europe between East and West", *Helsinki Monitor* (No. 1, 1999), pp. 7–17, at 12 (see also p. 11).

2.2.3 Framework Convention for the Protection of National Minorities (FCNM)[137]

The Preamble to the Framework Convention states that it was conceived of pursuant to the Declaration of the Heads of State and Government of the Member States of the Council of Europe adopted in Vienna on 9 October 1993. It goes on to list – "in a non-exhaustive way" – "three further sources of inspiration for the content" of the Framework Convention, i.e., the ECHR and various relevant United Nations (UN) and C/OSCE instruments containing commitments for the protection of national minorities.[138] The relevant documentary corpus within the UN and OSCE systems is by no means negligible (notwithstanding the fact that some documents are more political than legal in their coloration). But, as already mentioned, the crucible of inspiration has a broader circumference than merely the span of the UN and OSCE systems.

This point is of cardinal importance for the organic growth of the FCNM, as it anticipates (however implicitly) the practice of explicitly referring to international standards in the monitoring process (see further, *infra*). In this practice, pertinence should be the guiding principle, thereby inviting the invocation (where appropriate) of other types of hard and "soft law", where appropriate. This point is further reinforced when considered in light of Article 22, which reads:

> Nothing in the present framework Convention shall be construed as limiting or derogating from any of the human rights and fundamental freedoms which may be ensured under the laws of any Contracting Party or under any other agreement to which it is a Party.

The potential of Article 22 for the future development of minority rights protection is rather understated. Most States Parties to the FCNM are also subject to the ICCPR and other international treaties. In instances where Article 27, ICCPR, for example, is more generous than the FCNM in the protection it guarantees for particular minority rights, one could conceivably argue – on the basis of Article 22, FCNM – that the particular protection provided under the FCNM ought to be raised to match that of the ICCPR. Whatever about the resistance it would be likely to meet from States Parties if it were to be translated into practice, this argument does boast certain theoretical appeal.

---

137 For academic commentaries on the FCNM, see: Marc Weller, Ed., *The Rights of Minorities in Europe: A Commentary on the European Framework Convention for the Protection of National Minorities* (Oxford and New York, Oxford University Press, 2005); Patrick Thornberry and María Amor Martín Estébanez, *Minority Rights in Europe*, *op. cit.*, Chapter 2.

138 Explanatory Report to the Framework Convention, *op. cit.*, para. 23.

Any analysis of the FCNM must necessarily begin with its name, which points to the type of convention it actually is: a framework; lexically, a support structure to be built upon, a structural plan or basis of a project. Key to this conception is the leeway accorded States Parties in their honouring of the commitments entered into under the Convention. This is rendered explicit by para. 11 of the Explanatory Report to the FCNM:

> In view of the range of different situations and problems to be resolved, a choice was made for a framework Convention which contains mostly programme-type provisions setting out objectives which the Parties undertake to pursue. These provisions, which will not be directly applicable, leave the States concerned a measure of discretion in the implementation of the objectives which they have undertaken to achieve, thus enabling them to take particular circumstances into account.

The discretion conferred on States as a matter of principle is compounded firstly in the consistently cautious language used throughout the FCNM and secondly in the choice of monitoring structures and processes (see further, *infra*). As noted by the PACE, the FCNM "formulates a number of vaguely defined objectives and principles, the observation of which will be an obligation of the contracting states but not a right which individuals may invoke".[139] Conversely, apologists for the "framework" approach underline the situational diversity among States, and the consequent need for reliance on the margin of appreciation doctrine rather than a stricter, more normative type of approach.[140] This view favours placing the onus on States Parties to secure appropriate legislation and other measures in order to give domestic effect to the provisions of the FCNM.

It should be noted that to read potential for flexibility into the "vaguely defined objectives and principles" of the FCNM might well constitute no more than misplaced optimism. While one swallow does not make a summer, such a reading of the Convention backfired in *Chapman v. United Kingdom*. Significantly, the European Court of Human Rights observed that:

> there may be said to be an emerging international consensus amongst the Contracting States of the Council of Europe recognising the special needs of minorities and an obligation to protect their security, identity and lifestyles ([...] in particular the Framework Convention for the Protection of National Minorities), not only for the

139 Para. 7, PACE Recommendation 1255 (1995) on the protection of the rights of national minorities.

140 Frank Steketee, "The Framework Convention: A Piece of Art or a Tool for Action?", 8 *International Journal on Minority and Group Rights* (2001), pp. 1–15, at 4.

> purpose of safeguarding the interests of the minorities themselves but to preserve a cultural diversity of value to the whole community.[141]

Nevertheless, in a somewhat disingenuous *non-sequitur*, the Court then went on to state that is was not persuaded that:

> the consensus is sufficiently concrete for it to derive any guidance as to the conduct or standards which Contracting States consider desirable in any particular situation. The framework convention, for example, sets out general principles and goals but the signatory States were unable to agree on means of implementation. This reinforces the Court's view that the complexity and sensitivity of the issues involved in policies balancing the interests of the general population, in particular with regard to environmental protection, and the interests of a minority with possibly conflicting requirements renders the Court's role a strictly supervisory one.[142]

Thus, the Court spurned the opportunity at hand to engage with substantive rights envisaged by the FCNM by interpreting the vague and general wording as evidence of a lack of consensus among Contracting States. This reasoning is unsatisfactory, as the large number of ratifications (notwithstanding a certain number of interpretative declarations/reservations), must surely be persuasive evidence of a certain commonality of understanding and purpose. Whereas the Court has not repeated its apparent doubts about the solidity of the nascent consensus in certain subsequent considerations of the question,[143] its reluctance to engage with the implications of the consensus is a source of concern. In the past, the Court has been slow to acknowledge swells of similar practice across growing numbers of States in respect of other rights too. The Court's judgment in *Sirbu v. Moldova*[144] (a case concerning, *inter alia*, Article 10, ECHR and public access to official governmental information) has been criticised for failing to give due cognisance to the fact that "[A]t the present time, most if not all Member States of the Council of Europe have put in place laws and structures allowing for varying levels of access to official documents".[145] As such, the Court's judgment "did not give any in-depth exploration to the developing nature of the right to information at the national level".[146] It

141 *Chapman v. United Kingdom*, *op. cit.*, para. 93. See also, *D.H. & others v. Czech Republic*, *op. cit.*, para. 181.

142 *Ibid.*, para. 94.

143 See, for example, *D.H. & others v. Czech Republic*, *op. cit.*, para. 181, and *Sampanis & others v. Greece*, Judgment of the European Court of Human Rights (First Section) of 5 June 2008, para. 73.

144 *Sirbu and others v. Moldova*, Judgment of the European Court of Human Rights (Fourth Section) of 15 June 2004.

145 Tarlach McGonagle, "Workshop Report: the Changing Hues of Political Expression in the Media", in Susanne Nikoltchev, Ed., *IRIS Special: Political Debate and the Role of the Media – The Fragility of Free Speech* (European Audiovisual Observatory, Strasbourg, 2005), pp. 1–30, at 8.

146 *Ibid.*

was another few years before the Court began to show a real willingness to give legal recognition to a right of access to (State-held) information.[147]

Definitional uncertainty dogs the FCNM, just as it does other leading international instruments dealing with minority rights protection. The drafters of the FCNM deliberately eschewed the opportunity to fashion a definition of (national) minority, opting for a "pragmatic approach" as it was evident to them that it would have been impossible at that point in time "to arrive at a definition capable of mustering general support of all Council of Europe member States".[148] One of the prevailing currents of thought amongst the drafters was that it would be better to forge ahead even without the desired ballast of a definition.

In other words, progress on minority rights protection should not be held hostage to reaching (political) consensus on an apposite definition, especially given the fear that any such definition "would most likely be based on the lowest common denominator and would, by definition, exclude any evolution".[149] A closely related – if somewhat starker – argument is that any progress on minority rights protection should not be jeopardised by insistence on the prior resolution of definitional disagreements.[150]

Given the insoluble nature of the definitional question, this example of *realpolitik* is understandable. Furthermore, it will be recalled that a number of IGOs and academic commentators subscribe to the view that minorities are generally recognisable and that borderline cases can be determined on an *ad hoc* basis.

It is widely accepted that there is no consensus as to the meaning of the term "national minority",[151] and as has already been noted, the term is particularly troublesome. Geoff Gilbert has usefully explored the essential distinction between the two "discrete meanings" of the term "national minority".[152] The first,

---

147 Relevant jurisprudential developments can be traced through: *Sdružení Jihočeské Matky v. Czech Republic*, Admissibility Decision of the European Court of Human Rights (Fifth Section) of 10 July 2006, Application No. 19101/03; *Társaság a Szabadságjogokért v. Hungary*, Judgment of the European Court of Human Rights (Second Section) of 14 April 2009; *Kenedi v. Hungary*, Judgment of the European Court of Human Rights (Second Section) of 26 May 2009.

148 Para. 12, Explanatory Report to the FCNM.

149 Frank Steketee, "The Framework Convention: A Piece of Art or a Tool for Action?", *op. cit.*, at 6.

150 Heinrich Klebes, "The Council of Europe's Framework Convention for the Protection of National Minorities", *op. cit.*, at 93.

151 This was a conclusion of the Steering Committee for Human Rights (CDDH) which played an instrumental role in the drafting of the FCNM: see para. 4, Explanatory Report to the FCNM.

152 Geoff Gilbert, "The Council of Europe and Minority Rights", 18 *Human Rights Quarterly* (1996) pp. 160–189, at 165–166; 169–170.

"nationality as a precondition", insists that the recognition of minority status within a given State is contingent on members of the group being nationals of that State. In the second sense, the adjective is used rather to designate a particular type of minority in the context of a broader classification scheme. So understood, a national minority "is one that can be distinguished due to its ethnicity, religion, language, culture, or traditions, but which might also have either autonomist aspirations or, more likely, a kin-state".[153]

Heinrich Klebes, in his commentary on the Convention, argues that 'national minority' "refers to a minority on the national territory (the territory of the State)".[154] He continues by discounting the suggestion that the notion involves an ethnic link with another nation. Gilbert, on the other hand, posits that the term, when used in a European context, has traditionally "referred to those minorities with a kin-state".[155]

Another attempt to decipher the meaning of the term "national minority" could be built on extrapolation from contiguous debates waged in the United Nations. Such an approach, however, is a hopeless *cul-de-sac*. Rosalyn Higgins has posited that the UN Human Rights Committee interprets "ethnic" as subsuming "national", but the inclusion of the latter adjective in the UN Declaration on the Rights of Persons Belonging to National or Ethnic, Religious and Linguistic Minorities suggests that the terms tend towards synonymity, or at the very least have a high degree of conceptual/semantic congruence.

Given that Higgins understands "national" as being narrower than "ethnic", she is concerned that this could lead to a more restrictive reading of relevant provisions.[156] In this vein of logic, such concerns could equally arise, *mutatis mutandis*, from the wording employed in the FCNM. However, it has conversely been argued that on the basis of contextual analysis that "national" can only be taken in the UN Declaration as intended for the purposes of classification.[157]

---

153 *Ibid.*, p. 169.

154 Heinrich Klebes, "The Council of Europe's Framework Convention on National Minorities", *op. cit.*, p. 93.

155 Geoff Gilbert, "The Council of Europe and Minority Rights", *op. cit.*, at 169.

156 Rosalyn Higgins, "Minority Rights: Discrepancies and Divergencies Between the International Covenant and the Council of Europe System", in Rick Lawson & Matthijs de Blois, Eds., *The Dynamics of the Protection of Human Rights in Europe: Essays in Honour of Henry G. Schermers (Vol. III)* (Dordrecht, Martinus Nijhoff Publishers, 1994), pp. 195–209, at 202.

157 Geoff Gilbert, "The Council of Europe and Minority Rights", *op. cit.*, at 166.

2.2.3(i) Ceci n'est pas une minorité!

The definitional vacuum and the introduction of the notoriously unclear term "national" minority have together given rise to a phenomenon which could be termed, after the famous painter René Magritte, "*ceci n'est pas une minorité*".[158] This involves a notable tendency among States to enter (interpretative) declarations of the term (national) minority upon ratification of the FCNM (eg. Austria, Belgium, Denmark, Estonia, Germany, Luxembourg, Poland, Russia, Sweden, Switzerland and the former Yugoslav Republic of Macedonia). All but one of these declarations are similar in tenor, explaining how the FCNM will apply *ratione personae* on their respective territories.

The exception is the Russian declaration, which has been called an "anti-declaration" by one commentator[159] because it categorically opposes the unilateral determination of which national minorities should be entitled to protection under the FCNM. This declaration would appear to have been motivated by concern for the fate of Russian minorities in a number of ex-Soviet States. Its integral text is as follows:

> The Russian Federation considers that none [*sic*] is entitled to include unilaterally in reservations or declarations, made while signing or ratifying the Framework Convention for the Protection of National Minorities, a definition of the term "national minority", which is not contained in the Framework Convention. In the opinion of the Russian Federation, attempts to exclude from the scope of the Framework Convention the persons who permanently reside in the territory of States Parties to the Framework Convention and previously had a citizenship but have been arbitrarily deprived of it, contradict the purpose of the Framework Convention for the Protection of National Minorities.[160]

Some controversy has surrounded the question of whether these declarations should be regarded as (interpretative) declarations *stricto sensu*, or reservations from the perspective of international law.[161] Given the silence of the FCNM on declarations and reservations thereto, recourse must be had to the Vienna Convention on the

158 For a discussion of Magritte's famous series of paintings, *La trahison des images* (1928/9), *Ceci n'est pas une pomme* (1964) and *Les deux mystères* (1966), see: Jacques Meuris, *Magritte* (Cologne, Taschen GmbH, 2004), pp. 128–132.

159 Stefan Troebst, "From paper to practice: The Council of Europe's Framework Convention for the protection of national minorities", 10 *Helsinki Monitor* (No. 1, 1999), pp. 19–26, at 24.

160 Declaration contained in the instrument of ratification deposited by the Russian Federation on 21 August 1998.

161 For a detailed discussion of this question, see: Maria Telalian, "European Framework Convention for the Protection of National Minorities and its Personal Scope of Application", in Gudmundur Alfredsson & Maria Stavropoulou, Eds., *Justice Pending: Indigenous Peoples and Other Good Causes* (The Hague, Martinus Nijhoff Publishers, 2002), pp. 117–135, esp. at 125–134.

Law of Treaties.[162] The Vienna Convention does not provide a definition of the term 'declaration', but it does set out that a 'reservation' is "a unilateral statement, however phrased or named, made by a State, when signing, ratifying, accepting, approving or acceding to a treaty, whereby it purports to exclude or to modify the legal effect of certain provisions of the treaty in their application to that State".[163] It would appear (*inter alia* from the *jurisprudence constante* of the International Court of Justice) that a declaration is non-binding and only aims to interpret a treaty and not to modify its legal effect. According to Maria Telalian:

> It is obvious that the decisive element for making a distinction between an interpretative declaration and a reservation is to be found in the intention of the states that have made the declaration. If that intention is to simply clarify the meaning of the treaty and not to exclude or modify its legal effect in its application to that state, then the said declaration is an interpretative one.[164]

Telalian concludes – on the basis of an analysis of the wording of the (interpretative) statements in light of the underlying objectives of the FCNM – that one can best speak of "declarations" here, as the proposed interpretations do not go against the grain of the Convention. Declarations entered to date have tended to reinforce certain aspects of the FCNM, deny the existence of national minorities on their territories, list the various national minorities within their jurisdiction to be protected under the HCNM and link definitions of national minorities to citizenship.[165] As pointed out by Alan Phillips, the last-named qualification is not referred to in either the FCNM or its Explanatory Report.[166] Such linkage is a source of concern for this reason alone, not to mention the general controversy surrounding attempts to premise the recognition of minority groups on the criterion of citizenship.[167]

The controversy pits polarised viewpoints against one another. Some argue vehemently that human rights are not about citizenship, whereas others consider the

---

162 United Nations Treaty Series, Vol. 1155, p. 331, adopted on 22 May 1969; entry into force on 27 January 1980.

163 Article 2(1)(d), *ibid.*

164 Maria Telalian, "European Framework Convention for the Protection of National Minorities and its Personal Scope", *op. cit.*, at 129.

165 See: Alan Phillips, *The Framework Convention for the Protection of National Minorities: A Policy Analysis* (London, Minority Rights Group International, 2002), p. 4.

166 *Ibid.*

167 Of relevance in this connection is the likely motivation behind Russia's Declaration, *supra*, i.e. the fate of Russians in Baltic countries, where the denial of citizenship has proved a *de facto* means of exclusion.

criterion of citizenship to be "a foundational thesis"[168] of minority rights protection. As to the former, John Packer has argued:

> [...] human rights are the entitlements of human beings, and exactly not (as a general matter) to be conditioned on citizenship. Indeed, this is one of the great achievements of the post-second world war order – that it is a matter of international concern that the State respect, protect and ensure the inherent and inalienable rights of all *human beings* within its jurisdiction, no longer leaving citizens at the mercy of their governments or aliens to depend upon the possibility (not entitlement) of diplomatic protection. Still, citizenship may be relevant for certain rights [...].[169]

The conflicting stance is summed up by André Liebich as: "[...] a foundational thesis, implicitly or explicitly accepted in international instruments, has been that minorities can only be composed of citizens of the state in question".[170] The present analysis favours and follows Packer's stance.

Without a definition of the foggy term 'national minority', there was a certain inevitability about the subsequent uncoordinated spate of unilateral interpretations by States Parties. It should be noted that the expression of such interpretations is not limited to those statements made by States Parties upon signature or ratification of the FCNM. A number of States Reports also contain further stipulations on the ambit of application of the FCNM in their countries. However, the trend towards unilateral interpretations must give rise to concerns for the consistent interpretation and application of the FCNM at the national level. Another cause of concern is that States are left with too much freedom to determine the minorities to be covered under the FCNM, thereby deviating from the crucial principle established by the PCIJ in the *Minority Schools in Albania* case, namely that a minority is a question of fact (see *supra*).

The device of (interpretative) declarations is a very useful means for States to set themselves up as the ultimate arbiters of which minorities would enjoy the benefits of the FCNM within their own State boundaries. In particular, it offers them a less heavy-handed way of seeking to restrict the scope of application of the treaty to their own jurisdiction than a reservation (which involves a series of procedural formalities,[171] as well as carrying greater import). The usefulness of such

168 André Liebich, "Janus at Strasbourg: The Council of Europe between East and West", *op. cit.*, at 14.

169 John Packer, "Situating the Framework Convention in a wider context", in *Filling the Frame: Five years of monitoring the Framework Convention for the Protection of National Minorities*, *op. cit.*, pp. 43–51, at 45.

170 André Liebich, "Janus at Strasbourg: The Council of Europe between East and West", *op. cit.*, at 14.

171 See further, Articles 19–23 of the Vienna Convention on the Law of Treaties.

declarations must not, however, be abused by States authorities. By employing "different labels" or "additional criteria", declarations must not be allowed to insidiously serve as smoke-screens for the real exclusionary intent of States Parties.[172]

One would, however, naturally expect any excesses to be checked by the monitoring procedures. According to Frank Steketee, notwithstanding States' margin of appreciation in such matters, "it is incumbent on the monitoring mechanism at international level, and notably the Committee of Ministers, when 'evaluating the adequacy of the measures taken by the Parties to give effect to the principles set out in the framework Convention', also to assess the proper application *ratione personae* and to guard against any discriminatory or arbitrary exclusions".[173] The Committee of Ministers has been reluctant to pronounce its disapproval of any of the declarations submitted by States Parties to the FCNM and it would conceivably be loath to do so, given its highly political and politicised nature (see further *infra*). Nevertheless, it has urged States to exercise caution when considering whether to submit reservations and declarations, and to do so sparingly.[174] The Advisory Committee also scrutinises Declarations, with a view to verifying that they do not involve either arbitrary or unjustified distinctions between groups.[175] To date, it has "noted" a number of Declarations.[176] Vigilance has also been called for on the part of civil society in the policing of State declarations.[177]

A few words about the nature of the substantive rights set forth in the FCNM are now in order. First of all, the phraseology broadly follows trends established by other relevant international instruments. Article 3(2), for instance, reads: "Persons belonging to national minorities may exercise the rights and enjoy the freedoms flowing from the principles enshrined in the present framework Convention individually as well as in community with others". While Article 3(2) does give a favourable nod in the direction of the collective exercise of individual rights, the

---

172 See further, Gudmundur Alfredsson, "A Frame an Incomplete Painting: Comparison of the Framework Convention for the Protection of National Minorities with International Standards and Monitoring Procedures", 7 *International Journal on Minority and Group Rights* (2000), pp. 291–304, at 296.

173 Frank Steketee, "The Framework Convention: A Piece of Art or a Tool for Action?", *op. cit.*, at 6.

174 See further: Rights of national minorities, PACE Recommendation 1623 (2003), *op. cit.*, para. 6.

175 Rainer Hofmann, "Protecting the Rights of National Minorities in Europe. First Experiences with the Council of Europe Framework Convention for the Protection of National Minorities", 44 *German Yearbook of International Law/Jahrbuch für Internationales Recht* (2001), pp. 237–269, at 254–256.

176 See further, Kristin Henrard, "Charting the gradual emergence of a more robust level of minority protection: minority specific instruments and the European Union", *op. cit.*, at 567 *et seq.*

177 Alan Phillips, *The Framework Convention for the Protection of National Minorities: A Policy Analysis*, *op. cit.*, p. 4.

Explanatory Report to the FCNM curtly states that group rights as such are not countenanced.[178]

Gudmundur Alfredsson laments the terseness of the Explanatory Report's elaboration on the FCNM's exclusive recognition of individual rights.[179] It merely states: "[i]n this respect, the framework Convention follows the approach of texts adopted by other international organisations".[180] Terseness is never an obvious bedfellow of accuracy, and Alfredsson would appear to be suggesting – correctly, it must be added – that this explanation is disingenuously short. The "texts" (a very vague term) referred to are not identified, nor are the relevant international organisations specified either. Even if one were to take the explanation at face value or on a very general plane, it is not totally accurate. Collective rights are envisaged in the legal and political standards of a number of organisations.[181]

2.2.3(ii) Water in the wine and holes in the cheese[182]

The programmatic character of the FCNM has resulted in the language chosen prioritising progress and performance over end-results. State obligations are not styled as imperatives, but usually as undertakings and endeavours. This undeniably weakens the force of the commitments.

Moreover, the potential of many substantive provisions in the FCNM is considerably diluted (see Table 2 for examples), thereby attesting to the fact that it was begotten of political compromise.[183]

---

178 Explanatory Report to the FCNM, *op. cit.*, para. 13: "It [the FCNM] does not imply the recognition of collective rights".

179 Gudmundur Alfredsson, "A Frame an Incomplete Painting: Comparison of the Framework Convention for the Protection of National Minorities with International Standards and Monitoring Procedures", *op. cit.*, at 295 (footnote no. 10).

180 *Ibid.*

181 See, by way of example: the African Charter on Human and Peoples' Rights; ILO Convention 169; Article 1, ICCPR, and Article 1, ICESCR (both of which deal with peoples' right of self-determination).

182 Frank Steketee concedes that the "tortuous phraseology" of some provisions in the FCNM could be said to "read like a Swiss cheese", "The Framework Convention: A Piece of Art or a Tool for Action", *op. cit.*, at 4.

183 See further, Rainer Hofmann, "Protecting the Rights of National Minorities in Europe. First Experiences with the Council of Europe Framework Convention for the Protection of National Minorities", *op. cit.*, at 240.

Table 2[184]

Qualification	Articles
substantial numbers	10(2), 11(3) & 14(2)
sufficient demand	11(3) & 14(2)
if those persons so request	10(2)
a real need	10(2)
where necessary	4(2), 18(1) & 19
where appropriate	11(3) & 12(1)
as far as possible	9(3), 10(2) & 14(2)
where relevant/in so far as […] relevant	18(2)/19

Such dilutions typically water down the possible content of the rights provided for by a series of qualifications.[185] Article 11(3) is an old chestnut for the purposes of making this point. Containing seven qualifications or escape clauses, the basic right envisaged, *viz.* to display traditional names on public signposts, etc., is qualified and conditionalised almost into insipidity. It reads:

> In areas traditionally inhabited by substantial numbers of persons belonging to a national minority, the Parties shall endeavour, in the framework of their legal system, including, where appropriate, agreements with other States, and taking into account their specific conditions, to display traditional local names, street names and other topographical indications intended for the public also in the minority language when there is a sufficient demand for such indications.

Another example is Article 10(2). It reads:

> In areas inhabited by persons belonging to national minorities traditionally or in substantial numbers, if those persons so request and where such a request corresponds to a real need, the Parties shall endeavour to ensure, as far as possible, the conditions which would make it possible to use the minority language in relations between those persons and the administrative authorities.

The basic right in Article 10(2) is to use a minority language in dealings with administrative authorities. The basic limitation is the commonsensical realisation that assuring such a right in practice could involve significant financial and logistical expense for States authorities, and that factors such as demand, geographical

184 This table amends and supplements information provided in Alan Phillips, *The Framework Convention for the Protection of National Minorities: A Policy Analysis*, *op. cit.*, p. 3.

185 See, for example, Heinrich Klebes, "The Council of Europe's Framework Convention for the Protection of National Minorities", *op. cit.*, at 94.

concentration and available means will all be *relevant* to States' attempts to guarantee the core right. However, all rights – civil and political as well as social and economic – imply financial commitments by States. It is beyond dispute that a lack of means can never be accepted as justification for failing to strive to implement human rights obligations at the domestic level.[186] As pointed out by the UN Human Rights Committee in the context of the ICCPR, "failure to comply with [the obligation under Article 2(2) to give effect to the Covenant rights] cannot be justified by reference to political, social, cultural or economic considerations within the State".[187] This is a well-established principle of international human rights law and in practice, treaty-monitoring bodies, as well as independent human rights organisations, rely increasingly on human rights indicators and various benchmarks to monitor governmental performance as regards the (progressive) implementation of (economic, social and cultural) rights. This approach involves measuring the willingness of a government to implement human rights against its capacity to do so; the dissociation of a lack of moral or political commitment from financial or technical incapacity reveals any real progress or regression.[188]

The excessively diffident tone of Article 10(2) is unhelpful as it simply invites States to excuse their failure to honour the right by pointing towards inadequate means at their disposal or subjective assessments of the need for such a right to be facilitated. A further aggravating textual shortcoming is highlighted by Mark Lattimer in his critical dissection of this provision: "[...] the obligation is not to ensure that the minority language can be used; it is to 'endeavour to ensure [...] the conditions which would make it possible to use' the language, and all this only 'as far as possible'".[189] The ineffectual consequences of such wording can be measured by applying it analogously (as Lattimer does) to personal tax returns:

---

186 See, for example, CESCR General Comment No. 3 The nature of States parties obligations (Art. 2, para. 1 of the Covenant), adopted on 14 December 1990, para. 11 of which reads: "[...] even where the available resources are demonstrably inadequate, the obligation remains for a State party to strive to ensure the widest possible enjoyment of the relevant rights under the prevailing circumstances. Moreover, the obligations to monitor the extent of the realization, or more especially of the non-realization, of economic, social and cultural rights, and to devise strategies and programmes for their promotion, are not in any way eliminated as a result of resource constraints [...]". See also, paras. 1, 10, *ibid.*

187 General Comment No. 31 [80] Nature of the General Legal Obligation Imposed on States Parties to the Covenant, adopted on 26 May 2004, para. 14.

188 See further, Katarina Tomasevski, "Indicators", in Asbjorn Eide, Catarina Krause & Allan Rosas, Eds., *Economic, Social and Cultural Rights: A Textbook (Second Revised Edition)* (The Netherlands, Kluwer Law International, 2001), pp. 531–543; Asbjorn Eide, "The Use of Indicators in the Practice of the Committee on Economic, Social and Cultural Rights", in *ibid.*, pp. 545–551.

189 Mark Lattimer, "The Framework Convention as a catalyst for action at domestic level: the NGO perspective", in *Filling the Frame: Five years of monitoring the Framework Convention for the Protection of National Minorities*, *op. cit.*, pp. 58–61, at 58.

> If you were not strictly required to submit a tax return, but only required to endeavour to ensure the conditions which would make it possible, if in your opinion there was a real need, and only as far as was possible, would you do it? Life is busy, and you might just not get round to it…[190]

Obviously, the more limiting clauses that govern a specific right or obligation, the more severe its emasculation will be. These two examples admittedly contain more limiting clauses than most other provisions of the FCNM, but they nevertheless constitute the best illustration of the point that limitations on a right or obligation can seriously curtail the faithfulness of its realisation to its intended purpose.

The traditional conceptual tug-of-war between advocates of the flexibility of formulations and those who would favour firmer phraseology is well-documented. While both stances undoubtedly boast competing merits, the approach adopted here proceeds from the *lex lata*, arguing that the effectiveness of the flexible wording of relevant provisions is contingent on the firmness with which they are applied.

Section III of the FCNM (Articles 20–23)[191] deals with the interpretation and application of the Convention. In particular, it seeks to situate the FCNM in a broader international law context. The section opens with the requirement that persons belonging to a national minority and relying on the FCNM respect "the national legislation and the rights of others, in particular those of persons belonging to the majority or to other national minorities" (Article 20). However, it stops short of requiring that members of national minorities pledge or demonstrate loyalty to the State. According to the Explanatory Report to the FCNM, it is clearly the intention of Article 20 to draw attention to situations in which national minorities constitute a majority within specific geographical areas (so-called "internal minorities").[192] Article 21 was designed to allay the fears of States Parties as regards possible "doomsday" scenarios resulting from minority rights, i.e., the undermining of "the fundamental principles of international law and in particular of the sovereign equality, territorial integrity and political independence of States".

Article 23 asserts the primacy of the ECHR by stating that in the event of "the rights and freedoms flowing from the principles enshrined in" the FCNM being the subject of corresponding provisions in the ECHR, the former will be understood as conforming to the latter. Some of the positive obligations envisaged for State Parties under the FCNM go further than those set out in the ECHR, as interpreted by the European Court of Human Rights in its case-law. Article 23 therefore contributes to the interpretative grey area created by the non-justiciability of the provisions of the

190 *Ibid.*, at 59.
191 Note: Article 22 has already been considered *supra*.
192 Para. 89, Explanatory Report to the FCNM, *op. cit.*

FCNM. If the FCNM's provisions could be examined by the European Court of Human Rights, straightforward balancing tests could be engaged in. However, to date, the Court has exhibited a clear reluctance to do so – as demonstrated by the discussion of the *Chapman* case, *supra.*

2.2.3(iii) Proof of the pudding

The absence in Council of Europe instruments of any express provision for the justiciability of minority rights is widely criticised as being one of the great failings of efforts towards minority rights protection in Europe today.[193] Such criticism is without prejudice to the usefulness of other international legal and political mechanisms for the enforcement of minority rights.[194] The failure of the FCNM to render minority rights justiciable is particularly disappointing. The PACE did not mince its words when giving its view on the same: "[i]ts implementation machinery is feeble and there is a danger that, in fact, the monitoring procedures may be left entirely to the governments".[195] Given his insights into the drafting process and relevant behind-the-scenes politics, Heinrich Klebes' fear that the PACE's assessment could turn out to be an "understatement"[196] is another serious indictment.

The monitoring procedures of the FCNM are set out in Articles 24–26. Article 24 assigns responsibility for monitoring the implementation of the FCNM exclusively to the Committee of Ministers and Article 26 outlines the Advisory Committee's role of assistance in this regard.[197] Article 25 concerns the mechanics of the reporting system.

---

193 Kristin Henrard, *Devising an Adequate System of Minority Protection: Individual Human Rights, Minority Rights and the Right to Self-Determination* (The Hague, Martinus Nijhoff Publishers, 2000).

194 For a comprehensive overview of those mechanisms, see generally: *Mechanisms for the implementation of minority rights* (Germany, Council of Europe Publishing/European Centre for Minority Issues, 2004).

195 Para. 7, PACE Recommendation 1255 (1995) on the protection of the rights of national minorities.

196 Heinrich Klebes, "The Council of Europe's Framework Convention for the Protection of National Minorities", *op. cit.*, at 94.

197 Article 26 is quoted here for the sake of convenience:
"1. In evaluating the adequacy of the measures taken by the Parties to give effect to the principles set out in this framework Convention the Committee of Ministers shall be assisted by an advisory committee, the members of which shall have recognised expertise in the field of the protection of national minorities.
2. The composition of this advisory committee and its procedure shall be determined by the Committee of Ministers within a period of one year following the entry into force of this framework Convention."

Thus, as far as the monitoring of the FCNM is concerned, ultimate control and responsibility rests with the Committee of Ministers,[198] thereby prompting descriptions of the relationship between the two committees as one of "tutelage".[199] However, notwithstanding its officially ascribed role of "assistance" in the monitoring process, the Advisory Committee remains the *de facto* power-house for the monitoring activities. This is true by virtue of the extent of its procedural/ administrative involvement; its sheer hard graft and its engagement with substantive matters. It is therefore imperative that the Committee of Ministers makes greater efforts to harness the full potential for involving the Advisory Committee "in the monitoring of the follow-up to the conclusions and recommendations on an *ad hoc* basis, as instructed by the Committee of Ministers".[200]

The lack of a strong enforcement mechanism for the FCNM is often identified as its Achilles heel.[201] The question of legal enforceability is of crucial importance here. While justiciable rights generally tend to enjoy more robust protection than non-justiciable rights, it is widely recognised that justiciability, too, has its limitations and that other supplementary means of monitoring and protection are often required to shore up judicial solutions.[202] The drafters of the FCNM eschewed the opportunity to render the rights to be contained therein justiciable, opting instead to rely on other forms of control. As such, it continued in the vein of earlier CoE initiatives. The Venice Commission, for instance, has consistently subscribed to the view that "flexible, diplomatic solutions applied by a non-judicial body may prove more effective in this tricky field".[203] This stance is based on the argument that the political dimension to minority rights impinges to quite an extent on State sovereignty and is therefore less suited to traditional adjudication before the courts. The Commission has also posited that not all minority rights are justiciable, eg. statements of principle or hortatory goals and those rights that are formulated as State obligations rather than minority rights as such.[204]

---

198 See Articles 24–26, FCNM.

199 Stefan Troebst, "From paper to practice: The Council of Europe's Framework Convention for the Protection of National Minorities", *op. cit.*, at 25.

200 Committee of Ministers Resolution (97) 10, *op. cit.*, para. 36.

201 Charles F. Furtado, "Guess Who's Coming to Dinner? Protection for National Minorities in Eastern and Central Europe under the Council of Europe", *op. cit.*, at 352.

202 See generally, Geoff Gilbert, "The Council of Europe and Minority Rights", *op. cit.*, at 172; 188–189.

203 Section II, para. 4 bb), Opinion of the European Commission for Democracy through Law on the proposal drawn up by the Committee on Legal Affairs and Human Rights for an additional protocol to the European Convention on Human Rights, *op. cit.*

204 However, as already mentioned, optimal protection for minority rights is best guaranteed by complementary judicial and non-judicial approaches, and it is worth noting that such complementarity was not ruled out by the Venice Commission either. "An 'intermediate' solution may eventually lie in recourse to the advisory competence of the [European] Court [of Human Rights], as provided for in additional Protocol No. 2 to the ECHR [...]. [...] for example, [...] either the European Committee for the Protection of Minorities (Art. 18 of the draft) or the

Not only is the monitoring system constructed by the text of the FCNM overtly political in character, the *modus operandi* of the Advisory Committee – agreed upon by the Committee of Ministers even before the Advisory Committee was constituted – also turned out to be highly political. At the time of its inception, it is little wonder that scepticism abounded about the Advisory Committee's ability to overcome what seemed on paper to be formidable restrictions on the latitude within which it would have to operate.[205] There was a general – and well-founded – fear that the baby might be strangled at birth. Some of the anxiety stemmed from the following provisions:

> 29. The Advisory Committee may request additional information from the Party whose report is under consideration.
>
> 30. The Advisory Committee may receive information from sources other than state reports.
>
> 31. Unless otherwise directed by the Committee of Ministers, the Advisory Committee may invite information from other sources after notifying the Committee of Ministers of its intention to do so.
>
> 32. The Advisory Committee may hold meetings with representatives of the government whose report is being considered and shall hold a meeting if the government concerned so requests.
>
> A specific mandate shall be obtained from the Committee of Ministers if the Advisory Committee wishes to hold meetings for the purpose of seeking information from other sources.
>
> These meetings shall be held in closed session.

Since then, the Advisory Committee – through its own pro-activeness and the support of the Committee of Ministers – has managed to carve out increased operational autonomy for itself. Follow-up questionnaires to States Parties have become a standard feature of its work, thereby maximising the potential of Rule 29. Without the support of the Committee of Ministers, Rule 31 would have been a

---

Committee of Ministers of the Council of Europe could request an advisory opinion from the Court on a question of law concerning interpretation of the Convention." Giorgio Malinverni, "The draft Convention for the Protection of Minorities – The Proposal of the European Commission for Democracy through Law", *op. cit.*, at 268. On the topic of advisory opinions from the ECtHRs, see: Para. 12(i), Rights of national minorities, PACE Recommendation 1623 (2003), *op. cit.*; Boriss Cilevics, "The Framework Convention within the context of the Council of Europe", in *Filling the Frame: Five years of monitoring the Framework Convention for the Protection of National Minorities*, *op. cit.*, pp. 28–37, at 33.

205 See, for example, the Council of Europe Committee of Ministers Resolution (97) 10: Rules adopted by the Committee of Ministers on the monitoring arrangements under Articles 24 to 26 of the Framework Convention for the Protection of National Minorities, 17 September 1997 (especially paras. 29–32; 35–37).

dead-letter. The Advisory Committee has reported its satisfaction with the backing it has received from the Committee of Ministers in this regard. Meetings with State and non-State representatives have increasingly been relied upon by the Advisory Committee in its monitoring work to great effect. Again, the support of the Committee of Ministers was needed for the Advisory Committee to breathe life into Rule 32: it gave the Advisory Committee blanket authorisation for the entire initial monitoring cycle to hold meetings with representatives of non-governmental organisations and representatives of civil society in the context of its country visits conducted upon the invitation of States Parties. This relieved the Advisory Committee of "the obligation to request a separate mandate for each such meeting as normally required under Rule 32, paragraph 2".[206] In addition, follow-up seminars and other activities, aiming to generate "dialogue on the implementation of the findings of the monitoring mechanism between the reporting cycles", are now organised regularly in States Parties to the FCNM.[207]

The individual State reports constitute the lynchpin of the monitoring system, thus enhancing the importance of ensuring that the reporting guidelines are clear[208] and that the content of the reports themselves is both accurate and comprehensive.[209] While the Advisory Committee has made a point of commending the level of detail generally included in State reports,[210] it has nevertheless deemed it necessary to stress the need for even greater attention to detail. This has come about in two ways. First, it has now become a standard feature of the reporting process for the Advisory Committee to issue States Parties with questionnaires requiring more specific information concerning various aspects of their original reports.[211] The Advisory

206 See further, para. 25 of Activity Report 2, which refers to the relevant decision adopted by the Committee of Ministers on 3 May 2000.

207 Advisory Committee Activity Reports: No. 3, paras. 33–40; No. 4, paras. 18–20; No. 5, paras. 23–27; No. 6, paras. 27–29; No. 7, paras. 59–63.

208 The original outline for State reports for the first monitoring cycle of the FCNM was set out in Appendix 3 to CM Resolution (97) 10 and adopted by the Committee of Ministers on 30 September 1998: paras. 10, 11 (mentioning the possible need to modify them later – para. 15, Activity Report 3), Activity Report 1). The outline for State reports for the second cycle of monitoring (para. 15, Activity Report 3) was adopted by the Committee of Ministers on 15 January 2003. See also, paras. 21, 22, Activity Report 4. Reports for the second cycle should build on those submitted in the course of the first cycle and thereby avoid any unnecessary repetition; States should give details of their efforts to apply the conclusions of the Committee of Ministers on the first cycle of monitoring and on the extent to which they have taken appropriate account of the various comments in the Advisory Committee's Opinion on an article-by-article basis. The reports should also provide responses to specific questions addressed separately to States Parties by the Advisory Committee in the framework of continuing dialogue between them. The outline for State reports for the third monitoring cycle "follows quite closely the approach chosen for the second cycle" because that approach had proved successful (para. 32, Activity Report 6).

209 Para. 12, Activity Report 2.

210 Para. 12, Activity Report 2; para. 12, Activity Report 3.

211 (para. 17, Activity Report 1); para. 18, Activity Report 2; para. 15, Activity Report 3.

Committee has, however, been quick to point out that such requests for additional information do not have any undertones of criticism, and should rather be viewed as part of the broader process of "constructive dialogue between the Advisory Committee and the States Parties".[212] Indeed, it has saluted the quality and quantity of information contained in States' responses to these follow-up questionnaires,[213] noting that "in some cases, such responses have constituted a source of information comparable to the state report itself".[214] For the duration of the second monitoring cycle, the Advisory Committee adopted the practice of also submitting preliminary questions to States in an attempt to "limit the need to draw up lengthy questionnaires following the submission of the report [...] and to speed up the monitoring procedure".[215] This practice has not been continued in a routine manner during the third monitoring cycle – only on a case-by-case basis, if and when the Advisory Committee considers it necessary.[216]

Second, in its Activity Reports, the Advisory Committee has consistently urged States Parties to make particular efforts to provide information on the implementation of the various rights vouchsafed by the Framework Convention[217] and "pertinent statistical data".[218] As mentioned *supra*, such information is expressly required by the outlines for State reports. These requests were born of an over-reliance in State reports on legislative frameworks and a concomitant neglect of the relevant practice.

The Advisory Committee also realised at a very early stage that "in order to carry out its task effectively and in a balanced and consistent way, it may also need to seek information from sources other than the reporting States".[219] It recognised the vital role which information from independent sources could play in complementing and clarifying information contained in initial State reports and thereby helping it to form a "comprehensive picture of country situations".[220] The procedural decisions taken by the Committee of Ministers which have enabled the Advisory Committee "to establish and maintain free and frequent contacts"[221] with independent sources of information paid instant dividends, as was acknowledged by the Advisory Committee in its Activity Reports.[222] The Advisory Committee has also developed a so-called "*ad hoc*" contact procedure in order to add another string to its

212 Para. 17, Activity Report 1; para. 19, Activity Report 2; para. 15, Activity Report 3.
213 Para. 19, Activity Report 2.
214 *Ibid.*
215 Para. 21, Activity Report 4.
216 See para. 32, Activity Report 6.
217 Para. 17, Activity Report 1; para. 13, Activity Report 2; para. 12, Activity Report 3.
218 Para. 12, Activity Report 3.
219 Para. 18, Activity Report 1.
220 Para. 23, Activity Report 2.
221 Para. 23, Activity Report 2.
222 Para 24, Activity Report 2 and para. 16, Activity Report 3.

information-gathering bow.[223] The Advisory Committee continues to benefit from "excellent cooperation" with NGOs, minority associations and civil society generally, which it acknowledges as being indispensable for effective monitoring.[224] Contact and cooperation with other branches of the Council of Europe and other IGO bodies is also extensive and fruitful.

All of the foregoing demonstrates that there are at least four junctures at which greater attention could be paid to detail: in the State reports themselves; in the follow-up questionnaires addressed by the Advisory Committee to the States Parties; in the inward information flow from independent sources; in meetings with State and non-State actors. Each of these stages offers opportunities to prise open the very centre of pressing questions and situations. Three of them offer the Advisory Committee the opportunity to play a pro-active role in eliciting key information from States Parties, i.e., in the State reports, questionnaires and meetings with State representatives. Any reliable information received from independent sources would obviously feed into the formulation of questions for submission in writing to the States Parties or for raising in meetings with State representatives. Reliable information is therefore the lifeblood of the Advisory Committee, irrespective of whether it is received from the States themselves or from independent third parties. It is of cardinal importance that the Advisory Committee not be restricted in any way in seeking out and using information that is relevant to its work.

In a case of insult having been added to injury, one other problem trammelling the operational potential of the Advisory Committee is the problem of parsimonious funding, which has led to it being severely under-resourced. The Advisory Committee has consistently been stressing – and quite rightly with increasing urgency – its dire need for greater financial and human resources. It has warned that greater financial *largesse* would be required in order to preclude the danger that the quality of its work would be further compromised due to under-resourcing, thereby jeopardising the effectiveness of the entire monitoring process.[225] The spiralling workload has not been matched by adequate additional resources and the situation was described as "increasingly acute" just before the commencement of the second monitoring cycle.[226] Calls for greater funding have also emanated from a variety of other sources.[227]

---

223 For details, see: paras. 28–30, Activity Report 5.

224 Para. 37, Activity Report 4.

225 Advisory Committee Activity Reports: No. 1, paras. 30 and 36; No. 2, paras. 42 and 44; No. 3, paras. 48–54 and 58; No. 4, paras. 43, 44 and 46; No. 5, paras. 56 and 57; No. 6, paras. 70 and 74, and No. 7, para. 110.

226 Para. 43, Activity Report 4. See also para. 44, *ibid.*

227 Eg. Rights of national minorities, PACE Recommendation 1623 (2003), *op. cit.*, para. 12(v).

To sum up, granted much can and has been achieved despite textual and procedural limitations and "despite" is the key word here. This is a testament to the commitment and resourcefulness of those at the coal-face of the monitoring exercise and not an exoneration of the substantive and structural weaknesses of the FCNM. As pointed out by John Packer on the occasion of the fifth anniversary of the entry into force of the FCNM, this is not a time for resting on laurels.[228] Much more could be achieved:

- Consolidation of one of the AC's ongoing achievements, *viz.*, the *de facto* provision of interpretive guidance on the content of the FCNM's (largely) programmatic provisions,[229] thereby facilitating their implementation. This could be achieved, for example, through the elaboration of a new thematic commentary on the theme, minorities and the media.
- A distillation of principles from the "soft jurisprudence" of the Advisory Committee.
- Greater attention to the preambular affirmation of the FCNM's sources of inspiration and more frequent invocation of same.
- Greater attention to conceptual precision and linguistic consistency in Opinions
- Increased openness and transparency of procedures.
- More interaction with interested parties, especially representatives of minority groups.
- Timeliness of reporting and measures for dealing with persistent delays.[230]

In 2003, the PACE continued its criticism of certain CoE States for failing to ratify,[231] or sign and ratify,[232] the FCNM without debilitating reservations, and exhorted them to do so "swiftly".[233] These are familiar refrains in relevant PACE Recommendations, some of which have gone a step further.

In the same vein, Boriss Cilevics has argued that "not only ratification, but also fair implementation of the Framework Convention must become a necessary precondition for membership in [*sic*] the Council of Europe, as is the case today

---

228 John Packer, "Situating the Framework Convention in a wider context: achievements and challenges", *op. cit.*, at 51.

229 See further, on this observation, Rianne M. Letschert, *The Impact of Minority Rights Mechanisms*, *op. cit.*, p. 218.

230 See, in this connection, Decision of the Committee of Ministers of 19 March 2003 authorising the Advisory Committee to "submit a proposal regarding the commencement of the monitoring of the Framework Convention without a state report when a state is more than 24 months behind in submitting a state report [...]".

231 In this respect, it named: Belgium, Georgia, Greece, Iceland, Latvia, Luxembourg and the Netherlands). See further: PACE Resolution 1301 (2002) on the protection of minorities in Belgium.

232 In this respect, it named: Andorra, France and Turkey.

233 Para. 11, Rights of national minorities, PACE Recommedation 1623 (2003), *op. cit.*

with the European Convention of [*sic*] Human Rights and its Protocol No. 6".[234] A useful appendix to this recommendation would be that States Parties' adherence to the FCNM should be kept under continuous and vigilant scrutiny by the PACE and CoE Secretary General's monitoring mechanisms.[235] Such scrutiny serves as an extra source of pressure for States to comply with their obligations under the Convention. While States are under a presumptive commitment to implement their obligations under international law in good faith – in accordance with the principle of *pacta sunt servanda*, as enshrined, *inter alia*, in Article 26 of the Vienna Convention on the Law of Treaties[236] – measures adopted to give effect to specific conventional provisions do not always live up to the expectations generated by the act of ratification. In this sense, in the absence of effective enforcement/monitoring mechanisms, there is a danger that States will, in practice, be no more than "international street angels and domestic house devils".[237]

2.2.4 Organization for Security and Co-operation in Europe standards

The Organization for Security and Co-operation in Europe (OSCE), which currently comprises 56 Participating States, has also been in the vanguard of minority rights protection. After an earlier emphasis on standard-setting initiatives at IGO summits, OSCE activities in the domain of minority rights protection have in recent years tended to be channelled through the Office of the OSCE High Commissioner on National Minorities (HCNM) (see further, *infra*).

The seeds of OSCE protection for minority rights were sown in the Final Act of the CSCE Summit held in Helsinki in 1975. The Helsinki Final Act is divided into four main categories or "Baskets",[238] the first of which is entitled 'Questions relating to Security in Europe'. This Basket includes a Declaration on Principles Guiding Relations between Participating States. Principle VII of this Declaration, entitled "Respect for human rights and fundamental freedoms, including the freedom of thought, conscience, religion or belief", and Principle VIII, entitled "Equal rights

---

234 Boriss Cilevics, "The Framework Convention within the context of the Council of Europe", *op. cit.*, at 33. See also, *ibid.*, at 32.

235 This is already routinely taking place.

236 Article 26 (*Pacta sunt sevanda*) reads in its entirety: "[e]very treaty in force is binding upon the parties to it and must be performed by them in good faith".

237 Donncha O'Connell, "Beyond rights – towards interests", *Céide – A Review from the Margins* p. 17 (January/February 1999), at 17–18.

238 Basket I is "Questions relating to Security in Europe"; Basket II is "Co-operation in the fields of Economics, of Science and Technology and of the Environment"; Basket III is "Co-operation in humanitarian and other fields" and Basket IV is "Follow-up to the Conference". See further: Jane Wright, "The OSCE and the Protection of Minority Rights", 18 *Human Rights Quarterly* (1996), pp. 190–205; Jane Wright, "The Protection of Minority Rights in Europe: From Conference to Implementation", 2 *The International Journal of Human Rights* (No. 1, Spring 1998), pp. 1–31.

and self-determination of peoples" are the Principles most directly concerned with human – and specifically minority – rights. Principle VII, para. 4, contains the most explicit reference to minority rights:

> The participating States on whose territory national minorities exist will respect the right of persons belonging to such minorities to equality before the law, will afford them the full opportunity for the actual enjoyment of human rights and fundamental freedoms and will, in this manner, protect their legitimate interests in this sphere.

The wording employed is clearly redolent of Article 27, ICCPR, but boasts greater suppleness. In the first place, Principle VII, para. 4, is not couched in the same negative terms as Article 27, ICCPR. The extreme caution of the "shall not be denied" formula in Article 27, ICCPR, was not considered to be necessary, given that the resultant text would be political in character, and without legal consequences for Participating States.[239] The importance of this shift is more symbolic than semantic. As already noted, *supra*, the negative wording of Article 27, ICCPR, belies its positive import. Moreover, it was important to send out positive signals of intent as regards minority rights protection.

The wording of Principle VII, para. 4, is also more supple by its refusal to follow the precedent of Article 27, ICCPR, of particularising certain categories of minority and ear-marking them for special protection, to the possible exclusion of other categories. The references to "full opportunity for the actual enjoyment" and "their legitimate interests" are preferable on this score. "Full opportunity for the actual enjoyment..." implies a broad conception of equality that embraces the possibility of affirmative action in order to achieve equality in fact. "Legitimate interests" creates a broader base of possible associative motivations of members of minority groups than the restrictive platform of ethnic, linguistic and religious features/interests/objectives.

Follow-up to the Helsinki Final Act (and subsequent meetings) was assured by a number of intergovernmental procedures which were progressively strengthened, notably by the Vienna and Moscow Mechanisms.

The next real milestone for minority rights protection within the OSCE system was the Copenhagen Document, 1990. As would later be the case in the UN system, a catalogue of differentiated rights grew from the seed of a solitary article planted in a more general text. The fact that this was the first standard-setting exercise for minority rights to prove successful at the international level undoubtedly lent it

239 This is perhaps also the reason why the drafters did not become sucked into the debate on the competing merits of individual and group-oriented rights and protection.

extra importance and influence.[240] One of the five sections in the Document, Section IV, is devoted partly to the rights of persons belonging to national minorities (as they were now called) (paras. 30–39), and partly to the adjacent objective of combating “totalitarianism, racial and ethnic hatred, anti-semitism, xenophobia and discrimination against anyone as well as persecution on religious and ideological grounds” (para. 40).

Para. 30 positions the rights of persons belonging to national minorities firmly within respect for human rights, democracy, rule of law, pluralism, tolerance and other laudable societal values. Para. 31 deals with non-discrimination and factual equality for persons belonging to national minorities, and envisages special measures being adopted by States where necessary in order to achieve these ends. Para. 32 begins with the assurance that membership of a national minority is a matter of individual choice and shall not lead to adverse consequences for individuals exercising that choice. The sub-paragraphs in para. 32 then proceed to list specific rights intended for enjoyment by persons belonging to national minorities, such as: to use their mother tongue in public and in private; to establish and maintain educational, cultural and religious organisations; to profess and practise their religion; the pursuit of unimpeded national and transfrontier connections; to receive and impart information in their mother tongue; organisational participation, both nationally and internationally. This paragraph concludes with the reminder that the rights of persons belonging to national minorities may be exercised individually or in community with other group members.

Para. 33 provides for the promotion of national minority identities and Para. 34 sets out a number of linguistic rights, such as the right to education of or in one’s mother tongue (alongside learning of official State languages) and the right to use one’s mother tongue in dealings with public authorities. The right of minorities to participate in public affairs is underscored in para. 35. The following paragraph, 36, emphasises the importance of inter-State cooperation regarding issues relating to national minorities. Para. 37 is a pretty standard “prohibition of abuse of rights” provision; Para. 38 calls on States to honour commitments towards minorities arising out of relevant treaties to which they are already party and to accede to others to which they are not, “including those providing for a right of complaint by individuals”. It is particularly noteworthy that the Document should expressly draw attention to the question of the justiciability of minority rights and, more specifically, the possibility of individual petition. Para. 39 mentions, *inter alia*, the need for cooperation between States within various international fora.

---

240 See, in this connection, its influence on the UN Declaration on the Rights of Persons Belonging to National or Ethnic, Religious and Linguistic Minorities and the FCNM.

The foregoing brief bird's-eye view of the extent of relevant provisions in the Copenhagen Document should suffice to explain the impact it has had on the drafting of subsequent international instruments.[241] Obviously, the fact that it was a forerunner of other major texts contributed to its impact, but it is too easy to explain impact merely in terms of happenstance. The provisions themselves are phrased in relatively straightforward language, not the stodgy, arch-conservative bureaucratic legalese that tends to rob legal texts of much of their potential. Nor was it bound by legal or other historical baggage, as could be argued about comparable UN efforts: it was pretty much a self-propelled initiative, without complicated ties to precedent. Nor were there complex administrative impediments to the realisation of the drafting exercise: instead of sub-committees interminably exchanging draft documents over periods of years, this was a text adopted by heads of States.

2.2.4(i) OSCE High Commissioner on National Minorities (HCNM)

The Office of the OSCE HCNM was established in 1992, pursuant to the mandate set out in the CSCE Helsinki Document ("The Challenges of Change") of that year.[242] The first incumbent of the Office was the former Dutch Foreign Minister, Max van der Stoel (1993–2001)[243] and he was succeeded by Rolf Ekeus (2001–2007), who in turn was succeeded by Knut Vollebaek, the current incumbent. The Mandate sets out that the HCNM should be "an instrument of conflict prevention at the earliest possible stage",[244] and charges the incumbent with the task of providing "'early warning' and, as appropriate, 'early action' at the earliest possible stage in regard to tensions involving national minority issues which have not yet developed beyond an early warning stage", but in his/her judgment have the potential to do so.[245]

The HCNM's mandate has therefore designed an Office with a very specific remit. In formal terms, this remit is strictly one of conflict prevention, in contradistinction to the earlier, overarching OSCE principles (or contiguous Council of Europe mission statements) discussed *supra*, which are grounded in democratic values of

241 For example, the UN Declaration on the Rights of Persons Belonging to National or Ethnic, Religious and Linguistic Minorities, Council of Europe texts, including PACE Recommendation 1201 and the FCNM.

242 Section II – CSCE High Commissioner on National Minorities, "The Challenges of Change", CSCE Helsinki Document 1992 (adopted on 9–10 July 1992).

243 For an overview of his activities in this capacity, see *inter alia*: Walter A. Kemp, Ed., *Quiet Diplomacy in Action: The OSCE High Commissioner on National Minorities* (The Hague/London/Boston, Kluwer Law International, 2001); Wolfgang Zellner and Falk Lange, Eds., *Peace and Stability through Human and Minority Rights: Speeches by the OSCE High Commissioner on National Minorities* (Baden-Baden, Nomos, 1999).

244 Section II – CSCE High Commissioner on National Minorities, "The Challenges of Change", CSCE Helsinki Document 1992, *op. cit.*, para. (2).

245 *Ibid.*, para. (3).

pluralism, tolerance, etc., and thereby leave greater scope for the promotion of minority rights. Such typical democracy-enhancing goals might *prima facie* seem broader than the goal of conflict prevention. However, in practice, the HCNM has tended to interpret his mandate in a pro-active manner, tracing potential for conflict to its source in States authorities' denial of, inadequate provision for, or insufficient accommodation of, minority rights and interests (as the case may be). The deliberately purposive interpretation of the HCNM's mandate has contributed in large measure to the achievements of the Office to date.

The HCNM is required to "work in confidence" and to "act independently of *all* parties directly involved in the tensions".[246] The impartiality with which the HCNM's duties must be discharged would seem to rule out the possibility of interventions on behalf of minority groups, hence the importance of the choice of preposition in the HCNM's title. "On" was preferred to "for", in order to reflect the objectives of the mandate, *viz.*, impartial conflict prevention. In practice, though, the HCNM's interventions very often favour national minorities, but this results from the HCNM's assessment of the specific facts of given situations, rather than a pre-determined mandate to advance the minority cause.

The HCNM is answerable to the Chairman-in-Office of the OSCE and the Committee of Senior Officials (CSO),[247] but enjoys considerable operational autonomy. There are three main limitations to the permissibility of the HCNM's engagement. First, without the express consent of all parties involved (including the State), the HCNM is prevented from considering national minority issues in a State "of which the High Commissioner is a national or a resident, or involving a national minority to which the High Commissioner belongs".[248] Second, the HCNM may not "consider national minority issues in situations involving organized acts of terrorism".[249] This reinforces the overall preoccupation of the HCNM's mandate with conflict *prevention.* Third, the HCNM is precluded from considering "violations of CSCE commitments with regard to an individual person belonging to a national minority".[250] The purpose of this restriction is presumably to ensure that the HCNM's duties are discharged in a non-partisan and non-particularised manner. The concern for conflict prevention is generally more acute where group situations are implicated, rather than single individuals belonging to groups.

---

246 (emphasis added) *ibid.*, para. (4).

247 Note: as a result of the Budapest Summit ("Towards a Genuine Partnership in a New Era"), 5–6 December 1994, the CSO was succeeded by the Senior Council. See further, *ibid.*, paras. (13)–(22).

248 *Ibid.*, para. (5a).

249 *Ibid.*, para. (5b).

250 *Ibid.*, para. (5c).

The HCNM is relatively unhampered in its ability to draw on a wide range of information sources;[251] to consult a wide range of parties directly concerned in tensions;[252] to conduct country visits,[253] and to involve experts in relevant work and/or country visits.[254] Information about a situation involving a national minority or about any of the parties directly involved in such a situation can be collected or received by the HCNM "from any source, including the media and non-governmental organizations".[255] Parties directly involved in such situations may draw up and submit specific reports on relevant matters.[256] The only across-the-board restriction in respect of the HCNM's communications is set out in para. (25) of the Mandate:

> The High Commissioner will not communicate with and will not acknowledge communications from any person or organization which practises or publicly condones terrorism or violence.

Para. 26 of the Mandate stipulates the parties directly concerned in tensions who can provide specific reports to the HCNM and with whom the HCNM will endeavour to communicate during visits to a participating State. The parties can be bracketed into two main categories: State governments (including, where appropriate, regional and local ramifications of government in areas of residence of national minorities);[257] authorised representatives of associations, NGOs, religious and other groups of national minorities directly concerned and in the area of tension.[258]

The HCNM is required to submit specific information about the purpose of any proposed visit to an OSCE Participating State before it is due to take place. The State authorities are then given two weeks to liaise with the HCNM in connection with the same.[259] Para. 25 governs all of the various activities of the HCNM during visits to Participating States.[260] Once *sur place*, the State authorities are to facilitate the HCNM's travel and communications.[261] The HCNM may consult the parties involved and receive information in confidence from any individual, group or organisation directly concerned about the questions under immediate scrutiny.

---

251 *Ibid.*, paras. (23)-(25).
252 *Ibid.*, paras. (26), (26a) & (26b).
253 *Ibid.*, paras. (27)-(30).
254 *Ibid.*, paras. (31)-(36).
255 *Ibid.*, para. (23a).
256 *Ibid.*, para. (23b).
257 *Ibid.*, para. (26a).
258 *Ibid.*, para (26b).
259 *Ibid.*, para. (27).
260 *Ibid.*, paras. (27) & (29).
261 *Ibid.*, para. (27). Failure to allow the HCNM entry into a State or to assure free travel and communication, will lead to the HCNM informing the CSO of the same: *ibid.*, para. (28).

When information provided is confidential in character, the HCNM will respect its confidentiality.[262] States authorities may not take any measures against persons or organisations on the grounds that they have had contact with the HCNM.[263] Finally, as regards the HCNM's operational autonomy, up to three experts may be engaged by the HCNM in order to provide specific advice.[264] Criteria and circumstances governing the selection of experts are quite lenient, but the HCNM is required to "set a clearly defined mandate and time-frame for the activities of the experts".[265] The possibility of experts visiting a Participating State (only) at the same time as the HCNM is also provided for.[266]

Since its inception, the HCNM has been an effective agent of discreet, behind-the-scenes diplomacy. Not being hide-bound by a restrictive mandate, definitional rigidity or legal formulae certainly facilitated the adoption of a case-by-case approach. It also ensured tactical flexibility for the achievement of the HCNM's wider goals. The OSCE HCNM has also taken standard-setting initiatives concerning specific (aspects of) minority rights, thereby adding another important string to its bow.

The initiatives in question have led to the elaboration of: the Bolzano/Bozen Recommendations on National Minorities in Inter-State Relations (June 2008); the Recommendations on Policing in Multi-Ethnic Societies (February 2006); the Guidelines on the use of Minority Languages in the Broadcast Media (October 2003); the Lund Recommendations on the Effective Participation of National Minorities in Public Life (September 1999);[267] the Oslo Recommendations Regarding the Linguistic Rights of National Minorities (February 1998) and The Hague Recommendations on the Education Rights of National Minorities (October 1996). In addition, the HCNM has also issued recommendations for the Roma and Sinti communities. The so-called "Roma Recommendations" comprise a miscellany of reports and other statements developed over the years, rather than a single set of recommendations.

A point often made about OSCE minority rights standards is that they are an important source of soft law, of *de lege feranda*. The point is supported by the

262 *Ibid.*, para. (29).
263 *Ibid.*, para. (30).
264 *Ibid.*, para. (31).
265 *Ibid.*, para. (32).
266 *Ibid.*, para. (33).
267 It is worth noting in this connection that the OSCE Office for Democratic Institutions and Human Rights (ODIHR), in conjunction with the International Institute for Democracy and Electoral Assistance and the Office of the OSCE HCNM, has developed the Warsaw Guidelines to Assist National Minority Participation in the Electoral Process (January 2001). These Guidelines focus on the implementation of the Lund Recommendations that specifically "relate to the work of the ODIHR in respect of elections" – *ibid.*, p. 1.

example of the cross-fertilisation that has taken place in the drafting of relevant standards by various international organisations. OSCE commitments have in the past been a source of inspiration and influence for other (legal) texts and a reference point for international and national courts.[268] OSCE commitments have also penetrated sub-regional, bilateral treaties to very good effect, and they have been incorporated into a number of national constitutions and legislation. This tendency is sometimes referred to as the "upgrading" of political commitments.

This last statement taps into a wider discussion revolving around the competing advantages of political and legal standards. Obviously, this is a case of "horses for courses": each set of standards is designed differently to achieve different aims. Political commitments certainly have the potential to be more far-reaching than legal standards, and this potential often manifests itself in their wording. Nevertheless, it has persuasively been argued that in practice, politically binding standards can prove just as effective as their legally binding counterparts.[269]

The OSCE has provided an extra dimension to minority rights protection in Europe and hitherto, it has proved a dynamic one. It remains to be seen, however, whether the initial vigour and momentum will be maintained in a rapidly evolving and thus markedly different political environment. It is too early to evaluate the extent to which OSCE commitments such as those contained in the Copenhagen Document are a product of their times, a reaction to the collapse of the Soviet Block in Central and Eastern Europe. Another relevant question concerns the evolutionary curve that is likely to be traced by the Office of the HCNM itself and whether its erstwhile pro-active approach can be maintained under different stewardships.

At one juncture the suggestion that the OSCE could "loan" the European human rights organs of the Council of Europe was mooted.[270] This suggestion drew on the concept of "*Organleihe*", or organ-sharing, which has been developed in German administrative law. The central idea was that under a proposed additional protocol to the ECHR, the standards for minority rights protection being developed by the OSCE would become reviewable by the judicial organs of the ECHR in Strasbourg. The proposal was procedurally complicated and would have led to a potentially messy, tiered approach to minority rights protection (some CSCE States were not parties to the ECHR, and the protocol would have had to provide for such States to incorporate the entire ECHR…).[271] It ought to be stressed, however, that this

---

268 See, for example, *Sidiropoulos v. Greece*, *op. cit.*, para. 44.

269 Arie Bloed, Ed., *The Conference on Cooperation and Security in Europe: Analysis and Basic Documents*, 1972–1993 (Dordrecht, Martinus Nijhoff Publishers, 1993), pp. 22–25.

270 Stephan Breitenmoser and Dagmar Richter, "Proposal for an Additional Protocol to the European Convention on Human Rights Concerning the Protection of Minorities in the Participating States of the CSCE", 12 *Human Rights Law Journal* (No. 6–7, 1991), pp. 262–265.

271 Note however, that the complexity of the mechanism proposed by Breitenmoser and Richter has made a more positive impression on other commentators. See, for example, Geoff Gilbert, "The

proposal was floated while the OSCE standards were very much in their infancy, even predating the establishment of the Office of the OSCE HCNM.

Perhaps, then, the only element of the proposal that is worth retaining for more general contemporary debate is the possibility or desirability of organ-sharing *per se*. The main *forte* of any prospective organ-sharing arrangement between different IGOs would be its ability to maximise the experience and potential of existing bodies, thereby avoiding any unnecessary duplication of their efforts to achieve similar objectives. While it is always desirable to avoid pointless overlapping between institutions, this is usually achieved through the encouragement of complementary and synergic approaches between institutions. Indeed, the PACE has stressed the importance of synergic cooperation between the CoE and the HCNM in the domain of minority rights protection.[272]

As the approaches of the CoE and the HCNM to minority rights protection have – since the heady and formative days of the early 1990s – become rather consolidated, essential differences of substance and process are now more easily identifiable. By now, the relevant limbs of both IGOs have managed to carve out their own institutional space. This makes it easier to distinguish between the respective approaches and, by way of corollary, to determine areas of potential cooperation. Furthermore, given that no additional protocol to the ECHR has ever materialised, the possibility of the OSCE "organ-loaning" the Strasbourg judicial arms of the ECHR remains fanciful. Indeed, it is no longer desirable: the *modus operandi* of the HCNM has been developed along clear lines; it plays to its strengths and the aim of rendering OSCE commitments justiciable does not seem to inform relevant policy at all. As stressed by John Packer:

> [...] the HCNM is not a supervisory mechanism and does not concern himself with the protection of minority rights *in general*. The HCNM is limited to acting in situations where, to use the analysis of Gurr, there is 'the mobilization of grievance' through the 'coherent expression by leaders of political movements' causing tensions which threaten international peace and stability.[273]

In sum, the OSCE commitments relating to minority rights protection remain primarily political in character (despite instances of their "upgrading" to legal status), as do the channels for their enforcement. They continue to wield considerable influence among policy and law-makers throughout Europe. The various sets of

Legal Protection Accorded to Minority Groups in Europe", XXIII *Netherlands Yearbook of International Law* 1992, pp. 67–104, at 94–104.

272 PACE Recommendation 1773 (2006), "The 2003 guidelines on the use of minority languages in the broadcast media and the Council of Europe standards: need to enhance cooperation and synergy with the OSCE", 21 November 2006.

273 (footnotes omitted) John Packer, "Problems in Defining Minorities", *op. cit.*, at 238.

principles elaborated by the HCNM further edify earlier OSCE commitments. Applied and programmatic approaches to such principles have been instrumental in promoting their implementation. The overall OSCE contribution to minority rights protection must, however, also be viewed in terms of its limitations. The standards it promotes are not – of themselves – enforceable rights; their adoption is entirely contingent on the goodwill of States authorities.

2.2.5 European Union

The erstwhile goals of the European Economic Communities (as the European Union (EU) was then known) were primarily economic cooperation and the consolidation of peace through trade. However, as consistently held by the Court of Justice of the European Communities[274] and as was laid down explicitly in the Treaty of Amsterdam, 1997, the EU is bound by the fundamental rights regime of the ECHR. This growing commitment to the upholding of human rights was further consolidated by the proclamation of the Charter of Fundamental Rights of the European Union at the Nice European Council on 7 December 2000, as repeated and adapted in 2007.[275] Since then, the Treaty of Lisbon has strengthened the EU's commitments to human rights (including the rights of persons belonging to minorities) considerably. For instance, Article 2 of the Treaty on European Union now reads:

> The Union is founded on the values of respect for human dignity, freedom, democracy, equality, the rule of law and respect for human rights, including the rights of persons belonging to minorities. These values are common to the Member States in a society in which pluralism, non-discrimination, tolerance, justice, solidarity and equality between women and men prevail.

Relatedly, Article 3(3) states that the Union "shall respect its rich cultural and linguistic diversity, and shall ensure that Europe's cultural heritage is safeguarded and enhanced". Very significantly, Article 6.1 accords the Charter of Fundamental Rights of the European Union "the same legal value as the Treaties".[276] Under Article 6.2, the EU "shall accede" to the ECHR.[277] Article 6.3 affirms that

---

274 See, for example, Case 4/73, *Nold v. Commission* [1974], Judgment of 14 May 1974, ECR 491, para. 13; Case C-260/89, *Elliniki Radiophonia Tileorasi* [1991], Judgment of 18 June 1991, ECR I-2925, para. 41; Case C-353/89, *Commission v. The Netherlands* [1991], Judgment of 25 July 1991, ECR I-4069, para. 30.

275 Charter of Fundamental Rights of the European Union, Nice, 7 December 2000, as proclaimed by the European Parliament, the Council and the Commission, 12 December 2007, OJ C 303 of 14 December 2007, p.1.

276 See further in this connection: Declaration concerning the Charter of Fundamental Rights of the European Union, OJ C 306/249 of 17 December 2007.

277 See further in this connection: Protocol relating to Article 6(2) of the Treaty on European Union on the accession of the Union to the European Convention on the Protection of Human Rights

fundamental rights, as guaranteed by the ECHR and resulting from the constitutional traditions of Member States, "shall constitute general principles of the Union's law".

The express recognition of the rights of persons belonging to minorities as one of the founding values of the EU gives them firm constitutional grounding, which will greatly facilitate their development in the fullness of time. It is also significant that the reference is to "minorities" and not the more restrictive formula, "national minorities". The provision conferring legally-binding force on the Charter will advance the mainstreaming and consolidation of human rights within the EU and in its activities. Although the Charter does not contain provisions dealing explicitly with the rights of persons belonging to minorities, a number of its provisions are indirectly relevant.[278] Finally, the envisaged accession of the EU to the ECHR ought to make for the more consistent interpretation of human rights norms at the European level. The general upshot of these pending developments is that the EU's approach to human rights and the rights of persons belonging to minorities will no longer be largely confined to the political realm.[279] A more legal approach will be facilitated and necessitated.

In recent years, the EU's main focus on minority rights had been their inclusion as one of the so-called Copenhagen criteria[280] governing EU enlargement. The

and Fundamental Freedoms, OJ C 306/155 of 17 December 2007; Declaration on Article 6(2) of the Treaty on European Union, OJ C 306/249 of 17 December 2007.

278 See also in this connection: Guido Schwellnus, "'Much ado about nothing?' Minority Protection and the EU Charter of Fundamental Rights", Constitutionalism Web-Papers, ConWEB No. 5/2001.

279 See further: Olivier De Schutter, "The Framework Convention on the Protection of National Minorities and the Law of the European Union", in Kristin Henrard, Ed., *Double Standards Pertaining to Minority Protection*, *op. cit.*, pp. 71–116; Olivier De Schutter, "The Framework Convention on the Protection of National Minorities and the Law of the European Union", in Annelies Verstichel, Andre Alen, Bruno De Witte & Paul Lemmens, Eds., *The Framework Convention for the Protection of National Minorities: A Useful Pan-European Instrument?* (Antwerp/Oxford/Portland, Intersentia, 2008), pp. 231–272; Bruno De Witte & Eniko Horvath, "The many faces of minority policy in the European Union", in Kristin Henrard & Robert Dunbar, Eds., *Synergies in Minority Protection*, *op. cit.*, pp. 365–384; Bruno De Witte, "Politics versus law in the EU's approach to ethnic minorities", in Jan Zielonka, Ed., *Europe Unbound: Enlarging and reshaping the boundaries of the European Union* (London & New York, Routledge, 2002), pp. 137–160; Bruno De Witte, *Politics Versus Law in the EU's Approach to Ethnic Minorities*, EUI Working Paper RSC No. 2000/4; Kyriaki Topidi, "European Union standards and mechanisms for the protection of minorities and the prevention of discrimination", in Council of Europe, *Mechanisms for the implementation of minority rights* (Strasbourg, Council of Europe Publishing, 2004), pp. 183–202.

280 For further commentary on relevant issues, see: Manfred Nowak, "Human Rights 'Conditionality' in Relation to Entry to, and Full Participation in, the EU", in Philip Alston *et al.*, Eds., *The EU and Human Rights* (New York, Oxford University Press, Inc., 1999), pp. 687–698; Bruno De Witte & Gabriel N. Toggenburg, "Human Rights and Membership of the

European Council's conclusions adopted in Copenhagen in 1993 set out that membership of the EU "requires that the candidate country has achieved stability of institutions guaranteeing democracy, the rule of law, human rights and respect for and protection of minorities".[281] It has been noted that whereas the other criteria had already been recognised "as fundamental values in the European Union's internal development *and* for the purpose of its enlargement", "minority protection is *only* mentioned in the latter context".[282] This discrepancy has been criticised for imposing on aspirant Member States additional standards to those actually recognised within the EU by existing Member States.[283] Nevertheless, the inclusion of minority protection in the Copenhagen Criteria had a longer-term effect of publicising and institutionalising the issue.[284] As the EU did not have its own standards on minority protection, the process of pre-accession monitoring of candidate States, necessarily drew on relevant standards, reporting and monitoring, carried out in other fora. There was particular reliance on the work of the Council of Europe, especially its work relating to the FCNM. As such, the EU enlargement process proved an important catalyst for aspirant Member States to develop their laws, policies and practices concerning minority protection and bring them into line with FCNM standards.[285]

Of the various EU institutions, it is the European Parliament that has traditionally been the most sympathetic and sensitive to the objective of advancing minority rights protection within and by the EU. The need to develop a coherent EU policy on minority rights is one of the central emphases of its 2005 Resolution entitled

European Union", in Steve Peers & Angela Ward, Eds., *The European Union Charter of Fundamental Rights* (Oxford and Portland Oregon, Hart Publishing, 2004), pp. 59–82; Christophe Hillion, "Enlargement of the European Union: A Legal Analysis", in Anthony Arnull & Daniel Wincott, Eds., *Accountability and Legitimacy in the European Union* (Oxford University Press, 2002), pp. 401–418.

281 Conclusions of the Copenhagen European Council, *Bulletin of the European Communities* 6–1993, Point I.13.

282 (emphasis per original). Bruno De Witte, "Politics versus law in the EU's approach to ethnic minorities", *op. cit.*, at 140.

283 See, *inter alia, ibid.*

284 See further: Christophe Hillion, "Enlargement of the European Union: A Legal Analysis", *op. cit.*, at 408–409.

285 See further: James Hughes & Gwendolyn Sasse, "Monitoring the Monitors: EU Enlargement Conditionality and Minority Protection in the CEECs", *Journal on Ethnopolitics and Minority Issues in Europe (JEMIE)* (No. 1, 2003); André Liebich, "Ethnic minorities and long-term implications of EU enlargement", in Jan Zielonka, Ed., *Europe Unbound: Enlarging and reshaping the boundaries of the European Union, op. cit.*, pp. 117–136; Gabriel N. Toggenburg, Ed., *Minority Protection and the Enlarged European Union: The Way Forward* (Hungary, Open Society Institute, 2004); Antje Wiener & Guido Schwellnus, "Contested Norms in the Process of EU Enlargement: Non-Discrimination and Minority Rights", Constitutionalism Web-Papers, ConWEB No. 2/2004; Gwendolyn Sasse, "The Political Rights of National Minorities: Lessons from Central and Eastern Europe", in Wojciech Sadurski, Ed., *Political Rights under Stress in 21st Century Europe* (New York, Oxford University Press Inc., 2006), pp. 239–281.

"Protection of minorities and anti-discrimination policies in an enlarged Europe".[286] In the Resolution, it urges the European Commission to "establish a policy standard for the protection of national minorities", based on the FCNM.[287] It also provides a detailed list of international texts which could usefully inform the exercise of developing "some common and minimum objectives for public authorities in the EU" concerning the protection of minority rights.[288]

Recent developments concerning human rights protection in and by the EU include the establishment of the European Union Agency for Fundamental Rights[289] and the adoption of a Multi-annual Framework (MAF) for the Agency.[290] The MAF for the Agency is sure to disappoint persons belonging to minoritites. The thematic areas covered by the MAF do not include the rights of persons belonging to minorities as a separate item.[291] Discrimination against persons belonging to minorities is included in a wide-ranging, general focus on discrimination, but the further relevance of other focuses for persons belonging to minorities is, at best, no more than implicit. The failure to prioritise the rights of persons belonging to minorities cannot be dismissed as mere oversight, because the importance of those rights was raised at several junctures during the drafting process. First, in the proposal for the Council Decision initially put forward by the European Commission, it was acknowledged that, *inter alia*, the "protection of national minorities, minority rights and Roma issues" and "respect for cultural, religious and linguistic diversity" had been dealt with in recent European Parliament Resolutions and Council conclusions concerning fundamental rights.[292] The Commission's document also acknowledged that during the public consultation on future thematic priorities for the Agency, "minority rights" was one of the issues that had been mentioned "in particular".[293] Notwithstanding those acknowledgements, the Commission did not include minority rights (or specific aspects thereof) in its initial

---

286 European Parliament resolution on the protection of minorities and anti-discrimination policies in an enlarged Europe (2005/2008(INI)), 8 June 2005, OJ C 124 E/405 of 25 May 2006.

287 *Ibid.*, para. 6.

288 *Ibid.*, para. 8.

289 Council Regulation (EC) No. 168/2007 of 15 February 2007 establishing a European Union Agency for Fundamental Rights, OJ L 53/1, 22 February 2007. See generally: Philip Alston & Olivier De Schutter, Eds., *Monitoring Fundamental Rights in the EU: The Contribution of the Fundamental Rights Agency* (Oxford & Portland Oregon, Hart Publishing, 2005).

290 Council Decision of 28 February 2008 implementing Regulation (EC) No 168/2007 as regards the adoption of a Multi-annual Framework for the European Union Agency for Fundamental Rights for 2007–2012 (2008/203/EC), OJ L 63, 7 March 2008, p. 14.

291 Article 2, Council Decision implementing Regulation (EC) No 168/2007 as regards the adoption of a Multi-annual Framework for the European Union Agency for Fundamental Rights for 2007–2012, *op. cit.*

292 European Commission, Proposal for a Council Decision implementing Regulation (EC) No 168(2007 [sic] as regards the adoption of a Multiannual Framework for the European Union Agency for Fundamental Rights for 2007–2012, 12 September 2007, COM(2007) 515 final, p. 3.

293 *Ibid.*, p. 4.

list of ten thematic areas to be included in the MAF, as set out in that very same document.[294] In its "Detailed explanation of the proposal", the Commission only explained the relevance of the proposed focuses; no explanation was given as to why other focuses (eg. minority rights) had been omitted.[295]

In its response to the Commission's proposal, the European Parliament suggested an amendment to Recital 2 of the draft Council Decision in order to explicitly refer to the protection of minority rights, as follows:

> (2) The Framework should include the fight against racism, xenophobia and related intolerance amongst the thematic areas of the Agency's activity ***and the protection of the rights of persons belonging to ethnic or national minorities***.[296]

The European Parliament's proposed amendment was not included in the text ultimately adopted as the Council Decision, even though it had justified its proposal by referring to Recital 10 of the Council Regulation establishing the Agency, which requires that the protection of the rights of persons belonging to minorities be included in the permanent programme of the Agency.[297]

Finally, it should be noted that the EU Network of Independent Experts on Fundamental Rights' Thematic Comment No. 3, *The Protection of Minorities in the European Union*, comprised major research and performed a very important mapping function concerning relevant standards within the EU.[298]

Conclusions

This Chapter conducts an exploration of the main legal and institutional frameworks guaranteeing the rights of persons belonging to minorities at the international and European levels. Those frameworks exert a determinant influence on the shaping of legal and institutional frameworks at national and sub-national levels and are therefore of crucial importance for the realisation of the rights of persons belonging to minorities in practice.

---

294 *Ibid.*, pp. 5–6.

295 *Ibid.*, pp. 6–7.

296 (The text in bold italics is the amendment proposed by the European Parliament) European Parliament legislative resolution of 17 January 2008 on the proposal for a Council decision implementing Regulation (EC) No 168/2007 as regards the adoption of a Multiannual Framework for the European Union Agency for Fundamental Rights for 2007–2012, Amendment 2. This text was based on an identically-titled report adopted by the Parliament's Committee on Civil Liberties, Justice and Home Affairs (Rapporteur: Michael Cashman) on 20 December 2007 ('Cashman Report').

297 Cashman Report, *op. cit.*, p. 6.

298 EU Network of Independent Experts on Fundamental Rights' Thematic Comment No. 3, The Protection of Minorities in the European Union, 25 April 2005.

This Chapter seeks, not to be exhaustive, but to provide a level of detail that is necessary to understand the legal and political frameworks and dynamics that create the matrix for the protection and promotion of minority rights at the international and European levels. Its aim is to complement Chapter 1's thematic scene-setting in respect of minority rights with relevant normative scene-setting. The theoretical tensions that are are so strident in Chapter 1 continue to reverberate across Chapter 2.

Part II

Theoretical and normative approaches to freedom of expression and minority rights

Chapter 3
Minorities, freedom of expression and of the media

Introduction

This Chapter examines the added value of a minority rights dimension to the right to freedom of expression. It commences with a rehearsal of some of the more common rationales for freedom of expression and lends them different emphases reflecting various specificities of the minority dimension to the right. The instrumental role of the media in the realisation of the right to freedom of expression is then examined, first in general terms and subsequently from the perspective of persons belonging to minorities.

The media perform a number of crucial functions in a healthy democratic society. For instance, they play the role of a public watchdog sniffing out (governmental) corruption and shortcomings; contribute to the formation of public and individual opinions, and create fora for public deliberation and debate. If the media do not operate in a favourable (constitutional, legal, political and societal) environment, it is unlikely that they will be able to perform the various democracy-enhancing functions ascribed to them.

The need to engage with media functionality and to differentiate between different media types is also stressed. Particular attention is paid to the suitability of community, public service, commercial and transnational media for fulfilling the diverse communicative and informational needs and preferences of persons belonging to minorities.

The final focus of this chapter is the extent to which technology-driven changes have conditioned new communicative realities and possibilities, behavioural patterns of media usage and consequently the emergence of new regulatory paradigms.

3.1 Theories of freedom of expression and of the media

As a general rule, the right to freedom of expression does not discriminate. It is a fundamental right for everyone. Therefore, any attempts to plead the case for an enhanced right to freedom of expression for members of certain groups in society, for example minorities, would appear to be misguided and problematic *ab initio*. A more promising way to ensure that the right to freedom of expression for minorities is not just sterile and theoretical, but real and effective, would be to examine the interplay between the right to freedom of expression, specific minority rights and general rights with particular relevance for minorities. To do so, our enquiry must first be situated in an appropriate frame of reference.

The frame of reference chosen for present purposes is that of international human rights law, where freedom of expression takes its place in a catalogue of rights. It has already been explained in the Introduction that freedom of expression is not only a constitutive right, but an instrumental one as well. As such, its interaction with a number of other rights vouchsafed by international human rights law is notably dynamic. Although there is a tendency to perceive the interaction of freedom of expression with other rights as frictional (eg. the right to enjoy one's good name, the right to privacy, the right not to be subjected to racism, etc.), this is a lop-sided perspective and an unfortunate tendency. The interactional relationship between freedom of expression and other rights often generates enhanced understandings and applications of the rights in question. The focus here will, however, be limited to the impact of such interaction in respect of minority rights. As will be discussed in Chapter 4.4, the potential for synchronicity and synergy, rather than competition and conflict, is particularly evident in the case of the interaction of the right to freedom of expression with religious, linguistic, cultural and educational rights.

Before exploring some of the particular interfaces between freedom of expression and other rights, it is important to stress that the grounding of the right alongside other human rights enshrined in international law makes for welcome internal and external consistency in the interpretation and implementation of human rights. In other words, it is conducive to the coherent interpretation of discrete instruments setting forth guarantees of human rights, but also facilitates heightened levels of coherence across such instruments. To the extent that freedom of expression is interpreted in keeping with this perspective, it serves to underscore the universal, indivisible, interdependent and interrelated nature of human rights, as affirmed *inter alia* in the Vienna Declaration of 1993 (see further, Chapter 4.4).[1]

---

1 World Conference on Human Rights – The Vienna Declaration and Programme of Action (1993). See, in particular, Article 5 of the Declaration, which reads: "All human rights are universal, indivisible and interdependent and interrelated. The international community must treat human rights globally in a fair and equal manner, on the same footing, and with the same emphasis. While the significance of national and regional particularities and various historical, cultural and religious backgrounds must be borne in mind, it is the duty of States, regardless of their political, economic and cultural systems, to promote and protect all human rights and fundamental freedoms."

Rationales for the protection of freedom of expression are numerous, rich and varied.[2] As noted by Lucas A. Powe, Jr.:

> Each of the theories has explanatory power. Each has serious weaknesses. Each one, taken on its own, fails to provide an adequate basis for heightened protection of freedom of expression. [...] the whole is stronger than the sum of its parts. There is a synergy among the various explanations for freedom of expression that is lost when the discussion deals with the strengths and weaknesses of a single theory. Hence, when only one theory of freedom of expression is put forward, the claim for heightened protection will be weaker than if the full panoply of justifications were brought to bear on the problem [...][3]

Rather than have to choose between the various theories and to seek to ground freedom of expression in any "unitary principle"[4] (which would be a very subjective, ambitious and futile exercise anyway[5]), the analytical framework of positive international human rights law has much pragmatic appeal. It provides a context that is well-suited to conducting legal analysis, while at the same time offering the possibility to draw eclectically on the philosophical sophistication of distinct theories of freedom of expression. Given that the various theoretical justifications of the right to freedom of expression are "occasionally mutually exclusive, but more often just compatibly different" and that the right serves a number of purposes, it would not be unusual if several of those purposes were to "coalesce around a particular grouping of circumstances".[6] In such a scenario, the right to freedom of expression and other rights could be implicated, thereby emphasising their

---

2 See generally: Eric Barendt, *Freedom of Speech* (2nd Edition) (Oxford, Oxford University Press, 2005); Frederick Schauer, *Free speech: a philosophical enquiry* (Cambridge, etc., Cambridge University Press, 1982); Wojciech Sadurski, *Freedom of Speech and Its Limits* (Dordrecht/Boston/London, Kluwer Academic Publishers, 1999); Tom Scanlon, "A theory of freedom of expression", in T.M. Scanlon, *The Difficulty of Tolerance* (Cambridge, Cambridge University Press, 2003), pp. 6–25; Thomas I. Emerson, *Toward a General Theory of the First Amendment* (New York, Random House, 1966).

3 Lucas A. Powe, Jr., *The Fourth Estate and the Constitution: Freedom of the Press in America* (Berkeley & Los Angeles, University of California Press, 1991), p. 240.

4 Frederick Schauer, "Free Speech and the Argument from Democracy", in J. Roland Pennock & John W. Chapman, Eds., *Liberal Democracy: Nomos XXV* (USA, New York University Press, 1983), pp. 241–256, at 242. He continues: "But it is more likely that 'freedom of speech' is a bundle of interrelated principles, related by no more than a family resemblance. These principles may each have their own justification, and the scope and strength of the principles will be determined by those justifications." See also, Frederick Schauer, *Free speech: a philosophical enquiry, op. cit.*, p. 14.

5 Some authors have, nevertheless, sought to group relevant rationales for freedom of expression under an expansive version of particular rationales, eg. the autonomy-based "persuasion" principle (i.e., the State may not restrict expression on the basis of its ability to persuade those encountering it to act in ways contrary to the State's interests). See, for example, David A. Strauss, "Persuasion, Autonomy, and Freedom of Expression", 91 *Colum. L. Rev.* 334.

6 Frederick Schauer, "Public Figures", 25 *William and Mary Law Review* p. 905 (1984), at p. 930.

interdependent character. This choice of framework does not negate or even diminish the importance of the right to freedom of expression; as already stated, it merely ensures a particular contextualisation.

A venerable line of scholars have – in their own ways – argued that freedom of expression merits special consideration, even compared with other freedoms. This argument is grafted onto one of the quintessential liberalist theses of a negative conception of rights.[7] Under this conception of rights, special reasons must be adduced in order to justify the imposition of any constraint on individual rights. It demands "a maximum degree of non-interference [with individual liberty] compatible with the minimum demands of social life".[8] As Ronald Dworkin has argued, for example, "once a right is recognized in clear-cut cases, then the Government should act to cut off that right only when some compelling reason is presented, some reason that is consistent with the suppositions on which the original right must be based".[9]

More specifically, as regards freedom of expression, Dworkin rejects "the suggested principle that the Government can simply ignore rights to speak when life and property are in question", continuing: "[s]o long as the impact of speech on these other rights remains speculative and marginal, it must look elsewhere for levers to pull".[10] This is central to his famous "rights-as-trumps" approach; an approach which, incidentally, should not be mistaken as absolutist. Dworkin himself willingly concedes that "arguments of principle, which support a particular constraint on liberty on the argument that the constraint is required to protect the distinct right of some individual who will be injured by the exercise of the liberty".[11] Frederick Schauer, too, has utilised the same metaphor to make essentially the same point: under a "Free Speech Principle", "free speech is a good card to hold"; "[i]t does not mean that free speech is the ace of trumps".[12]

When other interests (as opposed to specific individual rights) are pitted against the right to freedom of expression, however, the superior weighting attached to the latter ought to be readily brought to bear on the balancing exercise. Thus, whenever

---

7 For a more extensive discussion of this concept – and its implications for freedom of expression, see Chapter 4.1.2.

8 Isaiah Berlin, "Two Concepts of Liberty", in Isaiah Berlin, *Liberty* (Ed. Henry Hardy) (Oxford University Press), pp. 166–217, at 207. Berlin associates this demand in particular with Mill and Constant, to whom he refers as "the fathers of liberalism", *ibid.*

9 Ronald Dworkin, *Taking Rights Seriously* (London, Duckworth & Co. Ltd., 1977), p. 200.

10 *Ibid.*, p. 204.

11 *Ibid.*, p. 274. Frederick Schauer makes a similar point: "The Free Speech Principle is important in all cases within its scope, but it is only necessarily more important in cases where no identifiable individual right is present on the other side of the balance.", *Free speech: a philosophical enquiry*, *op. cit.*, p. 134.

12 Frederick Schauer, *Free speech: a philosophical enquiry*, *op. cit.*, p. 9.

the (perceived) competing interest is based on an "argument of policy" (as opposed to "an argument of principle"),[13] to use Dworkin's phrase, the balancing exercise is conducted "with our thumbs on the free speech side of the scales",[14] to use Schauer's. The conclusion prompted by this qualitative distinction between rights and interests is that rights can act as veritable side-constraints on the right to freedom of expression, whereas it is considerably more difficult for assumed societal or public interests to lay claim to such a power of curtailment.[15]

The special consideration afforded to the right to freedom of expression results from the strength of the conceptual premises on which it rests. All those premises – varied as they are – style freedom of expression as a vital vector for the advancement of individual autonomy or self-fulfilment, or for the advancement of democratic practices or societal interests. The main rationales for freedom of expression could be briefly (but non-exhaustively) summarised as:

- self-fulfilment/self-realisation/self-actualisation/individual autonomy;[16]
- the advancement of knowledge/discovery of truth/avoidance of error;
- effective participation in democratic society; self-government;[17]
- distrust of government/slippery slope or camel's nose in the tent arguments;
- societal stability and progress;
- tolerance and understanding/conflict prevention;
- the enablement of other human rights, and
- a variety of derivative rationales.[18]

It is the argument from democracy that dove-tails with the present argument from inter-related human rights to the greatest extent. Furthermore, it is Eric Barendt's elaboration of the argument from democracy that most approximates the argument from inter-related human rights. Barendt's characterisation of the argument as being

---

13 Ronald Dworkin, *Taking Rights Seriously*, *op. cit.*, p. 274. See also, Ronald Dworkin, "Is the Press Losing the First Amendment?", 27 *New York Review of Books* (No. 19, 4 December 1980), pp. 49–57.

14 Frederick Schauer, *Free speech: a philosophical enquiry*, *op. cit.*, p. 133.

15 For a topical example, see the discussion on offence based on religious convictions, Chapter 7, *infra*.

16 See, for example: Susan J. Brison, "The Autonomy Defense of Free Speech", *Ethics* 108 (January 1998): 312–339.

17 See, for example: Alexander Meiklejohn, *Free Speech And Its Relation to Self-Government* (New York, Harper & Bros., 1948); William J. Brennan, "The Supreme Court and the Meiklejohnian Interpretation of the First Amendment", 79 Harv. L. Rev. 1 (1965).

18 For a concise elaboration of the content of these theories, see Tom Campbell, "Rationales for Freedom of Communication", in Tom Campbell & Wojciech Sadurski, Eds., *Freedom of Communication* (England, Dartmouth Publishing Co. Ltd., 1994), pp. 17–44. For a more detailed exposition of their content, see: Frederick Schauer, *Free speech: a philosophical enquiry*, *op. cit.*, pp. 3–86; Eric Barendt, *Freedom of Speech* (2nd Edition), *op. cit.*, pp. 1–23.

"from citizen participation in a democracy"[19] is more refined than the conventional treatment given to the argument, which tends to be limited to the importance of ideas and information for the processes of opinion-forming and decision-making by the body politic. As such, Barendt deep-links to the essential features of the argument, *viz.*, equality and participation. However, he stops short of incorporating them into a broader rights-based argument, such as the one advanced here.

Nevertheless, it is useful to reflect on the specific structural connection between the rights to non-discrimination/equality and participation (see further, Chapter 11.1). Within "the liberal conception of equality", Ronald Dworkin discerns the existence of two different rights: to equal treatment and to treatment as an equal. The right to equal treatment entails a right "to the same distribution of goods or opportunities as anyone else has or is given".[20] The right to treatment as an equal, on the other hand, involves a right "to equal concern and respect in the political decision about how these goods and opportunities are to be distributed"[21] – participatory rights, for want of a better description. Dworkin regards the right to treatment as an equal as more fundamental to the right to equal treatment.

It is also useful to dwell on the specific role of the rights to non-discrimination/equality and participation in strengthening the flanks of the right to freedom of expression. The central thesis here is that other rights – especially those process-oriented rights of non-discrimination/equality and of participation – when deployed in conjunction with the right to freedom of expression, can serve to reinvigorate the exercise of that right for members of minority groups, without adulterating the indiscriminate character of the right itself. Under international human rights law, operative notions of "equality" and "participation" are better described as "effective equality" and "effective participation". In order for both notions to be effective in the context of freedom of expression, they will have to be applied in such a way as to furnish and safeguard expressive opportunities for minorities. This will usually involve engaging with impediments to the realisation of freedom of expression that are deeply embedded in societal and institutional structures (see further, Chapter 11).

A conflation of socio-political and economic circumstances can have a determinant effect on individuals' ability to exercise their right to freedom of expression. The high incidence of members of minority groups suffering socio-political and economic disadvantage makes it more difficult for them to enjoy access to the media, thereby compounding their political disenfranchisement, social exclusion and inability to effectively exercise their right to freedom of expression. However,

---

19 Eric Barendt, *Freedom of Speech* (2nd Edition), *op. cit.*, pp. 18–21.

20 Ronald Dworkin, *Taking Rights Seriously*, *op. cit.*, p. 273.

21 *Ibid.*

of themselves, those adverse circumstances militating against minorities' ability to fully exercise their right to freedom of expression do not amount to an infringement of that right. Factual circumstances may leave the subjects of the right in a position of incapacity, but incapacity cannot ordinarily be construed as an infringement of rights, absent other considerations that might transform the evaluation.

Examples of transformative considerations would include situational inequality directly resulting from exclusionary or discriminatory institutional practices or a history of persecution. Degrees of intensity and permanency are highly relevant here. This can be usefully elucidated by drawing on the concept of "durable inequality",[22] or better, "durable but preventable inequality", from which certain minority groups suffer. Michael Walzer describes the "deepest and most enduring inequalities" as being "not primarily economic in their origins", but as having "their roots in cultural and racial/ethnic differences and in the political exploitation of these differences".[23] Members of groups disadvantaged by "durable inequality" are "categorized and stigmatized collectively, not individually, and then they are systematically discriminated against socially and economically",[24] according to Walzer. The right to non-discrimination/equality is triggered – in a strictly legal sense – by any of a combination of factors: when the discrimination/inequality is perpetrated institutionally (thereby implicating the vicarious liability of the State for the actions of its civil servants); repetitive patterns of preventable discrimination/inequality (thereby implicating State liability for acquiescence or failure to take positive measures to prevent the discrimination/inequality), etc.

The relationship between the issues broached in the preceding two paragraphs and freedom of expression for minorities will be discussed in greater detail in Chapters 5–8. What is important for immediate purposes is to make clear that the right to non-discrimination/equality, notwithstanding its cross-cutting tendencies, should not be perceived as a panacea for all the ills and injustices of society – a certain circumstantial threshold must be reached before the right will take effect in such a way as to impose positive obligations on States authorities.[25] Thus, while it may have been characteristically astute of Rousseau to posit that, "[p]recisely because the force of circumstance tends always to destroy equality, the force of legislation ought always to tend to preserve it",[26] from the perspective of the international

22 Michael Walzer develops this concept, the coinage of which he attributes to Charles Tilly, *Durable Inequality* (Berkeley, University of California Press, 1998). See further: Michael Walzer, *Politics and Passion: Toward a More Egalitarian Liberalism* (New Haven & London, Yale University Press, 2004), pp. 29 *et seq.*

23 *Ibid.*, p. 29.

24 *Ibid.*, p. 30.

25 See further, the discussion on negative and positive conceptions of liberty in Chapter 4.1.2.

26 Jean-Jacques Rousseau, *The Social Contract* (Trans. Maurice Cranston) (England, Penguin, 2004), p. 59.

protection of human rights, the question is unfortunately not quite so straightforward.

3.1.1 Rationales for minorities' access to expressive opportunities

The importance of active access to the media can be grounded in several rationales, including participation in democratic procedures and public debate, and the advancement of cultural and linguistic objectives. Flowing from these two rationales, in particular, access can be taken as having a crucial, controlling influence on expressive opportunities, the breadth and depth of public debate and the shaping of cultural and political narratives.[27] Effective access to the media therefore facilitates countermajoritarian posturing by minority groups, as well as the correction of biases in dominant cultural and political discourse. This line of reasoning prompts the conclusion that the kind of pluralism regarded as a hallmark of democratic society is well-served by effective, active access to viable expressive opportunities (see further, Chapter 11).

3.1.1(i) Democratic participation in public life

A vibrant public sphere cannot exist without freedom of expression and participation. Its existence is also predicated on the existence of free, independent and pluralistic media. This is because of the media's public watchdog role on the one hand, and their forum-providing role on the other hand. In modern democratic society, the media provide vital fora for public discussion to take place. When they assume such a role or when such a role is thrust upon them, they become powerful gate-keepers to the extent that they can control access to public debate. Their power also derives from their ability to mediate and thereby influence content. These observations explain the edginess about concentrations of media power and the absence of media-related pluralism which prevails in Chapter 9.

It is hard to come up with a more lucid articulation of the importance of access to the media for the principle of participation in democratic society than that provided by T.M. Scanlon:

> Access to means of expression is in many cases a necessary condition for participation in the political process of the country, and therefore something to which citizens have an independent right. At the very least the recognition of such rights will require governments to insure that means of expression are readily available

27 See, *inter alia*, Owen M. Fiss, "Silence on the Street Corner", XXVI *Suffolk University Law Review* (No. 1, Spring 1992), pp. 1–20, at 19; Monroe E. Price, *Television, the Public Sphere and National Identity*, (Oxford, Clarendon Press, 1995).

> through which individuals and small groups can make their views on political issues known, and to insure that the principal means of expression in the society do not fall under the control of any particular segment of the community.[28]

In his seminal article, "Access to the Press – A New First Amendment Right",[29] Jerome Barron likens the denial of access rights to prior or previous censorship,[30] which is generally anathema to most stalwart proponents of freedom of expression.[31] The reason for taking such a dim view of *ex ante* censorship is its drastic nature; its ability to totally foreclose both expression and expressive opportunities. In both cases – denial of access to the media and prior censorship – information and ideas are prevented from being aired or heard. However, denial of access, especially if systemic in nature, is the more drastic of the two, because prior censorship is usually directed at specific types of content, whereas the (systemic) denial of access is more likely to be content-neutral. The denial of access to the media – when no alternative expressive opportunities are available – can lead to information and ideas being nipped in the bud and the right to freedom of expression being thwarted.

Barron's central argument – that the interests of fairness dictate that some form of mandatory access to the media should be available to counter information and ideas purveyed by the media – is cogent and merits careful consideration, but it becomes more difficult to sustain when the denial of access is not blanket in nature, but applicable only to particular media. As explained in Chapter 11.1.1, international law does not recognise a right of individuals or groups to access particular media. Only "contingent" rights of access are admitted, otherwise – to formulate the pragmatic argument for this state of affairs – the way would be open "for such overload and chaos as to constitute a virtual reductio ad absurdum".[32] This is particularly true because every medium has its own inherent restrictions (such as traditional temporal and spatial restrictions in the case of broadcasting and the printed press, respectively) and under what Owen Fiss has termed the "dynamic of displacement",[33] a decision to broadcast particular content necessarily entails a

---

28 T.M. Scanlon, "A theory of freedom of expression", *op. cit.*, at 22.

29 Jerome A. Barron, "Access to the Press – A New First Amendment Right", 80 Harv. L. Rev. 1641 (1967). Barron is often credited with being the first (academic) to develop the case for access rights under the US First Amendment; this article was repeatedly referred to by the US Supreme Court in the *Red Lion* case (*Red Lion Broadcasting Co., Inc. v. Federal Communications Commission*, 395 US 367 (1969)) and in its jurisprudential progeny. See also: Jerome A. Barron, "Access to the Media – A Contemporary Appraisal", 35 Hofstra L. Rev. 937 (2006–2007).

30 See also in this connection, Owen M. Fiss, "Silence on the Street Corner", *op. cit.*

31 For example, Alexander Bickel has quipped that a "criminal statute chills, prior restraint freezes" – Alexander Bickel, *The Morality of Consent* (New Haven, Yale University Press, 1975), p. 61.

32 Judith Lichtenberg, "Introduction", in Judith Lichtenberg, Ed., *Democracy and the mass media* (USA, Cambridge University Press, 1990), pp. 1–20, at 17.

33 Owen M. Fiss, "Free Speech and Social Structure", 71 *Iowa Law Review* 1405 (1986), at 1415.

decision not to broadcast other content. As such, the power of the media to determine what to broadcast or publish "subtracts from public debate at the very moment that it adds to it".[34]

From the point of view of democratic theory, a deeper-scooping and more purposive argument would focus on the Meiklejohnian assertion that: "[w]hat is essential is not that everyone shall speak, but that everything worth saying shall be said".[35] Moderation or mediation is therefore required in order to ensure effective public deliberation though the avoidance of "unregulated talkativeness".[36]

Although Meiklejohn envisaged the State as playing the role of moderator of public debate, it should not be precluded that the media – as majorly significant agents for the propagation of information and ideas – could provide mediation in public debate. Indeed, *de facto*, one of their quintessential roles – the selection, presentation and treatment of issues – is inescapably mediatory in nature. The outstanding issue is therefore whether their mediation in public debate is grounded in altruism: "[t]he free press must be free to all who have something worth saying to the public, since the essential object for which a free press is valued is that ideas deserving a public hearing shall have a public hearing".[37] However, it should be noted that such an ascribed role for the media is changing (at least for some media) due to technological developments and resultant changes in patterns of media usage (see further, Chapter 3.3).

3.1.1(ii) Creating alternative discursive spaces

The importance of the media can also be gauged in terms of their discussion-fostering/forum-providing role. In modern democratic society, the media provide vital fora for public discussion to take place. When they assume such a role or when such a role is thrust upon them, they become powerful gate-keepers to the extent that they can control (the terms of) access to public debate.

Furthermore, the power of the media also stems from their ability to influence public debate – through initial agenda-setting, but also through their mediation of ensuing discussion. Roger Silverstone and Myria Georgiou have elucidated the dynamics at play in the mediation of public debate by the media as follows:

---

34 *Ibid.*

35 Alexander Meiklejohn, *Free Speech And Its Relation to Self-Government* (New York, Harper & Bros., 1948), p. 25.

36 *Ibid.*

37 The [Hutchins] Commission on Freedom of the Press, *A Free and Responsible Press* (Chicago, University of Chicago Press, 1947), p. 129 (Appendix).

> Mediation is a political process in so far as control over mediated narratives and representations is denied to individuals and groups by virtue of their status or their capacity to mobilise material and symbolic resources in their own interests. Mediation is also a political process in so far as dominant forms of imaging and story-telling can be resisted, appropriated or countered by others both inside media space, that is through minority media of one kind or another, or on the edge of it, through the everyday tactics of symbolic engagement, in gossip, talk or stubborn refusal.[38]

Silverstone and Georgiu then argue that "minorities and their media need to be understood" in the context of "these contested processes" which reveal the ability of the media to "provide frameworks for identity and community".[39]

Given the far-reaching influence of the media on public deliberation and – by extension – the formation of public opinion, concerns about the implications for democracy of concentrations of media power and the absence of media-related pluralism seem well-founded. The threats posed by such concentrations of media power to the workings of democracy are blatant and they are often invoked as a principal justification for the need to safeguard media pluralism and diversity.

3.1.1(iii) Creating and sustaining (cultural) identities

"Identity", as posited by Asbjorn Eide, "is essentially cultural",[40] but coupling together the concepts of "culture" and "identity" does not make the sum of their parts any easier to define. Cultural identity is the product of an attempted synthesis of elements that are – all at once – subjective and objective; factual and aspirational; latent and active; historical and contemporary. To compound matters further, in order to determine the nature of the relationship of individual identity to group identity, the concept of the situated self must also lock horns with the notion of libertarian individualism. While the Sisyphean task of reaching an adequate definition of cultural identity is beyond the scope of this book, a selection of relevant general remarks and references would nevertheless offer welcome conceptual contextualisation.

---

38 Roger Silverstone & Myria Georgiou, "Editorial Introduction: Media and Minorities in Multicultural Europe", 31 *Journal of Ethnic and Migration Studies* (No. 3, May 2005), pp. 433–441, at 434. For a lengthier discussion of relevant issues, see generally: Monroe E. Price, *Television, The Public Sphere, and National Identity, op. cit.*

39 *Ibid.*

40 Asbjorn Eide, "Cultural Rights and Minorities: Essay in Honour of Erica-Irene Daes", in Gudmundur Alfredsson & Maria Stavropoulou, Eds., *Justice Pending: Indigenous Peoples and Other Good Causes* (The Hague, Martinus Nijhoff Publishers, 2002), pp. 83–97, at 97.

Benedict Anderson has famously defined/described a nation as "an imagined political community" that is limited [by physical boundaries] and sovereign.[41] Anderson's description of a nation as "imagined", places it very consciously in oppositon to Ernest Gellner's characterisation of a nation as an invention.[42] For Anderson, invention rhymes with fabrication and falsity, whereas imagining and creation would actually be closer to the mark. He explains: "[i]n fact, all communities larger than primordial villages of face-to-face contact (and perhaps even these) are imagined. Communities are to be distinguished, not by their falsity/genuineness, but by the style in which they are imagined".[43]

But nations – and indeed other communities – can be imagined in different ways, including ways which are less contingent on geo-political limitations. These imaginings can incorporate a diasporic dimension,[44] a term which itself comprises a high level of internal differentiation. Whether communities are imagined as nations, or in sub-, inter-, or extra-national terms, or whether groups are constituted on the basis of ideological or other affinities or objectives, an appropriate, formal framework is necessary to ensure the protection and promotion of their identities.[45]

Discrete group identities are optimally engendered against a background of not only tolerance, "but also a positive attitude of cultural pluralism by the state and the larger society",[46] according to Eide. Both the acceptance of, and respect for, "the distinctive characteristics and contribution of minorities in the life of the national society as a whole"[47] are required, in his view. The importance of this triumvirate of pluralism, tolerance and participation for minority rights generally can hardly be overstated. Indeed, some commentators regard participation as one of the best gauges of tolerance in pluralist society.[48]

---

41 Benedict Anderson, *Imagined Communities: Reflections on the Origin and Spread of Nationalism* (Revised Edition) (USA, Verso, 1991), p. 6.

42 Ernest Gellner, *Thought and Change* (Repr.) (Chicago, University of Chicago Press, 1974), p. 169.

43 Benedict Anderson, *Imagined Communities: Reflections on the Origin and Spread of Nationalism, op. cit.*, p. 6.

44 See further: Kevin Robins, "Beyond Imagined Community? Transnational Media and Turkish Migrants in Europe", in Stig Hjarvard, Ed., *Media in a Globalized Society* (Denmark, Museum Tusculanum Press/University of Copenhagen, 2003), pp. 187–205. See also: David Morley & Kevin Robins, *Spaces of Identity: Global Media, Electronic Landscapes and Cultural Boundaries* (London, Routledge, 1995).

45 Stig Hjarvard, "Introduction", in Stig Hjarvard, Ed., *Media in a Globalized Society, op. cit.*, pp. 7–14, at p. 11.

46 Asbjorn Eide, "Cultural Rights and Minorities: Essay in Honour of Erica-Irene Daes", *op. cit.*, p. 97.

47 *Ibid.*

48 See, for example, T.M. Scanlon, *The Difficulty of Tolerance, op. cit.*, esp. pp. 194–195.

States have a particularly high level of responsibility for assuring the protection and promotion of their component cultural identities. As regards protection, policies and measures with harmful or assimilatory aims or effects must be avoided, or if already in place, discontinued. As regards promotion, States can reasonably be expected to actively and purposefully faciltitate "the maintenance, reproduction and further development of the culture of the minorities".[49] Appropriate facilitative initiatives should be pursued across the spread of areas falling within State competence.

The media, for their part, can play a crucial role in the consolidation and legitimisation of group identity. They can, for instance, become agents of "cultural consecration" in the sense of the term intended by Pierre Bourdieu.[50] The foregoing characterisation of the media as autonomous discursive spaces suggests that the media are a logical choice of locus for the pursuit of the project of imagining a community's identity. They constitute a forum in which various – and often competing – visions and versions of shared elements of identity can be put forward, explored, debated and ultimately rejected or validated. The media are often the handmaidens of – especially fledgling or divided – States seeking to assert national identities. As such, they can be saddled with the responsibility of propagating a politically-determined image of the nation or community.

According to Anderson, there are "processes by which the nation came to be imagined, and, once imagined, modelled, adapted and transformed".[51] In other words, what is involved here is an ongoing process of imagining; a dynamic force. Inherent in any definition of culture is its propensity for further development. As such, the media must prove responsive to the changing identities of groups, to imaginative alterations/revisions and adjustments.

By running their own media outlets, minorities and other communities of shared interests acquire considerable autonomy. In itself, this is an important step towards the realisation of such groups' rights to participation and the enjoyment of cultural life, in particular, as well as their rights to non-discrimination and equality. It presents them with the opportunities and space in which they can explore and define their identities. However, minority media and the discursive spaces which they are instrumental in creating, tend to be distinctive and self-contained. As such, they – by and large – do little to inform or educate society as a whole about the particular identities of the groups in question. They are also of limited value in advancing the

---

49 Asbjorn Eide, "Cultural Rights and Minorities: Essay in Honour of Erica-Irene Daes", *op. cit.*, p. 97.

50 Pierre Bourdieu, *Language and Symbolic Power* (United Kingdom, Polity Press, 1991), p. 121.

51 Benedict Anderson, *Imagined Communities: Reflections on the Origin and Spread of Nationalism*, *op. cit.*, p. 141.

goals of inter-community communication and the promotion of tolerance. They are not designed to build societal bridges. However, that is not to say that they cannot and do not build such bridges. Cooperation between minority and majority groups, or various minority groups can prove workable and mutually beneficial (eg. in television broadcasting: *TG4* in Ireland and *Omrop Fryslan* in the Netherlands). In some instances, minority broadcasters may even pursue deliberate strategies of securing "a hybrid audience beyond the grassroots ghetto":[52] in the interests of broader cultural legitimation as well as for economic reasons.

Linguistic identity

Tensions between the freedom and regulation of language use (especially where the latter rhymes with restriction) have great capacity for creating unity and division (if not polarisation) in society. This is hardly surprising, for a variety of reasons. First, it is a well-established tenet of international law that language is an impermissible ground for discrimination.[53] It is often argued, however, that non-discrimination should not be seen as an end-goal in itself and that equality is the preferred paradigm to be strived for. The notion of "effective equality" which permeates the Council of Europe's Framework Convention for the Protection of National Minorities (FCNM) is increasingly *de rigueur*. Allied to this is the particular reading of relevant international law provisions which holds that the purpose of such provisions is "to go beyond a guarantee of non-discrimination towards a more positive notion of conservation of linguistic identity".[54] In short, all of this leads to a more assertive, pro-active role for the law in the protection of language.

Second, language can be a vehicle for consolidating a sense of national identity or, more accurately, perhaps, the majoritarian identity of a given State. On the other hand, it can equally be a mechanism for asserting minority or non-majoritarian identitites. A third reason is that language is inextricably bound up in cultural matters. Indeed, the same is also true of the relationship between language and education; language and the media, and language and participation in public life generally. The nature of these highly sensitive relationships can have a determinative effect on society, leading alternately to greater cohesion or fragmentation (or even ghettoisation), depending on the line of argumentation pursued. The writer, Hugo Hamilton, epigrammatically captures the immanent complexities, sensitivities and symbolisms of these relationships, when he quotes his father as averring: "your

52 Chris Atton, *Alternative Media* (London, SAGE Publications, 2002), p. 144.

53 Ample evidence of this is provided by Article 2(2), ICCPR and ICESCR; Article 14, ECHR and Protocol No. 12 to the ECHR; Article 21 of the Charter of Fundamental Rights of the European Union, all of which cite language as one of the prohibited grounds for discrimination.

54 Patrick Thornberry, *International Law and the Rights of Minorities* (Oxford, Clarendon Press, 1991), p. 197.

language is your home and your country is your language and your language is your flag".[55]

3.1.2 Enhanced liberty for the media/the Fourth Estate

The foregoing sections have attempted to explicate the most important rationales for access to expressive opportunities. As the media very often constitute the most effective expressive opportunities available, this section will largely synthesise and synopsise the rationales already outlined and consider them in terms of the media as an institutional force in democratic society. Roger Silverstone has captured the multi-layered importance of the media with characteristic verve:

> It's all about power, of course. In the end. The power the media have to set an agenda. The power they have to destroy one. The power they have to influence and change the political process. The power to enable, to inform. The power to deceive. The power to shift the balance of power: between state and citizen; between country and country; between producer and consumer. And the power that they are denied: by the state, by the market, by the resistant or resisting audience, citizen, consumer. It is all about ownership and control: the who and the what and the how of it. And it is about the drip, drip, drip of ideology as well as the shock of the luminous event. It is about the media's power to create and sustain meanings; to persuade, endorse and reinforce. The power to undermine and reassure. It is about reach. And it is about representation: the ability to present, reveal, explain; and also the ability to grant access and participation. It is about the power to listen and the power to speak and be heard. The power to prompt and guide reflection and reflexivity. The power to tell tales and articulate memories.[56]

The foregoing points clearly to the need to study and comprehend the media's "power of definition, of incitement, of enlightenment, of seduction, of judgement".[57]

One of the profound paradoxes of democracy is that if it functions well, criticism of it will thrive. Criticism should pervade throughout society, but it is rooted in the media and, increasingly, civil libertarian and other non-governmental organisations.[58] It is not without reason that many people have come to regard the media as the Fourth Estate; a would-be extra pillar in a radical reworking of

---

55 Hugo Hamilton, *The Speckled People* (London, Fourth Estate, 2003), p. 3.

56 Roger Silverstone, *Why Study the Media?* (London/Thousand Oaks, CA/New Delhi, SAGE Publications, 1999), p. 143.

57 *Ibid.*

58 The European Court of Human Rights has recognised as much, *inter alia*, in *Steel & Morris v. United Kingdom*, when it referred to "the legitimate and important role that campaign groups can play in stimulating public discussion" – Judgment of 25 January 2005, para. 95.

Montesquieu's tripartite division of powers. The term, "the Fourth Estate", is one of notoriously imprecise metes and bounds,[59] which perhaps explains why the European Court of Human Rights has never actually used the term even though it has consistently shown great deference to the concept.

The coinage of the term is generally attributed to Edmund Burke, who – the story goes – used it to refer disparagingly to a group of parliamentary reporters in 1787.[60] The evolution of the doctrine has – since the very beginning – been dogged with questions about the democratic credentials of the media. Nowadays, such questions tend to be framed in terms of transparency, accountability and self-regulatory journalistic standards generally. The democratic aspirations and commercial realities (of ownership, market, etc.) make for very uneasy bedfellows.

The centrality of the (mass) media to the dynamics of democracy has been recognised time and again by the European Court of Human Rights, having ascribed to the media the "vital role of public watchdog".[61] The Court has stated that it is incumbent on the media to impart information and ideas on all matters of public interest. It has also consistently held that "[n]ot only do the media have the task of imparting such information and ideas: the public also has a right to receive them".[62] In light of this function of the media (corrective, curative, supervisory, stabilising – call it what you will), the Court has tended to carve out a zone of protection for the media's right to freedom of expression that is even greater than that of ordinary individuals.[63] This vision of the media ascribes to them an important critical role in democratic society; it envisages them as "criticasters".[64]

One hallmark of the expanded zone of the media's freedom of expression is the notion of journalistic independence. Importantly, this independence filters from the editorial level down to front-line journalism and reporting. A key pronouncement in this regard reads: "the methods of objective and balanced reporting may vary considerably, depending among other things on the medium in question; it is not for the Court, any more than it is for the national courts, to substitute its own views for those of the press as to what techniques of reporting should be adopted by

---

59 See generally: Julianne Schultz, *Reviving the Fourth Estate: Democracy, Accountability and the Media* (Australia, Cambridge University Press, 1998), Chapters 1 and 2.

60 *Ibid.*, pp. 49 and 97.

61 *The Observer & Guardian Newspapers Ltd. v. United Kingdom*, Judgment of the European Court of Human Rights of 26 November 1991, Series A, No. 216, para. 59.

62 *The Sunday Times (No. 1) v. United Kingdom*, Judgment of the European Court of Human Rights of 26 April 1979, Series A, No. 30, para. 65.

63 This approach by the Court is without prejudice to the level of freedom of expression enjoyed by individuals: *Steel & Morris v. United Kingdom*, *op. cit.*, para. 89.

64 Criticaster is a Dutch word meaning "fault-finder"; it is used here as a neologism meaning media (or media-like) disseminators of criticism.

journalists".[65] This commitment to the autonomy of the media in a democratic society goes a long way to guaranteeing operational latitude for journalists. Moreover, this operational latitude stretches to include "possible recourse to a degree of exaggeration, or even provocation".[66]

However, alongside the enjoyment of journalistic freedom – as defined by the Court – are concomitant duties and responsibilities[67] (discussed further in Chapter 4 (Section 1)). Speaking extra-judicially, the former President of the European Court of Human Rights, Luzius Wildhaber, has stated that: "[w]hile the Court has rightly stressed the potentially chilling effect of placing restrictions on speech that may be offensive to individuals or sectors of the community, genuine debate may also be stifled by over-aggressive and inadequately researched journalism".[68]

This is the nub of the problem concerning public resistance to a wider endorsement of the Fourth Estate doctrine. More principled scions of the media argue and crave for the media to be defined according to their vigilance in monitoring and divulging the excesses of various branches of State and society.[69] Or at least, that is the theory; or, some would say, "the fiction". It is also a theory according to which the defining goal of the media is to leave no stone unturned in their quest for "the best obtainable version of the truth".[70] It is a theory that is perhaps out of kilter with the reality of media professionals chasing sex and sleaze and sensationalism and salaciousness. This prompts the question, paraphrasing Lucas A. Powe: how well does [media] promise match performance? "How well", he asks, "is the press exercising its informing function? Is the press meeting its responsibilities, indeed its sole purpose, in vindicating the public's right to know?"[71] In addressing these questions, it is useful to distinguish between different types of media in terms of their purpose, functionality and reach (see Chapter 3.2).

---

65 *Bladet Tromso & Stensaas v. Norway*, Judgment of the European Court of Human Rights of 20 May 1999, Reports of Judgments and Decisions, 1999-III, para. 63, drawing on *Jersild v. Denmark*, Judgment of the European Court of Human Rights of 23 September 1994, Series A, No. 298, para. 31.

66 *Prager & Oberschlick v. Austria*, Judgment of the European Court of Human Rights of 26 April 1995, Series A, No. 313, para. 38.

67 See Article 10(2) of the European Convention on Human Rights.

68 Luzius Wildhaber, "The right to offend, shock or disturb? – aspects of freedom of expression under the European Convention on Human Rights", Sixth Annual RTE/UCD Lecture in the series: Broadcasting, Society and the Law, Dublin, 11 October 2001; also published in (2001) 36 *Irish Jurist* 17.

69 See further: Aidan White, *To Tell You the Truth: The Ethical Journalism Initiative* (Brussels, International Federation of Journalists, 2008).

70 Carl Bernstein, in Ellen Hazelcorn & Patrick Smyth, Eds., *Let in the Light: Censorship, secrecy and democracy* (Dingle, Ireland, Brandon Book Publishers Ltd., 1993), pp. 17–25, at p. 19.

71 Lucas A. Powe, Jr., *The Fourth Estate and the Constitution: Freedom of the Press in America*, *op. cit.*, p. 257.

3.1.3 An enabling environment for media freedom

The concept of "enabling environment" provides an extremely useful analytical frame for issues relating to media freedom.[72] It allows for full-scale ecological examination of the broader legal and policy environment in which the media operate. The concept is also sufficiently capacious to include scope for the evaluation of other extraneous factors affecting media performance, in particular political, socio-economic and cultural factors. The healthiness of the enabling environment in which media operate can be largely determinative of whether or not the media effectively realise their stated goals.

The realisation of an optimal, or at least favourable, enabling environment *for media freedom* is only possible when an optimal or favourable enabling environment *for human rights* in general has already been achieved. The extent to which freedom of expression is protected and promoted in a given society is often regarded both as a prerequisite for other media freedom(s) and as an informal barometer for the existence of other human rights. As consistently argued throughout this book, however, the right to freedom of expression is inextricably linked to a broad range of other human rights, in particular the rights of non-discrimination/equality, participation, freedom of religion or belief, cultural identity and heritage, language and education. According to the inter-related and interdependent conceptualisation of human rights espoused here, the antecedent enabling environment for human rights would also necessarily include minority rights. Furthermore, an enabling environment for human rights is necessarily shaped by principles, structures and practices of democracy and the upholding of the rule of law.

A favourable enabling environment for media freedom needs to rest on firm foundations. As well as the human rights grounding already described, it is also influenced in important ways by the operative public values of a given society. Typically, such values would include pluralism and tolerance.

The constitutional enshrinement of freedom of expression and other media freedoms are crucial features of a favourable enabling environment for media freedom. Relevant statutory provisions are also very important, but constitutional provisions boast superior legitimacy and permanency. Media objectives, practices and structures all generally tend to be regulated. The impact of that regulation can be

---

72 For a comprehensive exploration of the concept, see, Peter Krug & Monroe E. Price, "The Enabling Environment for Free and Independent Media: Contribution to Transparent and Accountable Governance", The USAID Office of Democracy and Governance Occasional Paper Series, January 2002, Doc. No. PN-ACM-006, and more recently and succinctly, Monroe Price & Peter Krug, "The Enabling Environment For Free and Independent Media" in Mark Harvey, Ed., *Media Matters: Perspectives on Advancing Governance & Development from the Global Forum for Media Development* (Beijing, Internews Europe, 2007), pp. 94–101.

assessed in micro and macro terms. The particular effects of individual regulatory provisions (eg. on journalistic freedoms, security of journalists (professional and physical), access to information, protection of sources, media ownership, competition, State subsidies for the promotion of certain public interest objectives, etc.) also have an aggregative effect which is a primary force in the shaping of the enabling environment.

The architecture of State institutions is also very important in this respect: they should ideally be democratic, transparent and accountable and foster interaction with the public. Media regulatory authorities should be independent and representative. Their structures and *modi operandi* should ensure transparency, accountability, participation in policy-formulation and effective appeals mechanisms against official decisions. They should broadly conform to the principles of good governance.

Factors other than the formal laws and institutions of State also shape the enabling environment for media freedom. As Monroe Price and Peter Krug have noted, "there is a close interaction between what might be called the legal-institutional and the socio-cultural, the interaction between law and how it is interpreted and implemented, how it is respected and received".[73] The prevailing political culture can also exercise a decisive influence on the ability of the media to carry out their objectives. In democratic countries, traditions of political stability are generally conducive to the existence of free and independent media. In conflict or (immediate) post-conflict situations, a different paradigm operates, in which different roles are assumed by or thrust upon the media.[74] Regulation (to the extent that it can withstand the conflict-related pressures) and public attitudes and expectations are coloured by the ambient political situation. In transitional democracies, too, the media may be susceptible to political vicissitudes and interference.[75] It is important that regulatory measures be tailored to the exigencies of prevailing situations. Very different kinds of regulation are required in very different political contexts.

---

73 Monroe Price & Peter Krug, "The Enabling Environment For Free and Independent Media", *op. cit.*, at 96.

74 See generally, Monroe E. Price & Mark Thompson, Eds., *Forging Peace: Intervention, Human Rights and the Management of Media Space* (Edinburgh, Edinburgh University Press, 2002).

75 See further: Jan van Cuilenburg & Richard van der Wurff, Eds., *Media and Open Societies: Cultural, Economic and Policy Foundations for Media Openness and Diversity in East and West* (Amsterdam, Het Spinhuis, 2000); Karol Jakubowicz, *Rude Awakening: Social and Media Change in Central and Eastern Europe* (New Jersey, Hampton Press, Inc., 2007); David L. Paletz & Karol Jakubowicz, Eds., *Business as Usual: Continuity and Change in Central and Eastern European Media* (New Jersey, Hampton Press, Inc., 2003); Monroe E. Price, Beata Rozumilowicz, and Stefaan G. Verhulst, Eds., *Media Reform: Democratizing the media, democratizing the state* (London, Routledge, 2002); Andrei Richter, *Post-Soviet perspective on censorship and freedom of the media* (Moscow, UNESCO, 2007).

All too often, the great importance attaching to the enabling environment for media development is understated. The securing in society of the rule of law, freedom of expression (including independence of the media and other related freedoms), human rights generally, democracy, pluralism, tolerance, etc., are necessary prerequisites for media development. This general rule is equally applicable to the use of media by minorities. The Advisory Committee on the FCNM has, on occasion, found that "problems pertaining to freedom of the media and the rights and situation of journalists *in general* may also affect the environment surrounding the media of persons belonging to national minorities".[76]

Guarantees of media-related pluralism are also important for minorities. Thomas Gibbons, in disaggregating the term, has usefully distinguished between three distinct levels of media-related pluralism: content, source and outlet.[77] Of these, content is the most substantive in character, whereas source and outlet are more instrumental (to achieving the aim of securing pluralism at the content level). Minorities have a clear interest in pluralism being guaranteed at all three levels. Pluralism of content ensures that they can draw on a wide range of diverse information, which is particularly important for opinion-forming and decision-making processes and political empowerment. The absence of pluralism at the level of sources (i.e., media ownership) can lead to the constriction of public debate and its domination by powerful political and commercial interests. These dangers have already been alluded to in the previous section, *supra*. The interest of minorities in the maintenance of pluralism among outlets is tied in with what is sometimes referred to as the media functionality principle. The ability to choose between different outlets or types of media increases the likelihood of effectively communicating one's message. In short, the media offer available to the general public is only meaningful for minorities to the extent that the offer includes media outlets that correspond to their real communicative needs.

Concerns for market sustainability are always present in minority media circles. Nowadays, the media have to operate in an increasingly competitive and commercialised environment. This is especially true of the broadcasting sector. In consequence, the need to boost audience shares is growing steadily as a driver of broadcasting policy. Public service media (PSM) are also willy-nilly caught up in this vortex, despite the specificity of their mandate. The stark reality is that minority-interest programmes (and especially minority-interest programmes in

---

76 (emphasis added) Advisory Committee Opinion on Ukraine (First Monitoring Cycle), adopted on 1 March 2002, para. 96. See also in this connection: Advisory Committee Opinion on Azerbaijan (First Monitoring Cycle), adopted on 22 May 2003, paras. 43 & 52.

77 Thomas Gibbons, "Concentrations of Ownership and Control in a Converging Media Industry", in Chris Marsden & Stefaan Verhulst, Eds., *Convergence in European Digital TV Regulation* (London, Blackstone Press Ltd., 1999), pp. 155–173, at 157.

"less prevalent (national or regional) languages"[78]) rarely command large audience shares. This can have adverse effects on advertising revenues, which in turn can lead to a general reluctance to broadcast minority-language programmes, particularly at peak viewing/listening times. In such an inhospitable climate, a persuasive case can be made for contemplating prescriptive regulation; financial stimulation; administrative relaxation, all with a view to adequately catering for the needs and interests of persons belonging to national minorities.

Another important feature of the enabling environment, also stressed by Price and Krug, and which is also central to any conceptualisation of the role of the media in any healthy democratic society, is the level of public awareness, understanding, credibility and appreciation of the socio-political role and relevance of the media. This demands the generation of "a special kind of literacy [...] that encompasses a desire to acquire, interpret, and apply information as part of a civil society".[79]

Finally, it should be noted that the concept of "enabling environment" is increasingly being relied upon in international policy-making circles. A very pertinent example is the World Summit on the Information Society (WSIS), the concluding documents of which give detailed consideration to the importance of favourable enabling enivornment for ICTs.[80] Those documents affirm the importance of ensuring a suitable enabling environment for the Information Society at national and international levels.[81] A key paragraph in the Geneva Declaration of Principles reads:

> The rule of law, accompanied by a supportive, transparent, pro-competitive, technologically neutral and predictable policy and regulatory framework reflecting national realities, is essential for building a people-centred Information Society. Governments should intervene, as appropriate, to correct market failures, to maintain fair competition, to attract investment, to enhance the development of the ICT infrastructure and applications, to maximize economic and social benefits, and to serve national priorities.[82]

78 Bruno de Witte, "Surviving in Babel? Language Rights and European Integration", in Yoram Dinstein & Mala Tabory, Eds., *The Protection of Minorities and Human Rights* (Dordrecht, Martinus Nijhoff, 1992), pp. 277–300, at p. 299.

79 Monroe Price & Peter Krug, "The Enabling Environment For Free and Independent Media", *op. cit.* at 99.

80 See, in particular, "Building the Information Society: a global challenge in the new Millennium", Declaration of Principles, World Summit on the Information Society, Geneva, 12 December 2003, Doc. WSIS-03/GENEVA/DOC/4-E, s. 6 (paras. 38–50).

81 *Ibid.*, para. 38; Tunis Commitment, World Summit on the Information Society, Tunis, 18 November 2005, Doc. No. WSIS-05/TUNIS/DOC/7-E, para. 9.

82 "Building the Information Society: a global challenge in the new Millennium", *op. cit.*, para. 39.

As such, the WSIS documents go beyond pure human rights and legal issues, to address economic and technological issues as well. This makes for comprehensiveness and connectedness in its approach. It is extremely important to include these additional dimensions in the formulation of policies to promote favourable enabling environments for communicative activities.

The foregoing discussion has shown the importance of a favourable enabling environment for the realisation of media freedoms. Its importance can also be gauged in terms of the realisation of freedoms enjoyed, or aspired to, by minority media. The focus will now shift to lines of thinking and normative provisions which recognise the importance of media objectives and seek to enhance the enabling environment for media freedom in light of those objectives.

3.2 Media functionality and media types

3.2.1 Media functionality

Assessments of the media's pervasiveness, power and influence are often prone to hyperbolic descriptions. Nevertheless, strong statements may very well be required to capture the full extent of their reach and impact in all three of the aforementioned respects. If not totally ubiquitous, the media certainly come close to ubiquity and have properly been described by Roger Silverstone as "an essential dimension of contemporary experience".[83] Furthermore, as Silverstone has also noted, "[o]ur daily passage involves movement across different media spaces and in and out of media space".[84] It is perhaps axiomatic to state that different media can and do perform different functions, and that they do so with varying degrees of effectiveness. It is precisely this differentiated functionality of various types of media that explains our daily "movement[s] across different media". The choice of media used at any given moment is influenced by purposive and behavioural considerations. Time-use and other studies tend to show that different media are used for different purposes and with different levels of intensity, depending on the setting and time of day.[85]

Without wishing to detract from the idiosyncratic nature of individual preferences for particular media, it is also relevant to consider preferential patterns of media

83 Roger Silverstone, *Why Study the Media?*, *op. cit.*, p. 1. See also, Peter Dahlgren, *Television and the Public Sphere: Citizenship, Democracy and the Media* (London, SAGE Publications, 1995), p. 155.

84 *Ibid.*, p. 8.

85 Tom Moring, "Functional Completeness in Minority Language Media", in Mike Cormack & Niamh Hourigan, Eds., *Minority Language Media: Concepts, Critiques and Case Studies* (Clevedon, Multilingual Matters Ltd., forthcoming: May 2007), pp. 17–33, at p. 23.

usage among groups, notably minorities. Such a group-oriented enquiry is relevant to the extent that persons belonging to minorities may share certain collective characteristics that would profoundly influence their individual media preferences. A shared language would be the best example of such a characteristic. The linguistic specificity of particular group inevitably shapes the media preferences of persons belonging to such groups – one way or another. Most people in a linguistic group may very well prefer to use media in their own language – to the extent that such media are available (although it cannot be discounted that some members of such groups may – for various reasons – have a preference for media employing dominant societal languages). This can facilitate their access to information, on the one hand, or their access to, and ability to participate effectively in, discursive fora on the other.

Such a group-oriented enquiry is also relevant to the extent that persons belonging to minorities are similarly structured in social terms and are therefore similarly affected by situational factors. General literacy levels within particular groups would be a good example of a situational factor of this kind: if average literacy levels within a particular minority group are very low, print media could be considered a less viable type of media than various broadcasting options. The same arguments apply *mutatis mutandis* to levels of familiarity with new media technologies (and of course the extent of their penetration in minority groups). Groups with strong oral traditions might conceivably exhibit preferences for types of media that best accommodate orality. Another example would be whether the group is territorially compact or dispersed, as such geographical facts could influence the suitability of different media for the entire group.

A further group-oriented approach has been developed by Tom Moring. He usefully applies the general notion of "institutional completeness", defined by Will Kymlicka as a minority group having "a full range of social, educational, economic, and political institutions, encompassing both public and private life",[86] specifically to the media sector.[87] For Moring, institutional completeness in respect of the media denotes "the level of completeness of a media system that serves a particular minority" and he proposes that such completeness is best measured in terms of: (i) the availability of different types of media, and (ii) the availability of different

86 Will Kymlicka, *Multicultural Citizenship: A liberal theory of minority rights* (New York, Oxford University Press, 1995), p. 78. Similarly, Raymond Breton has described the notion as the ability of a community to "perform all the services required by its members": Raymond Breton, "Institutional Completeness of Ethnic Communities and the Personal Relations of Immigrants", Vol. LXX *The American Journal of Sociology* (No. 2, 1964), pp. 193–205, at 194.

87 Tom Moring, *Access of National Minorities to the Media: New Challenges*, Report for the Committee of Experts on Issues Relating to the Protection of National Minorities (DH-MIN), Doc. DH-MIN(2006)015, 20 November 2006, p. 9. For a lengthier discussion, see generally: Tom Moring, "Functional Completeness in Minority Language Media", *op. cit.*

formats [within available media types].[88] To the extent that it is not already included in the notion of "formats", an additional means of measurement could be thematic orientations of content. The focus on formats/thematic orientations of content is important in the context of minority media (especially in minority-language broadcasting) because in the context of limited airtime and scarce financial resources, there is a tendency to prioritise certain formats/themes. In practice, this generally leads to the predominance of news/information programmes, programmes about cultural events of relevance to minorities and sometimes educational or children's programmes too.[89] To the extent that other formats/themes are neglected, it is not realistic to speak about full institutional completeness in the media sector (or functional completeness – see further, *infra*).

Returning briefly to the more general notion of institutional completeness, it is important to note that the notion is sometimes perceived to be a crucial feature of schemes for minority rights protection. Although not legally-binding, the Advisory Opinion of the Permanent International Court of Justice in the *Minority Schools in Albania* case[90] provides valuable insights into relevant thinking. It expressly links the need to achieve "perfect equality" between minority and majority sections of the population with the need to ensure for minorities "suitable means for the preservation of their racial peculiarities, their traditions and their national characteristics".[91] It reasons:

> These two requirements are indeed closely interlocked, for there would be no true equality between a majority and a minority if the latter were deprived of its own institutions, and were consequently compelled to renounce that which constitutes the very essence of its being as a minority.[92]

Later in the same Advisory Opinion, the Court refers to the minority institutions as being those "which alone can satisfy the special requirements of the minority groups".[93] Obviously, the quoted statements relate first and foremost to the facts of the case under consideration by the Court. Nevertheless, the general line of argumentation does have broader appeal. It argues that it is indispensable for minorities to have their own key institutions in the interests of ensuring equality for members of the minority group with members of the majority population and of sustaining the minority group as a group. Such an approach could be described as being based on principles of group autonomy or internal self-determination.

---

88 *Ibid.*

89 Tom Moring, "Functional Completeness in Minority Language Media", *op. cit.*, at 25.

90 *Minority Schools in Albania*, PCIJ, Advisory Opinion, 6 April 1935, Series A/B, No. 64, pp. 4–36.

91 *Ibid.*, p. 17.

92 *Ibid.*

93 *Ibid.*, p. 20.

The goals of this reading of institutional completeness can also be applied to institutional completeness in the media sector. However, the question of whether or not those (and other relevant) goals are realised in practice does not depend solely on the extent of a minority group's institutional completeness. To complement the quantitative focus of the notion of "institutional completeness", Moring introduces the notion of "functional completeness" as its qualitative counterpart. The latter notion refers to "the extent to which people within a target group actually lean on the media supply that is produced for them (in their language or for their community).[94] In practice, for a host of reasons – not least linguistic, political and economic, minority groups are unlikely to enjoy "perfect" institutional completeness in the media sector. Only in very rare cases will the degree of institutional completeness actually attained correspond to functional completeness for members of a minority group.[95] This is because the question of functionality depends on the viability of the overall range of media types and formats (including thematic orientations) for the fulfillment of the minority group's various communicative needs. If the overall range of media types and formats is *a priori* incomplete, the likelihood of the range being functionally sufficient is reduced accordingly. This would obviously not hold true if the limited range of media types and formats available correspond to the media preferences of members of the minority group – whether by virtue of a well-conceived media policy for the minority group, or simply by happenstance.

Finally, as regards functional completeness in the media sector, consideration should additionally be given to the concepts of needs and preference.[96] Needs in respect of the media vary per group and within groups. Any evaluation of the functionality of available media will inevitably be contingent on whether relevant needs are understood as giving primacy to the minority language in broadcasting, setting it on an equal footing with the majority language, or using it as a complementary language. Individual media preferences have already been discussed, *supra*, but consideration should also be given to preferences of groups (to the extent that they are ascertainable): if a majority of members of a minority group are not in favour of sustaining certain levels of minority-language broadcasting, the viability of measures geared towards such ends might be brought into question. This has been referred to as the "strict preference condition".[97]

94 Tom Moring, *Access of National Minorities to the Media: New Challenges*, *op. cit.*, p. 9.

95 Tom Moring, "Functional Completeness in Minority Language Media", *op. cit.*, at 19.

96 Tom Moring, *Access of National Minorities to the Media: New Challenges*, *op. cit.*, p. 10.

97 *Ibid.* and more extensively in Tom Moring, "Functional Completeness in Minority Language Media", *op. cit.*, at 28–30, and in François Grin & Tom Moring, with Durk Gorter, Johan Häggman, Dónall Ó Riagáin and Miquel Strubell, Support for Minority Languages in Europe, Final Report on a project financed by the European Commission, Directorate Education and Culture, 2003, p. 190.

If, in practice, the range of media types and formats that is available to a particular minority group is not viable for the fulfilment of their various communicative needs, this could give rise to a violation of a State's obligations both in terms of freedom of expression and minority rights (see further: Chapters 4.1, 10.1.1 and 10.3.1). Under such an approach, functional completeness could be used as a means of assessing whether members of a minority group enjoy an *effective* right to receive and impart information.

3.2.2 Media types

The notion of mass media rests on the prior notion, widely used in sociological studies, of *Gesellschaft* – a large, undifferentiated and impersonal society. The term, coined by Ferdinand Tönnies, is generally used in its dichotomization of *Gemeinschaft*, a community or "primary group bound by intimate ties regulating itself through the force of tradition and opinion".[98] "Mass" is capable of multiple – often evaluative and politically-tinctured – interpretations,[99] but for present purposes, it is its descriptive function that must be retained. It describes, first and foremost, the ability of the media to reach a societal mass. As such, it emphasises the point-to-multipoint nature of the media. This consideration is vitally important when it comes to assessing the influence of the media and the development of regulatory policies and measures. Although the term, "mass", usefully conveys the idea of wide reach, at the same time, it also suffers from one of the general shortcomings of theories of mass society[100] by its inability to illuminate relational dynamics within the "mass" to which it refers. The term does not lend itself to recognition of, or responsiveness to, the compositional complexities of the societal mass which is its object.

But even without being qualified by "mass", the "media" is an amalgamated concept and it would be methodoligcally remiss to attempt to analyse its objectives and impact in macro terms. Instead, it is necessary to disaggregate the concept and essentialise its constituent parts in order to emphasise the different objectives pursued by each. These objectives span an entire spectrum: informational, social, cultural, (politically) deliberative, creative, entertainment, etc. The effectiveness of particular media can only be assessed in terms of their specific objectives and any discussion of the equivalence of particular media should avoid comparing apples and pears.

---

98 Daniel Bell, *The Coming of Post-Industrial Society: A Venture in Social Forecasting* (USA, Basic Books, 1999), p. 383. See further: Daniel Bell, *The End of Ideology: On the Exhaustion of Political Ideas in the Fifties* (Revised Edition) (New York, The Free Press, 1962), p. 27.

99 Daniel Bell, for instance, distinguishes between mass as: undifferentiated number; the judgment by the incompetent; the mechanized society; the bureaucratized society, and mob – *The End of Ideology*, *op. cit.*, p. 22.

100 Daniel Bell, *The End of Ideology*, *op. cit.*, p. 38.

First of all, one may distinguish between mainstream and alternative media, with radical media[101] being counted as a subset of the latter. Distinctions between levels of geographical operation are also pertinent: international, national, regional, local and community. The last-named category is, however, rarely understood in a purely geographical sense: it is also laden with additional qualitative goals and features which frequently happen to coincide with its geographical reach (see further, Chapter 3.2.2(i)). A final cleavage involves majority and minority media. These two appelations are vague, expansive terms, and as such are more suited as short-hand phrases than tools for clinical definition. Nevertheless, the distinction that they point up is important for the purposes of analytical orientation. The expressive objectives and strategies of persons belonging to minorities can differ hugely, depending on whether mainstream or minority media are used. This is illustrated by the non-exhaustive selections of features[102] of mainstream and minority media listed below. The strategic importance of mainstream and minority media – and the dilemma of choosing which one to espouse – is captured well by Silverstone and Georgiou:

> Media representation involves both participation and recognition. And participation is a matter of the capacity to contribute to the mainstream, to enable the minority voice or visibility on national channels or the national press, but it is also a matter of the capacity to gain a presence on one's own terms on the nationally owned spectrum or on the global commons of the internet. Participation ultimately involves the equal sharing of a common cultural space. There are different issues here, and different politics, but both raise the questions of whether or how to enable minorities to speak, but also, and this is crucial, to enable them to be heard. Who is speaking and on behalf of whom? Do journalists from ethnic minorities speak as members of that ethnic group or as disinterested and professional journalists? But we must ask, too, who is listening and with what consequences?[103]

Mainstream and minority media

Given the documented shortcomings of the classic, unitary public sphere as elaborated by Habermas, much critical thinking and writing has been devoted to the co-existence of a variety of public spheres. Against this backdrop, the contrasting merits of majority and minority media will now be considered, as well as the necessary complementarity between them. Different rights and interests, aims and strategies are at play on each level, but as we shall see, this does not mean that they are mutually exclusive.

---

101 See, for example, John Downing, *Radical Media: the Political Experience of Alternative Communication* (Boston, MA, South End Press, 1984).

102 Not all of these features necessarily apply in all cases – the purpose of the lists is to be illustrative rather than prescriptive or exhaustive.

103 Roger Silverstone & Myria Georgiou, "Editorial Introduction: Media and Minorities in Multicultural Europe", *op. cit.*, at 436–437.

Mainstream media

- Public sphere – more opinions leads to debate that is more inclusive and more representative
- Elimination of discrimination and promotion of equality
- Participation in general affairs of State and society
- Intercommunity communication
- Fostering of mutual understanding and tolerance
- Expression of distinct cultural identities and challenging of (negative) stereotypes
- Promotion and validation of (minority) ways of life and traditions

Minority media

- Creation of alternative public spheres/own discursive spaces
- Empowerment of minority groups at local level
- Participation in own affairs
- Own institutions as a means of eliminating discrimination and promoting equality
- Promotion of language, culture and religion of minorities
- Validation of history, heritage and creative activities of minorities
- Positive impact on minority communities – creation of network of information exchange; social capital, etc.
- Employment opportunities and economic spin-offs

By providing for the expression of increasingly varied opinions, the media render the public sphere more inclusive and representative of diverse societal elements. Mainstream media should therefore strive to achieve a state of discursive toing and froing. This involves accommodating as wide a spectrum of minority views and interests as possible within majoritarian structures. Proponents of such accommodations frequently point out the risks of intellectual and cultural ghettoisation and isolation that inhere in alternative or minority media structures.[104]

It is widely accepted that the main motivation for the establishment and maintenance of minority media is to prevent assimilation and shape distinctive discursive spaces for minorities and other groups in society. A discursive space can be defined as: "a site of cultural production where the process of representation is shaped by the discursive construction of power relations between producers, participants,

[104] See, for example, Milica Pesic, "Commentary: Media representation of national minorities and the promotion of a spirit of tolerance and intercultural dialogue", in *Filling the frame: Five years of monitoring the Framework Convention for the Protection of National Minorities* (Strasbourg, Council of Europe Publishing, 2004), pp. 139–143, esp. at 140.

audiences and regional, national and international flows within a global mediascape".[105] As such, the independence of such discursive spaces is of paramount importance. So, too, is the number of actors required to give shape to discursive spaces. These spaces are shaped and controlled by the groups themselves, and not by dominant societal groups. Within such spaces, cultural identities can blossom without being in the shadow of dominant cultures. In the same vein, ideologies and stereotypes nurtured and reinforced by dominant groups and the mainstream media can be countered. Furthermore, minority languages can be promoted as the medium of programming and communication. In short, the goal of advancing intra- and inter-group definition is well-served by the existence of autonomous discursive spaces.

3.2.2(i) Community media

Certain types of minority broadcasting can be considered to be "community broadcasting" by virtue of the objectives and strategies they have in common. Various definitions of community broadcasting have been propounded in academic and NGO circles and among broadcasters themselves. Although the terms "community broadcasting" and "community media" are sometimes defined, and their practice regulated, by legislation at the national level, there are no authoritative, legally-binding definitions of the terms at the international level (notwithstanding UNESCO's extensive engagement with the topic). Nevertheless, a broad consistency can be detected across the variety of definitions emanating from the various contexts just mentioned. For instance, community broadcasting has been described as:

> independent broadcasting that is provided by and for the members of a community in a particular geographical location or belonging to a particular community of interest. Its primary purpose is to deliver social benefit and not to operate for private commercial profit. It should be owned by and accountable to the community that it seeks to serve and it should provide for participation by the community in the making of programs and in management.[106]

The World Association of Community Radio Broadcasters (AMARC), an association "favouring consultation, coordination, cooperation, exchange and promotion of community radio broadcasters", explains in its Articles of Association that the term "community radio broadcaster" means: "a non-profit radio broadcaster who, in accordance with the fundamental principles of AMARC, offers a service to the community in which it is located or which it serves, while promoting community

---

105 Niamh Hourigan, *Escaping the Global Village: Media, Language & Protest* (USA, Lexington Books, 2003), p. 143.

106 Steve Buckley, Kreszentia Duer, Toby Mendel & Seán Ó Siochrú, *Broadcasting, Voice, and Accountability: A Public Interest Approach to Policy, Law, and Regulation* (Ann Arbor, The University of Michigan Press/The World Bank, 2008), p. 212.

expression and participation". AMARC's Declaration of Principles, alluded to in the foregoing quotation, states, *inter alia*, that members of AMARC:

- Contribute to the expression of different social, political and cultural movements, and to the promotion of all initiatives supporting peace, friendship among peoples.
- Recognize the fundamental and specific role of women in establishing new communication practices.
- Express through their programming:
  - The sovereignty and independence of all peoples;
  - Solidarity and non-intervention in the internal affairs of other countries;
  - International cooperation based on the creation of permanent and widespread ties based on equality, reciprocity, and mutual respect;
  - Non-discrimination on the basis of race, sex, sexual preference or religion;
  - And respect for the cultural identity of peoples.

On the basis of the foregoing (and other) definitions and descriptions of community (radio) broadcasting, its key features can be said to include:

- In service of community (both local communities and communities of interest)
- Individual participation in all stages of broadcasting
- Independent and non-profit status

"Community media", it has been noted, "have at their heart the concepts of access and participation".[107] Three prime advantages of community broadcasting for minority communities are: (i) autonomy over all stages of the broadcasting process, the preparation and transmission of programmes; (ii) fostering of community cohesion; (iii) democratisation of intra-community communicative structures and processes. All of these advantages flow from one of the central underlying assumptions about community communication, i.e., "the assumption of a shared relevance that community issues have for both parties, both senders and receivers, because they all participate in the same community and because the community serves as a frame of reference for a shared interpretation of the relevance of the topics communicated within the community".[108] As community broadcasting is generally less institutionalised than other forms of broadcasting, the accessibility of its structures and operations to members of the community is more easily assured.

---

107 *Chris Atton, Alternative Media*, *op. cit.*, p. 17.

108 Ed Hollander, James Stappers, and Nicholas Jankowski, "Community Media and Community Communication", in Nicholas W. Jankowski, Ed., *Community Media in the Information Age: Perspectives and Prospects* (Cresskill, New Jersey, Hampton Press, Inc., 2002), pp. 19–30, at 23.

In practice, licensing authorities often apply different criteria to applications for community licences than to other types of licences.[109] They tend to focus on the extent to which the proposed service matches identifiable or expressed community interests, the representativeness of those proposing the service *vis-à-vis* the community as a whole, provision for inclusive participation, and the feasibility of management and financial structures and plans. The assessment of prospective services is sometimes carried out in consultation with representatives of the communities themselves. Performative standards are also usually different in respect of community broadcasting, thereby reflecting the specificity of its objectives and strategies. Impact assessment, again frequently involving representatives of the target communities, is also a common procedural feature of regulatory supervision of licensed community broadcasters.

The development of community media as a distinct media type or sector has traditionally been hampered by a lack of (legal) recognition, financial support and administrative facilitation. The importance of (legal) recognition of the distinctiveness of community media should not be underestimated as it can form a basis for instituting financial support or administrative facilitation. In recent years, however, the "long march"[110] of community media towards legal recognition has passed significant milestones, prompting Karol Jakubowicz to describe community media as "flavour of the decade worldwide".[111]

In December 2007, the IGO Special Mandates on Freedom of Expression/the Media called resolutely for community broadcasting to be "explicitly recognised in law as a distinct form of broadcasting", while expressing their concern that "the failure of many countries" to do so was adversely affecting the potential of the sector to contribute to media diversity.[112] They further stated that community broadcasting "should benefit from fair and simple licensing procedures, should not have to meet stringent technological or other licence criteria, should benefit from concessionary licence fees and should have access to advertising".

In September 2008, the European Parliament adopted two Resolutions that considerably enhanced the status of community broadcasting at the European level.

---

109 For a (now dated) survey of the theory and practice of community broadcasting across a wide sample of European countries, see: Nick Jankowski, Ole Prehn & James Stappers, Eds., *The People's Voice: Local radio and television in Europe* (London, John Libbey & Co. Ltd., 1992).

110 Nico Carpentier and Salvatore Scifo, "Introduction: Community media's long march", 27 *Telematics and Informatics* (2010), pp. 115–118.

111 Karol Jakubowicz, "Community media: 'Flavour of the decade' worldwide. A keynote address at the AMARC Europe Conference", 27 *Telematics and Informatics* (2010), pp. 119–121.

112 Joint Declaration on Diversity in Broadcasting, adopted by the UN Special Rapporteur on Freedom of Opinion and Expression, the OSCE RFOM, the OAS Special Rapporteur on Freedom of Expression and the ACHPR Special Rapporteur on Freedom of Expression and Access to Information, 12 December 2007.

The Resolution entitled 'Community media in Europe' provides extensive analysis of the objectives, features and importance of community media.[113] The Resolution, 'Concentration and pluralism in the media in the European Union', recognises community media as a distinct media type and underlines the importance of community media for ensuring overall pluralism in the European media landscape.[114]

In February 2009, the Council of Europe's Committee of Ministers' adopted a Declaration on the role of community media in promoting social cohesion and intercultural dialogue. It recognises "community media as a distinct media sector, alongside public service and private commercial media" and stresses the need to examine ways in which legal frameworks could be adapted in order to facilitate the development and optimal functioning of community media. It favours allocating a sufficient number of (analogue and digital) frequencies to community media and ensuring that community media are not disadvantaged by the digital switch-over. It advocates educational and vocational measures geared towards maximising all communities' use of available technological platforms.

The Declaration also stresses the "desirability" of:

- exploring various funding possibilities for the community media sector;
- promoting good practice in community media, *inter alia*, through conducting studies, exchanging information, developing exchange programmes and other collaborative projects;
- facilitating appropriate capacity-building and training of community media workers;
- "encouraging the media's contribution to intercultural dialogue", eg. by establishing networks in which to exchange information.

3.2.2(ii) Public service media/content

Broadcasting and public service in the broadest sense of the term can both boast long and strong traditions in Europe. They are capable of mutually-exclusive existence, owing to their distinctive aims, yet interaction between the two has great synergic effects on society and democracy. As posited by one commentator: "[p]ublic service in the spirit of democracy demands an unqualified commitment to the common good. Nothing less will do; nothing more is needed".[115] Of course, it is the

---

113 European Parliament Resolution of 25 September 2008 on Community Media in Europe (2008/2011(INI)).

114 European Parliament Resolution of 25 September 2008 on concentration and pluralism in the media in the European Union (2007/2253(INI)).

115 Louis C. Gawthrop, *Public Service and Democracy: Ethical Imperatives for the 21st Century* (New York, Seven Bridges Press, LLC, 1998), p. 101.

ascertainment of "the common good" that remains vexing. How public service is assured via broadcasting can be explained to the philosophies animating public service broadcasting.

The extensive traditional rationales for public service broadcasting have been elaborated authoritatively by many commentators[116] and it is not intended to reproduce the full extent of other analyses here. It would, however, be useful to note that Georgina Born and Tony Prosser identify three essential normative criteria for public service broadcasting: citizenship ("enhancing, developing and serving social, political and cultural citizenship"), universality and quality of services and of output.[117] Eric Barendt, for his part, identifies six basic features of public service broadcasting:

- general geographical availability;
- concern for national identity and culture;
- independence from both the state and commercial interests;
- impartiality of programmes;
- range and variety of programmes and
- substantial financing by a general charge on users.[118]

A more detailed recipe for public service broadcasting is also given by Born and Prosser (while acknowledging that not all of the proposed ingredients would command universal support):

- universal access or availability;
- mixed programming or universality of genres;
- high quality programming in each genre, including innovation, originality and risk-taking;
- a mission to inform, educate and entertain; programming to support social integration and national identity;
- diverse programming catering to minorities and special interest groups, to foster belonging and counteract segregation and discrimination;
- programming reflecting regional identities;
- provision of independent and impartial news and fora for public debate and plurality of opinion;
- commitment to national and regional production, and to local talent;

---

116 See, for example, Eric Barendt, *Broadcasting Law: A Comparative Study* (Oxford, Clarendon Press, 1993), Chapter III 'Public Broadcasting', pp. 50–74 and Toby Mendel, *Public Service Broadcasting: A Comparative Legal Survey* (Second Edition) (France, UNESCO, 2011).

117 Georgina Born & Tony Prosser, "Culture and Consumerism: Citizenship, Public Service Broadcasting and the BBC's Fair Trading Obligations", 64 *The Modern Law Review* (Issue No. 5, September 2001), pp. 657–687, at 671.

118 Eric Barendt, *Broadcasting Law: A Comparative Study*, *op. cit.*, p. 52.

- a mission to complement other broadcasters to enrich the broadcasting ecology;
- affordability; and
- limited, if any, advertising.[119]

The foregoing provides a clear idea of what public service broadcasting entails and of its potential for minorities in terms of accessibility of participatory mechanisms and the availability of targeted programming. The details of specific structures and practices to enhance the value of PSM for minorities are explored by the monitoring mechanisms of the FCNM and the ECRML, as documented in Chapters 10 and 11. Two major issues currently faced by PSM are the extent to which its remit ought to be developed in respect of new media platforms and the nature of its relationship to media markets (and its ultimate position and role in those markets). The resolution of these issues will affect the future shape of PSM and its relevance as a primary source of broadcasting for minorities.

One of the most vigorous sources of encouragement for public service broadcasters to harness the full potential of new media services has been the (not distinterested) European Broadcasting Union. It stated in the early days of new media services:

> Public broadcasting organizations have always been at the forefront of innovation in the broadcasting field, both on the technical side and in terms of diversifying their programming offer. In line with this tradition, and except where expressly and exceptionally stipulated otherwise, they continue to be entitled, and indeed are obliged, to make their programme offer available to the public in the most appropriate manner and form suggested by the changing viewing and listening habits of the public in an evolving audiovisual environment. This includes a complementary and diversified programme offer (thematic channels), its technical delivery (digital transmission, bouquets, on-line delivery) and its mode of funding (pay-TV, pay-per-view). As long as the additional programme offer is provided by the public broadcasting organization itself, the same legal principles of funding apply as in the case of its traditional core service.[120]

PSB's position in relevant markets could be: (i) a neo-liberal approach trumpeting the primacy of the market and calling for the abolition of PSB; (ii) pure PSB as a niche broadcaster, "offering only broadcast content and services which private broadcasters find commercially unrewarding",[121] and "whatever the market may

119 Georgina Born & Tony Prosser, "Culture and Consumerism: Citizenship, Public Service Broadcasting and the BBC's Fair Trading Obligations", *op. cit.*, at 671.

120 "The Public Service Broadcasting Remit: Today and Tomorrow", Statement by the European Broadcasting Union (Legal Department) of 29 April 1998.

121 Karol Jakubowicz, "Public Service Broadcasting: A Pawn on an Ideological Chessboard", in Els de Bens, Ed., *Media Between Culture and Commerce* (Bristol, UK/Chicago, USA, Intellect Books, 2007), pp. 115–141, at 115.

offer, the community still has a duty to provide broadcasting services free from the effect of the profit motive, offering the individual a 'basic supply' of what he/she needs as a member of a particular society and culture, and of a particular polity and democratic system".[122] The abolition of PSB would, needless to say, have drastic consequences for minorities, but either of the other two approaches would preserve its potential.

The following two sub-sections provide an overview of the detailed regulatory provisions governing PSB at the European level, first those developed by the EU and secondly those developed by the Council of Europe.

European Union

A regulatory framework for PSB does exist at the European level, but it really is no more than a framework: the Protocol to the Treaty of Amsterdam on the system of public broadcasting in the Member States recognises that it is largely for each Member State to confer, design and organise the remit for PSB in their own countries.[123] This is because "the system of public broadcasting in the Member States is directly related to the democratic, social and cultural needs of each society and to the need to preserve media pluralism".[124] The Protocol also sets out that State funding for PSB must be tied to the fulfilment of the broadcasters' public service remit.

A Resolution concerning public service broadcasting adopted by the Council of the European Union in 1999 was more expansive when outlining the importance of PSB.[125] It notes that "in view of [PSB's] cultural, social and democratic functions which it discharges for the common good, [it] has a vital significance for ensuring democracy, pluralism, social cohesion, cultural and linguistic diversity". It continues by "stressing that the increased diversification of the programmes on offer in the new media environment reinforces the importance of the comprehensive mission of public service broadcasters". In consequence, it positively encourages PSB to branch out into new media services and to exploit the potential of the new technological opportunities on offer in furtherance of their mandate.

122 *Ibid.*, at 116.

123 Protocol to the Treaty of Amsterdam amending the Treaty on European Union, the Treaties establishing the European Communities and certain related acts, signed at Amsterdam, 2 October 1997, OJ C 340/109 of 10 November 1997.

124 *Ibid.*

125 Resolution of the Council and of the Representatives of the Governments of the Member States, meeting within the Council of 25 January 1999 concerning public service broadcasting, OJ C 30/1 of 5 February 1999.

Further guidance on the question of State funding for PSB is provided by the aforementioned Council Resolution (1999) and, in greater detail, the European Commission's 2001 Communication on the application of State aid rules to public service broadcasting.[126] The Communication required States to provide a clear and precise definition of the public service remit, where such a definition was not already in existence. It allowed States to define this remit, and to provide for the financing and general organisation of the public broadcasting sector, in a manner that would give due recognition to relevant national specificities. All of this was, however, subject to the important proviso that any measures adopted for the financing of public service broadcasters would have to conform to certain standards of transparency in order to allow for the assessment of the proportionality of such measures.[127]

The criteria established by the ECJ in its *Altmark* judgment are also crucial – they reiterate and build on the aforementioned requirements:[128]

- first, the recipient undertaking is actually required to discharge public service obligations and those obligations have been clearly defined;
- second, the parameters on the basis of which the compensation is calculated have been established beforehand in an objective and transparent manner;
- third, the compensation does not exceed what is necessary to cover all or part of the costs incurred in discharging the public service obligations, taking into account the relevant receipts and a reasonable profit for discharging those options;
- fourth, where the undertaking which is to discharge public service obligations is not chosen in a public procurement procedure, the level of compensation needed has been determined on the basis of an analysis of the costs which a typical undertaking, well run and adequately provided with means of transport so as to be able to meet the necessary public service requirements, would have incurred in discharging those obligations, taking into account the relevant receipts and a reasonable profit for discharging the obligations.

In 2008 the Commission launched a public consultation on the future framework for State funding of PSB.[129] The development of the public service remit in the new

126 Communication from the Commission on the application of State aid rules to public service broadcasting (2001/C 320/04).

127 See further, T. McGonagle, "European Commission – State Aid Rules to Public Service Broadcasters Clarified", *IRIS* 2001–10: 4.

128 Case C-280/00, *Altmark Trans GmbH, Regierungspräsidium Magdeburg v. Nahverkehrsgesellschaft Altmark GmbH*, Judgment of the Court of Justice of the European Communities of 24 July 2003, Rec. 2003, p. I-7747, esp. paras. (87, 88), 89–94.

129 As announced in the European Commission's press release, "State aid: Commission launches public consultation on the future framework for State funding of public service broadcasting", IP/08/24, 10 January 2008.

media environment was one of the important focuses of the consultation exercise.[130] Following the consultation, in 2009, the Commission adopted a new Communication on the application of State aid rules to public service broadcasting.[131] The new Communication seeks, *inter alia*, to clarify accountability and control issues at national level and it has replaced the identically-titled 2001 Communication.

The regulatory picture that has been sketched here shows that it is largely for Member States to define and develop the remit of PSB in their own countries and that they may finance PSB as long as a certain number of procedural and other criteria are met. There is strong encouragement for the continuation and development of PSB activities on new media platforms.

Council of Europe

The approach to PSB taken by the Council of Europe is determined primarily by relevant standard-setting texts adopted by the Committee of Ministers. Numerous Recommendations are relevant, and the key definitional elements were conveniently synthesised in a 2007 Recommendation on the remit of public service media in the information society[132] and portray PSM as:

a) a reference point for all members of the public, offering universal access;
b) a factor for social cohesion and integration of all individuals, groups and communities;
c) a source of impartial and independent information and comment, and of innovatory and varied content which complies with high ethical and quality standards;
d) a forum for pluralistic public discussion and a means of promoting broader democratic participation of individuals;
e) an active contributor to audiovisual creation and production and greater appreciation and dissemination of the diversity of national and European cultural heritage.

These "key elements underpinning the traditional public service remit" are broadly consistent with the theoretical discussion *supra*. Each of them is elaborated upon in the Recommendation and the section on diversity is discussed in greater detail in Chapter 10.3.2. It is noteworthy that the title of the Recommendation refers to "public service media", which acknowledges that other media platforms are

130 *Ibid.* See, in particular, s.2.2.1 of the second-named document in the previous footnote.

131 Communication from the Commission on the application of State aid rules to public service broadcasting of 2 July 2009 (2009/C 257/01).

132 Recommendation Rec(2007)3 of the Committee of Ministers to member states on the remit of public service media in the information society, 31 January 2007.

increasingly being used to pursue public service objectives.[133] Further recognition of that trend is provided by a subsequent Recommendation adopted by the Committee of Ministers – on measures to promote the public service value of the Internet.[134]

The Recommendation's central objective is to prompt States authorities, where appropriate in cooperation with all interested parties, to take all necessary measures to promote the public service value of the Internet, *inter alia* by:

- "upholding human rights, democracy and the rule of law [...] and promoting social cohesion, respect for cultural diversity and trust" in respect of the Internet and other ICTs;
- setting out parameters for the roles and responsibilities of all key stakeholders within clear legal and other regulatory frameworks;
- promoting awareness in the private sector of the ethical dimension to relevant activities and the adjustment of practices in light of human rights concerns;
- encouraging, where appropriate and on an inclusive basis, "new forms of open and transparent self- and co-regulation" enhancing accountability for key actors.

The suggested measures for attaining the central objective of the Recommendation should be considered in light of the guidelines elaborated in the detailed and extensive appendix to the Recommendation. The guidelines focus first on human rights and democracy. In order to uphold human rights in the specific context of the Internet and ICTs, the rights to freedom of expression and association and assembly should not be subject to any restrictions beyond those provided for in the European Convention on Human Rights. The need to uphold the right to private life and correspondence on the Internet, proprietary rights (including intellectual property) and educational rights (including "media and information literacy") is similarly stressed. So too is the importance of other values and interests, such as "pluralism, cultural and linguistic diversity, and non-discriminatory access to different means of communication via the Internet and other ICTs". Civic engagement in e-democracy, e-participation and e-government, and the development by public administrations of diverse communicative possibilities, are advocated under the rubric, 'Democracy'.

The second structured focus of the guidelines is 'Access'. It calls for: strategies promoting affordable access to ICT infrastructure, including the Internet; "technical

---

133 See further, in this connection: OFCOM, *A new approach to public service content in the digital media age: The potential role of the Public Service Publisher*, Discussion Paper, 24 January 2007 & Summary of responses, 13 June 2007.

134 Recommendation CM/Rec(2007)16 of the Committee of Ministers to member states on measures to promote the public service value of the Internet, 7 November 2007.

interoperability, open standards and cultural diversity in ICT policy covering telecommunications, broadcasting and the Internet"; diversification of software models, including proprietary, free and open source software; affordable Internet access for everyone, especially those with particular needs arising from various situational specificities; public access points to the Internet and other ICT services; integration of ICTs into education; media and information literacy and training.

The guidelines then address 'Openness'. The key concern here is to safeguard freedom of expression and the free circulation of information on the Internet. To this end, they promote: active public participation in the creation of content on the Internet and other ICTs (specifically by refraining from imposing licensing requirements on individuals and from applying general blocking or filtering measures; facilitating re-use of existing digital content resources in accordance with intellectual property rights and of public data); "public domain information accessibility via the Internet"; adaptation and extension of the remit of public service media specifically to the Internet and other ICTs.

'Diversity' is the fourth main focus of the guidelines and it strives for equitable and universal involvement in the development of Internet and ICT content. As such, it encourages: developing a cultural dimension to digital content production, including by public service media; preserving the digital heritage; participation in "the creation, modification and remixing of interactive content"; measures for the production and distribution of user- and community-generated content; capacity-building for local and indigenous content on the Internet; multilingualism on the Internet.

The final focus of the guidelines is 'Security' – a more catch-all category than its title suggests. It underscores the importance of: the Council of Europe's Cybercrime Convention and its Additional Protocol focusing on racist and xenophobic acts; network and information security; legislative measures and appropriate enforcement agencies to deal with spam; enhanced cooperation between ISPs; protection of personal data and privacy; combating piracy in the field of copyright and neighbouring rights; improving transparent and effective consumer protection; promoting safer use of the Internet and ICTs, especially for children.

This synopsised overview of some of the main strands to the Council of Europe's approach to PSB/PSM confirms its suitability for the advancement of the communicative and informational needs and interests of minorities. This is clear from the objectives and strategies involved.

3.2.2(iii) Commercial media

Whereas media with purely commercial objectives are not usually vaunted for their contribution to the advancement of the right to freedom of expression of persons belonging to minorities, that does not mean that they are without importance for the realisation of that goal.

First, in some countries, commercial media (especially broadcasters) are subject to certain public service commitments. These can be public service obligations set out in regulation and applicable to all (or a wide selection of) broadcasters, or they can be specific obligations taken on voluntarily by individual broadcasters in return for remuneration. The former practice has always existed (to varying degrees) and the latter appears to be becoming more commonplace of late. Despite the extension of public service obligations to the commercial sector by broadcasters' voluntary subscription to contractual obligations, there remains, as Monroe Price has correctly pointed out, a certain tension or contradiction between the forced cohabitation of overall commercial objectives and a limited amount of public service objectives.[135] In concrete instances of both sets of objectives conflicting with one another, it is far from certain that the public service objectives would be able to hold their own, to the extent that they only account for a small, contractually-defined portion of the broadcaster's overall activities and services.

Second, the prioritisation of profits does not presumptively favour the informational preferences of minoritites, but at the same time, it does not preclude the possibility that minority preferences could be served by them. As John Keane has noted, commercial publishers of opinion are "primarily concerned to satisfy the demands of audiences within the boundaries of market competition".[136] Thus, "[m]edia entrepreneurs certainly provide choices, but they are always within the framework of *commercially viable* alternatives".[137] It is well-documented that certain minority groups can constitute lucrative niches in the broadcasting market, eg. satellite channels serving certain ethnic groups in the UK. The commercial attractiveness of a particular group is then determined by commercial calculations: critical mass; definable interests that are translatable into content terms; established patterns of media usage; general level of affluence, etc. Presence on commercial media (whether as slots on general/mainstream channels or as dedicated channels) can often enhance the public prestige of the interests/languages/cultures involved to a greater extent than comparable presence on PSB channels. While the general potential of commercial media to advance minority preferences in media output should not be overlooked, it should not be overstated either. The coincidence of minority interests

---

135 Monroe Price, *Television, the Public Sphere, and National Identity*, *op. cit.*, p. 234.
136 John Keane, *The Media and Democracy* (UK, Polity Press, 1991), p. 91.
137 *Ibid.*

and commercial viability is the exception rather than the rule and commercial media rarely provide proactively for unpopular programming based on altruistic motivations.

Third, it is important to recognise the negative impact that the failure of commercial media to cater for minorities' programming preferences can have. As commercial media very often reach large audiences, their influence on the formation of public opinion and indeed, the framing of issues for public discussion, is significant. The non-inclusion of programming involving and directed at minorities has ramifications far beyond the act of exclusion: questions of participation, equality and non-discrimination, cultural, linguistic, religious and other identities are all implicated. As explained by Myria Georgiu: "[i]dentities are not shaped only through positive and creative processes of participation and communion, but also in processes of exclusion, marginalization and regressive ideologies".[138] This third general observation can be related back to the reference at the beginning of this subsection to certain obligations and standards that apply across the board to all media or all media within a given sector (eg. broadcasting). Such measures can help to prevent exclusionary tendencies and practices in respect of commercial broadcasting.

3.2.2(iv) Transnational media

Given the political economy of international media, it is little wonder that there should be scepticism about their ability to enhance the right to freedom of expression of persons belonging to minorities. The business plans on which their economic and political might depend are often rightly perceived as anathema to the communicative needs and interests of persons belonging to minorities. Moreover, objectives of cultural imperialism are also imputed to dominant players on the international media scene. These issues are considered in further detail in Chapter 9 in the context of diversity in the media. For present purposes, however, the dangers posed by the globalising and homogenising potential of international media are not contested as such, but the attention will focus instead on the countervailing potential of international media to satisfy *certain* communicative needs of *certain* minority groups. Some of the reluctance to accept the validity of this proposition is clearly the result of conceptual associations with particular terminological choices.

By way of illustration, references to the international media instantly evoke dominant media players, such as the "Big Five".[139] On the other hand, references to "transfrontier" media conjure up an alternative framework, especially in Europe, where the term takes on a specific meaning given the traditional regulatory

---

138 Myria Georgiou, *Diaspora, Identity and the Media: Diasporic Transnationalism and Mediated Spatialities* (Cresskill, New Jersey, Hampton Press, Inc., 2006), p. 9.

139 Ben H. Bagdikian, *The New Media Monopoly* (Boston, Beacon Press, 2004), p. 3 – discussed at greater length, *infra*.

predominance of the EU's Television without Frontiers Directive and the Council of Europe's European Convention on Transfrontier Television. Another terminological variant is "transnational" media, which is (at least in European academic writing) increasingly being used in respect of media products and services originating outside of Europe, but which can be received within Europe.[140] The reason for alluding to these terminological differences is to advance three related points. First, each of the terms mentioned could be taken to the mean essentially the same thing, i.e., media that operate across State borders. Second, patterns of usage have emerged which have, in effect, attached different connotations to different terms. Thus, while there is considerable potential overlap between the different terms, in practice, each has its own distinctive conceptual ballast. Third, once these (admittedly imperfect) distinctions between the relevant terms have been flagged, and their acquired emphases explained, the question of whether "international media" can be considered suitable communicative outlets for persons belonging to minorities, becomes much more nuanced and meaningful.

The importance of these media can be gauged, *inter alia*, by their ability to satisfy informational needs of minorities no longer resident in their kin-States or of diasporic minorities. Another important dimension to transnational media concerns cultural representation and identity-formation. In this respect, the transnational "recognizes both the possibilities of networks and communities to surpass national boundaries, as well as the continuing significance of the national borders in partly framing and restricting social actions and their meanings".[141] Furthermore, the importance of the transnational dimension is crucial for the universality of human rights, in general, but the right to freedom of expression, in particular.[142] Its importance is also attested to by the inclusion of express provisions safeguarding cross-border exchanges in both the FCNM and the ECRML. The specific importance of the media has been explained in terms of their ability to "renegotiate and represent diasporic copresence and a common past through images, which shape the (selective) renewed and contemporary collective memory and provide

140 See generally: Jean K. Chalaby, "Deconstructing the transnational: a typology of cross-border television channels in Europe", 7 *New Media & Society* (No. 2, 2005), pp. 155–175; Philip Schlesinger, "Wishful Thinking: Cultural Politics, Media, and Collective Identities in Europe", 43 *Journal of Communication* (No. 2, Spring 1993), pp. 6–17; Jean K. Chalaby, Ed., *Transnational Television Worldwide: Towards a New Media Order* (I.B. Tauris, London/New York, 2005); Jean K. Chalaby, "Television for a New Global Order: Transnational Television Networks and the Formation of Global Systems", 65 *International Communication Gazette* (No. 6, 2003), pp. 457–472; John Sinclair, Elizabeth Jacka & Stuart Cunningham, *New Patterns in Global Television* (Great Britain, Oxford University Press, 1996).

141 Myria Georgiou, *Diaspora, Identity and the Media: Diasporic Transnationalism and Mediated Spatialities*, *op. cit.*, p. 10.

142 Article 10(1), ECHR and Article 19(2), ICCPR both use the formula, "regardless of frontiers".

repertoires for the construction of new individual and communal identities".[143] This explanation also holds true in respect of kin-State minorities.

Finally, it should be noted that to the extent that certain minority groups rely heavily on the informational output of transfrontier media, it can be argued that such media make viable contributions to existing diversity in terms of source, outlet and content. To borrow a couple of very valid observations made by Charles Husband in the more general context of "ethnic media organisations": (i) these media "are part of a creative topography that has followed upon global migration patterns", and (ii) "[t]hey are not alternative media: for many of their consumers they *are* the media".[144]

3.2.2(v) Other types of media

The list of different types of media presented above is by no means exhaustive. The Internet and other new media technologies may appear conspicuous by their absence, but they are considered in detail in Chapter 3.3. Other omissions include "alternative media" (including grassroots and alternative advocacy media[145]) and "radical media" (i.e., media that are "generally small-scale and in many different forms, that express an alternative vision to hegemonic policies, prioirities, and perspectives"[146]), both of which[147] are linked to social movement theory.[148] Their omission is explained by the fact that they are not dealt with as distinct types of media in relevant international legal instruments.

The purpose of the above selection is to highlight the differences between common types of media in terms of their purpose, functionality and reach. The foregoing discussion reveals that each of the media types surveyed can contribute in different ways to rendering the right to freedom of expression (in all its component parts)

143 Myria Georgiou, *Diaspora, Identity and the Media: Diasporic Transnationalism and Mediated Spatialities*, *op. cit.*, p. 13.

144 (emphasis per original) Charles Husband, "Minority Ethnic Media As Communities Of Practice: Professionalism and Identity Politics in Interaction", 31 *Journal of Ethnic and Migration Studies* (No. 3, May 2005), pp. 461–479, at 477.

145 Chris Atton, *Alternative Media*, *op. cit.*, p. 16 (drawing, *inter alia*, on the work of Michael Traber).

146 John D.H. Downing *et al.*, *Radical Media: Rebellious Communication and Social Movements* (Thousand Oaks/London/New Delhi, Sage Publications Ltd., 2001), p. v.

147 For a typology of alternative and radical media, see: Chris Atton, *Alternative Media*, *op. cit.*, p. 27.

148 See further, in this connection: Alberto Melucci, *Challenging codes: Collective action in the information age* (UK, Cambridge University Press, 1996); Doug McAdam, Sidney Tarrow & Charles Tilly, *Dynamics of Contention* (USA, Cambridge University Press, 2001); Doug McAdam, John D. McCarthy, Mayer N. Zald, Eds., *Comparative perspectives on social movements: Political opportunities, mobilizing structures, and cultural framings* (USA, Cambridge University Press, 1996).

effective for persons belonging to minorities. It should not be overlooked that other, less structured media can also play an important role in realising this objective. The foregoing discussion is also important because the enforcement and oversight bodies of relevant international treaties have so far revealed limited awareness of the functional differences between different types of media. When the communicative needs and preferences of persons belonging to minorities are optimally served by the functional features of particular types of media, there is a greater likelihood that they will exercise their right to freedom of expression in an effective manner.

3.3 New media and new regulatory paradigms

The growth and maturation of the European Court's attitude towards the media can largely be attributed to the media's function to serve the public interest through the provision of information and the facilitation and stimulation of public debate. The Court's attitude would appear to be premised at least in part on the point-to-multipoint nature of mass media communications; on the understanding that information purveyed and disseminated by the mass media will reach a larger section of society than communications between ordinary individuals. The contiguous considerations of impact and influence are key to this conception of the role and activities of the media.

Could or should this state of affairs under which the media enjoy preferential status change in the online world (as broadly defined)? Or, in other words, in a world where the barriers to mass communication are drastically diminished? Or in a world where communications services are becoming increasingly customised, personalised and individualised? Or in a world where the "proliferation of niche markets, the waning of public reliance on general interest intermediaries and the growing incidence of advance individual selection of news sources are all serving to insulate citizens from broader influences and ideas";[149] cutting them off from the rough and tumble of democracy; denying them the formative experience of being confronted with unwanted ideas; denying them exposure to situations where tolerance has to be learnt? Or, more poetically, in a world with a diminished incidence of "serendipitous encounters"?[150]

Some of these highlighted trends can contribute to the erosion of shared, collective experience and the reduction of common reference points; thus negatively affecting participatory democracy and engendering social fragmentation.[151] The net result of these trends and tendencies is that individuals are increasingly cocooning

---

149 Tarlach McGonagle, "Changing Aspects of Broadcasting: New Territory and New Challenges", *IRIS plus* 2001–10, p. 5. For a more expansive treatment of these issues, see generally, Cass R. Sunstein, *Republic.com 2.0* (Princeton NJ, Princeton University Press, 2007).

150 Andrew L. Shapiro, *The Control Revolution* (USA, Public Affairs, 1999), p. (xvi).

151 See further, Cass R. Sunstein, *Republic.com 2.0, op. cit.*, especially Chapter 1, "the daily me".

themselves in informational and communicational universes of their own creation; potentially leading to a Hall-of-Versailles type of effect where their own views are merely mirrored on all sides and distorted somewhat by virtue of excessive amplification. This stark prognosis is one of the arguments frequently invoked in favour of prohibition of websites and chat-groups dedicated to the propagation of hate speech and other types of extremist activities, for example.

Its starkness should not, however, be exaggerated. Filtering trends and proclivities towards self-insulation in the comforting surrounds of like-minded opinions are age-old practices and tendencies respectively. The Internet, like all of its forerunner communications technologies, will take some getting used to, particularly given the sheer diversity of communicative forms involved and the sheer diversity of information and opinions it makes available.[152] It is typical for pioneering technological changes to set a blistering pace; for regulatory responses to lag somewhat behind this *peloton*, gasping for breath, and for cultural changes to remain largely out of the picture, with much ground to make up. Familiarity with the workings and potential of the online world will eventually harness much of the awe and apprehension that have characterised the debate thus far.[153]

Quo vadis, then, for the media? First, is the cherished freedom of expression of the media – as staked out by the European Convention on Human Rights and the European Court of Human Rights – likely to be transposed *en bloc* to the online world? This is by no means sure. Crucially, though, the enjoyment of relevant freedoms by media actors in the off-line world has always been contingent on the simultaneous exercise of certain duties and responsibilities (including, first and foremost, that journalists – in principle – "obey the ordinary criminal law",[154] and also that they act "in good faith in order to provide accurate and reliable information in accordance with the ethics of journalism"[155]). There is nothing to suggest that such a proviso would not (or does not already) apply online as well.

This line of analysis begs further questions: first, in the online world, where it is much easier for individuals to engage in mass communication, are the above-

152 See further, the discussion of novel communicative and informational features of the Internet in *ACLU v. Reno*, 929 F.Supp. 824 (11 June 1996), at 842–844.

153 See generally, Ithiel de Sola Pool, *Technologies of Freedom* (Massachusetts and London, England, The Belknap Press of Harvard University Press, Cambridge, 1983).

154 *Fressoz & Roire v. France*, Judgment of the European Court of Human Rights of 21 January 1999, Reports of Judgments and Decisions, 1999-I, para. 52; see also, *Dupuis & others v. France*, Judgment of the European Court of Human Rights of 12 November 2007, para. 43. It should be noted that the Court found that there had been a violation of Article 10 in the particular circumstances of both these cases.

155 *Bergens Tidende & Others v. Norway*, Judgment of the European Court of Human Rights of 2 May 2000, Reports of Judgments and Decisions, 2000-IV, para. 53, drawing on *Goodwin v. United Kingdom*, Judgment of the European Court of Human Rights of 27 March 1996, Reports of Judgments and Decisions, 1996-II, para. 39.

mentioned distinctions between media actors and ordinary citizens *qua* communicators still valid? Alan Rusbridger captures the nature of ongoing shifts in public communication paradigms when he aptly refers to the "Splintering of the Fourth Estate".[156] In his influential and comprehensive study, *A new notion of media?*, Karol Jakubowicz distinguishes three new notions of media: (i) all media are new-media-to-be (see further, *infra*); (ii) forms of media created by new actors, and (iii) media or media-like activities performed by non-media actors.[157]

Blogging on topics of public interest, with the intention of contributing to public debate is a perfect example of a communicative practice of major societal significance and which forces a re-appraisal of activities that were hitherto the preserve of the traditional media.[158] On what grounds could such distinctions then be sustained? Would the rationales of impact, influence and service of the public interest, discussed above, be able to survive the transition to the online world?

In any case, it is patent that the Internet holds unprecedented potential for multi-directional communicative activity: unlike traditional media, it entails relatively low entry-barriers for speakers and listeners/viewers and it blurs/reduces the distinction between receiving and providing information and other types of content. This has prompted the oft-quoted observation that the Internet is "the most participatory marketplace of mass speech that [...] the world" has ever seen. The quotation is perhaps somewhat clumsily formulated, but its essence is certainly accurate. Whether its participatory promise is upheld in practice will depend in part on trends of commodification of information and content and the success of counter-currents at the interface of intellectual property and technology.[159]

The second line of analysis is more oriented towards the practice of journalism in an online environment. With the ease of direct access to original sources of information, including official information and in any case, the information which shapes the news of the day, there may be less of a role to be played by media professionals according to traditional conceptions of straight reporting. However, not everyone will invest the time and effort in checking original sources. Those who do will have to re-examine their approach to the intake and digestion of news and information available online. This need is prompted not only by the explosion of information caused by the advent of Internet-technology, its abundance and

---

156 Alan Rusbridger, "The Splintering of the Fourth Estate", 2010 Andrew Olle Media Lecture, Sydney, 19 November 2010.

157 Karol Jakubowicz, *A new notion of media?: Media and media-like content and activities on new communications services* (Strasbourg, Council of Europe, April 2009), pp. 19 *et seq.*

158 See further in this connection: Anne Flanagan, "Blogging: A Journal Need Not A Journalist Make", 16 Fordham Intell. Prop. Media & Ent. L.J. 395; Anne Flanagan, "The blogger as journalist under UK law", 10 *Communications Law* (No. 4, 2005), pp. 125–129.

159 See generally: Niva Elkin-Koren & Neil Weinstock Netanel, Eds., *The Commodification of Information* (The Hague, Kluwer Law International, 2002).

availability.[160] This informational boon is captured in the sloganistically-appealing remark: "[i]t is no exaggeration to conclude that the content on the Internet is as diverse as human thought".[161] The need is also prompted by various qualitative features of that information: anonymity of, or lack of information about, the provider; lack of traditional intermediaries processing/providing/packaging the information; resultant difficulties in assessing the credibility of the information, especially when it originates in foreign or unfamiliar institutions, organisations or cultural contexts.[162]

A particular role could perhaps be envisaged here for public service media if they were to assume the role of intermediaries or trustees by pointing the public towards other online material (extraneous to their own sites) to which they would have awarded a sort of "seal of approval". By doing so, they would vouch for the reliability of content on other websites as being of the same high standards as on their own websites. Such a public-service kite-marking initiative could develop to become a useful navigational tool in the online world; enabling the website of the broadcaster to become a portal which would confer credibility on external content.[163] This "reliability-enhancing"[164] initiative would lead any reputable public service broadcaster to be identified as a "beacon of trust"[165] in the online world.[166]

Overall, the media will have to take on a more intermediary role; place greater emphasis on analysis and interpretation; counter the self-interested agenda of organisations providing information; help to sift facts from rhetoric and comment on the extracted matter. This is no mean challenge for a sector which arguably bears the most responsibility for "the triumph of idiot culture" (i.e., the rise of a media culture in which serious journalism is eclipsed by an obsession with sensation and scandal).[167] This is a call for the media to rediscover their roots; their informative, dissident tradition. The International Federation of Journalists has responded to this call through the development of its Ethical Journalism Initiative.[168] It will have its work cut out for it.

---

160 See, for example, *ACLU v. Reno*, 929 F. Supp. 824 (11 June 1996), p. 881.

161 *Ibid.*, p. 842, para. 74.

162 See further, Anton Vedder, "Misinformation through the Internet: Epistemology and Ethics", in Anton Vedder, Ed., *Ethics and the Internet* (Antwerpen/Groningen, Intersentia, 2001), pp. 125–132, at 128.

163 *Ibid.*, p. 130.

164 *Ibid.*, p. 131.

165 D. Docherty, "Empires and evolution: public service content in the new media", 27 *Intermedia* (Issue No. 2, May 1999), pp. 20–23, at p. 23.

166 See further, Tarlach McGonagle, "Changing Aspects of Broadcasting: New Territory and New Challenges", *op. cit.*, pp. 6–7.

167 Carl Bernstein, in Ellen Hazelcorn & Patrick Smyth, Eds., *Let in the Light: Censorship, secrecy and democracy*, *op. cit.*, pp. 17–25, at p. 20.

168 See further: Aidan White, *To Tell You the Truth: The Ethical Journalism Initiative*, *op. cit.*

An interesting corollary question is often overlooked: what is the likely impact of the inexorable rise of Internet-related communication on the more traditional, off-line media? Will Darwinian theories apply? Will adaptation solely within the confines of the off-line world prove possible? Or will virtually all (mass) media concerns have to reinvent themselves in such a way as to secure footholds in the off- and online worlds?[169] As observed by a leading commentator in the early 1980s, the "new media are not only competing with the old media for attention, but are also changing the very system under which the old media operate".[170] That observation now seems prescient, given its continued validity in respect of the Internet.

It is also clear that the relationship between new and traditionally-used media is complex and evolutive and not simply either one of displacement or reinforcement.[171] Karol Jakubowicz has described a future scenario whereby all media will ultimately become "new-media-to-be". He writes: "[w]ith the digitisation of all media, they may all be transformed into convergent media distributed on broadband networks. Older media will not be substituted for and disappear, but may re-emerge in changed form, as another source of content available on broadband Internet and other broadband networks".[172] Whether the impact of new media on existing media will be predominantly additive or substitutive depends in no small measure on the functionality of the technology in question and its ability to fulfil the communicative needs and interests of its users. It also depends on the comparable levels of functionality of different media.[173]

Having "developed by accretion, as piecemeal responses to new technology", contemporary media regulation can be considered "complex and unwieldy".[174] Different regimes often apply to different media and each regime is characterised by its own specificities. In consequence, it can prove difficult to identify or achieve consistency in these different regimes. The reality of ongoing and projected technological changes has already precipitated fresh thinking about the best (regulatory) means of attaining desired objectives; of honouring specific values. This is particularly true in light of trends of convergence and individualisation.[175]

---

169 See further, on these questions, Colin Sparks, "The Impact of the Internet on the Existing Media", in Andrew Calabrese & Colin Sparks, Eds., *Toward a Political Economy of Culture: Capitalism and Communication in the Twenty-First Century* (Lanham, etc., Rowman & Littlefield Publishers, Inc., 2004), pp. 307–326.

170 Ithiel de Sola Pool, *Technologies of Freedom*, *op. cit.*, p. 22.

171 *Ibid.*, at 39–40.

172 Karol Jakubowicz, *A new notion of media?: Media and media-like content and activities on new communications services, op. cit.*, p. 19.

173 *Ibid.*, p. 40.

174 Thomas Gibbons, *Regulating the Media* (2nd Edition) (London, Sweet & Maxwell, 1998), p. 300.

175 See further, Tarlach McGonagle, "Co-Regulation of the Media in Europe: The Potential for Practice of an Intangible Idea", *IRIS plus* 2002–10, p. 2.

Such is the global and complicated nature of information technology and the modern media in general, that a multitude of additional regulatory difficulties (many of them unprecedented) has arisen. As concisely stated by Lawrence Lessig: "[R]elative anonymity, decentralized distribution, multiple points of access, no necessary tie to geography, no simple system to identify content, tools of encryption – all these features and consequences of the Internet protocol make it difficult to control speech in cyberspace".[176] Coupled with this detailed observation is the fact that the innovative features of new information technologies[177] have heightened the exposure of the traditional shortcomings of already-existing regulatory structures. It is at this juncture that the notions of self- and co-regulation (S&CR) have been introduced into the debate.

Another impetus for the emergence of the notions of S&CR has been the continuing debate on, and quest for, better governance at the European level.[178] In this context, the European Commission's White Paper on European Governance enumerated five key principles of good governance: openness, participation, accountability, effectiveness and coherence.[179] S&CR have been mooted as suitable means of helping to honour these principles in practice.

As demonstrated elsewhere,[180] the notions of S&CR are characterised by their fluidity. This definitional dilemma has been compounded by a lack of consistency in interpretations of the relevant (and other proximate) terms. (Pure) self-regulation is widely regarded as the "control of activities by the private parties concerned without the direct involvement of public authorities".[181] Co-regulation, for its part, refers to the "control of activities by a combination of action from private parties and public authorities".[182] Another term, coined to embrace as wide a selection of co-regulatory practices as possible, is "regulated self-regulation", which describes "a form of self-regulation that fits in with a framework set by the state to achieve

---

176 Lawrence Lessig, *Code and other laws of cyberspace* (New York, Basic Books, 1999), p. 166.

177 See, briefly, *supra*, and very extensively in *ACLU v. Reno*, *op. cit.*

178 See, in this connection, European Governance: A White Paper, Commission of the European Communities, 25 July 2001, COM(2001) 428 final; Mandelkern Group on Better Regulation Final Report, 13 November 2001; both of which were welcomed by the Laeken European Council, 14–15 December 2001.

179 White Paper on European Governance, *op. cit.*, p. 10.

180 Tarlach McGonagle, "Co-regulation of the Media in Europe: The Potential for Practice of an Intangible Idea", *op. cit.*; Carmen Palzer, "Co-Regulation of the Media in Europe: European Provisions for the Establishment of Co-regulation Frameworks", *IRIS plus* 2002–6; Wolfgang Schulz & Thorsten Held, "Regulated Self-Regulation as a Form of Modern Government", Study commissioned by the German Federal Commissioner for Cultural and Media Affairs, Interim Report (October 2001).

181 Mandelkern Group Report, *op. cit.*, p. 83.

182 *Ibid.*, p. 81; see also, *ibid.*, p. 17.

the respective regulatory objectives".[183] Another variant on the co-regulatory terminology is "audited self-regulation",[184] a term which tends to enjoy greater currency in the US than in Europe. The least that can be stated with certainty is that the terms indicate "lighter-touch" forms of regulation than the traditional State-dominated regulatory prototype.

It is imperative, however, that one avoids getting bogged down in definitional minutiae. What *is* important, though, is that one grasps that the principle of co-regulation implies a novel approach to regulation, by virtue of its in-built potential for involving an increased number of interested parties (to a greater or lesser extent) in a flexible regulatory process. It might be useful if one were to conceive of regulation in terms of a continuum stretching from the traditional State-dominated model through co-regulation to self-regulation.

Figure 1. Regulatory continuum

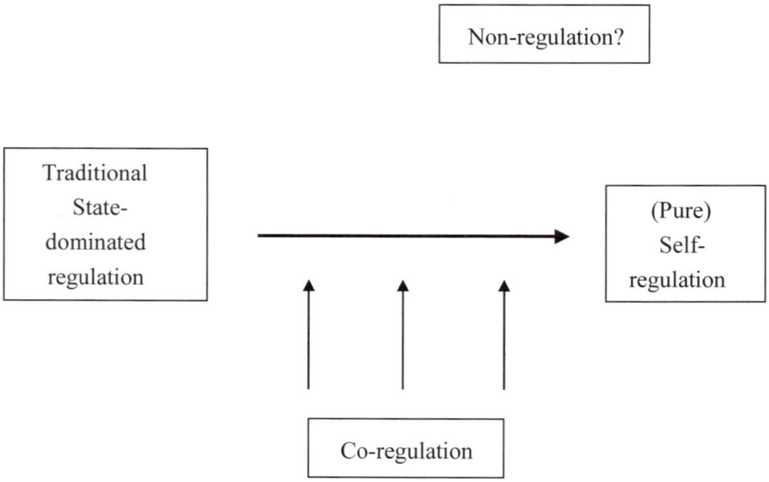

The vagueness of what exactly co-regulation entails and the relative shortage of tried and tested models to examine have served to stymie its development, both as a concept and as a practice. While it is understandably difficult to conceive of and

183 Wolfgang Schulz & Thorsten Held,, "Regulated Self-Regulation as a Form of Modern Government", *op. cit.*, p. 85. The coiners of the term elaborate on its flexibility in the following manner: "[t]hus, all means of governmental influence on self-regulatory processes can be described and phenomena referred to as co-regulation in other contexts are covered as well."

184 Audited self-regulation has been described as: "the delegation by Congress or a federal agency to a nongovernmental entity the power to implement laws or agency regulations, with powers of review and independent action retained by a federal agency" – D.C. Michael, "Federal Agency Use of Audited Self-Regulation as a Regulatory Technique", 47 *Administrative Law Review* (Spring 1995), pp. 171–254, at 176.

develop practical guidelines for co-regulation *in abstracto*, some focused research is likely to make a significant contribution to the concretisation of relevant discussions.[185] One research project examined a variety of S&CR models from different jurisdictions and from that starting point, came up with a "tool-box" of appropriate instruments for "the regulation of self-regulation".[186] Subsequently, some of the persons involved in that research had a central role in the elaboration of a *Study on Co-Regulation Measures in the Media Sector*.[187] This study surveyed existing co-regulatory practices concerning press, broadcasting, online and mobile services and film and interactive games in the (then) 25 EU Member States.[188] The study also spanned the following regulatory objectives: protection of minors and human dignity; advertising; quality ethics, diversity of private media; access, setting of standards. As such, it represents a wealth of descriptive material, facilitating both thematic and geographical comparisons and analysis. A section focusing on impact assessment is a useful empirical component to the study, permitting evaluations of actual co-regulatory practices.[189] Contextualisation is provided by a discussion of co-regulation under the ECHR and under EU law.[190] Notwithstanding the contribution of these and other research projects to general comprehension of the concept of S&CR, a related and perhaps self-evident observation is that some areas and political/legal contexts are better suited to S&CR than others.[191] But the vagueness that has characterised – and to an extent hampered – the debate on co-regulation so far should not be perceived uniquely in a negative light. It is precisely the same vagueness or intangibility that enables the notion to offer so much potential for milking.

---

185 Wolfgang Schulz *et al.*, *Study on Co-Regulation Measures in the Media Sector: Final Report* (Study for the European Commission, Directorate Information Society and Media Unit A1 Audiovisual and Media Policies Tender DG EAC 03/04), June 2006. See also: Christopher T. Marsden, "Co-Regulation in European Media and Internet Sectors", 8 *MultiMedia und Recht* (No. 1, 2005), pp. 3–7; Christopher T. Marsden, "Co- and self-regulation in European media and Internet sectors: The results of Oxford University's study www.selfregulation.info", 9 *Communications Law* (No. 5, 2004), pp. 187–195; Scott G. Dacko & Martin Hart, "Critically Examining Theory and Practice: Implications for Coregulation and Coregulating Broadcast Advertising in the United Kingdom", 7 *The International Journal on Media Management* (Nos. 1&2, 2006), pp. 2–15.

186 Wolfgang Schulz & Thorsten Held, "Regulated Self-Regulation as a Form of Modern Government", *op. cit.*

187 Wolfgang Schulz *et al.*, *Study on Co-Regulation Measures in the Media Sector*, *op. cit.*

188 *Ibid.*, pp. 1–2.

189 *Ibid.*, Chapter 4 – Impact Assessment.

190 *Ibid.*, Chapter 5 – Implementation: ss. 5.1 and 5.2, respectively.

191 For a fuller discussion of the possible thematic ambit of S&CR (including with respect to the independence of journalists; tackling hate speech; the protection of minors; advertising, and technical standards), see Tarlach McGonagle, "Co-Regulation of the Media in Europe: The Potential for Practice of an Intangible Idea", *op. cit.* See also, Susanne Nikoltchev, Ed., *IRIS Special: Co-Regulation of the Media in Europe* (Strasbourg, the European Audiovisual Observatory, 2003).

The advantages of a committed co-regulatory system are numerous: greater representation and participation would result in the guiding documents commanding the confidence of all parties; the channelling of industry expertise into the regulatory drafting process would lead to greater sensitivity to the realities of the media world; an efficient system of sanctions, again elaborated multilaterally, would also enhance the credibility of the system (unlike State-devised equivalent structures which have traditionally tended to elicit resistance from industry players); procedural efficiency and expeditiousness; regulation would be more flexible, more easily and swiftly adapted to changing realities ushered in by technological and societal developments.

At the European level, there are increasing indications of enthusiasm in regulatory- and policy-making circles for the exploration of S&CR techniques specifically in relation to the media. As regards the European Union, the Audiovisual Media Services (AVMS) Directive[192] provides a good example of how the erstwhile cautious support for S&CR has quickly grown more confident.[193] Article 4.7 reads:

> Member States shall encourage co-regulation and/or self-regulatory regimes at national level in the fields coordinated by this Directive to the extent permitted by their legal systems. These regimes shall be such that they are broadly accepted by the main stakeholders in the Member States concerned and provide for effective enforcement.

Of itself, Article 4.7 is of limited substantive relevance. The core obligation it places on Member States – merely to encourage co-regulation and/or self-regulatory regimes [...] – is tame. The nature of S&CR is not explained in the Article, nor are any of its key features alluded to. Recital 44 discusses S&CR at greater length, but its explanatory power is also limited. It points to the suitability of S&CR for advancing consumer protection and for the attainment of public interest objectives. Co-regulation is dealt with explicitly in the second paragraph of Recital 44's second paragraph. It reads:

> Co-regulation gives, in its minimal form, a legal link between self-regulation and the national legislator in accordance with the legal traditions of the Member States. Co-regulation should allow for the possibility of State intervention in the event of its objectives not being met. Without prejudice to formal obligations of the Member States regarding transposition, this Directive encourages the use of co-regulation

192 Directive 2010/13/EU of the European Parliament and of the Council of 10 March 2010 on the coordination of certain provisions laid down by law, regulation or administrative action in member states concerning the provision of audiovisual media services (codified version), OJ L 95/2 of 15 April 2010.

193 Fourth Report from the Commission to the Council, the European Parliament, the European Economic and Social Committee and the Committee of the Regions on the application of Directive 89/552/EEC "Television without Frontiers", COM (2002) 778 final, 6 January 2003.

> and self-regulation. This should neither oblige Member States to set up co- and/or self-regulatory regimes nor disrupt or jeopardise current co-regulation or self-regulatory initiatives which are already in place within Member States and which are working effectively.

In addition, both the Directive on electronic commerce (Article 16)[194] and the Data Protection Directive (Article 27)[195] have stressed the importance of codes of conduct; an approach which represents a tentative move away from traditional regulatory techniques and arguably in the direction of co-regulation.

As regards the Council of Europe, while the formal review of the European Convention on Transfrontier Television has been discontinued,[196] a 2003 report[197] concludes with a consideration of the architecture of future regulation, including S&CR as possible options. There has been a growing willingness to countenance S&CR at successive European Ministerial Conferences on Mass Media Policy (eg. Prague, 1994; Thessaloniki, 1997; Cracow, 2000; Kyiv, 2005) and on Media and New Communication Services (Reykjavik, 2009).[198] The prospect has also been broached in the Committee of Ministers' Recommendation on self-regulation concerning cyber content;[199] the Standing Committee's Statement on human dignity and fundamental rights of others,[200] and perhaps most explicitly, the Council of Europe's Submission to the 2nd Preparatory Committee for the World Summit on the Information Society;[201] the Committee of Ministers' Declaration on freedom of

---

194 Directive 2000/31/EC of the European Parliament and of the Council of 8 June 2000 on certain legal aspects of information society services, in particular electronic commerce, in the Internal Market (Directive on electronic commerce), OJ L 178, 17 July 2000, p. 1.

195 Directive 95/46/EC of the European Parliament and of the Council of 24 October 1995 on the protection of individuals with regard to the processing of personal data and on the free movement of such data, OJ L 281, 23 November 1995, p. 31.

196 Council of Europe Press Release, "Transfrontier television: the revision of the Convention discontinued", 4 February 2011.

197 Report by Dr Andreas Grünwald on possible options for the review of the European Convention on Transfrontier Television, Standing Committee on Transfrontier Television of the Council of Europe, Doc. T-TT(2003)002, 24 April 2003.

198 In 2009, the ministerial conference was titled and calibrated differently in order to reflect changing notions of the media. For analysis, see: Tarlach McGonagle & Kim de Beer, "*A brave new media world?* Een kritische blik op het nieuwe mediabeleid van de Raad van Europa", 22 *Mediaforum* 2010–5, pp. 146–156.

199 Recommendation Rec(2001)8 of the Committee of Ministers to member states on self-regulation concerning cyber content (self-regulation and user protection against illegal or harmful content on new communications and information services), 5 September 2001.

200 Statement (2002)1 on Human Dignity and the Fundamental Rights of Others, Standing Committee on Transfrontier Television of the Council of Europe, 12–13 September 2002. For a fuller discussion of the relevant provisions of these texts, see Tarlach McGonagle, "Co-Regulation of the Media in Europe: The Potential for Practice of an Intangible Idea", *op. cit.*

201 Democracy, human rights and the rule of law in the Information Society, Contribution by the Council of Europe to the 2nd Preparatory Committee for the World Summit on the Information Society, Doc. WSIS/PC-2/CONTR/32-E of 9 December 2002.

communication on the Internet;[202] the Committee of Ministers' Recommendation on the right of reply in the new media environment;[203] the Committee of Ministers' Declaration on human rights and the rule of law in the Information Society;[204] the Committee of Ministers' Declaration on protecting the role of the media in democracy and in the context of media concentration;[205] the Committee of Ministers' Recommendation on promoting freedom of expression and information in the new information and communications environment.[206]

The level of politico-legal support for S&CR as sketched above seems to be growing independently of any accompanying attempts to define its scope. This has predictably fuelled the criticism that passing textual references to S&CR are no more than lip-service on the part of governmental and intergovernmental organisations in their purported quest to attain high-minded principles for the enhancement of participatory practices in their decision-making processes. It has also fuelled scepticism about the practical appeal of S&CR. While this criticism is persuasive and this scepticism is not without foundation, neither should lead to the routine dismissal of S&CR as regulatory alternatives, without first attempting to engage meaningfully with the substantive issues involved.

Finally, it should be reiterated that the underlying objectives of S&CR can be addressed effectively even without having been formulated in the idiom of S&CR as such. This point is demonstrated by the concern for inclusive, participatory governance of the Internet and its inherent goal-setting, as articulated in the concluding documents of the World Summit on the Information Society:

> The Internet has evolved into a global facility available to the public and its governance should constitute a core issue of the Information Society agenda. The international management of the Internet should be multilateral, transparent and democratic, with the full involvement of governments, the private sector, civil society and international organizations. It should ensure an equitable distribution of resources, facilitate access for all and ensure a stable and secure functioning of the Internet, taking into account multilingualism.[207]

Having canvassed a number of so-called regulatory alternatives, another, more fundamental question, must be addressed, *viz.* whether there should be regulation at all. Or more aptly, whether there should be additional regulation, for much time and

202 Adopted on 28 May 2003.

203 Recommendation Rec (2004) 16 on the right of reply in the new media environment, 15 December 2004.

204 Adopted on 13 May 2005.

205 Adopted on 31 January 2007.

206 Recommendation CM/Rec(2007)11 on promoting freedom of expression and information in the new information and communications environment, 26 September 2007.

207 "Building the Information Society: a global challenge in the new Millennium", *op. cit.* para. 48.

effort have thankfully been spent debunking the all-too-frequently recurring misperception that the online world is unregulated. In regulatory matters, reflex should be replaced by reflection. It is only once the need for specific regulation has been convincingly established that its possible mechanics should be considered. There is a certain unease among critics of S&CR about the sharing (or partial transfer) of regulatory responsibilities that have traditionally been the preserve of the State. The fear that S&CR bodies would lack the authority, accountability and a host of other (procedural) safeguards necessary for ensuring the public service role they would be expected to fulfil is also very palpable.

In response to these concerns, it ought to be pointed out that co-regulation, in particular, should not be perceived as a result-driven phenomenon. One of the most attractive features of co-regulation is that its structures are designed to optimise quality of governance and it attaches paramount importance to process values. Greater representation and participation in regulatory structures is one of the first of these process values that comes to mind; an inclusiveness of a greater selection of parties, including minorities. In the same vein, responsiveness to the public and an ability to serve the stated interests and needs of diverse societal groups is another prerequisite. The process should remain transparent and easily accessible to the public. Structures should be in place ensuring user-friendliness as regards complaints and appeals mechanisms, with the possibility of ultimate recourse to an independent arbiter or the courts. Co-regulation offers a structural framework that is particularly conducive to guaranteeing these – and other – process values.

Operational autonomy for the co-regulatory body is also crucial, and adequate, independent financing is a *sine qua non* for the same if the body is to be insulated from powerful political and commercial interests. A co-regulatory system's accountability to the public could be safeguarded by structured evaluation processes (eg. governing the start-up phase which would include the drafting of codes, guidelines, etc., and equally once the system is up and running and the codes, etc., are being implemented). An earnest espousal of these principles – which could be set out in the enabling legislation that would set up the co-regulatory system – would go a long way towards meeting some of the ideals of good governance as set out in the European Commission's White Paper, such as the creation of "a reinforced culture of consultation and dialogue".[208]

An increasing openness to the potential of S&CR is now very much a feature of the regulatory *Zeitgeist.* For co-regulation to establish itself as a viable regulatory model, it will need to bridge the gap between theory and practice; a gap of considerable scepticism and resistance. In order to do so, its drivers will have to keep a resolute focus on the primary goal to be achieved: to ensure a more equitable

208 European Commission, "European Governance: A White Paper", *op. cit.*, p. 16.

type of regulation which would enhance opportunities for freedom of expression, not curtail them.

Finally, although already mentioned, *supra*, the potential of S&CR for ensuring the effective participation of persons belonging to minorities in regulatory structures and processes governing the media merits reiteration. Effective participation in S&CR mechanisms clearly ripples into the exercise of the right to freedom of expression by persons belonging to minorities. At a general level, Karol Jakubowicz has noted that a "major role can be played by problem definition: whoever defines the problem under discussion can then control the process – set the agenda, determine policy framing and formulation, develop solutions, etc."[209] This is true, *a fortiori*, in respect of problem and issue definition in the realm of media regulation, as was demonstrated in the discussion in Chapter 3.1.3 of the features of an appropriate enabling environment for freedom of expression. Effective participation in S&CR would therefore create equitable opportunities for representatives of persons belonging to minorities to contribute to the setting of parameters for policy formulation and thereby the terms of conceptual and substantive engagement with particular issues, especially those of greatest relevance for their own needs and interests.[210]

Conclusions

This chapter follows through on the rationales for the rights of persons belonging to minorities and examines their relevance in respect of freedom of expression. It sets out the minority-specific dimension to the main theories for freedom of expression. It thereby shows that is particularly important for minorities to be able to participate in public life/debate, contest dominant orthodoxies in society, and create, sustain and develop their identities. These particular interests in expressive rights are, of course, shared with non-minority groups, but their importance is appropriately accentuated in respect of minorities owing to their situational specificities (eg. prevalent societal discrimination against them could hinder their access to the media and other communicative fora) or the specificities of their identities (eg. linguistic distinctiveness from other societal groups: specific features of cultural identity may restrict the range of communicative fora or media via which it can viably be transmitted). This discussion provides clear linkage between minority-specific aspects of theory and practice.

The right to freedom of expression clearly cannot be exercised in an effective manner in the absence of expressive opportunities and outlets, the *primus inter*

209 Karol Jakubowicz, "Media Governance Structures in Europe", in Els de Bens, Ed., *Media Between Culture and Commerce*, op. cit., pp. 197–223, at 197.
210 See further, in this connection, Chapter 11.3.

pares of which is the media (which are capable of providing fora and content alike). However, the media is a term that is too general and too amalgamated to be analytically meaningful for present purposes. Different types of media correspond to varying degrees to the various but specific communicative needs and preferences of different groups in different situations. Inevitably, in different sets of circumstances, certain media will therefore be more effective than others. The notion of media functionality is of great analytical value in this connection. This Chapter examines the various dimensions to media functionality, first in the context of different types of media, and second, in relation to the specific communicative needs and interests of minorities. The double disaggregation involved in this theoretical approach opens up a level of detail and specificity that is largely absent from conventional interpretive and monitoring approaches to relevant international instruments. As such, its application in practice could greatly enhance interpretive and monitoring approaches and especially assessments of whether the right to freedom of expression of persons belonging to minorities is effective in concrete cases.

Despite the importance of media functionality as a factor influencing the ability of different types of media to render the exercise of the right to freedom of expression effective, other important – and prior – influences must also be considered. The media (in general) are best able to carry out the democracy-oriented tasks ascribed to them in a favourable enabling environment. The existence of such an environment implies, at a minimum, respect for rule of law and human rights generally and for the right to freedom of expression and minority rights in particular. Key elements of an appropriate enabling environment include constitutional, legislative and other regulatory standards guaranteeing relevant freedoms, reinforced by official state policies concerning media regulation and minority rights and societal attitudes to both. The extent to which operative public values such as pluralistic tolerance are upheld is also of central importance.

The final focus of this Chapter is on the advent of new communications technologies. These new technologies entail a combination of novel qualitative and quantitative features which have led to new practices and patterns of communication in society, which in turn have given rise to new communicative needs and interests. The impact of these new technologies has affected all groups in society, but not necessarily in identical ways. The most pertinent technology-driven changes include media convergence, participatory models for generation of content, commodification of information, individualisation of choice, explosion of available information. As with the so-called "traditional" media (eg. print media, broadcasting), the suitability of particular technological opportunities for minority groups depends on considerations of media functionality and on their ability to afford and use the technology in question.

Another decisive change concerns a new direction in regulatory thinking, prompted by technological developments and an apparent willingness by States authorities to engage with industry and civil society actors. New co-regulatory approaches to media regulation offer considerable potential for the inclusion of minority perspectives in law- and policy-making exercises and that potential should be thoroughly explored with a view to its maximisation by all interested parties.

There are a number of upshots to the foregoing. The emergence of new technological possibilities and practices has occasioned the need for reappraisals of existing understandings of media functionality and regulatory policy. Chapters 4 and 11 make the case for those reappraisals to be applied to interpretive and monitoring processes of international instruments containing provisions dealing with freedom of expression.

Chapter 4
The coupling of freedom of expression and minority rights

Introduction

Chapter 3 explores a selection of theories on freedom of expression and the media, particularly from the perspective of persons belonging to minorities. The present chapter will demonstrate that many of the principles, theories and issues addressed in Chapter 3 are also reflected in the various provisions guaranteeing the right to freedom of expression under international law. It will also consider a selection of unsuccessful attempts to integrate those principles, theories and issues into international legal standards.

With customary eloquence, the Nobel Laureate, Séamus Heaney, has challenged the suggestion that "first line and the last line of any poem" are "where the poem begins and ends".[1] His remarks are equally applicable to international legal treaties. The consideration of such treaties does not begin or end with textual formulations. It incorporates – to varying extents – drafting processes, historical and teleological purposes and their normative and societal impact. This premise explains the inclusion of the forthcoming focuses on such peri-textual aspects of international legal standards.

4.1 An underexplored nexus of international law

The leading provisions in international law concerning the right to freedom of expression will be subjected to close scrutiny at various junctures in Chapters 6–11. For present purposes, it is sufficient to note that the most important of those provisions are Article 19, UDHR, Article 19, ICCPR and Article 10, ECHR. As already noted in Chapter 2, Article 27, ICCPR, is the leading provision concerning minority rights. However, under international human rights law, the nexus between freedom of expression on the one hand, and minority rights on the other hand, remains surprisingly understated.

The UN Human Rights Committee, however, is showing increasing interest in the linkage between Articles 19 and 27, ICCPR. The occasion of drafting a new General Comment on Article 19 presented the Committee with the opportunity to underscore that linkage and thereby compensate for the terseness of the original textual

1 Séamus Heaney, "The Fragment", in *Electric Light* (London, Faber & Faber Ltd., 2001), p. 57.

provisions. It seized the opportunity by explicitly mentioning Article 27 – alongside Articles 17, 18 and 25 – as containing "guarantees for freedom of opinion and, or expression".[2] It further reaffirms that Article 19(2) "protects all forms of expression and the means of their dissemination" and that "[s]uch forms include, the spoken, written and sign language [and various forms of non-verbal expression]".[3]

Earlier, in its Views on the Communication, *Ballantyne and others v. Canada*, the Human Rights Committee found that a State "may choose one or more official languages, but it may not exclude, outside the spheres of public life, the freedom to express oneself in a language of one's choice".[4] The Communication involved a challenge to a legislative prohibition on the use of languages other than French in, *inter alia*, public billposting and outdoor commercial advertising in Quebec. The above-cited finding was central to the Committee's conclusion that there had been a violation of Article 19(2), ICCPR. It also offers persons belonging to linguistic minorities a modest, but nevertheless important, safeguard of their right to freedom of expression in their own languages.

In the case of *Mavlonov and Sa'di v. Uzbekistan*, the denial of (re-)registration of a minority-language newspaper, thereby preventing it from being able to publish, was at issue.[5] Noteworthy factual details include the status of the newspaper in question as the only non-governmental Tajik-language publication in the Samarkand region of Uzbekistan and its coverage of educational, cultural and other matters of interest to the Tajik minority in the region. The Committee found that there had been a violation of the first applicant's right to impart information (as editor of the newspaper) and a violation of the second applicant's right to receive information and ideas in print (as a reader of the newspaper).[6] It also found that there had been a violation of Article 27 (read with Article 2) as – in the circumstances of the case – "the use of a minority language press as means [*sic*] of airing issues of significance and importance to the Tajik minority community in Uzbekistan, by both editors and readers, is an essential element of the Tajik minority's culture".[7] While the simultaneous, separate violations of Articles 19 and 27 in the same case is interesting in the context of the present discussion, even more interesting is the Separate opinion of Committee members Sir Nigel Rodley and Mr. Rafael Rivas Posada.[8] They were of the opinion that the Committee's finding of a "self standing

2 Draft General Comment No. 34 (Upon completion of the first reading by the Human Rights Committee), Doc. No. CCPR/C/GC/34/CRP.6, 3 May 2011, para. 3.

3 *Ibid.*, para. 11.

4 *Ballantyne, Davidson & McIntyre v. Canada*, Communication Nos. 359/1989 & 385/1989, 31 March 1993, para. 11.4.

5 *Mavlonov & Sa'di v. Uzbekistan*, Communication No. 1334/2004, 19 March 2009.

6 *Ibid.*, para. 8.4.

7 *Ibid.*, para. 8.7.

8 Appendix to *ibid.*

violation" of Article 19(2) in respect of the second applicant – a reader of the newspaper – was too "far-reaching". They favoured a finding of a violation of Article 19 *juncto* 27 "because of the special nature of article 27 which envisages the enjoyment of rights by persons as members of minority communities". It is submitted here that that is a preferable assessment of the key issues in the case.

The absence of explicit and extensive linkage between the aforementioned normative provisions guaranteeing freedom of expression and minority rights, can be explained largely by historical and political reasons. Whereas the US (along with Britain and France) championed the cause of freedom of expression (or "freedom of information", to use the UN parlance of the time), the USSR and its allies championed the rights of minorities. The ideological polarisation that defined the Cold War also precluded the possibility of the synergic application of freedom of expression and minority rights. Early evidence of this polarisation was to be found in the political pressure brought to bear by both sides concerning the creation of sub-commissions of the UN Commission on Human Rights. This pressure was applied along the above-mentioned lines and resulted in the establishment of a Sub-Commission on Freedom of Information and of the Press, on the one hand, and a Sub-Commission on the Prevention of Discrimination and the Protection of Minorities, on the other hand.[9] It has been noted that "[t]his was but the beginning of continual finger-pointing by American and Soviet UN representatives at the respective weaknesses of their countries".[10]

4.1.1 Tentative tendencies and attempted couplings in international law

4.1.1(i) Actual couplings

No provision of *generalist* international human rights treaty law couples the right to freedom of expression and the rights of minorities *in an explicit and detailed way.*[11] Article 17(d) of the UN Convention on the Rights of the Child comes closest, by requiring States Parties to "encourage the mass media to have particular regard to the linguistic needs of the child who belongs to a minority group or who is indigenous". The provision did not enjoy an entirely smooth passage through the drafting process, however. From the introduction of the draft proposal to "[e]ncourage the mass media agencies to have particular regard to the linguistic

9 For commentary, see: John P. Humphrey, *Human Rights & the United Nations: a great adventure*, (New York, Transnational Publishers, Inc., 1984), p. 20.

10 Mary Ann Glendon, *A World Made New: Eleanor Roosevelt and the Universal Declaration of Human Rights* (New York, Random House, Inc., 2001), p. 36.

11 Article 27, ICCPR, of course, states *inter alia* that persons belonging to minorities shall not be denied the right "to use their own language". That provision could therefore be described as "explicit", but not as "detailed" insofar as it does not explore or reflect the (potential) extent of the intersectionality of the rights in question.

needs of minority groups",[12] quibbling began over the most appropriate wording to designate "minority groups". In due course, the relevant *termini technicus* evolved to refer to the linguistic needs of "the child who belongs to a minority group or an indigenous population",[13] before its final wording was settled on.

Whereas proposed alternative wordings such as "indigenous population" and "indigenous child" drew criticisms from various quarters, it was an intervention by the Turkish observer specifically targetting the formulations, "minority group" and "indigenous population", that proved the most pointed.[14] He argued that the failure in various international fora to reach consensual definitions of those concepts meant that the proposed subparagraph would be "non-applicable".[15] He deployed this argument in the context of his more general view that the subparagraphs in the draft article were superfluous to its introductory part and argued that "it should not be the role of this Convention to give detailed guidance as to what the States Parties should do in implementing the article". Thus, he urged the deletion of all subparagraphs, or as a second-best option, the deletion of subparagraph (d) at least. When the draft text was adopted without accepting his suggestions, the observer for Turkey reiterated his position and added that "there would be no alternative by States Parties but to interpret, under the circumstances, these terms according to their national law". He rounded off his intervention by mooting the possibility of adopting a reservation to that effect when the Convention would be opened for signature.[16]

The coupling of freedom of expression and minority rights in Article 17(d) is shored up to a limited extent by other sub-sections of Article 17. For example, Article 17(a) obliges States Parties to "encourage the mass media to disseminate information and material of social and cultural benefit to the child and in accordance with the spirit of article 29". In turn, Article 29 – which focuses on the goals of education – explicitly recognises the importance of developing respect for a child's "own

12 The Baha'i International Community (an NGO with consultative status with ECOSOC) submitted a proposed wording on the topic which included the following provision: "encourage mass media agencies to disseminate their child-oriented programmes not only in the official language(s) of the State but also in the language(s) of the State's minority and indigenous groups". However, this proposal was not considered by the 1983 Working Group. See further: E/CN.4/1983/62, Annex II (E/CN.4/1983/WG.1/WP.2/WP.29); Sharon Detrick, Jaap Doek & Nigel Cantwell, Eds., *The United Nations Convention on the Rights of the Child: A Guide to the "Travaux Préparatoires"* (The Netherlands, Martinus Nijhoff Publishers, 1992), p. 281.

13 Text as adopted by the Working Group at first reading, E/CN.4/1988/WG.1/WP.1/Rev.2, pp. 14–15; Sharon Detrick *et al.*, *The United Nations Convention on the Rights of the Child: A Guide to the "Travaux Préparatoires"*, *op. cit.*, p. 288.

14 Considerations 1989 Working Group, E/CN.4/1989/48, pp. 53–55; Sharon Detrick *et al.*, *The United Nations Convention on the Rights of the Child: A Guide to the "Travaux Préparatoires"*, *op. cit.*, p. 289.

15 *Ibid.*; Sharon Detrick *et al.*, *The United Nations Convention on the Rights of the Child: A Guide to the "Travaux Préparatoires"*, *op. cit.*, p. 290.

16 *Ibid.*

cultural identity, language and values [...]",[17] and of cultivating understanding, tolerance and other virtues.[18] Finally in this connection, Article 17(b) requires States to "encourage international co-operation in the production, exchange and dissemination of such information and material from a diversity of cultural, national and international sources".

Despite the dearth of successful couplings of the right to freedom of expression and minority rights in international human rights treaties, there have been a few examples of "near misses", both in the context of the United Nations and the Council of Europe.

4.1.1(ii) Attempted couplings: United Nations

In 1948, a draft Convention on Freedom of Information was drawn up by a United Nations Conference on Freedom of Information.[19] Some of the exchanges at the Conference were no more than early rehearsals of ideological stances *vis-à-vis* freedom of information/expression that would soon come to typify relevant debates in the Cold War era.[20] As such, some of the conference proceedings have been disparagingly described as a "dialogue between the deaf".[21] Despite this criticism, the conference was "hailed as a great success"[22] – at the time – due to its adoption of three draft conventions,[23] 43 resolutions and draft articles for the international bill of rights. Subsequent procedures and events quickly altered enthusiasm for the achievements of the conference. John P. Humphrey, who was the executive secretary of the conference, believed that the conference would indeed have been a "great success" if the three draft conventions had been opened for signature and ratification immediately after the conclusion of the conference. He explained the failings of the post-conference procedures as follows:

> If the countries invited to the conference had been asked to give their delegations full powers to sign any conventions approved by it, the three conventions would undoubtedly be in force today. But because it was thought that their prestige and authority would be enhanced if the conventions were approved by the United Nations before they were opened for signature, the three drafts together with the rest of the

17 Article 29.1(c), CRC.

18 Article 29.1(d), CRC.

19 United Nations Conference on Freedom of Information: Final Act (Lake Success, New York, United Nations Publishing, 1948).

20 John P. Humphrey, *Human Rights & the United Nations: a great adventure*, *op. cit.*, p. 35.

21 *Ibid.*, p. 53.

22 *Ibid.*

23 The three draft conventions focused on: the gathering and international transmission of news; the institution of an international right of correction, and freedom of information. Of the three, only the convention concerning the institution of the international right of correction was formally adopted and entered into force.

> final act were sent to the Economic and Social Council for further action. This gave the opposition the time to organize its forces as well as unlimited time in which to press its point of view. In ECOSOC and later in the General Assembly, there began a long and frustrating process of discussion and amendment. In brief, the amendments which the communist and developing countries forced on the United Nations were from the Western point of view so radical that the draft conventions became unacceptable. What was coming to the surface was the resentment felt in many countries toward the monopolistic practices of the great news-gathering agencies, and the too simple concept of freedom of information current in the West, particularly among professional journalists. And as so often happens, the opposition overreacted.[24]

Thus, the draft Convention on Freedom of Information came to be further discussed in ECOSOC and the General Assembly. If ever a drafting process was going nowhere in a hurry, this was it! Ultimately, the draft convention never saw the light of day.[25] Nevertheless, the draft text, as originally drawn up in 1948, contained some provisions that were of particular relevance to minorities. For instance, the following excerpt from Article 3 of the draft Convention merits consideration:

> Each Contracting State shall encourage the establishment and functioning within its territory of one or more non-official organizations of persons employed in the dissemination of information to the public, in order to promote the observance by such persons of high standards of professional conduct, and in particular:
> [...]
> (e) To counteract the persistent spreading of false or distorted reports which promote hatred or prejudice against States, persons or groups of different race, language, religion or philosophical conviction.[26]

If adopted, this provision would have accorded minorities a measure of protection which they do not enjoy under contemporary international law. The wording of the introductory sentence is somewhat abstruse, but it seems to concern the free (i.e., unhindered) operation of media entities which are independent of State control. The defining purpose of such media entities would be the promotion of professional

---

24 *Ibid.*

25 In 1951, the draft Convention was revised by an *ad hoc* committee of the UN General Assembly and in 1959, the Third (Social, Humanitarian and Cultural) Committee of the General Assembly proceeded to have a detailed discussion of the *ad hoc* committee's revised text (now comprising 19 articles). From 1959 through 1961, the Third Committee managed to approve the text of the Preamble to the draft Convention, as well as Articles 1–4. Lack of time prevented further discussion of, or progress on, the remainder of the *ad hoc* committee's revised draft text. Further discussion of the draft text was postponed therefore until the following year's session, and that self-same exercise in procrastination was repeated every year until 1973, whereafter the agenda item completely disappeared without explanation!

26 Draft Convention on Freedom of Information, *Yearbook of the United Nations 1947–48*, pp. 593–595.

quality in the media sector. The description of the State duty ("shall encourage") is not necessarily oxymoronic: rather, it insists that the obligation on States is an imperative one, but that the obligation is merely to "encourage" the creation and operation of media entities.

It is, however, para. (e) that would have filled a gap in international law, by virtue of its focus on "false or distorted reports which promote hatred or prejudice against" particular groups. Promotion would – most likely – involve a lower evidentiary standard than "incitement" – the *ne plus ultra* of free expression according to the current canon of international law and a term which has a distinct meaning in criminal law generally. The elements of falsity or distortion would also cover sensationalist reporting, stereotyping, and a range of other journalistic and presentational styles not currently covered *per se* by existing standards (see further, Chapter 6).

So far, so good, but what about the likely consistency of this enhanced protection for minorities (as the subjects of particular types of reporting) with a robust system of free expression? A crucial consideration would be whether the promotion of hatred or prejudice would be judged subjectively or objectively. Second, while the lower evidentiary standard implied by promotion could diminish the level of protection for vigorous, abrasive types of expression, the extent to which this would be so could, perhaps be offset by a strict insistence on the persistency with which the false or distorted reports would be spread. A final – and empirically verifiable – cause for concern is the danger that States authorities would seek to (ab)use the criteria of falsity and distortion in order to silence opponents of governmental authority or policy.

Whereas Article 3(e) may have had the potential to influence practices of portraying minorities in the media, the manna of participatory rights of access to the media was not to be found elsewhere in the draft Convention. On the contrary, Article 5, for example, stated that: "Nothing in the present Convention shall prevent a Contracting State from reserving under its legislation to its own nationals the right to edit newspapers or news periodicals produced within its territory". The naked fear of foreign influence on the shaping of news or public opinion is exposed by this provision; a fear that has not fully been dispelled, as shown by the drafting of the FCNM (see further, Chapter 2.2.3).

4.1.1(iii) Attempted couplings: Council of Europe

A number of attempts were also made to explicitly couple the right to freedom of expression with the rights of minorities in the European Convention on Human Rights. The first occurred during the drafting process of the Convention and the second (discussed *infra* in the context of Article 9, FCNM (Chapter 4.3.1)) concerned a proposal to review Article 10 of the Convention in the mid-1990s.

The *travaux préparatoires* of the European Convention on Human Rights document efforts to ensure that the final text of the provision on freedom of expression would expressly refer to certain particularised interests of minorities. At an early stage in the drafting process, one of the Irish representatives, James Everett, submitted that the Convention should secure for all citizens "and particularly for any minority in their country [...] freedom of speech and expression of opinion generally; freedom of association and assembly; freedom from discrimination on account of religion or other political opinion".[27]

More specifically, at a later stage in the drafting process, another one of the Irish representatives,[28] William Norton, pressed *inter alia* for the amendment of Article 10(2) of the draft Convention so that it would "stipulate that no restriction should be imposed on the right of national minorities to give expression to their aspirations by democratic means".[29]

While the *travaux* do not reveal any conscionable objections to this proposal, it seems that its ultimate omission from the final text can be best explained by the fact that it hitched its fortunes on those of the agenda to secure broader and stronger protection for minority rights in the nascent Convention. That agenda was set out in specific, formal terms as "the need for an examination of the problem of the wider protection of the rights of national minorities, with a view to a more precise definition of the rights of these minorities".[30] When that broader agenda failed to

---

27 A. H. Robertson, Ed., *Collected edition of the Travaux préparatoires of the European Convention on Human Rights* (The Hague, etc., Martinus Nijhoff, 1975–1985) (hereafter "*Collected edition of the Travaux préparatoires of the European Convention on Human Rights*"), Vol. I, p. 104.

28 Although Everett and Norton were both members of the same political party (the Labour Party), it is unclear to what extend their respective interventions were synchronised. As Ireland was extremely homogeneous at the time, it might appear here to be an unlikely champion of minority rights. However, it is most likely that the interventions were born out of concern for the interests and welfare of the Catholic/nationalist minority in Northern Ireland (this theory has been given credence by other commentators, especially in respect of Everett, see: Michael Kennedy and Eunan O'Halpin, *Ireland and the Council of Europe: from isolation towards integration* (Strasbourg, Council of Europe Publishing, 2000), p. 51).

29 *Collected Edition of the Travaux Préparatoires of the European Convention on Human Rights*, Vol. V, p. 60. See also, *ibid.*, p. 274, where this shortcoming is criticised in same breath as omission of right of political opposition.

30 Letter by Sir David Maxwell-Fyfe, Chairman of the Committee on Legal and Administrative Questions [of the Consultative Assembly] to the Chairman of the Committee of Ministers, 24 June 1950. The need to address the issue of minority rights was pointed out in a Report by the Committee on Legal and Administrative Questions to the Consultative Assembly (Doc. 77, para. II) and Maxwell-Fyfe's letter duly reminded the Committee of Ministers of that fact. See further, *ibid.*, Vol. V, p. 40.

prevail, the specific proposal to amend Article 10(2) was, in effect, similarly doomed.[31]

What would have been the impact of such wording, had it been adopted? Any attempt to answer this question will be necessarily speculative, but there are good grounds for believing that its impact could have been far-reaching, not least if it had been embedded in the constellation of broader minority rights that was simultaneously being lobbied for in the drafting process.[32] One likely consequence of the proposal would have been to give firm protection to the expression of minorities' secessionist aspirations, as long as they would be articulated in accordance with the precepts of democracy. The safeguarding of such a right for minorities would enter into direct collision with the entitlement of States authorities – specified in Article 10(2) – to restrict the exercise of the right to freedom of expression in the interests of "territorial integrity". *Prima facie*, it is very difficult to see how these conflicting standpoints could be reconciled in practice, without leading to the neutering of one or the other. If the freedom of expression of minorities were to trump the legitimate restriction of expression on the grounds of "territorial integrity", States comprising volatile political enclaves where independence/secession movements enjoy widespread support, would be deprived of one of their most convenient justifications for political repression and censorship of expression. The European Court of Human Rights has found time and again that State measures interfering with the right to freedom of expression based on the objective of preserving territorial integrity can be a mere sham for discrimination against, or repression of, political opposition.[33] The coincidence of political opposition and secessionist minorities is not unusual, thus rendering minorities more susceptible than other sections of the population to measures clamping down on expression that could jeopardise territorial integrity.

4.1.1(iv) Attempted couplings: assessment

The purpose of documenting these "near misses" in international law can hardly be dismissed as mere academic indulgence. They provide very valuable insights into:

---

31 This reading of events is seemingly corroborated by comments by another Irish delegate, to the effect that the signing of the draft Convention was intended as an "instalment on what the peoples of Europe want" – T.F. O'Higgins, *The Irish Independent*, 17 August 1950, quoted in Michael Kennedy and Eunan O'Halpin, *Ireland and the Council of Europe: from isolation towards integration*, *op. cit.*, p. 72.

32 In general terms, the case for greater protection of minority rights was consistently championed throughout the drafting process by a Danish representative, Mr. Lannung. See, *Collected edition of the Travaux préparatoires of the European Convention on Human Rights*, in particular, Vol. I, p. 54; Vol. V, p. 22.

33 See, among many other cases, *Arslan v. Turkey*, Judgment of the European Court of Human Rights of 8 July 1999 and *Ceylan v. Turkey*, Judgment of the European Court of Human Rights of 8 July 1999.

(a) the general sensitivity of minority issues in the immediate post-World War II period; (b) the fearful determination of States to restrict the freedom of expression of certain (often minority) groups on account of the clear nexus between strong protection for freedom of expression and effective political participation.

(a) As has already been seen in Chapter 2, the Universal Declaration of Human Rights contains no provisions explicitly protecting minority rights. Another Resolution, entitled "Fate of Minorities",[34] was adopted by the UN General Assembly on the same day as the Resolution proclaiming the Universal Declaration.[35] The Resolution, "Fate of Minorities", called for a "thorough study of the problem [*sic*!] of minorities" so as to enable the UN to "take effective measures for the protection of racial, national, religious or linguistic minorities". Thus, in one fell swoop, the importance of minority rights was recognised (at least nominally) and sidelined.

One could argue that the collapse of the League of Nations system, compounded by the atrocities of the Second World War, had left a gaping void in the international law-making arena. In such a standardless and structureless context, it was – perhaps – not unreasonable to insist that any novel approach to the protection of minority rights (which, we must not forget, was an even more contentious concept then than it is nowadays) be grounded in a "thorough study of the problem of minorities". However, given the widespread political apprehensiveness-*cum*-nervousness about explicitly recognising and protecting minority rights (especially without clearly defining their content in advance), this insistence could not but have had dilatory consequences and led to a *de facto* sidelining of the issue of minority rights.

The "fate" of proposals to explicitly enshrine minority rights protection in the draft European Convention on Human Rights proved similarly inauspicious. Mr Lannung, a Danish representative, presented a Report on "the problem of the wider protection of the rights of national minorities"[36] and the Committee on Legal and Administrative Questions of the Consultative Assembly of the Council of Europe "unanimously recognised the importance of [the] problem".[37] However, stressing that its task was "to draw up a list, not of fundamental rights, which must be defined in a general declaration, but only of those which appeared suitable for inclusion in an immediate international guarantee",[38] the Committee decided to adhere to the

---

34 UN General Assembly Resolution 217 C (III) of 10 December 1948.

35 UN General Assembly Resolution 217 A (III) of 10 December 1948.

36 First Session of the Consultative Assembly of the Council of Europe, Strasbourg, 10 August – 8 September 1949; Sitting of the Committee on Legal and Administrative Questions, 5 September 1949: *Collected edition of the Travaux préparatoires of the European Convention on Human Rights,* Vol. I, p. 200 (see also Eighth Sitting of the Consultative Assembly, 19 August 1949, p. 54).

37 *Ibid*., p. 200; Fifteenth sitting of the Consultative Assembly, 5 September 1949, *ibid*., p. 220.

38 *Ibid*., p. 222; see also, *ibid*., p. 200.

fundamental rights listed in the operative article [Article 2] of the draft Resolution under consideration – which did not include minority rights *per se*. Again tracking the course of events in the UN General Assembly, the Committee also decided to put on formal record, its "approval in principle of M. Lannung's declarations" and to "draw the attention of the Committee of Ministers to the need for a subsequent examination of the problem, with a view to defining more exactly the rights of national minorities".[39]

The foregoing historical perspectives reveal clear instances of parallelism in UN and Council of Europe approaches to the protection of minority rights. Essentially, the parallelism may be summarised as prioritisation in principle being reduced to procrastination in practice. Political wariness towards the active development of minority rights was very much the order of the day in both IGOs. Any effective attention paid to minority rights was largely subsumed in wider focuses on equality.

(b) The second useful purpose of analysing the aforementioned "near misses" of international treaty law is the opportunity this affords to explore relevant issues and interlinkages. By way of brief review, the main examples given *supra* involved: additional protection for certain groups from false or distorted reports promoting hatred or prejudice; prohibiting non-nationals from editing newspapers or news periodicals, and the right of minorities to express their aspirations by democratic means. Individually and collectively, these examples implicate not only the right to freedom of expression and minority rights, but several of other fundamental rights that qualitatively strengthen the right to freedom of expression (see further, Chapter 4.4). The first example – enhanced group protection from hatred and prejudice – clearly lies at the heart of the right to non-discrimination and equality (see, in particular, Chapter 5). The second example is not only discriminatory, but restrictive of participatory rights. The third example also involves participatory rights and implicitly the right to self-determination (for the second and third examples, see, in particular, Chapter 11).

A number of underlying concerns can be detected. Firstly, there is the societal imperative of countering hatred and prejudice. Secondly, one can sense across the other two examples a fear of/respect for the ability of the media to influence and shape public opinion. Hence, States' determination to retain control of political and cultural narratives on their own territory and to prevent non-nationals from influencing those narratives by taking up editorial positions in newspapers. While the third example need not necessarily involve the media, it does pay homage to the importance of being able to contribute to the shaping of public debate and relevant (national) narratives. Once again, two key axes are discernible here: the axis of

---

39 *Ibid.*, pp. 222; 200.

expression and its perlocutionary effect of influencing public opinion, on the one hand, and the axis of expression and effective political participation, on the other hand.

4.1.2 Qualifying State obligations

It is useful to explore the relationship between freedom of expression and minority rights not only through an examination of general and specific provisions of international law, but also through an examination of the nature of State obligations under those provisions.

Traditionally, discussions about civil and political rights have been presumptively framed in terms of negative liberty. This is a notion which has been given much of its contemporary theoretical shape by Isaiah Berlin. Drawing on the intellectual tradition of Locke, Mill, Constant, de Tocqueville and others, Berlin has articulated one of the key tenets of the notion as follows:

> there ought to exist a certain minimum area of personal freedom which must on no account be violated; for if it is overstepped, the individual will find himself in an area too narrow for even that minimum development of his natural faculties which alone makes it possible to pursue, and even to conceive, the various ends which men hold good or right or sacred. It follows that a frontier must be drawn between the area of private life and that of public authority. Where it is to be drawn is a matter of argument, indeed of haggling.[40]

The notion of negative liberty is therefore centrally concerned with the demarcation of zones of personal autonomy and agency on the one hand, and legitimate State action on the other. Essentialising the concept, Berlin describes the zone of non-interference by the State as "liberty *from*; absence of interference beyond the shifting, but always recognisable, frontier".[41]

Often associated with civil libertarianism, hostility to intervention by State authorities has particularly strong resonance in the realm of freedom of expression. This is a hostility of principle: a distrust of governmental motivation for the regulation (read: restriction) of expression,[42] and a fear that paternalistic State impulses would encroach on moral and intellectual freedom. It inevitably draws on

---

40 Isaiah Berlin, "Two Concepts of Liberty", in *Liberty* (Ed. Henry Hardy) (Oxford University Press), p. 171.

41 (emphasis per original) *Ibid.*, p. 174.

42 See, for example: Geoffrey R. Stone, "Democracy and Distrust", 64 *Colorado Law Review* 1171 (1993).

a variety of slippery slope arguments, such as: "repression has no stopping place"; "[o]nce begun, it can quickly move all the way to a totalitarian system".[43]

History provides ample evidence that these arguments of principle and these fears have a very real basis. This historical legitimacy, in turn, lends much persuasive force to the negative conception of civil and political rights generally and of freedom of expression in particular. Yet, such an exclusively negative conception is necessarily incomplete. A positive conception of liberty – with its implicit recognition of positive State obligations – is not only possible, but actually complementary to its negative counterpart.

In order to appreciate that there is no inherent contradiction or necessary tension in the compossibility of negative and positive conceptions of liberty (and *a posteriori* negative and positive State obligations), it is important to understand and distinguish between the different roles played by the State in the system of freedom of expression (see further the detailed discussion of these roles at the end of this section, *infra*).

The complementarity between both conceptions of liberty (or sets of State obligations) can be justified by substantive and instrumental arguments. When exclusion and discrimination are institutionally and societally entrenched, *negative* liberty may be inadequate to render certain rights – notably freedom of expression – meaningful for the victims of such exclusion and discrimination. *Positive*, equalising measures are then called for in order to realise such rights. *Positive* rights – such as effective participation; equality of access to institutionalised forms of communication, etc. – are often, as Berlin himself assures us, a means for protecting the negatively conceived liberty of individuals (and groups).[44]

The recognition of certain positive State duties in certain concatenations of circumstances should not be construed as implying that States are somehow obliged to remove all impediments – including all kinds of social and economic disadvantage – to the maximal realisation of rights. Such an ambitious claim – for the doctrine of positive State obligations to be a panacea for all the ills of society – could never be sustained. As Berlin points out, for one's liberty to be breached, some kind of agency – either governmental or third-party – must be involved; "[m]ere incapacity

43 Thomas I. Emerson, *The System of Freedom of Expression* (Random House, New York, 1970), p. 724. See also Salman Rushdie's comment: "[y]ou think you can give away one per cent of your freedom and you've still got 99 per cent, but actually, once you give away the first one per cent it's very remarkable how fast the other 99 per cent goes", Salman Rushdie, "Secrecy and Censorship"? in Ellen Hazelcorn & Patrick Smyth, Eds., *Let in the Light: Censorship, secrecy and democracy* (Dingle, Ireland, Brandon Book Publishers Ltd., 1993), pp. 26–38, at 29.

44 Isaiah Berlin, "Two Concepts of Liberty", *op. cit.*, p. 211.

to attain a goal" is not sufficient.[45] He illustrates the point colourfully with the quip: "[i]t is not lack of freedom not to fly like an eagle or swim like a whale".[46] Attention must rather focus on specific circumstances which impede sections of the population from exercising their right to freedom of expression and which clearly do fall within the zone of legitimate State responsibility (or "interference", to continue to apply Berlin's terminology). As Eric Barendt has argued, the suggestion that "government should ensure that all individuals and groups are in a position to communicate their views muddles freedom, or liberty, of speech with the conditions for its exercise".[47] This is a difficult point and it will be revisited in greater detail in the following sub-section.

For reasons of conceptual convenience, the duties of States which correlate to human rights are frequently styled as those which are "positive" or "affirmative" on the one hand and those which are "negative" or "restrictive" on the other hand. Technically speaking, though, such qualifiers more accurately describe the kind of action required of States in order to fulfil their duties in respect of human rights.[48] The distinction between positive and negative State obligations has considerable appeal as an organising principle and this is reflected in the structure of subsequent chapters of this book. In order to structure the forthcoming discussion of various State obligations, the distinction provides a convenient (if somewhat rough) way of separating two broad categories of obligations. Chapter 6 focuses on negative State obligations whereas Chapters 9–11 focus on positive State obligations. Within each chapter, greater specificity emerges, both in terms of the obligations identified and the rigour with which they are analysed.

One of the main conceptual limitations of the distinction is that it suggests a (complete) separation of negative and positive State obligations. This is why it will be relied on here for the purpose of imposing structural order on the discussion and not as the guiding analytical principle. In reality, although negative and positive State obligations are often readily distinguishable, it can also be difficult to pinpoint where one category ends and the other begins. Intersection and overlap between the two are not uncommon. By way of illustration: the negative State obligation to protect persons belonging to minoritites from "hate speech" can logically flow into the positive State obligation to facilitate access for such persons to the media. This logical flow is explored in considerable detail in Chapter 8, but it can be summarised here by saying that an effective and comprehensive approach to combating "hate speech" would ordinarily involve preventive measures, including pro-active policies to secure minority involvement in media activities. In the same vein, the negative

45 *Ibid.*, p. 169.

46 *Ibid.*

47 Eric Barendt, *Freedom of Speech* (2nd Edition), (Oxford, Oxford University Press, 2005), p. 104.

48 Henry Shue, *Basic Rights: Subsistence, Affluence, and U.S. Foreign Policy* (Princeton, New Jersey, Princeton University Press, 1980), p. 52; see also p. 53.

obligation to counter hate speech and severe forms of negative (ethnic) stereotyping by the media is logically and seamlessly connected to the positive obligation to promote tolerance and intercultural understanding. Viewed as such, it seems more accurate to conceptualise negative and positive State obligations as being situated on a continuum or a sliding scale, rather than as being mutually exclusive.

The conceptual limitation described in the previous paragraph is by no means fatal to the utility of the distinction between negative and positive State obligations for broad categorising purposes. The complete separation of the two categories is not explicit, after all: it is merely one possible reading of the inter-categorical relationship.

4.1.2(i) International human rights treaty law

All international human rights treaties share the primary objective of ensuring that the rights enshrined therein are rendered effective for everyone. However, the formulae and approaches relied upon to realise that objective tend to vary per treaty. Each human rights treaty has its own standard of metricity, but conversion is possible between the different metric systems because of the broad congruence of their underlying objectives, *viz.* the effective universal realisation of human rights for everyone. Conversion is also facilitated by the interdependent and inter-related character of human rights, meaning that a general presumption of consistency applies across specific treaties and their specialised focuses. In the following paragraphs, a sample of international treaties (i.e., the ICCPR and the ECHR) will be surveyed to illustrate the different but comparable approaches to ensure that human rights are effective in practice.

ICCPR

Under Article 2(1) of the ICCPR,[49] States Parties must "respect" and "ensure" to all individuals subject to its jurisdiction the rights recognised in the Covenant in a non-discriminatory manner. The obligation undertaken by States Parties is therefore twofold. First, "to respect" all of the rights recognised in the ICCPR, States must not violate them. Second, "to ensure" those rights is a more far-reaching undertaking and, according to one leading commentator, it "implies an affirmative obligation by the state to take whatever measures are necessary to enable individuals to enjoy or exercise the rights guaranteed in the Covenant, including the removal of governmental and possibly also some private obstacles to the enjoyment of these

---

49 It reads: "Each State Party to the present Covenant undertakes to respect and to ensure to all individuals within its territory and subject to its jurisdiction the rights recognized in the present Covenant, without distinction of any kind, such as race, colour, sex, language, religion, political or other opinion, national or social origin, property, birth or other status".

rights".[50] The reading of affirmative State obligations into Article 2, ICCPR, is borne out by subsequent paragraphs of the Article and the interpretive clarifications offered, *inter alia*, by the UN Human Rights Committee's General Comment No. 31 – "The Nature of the General Legal Obligation Imposed on States Parties to the Covenant".

Article 2(2) requires States "to take the necessary steps, in accordance with its constitutional processes and with the provisions of the present Covenant, to adopt such laws or other measures as may be necessary to give effect to the rights recognized in the present Covenant". This requirement is "unqualified and of immediate effect".[51] In addition, pursuant to Article 2(3), States "must ensure that individuals also have accessible and effective remedies to vindicate those rights".[52] Importantly for persons belonging to minorities, the envisaged remedies "should be appropriately adapted so as to take account of the special vulnerability of certain categories of person [...]".[53]

European Convention on Human Rights

One of the foundational premises for the European Court of Human Rights' general approach to positive State obligations[54] is its concern that the purpose of the ECHR is to "guarantee not rights that are theoretical or illusory but rights that are practical and effective".[55] Based on an analysis of the Court's relevant case-law, Alastair Mowbray has concluded that "various forms of positive obligations have been imposed upon different governmental bodies in order to secure a realistic guarantee

---

50 Thomas Buergenthal, "To Respect and Ensure: State Obligations and Permissible Derogations", in Louis Henkin, Ed., *The International Bill of Rights* (New York, Columbia University Press, 1981), pp. 72–91, at 77. Buergenthal also notes that such affirmative obligations could include "providing some access to places and media for public assembly or expression" – *ibid.*

51 General Comment No. 31 [80] – "The Nature of the General Legal Obligations Imposed on States Parties to the Covenant", 29 March 2004, para. 14.

52 *Ibid.*, para. 15.

53 *Ibid.*

54 Another central premise is the "living instrument" doctrine generally followed by the Court (see further, Chapter 4.2.2). This premise (also known as the "dynamic and evolutive" approach) is sometimes invoked in tandem with the "practical and effective rights" premise (eg. in *Stafford v. the UK*, Judgment of the European Court of Human Rights of 28 May 2002, para. 68 and *Christine Goodwin v. the UK*, Judgment of the European Court of Human Rights of 11 July 2002, para. 74). If the ECHR is interpreted in a dynamic manner, there is always a possibility of expanding the scope of positive State obligations.

55 *Airey v. Ireland*, Judgment of the European Court of Human Rights of 9 October 1979, para. 24. See also, *mutatis mutandis*, the *"Belgian Linguistic"* judgment of the European Court of Human Rights of 23 July 1968, p. 31, paras. 3 and 4; *Marckx v. Belgium*, Judgment of the European Court of Human Rights of 13 June 1979, p. 15, para. 31.

of Convention rights and freedoms".[56] What exactly a "realistic guarantee" entails is best determined on a case-by-case basis, although certain trends can tentatively be identified per Convention article.

In its *Airey* judgment, the Court stated that "although the object of Article 8 (art. 8) is essentially that of protecting the individual against arbitrary interference by the public authorities, it does not merely compel the State to abstain from such interference: in addition to this primarily negative undertaking, there may be positive obligations inherent in an effective respect for private or family life".[57] In *X. & Y. v. The Netherlands*, it supplemented that statement by admitting that such "obligations may involve the adoption of measures designed to secure respect for private life even in the sphere of the relations of individuals between themselves".[58] This is an important extension of the principle as articulated in anterior case-law; it confirms a degree of horizontal applicability of relevant rights.

The Court has deliberately adopted similar reasoning regarding the right to freedom of assembly; it held that "genuine, effective freedom of peaceful assembly" cannot:

> be reduced to a mere duty on the part of the State not to interfere: a purely negative conception would not be compatible with the object and purpose of Article 11. Like Article 8, Article 11 sometimes requires positive measures to be taken, even in the sphere of relations between individuals, if need be [...].[59]

The pattern of recognising that positive State duties are sometimes necessary in order to render rights effective can also be detected in respect of Article 10. Such positive State duties apply to substantive and procedural matters alike. In David-versus-Goliath-type situations, where negligibly-funded informational campaigns aiming to influence debate on matters of public interest are pitted against the muscular financial might of multinational corporations, fairness requires that some approximate equality of arms be strived for. In the Court's own words:

> If, however, a State decides to provide such a remedy [against defamation] to a corporate body, it is essential, in order to safeguard the countervailing interests in free expression and open debate, that a measure of procedural fairness and equality of arms is provided for.[60]

---

56 Alastair Mowbray, "The Creativity of the European Court of Human Rights", *Human Rights Law Review* 5: 1 (2005), 57–79, at 78.

57 *Airey v. Ireland*, *op. cit.*, para. 32. See also: (see the above-mentioned *Marckx* judgment, p. 15, para. 31).

58 Judgment of the European Court of Human Rights (Chamber) of 26 March 1985, para. 23.

59 *Plattform "Ärzte für das Leben" v. Austria*, Judgment of the European Court of Human Rights (Chamber) of 21 June 1988, para. 32.

60 *Steel & Morris v. UK*, Judgment of the European Court of Human Rights (Fourth Section) of 15 February 2005, para. 95.

Although the Court does not go to the trouble of spelling out the (self-evident?) implications of its pronouncement, it seems logical that it would be for the State to guarantee the requisite measure of procedural fairness and equality of arms. No other actor is appropriately placed or vested with the necessary authority to do so.

As regards more substantive concerns, the Court has accepted in principle that positive measures may be required of States in order to give effect to the right to freedom of expression (as with Articles 8 and 11, including the protection of the right in the sphere of relations between individuals[61]), but it has yet to meaningfully explore the practical workings of the principle. For instance, in *Özgür Gündem v. Turkey*, taking as its starting point, "the key importance of freedom of expression as one of the preconditions for a functioning democracy", the Court recognised that:

> Genuine, effective exercise of this freedom does not depend merely on the State's duty not to interfere, but may require positive measures of protection, even in the sphere of relations between individuals [...]. In determining whether or not a positive obligation exists, regard must be had to the fair balance that has to be struck between the general interest of the community and the interests of the individual, the search for which is inherent throughout the Convention.[62]

This recognition amounts to an important statement of principle, even if the Court does immediately go on to concede:

> The scope of this obligation will inevitably vary, having regard to the diversity of situations obtaining in Contracting States, the difficulties involved in policing modern societies and the choices which must be made in terms of priorities and resources. Nor must such an obligation be interpreted in such a way as to impose an impossible or disproportionate burden on the authorities [...].[63]

4.1.2(ii) Differentiated roles and duties of States regarding expression

It should be obvious by now that as well as placing States under a general duty of non-interference, the right to freedom of expression also gives rise to positive obligations for States. It requires them to stimulate freedom of expression and information by assuring broader societal circumstances that are conducive to

---

61 See, among other authorities, *Fuentes Bobo v. Spain*, Judgment of the European Court of Human Rights of 29 February 2000, para. 38.

62 *Özgür Gündem v. Turkey*, Judgment of the European Court of Human Rights (Fourth Section) of 16 March 2000, para. 43.

63 *Ibid.*

freedom of expression and pluralism generally.[64] Eric Barendt takes the view that as freedom of expression is "primarily a negative liberty", there are persuasive arguments against "the recognition of general positive free speech rights".[65] Thus, he cautions against the acceptance of "broad propositions of principle about positive free speech rights" out of fear for the "range of possible implications" that could flow from such propositions.[66] Nevertheless, he does concede that "in some contexts, there is a convincing case for upholding narrowly defined positive free speech rights".[67] It is submitted here that positive State obligations in respect of the right to freedom of expression can be slotted into two main categories: (i) pluralism and diversity, and (ii) non-discrimination, equality and access rights. These categories will be the focus of Chapters 9–11.

As already mentioned, the State can and does assume different roles in relation to the protection and furtherance of free expression. An exploration of those roles usefully elucidates the extent of concomitant State responsibilities. Zechariah Chafee, Jr. has characterised the relationship between the State and expression as being threefold: "(1) the use of governmental power to limit or to suppress discussion, (2) affirmative governmental action to encourage better and more extensive communication, and (3) government as a party to communication".[68] State responsibilities vary in accordance with the role being performed. Arguably, so too does the level of scrutiny to which State measures are subjected.[69]

(1) Limitation or suppression of discussion

It is in respect of this particular role that the State should pursue a presumptively – or generally – abstentionist line. The central reason for this is distrust of governmental intentions and actions. This sense of distrust has nourished US First Amendment doctrine more than it has European standards concerning freedom of expression, and is well captured in the following citation: "if there is any fixed star

64 See, for example, Dirk Voorhoof, "Guaranteeing the freedom and independence of the media", in Karol Jakubowicz, Ed., *Media and democracy* (Strasbourg, Council of Europe Publishing, 1998), pp. 35–57, at 42–43.

65 Eric Barendt, *Freedom of Speech* (2nd Edition), *op. cit.*, p. 105.

66 *Ibid.*, p. 103.

67 *Ibid.*, p. 105.

68 Cited in The Commission on Freedom of the Press, *A Free and Responsible Press* (Chicago, University of Chicago Press, 1947), p. 136 [summary of Zechariah Chafee, Jr., *Government and Mass Communications*]. See also: Thomas I. Emerson, *The System of Freedom of Expression* (New York, Random House, 1970), p. 4; Robert C. Post, *Constitutional Domains: Democracy, Community, Management* (Cambridge, Massachusetts, Harvard University Press, 1995) (generally).

69 Owen Fiss, for example, enquires as to "whether the allocative state should be subjected to the same strict scrutiny as the regulatory one when it comes to speech": Owen M. Fiss, *The Irony of Free Speech* (Cambridge & London, Harvard University Press, 1996), p. 29.

in our constitutional constellation, it is that no official, high or petty, can prescribe what shall be orthodox in politics, nationalism, religion or other matters of opinion".[70]

This is an iron-plated argument from classical liberalism that regards the importance of negative liberty or non-interference by the State as fundamental. However, as will be demonstrated in the next Chapters, this presumption of non-interference is rebuttable, and there are clearly situations in which State intervention is not only desirable, but also necessary, in order to limit or suppress certain types of particularly harmful expression.

(2) Facilitation or encouragement of expression

The goal of facilitation and creation of expressive opportunities can be achieved in a variety of ways. For instance, the State could play the role of arbiter, ensuring, to take the famous Meiklejohnian example,[71] that all parties in a town-hall meeting are given adequate opportunity to express themselves. Central to the moderating task is the conviction that the purpose of freedom of expression is not to ensure "unregulated talkativeness".[72] Rather, "[w]hat is essential is not that everyone shall speak, but that everything worth saying shall be said".[73] In its capacity as arbiter of the fairness of public debate, the creation and upholding of certain rights of access to the media could be seen as modern-day policy objectives for the State. Alternatively, the pursuit of this objective could also be more far-reaching, if conceived of as the promotion of media- and information-related pluralism. Such a conceptualisation would point towards a more allocative or distributory role for the State.

An allocative role for the State as regards expression is by no means uncontested, however. Some commentators express uneasiness about subsidising speech, whether artistic, educational or other.[74] Their unease stems from a typical and deep-seated liberalist suspicion of governmental intervention:

---

70 Robert Jackson, J., in *West Virginia State Board of Education v. Barnette*, 319 US 624 (1943). Cited in Samuel Walker, *Hate Speech: The History of an American Controversy* (USA, University of Nebraska Press, 1994), p. 2 and p. 166.

71 See generally, Alexander Meiklejohn, *Free Speech And Its Relation to Self-Government* (New York, Harper & Bros., 1948), and esp. p. 25.

72 *Ibid.*, p. 25.

73 *Ibid.*, p. 25.

74 See generally: Robert C. Post, Ed., *Censorship and Silencing: Practices of Cultural Regulation* (Los Angeles, The Getty Institute for the History of Art and the Humanities, 1998).

> The official patron easily turns into the authoritative regulator. Further, the view that government is needed, by subsidy and regulation, to establish or enable the expression of the disadvantaged or the unequal, signifies a disturbing reliance on government. Rights undergo a self-inconsistent transformation when they are conceptualized as what government policy must positively provide or promote.[75]

(3) Participation in communicative process

Government speech or government-sponsored speech could serve the purpose of countering harmful speech from third-party quarters, or it could serve the purpose of advancing perspectives that are either neglected or discriminated against. In these senses, the government's role as a speaker could be viewed as closely related to its other two roles in relation to speech. But government speech, *qua* speech, could have – and often does have – the additional characteristic of providing information on matters of importance to society. Needless to say, in no circumstances should messages concerning matters of importance to governmental parties be twisted into or disguised as matters of importance to society.

4.2 New trends in the development of the nexus under international treaty law

4.2.1 Filling the interstices of international treaty law

The foregoing sections have demonstrated that the international protection accorded to minorities' freedom of expression is – overall – quite erratic. That is why, as noted in the introduction to this book, it is extremely important to identify and group the disparate provisions in international instruments dealing with the topic. It is only through the documentation and analysis of the numerous relevant provisions that key features of the overall picture can be extracted. In light of these considerations, it is useful to consider Karol Jakubowicz's proposed "full matrix of the rights of national minorities in the media field":[76]

---

75 George Kateb, "The Freedom of Worthless and Harmful Speech", in Bernard Yack, Ed., *Liberalism without Illusions* (Chicago, University of Chicago Press, 1996), pp. 220–240, at 238.

76 (reproduced in its original tabular form here) Karol Jakubowicz, "Report: A critical evaluation of the first results of the monitoring of the Framework Convention on the issue of persons belonging to national minorities and the media (1998–2003)" in *Filling the Frame: Five years of monitoring the Framework Convention for the Protection of National Minorities* (Strasbourg, Council of Europe Publishing, 2004), pp. 113–138, at 118.

Negative goals	Positive goals	
I. "Ban, combat"	II. "Assist"	III. "Empower"
State action to prohibit, disavow, marginalise, counteract all forms of discrimination and inequality	State action to develop public policy and regulation and provide assistance and funds to guarantee the right of minorities to media in their own languages, to access to media from kin and/or neighbouring countries and to a proper representation of their identity, culture, history and interests in media content, as well as action to promote inter-cultural and inter-ethnic dialogue and understanding	State not to hinder, or take action to ensure minority access to, and participation in, the media at the level of: 1. Programming 2. Work-force 3. Editorial control and management 4. Ownership of media 5. Regulation and oversight 6. Legislation, public policy

The usefulness of this proposed matrix derives from a number of its features. First, it identifies a wide range of specific State obligations, as developed by, or inferred from, a number of international instruments.[77] Second, it points to the purposes of those State obligations and how they benefit persons belonging to minorities. The matrix offers a useful analytical framework. It facilitates the break-down of relevant State obligations and their categorisation in purposive terms, thereby elucidating the substantive specificities of the right and enabling a more accurate determination of whether the right is being effectively realised in practice.

It has already been shown that the relationship between the right to freedom of expression and minority rights in international treaties of a generalist nature has not been particularly fecund. There is perhaps a certain inevitability about this: by their very nature, generalist human rights treaties can hardly be expected to provide detailed or sophisticated protection for specific niche rights or for interfaces between specific rights. Rather, such detailed or elaborate provisions could be more logically included in specialised treaties, where the targeted thematic focus would be more conducive to the exploration and elaboration of details, nuances and technicalities. Notwithstanding the role that could be played by specialised treaties in this respect, some commentators remain reluctant to accept that international law could have the capacity to negotiate the specific exigencies of discrete minority rights at all. The various arguments and general reasoning that coalesce into this reluctance merit careful scrutiny.

---

77 *Ibid.*, at 118–119. Note that subsequent sections of this book examine an extensive range of State obligations in detailed fashion.

The essence of the case rejecting – or at least stringently querying – the appropriateness of international law as a vehicle for the protection and promotion of minority rights is captured by Will Kymlicka and Alan Patten:

> But it is doubtful that international law will ever be able to do more than specify the most minimal of standards. The members of various linguistic groups have quite different needs, desires, and capacities, depending on their size, territorial concentration, and historic roots. A set of guidelines that is satisfactory to a small, dispersed immigrant group will not satisfy a large, concentrated historic minority. [...] Any attempt to define a set of rights that applies to all linguistic groups, no matter how small and dispersed, is likely to end up focusing on relatively modest claims. [...] Both majority and minority groups want much more than is, or could reasonably be, guaranteed in international law.[78]

Kymlicka and Patten refer specifically to the rights and needs of members of linguistic groups, but one can easily extrapolate from the specificity of their chosen example and apply the concerns they outline to a broader range of discrete minority rights and needs. The central thrust of Kymlicka and Patten's case is twofold: international law is ill-equipped to deal with the issues at hand because of minimalistic tendencies in its scope and content (this will be considered in detail in the next section) and it is insufficiently attentive or responsive to *couleur nationale* or, better, *locale*.

The importance of local-level action, engagement, politics, etc., cannot be gainsaid. The proximity of law to its subjects generally favours heightened sensitivity to specificity. However, these truisms do not detract from the importance of underlying principles and paradigms, the articulation of which often takes place at another level. *Couleur locale* should inform the implementation of general principles in such a way as to maximise their efficiency in practice. The potential for synergic interaction is considerable. When Michael Ignatieff attributes the success of human rights in modern times (at least partly) to their ability to go global by going local,[79] this kind of synergy certainly deserves some of the accolades.

Nevertheless, even laws that are finely tuned to the specificities of local needs and circumstances can be found to be deficient. Legal provisions are but one instrument of social policy; others play different but no less valid – and even vital – roles in achieving social objectives. The dynamic interplay between legal and non-legal

---

78 Alan Patten & Will Kymlicka, "Introduction – Language Rights and Political Theory: Context, Issues, and Approaches" in Will Kymlicka & Alan Patten, Eds., *Language Rights and Political Theory* (New York, Oxford University Press, 2003), pp. 1–51, at 34–35.

79 Michael Ignatieff, Michael Ignatieff *et al.*, *Human Rights as Politics and Idolatry* (Princeton, Princeton University Press, 2001), p. 7. This point is picked up on later in the same volume by K. Anthony Appiah, *ibid.*, p. 106.

regulatory measures and other societal forces will be considered in detail in Chapter 11 (in particular).

International law is subject to a number of inherent limitations. For analytical purposes, it is desirable to identify and group the most salient of these limitations. One possible way of doing so would be to focus on: (i) the modest scope and content of international treaties – individually and collectively; (ii) the under-utilisation of existing international law instruments (i.e., inadequate implementation, monitoring and enforcement), and (iii) over-stretch in standard-setting, i.e., the reliance on international law – especially human rights instruments – in attempts to realise objectives for which they were not designed.[80]

4.2.2 Modesty of scope and content of international treaty law

It is perhaps easy to be sceptical or cynical about what international treaties can or seek to achieve, particularly given the *Realpolitik* of their drafting processes. More often than not, State representatives come to the drafting table with the narrow intention of preventing agreement on any measures that would curtail the action of their home States when action is needed to defend their States' "essential interests", or on measures that would adversely affect their home States' non-essential interests.[81] Drafting exercises are inevitably also infused with altruistic intentions and a resolve to advance shared interests, but it is doubtful that such commonality of principle and purpose between States representatives would always take precedence over more viscerally-felt, parochial anxieties. Given this *Realpolitik*, the sardonic quip by Philip Allott, that a "treaty is a disagreement reduced to writing",[82] does not seem misplaced.

The modest scope of international treaties can also be explained in less sceptical and less cynical ways. The tendency towards minimalism in international human rights treaties is at least in part due to the fact that "problems of agreement, interpretation, and enforcement inhere even in the most minimalist formulations of

---

80 At first glance, the distinction between (i) and (iii) may appear to be artificial, but in actual fact, that is not the case. The modest scope and content of treaties concerns arguments of legal formalism, whereas the focus on the overstretch of human rights instruments is more concerned with deviations from legal formalism and, indeed, a somewhat cavalier regard for its importance.

81 This point is a paraphrasal of a point made by Martti Koskenniemi in the specific context of the adoption by the UN General Assembly of a definition of "aggression": Martti Koskenniemi, "'The Lady Doth Protest Too Much': Kosovo, and the Turn to Ethics in International Law", 65 *The Modern Law Review* (No. 2, March 2002), pp. 159–175, at 168. I also attempt to extend the application of Koskenniemi's observation to the drafting of international treaties generally.

82 Philip Allott, "The Concept of International Law", EJIL 10 (1999), pp. 31 – 50, at 43.

human rights".[83] Kwame Anthony Appiah has described the basic, familiar dilemma as follows: "[a] conception of rights that's highly determinate in its application may not be thin enough to win widespread agreement; a conception of rights that's thin enough to win widespread agreement risks indeterminacy or impotence".[84] One can safely assume a general wariness on the part of States when it comes to taking on extra commitments that are legally binding and enforceable.

The tailoring of a treaty's objectives to realistic prospects of their achievability also seems central here. On such reasoning, the more ambitious, complicated or contentious the content of a draft convention is, the more difficult it will prove to broker agreement for it amongst a wide range of States. The detailed treatment of highly specific issues is often among the primary casualties of such a tendency towards minimalism. Even if these initial obstacles are cleared, potential interpretative and enforcement difficulties remain to be faced.

This modesty of ambition in positive international law can readily be detected in the main human rights instruments under discussion here. The Universal Declaration of Human Rights – admittedly a Declaration, but nevertheless one that lays very strong claims to being part of customary international law – consciously styles itself as nothing more than "a common standard of achievement for all peoples and all nations". This implies that there are higher standards than the common one. Similarly, as noted *supra*, the drafters of the ECHR saw it as a general declaration of rights for immediate application: they kept open the possibility of building protection for other rights (most notably, minority rights) at an ulterior date.

When the content of rights – as formulated in the provisions of a treaty – is indeed minimalistic, or even merely not inclusive enough or robust enough, the interpretive techniques employed can either compound or reduce a treaty's textual shortcomings. Articles 31 and 32 of the Vienna Convention on the Law of Treaties are crucially important in this connection. They read:

> **Article 31 – General rule of interpretation**
>
> 1. A treaty shall be interpreted in good faith and in accordance with the ordinary meaning to be given to the terms of the treaty in their context and in the light of its object and purpose.
>
> 2. The context for the purpose of the interpretation of a treaty shall comprise, in addition to the text, including its preamble and annexes:

[83] Amy Gutmann, "Introduction", in Michael Ignatieff *et al.*, *Human Rights as Politics and Idolatry*, *op. cit.*, pp. vii-xxviii, at xii.

[84] Kwame Anthony Appiah, *The Ethics of Identity* (Princeton and Oxford, Princeton University Press, 2005), pp. 263–264.

(a) any agreement relating to the treaty which was made between all the parties in connection with the conclusion of the treaty;
(b) any instrument which was made by one or more of the parties in connection with the conclusion of the treaty and accepted by the other parties as an instrument related to the treaty.

3. There shall be taken into account, together with the context:
(a) any subsequent agreement between the parties regarding the interpretation of the treaty or the application of its provisions;
(b) any subsequent practice in the application of the treaty which establishes the agreement of the parties regarding its interpretation;
(c) any relevant rules of international law applicable in the relations between the parties.

4. A special meaning shall be given to a term if it is established that the parties so intended.

Article 32 – Supplementary means of interpretation

Recourse may be had to supplementary means of interpretation, including the preparatory work of the treaty and the circumstances of its conclusion, in order to confirm the meaning resulting from the application of article 31, or to determine the meaning when the interpretation according to article 31:
(a) leaves the meaning ambiguous or obscure; or
(b) leads to a result which is manifestly absurd or unreasonable.

Thus, the core text of a treaty, along with its preambular affirmations and annexes are of clear contextual importance for its interpretation (Article 31.2). So too are any agreements or (multilaterally accepted) unilateral instruments adopted in connection with the conclusion of the treaty (Article 31.2(a) and (b)). Other, extra-contextual, considerations of relevance are: any subsequent agreement between parties concerning interpretation or application (Article 31.3(a)) and any subsequent practice in application which points towards interpretative consequences (Article 31.3(b)). The broader matrix of international law is alluded to in Article 31.3(c). This is an important allusion in respect of human rights provisions in international law. It recognises the existence of an anterior body of inter-State commitments; a recognition which is often undergirded by explicit treaty stipulations that existing State obligations relating to human rights shall not be diminished in any way by obligations imposed by new treaties. In this connection, efforts to crystallise and distil "relevant rules of international law applicable in the relations between the parties" can therefore help to clarify important extraneous considerations for the interpretation of individual treaties.[85] According to Article 32, the *travaux* of a

[85] See, for example, the Guidelines on the use of Minority Languages in the Broadcast Media (2003), *infra*.

treaty and the circumstances of its conclusion are to be regarded as supplementary means of interpretation that can be relied upon in situations of ambiguity, etc., in order to determine the correct meaning of certain treaty provisions.

Whenever the text of a treaty reveals ambiguities, inconsistencies or absurdities, it must then turn unto itself in order to unlock its own inner, deeper, concealed meaning. A literalist approach may not always suffice and guidance may have to be sought from the (drafting) history (as provided for by Article 32) or the *telos* of the treaty. However, to rely solely on the historical interpretation of a treaty can also prove of limited utility, especially when such an interpretative approach places inordinate emphasis on the need to decipher the "original intent" of its drafters (which may be obscure or incoherent). Paraphrasing two well-known maxims in US Consitutional interpretation, reliance on history should be limited to "broad purposes, not specific practices" because a treaty "is not a static document whose meaning on every detail is fixed for all time by the life experience of the Framers".[86]

These two maxims point inexorably towards a teleological approach to treaty-interpretation, not least because its responsive character can render the treaty more enduring and "future-proof" than alternative interpretive techniques. Such an approach provides continuous, evolutive compensation for any lack of prescience on part of the original negotiating parties/drafters. By interpreting the original vision or intent in light of modern-day societal standards, it drags the original vision out of potential desuetude and helps to reduce uncertainty about original intent. Socio-political changes can dramatically alter the broader context in which law is applied; hence another reason to favour an interpretive technique that is reflective of such changes. As regards the media, the speed of technological change also pleads for interpretive flexibility if treaty formulations are to maintain a relevant grip on their subject matter (see further, Chapter 11). This logic has prompted specific calls for the adoption of a new General Comment on Article 19, ICCPR, to reflect how new technological capabilities and uses have re-shaped contemporary communicative realities.[87] The foregoing assertion of the general suitability of teleological interpretation for international treaties is admittedly partisan, but a thorough – and academically satisfactory – exploration of the competing merits of leading techniques of treaty/constitutional interpretation is beyond the scope of the present analysis.[88] One main justification for the preferential treatment of teleological interpretation in the present discussion is that it is the favoured interpretive technique of a number of international human rights adjudicative bodies.

86 Brennan, J., in *Marsh v. Chambers*, 463 US 783 (1983), at 816.

87 See, for example, Jamie F. Metzl, "Information Technology and Human Rights", 18 *Human Rights Quarterly* (No. 4, 1996), 705–746, at 742–743.

88 One major critique of teleological interpretation is that it opens the door for judicial activism, a practice which in turn is susceptible to the politicisation of treaty/constitutional interpretation.

For instance, Harris, O'Boyle and Warbrick have noted that the Strasbourg adjudicative authorities have only made "occasional use" of the *travaux préparatoires* for interpretive purposes. This, they explain, "is partly because the *travaux* are not often helpful and partly because of the emphasis upon a dynamic and generally teleological interpretation of the Convention that focuses where relevant upon current European standards rather than the particular intentions of the drafting states".[89] Although allowing that differences of nuance are reflected by each, the notions of teleological, purposive and responsive interpretation can be described as roughly equivalent.

Although the European Court of Human Rights "generally eschews abstract theorising",[90] it has characterised its interpretive technique in terms of the "living instrument" doctrine.[91] Since the initial enunciation of the doctrine in *Tyrer v. UK*, the Court has consistently held that the ECHR is a "living instrument" which "must be interpreted in the light of present-day conditions".[92] In its present state of development, the doctrine applies to both the substance and the enforcement processes[93] of the Convention, and even to institutional bodies which did not exist and were not envisaged at the time of its drafting.[94] This "dynamic and evolutive"[95] interpretive approach constitutes an important safeguard against the risk that the Convention would ever become – to import a phrase from US First Amendment doctrine – "static and lifeless".[96]

By its adherence to this particular interpretive technique, the Court has put in place the procedural wherewithal for emphasising in its judgments what has been termed "the dialectical relationship of the law to its ambient culture".[97] Or "cultures", to be

---

89 [footnotes omitted] David Harris, Michael O'Boyle, Colin Warbrick, *et al.*, *Law of the European Convention on Human Rights* (Second Edition) (Oxford, Oxford University Press, 2009), p. 17.

90 Alastair Mowbray, "The Creativity of the European Court of Human Rights", *Human Rights Law Review* 5: 1 (2005), 57–79, at 61.

91 For an overview of the historical development of the "living instrument" doctrine (including recent developments) by the European Court of Human Rights, see: Alastair Mowbray, "The Creativity of the European Court of Human Rights", *op. cit.*

92 *Tyrer v. the United Kingdom*, Judgment of the European Court of Human Rights of 25 April 1978, Series A, no. 26, para. 31; *Matthews v. the United Kingdom*, Judgment of the European Court of Human Rights of 18 February 1999, para. 39.

93 *Loizidou v. Turkey*, Judgment of the European Court of Human Rights (preliminary objections) of 23 March 1995, Series A, no. 310, para. 71.

94 *Matthews v. the United Kingdom*, *op. cit.*, para. 39.

95 *Stafford v. the United Kingdom*, *op. cit.*, para. 68; *Christine Goodwin v. the United Kingdom*, *op. cit.*, para. 74. Mowbray has pointed out that the Court has recently been making references to the "living instrument" doctrine and the "dynamic and evolutive" interpretative approach pretty much interchangeably: *op. cit.*, p. 64.

96 Brennan, J., dissenting, in *Marsh v. Chambers*, *op. cit.*, at 817.

97 Robert C. Post, *Constitutional Domains: Democracy, Community, Management*, *op. cit.*, p. 17. It should be noted, though, that Post uses the term "responsive interpretation".

more accurate, given the extant cultural heterogeneity throughout the 47 Member States of the Council of Europe. This allows for adaptive doctrinal development; an ability to respond (as deemed appropriate) to developing legal standards in Member States, particularly in instances of emergent consensual, cross-national trends.[98] However, this interpretive approach is subject to certain limitations,[99] the most important of which is that "any interpretation must also accord with the fundamental objectives of the Convention and its coherence as a system of human rights protection".[100] In practice, judicial activism can also be checked by a certain caution/conservatism in its application.

4.2.3 Under-utilisation of international treaty law

The problem of inadequate enforcement of existing international human rights instruments frequently draws the critical ire of commentators, and rightly so.[101] The substantive merit of a treaty can be seriously undermined by its procedural shortcomings, both on paper and in practice. Conor Gearty is vehemently critical of the "combination of rhetorical confidence and feeble implementation [which] means that we can all live in a culture apparently unparalleled in its commitment to human rights and equality, without having to make – or be forced to make – any of the sacrifices that would and should be required of us to make such a set of allegiance matter to anybody other than ourselves".[102] This gives rise to a phenomenon infecting human rights which he terms "Standards That Are Merely Mirages".[103]

---

98 *Stafford v. the United Kingdom*, *op. cit.*, para. 68.

99 See further, Alastair Mowbray, "The Creativity of the European Court of Human Rights", *op. cit.*, at 67.

100 *Pretty v. the United Kingdom*, Judgment of the European Court of Human Rights of 29 April 2002, para. 54.

101 Philip Alston, "Conjuring up New Human Rights: A Proposal for Quality Control", 78 *American Journal of International Law* 607–621 (1984); Gudmundur Alfredsson, "Concluding Remarks: More Law and Less Politics", in Gudmundur Alfredsson *et al.*, Eds., *International Human Rights Monitoring Mechanisms* (Great Britain, Kluwer Law International, 2001), pp. 913–926.

102 Conor Gearty, "Is the idea of human rights now doing more harm than good?", Paper delivered at the London School of Economics, 12 October 2004, p. 6 of transcript. See also: Conor Gearty, "Reflections on Civil Liberties in an Age of Counterterrorism", 41 Osgoode Hall L.J. 185 (Summer/Fall, 2003); David Kennedy, "The International Human Rights Movement: Part of the Problem?", 15 *Harvard Human Rights Journal* (Spring 2002), 101–126; Tom Campbell, Keith Ewing & Adam Tomkins, Eds., *Sceptical Essays on Human Rights* (Oxford, Oxford University Press, 2001).

103 Actually, the metaphor he spins presents human rights "as a computer programme designed to do good", which is being threatened by three viruses, including the acronymic STAMM (i.e., "Standards That Are Merely Mirages") virus: Conor Gearty, "Is the idea of human rights now doing more harm than good?", *op. cit.*, p. 5 of transcript.

The ultimate goal of international treaties is to ensure the faithful enshrinement and effective implementation of their principles and provisions in national law.[104] Adjudication and monitoring typically play complementary roles in ensuring the enforcement of international law at the national level. Adjudication is generally a more heavy-hitting measure of enforcement than monitoring, and can constitute the culmination of a monitoring exercise. In another sense, though, adjudication can be a form of monitoring, for example the work of the European Court of Human Rights has been described as "'monitoring' *par excellence*".[105] In this sense, "*excellence*" is not an evaluative term of the quality of the Court's work, but an indication of its juridical – and therefore legally binding – character.

In recent years, monitoring has had its name dragged around in the proverbial mud. The often ineffectual outcomes of the monitoring of humanitarian crises and conflict situations and the inability of monitoring mechanisms to avert or prevent the escalation of such crises and conflicts have contributed to a general undermining of faith in the usefulness of the entire monitoring enterprise. The practice tends to be inextricably associated with the ills it is supposed to observe. The point can be made wryly by quoting one proposed definition of "monitor": "A verb meaning, To ignore, to do nothing about, to treat with apathy, as in 'We are monitoring the situation on a 24-hour basis'".[106] Such general cynicism should not, however, be allowed to detract from the merits of specific monitoring exercises. For Philip Alston and J.H.H. Weiler, monitoring is "an indispensable element in any human rights strategy".[107] They explain:

---

104 See further: Andrew Drzemczewski, "The European Human Rights Convention: Protocol No. 11 – Entry into Force and First Year of Application", 21 *Human Rights Law Journal* (No. 1–3, 2000), pp. 1–17, at 10. For an overview of the incorporation of the ECHR into the national legal systems of Council of Europe Member States, see: Robert Blackburn & Jörg Polakiewicz, Eds., *Fundamental Rights in Europe: The Europrean Convention on Human Rights and its Member States, 1950–2000* (England, Oxford University Press, 2001); for a more historical perspective, see: Andrew Drzemczewski, *European Human Rights Convention in Domestic Law: A Comparative Study* (United Kingdom, Clarendon Press, 1985).

105 Committee of Wise Persons, Final Report to the Committee of Ministers, Doc. No. CM(98)178, 20 October 1998, para. 69. The firm, original context of this phrase was the sentence: "*In addition to the "monitoring" par excellence undertaken in the proceedings before the European Court of Human Rights, an important task of the Council of Europe is to ensure that every member state respects the values and the important system of norms and standards developed by the Organisation over the years and embodied in some 170 conventions and a great number of recommendations.* […]" (italics per original).

106 Provided by Miles Kingston, *The Independent*, London, 17 February 1998. Cited in Andrew Drzemczewski, "Monitoring by the Committee of Ministers of the Council of Europe: A Useful 'Human Rights' Mechanism?", in I. Ziemele, Ed., *Baltic Yearbook of International Law*, Vol. 2, 2002, pp. 83–103, at 88.

107 Philip Alston & J.H.H. Weiler, "An 'Ever Closer Union' in Need of a Human Rights Policy: The European Union and Human Rights", in Philip Alston *et al.*, Eds., *The EU and Human Rights* (New York, Oxford University Press, 1999), pp. 3–66, at 55.

> Systematic, reliable, and focused information is the starting point for a clear understanding of the nature, extent, and location of the problems which exist and for the identification of possible solutions. It is also a necessary element in any strategy to garner the support of civil society and the community at large for measures to promote and protect the human rights of vulnerable groups.[108]

The mechanisms instituted by the Framework Convention for the Protection of National Minorities and the European Charter for Regional or Minority Languages, for instance, represent good examples of the primarily preventive character of monitoring mechanisms within the Council of Europe, according to Andrew Drzemczewski.[109] A detailed evaluation of the effectiveness of these two monitoring mechanisms in respect of both conventions' provisions on freedom of expression and the media, will now be provided.

4.3 Emergence of differentiated protection for minorities' right to freedom of expression

ECHR protection of the right to freedom of expression is guaranteed in the broader context of a particularly strong conception of democracy; one in which the principles of pluralism, tolerance and broadmindedness reign supreme.[110] It correctly perceives the right to freedom of expression, information and opinion as empowering and facilitative. Conceptually, it styles freedom of information as the "touchstone" of all other human rights;[111] a constitutive right which is instrumental in securing the realisation of other rights. This is a conception of democracy in which Article 10 of the (European) Convention for the Protection of Human Rights and Fundamental Freedoms (ECHR) plays a dominant role:

> **Article 10 – Freedom of expression**
>
> 1 Everyone has the right to freedom of expression. This right shall include freedom to hold opinions and to receive and impart information and ideas without interference by public authority and regardless of frontiers. This article shall not prevent States from requiring the licensing of broadcasting, television or cinema enterprises.
>
> 2 The exercise of these freedoms, since it carries with it duties and responsibilities, may be subject to such formalities, conditions, restrictions or penalties as are

108 *Ibid.*

109 Andrew Drzemczewski, "La prévention des violations des droits de l'homme: les mécanismes de suivi du Conseil de l'Europe", 11 *Revue trimestrielle des droits de l'homme* (no. 43, 2000), pp. 385–428, at 401.

110 *Handyside v. United Kingdom*, Judgment of the European Court of Human Rights of 7 December 1976, Series A, No. 24, para. 49.

111 United Nations General Assembly Resolution 59(1), 14 December 1946.

> prescribed by law and are necessary in a democratic society, in the interests of national security, territorial integrity or public safety, for the prevention of disorder or crime, for the protection of health or morals, for the protection of the reputation or rights of others, for preventing the disclosure of information received in confidence, or for maintaining the authority and impartiality of the judiciary.

Of course, this reference to Article 10 includes not only the letters set in stone, but the vast and vigorous case-law that has been developed by the European Court of Human Rights on freedom of expression and information. This has been described as "one of the great glories of the European Court".[112] Whether one agrees fully with this description or not, there can be no denying that it does contain a substantial truth. Many important battles in the war of principles have been won, such as: the public's interest in receiving information via responsible investigative media; in robust political debate, and in the free exchange of information or ideas "that offend, shock or disturb the State or any sector of the population".[113] It is likely that the next battles to be fought will be somewhat localised. This is not so much a reference to geographical localisation (although it remains a truism that more work on freedom of expression has to be done in some countries than in others); rather it refers to a kind of thematic localisation. Building on some of the advances already registered in the Article 10 case-law, issues such as technology, access and language are likely to feature more prominently on the Court's agenda in the future. Just as they are likely to feature increasingly in the context of minority rights and therefore on the agenda of the Advisory Committee as well.

4.3.1 Framework Convention for the Protection of National Minorities (FCNM)

The linkage between Article 10, ECHR and Article 9, FCNM, is very explicit. The latter was cast in the mould of the former, and the resultant textual similarities are acknowledged in the Explanatory Report to the Framework Convention.[114]

> **Article 9**
>
> 1 The Parties undertake to recognise that the right to freedom of expression of every person belonging to a national minority includes freedom to hold opinions and to receive and impart information and ideas in the minority language, without interference by public authorities and regardless of frontiers. The Parties shall

---

112 Gerard Hogan, "The Belfast Agreement and the Future Incorporation of the European Convention of Human Rights in the Republic of Ireland", 4 *The Bar Review* (No. 4, 1999), pp. 205–211, at 206.

113 *Handyside v. United Kingdom, op. cit.*

114 See the Explanatory Report to the Framework Convention for the Protection of National Minorities, in particular, paras. 56 & 58.

> ensure, within the framework of their legal systems, that persons belonging to a national minority are not discriminated against in their access to the media.
>
> 2 Paragraph 1 shall not prevent Parties from requiring the licensing, without discrimination and based on objective criteria, of sound radio and television broadcasting, or cinema enterprises.
>
> 3 The Parties shall not hinder the creation and the use of printed media by persons belonging to national minorities. In the legal framework of sound radio and television broadcasting, they shall ensure, as far as possible, and taking into account the provisions of paragraph 1, that persons belonging to national minorities are granted the possibility of creating and using their own media.
>
> 4 In the framework of their legal systems, the Parties shall adopt adequate measures in order to facilitate access to the media for persons belonging to national minorities and in order to promote tolerance and permit cultural pluralism.

However, Article 9 is not simply a carbon copy of the European prototype for freedom of expression. In some respects, it builds on the original model and introduces greater specificity as regards dimensions to the right to freedom of expression that could be of particular importance for persons belonging to national minorities.[115] Article 9(4) foregrounds, in an explicit manner, issues that are clearly of relevance to freedom of expression and to national minorities, but which have hitherto been subsumed in more general aspects of the Article 10 jurisprudence of the European Court.[116] The goals of striving towards tolerance and cultural pluralism – outcrops of the Article 10 jurisprudence of the European Court – are clearly remindful of Article 6, FCNM,[117] which reads:

> 1 The Parties shall encourage a spirit of tolerance and intercultural dialogue and take effective measures to promote mutual respect and understanding and co-operation among all persons living on their territory, irrespective of those persons' ethnic, cultural, linguistic or religious identity, in particular in the fields of education, culture and the media.
> 2 The Parties undertake to take appropriate measures to protect persons who may be subject to threats or acts of discrimination, hostility or violence as a result of their ethnic, cultural, linguistic or religious identity.

---

115 See, for example, *ibid.*, paras. 56 & 59.

116 See, in particular, *ibid.*, para. 62.

117 For commentary, see: Geoff Gilbert, "Article 6", in Marc Weller, Ed., *The Rights of Minorities in Europe: A Commentary on the European Framework Convention for the Protection of National Minorities* (Oxford and New York, Oxford University Press, 2005), pp. 177–191.

The main media-related provisions of the FCNM are summarised here in tabular form:

Provision	Summary details
Article 6.1	Encouragement of spirit of tolerance and intercultural dialogue; effective measures to promote mutual respect and understanding and cooperation among all persons, in particular ... in the media
Article 9.1	Linguistic freedom and non-discriminatory access to media
Article 9.2	Licensing of radio, television or cinema must be non-discriminatory and based on objective criteria
Article 9.3	Freedom to create and use print media without hindrance; possibility to create and use own broadcast media outlets
Article 9.4	States must adopt adequate measures to facilitate minorities' access to media and to promote tolerance and permit cultural pluralism

It is interesting to note that during the drafting of the FCNM, the *ad hoc* Committee of Experts for the Protection of National Minorities (CAHMIN) was "informed by the representative of the Steering Committee on the Mass Media (CDMM) that the latter committee had initiated discussions on the revision of Article 10 ECHR, with a view to adding journalistic and editorial freedom, access by various groups in society to the media, and copyright".[118] This was a reference to discussions based on a study commissioned by the CDMM as part of its contribution to the implementation of a Council of Europe project on "Human Rights and Genuine Democracy". The Study was entitled "Critical perspectives on the scope and interpretation of Article 10 of the European Convention on Human Rights" and it was written by Dirk Voorhoof.[119] The Study concluded as follows:

> Analysis of the case law on Art. 10 makes clear that Art. 10 E.C.H.R. is not a static rule but a living instrument of human rights' protection. The indefiniteness and open character of the formulation and construction of the Article leads to an ever developing, dynamic and expanding influence of it. The future impact of Art. 10 on information law and media policy in Europe will, to a considerable extent, depend on the manner in which the European Commission and the European Court leave a narrow or a wide margin of appreciation to the contracting States with regard to the justification of the "pressing social need" and of the manner in which they take account of the various factors and dimensions involved in the freedom of expression and information.[120]

Ultimately, the Bureau of the Council of Europe's Steering Committee on Human Rights (CDDH-BU), citing the first two sentences of the above excerpt from the

118 CAHMIN (94) 5, 1 February 1994, 1st meeting 25 January – 28 January 1994, Meeting Report: para. 36.

119 October 1993, Doc. No. CDMM (93) 36.

120 *Ibid.*, p. 65.

Study, endorsed Voorhoof's conclusions and stated that it "therefore did not consider it appropriate, at this juncture, to redraft Article 10 of the ECHR".[121] Had the CDDH-BU not followed Voorhoof's conclusions, it is a matter of speculation how far-reaching the proposed express provision for group access to the media might have been. Nevertheless, the very fact that the question was formally discussed at all could be taken as corroborating the observations *supra* that a paradigmatic development in thinking is beginning to emerge as regards freedom of expression. Qualitative considerations and the right to active participation in the media are likely to come increasingly to the fore.

Monitoring

(i) *General*

At the time of its inception, scepticism abounded about the Advisory Committee's ability to overcome what seemed on paper to be formidable restrictions on the latitude within which it would have to operate.[122] Since then, the Advisory Committee – through its own pro-activeness and the support of the Committee of Ministers – has managed to carve out increased operational autonomy for itself.

(ii) *Advisory Committee*

Thematic approach

When drafting the FCNM, the CAHMIN "considered that programme-type provisions should be included in the framework Convention establishing certain objectives without going into technical details".[123] The final text of Article 9, FCNM, shows that this decision was indeed adhered to. This decision shifted the responsibility for examining the compatibility of "technical details" with the standards set out in Article 9 to the Advisory Committee. This shift in responsibility has at least two logical corollaries. First, it points up the need for the Advisory Committee to develop or at least have access to a high level of expertise concerning the nature of technical details, if it is to evaluate their impact in an effective manner. Second, both of these points underscore the need for the Advisory Committee to be

121 Steering Committee on the Mass Media (CDMM), Secretariat Memorandum prepared by the Directorate of Human Rights, 11 May 1994, Doc. No. CDMM (94) 31. This document contains an excerpt from the Report of the 42nd Meeting of the Bureau of the CDDH-BU, including its Opinion on the Voorhoof Report.

122 See, for example, the Council of Europe Committee of Ministers Resolution (97) 10: Rules adopted by the Committee of Ministers on the monitoring arrangements under Articles 24 to 26 of the Framework Convention for the Protection of National Minorities, 17 September 1997 (especially paras. 29–32; 35–37).

123 CAHMIN (94) 5, 1 February 1994, 1st meeting 25 January – 28 January 1994, Meeting Report, p. 8, para. 37, ECMI docs. Art. 9.1.

able to maximise the potential knowledge and experience provided by external sources of information.

The treatment given to Article 9 as part of the Advisory Committee's article-by-article approach tends to be detailed and discursive and to offer a wealth of information about the prevailing situations in whatever country is under scrutiny. This information is wide-ranging in character: covering general context, legislation and its implementation and a miscellany of practical considerations. Or, to use the terminology of the Outline for the initial State reports: narrative, legal, state infrastructure, policy, factual.[124] As such, it reflects the numerous criteria, discussed in Chapter 11, which affect the access of persons belonging to national minorities to the media, including in their own languages. The comprehensive treatment of country-specific situations in the Advisory Committee's Opinions is their great strength. Ironically, however, the specificity of the analysis can also be a limiting factor, at least to the extent that the scrutiny provided is *prima facie* deprived of a more general character.

However, one can still find a number of interpretative diamonds in the rough. With a little bit of cutting and polishing, excerpts from Advisory Committee Opinions could be of considerably greater worth, in a wider context than that of the individual circumstances under scrutiny. What is required for each substantive issue addressed is the elaboration of a strong formula with maximum reach and for it to be consistently applied across different country situations. Such an approach would have the merit of enhancing predictability and elevating country-specific analysis to a higher, more general plane on which it would achieve greater impact. Of course, the obvious subtext here is that the quest for consistency, predictability and generality should not be allowed to ride roughshod over the subtleties and sensitivities of specific country-situations. Like in the jurisprudence of Article 10, ECHR, the challenge here is to strike a careful balance between lofty ideals and the hard political and social realities of individual cases. If met squarely, this challenge could lead to immensely instructive and immensely rewarding results, not least for the future monitoring of the FCNM. It should not be shirked.

The evolution of standards from a somewhat lapidary text is crucial and this is another example of parallelism between Article 10, ECHR, and Article 9, FCNM. Chapter 11's focus on how the text of Article 9 of the Framework Convention has been interpreted in the Opinions of the Advisory Committee is therefore appropriate, as it helps to improve our understanding of the full ambit of Article 9.[125] This is

---

124 Outline for reports to be submitted pursuant to Article 25 paragraph 1 of the Framework Convention for the Protection of National Minorities, Appendix 3 (item 4.1), Committee of Ministers Resolution (97) 10, *op. cit.*

125 See also, John Packer & Sally Holt, "Article 9", in Marc Weller, Ed., *The Rights of Minorities in Europe: A Commentary on the European Framework Convention for the Protection of National Minorities*, *op. cit.*, pp. 263–300.

particularly true in the continued absence of any other mechanisms for offering authoritative interpretations of the text of the Framework Convention, eg. direct justiciability before the European Court of Human Rights.

Although the Advisory Committee has begun the practice of developing thematic commentaries, the theme, minorities and the media, has not featured yet. To date, two thematic commentaries have been adopted – on educational rights[126] and participatory rights,[127] while work on a third – linguistic rights, is ongoing. However, minorities and the media has been – and continues to be – mooted as a suitable theme for one of the Advisory Committee's future thematic commentaries.[128] The importance of the theme was recognised at the *Filling the Frame* Conference that was organised to mark the fifth anniversary of the entry into force of the FCNM in 2003.[129] Participation, the media and education were the subjects of the Conference's three thematic workshops.

Intertextual references

Occasional references are made in the Opinions of the Advisory Committee to the Committee of Ministers Recommendation (97) 21 on the media and the promotion of a culture of tolerance, in particular, as well as other standard-setting texts with focuses on the media. It is submitted here that more frequent references in Advisory Committee Opinions to Committee of Ministers' Recommendations on relevant topics could prove extremely useful. Or, more ambitiously, this "import trade" would not even have to be limited to Committee of Ministers' Recommendations.

The Preamble to the Framework Convention states that it was conceived of pursuant to the Declaration of the Heads of State and Government of the Member States of

126 Advisory Committee on the Framework Convention for the Protection of National Minorities, Commentary on Education under the Framework Convention for the Protection of National Minorities, Doc. No. ACFC/25DOC(2006)002, 2 March 2006.

127 Advisory Committee on the Framework Convention for the Protection of National Minorities, Commentary on the Effective Participation of Persons Belonging to National Minorities in Cultural, Social and Economic Life and in Public Affairs, Doc. No. ACFC/31DOC(2008)001, 5 May 2008.

128 Asbjørn Eide, "The work of the Advisory Committee on the Framework Convention for the Protection of National Minorities on thematic commentaries, and the potential impact of these commentaries", pp. 6 and 14; Marc Weller, Rapporteur, "Workshop 3: The Advisory Committee's Thematic Work – Roundtable Discussion", p. 6; both papers presented at the conference, *Enhancing the Impact of the Framework Convention*, Strasbourg, 9–10 October 2008. See also: Rainer Hofmann, "Implementation of the FCNM: Substantive Challenges", in Annelies Verstichel, Andre Alen, Bruno De Witte & Paul Lemmens, Eds., *The Framework Convention for the Protection of National Minorities: A Useful Pan-European Instrument?* (Antwerp/Oxford/Portland, Intersentia, 2008), pp. 159–185, at 170.

129 The (revised) conference proceedings have been published as: *Filling the frame: Five years of monitoring the Framework Convention for the Protection of National Minorities, op. cit.*

the Council of Europe adopted in Vienna on 9 October 1993. It goes on to list – "in a non-exhaustive way" – "three further sources of inspiration for the content" of the Framework Convention, i.e., the ECHR and various relevant United Nations (UN) and C/OSCE instruments containing commitments for the protection of national minorities.[130] The relevant documentary corpus within the UN and OSCE systems is by no means negligible (notwithstanding the fact that some documents are more political than legal in their coloration). But as already mentioned, the crucible of inspiration has a broader circumference than merely the span of the UN and OSCE systems. This point is of cardinal importance.

Thus, insofar as the practice of explicitly referring to international standards is concerned, pertinence should be the guiding principle, thereby inviting the invocation (where appropriate) of other types of "soft law", for example, the Council of Europe Committee of Ministers' Declaration on the Freedom of Expression and Information of 1982; the Oslo Recommendations Regarding the Linguistic Rights of Persons belonging to National Minorities or the international Guidelines on the Use of Minority Languages in the Broadcast Media.[131] This could be a useful way of signposting exemplary or exhortatory standards elaborated in other fora, without having to incorporate large chunks of text from the same standards. In other words, this would involve an exercise of enrichment by reference or intertextuality. It has the further advantage of referring to standards already enjoying the endorsement of other international bodies and the authority that accrues from such endorsement.

The merits of referring to the aforementioned Guidelines on the Use of Minority Languages in the Broadcast Media deserve particular attention here because their subject matter comprises a range of issues that are instrumental in protecting and promoting the interests of persons belonging to national minorities as regards their access to the media (especially in their own languages) (see further, Chapter 11). The Guidelines would be eminently suited to achieving synchronicity with the FCNM – at least in terms of their programmatic character. The greater specificity of the Guidelines could help to fill the gaps in the more general wording of Article 9, FCNM; gaps which are inevitably present as a result of the treaty's broader, more sweeping thematic preoccupations. The complementarity quotient here is high.

Scope for use of more pro-active language

The largely article-by-article approach taken by the Advisory Committee in its country-specific Opinions facilitates in-depth engagement with the various issues addressed by Article 9, FCNM (and indeed, Article 6), as well as the task of

130 Explanatory Report to the Framework Convention, *op. cit.*, para. 23.

131 These Guidelines were elaborated by a group of international experts under the auspices of the OSCE High Commissioner on National Minorities and were first floated in public at a conference in Baden-bei-Wien, Austria, on 25 October 2003. See further, Chapter 4.3.4.

prioritising areas for future attention. The Advisory Committee's specific findings often go beyond merely pointing out a situation or practice that is unsatisfactory; they often prompt suggestions for lines of action to redress the situation or practice in question. While this forward-looking approach is very laudable, again, with a little extra journeying, it could perhaps gain further in effectiveness. In a similar vein, the suggestions advanced for following up on the Advisory Committee's findings tend to rely on calls to "examine", give "particular attention to", "identify", "take the necessary measures", "place emphasis", "try to meet expectations", etc.

An Irish proverb says that if you light the wick, you might as well burn the whole candle. By applying the proverb to this context, then, might it not be constructive to go further than identifying areas meriting attention or exploration or examination and to actually suggest possible ways in which such attention could be administered; such exploration or examination carried out? Of course, it would be imperative that such suggestions not be perceived by State representatives as being imposed as some kind of disguised *diktat*. Rather, the presentation of useful reference points (eg. identified best State practices) or palettes of options would be a preferred approach. Given the political acumen that has been displayed in the past by the Advisory Committee, confidence in its ability to rise to this challenge of persuasion would not be misplaced. Meetings with State representatives within the context of the monitoring process afford the Advisory Committee ideal opportunities for prising open the very centre of pressing questions and situations (including those relating to access to the media) and for assuming a pro-active role in the open and constructive discussion of possible measures to be taken.

(iii) *Committee of Ministers*

As far as the monitoring of the FCNM is concerned, ultimate control and responsibility rests with the Committee of Ministers.[132] This fact alone is not unproblematic in many respects. Most fundamentally, the process is essentially about States monitoring their own activities and this inevitably gives rise to *prima facie* concerns for the independence and objectivity of the exercise.[133] The summary and often bland content of Committee of Ministers' country-specific Recommendations concerning the application of the FCNM (see further, *infra*), furthermore does little to dispel such concerns.

132 See Articles 24–26, FCNM.

133 This scepticism has been conveyed by Andrew Drzemczewski in the context of other, general monitoring work by the Committee of Ministers, when he posed the question: "Is consensus-based confidential monitoring – in which the State being monitored is itself involved in the decision-making process and in which issues are not put to the vote – not intrinsically 'defective' *ab initio*?" – Andrew Drzemczewski, "Monitoring by the Committee of Ministers of the Council of Europe: A Useful 'Human Rights' Mechanism?", in I. Ziemele, Ed., *Baltic Yearbook of International Law*, Vol. 2, 2002, pp. 83–103, at 88.

However, notwithstanding its officially ascribed role of "assistance" in the monitoring process, the Advisory Committee remains the *de facto* power-house for the monitoring activities. This is true by virtue of the extent of its procedural/administrative involvement; its sheer hard graft and its serious engagement with substantive matters. It is therefore imperative that the Committee of Ministers makes greater efforts to harness the full potential for involving the Advisory Committee "in the monitoring of the follow-up to the conclusions and recommendations on an *ad hoc* basis, as instructed by the Committee of Ministers".[134]

Of the country-specific resolutions adopted by the Committee of Ministers in respect of its first monitoring cycle, 14 did not make specific reference to persons belonging to national minorities and the media.[135] In respect of the ongoing second monitoring cycle, the figure is five.[136] In respect of the ongoing third monitoring cycle, the figure is two.[137] However, of the country-specific Resolutions in which the media are mentioned, the relevant treatment of issues is rarely more than cursory. While it could be argued that the brevity of these Resolutions is par for the course because the Advisory Committee Opinions provide superior breadth and depth of analysis, it is nevertheless to be regretted that this opportunity for a more detailed approach to media-related (and other) issues has not been routinely seized by the Committee of Ministers.

Greater specificity is particularly required in the first part (conclusions) of the Committee of Ministers' country-specific Resolutions in the first monitoring cycle. While the recommendation in the second part of such Resolutions that the State Party take appropriate account of the various comments in the relevant Advisory Committee Opinion is laudable, there remains a danger – absent maximum specificity or maximum levels of detail – of individual concerns being inadvertently smothered in this blanket, catch-all approach. From the second monitoring cycle on, these country-specific Resolutions have been structured somewhat differently: 1) conclusions (comprising "Positive developments" and "Issues of concern"); 2) recommendations (focusing on specific minority groups, issues or situations), and 3) provision for continued communication about the monitoring process between the Advisory Committee and State authorities. In these Resolutions, increased detail could most aptly be introduced into the conclusions and recommendations. Finally,

134 Committee of Ministers Resolution (97) 10, *op. cit.*, para. 36.

135 The Resolutions in question concerned the following States: Denmark, Estonia, Hungary, Ireland, Liechtenstein, Lithuania, Malta, the Netherlands, Portugal, San Marino, the Slovak Republic, Spain, Switzerland and the United Kingdom. In order to avoid drawing disingenuous conclusions from statistics, it should be pointed out that the Resolutions in question on occasion give very summary treatment to the countries under scrutiny (particularly in the case of small countries, for which there may not even be any thematic treatment at all).

136 The States in question are:. Estonia, Liechtenstein, Malta, San Marino and the Slovak Republic.

137 The States in question are: Liechtenstein and San Marino.

it cannot be gainsaid that the Committee of Ministers ought to bring increased political pressure to bear in relevant quarters in order to ensure a significant strengthening of the Advisory Committee's financial and human resources.

To conclude this analysis of the monitoring of the FCNM, it must be reiterated that there is clearly a need to derive general principles from specific country situations in a more systematic way. The germ of such principles is already contained in the Advisory Committee's Opinions and if the relevant statements were to be elevated to a higher plane of general application and to constitute a more distinct corpus, they would then offer invaluable interpretative clarity for (Article 9 of) the FCNM. The challenge here would be to marry the goals of showing particular deference to *couleur locale*, while at the same time striving for formulae that would tend towards universal relevance or application.

Similarly, there is a need for terminological precision, the clarification of concepts and more attention to explaining new or unfamiliar technological features. It is also necessary to undergird the findings of the Advisory Committee by making increased references to relevant international standards (including so-called "soft law"). A pro-active role for the Advisory Committee in making suggestions to States Parties on how to address issues of concern would also be useful.

References to media-related issues in Committee of Ministers' country-specific Resolutions have, to date, been scant and when such references have been made, they have generally been found wanting in detail. A heightened role for the Advisory Committee in the monitoring process (with the backing of sufficient human and financial resources) could go some way towards offsetting the effect of this perceived shortcoming of Committee of Ministers' Resolutions.

4.3.2 European Charter for Regional or Minority Languages (ECRML)

The European Charter for Regional or Minority Languages also brings together certain key aspects of the right to freedom of expression and minority rights.[138] However, before examining relevant focuses, it is useful to recall the rather unique character of the Charter. Its "chief distinguishing feature is its purpose: the protection it seeks to give a European cultural asset, namely the linguistic diversity represented by regional and minority languages".[139] As such, it subjects contracting States to various legal obligations, but it does not set out to create rights for either individuals or groups. The extent to which rights for individuals or groups flow

138 For a general commentary on the Charter, see: Jean-Marie Woehrling, *The European Charter for Regional or Minority Languages: A critical commentary* (Strasbourg, Council of Europe Publishing, 2005). For commentary specifically on Article 11, see *ibid*., pp. 200–214.

139 *Ibid*., p. 27.

from, or are affirmed by, State obligations can therefore be regarded as incidental to the central purpose of the Charter. Article 11 is the Charter's principal article concerning the right to freedom of expression; it reads as follows:

Article 11 – Media

1 The Parties undertake, for the users of the regional or minority languages within the territories in which those languages are spoken, according to the situation of each language, to the extent that the public authorities, directly or indirectly, are competent, have power or play a role in this field, and respecting the principle of the independence and autonomy of the media:

a to the extent that radio and television carry out a public service mission:

i to ensure the creation of at least one radio station and one television channel in the regional or minority languages; or

ii to encourage and/or facilitate the creation of at least one radio station and one television channel in the regional or minority languages; or

iii to make adequate provision so that broadcasters offer programmes in the regional or minority languages;

b i to encourage and/or facilitate the creation of at least one radio station in the regional or minority languages; or

ii to encourage and/or facilitate the broadcasting of radio programmes in the regional or minority languages on a regular basis;

c i to encourage and/or facilitate the creation of at least one television channel in the regional or minority languages; or

ii to encourage and/or facilitate the broadcasting of television programmes in the regional or minority languages on a regular basis;

d to encourage and/or facilitate the production and distribution of audio and audiovisual works in the regional or minority languages;

e i to encourage and/or facilitate the creation and/or maintenance of at least one newspaper in the regional or minority languages; or

ii to encourage and/or facilitate the publication of newspaper articles in the regional or minority languages on a regular basis;

f i to cover the additional costs of those media which use regional or minority languages, wherever the law provides for financial assistance in general for the media; or

ii to apply existing measures for financial assistance also to audiovisual productions in the regional or minority languages;

g to support the training of journalists and other staff for media using regional or minority languages.

2 The Parties undertake to guarantee freedom of direct reception of radio and television broadcasts from neighbouring countries in a language used in identical or similar form to a regional or minority language, and not to oppose the retransmission of radio and television broadcasts from neighbouring countries in such a language. They further undertake to ensure that no restrictions will be placed on the freedom of expression and free circulation of information in the written press in a language used in identical or similar form to a regional or minority language. The exercise of the above-mentioned freedoms, since it carries with it duties and responsibilities, may be subject to such formalities, conditions, restrictions or penalties as are prescribed by law and are necessary in a democratic society, in the interests of national security, territorial integrity or public safety, for the prevention of disorder or crime, for the protection of health or morals, for the protection of the reputation or rights of others, for preventing disclosure of information received in confidence, or for maintaining the authority and impartiality of the judiciary.

3 The Parties undertake to ensure that the interests of the users of regional or minority languages are represented or taken into account within such bodies as may be established in accordance with the law with responsibility for guaranteeing the freedom and pluralism of the media.

Article 11 is a derivative formulation of Article 10, ECHR; the debt of the former to the latter is acknowledged in the Explanatory Report to the Charter (para. 112). Indeed, Article 11(2) of the Charter incorporates Article 10(2), ECHR, almost verbatim. Like other substantive Articles of the Charter, it is governed by Article 2, which sets out the requirements for undertakings entered into by States Parties:

1. Each Party undertakes to apply the provisions of Part II to all the regional or minority languages spoken within its territory and which comply with the definition in Article 1.

2. In respect of each language specified at the time of ratification, acceptance or approval, in accordance with Article 3, each Party undertakes to apply a minimum of thirty-five paragraphs or sub-paragraphs chosen from among the provisions of Part III of the Charter, including at least three chosen from each of the Articles 8 and 12 and one from each of the Articles 9, 10, 11 and 13.

No explanation is given either in the Charter proper or in the Explanatory Report thereto[140] as to why three paragraphs or sub-paragraphs must be chosen from Articles 8 (Education) and 12 (Cultural activities and facilities) and only one from Articles 9 (Judicial authorities), 10 (Administrative authorities and public services), 11 (Media) and 13 (Economic and social life). Even though the stipulated requirements are "minimum" and States are free to take on additional commitments *vis-à-vis* the media, the impression given by Article 2(2) is that the media belong to the poor(er) relations in the family of State obligations under the Charter. This impression is all the more puzzling when one considers the importance of the other, similarly designated "poor relations" (i.e., judicial and administrative authorities, public services, economic and social life). However, it must be added that any implicit belittlement of the role or importance of the media is offset by the Expert Committee's repeated insistence in its country-specific Reports that the media have a determinative influence on the future of regional and minority languages.

Monitoring

(i) *General*

A purely textual analysis of the Charter prompts a number of sceptical remarks concerning the impact it is likely to have in raising the level of protection and promotion of minority languages in Contracting States. First, the confidence exuded by the preambular affirmations of the Charter do not carry through to its substantive provisions. There is a clear scale of onerousness present in the range of commitments offered within Articles 8–13 of the Charter. As long as States comply with the requirements set out in Article 2(2), they are free to choose the level of onerousness of the commitments they enter into. This panders – perhaps inordinately – to the discretion and therefore good faith of States. This temerity of approach may very well have been designed to encourage wider ratification of the Charter by States, but due to its apparent potential for low-level commitments, there is no guarantee that it will lead to the achievement of meaningful results at the national and sub-national levels.[141]

It has been posited that the "*table d'hôte*" character of Charter's commitments offers a measure of flexibility to States Parties, without which there would be considerably greater reluctance to ratify the Charter. Dónall Ó Riagáin, for instance, has argued that a "less flexible formula would not work because of the greatly differing language situations obtaining in Europe".[142] The Charter's modest

140 See, in particular, paras. 41–47 of the Explanatory Report.

141 See further, Robert Dunbar, "Minority Language Rights in International Law", 50 ICLQ (2001) 90–120, at 113.

142 Dónall Ó Riagáin, "The Charter: An Overview", in François Grin, *Language policy evaluation and the European Charter for Regional or Minority Languages* (Palgrave Macmillan, 2003) pp. 55–68, at 64.

ambition could be summed up in the working principle that half a loaf is better than no bread; or, to emphasise the meagreness of expectations it generates, the equivalent proverb in Dutch: half an egg is better than an empty shell! Nevertheless, the wisdom of this logic has yet to be borne out in practice: the Charter's rate of uptake by States has been generally disappointing,[143] with only 25 ratifications to date.

(ii) *Expert Committee*

Thematic approach

The Expert Committee investigates whether the State is upholding its obligations by comparing the factual information at its disposal to the particular commitments entered into. The Reports home in on specific commitments undertaken by States: they do not adopt a simple article-by-article approach. This means that the Expert Committee does not necessarily examine the same commitments in respect of every State Party. Nevertheless, its pronouncements on substantive matters are frequently of wider interest/relevance than merely to the particular State to which they are addressed. This is more obviously and more frequently true of the Expert Committee's evaluations than those of the Advisory Committee to the FCNM. Despite the fact that the Expert Committee does not always consider the same commitments in respect of each State, its occasional references to findings in respect of other States does make for greater overall consistency in the evaluative work of the Committee.

On paper, the asserted realism of the Charter could seem more like resigned defeatism, but in practice, the Expert Committee has been striving to achieve maximum returns on what is *prima facie* a restrictively-designed text. This is illustrated by how the specificity of commitments entered into by States has bred specificity of analysis by the Expert Committee. Those trends towards specificity created a need for the Expert Committee to develop expertise on various aspects of the media (especially broadcasting), such as its sociological dimension and the impact of technological developments. By and large, the Committee has risen to that challenge and delivered in kind. As a result, the use of technical terminology is noticeably cleaner and clearer than, for example, by the AC FCNM (but it should also be acknowledged that the text of Article 9, FCNM, cannot boast exemplary clarity of formulation to start with). The Committee's comments have also borne out an awareness of the need for conceptual and linguistic precision.

143 See, for example, relevant remarks in the five Biennial reports by the Secretary General [of the Council of Europe] to the Parliamentary Assembly on the application of the European Charter for Regional or Minority Languages (21 June 2010 – Doc. 12300; 24 October 2007 – Doc. 11442; 3 September 2005 – Doc. 10659; 11 September 2002 – Doc. 9540; 18 October 2000 – Doc. 8879).

Intertextual references

At least as regards Article 11, the Expert Committee has not tended to routinely refer to other Council of Europe standard-setting texts, never mind other international instruments. The Preamble to the Charter considers "that the right to use a regional or minority language in private and public life is an inalienable right conforming to the principles embodied" in the ICCPR and "according to the spirit" of the ECHR, and it also has "regard to" relevant CSCE work (in particular the Helsinki Final Act of 1975 and the Copenhagen Meeting of 1990). However these are courtesy nods; acknowledgements of the existence of other standards developed in other international fora. They do not – on any reading – amount to the sourcing of inspiration for the Charter. This is a significant difference from the Preamble to the FCNM. Perhaps, then, given that there is no *ab initio* grounding of the Charter in anterior international law, it should come as no surprise that the Expert Committee would rarely (if ever) refer to prevailing international legal (and non-legal) standards that are extraneous to the Charter itself.

This may be partly to do with the nature of the Charter and the lack of provision for cross-fertilisation by other international law texts. The absence of such a provision should not necessarily preclude the Expert Committee from tactically or systematically invoking relevant references; indeed its purposive approach to its evaluative task suggests that it would not be adverse to doing so in the future. For the moment, though, its failure to enrich its own work by such invocations must be regarded as a missed opportunity, because, as was argued in connection with the AC to the FCNM, *supra*, it could be advantageous to regularly make such cross-linkage.

However, the Expert Committee does, on occasion, refer to the approach of the AC FCNM on matters of overlapping interest. Such cross-references are only made sporadically and even then as parenthetical remarks seeking to confirm or re-affirm stand-points already taken by the Expert Committee on particular issues. This tactic shows welcome awareness of the activities of a sibling Council of Europe body and is important for fostering certain thematic consistency across Council of Europe approaches. At the same time, though, the tactic also boasts a certain, calculated temerity: a more assertive policy of cross-referencing could risk leading to the entanglement of nets.

Scope for use of more pro-active language

A general perusal of Expert Committee country-specific Reports suggests that the Committee is also less likely to fudge its words than the AC. When it feels that commitments are not being properly honoured, it is quick to say so and indeed, to offer suggestions on how States Parties might consider ameliorating the situation. There are at least two plausible explanations for this:

(a) The specificity of commitments narrows down the scope of enquiry and the evaluation of detailed factual information means that it generally is possible to ascertain whether States are genuinely upholding their undertakings. The Expert Committee is sensitive to dichotomies between the meeting of obligations in formal and in real terms, and its comments frequently reflect this. It also frequently finds that certain obligations are only being partially fulfilled and indicates how outstanding issues should/might be addressed. Where it is not in a position to draw relevant conclusions (eg. due to a lack of information, or ambiguous information or conflicting information), it tends to state as much and request that the subsequent State Report provide the necessary clarification.

(b) From its inception, the Expert Committee appears to have been considerably freer than its FCNM counterpart in its ability to gather information other than that provided through official State channels. This refers not only to the erstwhile convoluted restrictions of mandate under which the AC had to operate, but also – to an extent – the cautious mindset engendered by such restrictions.

(iii) *Committee of Ministers*

As with the FCNM, CM Recommendations on the application of the Charter in specific countries tend to be rather terse and do little to elucidate the content of the State obligations under scrutiny. This, as also stated in the context of the FCNM, is more of an observation than a criticism, as these Recommendations – by nature – are not intended as explanatory texts. Rather, one would expect the Reports of the Expert Committee, on which the CM Recommendations are based, to fulfil such an explanatory role. As with the FCNM, the CM relies very heavily on the detail and quality of the Expert Committee's Reports.

Moreover, CM Recommendations do not always refer to the media in any case. Seven of the 20 Recommendations addressed to States Parties so far on the basis of their First Periodical Reports contained no specific media-related recommendations.[144] As regards the 16 Recommendations adopted to date on the basis of States' Second Periodical Reports, five contained no specific media-related recommendations.[145] In respect of Recommendations adopted in the third reporting cycle, the figure was similar.[146] The pattern is continuing in the ongoing fourth reporting cycle.[147] Such reductionism is disappointing, as a failure to mention issues relating to the media certainly does not mean that they are not pressing, nor is it necessarily in keeping with the findings of the Expert Committee.

144 Cyprus, Hungary, Montenegro, Norway, Serbia, Slovenia and Switzerland.

145 Cyprus, the Netherlands, Norway, Slovenia and Spain.

146 Four of the seven Recommendations adopted so far did not contain references to the media: the Netherlands, Norway, Switzerland and the United Kingdom.

147 One out of five: Switzerland.

(iv) Secretary General

A useful and rather unique innovation in the Charter monitoring mechanism is the requirement that the Secretary General of the Council of Europe "shall make a two-yearly detailed report to the Parliamentary Assembly on the application of the Charter".[148] The usefulness of this provision is that it keeps the parliamentary organ of the Council of Europe directly informed of how the Charter is faring (note the stipulation that the report should be "detailed"), thereby facilitating discussion by the parliamentarians.

4.3.3 Conceptual over-stretch and non-treaty-based standard-setting

Sections 2.2 and 2.3 of this chapter have dredged up the main observations concerning the limitations of generalist international law in terms of scope, content and enforcement. It is, of course, important not to understate the role that generalist international law does play in safeguarding the rights of persons belonging to minorities: piecemeal provisions and interventions can certainly make an impact.[149] Section 3 has so far examined the role played by thematically-specific international treaties in plugging the gaps in international law. In addition, it is also useful to reflect on the possible gap-filling or standard-setting role for instruments that are independent of treaty law.

Drawing on the foregoing, it can be argued forcefully that stronger enforcement mechanisms and practices would stimulate improved implementation and reduce the need for supplementary and complementary treaties. Without wishing to detract from the undoubted merits of this argument, a rejoinder thereto might point out that the elaboration of other, non-treaty, supplementary and complementary instruments (whether legal, quasi-legal or political in character – and leaving aside for the moment any consideration of the extent of their binding effects) could prove useful to the extent that they would pursue specific strategic goals. Basic to such an approach is a faith placed in the ability of a rising normative tide to lift all boats. In other words, to strive for the realisation of specific aims by simultaneously employing diverse strategies, enhances the probability of those aims being attained. Different strategies lend themselves better to different circumstances and are ultimately capable of registering different gains.

---

148 Article 16(5) of the Charter.

149 See, generally, the discussions of various international instruments that are not specifically devoted to the protection of minority rights in: Council of Europe, *Mechanisms for the implementation of minority rights* (Strasbourg, Council of Europe Publishing, 2004); Kristin Henrard & Robert Dunbar, Eds., *Synergies in Minority Protection: European and International Law Perspectives* (Cambridge, Cambridge University Press, 2008).

But we need to proceed cautiously in our development of this line of thinking: standards that are inadequately anchored in human rights law can lead to rights inflation and devaluation. At the theoretical level, as posited by Frederick Schauer: "when a list of rights becomes coextensive with the list of wants, or even with the list of fundamental needs, we lose any strong sense of having a right".[150] This is also one of Ronald Dworkin's themes of predilection. He distinguishes between the infringement and inflation of a (moral) right by government, stating that the former involves the definition of a right "more narrowly than justice requires", whereas in the latter case, a right is defined "more broadly than justice requires".[151] He regards the infringement of a right as being more serious than its inflation, because infringement constitutes a wrong to an individual, and *a fortiori*, the special character of rights means that they should only be curtailed by other rights or "when some compelling reason is presented, some reason that is consistent with the suppositions on which the original right must be based".[152] The adverse consequence of the inflation of a right is, to paraphrase Dworkin's own words, that society is thereby cheated of some general benefit.[153]

Also addressing the topic of rights inflation, Amy Gutmann has cautioned that:

> A human rights regime still needs to avoid overextending itself beyond what are reasonable aspirations. But it also needs to avoid a minimalism so sparing that its enforcement would leave the most vulnerable people without what is (minimally) necessary to protect their ability to live a minimally decent life by any reasonable standards.[154]

It is not obvious how these apparently antipodal objectives can be bridged in practice. A first step, however, might be to recognise that generally speaking, human rights instruments tend to vacillate between concrete, minimalist treaty law and more aspirational, exhortatory soft law (although treaties can and do have the latter characteristics as well). Both can be normative in character, of course, but they rest on very different kinds of legitimacy and their respective legal statuses should therefore not be confused.

"Soft law" is the catch-all rubric under which various kinds of standard-setting measures not directly related to treaty law are sometimes lumped together.[155] The

150 Frederick Schauer, *Free Speech: A Philosophical Enquiry* (Cambridge, Cambridge University Press, 1982), p. 56.

151 Ronald Dworkin, *Taking Rights Seriously* (London, Duckworth & Co. Ltd., 1977), p. 198.

152 *Ibid.*, p. 200.

153 *Ibid.*, p. 198.

154 Amy Gutmann, "Introduction", in Michael Ignatieff *et al.*, *Human Rights as Politics and Idolatry*, *op. cit.*, at xii.

155 See further: C.M. Chinkin, "The Challenge of Soft Law: Development and Change in International Law", 38 ICLQ (1989), pp. 850–866; Hartmut Hillgenberg, "A Fresh Look at Soft Law", 10 EJIL (No. 3, 1999), pp. 499–515.

use of scare quotes when denoting "soft law" is deliberate and is an indication of the contested nature of the term.[156] Many commentators are rightly critical of the term, firstly because its amorphous nature renders it pretty useless for the purposes of categorisation or meaningful analysis. A second and related criticism is that it masks a huge variety in the nature of the instruments and in the impact of those instruments on the development of international law. However, one should not throw out the baby with the bathwater. Rather, one should turn these criticisms to constructive ends. The relevance and importance of soft law can only be fully appreciated by exploring the full range of instruments that are included in its ambit. These instruments vary not only in character, as already mentioned, but also in terms of their legal status/significance.

The importance of their status can be determined by such factors as their purported objectives (interpretation or synthesis of existing standards; indicating emergent State practice in a particular area of law; facilitation of bench-marking practices; setting of new standards;[157] application of existing standards to new points of focus, etc.); the nature and standing of the issuing body; procedures by which they are adopted; enforcement and monitoring mechanisms provided for; subsequent uptake (i.e., adoption and implementation) by States and/or other addressees as well as any relevant third parties.

Thus, the usefulness of soft-law documents as standard-setting documents, is best considered in non-legal terms. To consider them as primarily political is by no means to deprive them of legitimacy or impact. The lessons of standard-setting in the area of minority rights bear ample testimony to the normative potential and usefulness of overtly political approaches.[158] This is, however, subject to the proviso (discussed *supra*) that attempts should not be made to stretch the scope of human rights beyond its elastic limit, or to put it – literally – in Machiavellian terms, to avoid the "error" of men "of not knowing when to limit their hopes".[159]

While it is generally regarded as a fruitful and instructive exercise to compare inter-institutional approaches to identified topics, it can be equally fruitful and instructive to examine various intra-institutional approaches. This is especially true of the Council of Europe, given the multiplicity of different sources of standard-setting

---

156 See, in this connection: Jan Klabbers, "The Redundancy of Soft Law", 65 *Nordic Journal of International Law* (1996), pp. 167–182; Jan Klabbers, "The Undesirability of Soft Law", 67 *Nordic Journal of International Law* (1998), pp. 381–391.

157 This possible function of soft law is controversial and the (generally) non-legal status of soft-law instruments should be stressed in no uncertain terms here.

158 See further, Chapter 2, including the discussion of the upgrading of OSCE standards into legal norms at national and international levels.

159 Cited in Daniel Bell, *The End of Ideology: On the Exhaustion of Political Ideas in the Fifties* (Revised Edition) (New York, The Free Press, 1962), p. 393.

texts on issues affecting the freedom of expression rights of minorities, both directly and indirectly. The various approaches tend to admit different side-constraints on the right to freedom of expression, reflecting the inherent biases of their particularised mandates. Furthermore, the various approaches rely on different mechanisms of enforcement and monitoring (if any). Their norm-making importance is determined largely by a combination of their substantive provisions and procedural mechanisms. When evaluating the effectiveness of the impact of various bodies, awareness must be shown of constitutive and procedural variations between them. Subsequent chapters will draw on texts and initiatives by a number of Council of Europe bodies: the Committee of Ministers (CM), Parliamentary Assembly (PACE), European Commission against Racism and Intolerance (ECRI), Venice Commission, and others, as appropriate.

The Committee of Ministers, the executive organ of the Council of Europe, has contributed in no small measure to the organisation's efforts to promote the diversification of opinion in the media,[160] with resultant benefits for minorities. It has, for instance, adopted a number of Recommendations and Declarations touching on relevant issues.[161] Such statements do not, however, legally bind Member States,[162] and as such, we can class them too under the broad rubric of "soft law". Recommendations deal with matters for which the CM has agreed "a common policy".[163] While these commitments may not be legally enforceable, they are politically authoritative[164] and their implementation at the national level is monitored at the international level.[165] The CM may ask States authorities "to

160 The efforts of the Parliamentary Assembly of the Council should also be praised at this juncture, even though constraints of space prevent an in-depth analysis of the same.

161 For a comprehensive overview of these and other international instruments, see Karol Jakubowicz, "Report: A critical evaluation of the first results of the monitoring of the Framework Convention on the issue of persons belonging to national minorities and the media (1998–2003)", in *Filling the frame: Five years of monitoring the Framework Convention for the Protection of National Minorities* (Strasbourg, Council of Europe Publishing, 2004), pp. 113–138.

162 Article 15(b), Statute of the Council of Europe.

163 Pursuant to Article 20 of the Statute, the adoption of a Recommendation by the CM requires: "a unanimous vote of all representatives present" and "a majority of those entitled to vote". However, in order to make their voting procedure more flexible, the Ministers' Deputies reached a gentleman's agreement at their 519*bis* meeting (November 1994) not to apply the unanimity rule to Recommendations.

164 See further: Jan Kleijssen, "Council of Europe Standard-setting in the Human Rights Field", in J.P. Loof & R.A. Lawson, Eds., *60 jaar Europees Verdrag voor de Rechten van de Mens – Een lichtend voorbeeld?* – Special Issue of *Nederlands Tijdschrift voor de Mensenrechten*, Vol. 35 [2010], No. 7, pp. 897–904; Florence Benoît-Rohmer & Heinrich Klebes, *Council of Europe law: Towards a pan-European legal area* (Strasbourg, Council of Europe Publishing, 2005), pp. 108–109.

165 Council of Europe Monitoring Processes: An Overview, Monitor/Inf (2004) 2, Document prepared by the Monitoring Department Directorate of Strategic Planning, Council of Europe, 5 April 2004 (replaces Monitor/Inf (2000) 1); Andrew Drzemczewski, "La prévention des violations des droits de l'homme: les mécanismes de suivi du Conseil de l'Europe", *op. cit.*;

inform it of the action taken by them" regarding Recommendations and it has formally emphasised the need for intergovernmental committees (steering committees and committees of experts) to improve their monitoring of the implementation of Recommendations and Resolutions.[166] One of the terms of reference for the Steering Committee on the Media and New Communication Services (CDMC) is to "monitor the implementation by member states of non-binding instruments prepared under its authority with a view, where necessary, to identifying and proposing further action".[167] This certainly includes thematically relevant Recommendations and Declarations adopted by the Committee of Ministers.

In the context of the monitoring activities of the Council of Europe, Andrew Drzemczewski has stressed that there is "a certain urgency to circumvent a potential turf-war that could undermine not only the work of both organs [i.e., the CM and the PACE] (and others) but also the credibility of the Organisation itself".[168] He has also called for "more in-house synergy" on the basis of very practical concerns, *viz.* the "real dangers of unnecessary duplication of work and unnecessary diversification of energies".[169] These cautionary words of advice are just as relevant to the duplicity of substantive, normative approaches to given issues as they are to the monitoring and miscellaneous follow-up processes. Efforts should be made to enhance consistency across the different approaches and to eliminate inter-sibling spats and rivalries. A centralised, uniform approach is not necessary, feasible or even desirable. Distinctive mandates preclude the possibility of uniformity, but they also furnish different angles of approach.

Despite the wary tone of the foregoing paragraphs, international standards that are not legally-binding on States *can* play a useful, but limited, role in relation to the development of international human rights law. For instance, it can have an interpretative function by fleshing out the details of hard-law provisions (which traditionally tend towards terseness) or it can be an indicator of emergent State practice in a particular area.

Andrew Drzemczewski, "Monitoring by the Committee of Ministers of the Council of Europe: a useful 'human rights' mechanism?", *op. cit.*; Andrew Drzemczewski, "Monitoring by the Council of Europe", in Gudmundur Alfredsson *et al.*, Eds., *International Human Rights Monitoring Mechanisms* (Great Britain, Kluwer Law International, 2001), pp. 525–532.

166 405th Meeting of the Ministers' Deputies, 1987. See also: Andrew Drzemczewski, "La prévention des violations des droits de l'homme: les mécanismes de suivi du Conseil de l'Europe", *op. cit.*, at 397.

167 Terms of reference of the Steering Committee on Media and New Communication Services (CDMC), adopted by the Committee of Ministers of the Council of Europe on 11 February 2009 (as revised on 9 November 2009), para. 4(ii).

168 Andrew Drzemczewski, "Monitoring by the Committee of Ministers of the Council of Europe: A Useful 'Human Rights' Mechanism?", *op. cit.*, at 88.

169 [footnote omitted] *Ibid.*, p. 102.

4.3.4 Guidelines on the use of Minority Languages in the Broadcast Media

A set of international Guidelines on the Use of Minority Languages in the Broadcast Media (2003) provide a concrete and relevant example of how legal standards can usefully be supplemented by non-legally-binding standards.[170] Elaborated by a group of experts under the auspices of the OSCE HCNM, the Guidelines draw inspiration from and seek to crystallise existing international legal and political standards dealing with the topic. Their usefulness derives from their elucidation of existing international standards and their suitability for benchmarking exercises by a variety of parties (including States authorities, IGOs and NGOs).

The Guidelines follow earlier standard-setting initiatives taken by the OSCE HCNM concerning specific aspects of minority rights. The initiatives in question led to the elaboration of The Hague Recommendations on the Education Rights of National Minorities (October 1996); the Oslo Recommendations Regarding the Linguistic Rights of National Minorities (February 1998), and the Lund Recommendations on the Effective Participation of National Minorities in Public Life (September 1999).[171] However, the character of the Guidelines on the Use of Minority Languages in the Broadcast Media is more programmatic than those of its forerunners, which explains why they are styled as Guidelines rather than Recommendations.

The first section of the Guidelines presents their underlying general principles: freedom of expression; cultural and linguistic diversity; protection of identity, and equality and non-discrimination.

The second section, entitled ‘Policy’, sets out that States should develop policy to address the use of minority languages in the broadcast media. The elaboration and application of such State policy should include the “effective participation” of persons belonging to national minorities. It ought to be supportive of public service broadcasting to the extent that such broadcasting caters, *inter alia*, for the linguistic needs of national minorities. State policy in this area should also “facilitate the establishment and maintenance by persons belonging to national minorities of broadcast media in their own language” (para. 8), and independent regulatory bodies should have responsibility for its implementation.

---

170 For detailed commentary, see: Tarlach McGonagle, “Regulating minority-language use in broadcasting: international law and the Dutch national experience”, 16 *Mediaforum* (No. 5, May 2004), pp. 155–160; Tarlach McGonagle & Andrei Richter, “Regulation of Minority-Language Broadcasting”, *IRIS plus* (Supplement to *IRIS – Legal Observations of the European Audiovisual Observatory*), 2004–2; George Jones (Series Editor), Sally Holt & John Packer (Guest Editors), *Mercator Media Forum 8* (Cardiff, University of Wales Press, 2005); John Packer & Sally Holt, “The use of minority languages in the broadcast media: Introducing new guidelines”, *Helsinki Monitor* (2004, No. 2), pp. 103–126.

171 Other Recommendations have been adopted by the OSCE HCNM since; see further, Chapter 2.2.4(i).

Regulation (including licensing) "must be prescribed by law, based on objective and non-discriminatory criteria and shall not aim to restrict or have the effect of restricting broadcasting in minority languages" (para. 9). States may not prohibit the use of any language in the broadcast media and any measures promoting one or more language(s) should not have restrictive repercussions for the use of other languages, or otherwise adversely affect the rights of persons belonging to national minorities. Furthermore, again drawing on the language of Article 10, ECHR, regulation must pursue a legitimate aim and be proportionate to that aim. The proportionality of regulation should be assessed in light of a wide range of factors, including the existing political, social, religious, cultural and linguistic environment; the number, variety, geographical reach, character, function and languages of available broadcasting services, and the rights, needs, expressed desires and nature of the audience(s) affected.

The Guidelines stipulate that onerous translation requirements should not be imposed on minority-language broadcasting and that transfrontier broadcasting must not be restricted (on the basis of language). Moreover, the availability of foreign broadcasting in a minority language does not obviate the need for States to facilitate the domestic production of programmes in that language, "nor does it justify a reduction of the broadcast time in that language" (para. 13).

The fourth section of the Guidelines countenances a number of facilitative measures aimed at stimulating broadcasting in minority languages, both qualitatively and quantitatively. These include States providing access to broadcasting technology and infrastructure; creating financial assistance schemes; pursuing advantageous fiscal policies and maintaining particular licensing and administrative regimes; all with a view to achieving "effective equality" for broadcasters operating (to varying degrees) in minority languages. As elsewhere in the Guidelines, providing incentives for minority language broadcasting and teasing out various possibilities for its realisation, are approached distinctly from public service and private broadcasting perspectives. The importance of capacity-building (eg. technical support for the distribution of productions in minority languages; education and training of personnel for minority-language broadcasting) is also emphasised.

To conclude, the Guidelines can be described as representing a synthesis of existing relevant international legal and political standards. As such, their content should be familiar because they reflect a body of diverse commitments already undertaken by most European States in their miscellaneous international treaty obligations. The novelty of the Guidelines is that, for the first time, those diverse commitments are brought together in a document of exemplary clarity and coherence. The Explanatory Note to the Guidelines enhances the clarity offered by the Guidelines, by sourcing each element in precise, pre-existent international standards. Another strength of the Guidelines is their comprehensive nature. As described in the Explanatory Note, the Guidelines draw not only on international treaty law, but also on relevant jurisprudence elaborated pursuant to the same. They also draw on an array of relevant international texts which are not legally binding on States, but which are nevertheless of considerable normative and political importance.

A crucial process that fed into the elaboration of the Guidelines was the compilation of the study, *Minority-Language Related Broadcasting and Legislation in the OSCE*.[172] It is a comprehensive survey of the regulation of minority-language use in the broadcasting sectors of each of the (then) 55 Participating States of the OSCE. The study provides keen insights into best relevant practices in operation at the national and sub-national levels across the sweep of OSCE Participating States. It is important to mention the study in order to demonstrate that vast first-hand research (comprising data and contextual analysis) also informs the Guidelines, thereby enhancing its credibility at the coal-face of human rights protection.

The Guidelines do not present a fixed blue-print for adoption in each and every European State. Rather, they offer a palette of options and examples which could usefully be adapted to meet the legal and cultural priorities and sensitivities of individual situations in individual States. The margin of appreciation for States is wide. As such, the drafting of the Guidelines was infused with the hope that they could constitute a proverbial rising tide which would lift at least some boats. Another intended purpose of the Guidelines is to map and clarify existing relevant legal and political standards at the international level.

While it can be difficult to assess the precise impact of non-binding texts such as these Guidelines, it is useful to document instances of their invocation or application. The OSCE HCNM has relied on the Guidelines in the course of his work[173] and the Parliamentary Assembly of the Council of Europe has also formally articulated the objective of furthering take-up of the Guidelines in its Recommendation 1773 (2006), entitled "The 2003 guidelines on the use of minority languages in the broadcast media and the Council of Europe standards: need to enhance cooperation and synergy with the OSCE" (see also, Chapter 2.2.2).[174] The Recommendation stresses the complementarity between Council of Europe and OSCE instruments

172 Tarlach McGonagle, Bethany Davis Noll & Monroe Price, Eds., *Minority-Language Related Broadcasting and Legislation in the OSCE*, Study commissioned by the OSCE High Commissioner on National Minorities, carried out by the Programme in Comparative Media Law and Policy (PCMLP), Oxford University and the Institute for Information Law (IViR) of the University of Amsterdam, April 2003 (published: September 2003).

173 Although this reliance has – to the knowledge of the author – yet to be documented in a systematic and comprehensive way.

174 The 2003 guidelines on the use of minority languages in the broadcast media and the Council of Europe standards: need to enhance cooperation and synergy with the OSCE, Recommendation 1773 (2006), Parliamentary Assembly of the Council of Europe, 17 November 2006. For an overview of the content of the Recommendation, see: Tarlach McGonagle, "Parliamentary

aiming to "guarantee that minorities can use their own languages and that these languages are broadcast by the media". The operative part of the text recommends, *inter alia*, that the Council of Europe's Committee of Ministers:

- invite States "to ensure that people belonging to national minorities or using regional or minority languages have a balanced access to public broadcast media and an effective right to establish and use private broadcast media", in accordance with Article 11, ECRML [entitled "Media"] and Article 9, FCNM [dealing with freedom of expression and access to the media], as elucidated by the work of both treaties' competent monitoring bodies; relevant PACE Recommendations and Resolutions, and the Guidelines on the use of Minority Languages in the Broadcast Media, and
- "regularly" take the 2003 Guidelines "into account" in the monitoring of the implementation of the ECRML and FCNM.

These recommendations are important because they recognise the obvious overlap between the Guidelines, Article 11, ECRML, and Article 9, FCNM. The explicit encouragement of cross-referencing these texts in relevant treaty-monitoring and other fora should greatly enhance the consistency with which relevant standards are interpreted and applied. Various cooperative and coordinating strategies and initiatives could be taken between relevant IGOs and between relevant bodies within relevant IGOs in order to generate further synergies in the promotion and application of the Guidelines. A number of possible measures are set out in PACE Recommendation 1773 (2006) and elsewhere.[175]

4.4 Interplay with other human rights

It is important to emphasise the overall coherence of all human rights as well as their interconnectedness. This is the interpretive context in which the interplay between the rights of persons belonging to minorities and the right to freedom of expression must be developed. In this connection, the added value of minority rights to a select number of rights with which the right to freedom of expression and minority rights enjoy a high level of valency, merits attention: non-discrimination/equality, participation, education, culture, religion and language. The specific importance of each of these rights within the freedom of expression/

Assembly: Recommendation on Minority Languages and Broadcasting and Inter-Institutional Cooperation", *IRIS* 2007–2: 3.

175 Suggested strategies are set out more fully in Tarlach McGonagle, 'Guidelines on the use of Minority Languages in the Broadcast Media: overview and prospects for further implementation', Hearing on the use of minority languages in the broadcast media, Parliamentary Assembly of the Council of Europe – Sub-Committee on Rights of Minorities, Committee on Legal Affairs and Human Rights, Eerste Kamer der Staten-Generaal, The Hague, 28 April 2006 (unpublished paper, on file with author).

minority rights interface will then be addressed at later stages in this book, as appropriate.

The conceptual framework for international human rights law is set out by the Vienna Declaration.[176] Article 5 of the Declaration forcefully states that:

> All human rights are universal, indivisible and interdependent and interrelated. The international community must treat human rights globally in a fair and equal manner, on the same footing, and with the same emphasis. While the significance of national and regional particularities and various historical, cultural and religious backgrounds must be borne in mind, it is the duty of States, regardless of their political, economic and cultural systems, to promote and protect all human rights and fundamental freedoms.

To insist on the interdependent and inter-related character of all human rights is not to deny that in practice, the exercise of various rights in certain situations can generate certain frictions, eg. the right to freedom of expression and the right to be free from racial discrimination. Rather, it is to insist on the presumptive coherence of rights.[177] Such an integrated conceptualisation of human rights facilitates the exploration of how other rights relate to the right to freedom of expression and minority rights.

The great *forte* of an approach to human rights that is based on their "universal, indivisible and interdependent and interrelated" character is that it is even-textured. To approach a particular problem, eg. racism, from one or two specific angles, eg. non-discrimination and protection of human dignity, entails a risk that other harms and remedies will not be adequately considered. An integrated approach to human rights, however, reduces the risk of particularism or sectionalism and their attendant limitations. It could be argued, for example, that an integrated human-rights approach to racism would not only emphasise protection against prejudice, discrimination and violence, but also promote "voluntary identification based on shared culture" and indigenous rights.[178] Such promotional strategies are not precluded by a sectional approach to racism (indeed they are already in evidence in ICERD, for example), but an integrated human-rights approach is *prima facie* more accommodating of such strategies because of its recognition of the continuity between negative and positive rights and corresponding State duties.

---

176 World Conference on Human Rights – The Vienna Declaration and Programme of Action (1993).

177 For a detailed conceptual exploration of this notion, see: Rolf Künnemann, "A Coherent Approach to Human Rights", 17 *Human Rights Quarterly* (No. 2, 1995), pp. 323–342.

178 Michael Banton, *The International Politics of Race* (Cambridge, Polity Press, 2002), p. 187.

The universal character of rights implies that minority rights are part of a broader scheme and cannot be considered or developed in isolation. To translate this somewhat abstract argument into practical terms: this means that the development of minority rights is conditioned by its dialectic relationship with "majority" rights.[179] The rights of one group in society cannot presumptively override those of another group. The promotion of rights for one group must reckon with consequences for rights of other groups. As already noted in Chapter 2, the European Court of Human Rights has stated:

> Although individual interests must on occasion be subordinated to those of a group, democracy does not simply mean that the views of a majority must always prevail: a balance must be achieved which ensures the fair and proper treatment of minorities and avoids any abuse of a dominant position.[180]

Another adjective frequently applied to human rights – most famously, perhaps, in the first preambular sentence of the Universal Declaration of Human Rights – but which is not mentioned in Article 5 of the Vienna Declaration, is "inalienable". It is important to recall its meaning and relevance at this juncture. It means that as a matter of principle, human rights cannot be taken away from their holders (i.e., everyone), either by States authorities or by third parties. Limitations on particular rights can, of course, be legitimate in certain circumstances, but the importance of insisting on the inalienability of rights is to emphasise their presumptive primacy and the restricted application to be given to permissible limitations.

Central to this conceptualisation of human rights are the values of "pluralism, tolerance and broadmindedness",[181] which are prerequisites of democratic society (as consistently held by the European Court of Human Rights). These are the kind of values described by Bhikhu Parekh as "operative public values", i.e., those values "that a society cherishes as part of its collective identity and in terms of which it regulates the relations between its members", and which "constitute the moral structure of its public life and give it coherence and stability".[182] Parekh's elaboration of the notion of "operative public values" furnishes us with an immensely helpful theoretical and practical model for the discussion of pluralistic tolerance in Chapter 5.

---

179 *Ibid.*, p. 170.

180 *Young, James & Webster v. United Kingdom*, Judgment of the European Court of Human Rights of 13 August 1981, Series A No. 44 p. 25, para. 63; *Chassagnou & Others v. France*, Judgment of the European Court of Human Rights of 29 April 1999, para. 112.

181 *Handyside v. United Kingdom*, Judgment of the European Court of Human Rights of 7 December 1976, Series A, No. 24, para. 49.

182 Bhikhu Parekh, *Rethinking Multiculturalism: Cultural Diversity and Political Theory* (2nd Edition) (New York, Palgrave Macmillan, 2006), p. 363.

4.4.1 Added value of minority dimension to human rights

The conceptualisation of human rights as an integrated, systemic whole reinforces the recognition that "the very same values behind universal human rights require specific attention and protection in respect of members of minorities".[183] However, the commonality of underlying values does not imply that the strategies adopted for the protection and promotion of those values will be similarly congruent. These observations are the inevitable corollaries of the dual nature of minority rights, which comprise individual and collective aspects.

In figurative terms, minority rights can aptly be described as offshoots from individual human rights. As was seen in Chapter 2, provisions for minority rights in positive international law stress that they stem from central human rights principles and that they include the panoply of human rights recognised internationally. While this tendency has resulted in some redundancies in the restatement of certain rights, restatement is – of itself – not necessarily an unwelcome feature. By reiterating that a particular right also applies to minorities could be tantamount to stating that it is likely to be exercised differently by members of minorities and other individuals in society. However, stemming from, and reaching further than, individual human rights *simpliciter*, minority rights yield added value and should be regarded as human rights "plus".[184] At the very least, minority rights should serve the purpose of clarification, reaffirmation and recalibration of existing rights *vis-à-vis* persons belonging to minority groups. In some cases, they should also expand existing rights or identify new areas of application, most importantly for rights specifically requiring communal exercise. This can often imply certain affirmative obligations for States. These considerations are important when assessing whether the right to freedom of expression of persons belonging to minorities is exercised effectively.

The added value of a minority dimension to the following rights is to be considered very important: non-discrimination/equality; participation in public life; education; culture; religion, and language. These rights[185] have been selected for closer examination because of their propensity for interaction with the right to freedom of expression.

---

183 Martin Scheinin, "Minority rights: additional rights or added protection?", in Morten Bergsmo, Ed., *Human Rights and Criminal Justice for the Downtrodden: Essays in Honour of Asbjorn Eide* (Leiden/Boston, Martinus Nijhoff Publishers, 2003), pp. 486–504, at 493.

184 See further, John Packer, "On the Content of Minority Rights", in Juha Räikkä, Ed., *Do We Need Minority Rights? Conceptual Issues* (The Hague, Martinus Nijhoff Publishers, 1996), pp. 121–178, at 153 *et seq.*

185 The classical civil and political rights of freedom of association and freedom of expression may at first glance appear conspicuous by their absence (as separate categories). However, freedom of association is treated in a number of the above categories (eg. culture, religion, participation, etc.).

Effective provisions of non-discrimination and equality are prerequisites for the attainment of pluralism in society, as true pluralism cannot be said to exist if (individuals belonging to) certain groups suffer from discrimination or are denied equality of opportunity, equality before the law, etc. An effective right of participation in public life for all sections of society is an important means of perpetuating equality of opportunity and safeguarding pluralism. Effective participation in all aspects of public life ensures that a plurality of views and interests necessarily inform decision-making processes.

From a functional perspective, education also has a significant role to play in guaranteeing pluralism in society. This is achieved by ensuring that the principles of neutrality and impartiality are upheld in the educational sector and by making it a sector that is receptive to and representative of all groups in society. As stated by the European Court of Human Rights, the objective of Article 2, Protocol 1 to the ECHR (right to education) is to safeguard "the possibility of pluralism in education which possibility is essential for the preservation of the 'democratic society' as conceived by the Convention".[186] This creates an obligation for States to "take care that information or knowledge included in the curriculum is conveyed in an objective, critical and pluralistic manner".[187] The principles of non-discrimination and equality and of participation all contribute to the realisation of this goal, thereby demonstrating how the purposes and effects of all three of these process-oriented rights are closely intertwined.

The greater the level of awareness of the precise content of each of the aforementioned rights, the easier it is to identify their potential synergies with the right to freedom of expression of persons belonging to minorities. A number of enquiries pursued later in this book draw on specific elements of these rights in order to elucidate important frictions and synergies involving the right to freedom of expression of persons belonging to minorities. For instance, the rights to non-discrimination/equality, participation and freedom of expression converge into a powerful synergy in respect of access to media. The principles of "availability, accessibility, acceptability and adaptability", developed in the context of primary education, retain much of their relevance for persons belonging to minorities in the context of more applied forms of education, eg. training of journalists, media literacy, etc. Another example of convergent rights involves cultural, educational, linguistic and expressive rights in the context of educational curricula and materials, or more specifically, the manner in which the lifestyles, cultures and languages of minorities are expressed therein. As the media are vital agents for the transmission of culture and language, considerations of media functionality are determinative in assessments of whether the right to freedom of expression of persons belonging to

186 *Kjeldsen, Busk Madsen & Pedersen v. Denmark*, Judgment of the European Court of Human Rights of 5 November 1976, para. 50.

187 *Ibid.*, para. 53.

minorities is effective in practice. As the question of effectiveness is tied to the suitability of various fora or media for the satisfaction of expressive needs, the centrality of cultural and linguistic rights is obvious. Finally, as regards religion: a detailed understanding of the content of the right to freedom of religion reveals that it does not extend to a right not to be offended on the basis of one's religious beliefs, thus rendering attempts to restrict the right to freedom of expression on that basis problematic.

Conclusions

Provisions in international law dealing pointedly with the right to freedom of expression of persons belonging to minorities are few and far between. This is particularly true of human rights treaties that are generalist in their thematic orientation, but also of treaties with a specialised focus. The effectiveness of relevant provisions, such as they are, is largely determined by the strength of their formulation, the clarity and detail of (official) interpretive texts and the rigour with which they are implemented, either by adjudicative or monitoring mechanisms and processes. In each of these respects, leading international instruments are to be found wanting.

Owing to the manifold sensibilities involved, formulations of minority rights in international treaties are rarely robust: the language in which they are formulated is usually heavily compromised by the deferential accommodation of relevant political and cultural sensitivities of States parties to the drafting processes. The same political sensitivities have also tended to limit the justiciability of minority rights under international treaties. In the same vein, the limiting effects of political sensitivities explain why, in specialised treaties such as the FCNM and the ECRML, the guarantees of freedom of expression extend only slightly beyond those explicitly provided for in generalist treaties.

The foregoing observations suggest that explicit provisions in international human rights treaties purporting to guarantee the right to freedom of expression for persons belonging to minorities are limited in terms of both scope and impact. Nevertheless, the generic obligation on States to ensure that all rights are secured for everyone also includes the right to freedom of expression for persons belonging to minorities. The latter obligation must therefore reinforce express provisions (however weakly worded) guaranteeing the right to freedom of expression for persons belonging to minorities to the extent necessary to render the exercise of the right effective in practice. This argument can be advanced by unparcelling the generic State duty to ensure the realisation of human rights into specific negative and positive State obligations. This allows for the introduction of greater nuance into State obligations to vouchsafe human rights. It also facilitates a more discerning approach to the right to freedom of expression for persons belonging to minorities by recognising that different expressive needs of minorities give rise to different types of duties for States, which in turn call for different levels of State action. The generic duty to ensure the realisation of the right in practice will only be discharged in a given situation when the requisite action has been taken.

Generalist human rights treaties are usefully supplemented by thematically-specific treaties, especially at the regional level. The true strength of guarantees for freedom of expression contained in treaties such as the FCNM and ECRML lies not in their actual wording (which, as noted above, are usually only minimal advances on the wording in generalist treaties), but in how they are interpreted by the treaties' designated monitoring bodies. The guarantees impose programmatic obligations on States, but the content of those obligations can be difficult to determine in the abstract. In practice, their real content must be elucidated through their operationalisation, i.e., their application to, or review in light of, concrete situations. This exercise ultimately helps to ascertain the precise nature and extent of State obligations to render the right to freedom of expression of persons belonging to minorities effective. What emerges from the monitoring exercise is a range of duties largely congruent with range of duties which will be discussed in more detail in subsequent chapters.

Although already evident to varying degrees, the systematic inclusion of the following considerations in the monitoring of the FCNM and ECRML, would greatly enhance the theoretical coherence and depth of the monitoring processes:

- recognition of particular minorities and assessment of their particular needs, based on salient group characteristics and situational specificities (Chapter 1);
- comprehensive pluralistic tolerance as an operative public value (Chapter 5);
- interplay between freedom of expression, minority rights and other human rights (Chapter 4);
- enabling environment, societal considerations, media functionality, etc. (Chapter 3).

Standard-setting work extraneous to treaty and enforcement mechanisms should also be mindful of the foregoing.

To build on the conclusions to Chapter 3: it is imperative that the adjustment of relevant theories to reflect new communicative realities also informs the interpretive and monitoring processes of international instruments containing provisions dealing with freedom of expression. The ability of authoritative adjudicatory and monitoring bodies to meet this challenge is crucial for ensuring the organic vitality of relevant instruments. It is also crucial for ensuring that the right to freedom of expression is effective in practice – not only for persons belonging to minorities, but for everyone. It is therefore welcome that the UN Human Rights Committee is finalising a new draft General Comment on Article 19, ICCPR, which is expected to reflect new realities affecting the exercise of the right to freedom of expression.[188] It is strongly recommended that the monitoring bodies of the FCNM and ECRML systematically factor considerations of media functionality and the impact of new technologies into their monitoring work. The same is true of the Committee of Ministers of the Council of Europe, and other non-treaty-based standard-setting bodies, such as ECRI. The role that could be played by the European Court of Human Rights in this connection is discussed in detail in Chapter 11.

Finally, it is useful to reiterate that the conventional theory that all human rights constitute an inter-related and interdependent whole holds enormous explanatory power. The presumptive coherence of all human rights does not, however, preclude the possibility that their actual interplay, in specific circumstances, could involve varying degrees of friction. This explains the importance of comprehensive pluralistic tolerance as an operative public value and as a guiding interpretive principle.

No matter how exhaustive an analysis of the right to freedom of expression may be, unless it contextualises the relationship of the right with other human rights, it remains inevitably incomplete. Thus, relational aspects of the right to freedom of expression and other human rights must be identified and appreciated. In this respect, the right to freedom of expression clearly intersects with the added value of the minority dimension to a number of selected rights, especially: non-discrimination/equality, participation, education, culture, religion and language. Again, comprehensive pluralistic tolerance serves as a foil to any resistance to the recognition of the minority dimension to these rights. That is the central focus of Chapter 5.

---

188 See further, Draft General Comment No. 34 (Upon completion of the first reading by the Human Rights Committee), Doc. No. CCPR/C/GC/34/CRP.6, 3 May 2011, especially paras. 11 and 14.

Part III

Regulation and Restriction of Expression to Protect Minority Rights

CHAPTER 5
THE PLURALISM *PROBLÉMATIQUE*

INTRODUCTION

The notion of pluralism was introduced at the beginning of Chapter 1 and it will now be appropriately revisited at the core of this book. Pluralism, as already noted, is a very amorphous concept. Its precise interpretation differs between ideologies, disciplines and, inevitably, individual normative texts, organisations and commentators. For instant purposes, the focus will primarily be on two distinct, but inextricably linked, types of pluralism: societal pluralism and value-pluralism. It will also note and seek to explain the inexorable gravitation of these kinds of pluralism towards notions of tolerance. Later, in Chapter 9, the analysis will turn to an applied pluralism which specifically concerns the media.

5.1 SELECTED THEORIES OF PLURALISM AND TOLERANCE

5.1.1 Pluralism

Pluralism has been described in a variety of ways. Incorrigible and a "messy reality"[1] are two of the more imaginative descriptors it has attracted. Its incorrigibility has already been commented on at the very beginning of Chapter 1, but it is useful to reiterate here that despite the negative connotations of the term, "incorrigible", it does serve to adequately describe the inherent, permanent and indelible nature of pluralism. Its incorrigibility is underscored by the ease of individual and group movement, most saliently illustrated by migration and mobility patterns, in contemporary, post-modern times. The familial and parochial anchorage of individual lifestyles, so typical in the past, is increasingly on the wane. Societal propensities towards individualisation are (at least) facilitated by developments in communications technologies.

The "messy reality" of pluralism has similarly negative connotations. It must be pointed out, however, that the messiness is not inevitable, which means that this choice of adjective is not entirely justified. It is not the reality of pluralism as such that is messy. Pluralism makes no pretensions toward coherence or orderliness; it does not purport or aspire to be unitary or systematic. Thus, any putative messiness

---

1 Nancy L. Rosenblum, "Pluralism and Self-Defense", in Nancy L. Rosenblum, Ed., *Liberalism and the Moral Life* (Massachusetts, Harvard University Press, 1989), pp. 207–226.

would more accurately describe the failure to adequately accommodate pluralism, thereby leading to messy (societal) consequences.

Michael Walzer resorts to a musical metaphor in his attempt to describe what pluralism entails: "[t]he voices are loud, the accents various, and the result is not harmony – as in the old image of pluralism as a symphony, with each group playing its own instrument (but who wrote the music?); the result is a jangling discord [...]".[2] Benjamin Barber also employs a similar musical metaphor, but one that reveals a different interpretive approach to pluralism:

> Noise is of course a concomitant of democratic politics, and the citizen has nothing to fear from a little high decibel cacophony. But the aim is harmony: the discovery of a common voice. Not unity, not voices disciplined into unison, but musical harmony in its technical meaning. [...] in music, harmony is not a matter of a single voice but of several voices, of distinct notes, which complement and support one another, creating not the ennui of unison but a pleasing plurality.[3]

It is futile to get caught up in metaphorical entanglement here. Both interpretive approaches can validly be upheld on their own terms. Indeed, in practice, pluralism can be more or less harmonious or acrimonious, depending on the structures that are in place to accommodate its different voices and notes. It is in that accommodation that societal and value-pluralism converge. It is also where the notion of tolerance begins to come into its own.

5.1.2 Tolerance

Tolerance/toleration operates at several levels – individual, group and State (at least).[4] Tolerance is a child of historical struggles for freedom of religion, but it has matured to outgrow its childhood features.[5] While still retaining great relevance for religious issues, it is nowadays readily related to a broader range of beliefs, ideas, expressions and (cultural) practices. The focus here will be less on tolerance in interpersonal relations than on tolerance between different societal groups, and especially between the State and different societal groups.

---

2 Michael Walzer, *On Toleration* (USA, Yale University Press, 1997), p. 96.

3 Benjamin R. Barber, "Liberal Democracy and the Costs of Consent", in Nancy L. Rosenblum, Ed., *Liberalism and the Moral Life*, *op. cit.*, pp. 54–68, at 65.

4 In this text, the terms are used interchangeably, although Jürgen Habermas has argued that "in English the word 'tolerance' as a form of behavior is distinguished from 'toleration,' the legal act with which a government grants more or less unrestricted permission to persons to practice their particular religion." – Jürgen Habermas, "Intolerance and discrimination", 1 *I.CON* (No. 1, 2003), pp. 2–12, at 2–3.

5 See further, *ibid.*, and Egbert Dommering, "Tolerantie, de vrijheid van meningsuiting en de Islam", in Aernout Nieuwenhuis and Wouter Hins, Eds., *Van ontvanger naar zender: opstellen aangeboden aan prof. mr. J.M. de Meij* (Amsterdam, Cramwinckel, 2003), pp. 89–108.

5.1.2(i) Notions of tolerance

Tolerance is a concept of complex, composite coloration: at least seven different shades of tolerance can be identified. These reflect, to a greater or lesser extent, the different intensities of meaning which the term conjures up for different people. Tolerance must begin with awareness; a consciousness of the other (person or opinion); but it must also go further than that. Mere awareness does not imply any degree of engagement with the other; it is still possible to damn him/her with indifference. The next shade of tolerance could therefore be said to be forbearance, which in turn leads on to a form of acceptance in the guise of non-discrimination. From this passivity, a more active form of acceptance – entailing affirmative efforts or measures – can emerge. Its manifestation is as equality. In its turn, equality is a precursor to full respect for the dignity of the other and full respect for the difference of the other.

Michael Walzer has also conceptualised a continuum of toleration, which can be summarised as: "any attitude on the continuum of resignation, indifference, stoicism, curiosity, and enthusiasm",[6] but which is preferable to cite more amply:

> Understood as an attitude or state of mind, toleration describes a number of possibilities. The first of these, which reflects the origins for religious toleration in the sixteenth and seventeenth centuries, is simply a resigned acceptance of difference for the sake of peace. People kill one another for years and years, and then, mercifully, exhaustion sets in, and we call this toleration. But we can trace a continuum of more substantive acceptances. A second possible attitude is passive, relaxed, benignly indifferent to difference: 'It takes all kinds to make a world.' A third follows from a kind of moral stoicism: a principled recognition that the 'others' have rights even if they exercise those rights in unattractive ways. A fourth expresses openness to the others; curiosity; perhaps even respect, a willingness to listen and learn. And, furthest along the continuum, there is the enthusiastic endorsement of difference [...].[7]

Rainer Forst, too, has identified a very insightful gradation of conceptions of tolerance, which move from permission, through co-existence and respect to esteem.[8] From these attempts to articulate the full span of tolerance/toleration, it is very clear that the exercise is firmly rooted in subjectivity. It can be taken as a given that all definitions of tolerance would have to comprise the notion of enduring practices or ideas to which one is personally opposed.

---

6 *Ibid.*, p. 92.

7 *Ibid.*, pp. 10–11.

8 Rainer Forst, "Toleration, justice and reason", in Catriona McKinnon & Dario Castiglione, Eds., *The culture of toleration in diverse societies: Reasonable tolerance* (Manchester & New York, Manchester University Press, 2003), pp. 71–85, at 73–75. See also for extra conceptual contextualisation, *ibid.*, at 71–73.

Tolerance is extolled because of the perceived (libertarian) values of self-restraint and of deference to the autonomy of others. But tolerance must be contained within certain limits, for everything that is tolerated contributes to the shaping of the society in which we live.[9] Otherwise, there would be a danger that what Karl Popper has termed the "paradox of tolerance" would materialise.[10] According to that paradox, unlimited tolerance leads inexorably to the disappearance of tolerance. Popper explains: "[i]f we extend unlimited tolerance even to those who are intolerant, if we are not prepared to defend a tolerant society against the onslaught of the intolerant, then the tolerant will be destroyed, and tolerance with them".[11] Thus, as noted by Umberto Eco, "to be tolerant, one must set the boundaries of the intolerable",[12] an apparently intractable challenge. What is required to meet this challenge is a certain measure of "rational intolerance"[13] or reasonable tolerance. As Rainer Forst has explained:

> Being tolerant thus means seeking reasonable justification, accepting reasonable disagreement within the limits of reciprocity and generality, and being aware of the different contexts of justification that persons are part of. It implies tolerating other beliefs within these limits by not rejecting them as unreasonable or immoral, though it does not imply a qualification of the ethical truth of one's own beliefs.[14]

It is important at this juncture to recall the allusion at the beginning of this section to beliefs, ideas, expression and (cultural) practices as various objects of tolerance. The delineation of tolerable *expression* is centrally important for minorities. Unanimity tends to prove elusive whenever efforts are made to trace the conceptual contours of the right to freedom of expression. While the existence of an impregnable inner zone of inoffensive speech is undisputed, disagreement tends to stymie attempts to fix the outer definitional demarcations of the right. Yet, as Ronald Dworkin has observed, "[I]t is the central, defining, premise of freedom of speech that the offensiveness of the ideas, or the challenge they offer to traditional ideas, cannot be a valid reason for censorship; once that premise is abandoned it is difficult to see what free speech means".[15] Thus, this intellectual gauntlet will have to be taken up before any attempts are made to accurately delineate the scope of the right

---

9 Alexander Bickel, *The Morality of Consent* (USA, Yale University Press, 1975), p. 74.

10 Karl Popper, *The Open Society and Its Enemies (Volume I: The Spell of Plato)* (New York & London, Routledge, 2005), p. 293.

11 *Ibid.*

12 Umberto Eco, "Tolerance and the Intolerable", *23 (1&2) Index on Censorship* 47 (1995), at p. 53.

13 Author's translation of "rationele intolerantie [van meningen]" – Egbert Dommering, "Tolerantie, de vrijheid van meningsuiting en de Islam", *op. cit.*, at 98.

14 Rainer Forst, "Toleration, justice and reason", *op. cit.*, at 81.

15 Ronald Dworkin, *Freedom's Law* (New York, Oxford University Press, 1996), p. 206.

to freedom of expression.[16] It has also been observed that: "[E]xtremist speech is the anvil on which our basic conception of free speech has been hammered out".[17]

Leaving aside definitional complexities and controversies for the moment,[18] it can be said that "hate speech" is generally regarded as the cut-off point between permissible and impermissible types of expression. Why should "hate speech" be tolerated? What factors should determine the level of our tolerance? "Is there", as Ursula Owen asks, "a moment where the *quantitative* consequences of hate speech change *qualitatively* the arguments about how we must deal with it?"[19] How tolerant should society be of extremist speech? The underlying concerns are reminiscent of Popper's "paradox of tolerance". Alexander Bickel picks up on these concerns in a stark manner when he warns against excessive tolerance because in an environment "[W]here nothing is unspeakable, nothing is undoable."[20]

5.1.2(ii) Normative articulations of tolerance

Whereas the attainment of tolerance is central goal common to all IGOs active in the realm of human rights protection, it is usually styled in relevant international instruments as a guiding principle rather than as an operative provision. This has much to do with the difficulty of defining such a vague concept. A notable exception in this regard is the Council of Europe's Framework Convention for the Protection of National Minorities (FCNM).[21] Article 6, FCNM, places States Parties under a programmatic obligation to promote tolerance and has led to the application of the notion in a variety of practical ways. Nevertheless, the general trend is for international conventions to refer to tolerance merely as a preambular principle, with attempts to explore its actual meaning more likely to arise in instruments that are not legally binding on States. The upshot of all of this is that in practical terms, attempts by IGO texts to explore the substance of the concept are of limited value

---

16 See T.I. Emerson, *The System of Freedom of Expression* (New York, Random House Publishing Company, 1970), p. 9: "In constructing and maintaining a system of freedom of expression the major controversies have arisen not over acceptance of the basic theory, but in attempting to fit its values and functions into a more comprehensive scheme of social goals. These issues have revolved around the question of what limitations, if any, ought to be imposed upon freedom of expression in order to reconcile that interest with other individual and social interests sought by the good society".

17 Lee C. Bollinger, *The Tolerant Society* (New York, Oxford University Press, 1989), p. 4.

18 These complexities and controversies are dealt with at length in Chapter 6, *infra*.

19 Ursula Owen, "Hate Speech – The Speech That Kills", *27(1) Index on Censorship* 32 (1998), at 37.

20 Alexander Bickel, *The Morality of Consent*, *op. cit.*, p. 73.

21 Relevant aspects of the FCNM are discussed in detail in Chapter 8.2.1, where it is presented as a major component in a case-study of the Council of Europe's comprehensive approach to "hate speech").

for the advancement of legal understandings of the meaning of tolerance. UNESCO's Declaration of Principles on Tolerance (1995), is a case in point.

The Declaration comprises a Preamble and six Articles ("Meaning of tolerance"; "State level"; "Social dimensions"; "Education", "Commitment to action" and "International Day for Tolerance"). The Preamble merits little critical analysis: as is the wont of preambular sections, it grounds the Declaration proper in relevant principles, international standards and relevant issues. As the Declaration was not drafted as a document purporting to create legal obligations for States, it is somewhat predictable that the language used in its operative part lacks the kind of clinical or technical precision that could legitimately be demanded of a legalistic text. As such, examples of loose usage of terminology will not be subjected to the rigorous analysis applied to legal texts elsewhere in this study. Rather, attention will focus on the spirit of the document and on some of its more useful aspirations and observations.

Article 1 comprises four paragraphs, which are rather disjointed. Article 1.1 is celebratory of the richness of cultural diversity in the world, "our forms of expression and ways of being human". It describes tolerance as, *inter alia*, "harmony in difference", "a moral duty" as well as "a political and legal requirement" and "the virtue that makes peace possible". These descriptions fail to elucidate the nature of tolerance, however. Article 1.2 points out that tolerance "is not concession, condescension or indulgence" but that it is "above all, an active attitude prompted by recognition of the universal human rights and fundamental freedoms of others". It also usefully points to the differentiated levels of application of tolerance, but the way it does so (by stating that tolerance "is to be exercised by individuals, groups and States") is potentially problematic. Its identification of groups as an intermediate category assumes that groups are structured units or at least that they have representative structures capable of making decisions and taking formal stances that could be characterised as tolerant. It is difficult to imagine how a group *qua* group could exercise tolerance, unless via representative decision-making structures. To hold otherwise would be to assume consensual attitudes among all group members, thereby ignoring inevitable heterogeneity within groups.

Article 1.3 links tolerance to "human rights, pluralism (including cultural pluralism), democracy and the rule of law". It then correctly states that it "involves the rejection of dogmatism and absolutism and affirms the standards set out in international human rights instruments". A puzzling inclusion in Article 1.4 is the statement that "the practice of tolerance does not mean toleration of social injustice or the abandonment or weakening of one's convictions". Perhaps the intention here was to close some perceived loophole that might have allowed tolerance to be misconstrued as condoning social injustice. The remainder of this paragraph then approximates a description of tolerance: "[i]t means that one is free to adhere to one's own convictions and accepts that others adhere to theirs. It means accepting the fact that human beings, naturally diverse in their appearance, situation, speech, behaviour and values, have the right to live in peace and to be as they are. It also means that one's views are not imposed on others".

To synopsise, Article 1, which purports to explain tolerance, does pick up on several key notions developed in the theoretical discussion, *supra*: tolerance can be considered from moral, political and legal perspectives; it is an active attitude that is respectful of the rights and differences of others; it is at home in an interrelated conceptualisation of human rights; it rejects fundamentalism; it recognises the value of the convictions and lifestyles of others.

Article 2 is concerned with one particular level of application of tolerance: the State-level. Basically, the case is made for a favourable enabling environment for the realisation of tolerance. This involves adherence to human rights norms, just laws and enforcement procedures, the availability of social and economic opportunities for everyone on a non-discriminatory basis, social and political inclusion.

The social dimensions of tolerance are explored in Article 3. It is noted that nowadays, "the globalization of the economy" and "rapidly increasing mobility, communication, integration and interdependence, large-scale migrations and displacements of populations, urbanization and changing social patterns" present additional challenges for the realisation of tolerance (Article 3.1). It recognises that tolerance can be promoted by education and the media. It reaffirms some of the socio-economic priorities of the UNESCO Declaration on Race and Racial Prejudice and advocates the use of scientific studies and networking for the advancement of international efforts to promote tolerance.

Article 4 describes education as "the most effective means of preventing intolerance" (para. 1). The importance of rights education is stressed, as is the need for education for tolerance to address the root causes of intolerance. In the same vein, education for tolerance "should aim at countering influences that lead to fear and exclusion of others, and should help young people to develop capacities for independent judgement, critical thinking and ethical reasoning" (Article 4.3). Relevant means for attaining these aims include the improvement of: "teacher training, curricula, the content of textbooks and lessons, and other educational materials including new educational technologies [...]" (Article 4.4).

In keeping with the overall mandate of UNESCO, Article 5 commits States to the promotion of "tolerance and non-violence through programmes and institutions in the fields of education, science, culture and communication". Article 6 proclaims 16 November as the annual International Day for Tolerance.

The Declaration clearly has a patchwork character: it is comprised of conceptual and practical elements as well as sociological ruminations and a measure of attention for State obligations. Its usefulness lies in its exploration of the different ramifications of tolerance and pluralism in a way that is hardly feasible within the strictures of legally-binding instruments. By tracing various strands of tolerance and pluralism, the Declaration contributes to their elucidation. The importance of conceptual clarification cannot be gainsaid given that, first of all, the concepts of tolerance and pluralism underlie and animate the entire system of human rights protection, and secondly, as already mentioned, attempts to explain the concepts simply are not forthcoming in legally-binding texts in which they are relied upon.

5.2 Towards a notion of comprehensive pluralistic tolerance

Having signalled the limited explanatory value of existing normative articulations of tolerance, the discussion will now continue with an exploration of relevant theories. The term, "pluralism", is much used and abused. It tends to be bandied about in a variety of contexts – philosophical, political and legal, to name but a few – as an *idée reçue*; with its premises usually taken for granted and seldom explained, much less, questioned. Indeed, the use of the term is bedevilled by a lack of definitional precision and consistency across international instruments and academic literature (and notoriously even within international instruments and in the works of individual authors). These inconsistencies and the despairing confusion which they have generated have been well-documented, not least in the context of freedom of expression and information (see further, Chapter 9). Some definitional decortication is therefore in order if we are to disabuse ourselves of prevalent misunderstandings arising from inconsistent applications of this term.

This exploration of "pluralism" will begin with some brief etymological musings; take a philosophical spin and then veer towards a more standard legal analysis of normative provisions in international human rights law.

In its ordinary, everyday usage, "pluralism" is a (value-)neutral term which is purely descriptive of a particular societal state – in this case, a heterogeneous one, in which different groups, often with distinctive cultural identities, espousing different moral values and leading different lifestyles, co-exist. However, at another interpretive level – the one that concerns us here – the term is vested with an additional, value-laden signification. By acquiring an evaluative moral element, the concept becomes more purposive; more normative. As such, it has alternately been referred to as "moral pluralism", "value-pluralism",[22] and, with superior clarity, "a pluralism of values".[23]

Thus conceived and interpreted, the notion of "pluralism" expands laterally in the direction of the adjacent notion of "tolerance". Taken to its logical ends, this lateral expansion ultimately leads to a kind of "pluralistic tolerance" (also referred to elsewhere as "pluralist toleration"[24] – but meaning essentially the same thing) – one of the most powerful animating principles of the European Convention on Human Rights. Time and again, the European Court of Human Rights has averred that [societal] pluralism has been hard-won over the ages and that it is indissociable with democratic life. In the same vein, it has consistently held that pluralism, along with its kindred concepts of tolerance and broadmindedness, constitutes one of the essential hallmarks of democratic society. The Court's case-law concerning Articles 9, 10 and 11 of the Convention has proved very fertile ground for the cultivation of "pluralistic tolerance".

The notion of pluralistic tolerance does not harbour any ambition to dissolve inter-community differences; rather, as is argued *infra*, its primary concern is to build and consolidate awareness and understanding of inter-community differences. In terms of democratic political theory, it could therefore be characterised as "integrationist" – as opposed to "assimilationist". Although connotatively sceptical, there is a relevant kern of validity in Frank Michelman's observations that pluralism involves "the deep mistrust of people's capacities to communicate *persuasively* to one another their diverse normative experiences: of needs and rights, values and interests, and, more broadly, interpretations of the world", and that it "doubts or denies our ability to communicate such material in ways that move each other's views on disputed normative issues toward felt (not merely strategic) agreement without deception, coercion, or other manipulation".[25] If the reconciliation of particular worldviews is a goal that is conceded to be ultimately unattainable, the default objective becomes the creation of structures and processes which provide for, or at least facilitate, the presentation and discussion of pertinent differences. The airing of such differences in democratic, discursive fora is a laudable societal goal in itself: the democratic merits of the structural and procedural facilitation of

---

22 Joseph Raz, *The Morality of Freedom* (New York, Oxford University Press, 1986), pp. 395 *et seq.*

23 Isaiah Berlin, "Two Concepts of Liberty", in Isaiah Berlin, *Liberty* (Ed. Henry Hardy) (Oxford University Press), pp. 166–217, at 217.

24 Joseph Raz, "Free Expression and Personal Identification", 11 *Oxford Journal of Legal Studies* (No. 3, 1991), pp. 303–324, at 322.

25 Frank Michelman, "Law's Republic", 97 *Yale Law Journal* 1493, at 1507 (1988). Also quoted in Kent Greenawalt, *Fighting Words: Individuals, Communities, and Liberties of Speech* (Princeton, Princeton University Press, 1995), p. 128.

disagreement are considerable, if often under-appreciated.[26] As one expert has noted, "debates can become pitched conflicts, whose constant recurrence indicates a lack of problem-solving capacity in the current deliberative framework".[27]

5.2.1 Minimum moral and ideological commonality

It is of crucial importance to insist that all of the foregoing assumes the (prior) existence of minimal foundations of ideological commonality, without which democratic society simply cannot exist.[28] There need not be agreement on all substantive values, but at least on the terms of democratic engagement; an *a priori* commitment by all communities to the animating philosophies and support structures of democratic society. There are many theoretical ways of describing this anterior commitment to the implied terms and conditions of democratic engagement. One could, for example, take a "social contract" style of approach, after Rousseau, or explore the niceties of other variations on the civil compact theme. Although academic literature on this topic is rich and varied and grapples with many problematic questions,[29] it need not detain us unduly here. The main point to be stressed is that tolerance expresses "a recognition of common membership that is deeper than these conflicts [i.e., serious conflicts – at the deepest level – about the nature and direction of society], a recognition of others as just as entitled as we are to contribute to the definition of our society".[30] This concern for "participatory parity" is regularly voiced by other experts.[31] As James Bohman has argued, "toleration in a deliberative democracy is based on the commitment to the principle of political egalitarianism: that is, the equal access to political influence of all citizens over all decisions that affect them".[32]

---

26 See further on this point: John Keane, *The Media and Democracy* (UK, Polity Press, 1991), pp. 176, 178 and 179.

27 James Bohman, "Reflexive toleration in a deliberative democracy", in Catriona McKinnon & Dario Castiglione, Eds., *The culture of toleration in diverse societies: Reasonable tolerance*, *op. cit.*, pp. 111–131, at 127.

28 See also, in this connection, Peter Dahlgren, *Television and the Public Sphere: Citizenship, Democracy and the Media* (London, SAGE Publications, 1995), pp. 20 and 141.

29 For example, firstly, is it necessary to (formally) ascertain group consent to be bound by the tenets of democracy be ascertained? How could it be ascertained? Would it have to be expressed actively (and if so on a once-off basis or regularly) or could it be inferred (and if so, from positive actions or merely passive behaviour)?

30 T.M. Scanlon, "The difficulty of tolerance", in T.M. Scanlon, *The Difficulty of Tolerance: Essays in Political Philosophy* (United Kingdom, Cambridge University Press, 2003), pp. 187–201, at 193.

31 Nancy Fraser, "Recognition without ethics?", in Catriona McKinnon & Dario Castiglione, Eds., *The culture of toleration in diverse societies: Reasonable tolerance*, *op. cit.*, pp. 86–108, at 95.

32 (footnote omitted) James Bohman, "Reflexive toleration in a deliberative democracy", *op. cit.*, at 118.

In any society, occasional incidents can strike raw community nerves, cause hurt and clamouring for vengeance. One must resign oneself to the inevitability of such occasional flash-points for society (while, of course, striving to minimise their incidence). One strategy for pre-empting the occurrence of such flash-points is to examine the underlying reasons for the "rawness" of inter-community nerves in the first place.

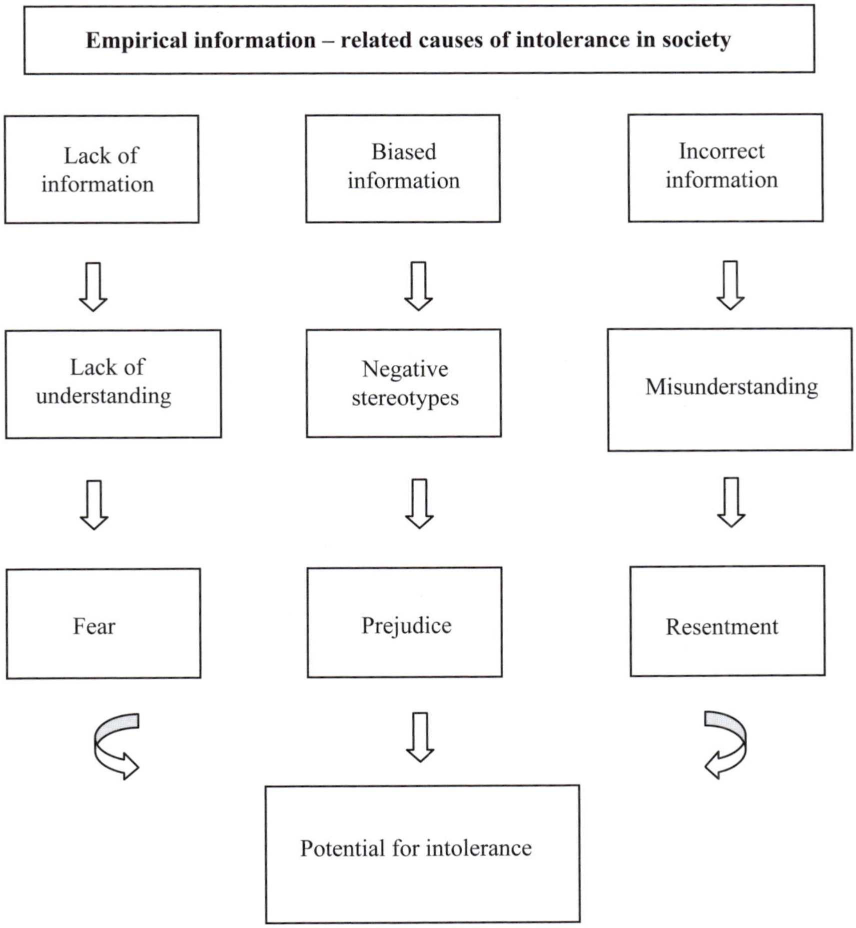

As discussed at the beginning of Chapter 1, individuals and groups exhibit intuitive uneasiness/distrust/dislike of that which is foreign and unfamiliar to them; that which lies outside the circle of their own experience. In philosophy and literature, the irruption of the alien is often discussed in terms of otherness. In religion, the appelation has traditionally been more emotionally charged and (ironically, perhaps) decidedly less charitable. Instinctive distrust of otherness or difference is one of the many reasons for intercommunity stand-offishness and/or hostility. This distrust feeds on lack of information about and consequent comprehension of, the other. The above diagram seeks to empirically set out a range of information-related causes of intolerance.

This diagram illustrates the importance in pluralistic democratic society of the adequacy and availability/accessibility of information and ideas in terms of their quantity, objectivity and accuracy. In this respect, questions of presentation and representation are extremely important. From the perspective of persons belonging to minorities, problematic practices in this regard include: "tokenism; negative stereotyping; unrealistic and simplistic portrayals of their community; negative or non-existent images of their countries or areas of origin".[33] Engagement with these practices and their underlying issues pursuant to international instruments will be examined in detail in Chapter 6.

The arguments, observations and speculations canvassed above all appear to gravitate towards, and indeed precipitate, the conclusion that greater inter-community communication would help to reduce tensions and to foster intercultural and intergroup understanding and tolerance. This preliminary conclusion – or better, working principle – is consistent with Eric Barendt's conceptualisation of freedom of expression as not only containing a set of rights, but also reflecting important public, societal values, especially pluralistic tolerance.[34] T.M. Scanlon goes even further by arguing that a commitment to freedom of expression actually implies "certain institutional arrangements as crucial means to those goals".[35]

If the notion of tolerance espoused here is to be in any way meaningful, then it has to necessarily be stronger than mere indifference to the identities, creeds and worldviews of other groups in society.[36] On such a reading, tolerance has to be conscious, informed and considered. This can only be achieved when there is effective communication and engagement between individuals and groups,[37] and as Lee C. Bollinger has noted, "free speech stands symbolically as the gateway to social intercourse".[38] Dialogical interaction across community lines provides various groups with opportunities to articulate and advance their identities, values and viewpoints, as well as commensurate opportunities for hearing and listening to

33 Andrea Millwood Hargrave, Ed., *Multicultural Broadcasting: concept and reality*, Report for the British Broadcasting Corporation, Broadcasting Standards Commission, Independent Television Commission and Radio Authority, November 2002, p. 2.

34 Eric Barendt, *Freedom of Speech* (2nd Edition) (Oxford, Oxford University Press, 2005), p. 36.

35 T.M. Scanlon, "The difficulty of tolerance", *op. cit.*, p. 189.

36 See further, s. 2.1.2(i), *supra*, for a more detailed discussion of the various shades of meaning ascribed to "tolerance".

37 See further, Eric Barendt, *Freedom of Speech* (2nd Edition), *op. cit.*, p. 36.

38 Lee C. Bollinger, *The Tolerant Society*, *op. cit.*, p. 238.

descriptions of the identities, values and viewpoints of other groups (which are often unfamiliar to them). Exchange and reciprocity of perspective are central here; the notion of tolerance involved is necessarily "deliberative".[39] Styled as such, tolerance is "connected to communication" in different ways: "an attitude toward the reason of others"; "an attitude toward the speakers", and a "communicative attitude toward the *perspectives* of those to whom one is attempting to justify a decision in deliberation".[40]

While undoubtedly of importance in instances of individualised communciation, the realisation of inter-community communication is also of considerable importance for society in general. Thus, a compelling case can be made for pursuing this objective in structural and systematic terms.[41] Furthermore, as posited by Jacob T. Levy: "[w]hether through the evolved rules or explicit agreement", different cultural communities "must develop a framework for interaction – the interactions of their members as well as the interactions of their traditions and norms and rules".[42] The significance of Levy's point lies in the fact that it looks beyond the specifically verbal preoccupation of most analyses of structural intercommunity dialogue. It probes the dialogical character of deeper cultural values and their non-verbal expression. Such an approach acknowledges that communicative channels are merely part of more pervasive societal structures. Bhikhu Parekh advocates a similarly coherent and comprehensive approach: intercommunity dialogue would be structured by what he terms "operative public values" (see further, Chapter 3.1.1), and there is a need to find "new institutional forums" in which such dialogue could be conducted.[43]

5.2.2 Pluralistic tolerance, democracy and freedom of expression

One of the most compelling arguments in favour of minority rights is the need to safeguard democratic society from what has been termed the "tyranny of the majority", a term first introduced into the lexicon of political theory by Alexis de Tocqueville.[44] The notion requires little explanation: it involves unchecked or insufficiently checked majoritarian tendencies and preferences which tend to ride roughshod over minority values and interests. Morally speaking, the legitimacy of majority rule is contingent on the existence of mechanisms allowing for the effective participation of minorities in deliberative political processes. Only such inclusive

39 See generally: James Bohman, "Deliberative Toleration", 31 *Political Theory* (No. 6, December 2003), pp. 757–779.

40 James Bohman, "Reflexive toleration in a deliberative democracy", *op. cit.*, at 120.

41 This point will be developed significantly, *infra*.

42 Jacob T. Levy, *The Multiculturalism of Fear* (New York, Oxford University Press, 2000), p. 41.

43 Bhikhu Parekh, *Rethinking Multiculturalism: Cultural Diversity and Political Theory* (Second Edition) (New York, Palgrave Macmillan, 2006), p. 306.

44 In his two-volume work, *Democracy in America* (1835, 1840).

participatory practices can provide "the moral basis for binding everyone to the rule ultimately adopted".[45] This point can easily be extended beyond decision-making and also applied to the legitimation of of ideas generally through effective participation in public debate. The key consideration is, as John Dewey has noted, that ideas be given the opportunity "to spread and become the possession of the multitude".[46] This is of clear relevance for information about minority groups as well as their views and interests. The underlying concern is for "the methods and conditions of debate, discussion and persuasion".[47]

But the workings of democracy can be distorted or subverted at the other extreme of the spectrum too. Unbridled contractarianism could, for instance, lead to vocal and influential minorities dictating in large measure the affairs of state.[48] Some minority groups might – just like their majoritarian counterparts – try to use the apparatus of state to extend the application of their values society-wide. One must also reckon with what has been termed the "displaced majority syndrome", a belief among dominant societal groups "that too much attention is being paid to the needs of ethnic communities, which are becoming more assertive".[49] Such tendencies, too, go against the grain of truly democratic ideals. As Isaiah Berlin has put it, "truth and justice" are not "the monopoly of the martyrs and the minorities" and society should "strive to remain fair even to the big battalions".[50]

Fears of majority tyranny or minority diktat are not confined to the political arena. Given the far-reaching influence of the media on public deliberation and the formation of public opinion, these fears also spill over into the media sector. Power in the media sector can yield significant influence in the political sector. The skewing of public debate is not at far remove from the skewing of political decision-making (see further, Chapter 3). This proximity between official and non-official institutions in the public sphere has already been underlined.

Thomas Emerson's understated fourth rationale for freedom of expression[51] – which has eloquently been described by another commentator as "a means of maintaining

---

45 Frederick Schauer, *Free speech: a philosophical enquiry* (Cambridge, etc., Cambridge University Press, 1982), p. 42.

46 John Dewey, *The Public and its Problems* (Chicago, The Swallow Press, Inc., 1954), p. 208.

47 *Ibid.* He describes the "essential need" for "the improvement of the methods and conditions of debate, discussion and persuasion" as "*the* problem of the public" (italics per original).

48 See further in this connection: Albert Weale, "Toleration, individual differences and respect for persons", in John Horton & Susan Mendus, Eds., *Aspects of Toleration* (London & New York, Metheun, 1985), pp. 16–35, at 23 *et seq.*

49 Roger Eatwell, "Why are Fascism and Racism Reviving in Western Europe?", 65 *Political Quarterly* (No. 3, July/September 1994), pp. 313–325, at 319.

50 Isaiah Berlin, "Historical Inevitability", in Isaiah Berlin, *Liberty*, *op. cit.*, pp. 94–165, at 151.

51 The three other rationales for freedom of expression put forward by Emerson describe freedom of expression as being essential: "as a means of assuring individual self-fulfillment"; as a

societal homeostasis and social cohesion"[52] – deserves special mention at this juncture. It explains the crucial importance of freedom of expression in the triangular relationship linking pluralistic tolerance, democracy and freedom of expression. He explicates:

> [...] freedom of expression is a method of achieving a more adaptable and hence a more stable community, of maintaining the precarious balance between healthy cleavage and necessary consensus. This follows because suppression of discussion makes a rational judgment impossible, substituting force for reason; because suppression promotes inflexibility and stultification, preventing society from adjusting to changing circumstances or developing new ideas; and because suppression conceals the real problems confronting a society, diverting public attention from the critical issues. At the same time the process of open discussion promotes greater cohesion in a society because people are more ready to accept decisions that go against them if they have a part in the decision-making process. [...] Freedom of expression thus provides a framework in which the conflict necessary to the progress of a society can take place without destroying the society. It is an essential mechanism for maintaining the balance between stability and change.[53]

John Rawls also places great store by "the stability of just institutions", reasoning that such "stability means that when tendencies to injustice arise other forces will be called into play that work to preserve the justice of the whole arrangement".[54] In other words, when democracy and justice enjoy firm institutional and societal anchorage, the dangers posed by anti-democratic forces can be more readily absorbed by the system. The strength of the democratic organism produces its own antibodies against anti-democratic infection, without needing to have recourse to more heavy-handed measures such as the antibiotics of coercive or repressive legislation.

5.3 Comprehensive pluralistic tolerance in practice

The purpose of this sub-section is to present a short selection of different instances in which the European Court of Human Rights has engaged with the notions of

---

"process for advancing knowledge and discovering truth", and "to provide for participation in decision making by all members of society": Thomas I. Emerson, *The System of Freedom of Expression*, *op. cit.*, pp. 6–7.

52 Thomas David Jones, *Human Rights: Group Defamation, Freedom of Expression and the Law of Nations* (The Netherlands, Martinus Nijhoff Publishers, 1998), pp. 65–66.

53 Thomas I. Emerson, *The System of Freedom of Expression*, *op. cit.*, p. 7. See also, for a fuller exposition of this rationale for freedom of expression, Thomas I. Emerson, *Toward a General Theory of the First Amendment* (New York, Random House, 1966).

54 John Rawls, *A Theory of Justice (Revised Edition)* (USA, Harvard University Press, 1999), p. 192.

pluralism and tolerance.[55] The selected examples demonstrate that the theoretical discussion in the foregoing sub-sections is consonant with actual judicial practice. Further examples of such engagement with these concepts are recurrent throughout Chapter 8.

Just as pluralism – and by extension, democracy – presuppose the absence of discrimination and the existence of effective equality, so too are they predicated on the existence of tolerance. Pluralism demands a certain balancing of majority/minority interests, leading to the tolerance and democratic accommodation of minority interests. This has been recognised by the European Court of Human Rights:

> Although individual interests must on occasion be subordinated to those of a group, democracy does not simply mean that the views of a majority must always prevail: a balance must be achieved which ensures the fair and proper treatment of minorities and avoids any abuse of a dominant position.[56]

The Court sees pluralism and tolerance very much as being in the service of effective political democracy:

> in a democratic society even small and informal campaign groups [...] must be able to carry on their activities effectively and [...] there exists a strong public interest in enabling such groups and individuals outside the mainstream to contribute to the public debate by disseminating information and ideas on matters of general public interest [...][57]

The precepts of pluralism and tolerance are also of central relevance to other rights and interests that are themselves crucial for the assertion of minority identities, such as culture and language, and religion. As regards participation, culture and language, the Court has noted that:

> While in the context of Article 11 ["Freedom of assembly and association"] the Court has often referred to the essential role played by political parties in ensuring pluralism and democracy, associations formed for other purposes, including those protecting cultural or spiritual heritage, pursuing various socio-economic aims, proclaiming or teaching religion, seeking an ethnic identity or asserting a minority

55 See further in this connection, Aernout Nieuwenhuis, "The Concept of Pluralism in the Case-Law of the European Court of Human Rights", *European Constitutional Law Review*, 2007–3, pp. 367–384.

56 *Young, James & Webster v. United Kingdom*, Judgment of the European Court of Human Rights of 13 August 1981, Series A No. 44 p. 25, para. 63; *Chassagnou & Others v. France*, Judgment of the European Court of Human Rights of 29 April 1999, para. 112.

57 *Steel & Morris v. United Kingdom*, Judgment of the European Court of Human Rights (Fourth Section) of 15 February 2005, para. 89.

> consciousness, are also important to the proper functioning of democracy. For pluralism is also built on the genuine recognition of, and respect for, diversity and the dynamics of cultural traditions, ethnic and cultural identities, religious beliefs, artistic, literary and socio-economic ideas and concepts. The harmonious interaction of persons and groups with varied identities is essential for achieving social cohesion. It is only natural that, where a civil society functions in a healthy manner, the participation of citizens in the democratic process is to a large extent achieved through belonging to associations in which they may integrate with each other and pursue common objectives collectively.[58]

The foundational importance of freedom of religion for democratic society cannot be gainsaid. The Court has repeatedly held that the "pluralism indissociable from a democratic society, which has been dearly won over the centuries depends on it".[59] However, solutions as to how potentially competing interests ought to be balanced are not always self-evident. Pluralism entails diversity and divergence, which in turn mean that the balancing exercise can often involve a certain amount of antagonism.[60] To continue with the example of freedom of religion:

> The Court reiterates that the autonomous existence of religious communities is indispensable for pluralism in a democratic society. While it may be necessary for the State to take action to reconcile the interests of the various religions and religious groups that coexist in a democratic society, the State has a duty to remain neutral and impartial in exercising its regulatory power and in its relations with the various religions, denominations and beliefs. What is at stake here is the preservation of pluralism and the proper functioning of democracy, one of the principal characteristics of which is the possibility it offers of resolving a country's problems through dialogue, even when they are irksome.[61]

Inherent in the protection and promotion of public debate and dialogue (especially concerning "irksome" issues or problems) is the risk that falsehoods will be floated and malice propagated. However, this is all part of the democratic experiment;[62] the

---

58 *Gorzelik & others v. Poland*, Judgment of the European Court of Human Rights (Grand Chamber) of 17 February 2004, para. 92.

59 *Hasan & Chaush v. Bulgaria*, Judgment of the European Court of Human Rights of 26 October 2000, para. 60.

60 *Kokkinakis v. Greece*, Judgment of the European Court of Human Rights of 19 April 1993, para. 33; *Metropolitan Church of Bessarabia and others v. Moldova*, Judgment of the European Court of Human Rights of 13 December 2001, para. 123; *Hasan & Chaush v. Bulgaria*, *op. cit.*, para. 78; *Serif v. Greece*, Judgment of the European Court of Human Rights of 14 December 1999, para. 49; *Agga v. Greece*, Judgment of the European Court of Human Rights of 17 October 2002, paras. 53, 56; *Manoussakis v. Greece*, Judgment of the European Court of Human Rights of 29 August 1996, para. 44; *Supreme Holy Council of the Muslim Community v. Bulgaria*, Judgment of the European Court of Human Rights of 16 December 2004, para. 93.

61 *Supreme Holy Council of the Muslim Community v. Bulgaria*, *op. cit.*, para. 93.

62 Paraphrasal of Holmes, J., dissenting, in *Abrams v US*, 250 US 616 (1919), at 630, when he described both the US Constitutional enterprise and life itself as being experimental.

cut and thrust of debate that is free, robust and uninhibited.[63] As stated in the *Handyside* case, information and ideas which "offend, shock or disturb the State or any sector of the population" must be allowed to circulate in order to safeguard the "pluralism, tolerance and broadmindedness" that underpin "democratic society".[64] Thus, the catch-cry of consumers, "let the buyer beware", is equally *de rigueur* in the domain of freedom of expression and information. The poet e.e. cummings has astutely extended the application of this slogan: "democ/ra(caveat emptor)cy".[65]

Conclusions

Pluralism and tolerance are complex concepts. It is very important to engage with their conceptual complexity in order to clarify precisely what is involved when they are invoked in international instruments. Such invocations tend to occur as preambular rather than operative provisions. As such, they serve as guiding principles which help to shape the interpretive context of human rights generally. The two concepts are brought together in this analysis and described as pluralistic tolerance, which in turn is presented as an "operative public value". To style pluralistic tolerance as an "operative public value" is to acknowledge the diverse practical implications of its conceptual complexity. It is also to articulate the actual approach of the European Court of Human Rights to pluralistic tolerance in democratic societies. This approach involves an appreciation of the societal benefits of vigorous debate, assured by effective communicative rights, equitable deliberative structures and processes, and viable communicative opportunities, including for persons belonging to minorities. This approach also involves engagement with minorities and their rights at the societal level and not in a compartmentalised fashion. Minorities are in a dialectical and dialogical relationship with other groups in society and the validation of their rights and interests needs to be realised in that broader, integrated perspective.

It is the very essence of pluralistic tolerance that the expression of differences in values, beliefs and opinions be tolerated – subject to certain limits elaborated in accordance with the abuse of rights doctrine. Pluralistic tolerance must not be understood as a passive attitude, but as the active recognition of the need for democratic society to foster the expression of difference. It is rendered "comprehensive" when it is meaningfully applied across the whole spectrum of human rights. A key purpose of pluralistic tolerance is to prevent the curbing or

63 Paraphrasal of the United States Supreme Court in *New York Times Co. v. Sullivan*, 376 U.S. 254 (1964).

64 *Handyside v. the United Kingdom*, Judgment of the European Court of Human Rights of 7 December 1976, Series A, No. 24, para. 49.

65 E.e. cummings, "a salesman is an it that stinks Excuse", in G.J. Firmage, Ed., *E.E. CUMMINGS COMPLETE POEMS 1904–1962* (New York, Liveright, 1994), p. 549.

chilling of public debate. Intolerant attitudes, or even genuine (but intensely subjective) grievances, should not be allowed to inflate restrictions on the right to freedom of expression that are enshrined in international law and (narrowly) interpreted by officially-designated authoritative bodies. Pluralistic tolerance must therefore serve as a brake on any illegitimate erosion of the right to freedom of expression. At the same time, it must also uphold other rights (eg. non-discrimination, participation, etc.) in order to ensure that any expression that does not fall under the limitations permitted by international law, but is nevertheless considered objectionable or offensive by discrete groups in society, can be vigorously contested on equitable terms of engagement.

The scrutiny and explication of the above considerations provided in this Chapter aim to offset the incantatory nature of invocations of pluralism and tolerance in international instruments. The analysis reveals that the theories underlying relevant provisions in international instruments are more multi-dimensional, and their implications more far-reaching, than is often appreciated. As an operative public value, the converged notion of pluralistic tolerance generally needs to be addressed in a more serious and focused way than heretofore. This demands renewed reflection on effective strategies for upholding and operationalising relevant values. It is particularly pertinent to enquire about the nature and extent of the obligations that such operationalisation would entail for States authorities and also for third parties, especially the media. Through its elucidation of the notion of pluralistic tolerance, this Chapter paves the way for a detailed examination of these questions in the following chapters.

Chapter 6
Delineating the limits of permissible expression under International Human Rights Law

Introduction

Having introduced the main international and European legal standards on freedom of expression in Chapter 4, and set out their general scope, the purpose of this chapter is to give an overview of States' relevant negative obligations. In other words, it will examine the extent to which international and European legal standards oblige States to limit the right to freedom of expression. More specifically, the focus will be on permissible limitations on the right to freedom of expression under international and European law which can serve to protect the rights of persons belonging to minorities. Inevitably, then, this chapter aims to assess the *main* provisions of international and European law that frame the struggle against racist ("hate") speech.[1] It will consider the implementation or development of a number of those provisions, as well as the actual interplay between them. Relevant non-legal standards will be considered to the extent that they complete the broader normative picture.

6.1 Global instruments: asymmetries and conundrums

A number of United Nations' treaties home in on various aspects of the right to freedom of expression and the imperative of combating racism. A selection of relevant provisions from those treaties will now be examined, commencing with the Genocide Convention because of the protection it seeks to secure for the *existence* of minorities.

6.1.1 Genocide Convention

Article II of the Convention on the Prevention and Punishment of the Crime of Genocide (the Genocide Convention), 1948, defines "genocide" as:

---

1 See also: Sandra Coliver, Ed., *Striking a Balance: Hate Speech, Freedom of Expression and Non-discrimination* (United Kingdom, ARTICLE 19/University of Essex, 1992); Stephanie Farrior, "Molding the Matrix: The Historical and Theoretical Foundations of International Law Concerning Hate Speech", 14 Berkeley J. Int'l L. 1; Tarlach McGonagle, "Wresting (Racial) Equality from Tolerance of Hate Speech", (2001) 23 *Dublin University Law Journal* (ns) 21, pp. 21–54.

> … any of the following acts committed with intent to destroy, in whole or in part, a national, ethnical, racial or religious group, as such:
> (a) Killing members of the group;
> (b) Causing serious bodily or mental harm to members of the group;
> (c) Deliberately inflicting on the group conditions of life calculated to bring about its physical destruction in whole or in part;
> (d) Imposing measures intended to prevent births within the group;
> (e) Forcibly transferring children of the group to another group.

Article III then lists the following five acts as being "punishable" under the Convention: "(a) genocide [as defined in Article II]; (b) conspiracy to commit genocide; (c) direct and public incitement to commit genocide; (d) attempt to commit genocide; (e) complicity in genocide".

Of the punishable acts, "direct and public incitement to commit genocide" is clearly the most relevant to freedom of expression. As noted by the International Criminal Tribunal for Rwanda (ICTR) in its *Akayesu* judgment, "[p]erhaps the most famous conviction for incitement to commit crimes of international dimension was that of Julius Streicher by the Nuremberg Tribunal for the virulently anti-Semitic articles which he had published in his weekly newspaper *Der Stürmer*".[2] Before proceeding to dissect the formula, "direct and public incitement to commit genocide" and its potential for curbing freedom of expression in the name of protecting minority rights, a few general remarks concerning, first, incitement, and second, the Genocide Convention, would be apposite.

In his dissenting opinion in *Gitlow v. New York*,[3] Justice Oliver Wendell Holmes famously asserted that "[e]very idea is an incitement".[4] While he may have overstated the point, the quip certainly does contain a grain of truth. Incitement does depend on the intensity with which one seeks to cause a desired result to be achieved via the agency of a third party. This is borne out by Holmes' subsequent comments in that same Dissent: "[every idea] offers itself for belief and if believed it is acted on unless some other belief outweighs it or some failure of energy stifles

2 *The Prosecutor v. Jean-Paul Akayesu*, Case No. ICTR-96–4-T, ICTR (Chamber I) Judgment of 2 September 1998, para. 550. It should be noted that Streicher's conviction predated the elaboration of the Genocide Convention and was based on the notion of war crimes as described in the London Charter of the International Military Tribunal (which set out the laws and procedures governing the Nuremberg Trials), 1945.

3 268 US 652 (1925); Justice Brandeis joined in Justice Holmes' dissenting opinion. In this case, the US Supreme Court upheld the constitutionality of a New York statute under which Benjamin Gitlow had been convicted of criminal anarchy for printing, publishing and knowingly circulating political writings calling, *inter alia*, for proletarian action to accomplish the Communist Revolution. The writings in question also favoured the replacement of the existing political order with a "proletarian dictatorship" and "the complete structure of Communist Socialism".

4 *Ibid.*, at 673.

the movement at its birth. The only difference between the expression of an opinion and an incitement in the narrower sense is the speaker's enthusiasm for the result".[5]

In keeping with Justice Holmes' assertion that "every idea is an incitement", notions such as advocacy and incitement could usefully be conceptualised as two points on a continuum of encouragement or persuasion.

Ordinarily, incitement is considered to be a so-called inchoate or preliminary offence (other examples of such offences are attempt and conspiracy).[6] The rationale for the offence is described by one leading academic commentator as being that "someone who instigates or encourages another person to commit an offence should be liable to conviction for those acts of incitement, both because he is culpable for trying to cause a crime and because such liability is a step towards crime prevention".[7] Furthermore, the "offence of incitement is committed irrespective of whether the person(s) incited respond by committing the offence concerned".[8] Incitement is therefore an offence distinct from whatever offence it promotes. Indeed, whenever incitement proves successful and the person incited carries out the substantive offence intended by the inciter, the latter is then properly regarded as an accomplice to the substantive offence, which also leads to criminal liability (albeit of a different nature).

As with almost all other types of crime,[9] incitement comprises a conduct element (the *actus reus*) and a fault element (the *mens rea*); the former involves "some form of encouragement or persuasion to commit an offence",[10] while the latter involves intent that the substantive offence be committed. The nature and implications of both elements of the offence will be given separate consideration, *infra*.

Andrew Ashworth endorses the tendency to include inchoate offences within the criminal law, "both on the consequentialist ground of the prevention of harm and on the 'desert' ground that the defendant has not merely formed a culpable and harm-directed mental attitude but has also manifested it".[11] He continues:

> However, shifting the focus to the occurrence or non-occurrence of harm attributes too much significance to matters of chance. This may be appropriate in a system of compensation, but not in a system of public censure such as the criminal law. There is a respectable conception of fairness, connected to principles of individual

5 *Ibid.*

6 Andrew Ashworth, *Principles of Criminal Law* (Second Edition), (Oxford, Clarendon Press, 1995), p. 442.

7 *Ibid.*, p. 462.

8 *Ibid.*

9 With the notable exception of strict-liability offences, which do not require *mens rea*.

10 *Ibid.*

11 *Ibid.*, p. 468.

> autonomy, that favours penalizing people who tried and failed – even if, because of some fact unknown to them, their attempt was bound to fail. The moral difference between those who fail and those who succeed in causing harm is too slender to justify exempting the former from criminal liability.[12]

The preventive and punitive features of the offence – thus sketched – argue persuasively for the appropriateness of its inclusion among the punishable acts enumerated in the Genocide Convention.

The Convention has not undergone the same organic growth as subsequent treaties elaborated under the auspices of the United Nations. Its failure to establish its own implementation machinery (notwithstanding the possibility for States to have recourse to the International Court of Justice under Article 9 of the Convention) has meant that it has not benefited from the interpretive development normally achieved through continuous monitoring scrutiny or adjudicative decisions. Similarly, unlike other treaties, it has no designated body to offer interpretive guidance, eg. by means of general comments, or to offer legal and technical advice to States regarding their implementation of the Convention's provisions. However, the direct incorporation of the Article III definition of genocide into the Statutes of the International Criminal Tribunal for the Former Yugoslavia (ICTY) (Article 4.3) and the ICTR (Article 2.3) has re-actualised the definition of genocide in international law.[13] The ICTR, in particular, has made important contributions to contemporary interpretations of "direct and public incitement to commit genocide". For instance, the Tribunal has endorsed the International Law Commission's characterisation of "public" incitement as "communicating the call for criminal action to a number of individuals in a public place or to members of the general public at large", by technical means of mass communication, such as by radio or television.[14] As for the definitional criterion of directness, the Tribunal again followed the International Law Commission, stating that "[t]he 'direct' element of incitement implies that the incitement assume a direct form and specifically provoke another to engage in a criminal act, and that more than mere vague or indirect suggestion goes to constitute direct incitement".[15] The requirement of directness does not rule out the possibility that incitement can be coded or veiled, as long as the intended meaning of the

---

12 *Ibid.*, pp. 468–469.

13 Article 4.3, Statute of the ICTY, as amended; Article 2.3, Statute of the ICTR, as amended; Rome Statute establishing International Criminal Court.

14 *Ibid.*, fn. 126; *The Prosecutor v. Ferdinand Nahimana, Jean-Bosco Barayagwiza & Hassan Ngeze* (the Media case), Case No. ICTR-99–52-T, ICTR (Trial Chamber I) Judgment of 3 December 2003, para. 1011. See also the judgment of the Appeals Chamber in the same case: *Ferdinand Nahimana, Jean-Bosco Barayagwiza & Hassan Ngeze v. The Prosecutor*, Case No. ICTR-99–52-A, ICTR (Appeals Chamber), Judgment of 28 November 2007.

15 The *Akayesu* case, *op. cit.*, para. 557; the Media case, *op. cit.*, para. 1011.

message is clear to its target audience. "Camouflaged incitement"[16] or "oblique incitement"[17] can be devastatingly potent, as is clearly illustrated by the transcripts of, for example, *The Media Case*. Although writing from the context of the *Brandenburg* test (see further, *infra*),[18] David Crump has compiled a test based on "eight evidentiary factors for determining whether an utterance is incitement",[19] notwithstanding its camouflaged appearance:

1. The express words or symbols uttered;
2. The pattern of the utterance, including any parts that both the speaker and the audience could be expected to understand in a sense different from the ordinary;
3. The context, including the medium, the audience, and the surrounding communications;
4. The predictability and anticipated seriousness of unlawful results, and whether they actually occurred;
5. The extent of the speaker's knowledge or reckless disregard of the likelihood of violent results;
6. The availability of alternate means of expressing a similar message, without encouragement of violence;
7. The inclusion of disclaimers, and
8. Whether the utterance has "serious literary, political, or scientific value" (or, alternatively, whether it is "speech on a matter of public concern").[20]

Crump's test is useful, but it would require some tweaking before it could be applied to international law provisions. As already noted, whether actual events occur as a result of the incitement (Factor 4) is not relevant to the commission of the offence. In Factor 8, the first formulation is based on First Amendment jurisprudence and is probably too parochial for wider international application, whereas the parenthetical alternative is closer to well-established concepts in the case-law of other international interpretative and adjudicative bodies, such as the European Court of Human Rights. Crump's test is one particular illustration of how carefully-devised methodologies for a case-by-case approach to "camouflaged incitement" (or, indeed, other kinds of contested expression) can unpack particular utterances as well as their illocutionary projects and determine whether, all things considered, they can legitimately be restricted. At the very least, adjudicative bodies should not be fixated on certain or particular words or formulae.

---

16 David Crump, "Camouflaged Incitement: Freedom of Speech, Communicative Torts, and the Borderland of the Brandenburg Test", 29 Ga. L. Rev. 1 (1994).

17 Larry Alexander, "Incitement and Freedom of Speech", in David Kretzmer and F. Kershman Hazan, Eds., *Freedom of Speech and Incitement Against Democracy* (The Netherlands, Kluwer Law International, 2000), pp. 101–118, at p. 106.

18 *Brandenburg v. Ohio*, 395 US 444 (1969).

19 David Crump, "Camouflaged Incitement: Freedom of Speech, Communicative Torts, and the Borderland of the Brandenburg Test", *op. cit.*, at 52.

20 *Ibid.*, at 54–69.

The relevant *mens rea* required for the crime of direct and public incitement has been held by the ICTR to involve: "the intent to directly prompt or provoke another to commit genocide. It implies a desire on the part of the perpetrator to create by his actions a particular state of mind necessary to commit such a crime in the minds of the person(s) he is so engaging. That is to say that the person who is inciting to commit genocide must have himself the specific intent to commit genocide [...]".[21] It is frequently pointed out that the definitional requirement of specific intent can, in practice, be difficult to prove – certainly in comparison to a test based on a more objective central criterion. Nevertheless, the subjectivity of the intent is an important and distinguishing feature of the Convention.[22] It is generally accepted that courts should be entitled to "infer the necessary intent from sufficient evidence",[23] and this view has indeed been borne out in practice.[24] The notion of intent was preferred to that of "motive" by the drafters of the Convention.[25]

It has been suggested that "the Convention's most conspicuous weakness is [perhaps] that it insufficiently formulates preventive measures" and that to meaningfully address that weakness, relevant "international short-term and long-term action would need to relate to different stages in the evolution of a genocidal process – anticipation of its happening; early warning of its commencement; and action to be taken at the outset of or during a genocide itself to stop it".[26] Any monitoring or early-warning work carried out on the basis of the Genocide Convention would necessarily have to reckon with "hate speech" as a contributory factor to genocidal events. It is widely recognised that various kinds of incendiary or inflammatory speech (commonly referred to as "hate speech") targeting specific groups which do not amount to "direct and public incitement to commit genocide" can nevertheless be instrumental in exacerbating inter-group tensions and thereby

---

21 The *Akayesu* case, *op. cit.*, para. 560; the Media case, *op. cit.*, para. 1012.

22 Nicodème Ruhashyankiko, Special Rapporteur, *Study of the Question of the Prevention and Punishment of the Crime of Genocide*, Commission on Human Rights, Sub-Commission on Prevention of Discrimination and Protection of Minorities, Doc. E/CN.4/Sub.2/416, 4 July 1978, para. 100; Josef L. Kunz, "The United Nations Convention on Genocide", 43 *The American Journal of International Law* (No. 4, October 1949), pp. 738–746, at p. 743.

23 Benjamin Whitaker, *Revised and updated report on the question of the prevention and punishment of the crime of genocide*, Commission on Human Rights, Sub-Commission on Prevention of Discrimination and Protection of Minorities, Doc. E/CN.4/Sub.2/1985/6, 2 July 1985, para. 39.

24 The *Akayesu* case, *op. cit.*

25 Benjamin Whitaker, *Revised and updated report on the question of the prevention and punishment of the crime of genocide*, *op. cit.*, para. 38; Nicodème Ruhashyankiko, Special Rapporteur, *Study of the Question of the Prevention and Punishment of the Crime of Genocide*, *op. cit.*, paras. 101–106.

26 Benjamin Whitaker, *Revised and updated report on the question of the prevention and punishment of the crime of genocide*, *op. cit.* (see also the Corrigendum thereto: UN Doc. No. E/CN.4/Sub.2/1985/6/Corr.1), para. 78.

creating the kind of social climate which is conducive to the perpetration of genocidal activities.

The term "hate speech" is commonly used in international politico-legal discourse, despite the fact that it is not authoritatively defined in any binding international treaty. As a consequence, the precise ambit of the term is uncertain (see further, *infra*). Whereas direct and public incitement to commit genocide could be considered a (very extreme) form of "hate speech", the converse is not necessarily true, i.e., it cannot be assumed that all forms of "hate speech" amount to direct and public incitement to commit genocide. A very exacting definitional threshold must be crossed for hate speech to constitute the latter. Nevertheless, hate speech remains of great concern in the context of the Convention because of its potential contribution to the creation of a climate of hatred in which genocidal activities are more likely to be carried out. William Schabas has referred to hate propaganda (which is also a definitional notch above ordinary hate speech) as the Convention's "blind spot".[27] This line of thinking prompts a number of important considerations, concerning, in particular: the reasons for the original omission of hate propaganda from the Genocide Convention; the extent to which other international legal instruments compensate for that omission, and the extent to which the potential negative effects of that omission are being overcome by current-day efforts to anticipate and prevent genocidal tendencies.

During the drafting of the Convention, an amendment was proposed that would have included in Article III a sub-paragraph rendering punishable as acts of genocide: "All forms of public propaganda (press, radio, cinema, etc.) aimed at inciting racial, national or religious enmities or hatreds or at provoking the commission of acts of genocide".[28] The arguments deployed against the proposed amendment prevailed.[29] First, it was submitted that propaganda for genocide would in virtually all cases also amount to incitement to genocide, so the enumeration of a separate offence of making propaganda for genocide would be superfluous. Second, it was submitted that the punishment of propaganda "aimed at inciting racial, national or religious enmities or hatreds" would go beyond the remit of the Convention insofar as "the intention to destroy a specific group, which was an essential part of the definition of genocide, would be absent".[30] The standard

27 William A. Schabas, "Hate Speech in Rwanda: The Road to Genocide", (2000) 46 McGill L.J. 141, at 162.

28 Amendment (A/C.6/215/Rev.1), cited in Nicodème Ruhashyankiko, Special Rapporteur, *Study of the Question of the Prevention and Punishment of the Crime of Genocide*, *op. cit.*, para. 117. Ruhashyankiko also notes that the Secretary-General's draft (E/447) "contained provisions whereby propaganda in favour of genocide was declared punishable" – *ibid.*

29 For a description of the drafting process concerning this particular item, see William Schabas, "Hate Speech in Rwanda: The Road to Genocide", *op. cit.*, at 163–167.

30 Nicodème Ruhashyankiko, Special Rapporteur, *Study of the Question of the Prevention and Punishment of the Crime of Genocide*, *op. cit.*, para. 119.

argument that measures seeking to punish propaganda might unduly encroach on freedom of expression was also invoked.

Although Schabas has identified the failure of the Genocide Convention to prohibit hate propaganda as its blind spot, he does readily concede that this failure has been corrected somewhat "by subsequent international human rights instruments dealing with racial discrimination".[31] In fact, international human rights instruments comprise a wide panoply of provisions – both generalistic and dealing specifically with racial discrimination – which extensively address hate speech (see *infra*). As such, there are ample measures available to the international community for dealing with the broader phenomenon of hate speech, and if they are used properly, i.e., coherently/synergically – and perhaps also imaginatively, there should be little ground for fears that hate speech which is unpunishable under the Genocide Convention would not be detected and dealt with under other international instruments.

To the extent that hate speech/propaganda is a relevant focus for early-warning mechanisms, the analysis needs to be both cautious and sophisticated. As noted by Benjamin Whitaker, any preventive international action "would need to relate to different stages in the evolution of a genocidal process – anticipation of its happening; early warning of its commencement; and action to be taken at the outset of or during a genocide itself to stop it".[32] In this connection, it is imperative not only to condemn the causes of genocidal activities, but to be analytical of various processes of causation too.[33] The causal relationship between speech and action is complex and contentious at the best of times, but it seems intuitively sound to assume that the nature of that relationship (whatever it may be) will vary depending on the stage of the evolving genocidal process. Catharine MacKinnon sums up many of the complexities involved in her praise for the approach of the ICTR in *the Media Case*:[34] "[i]nstead of trying to shoehorn the relation between expression and action into a single formulation, the Tribunal, sticking close to the factual record, recognized the many dynamic connections between word and deed that a complex social conflagration like genocide expectably generates".[35] MacKinnon also perspicaciously notes that the relevance of "[t]he strong but subtle principles articulated in *The Media Case*"[36] reaches beyond both the case at hand and the

31 William Schabas, "Hate Speech in Rwanda: The Road to Genocide", *op. cit.*, at pp. 162–163.

32 Benjamin Whitaker, *Revised and updated report on the question of the prevention and punishment of the crime of genocide*, *op. cit.*, para. 78.

33 *Ibid.*, para. 80.

34 Note: at the time of writing, the full text of the Appeal Judgment in this case was not publicly available.

35 Catharine A. MacKinnon, "Prosecutor v. Nahimana, Barayagwiza, & Ngeze. Case No. ICTR 99–52-T", 98 *The American Journal of International Law* (No. 2, April 2004), pp. 325–330, at 329.

36 *Ibid.*, at 330.

exceptional nature of (pre- or potentially) genocidal contexts. The principles in question are "applicable to many legal areas of speech regulation"[37] and are well-suited to the purposes of day-to-day adjudication and application.

The UN Committee on the Elimination of Racial Discrimination (CERD) has declared its "determination to provide the Special Adviser on the Prevention of Genocide (SAPG) with timely and relevant information on laws, policies and practices that may indicate systematic or systemic discrimination based on race, colour, descent, or national or ethnic origin which may potentially result in violent conflict and genocide".[38] For that purpose, it undertook "to develop a special set of indicators related to genocide, including the cultural and historic roots of genocide and the importance of recognizing the multicultural dimension of most societies".[39]

CERD then proceeded to develop a set of "key indicators" which could "serve as a tool for the Committee, when examining the situation in a State party under one of its procedures, to assess the existence of factors known to be important components of situations leading to conflict and genocide".[40] It explained its proposed approach as follows: "[i]f one or more of the following indicators are present, this should be clearly stated in the concluding observations or decision, and the Committee shall recommend that the State party report, within a fixed deadline, to the Committee under the follow-up procedure on what it intends to do to ameliorate the situation".[41] The collective scope of the indicators is broad, with discrete focuses of attention including: the lack of legislative and institutional frameworks to prevent racial discrimination and provide redress for victims; "[s]ystematic official denial of the existence of particular distinct groups"; systematic exclusion from participation in public life; serious patterns of targeted violence which is ethnically-motivated. The indicators focusing specifically on matters with implications for freedom of expression are the following:

> 5. Grossly biased versions of historical events in school textbooks and other educational materials as well as celebration of historical events that exacerbate tensions between groups and peoples.
>
> 8. Systematic and widespread use and acceptance of speech or propaganda promoting hatred and/or inciting violence against minority groups, particularly in the media.

---

37 *Ibid.*

38 Declaration on the prevention of genocide, Committee on the Elimination of Racial Discrimination, 17 October 2005, CERD/C/66/1, para. 3.

39 *Ibid.*

40 Decision on follow-up to the declaration on the prevention of genocide: indicators of patterns of systematic and massive racial discrimination, Committee on the Elimination of Racial Discrimination, 14 October 2005, CERD/C/67/1.

41 *Ibid.*

9. Grave statements by political leaders/prominent people that express support for affirmation of superiority of a race or an ethnic group, dehumanize and demonize minorities, or condone or justify violence against a minority.

The underlying concerns of these focuses, *viz.* the portrayal of historical events (which in turn raises broader questions about collective memory), the corrosive impact of hateful propaganda (and broader questions concerning the role and responsibilities of the media as regards the same), and the far-reaching effects of hateful statements by public figures and the legitimacy conferred on those statements by the status of those figures, are recurrent in debates concerning freedom of expression and minorities. They will be considered in greater depth, *infra*. In anticipation of that discussion, it suffices here to note that the importance of these concerns stems not only from their identification as possible indicators of situations which could degenerate into conflict or genocide. Equally, they are good markers of situations in which the objective of comprehensive pluralistic tolerance (discussed in Chapter 5) is not being attained. As such, these concerns routinely inform the monitoring process under the Framework Convention for the Protection of National Minorities, as will be demonstrated in Chapter 8.2.1. Similarly, the UN Independent Expert on minority issues has also adverted to the relevance of such indicators and stressed their importance for protecting the physical integrity of minorities (which she has identified as one of her main areas of concern).[42] CERD's already-mentioned intention to act as an early-warning mechanism for the SAPG also implies that office's engagement with the practical application of the indicators. The convergence of different institutional interests in the CERD Guidelines is clear evidence of their value as a tool for wide application (i.e., by other interested parties and not just in the formal context for which they were developed by CERD).[43]

Useful as these indicators are for monitoring and early-warning purposes, they should not be considered in isolation: their usefulness and importance would be greatly overstated if they were not assessed in light of the presence of other indicators and the overall contextual situation. CERD has been very forthright in its recognition of the risk that the reliability of its indicators could be compromised if their assessment was not sufficiently contextually embedded:

---

42 Specific Groups and Individuals: Minorities, Report of the independent expert on minority issues, Gay McDougall, Commission on Human Rights (62nd session, 6 January 2006), E/CN.4/2006/74, para. 71. See also in this connection, *ibid.*, paras. 50 (where the Independent Expert welcomes the CERD initiatives on genocide-prevention, discussed *supra*) and 22 (where she sets out the "four broad areas of concern relating to minorities around the world, based on the [UN] Declaration on the Rights of Minorities and other relevant international standards relating to minority rights").

43 See further: William A. Schabas, *Preventing Genocide and Mass Killing: The Challenge for the United Nations* (London, Minority Rights Group International, 2006), p. 20.

As these indicators may be present in States not moving towards violence or genocide, the assessment of their significance for the purpose of predicting genocide or violence against identifiable racial, ethnic or religious groups should be supplemented by consideration of the following subset of general indicators:

1. Prior history of genocide or violence against a group.
2. Policy or practice of impunity.
3. Existence of proactive communities abroad fostering extremism and/or providing arms.
4. Presence of external mitigating factors such as the United Nations or other recognized invited third parties.[44]

In order to summarise the essential points of the foregoing discussion, a number of penultimate overall observations will now be marshalled. First, as suggested by its full title, the Genocide Convention pursues the twin objectives of prevention and punishment of genocide. Measures seeking to advance its preventive remit – both tried and theoretical – necessarily have implications for other human rights, not least freedom of expression. The most obvious illustration of this involves offsetting the presumptive causal connection between incitement and virulent forms of "hate speech" and genocide against the presumptive interference with the right to freedom of expression that regulation of such forms of speech entails. The foregoing discussion has shown that this conundrum is not intractable, but that considerable circumspection is required for its resolution. Interpretive clarity as regards key legal terminology is indispensable, as is sensitive, contextualised analysis of impugned speech. Various specialised human rights mechanisms have undertaken formal action designed to prevent genocide; much of this action has been concerted and achieved in a spirit of cooperation, thereby demonstrating the conceptual proximity of the mandates in question and the interdependence of the rights they protect. Insofar as these measures deal with issues relating to freedom of expression, they have by and large tended to emphasise the positive, non-prescriptive role that media can play in this regard.

The only significant exception to this tendency is a practice known as "information intervention".[45] The term is perhaps deceptively euphemistic. The coiner of the term, Jamie Metzl, describes it as "a soft form of humanitarian intervention"[46] or a form of intermediate action "between neglect and armed intervention".[47] Its essence is the use by the international community of "information tactics" in an "aggressive

44 CERD Decision on follow-up to the declaration on the prevention of genocide: indicators of patterns of systematic and massive racial discrimination, *op.cit.*, p. 3.

45 Jamie F. Metzl, "Information Intervention: When Switching Channels Isn't Enough", 76 *Foreign Affairs* (No. 6, November/December 1997), pp. 15–20.

46 Mark Thompson, "Defining Information Intervention: An Interview with Jamie Metzl", in Monroe E. Price & Mark Thompson, Eds., *Forging Peace: Intervention, Human Rights and the Management of Media Space* (Edinburgh, Edinburgh University Press, 2002), pp. 41–65, at 41.

47 Jamie F. Metzl, "Information Intervention: When Switching Channels Isn't Enough", *op. cit.*, at 20.

manner" against a particular State or States "when this is justified on strong human rights grounds".[48] Given the involvement of the international community and the implications such action would have for the sovereignty of a targeted State, the legitimacy of "information intervention" must be assessed in light of relevant provisions of the UN Charter.

As set out in Article 2(1) of the Charter, the UN is "based on the principle of the sovereign equality of all its Members". Article 2(7) firms up this principle by stating:

> Nothing contained in the present Charter shall authorize the United Nations to intervene in matters which are essentially within the domestic jurisdiction of any state or shall require the Members to submit such matters to settlement under the present Charter; but this principle shall not prejudice the application of enforcement measures under Chapter VII.

Chapter VII, for its part, is entitled: "Action with respect to threats to the peace, breaches of the peace, and acts of aggression". Article 39 states that the Security Council "shall determine the existence of any threat to the peace, breach of the peace, or act of aggression and shall make recommendations, or decide what measures shall be taken in accordance with Articles 41 and 42, to maintain or restore international peace and security". Articles 41 and 42 read as follows:

> Article 41
> The Security Council may decide what measures not involving the use of armed force are to be employed to give effect to its decisions, and it may call upon the Members of the United Nations to apply such measures. These may include complete or partial interruption of economic relations and of rail, sea, air, postal, telegraphic, radio, and other means of communication, and the severance of diplomatic relations.
>
> Article 42
> Should the Security Council consider that measures provided for in Article 41 would be inadequate or have proved to be inadequate, it may take such action by air, sea, or land forces as may be necessary to maintain or restore international peace and security. Such action may include demonstrations, blockade, and other operations by air, sea, or land forces of Members of the United Nations.

These are the main pillars of the legal framework within which "information intervention" would have to manoeuvre.[49] The sponsorship of "information

---

48 Mark Thompson, "Defining Information Intervention: An Interview with Jamie Metzl", *op. cit.*, at 41.

49 See further in this connection: Alexander C. Dale, "Countering Hate Messages that Lead to Violence: The United Nations's Chapter VII Authority to Use Radio Jamming to Halt Incendiary Broadcasts", 11 Duke J. of Comp. & Int'l L. 109 (Fall – Winter 2001).

intervention" by Metzl and others is clearly the product of disillusionment at how politicised, selective and ultimately ineffective the UN Security Council's track record in humanitarian intervention has been. "Information intervention" is therefore presented as an alternative, but less radical, last-ditch attempt by the international community to prevent the outbreak of massive violence or genocide in a particular State or States. These are not measures which the present author would advocate lightly. They should only be countenanced in the most exceptional circumstances (eg., after the triggering of recognised early-warning mechanisms of legitimate international bodies with a mandate for genocide-prevention, or the concurrence of findings of a number of reputable independent expert bodies) and even then only after the most stringent legal safeguards have been met. Given the wide discretion of the Security Council for deciding what constitutes a "threat to the peace, breach of the peace, or act of aggression", it is vital to insist on the need for stringent objective safeguards. Metzl himself is also alert to the need for circumspection in this regard; after spelling out the importance of maintaining "relative consensus"[50] about the international definition[s] of incitement and the interpretation of Article 20, ICCPR (see further, *infra*), he states:

> As a precaution, there should be a strong presumption against jamming, with a narrowly defined and clearly delineated exception for broadcasts that constitute incitement where a genocidal act appears imminent. This determination could appropriately be made by the Security Council but might also be delegated to an international commission of political and human rights experts.[51]

In the past, techniques of information intervention have tended to focus on radio-jamming, a practice that has been defined as the deliberate interference with a broadcast "by transmitting *terrible noise* on the same frequency in order to make reception impossible".[52] Needless to say, other existing definitions offer greater technological precision than "terrible noise"; for example: "the deliberate emission of electromagnetic (EM) radiation to reduce or prevent hostile use of a portion of the EM spectrum".[53] This can involve introducing a "disrupting signal (causing just noise or 'fuzz') or an overriding signal (a different broadcast) into a specific frequency on the electromagnetic spectrum".[54] A further distinction can be made

---

50 Jamie F. Metzl, "Rwandan Genocide and the International Law of Radio Jamming", 91 *The American Journal of International Law* (No. 4, October 1997), pp. 628–651, at 648.

51 (footnote omitted) *Ibid.*, at p. 649.

52 (emphasis added) S. Leinwoll, cited in Arie Bloed & Pascale C.A.E. de Wouters d'Oplinter, "Jamming of Foreign Radio Broadcasts", in Arie Bloed and Pieter van Dijk, Eds., *Essays on Human Rights in the Helsinki Process* (Dordrecht, Martinus Nijhoff Publishers, 1985), pp. 163–180, at 163.

53 Don Herskovitz, cited in Alexander C. Dale, "Countering Hate Messages that Lead to Violence: The United Nations's Chapter VII Authority to Use Radio Jamming to Halt Incendiary Broadcasts", *op. cit.*, at 115.

54 *Ibid.*

between two further types of jamming. "Spot jamming" is a "pinpoint technique of jamming" whereby a receiver is used "to find the signal frequency transmitting the incendiary broadcasts and then tune a jamming signal to that frequency".[55] "Barrage jamming", on the other hand, involves the simultaneous jamming of a large number of frequencies, thereby preventing targeted broadcasters from circumventing the jamming by frequency-hopping. Each of these jamming techniques have their pros and cons, in terms of costs, expediency and efficiency. Barrage jamming is clearly the more invasive, but it also has the potential to affect broadcasts that are not incendiary by virtue of its blanketing tendencies.

Although to date, the theory and practice of information intervention have primarily concentrated on radio-jamming, this would not preclude the application of qualitatively comparable measures to the Internet in the future. Indeed, examples/ allegations of such Internet-based measures have already surfaced in various quarters.[56] Such measures would conceivably include denial-of-service (DOS) attacks, which can take various forms. Two general forms of DOS attacks have been identified: (i) "Force the victim computer(s) to reset or consume its resources such that it can no longer provide its intended service", and (ii) "Obstruct the communication media between the intended users and the victim so that they can no longer communicate adequately".[57] Examples of DOS attacks include:

- attempts to "flood" a network, thereby preventing legitimate network traffic;
- attempt to disrupt a server by sending more requests than it can possibly handle, thereby preventing access to a service;
- attempts to prevent a particular individual from accessing a service;
- attempts to disrupt service to a specific system or person.[58]

Finally, as regards technical details of DOS attacks, they take effect through the:

1. consumption of computational resources, such as bandwidth, disk space, or CPU time;
2. disruption of configuration information, such as routing information;
3. disruption of physical network components.[59]

---

55 *Ibid.*

56 See, for example, Ian Traynor, "Russia accused of unleashing cyberwar to disable Estonia", *The Guardian*, 17 May 2007. Similar accusations have been made against Russia in respect of Georgia; see further: John Markoff, "Before the Gunfire, Cyberattacks", *The New York Times*, 12 August 2008.

57 "Denial-of-service attack", *Wikipedia*, consulted on 12 February 2007.

58 *Ibid.*

59 *Ibid.*

In order to ensure the effective implementation of information intervention in practice, Metzl has recommended the establishment, under the auspices of the UN, of "an independent information intervention unit with three primary areas of responsibility: monitoring, peace broadcasting, and, in extreme cases, jamming radio and television broadcasts".[60] He envisages it as a "well-trained and equipped rapid information response team to address and challenge media activities in a given country when those activities are inciting people to commit mass abuses whose realization appears imminent".[61]

Finally, another issue with implications for freedom of expression concerns the status of genocide-denial. Under the Genocide Convention, this putative offence is not included among the enumerated "punishable" acts. Given that the prohibition of Holocaust denial is recognised as a legitimate restriction on freedom of expression, as guaranteed under international law, it is certainly a question deserving further exploration whether the scope of the Genocide Convention could or should be extended to include a more generic offence genocide-denial. This question is highly topical, both at international and national levels (see further, Chapter 7.3.1).[62] As will be seen below, only one international, legally-binding treaty expressly countenances the criminalisation of the denial of genocides other than/as well as the Holocaust.[63]

6.1.2 International Bill of Rights

The Universal Declaration of Human Rights, 1948, as well as being imbued with the importance of human dignity and non-discrimination, contains a specific Article devoted to the right to freedom of expression, Article 19: "Everyone has the right to freedom of opinion and expression; this right includes freedom to hold opinions without interference and to seek, receive and impart information and ideas through any media and regardless of frontiers". This right was subsequently enshrined – and indeed fleshed out – in Article 19 of the International Covenant on Civil and Political Rights (ICCPR), which reads:

---

60 Jamie F. Metzl, "Information Intervention: When Switching Channels Isn't Enough", *op. cit.*, at 17.

61 Jamie F. Metzl, "Rwandan Genocide and the International Law of Radio Jamming", *op. cit.*, at 649.

62 This is evidenced by the controversy generated by the passing at first reading by the French Assemblée Nationale of a Bill to prohibit the calling into question of the Armenian genocide (Proposition de Loi tendant à réprimer la contestation de l'existence du génocide arménien), 12 October 2006.

63 Additional Protocol to the Convention on Cybercrime, concerning the criminalisation of acts of a racist and xenophobic nature committed through computer systems: see, in particular, Article 6.

1. Everyone shall have the right to hold opinions without interference.
2. Everyone shall have the right to freedom of expression; this right shall include freedom to seek, receive and impart information and ideas of all kinds, regardless of frontiers, either orally, in writing or in print, in the form of art, or through any other media of his choice.
3. The exercise of the rights provided for in paragraph 2 of this article carries with it special duties and responsibilities. It may therefore be subject to certain restrictions, but these shall only be such as are provided by law and are necessary:
   (a) For respect of the rights or reputations of others;
   (b) For the protection of national security or of public order (ordre public), or of public health or morals.

The only restrictions on the right countenanced by this article are those which are "provided by law and are necessary: (a) For respect of the rights or reputations of others; (b) For the protection of national security or of public order (ordre public), or of public health or morals". Nevertheless, Article 19 must be read in conjunction with Article 20, which further trammels the scope of the right. It reads:

1. Any propaganda for war shall be prohibited by law.
2. Any advocacy of national, racial or religious hatred that constitutes incitement to discrimination, hostility or violence shall be prohibited by law.

Article 20(2) is crucial for the purposes of the present analysis, but before dispensing with Article 20(1) as being of lesser relevance to our central concerns, it is useful to note that it contains yet two more instances of definitionally problematic terms, i.e., "war" and "propaganda". To repeat a point made in respect of "hate speech", the term, "propaganda", is sufficiently broad to cover a range of different types of expression which vary in terms of the harmfulness of their content, the sophistication of their presentation and strategies of dissemination and the gravity of their effects. In order to avoid undue encroachment on the right to freedom of expression, it is necessary that States exercise great caution when circumscribing the ambit of the term in legislative prohibitions at the national level. This concern featured prominently in debates during the drafting process.[64]

Turning, then, to Article 20(2), the obligation imposed on States can be essentialised as the adoption of the necessary legislative measures to prohibit the advocacy of national, racial or religious hatred when – and this is the crucial threshold – such advocacy amounts to incitement to discrimination, hostility or violence. As already explained in Chapter 6.1.1, advocacy must attain a certain degree of intensity before it can be considered to amount to incitement. It was also pointed out in that

64 Marc J. Bossuyt, *Guide to the "Travaux Préparatoires" of the International Covenant on Civil and Political Rights* (Dordrecht, etc., Martinus Nijhoff Publishers, 1987), pp. 393–394.

discussion that the nature of incitement is qualified by what is being incited. In the context of Article 20(2), "[i]ncitement to 'discrimination' and 'violence' are legally defined (or definable) concepts".[65] The same cannot be said of "hostility" and this has led to serious interpretive difficulties.

Moreover, the term, "hatred", is also very difficult to define in legal terms, although one commendable attempt to do so describes hatred as "an active dislike, a feeling of antipathy or enmity connected with a disposition to injure".[66] Semantically, hatred is more intense than hostility, but the latter term (or at least some lexical variants thereof, eg. hostilities) does have a strong connotation of war. If Manfred Nowak's insistence that Article 20 is unique among other substantive provisions of the ICCPR in terms of its clear responsiveness to the atrocities carried out by the Nazis and the general horrors of World War II[67] is to be taken seriously, the association of hostility with belligerent (inter-State) behaviour should not be ignored. However, other – more conventional – attempts to distinguish the meanings of "hatred" and "hostility" have also been put forward. Karl Josef Partsch, for instance, has suggested that "perhaps 'hatred' has a strong subjective element while 'hostility' suggests an attitude displayed externally".[68]

Unfortunately, neither the *travaux préparatoires* nor the UN Human Rights Committee's General Comment No. 11 on Article 20 (discussed *infra*) offer much guidance for deciphering the precise meaning of the terms and thereby unlocking the nature of their relationship. Interpretive difficulties concerning the qualifiers "national, racial or religious" did arise in the drafting of Article 20, but followed similar patterns to those in other comparable treaties and were not quite as problematic as hostility and hatred (and war and propaganda). Legal interpretive difficulties aside, these notions can also prove philosophically problematic. For instance, Michael Banton, drawing on the work of Karl Popper, rhetorically asks: "[i]f observable behaviour is the outward form of some inward condition, how can one be certain about the nature of that condition?"[69] Affective states cannot be detected or defined with medical objectivity; the determination is therefore necessarily subjective.

---

65 Karl Josef Partsch, "Freedom of Conscience and Expression, and Political Freedoms", in Louis Henkin, Ed., *The International Bill of Rights: The Covenant on Civil and Political Rights* (New York, Columbia University Press, 1981), pp. 209–245, at 228.

66 Karl Josef Partsch, "Racial Speech and Human Rights: Article 4 of the Convention on the Elimination of All Forms of Racial Discrimination", in Sandra Coliver, Ed., *Striking a Balance: Hate Speech, Freedom of Expression and Non-discrimination*, *op. cit.*, pp. 21–28, at 26.

67 Manfred Nowak, *U.N. Covenant on Civil and Political Rights – CCPR Commentary* (2nd revised edition) (Kehl, N.P. Engel, 2005), pp. 468 and 475.

68 Karl Josef Partsch, "Freedom of Conscience and Expression, and Political Freedoms", *op. cit.*, at 228.

69 Michael Banton, *International Action Against Racial Discrimination* (Oxford, Clarendon Press, 1996), p. 53.

It is rarely disputed that Articles 19 and 20, ICCPR, are closely related. One leading commentator has even referred to Article 20 as being "practically a fourth paragraph to Article 19 and has to be read in close connection with the preceding article"[70] and another has written that it should be "understood as a *lex specialis* to" Article 19.[71] Indeed, during the drafting of the ICCPR, the draft article that ultimately became Article 20 was realigned so that it would immediately follow Article 19, thereby emphasising the contiguity of the two articles.[72] However, it is important to stress that the outcome of the drafting process was only achieved after much intense and divisive debate about the implications that restrictions such as those under discussion would be likely to have for the exercise of the right to freedom of expression. The intensity of States Parties' ideological *prises de position* on this question can also be gauged from the tenor of the numerous reservations and interpretive declarations entered in respect of Article 20 upon ratification of the Covenant.[73] Similar ideological intensity flared up in the UN Human Rights Committee (HRC) during the preparation of its General Comment on Article 20 and appeared to jeopardise the practice of adopting consensual General Comments before necessary compromises were eventually brokered.[74]

It is noteworthy that Article 20, unlike other substantive articles in the ICCPR, does not set out a right as such. Instead, it sets out further restrictions on other rights (most notably the right to freedom of expression), thereby prompting Nowak to label it "an alien element in the system of the Covenant".[75] It provides for further restrictions by explicitly requiring that certain conduct "shall be prohibited by law".[76] It does not prescribe "what kind of law" should assure prohibition at the national level and it would therefore appear that States enjoy some measure of discretion as to their choice of legislation.[77] It *is* clear, however, that some kind of

---

70 Karl Josef Partsch, "Freedom of Conscience and Expression, and Political Freedoms", *op. cit.*, at 227.

71 Manfred Nowak, *U.N. Covenant on Civil and Political Rights – CCPR Commentary* (2nd revised edition), *op. cit.*, p. 477.

72 Article 26 of the Human Rights Commission's draft of 1954 had originally been positioned at the very end of the substantive provisions contained in the draft text. See further: Manfred Nowak, *U.N. Covenant on Civil and Political Rights – CCPR Commentary* (2nd revised edition), *op. cit.*, p. 470; Marc Bossuyt, *Guide to the "Travaux Préparatoires" of the International Covenant on Civil and Political Rights*, *op. cit.*, p. 398.

73 Eg. Denmark, Finland, Iceland, Ireland, the Netherlands, Sweden and Switzerland.

74 For an illuminating discussion of the preparation of General Comment, see: Dominic McGoldrick, *The Human Rights Committee: Its Role in the Development of the International Covenant on Civil and Political Rights* (Second Edition) (Oxford, Clarendon Press, 1994), pp. 484–490.

75 Manfred Nowak, *U.N. Covenant on Civil and Political Rights – CCPR Commentary* (2nd revised edition), *op. cit.*, p. 468.

76 See further, Dominic McGoldrick, *The Human Rights Committee*, *op. cit.*, p. 480.

77 Karl Josef Partsch, "Freedom of Conscience and Expression, and Political Freedoms", *op. cit.*, at 228.

law is required and that educational and purely administrative measures will not suffice to discharge the obligation of prohibition *by law.* The extent of the obligations created under Article 20 is often misinterpreted. It is therefore necessary to spell out that while Article 20(2) requires States to *prohibit* by law hatred that incites to discrimination, hostility or violence, it does not necessarily require States to *criminalise* such hatred.[78] This point, far from being of mere academic interest, has very practical consequences, as will be demonstrated in the discussion of State obligations under Article 4, ICERD, *infra.*

General Comment No. 11

The UN HRC has attempted to elucidate the relationship between Articles 19 and 20 by declaring the required prohibitions enumerated in the latter to be "fully compatible" with the right to freedom of expression and indicating that such prohibitions are subsumed into the "special duties and responsibilities" upon which the exercise of the right (as *per* Article 19) is contingent.[79] It has also stated that "[f] or article 20 to become fully effective there ought to be a law making it clear that propaganda and advocacy as described therein are contrary to public policy and providing for an appropriate sanction in case of violation".[80]

A number of apposite analytical remarks should be made in relation to Article 20. First, its provisions are mandatory and "States parties are obliged to adopt the necessary legislative measures prohibiting the actions referred to therein".[81] Second, as pointed out by the UN Human Rights Committee's General Comment No. 11, "these required prohibitions are fully compatible with the right to freedom of expression as contained in article 19".[82] Moreover, as also pointed out by the same General Comment, there is an umbilical link between these required prohibitions and the "special duties and responsibilities" that inhere in (the exercise of) the right to freedom of expression.[83] Fourth, there is a transfrontier dimension to Article 20(2), as it covers "any advocacy of national, racial or religious hatred that constitutes incitement to discrimination, hostility or violence, whether such propaganda or advocacy has aims which are internal or external to the State concerned".[84]

---

78 *Ibid.*, at 229. Draft versions of the article would have obliged States to make incitement to racial hatred a crime, but such an approach did not prevail: Manfred Nowak, *U.N. Covenant on Civil and Political Rights – CCPR Commentary* (2nd revised edition), *op. cit.*, p. 470.

79 UN Human Rights Committee, General Comment No. 11 – Prohibition of propaganda for war and inciting national, racial or religious hatred (Article 20), 29 July 1983, para. 2.

80 *Ibid.*

81 *Ibid.*, para. 1.

82 *Ibid.*, para. 2.

83 *Ibid.*, para. 2.

84 *Ibid.*, para. 2.

In its draft General Comment No. 34 on freedom of opinion and expression,[85] the HRC revisits the relationship between Articles 19 and 20. It reaffirms that both articles are "compatible with and complement each other".[86] It clarifies that the acts addressed by Article 20 "are of such an extreme nature that they would all be subject to restriction" pursuant to Article 19(3).[87] Therefore, "a limitation that is justified on the basis of [A]rticle 20 must also comply with" Article 19(3).[88] The draft General Comment also qualifies the extent to which Article 20 can be seen as a *lex specialis* to Article 19 (as claimed by Nowak, see *supra*). It points out that the distinguishing features of the acts addressed in Article 20 (*vis-à-vis* other acts that may be subject to restrciction under Article 19(3)) is that "the Covenant indicates the specific response required from the State: their prohibition by law".[89] "It is only in this respect", according to the draft General Comment, that Article 20 "may be considered as *lex specialis*" with regard to Article 19.[90]

Analysis of HRC Jurisprudence

The jurisprudence of the HRC has, to date, provided only limited illumination of the relationship between Articles 19 and 20. For instance, in *J.R.T. and the W.G. Party v. Canada*,[91] the dissemination of anti-Semitic messages by telephonic means was adjudged by the HRC to "clearly constitute the advocacy of racial or religious hatred" under Article 20(2).[92] The HRC, in declaring the case inadmissible, concluded that was no apparent need to consider the nexus between Articles 19 and 20.

In this regard, Nowak takes issue with Dominic McGoldrick's conclusion that a "prohibition established in accordance with the terms of article 20 cannot found a violation of article 19".[93] The essence of Nowak's argument is that "the obligation in Art. 20 may not be interpreted in such a way as to establish for a State party the right to restrict other Covenant rights to an extent going beyond permissible interference therein".[94] This means that "legal prohibitions under Art. 20 are to be interpreted in conformity with the restrictions that are legitimate under Art.

---

85 UN HRC, Draft General Comment No. 34 (Upon completion of the first reading by the Human Rights Committee), Doc. No. CCPR/C/GC/34/CRP.6, 3 May 2011.

86 *Ibid.*, para. 52.

87 *Ibid.*

88 *Ibid.*

89 *Ibid.*, para. 53.

90 *Ibid.*

91 Communication No. 104/1981, Decision of 6 April 1983.

92 *Ibid.*, para. 8(b).

93 Dominic McGoldrick, *The Human Rights Committee*, *op. cit.*, p. 491.

94 Manfred Nowak, *U.N. Covenant on Civil and Political Rights – CCPR Commentary* (2nd revised edition), *op. cit.*, p. 477.

19(3)".[95] It is submitted here that Nowak's argument is correct and that it is also without prejudice to the thesis that Articles 19 and 20 are contiguous (indeed, Nowak's subsequent arguments – to the effect that the "specific purposes for interference" set out in Article 20 could "easily be included under those in Article 19(3)" – confirm this[96]). Article 20 obliges States Parties to prohibit certain conduct by law, but does not specify how they should do so. As such, there is – as the expression goes – plenty of room for a slip 'twixt the cup and the lip. In other words, the manner in which the prohibition is assured at the national level could give rise to an impermissible restriction on the right to freedom of expression, for example if disproportionate measures were employed. It therefore stands to reason that measures adopted pursuant to the obligation contained in Article 20 should also have to pass muster under Article 19(3). This interpretation is also borne out by the HRC's draft General Comment No. 34, as already discussed.

The case of *Faurisson v. France*[97] is one example of where the HRC could have grasped the definitional nettle more firmly, but failed to do so. The case arose from the conviction of Robert Faurisson, an academic, for the contestation of crimes against humanity (i.e., Holocaust denial). Crucial to the HRC's finding that Faurisson's conviction was not a violation of Article 19 were submissions by the French authorities that revisionist theses amounting to the denial of a universally-recognised historical reality constitute the principal [contemporary] vehicle for the dissemination of anti-Semitic views. The restriction on Faurisson's freedom of expression was grounded in the deference pledged to the "respect of the rights or reputations of others" in Article 19(3) and was specifically intended to serve "the respect of the Jewish community to live free from fear of an atmosphere of anti-semitism".[98] While one Individual Opinion in the instant case posited that the statements on which Faurisson's conviction was based remained outside the boundaries of "incitement" as envisaged by Article 20(2), it is submitted here that the issue could have been probed further.[99]

In *Ross v. Canada*,[100] the HRC held that the restrictions imposed on a school-teacher's freedom of expression did not violate Article 19, as they had the purpose of protecting the "rights or reputations" of persons of Jewish faith, in particular in the educational sphere. The teacher had been publishing anti-Semitic tracts outside

95 *Ibid.* This is view is shared by Karl Josef Partsch; see: "Freedom of Conscience and Expression, and Political Freedoms", *op. cit.*, at 230.

96 *Ibid.*

97 Communication No. 550/1993, HRC Decision of 8 November 1996.

98 *Ibid.*, para. 9.6.

99 *Ibid.*, Individual Opinion by Elizabeth Evatt and David Kretzmer, co-signed by Eckart Klein (concurring), para. 4. The Individual (concurring) Opinion of Cecilia Medina Quiroga also concurred in Evatt and Klein's Individual Opinion, but the Individual (concurring) Opinion by Rajsoomer Lallah considers the suitability of applying Article 20(2).

100 Communication No. 736/1997, HRC Decision of 18 October 2000.

of the classroom and was disciplined by being transferred to an administrative post. The HRC noted that "the rights or reputations of others for the protection of which restrictions may be permitted under article 19, may relate to other persons or to a community as a whole".[101] Citing its *Faurisson* decision, the HRC stated that "restrictions may be permitted on statements which are of a nature as to raise or strengthen anti-semitic feeling, in order to uphold the Jewish communities' right to be protected from religious hatred", and that such restrictions "also derive support from the principles reflected in article 20(2) of the Covenant".[102] The actual necessity of the restrictions was justified for the protection of "the right and freedom of Jewish children to have a school system free from bias, prejudice and intolerance".[103]

Article 20's relationship with other ICCPR rights

Article 20's connection with Article 19 is most obvious, but it is also connected to other articles in the ICCPR, even in fundamental ways. Article 20 can, for example, be "primarily conceived of as a special State obligation to take preventive measures at the horizontal level to enforce the rights to life (Art. 6) and equality (Art. 26)".[104] Because of the centrality of these two rights within the Covenant system, "it was decided to combat the roots of the main causes for their systematic violation (wars, as well as racial, national and religious discrimination) by way of preventive prohibitions in the area of formation of public opinion".[105] Article 20(2)'s connection with Article 26 is also of interpretive significance. Whereas Article 26 is concerned with the prohibition of, and provision of effective protection against, discriminatory acts, Article 20 is concerned with the prohibition of incitement to such acts.[106] This structural separation of incitement and principal acts reinforces the conceptual distinction between them which underscores the inchoate nature of incitement (see further, *supra*).

The restrictions set out in Article 20 can also have implications for other rights, such as freedom of religion, assembly and association, and minority rights. The link between Article 20 and Article 18 [the right to freedom of thought, conscience and religion] also merits scrutiny. The HRC has stated clearly that "no manifestation of religion or belief may amount to propaganda for war or advocacy of national, racial or religious hatred that constitutes incitement to discrimination, hostility or

101 *Ibid.*, para. 11.5.
102 *Ibid.*, para. 11.5.
103 *Ibid.*, para. 11.6.
104 Manfred Nowak, *U.N. Covenant on Civil and Political Rights – CCPR Commentary* (2nd revised edition), *op. cit.*, p. 468.
105 *Ibid.*
106 See further, Karl Josef Partsch, "Freedom of Conscience and Expression, and Political Freedoms", *op. cit.*, at 229.

violence".[107] Thus, advocacy of/incitement to such actions shall not be tolerated under the ICCPR, even if they are ostensible manifestations of religion or belief; in such circumstances, it is not only valid for States authorities to restrict the right to manifest religion or belief, they are obliged to do so.[108]

Article 20(2) also contemplates measures that "constitute important safeguards against infringement of the rights of religious minorities and of other religious groups to exercise the rights guaranteed by articles 18 and 27, and against acts of violence or persecution directed towards those groups".[109] Although the UN HRC is right to describe these safeguards as "important", it would be erroneous to seek to infer therefrom any putative right not to be offended in one's (religious) beliefs or sensibilities. This point is relevant to a broader argument to be developed *infra*.

There have been calls, including by the UN Special Rapporteurs on freedom of religion or belief and on contemporary forms of racism, racial discrimination, xenophobia and related intolerance, for the HRC to elaborate a new General Comment on Article 20 that would, *inter alia*, elucidate "the interrelations between freedom of expression, freedom of religion and non-discrimination".[110] While the HRC's new draft General Comment No. 34 formally focuses on Article 19, its final section examines the relationship between Articles 19 and 20 (see further, *supra*).

Comparative perspective

For comparative purposes, it is interesting to consider how the similarly-inclined Article 13(5) of the American Convention on Human Rights (ACHR) has been crafted.[111] Whereas Article 13(5), ACHR, borrows heavily from the wording of Article 20, ICCPR, it departs from that wording in one noteworthy respect: it recognises an explicit group element to general offences of hatred amounting to incitement to lawless violence or other similar illegal action:

---

107 UN Human Rights Committee, General Comment 22 – The right to freedom of thought, conscience and religion (Article 18) (48th session, 30 July 1993), para. 7.

108 See further, *Ross v. Canada*, *op. cit.*, paras. 11.5–11.8; Manfred Nowak, *U.N. Covenant on Civil and Political Rights – CCPR Commentary* (2nd revised edition), *op. cit.*, pp. 426–427; 430.

109 *Ibid.*, para. 9.

110 Report further to Human Rights Council decision 1/107 on incitement to racial and religious hatred and the promotion of tolerance, *op. cit.*, at para. 61. See also, in this connection, *ibid.*, paras. 44–50 & 60.

111 For detailed analysis, see: Eduardo Andres Bertoni, "The Inter-American Court of Human Rights and the European Court of Human Rights: A Dialogue on Freedom of Expression Standards", [2009] E.H.R.L.R. (No. 3), pp. 332–352.

Article 13(5)

> Any propaganda for war and any advocacy of national, racial, or religious hatred that constitute incitements to lawless violence or to any other similar illegal action against any person or group of persons on any grounds including those of race, color, religion, language, or national origin shall be considered as offenses punishable by law.

The focus of "incitement" here is on "lawless violence" or "any other similar illegal action"; the latter phrase is *prima facie* broad enough in scope to cover discrimination (specifically mentioned in Article 20(2), ICCPR), but it is doubtful whether it would also catch "hostility" (also specifically mentioned in Article 20(2), ICCPR), given the definition-resistant properties of the term and the resultant inconceivability that such a vague notion could be rendered illegal. Another significant difference is that Article 13(5), ACHR, refers to a non-exhaustive list of grounds for the advocacy in question. A structural difference between the two comparable provisions, which is not without substantive consequences, is that Article 13(5), ACHR, is incorporated into a more general article on the right to freedom of expression, thus explicitly recognising it as one of the permissible restrictions on that particular right. By way of contrast, Article 20, ICCPR, by virtue of its free-standing status, is applicable to other rights vouchsafed in the ICCPR as well (see further, *supra*).

6.1.3 ICERD

Article 4 of the International Convention on the Elimination of All Forms of Racial Discrimination (ICERD) is also a crucial reference point for any examination of the interaction between freedom of expression and the elimination of racism. It reads:

> States Parties condemn all propaganda and all organizations which are based on ideas or theories of superiority of one race or group of persons of one colour or ethnic origin, or which attempt to justify or promote racial hatred and discrimination in any form, and undertake to adopt immediate and positive measures designed to eradicate all incitement to, or acts of, such discrimination and, to this end, with due regard to the principles embodied in the Universal Declaration of Human Rights and the rights expressly set forth in article 5 of this Convention, inter alia:
>
> (a) Shall declare an offence punishable by law all dissemination of ideas based on racial superiority or hatred, incitement to racial discrimination, as well as all acts of violence or incitement to such acts against any race or group of persons of another colour or ethnic origin, and also the provision of any assistance to racist activities, including the financing thereof;
>
> (b) Shall declare illegal and prohibit organizations, and also organized and all other propaganda activities, which promote and incite racial discrimination, and shall

recognize participation in such organizations or activities as an offence punishable by law;

(c) Shall not permit public authorities or public institutions, national or local, to promote or incite racial discrimination.

Article 4, ICERD, is rightly considered to be "one of the most difficult and controversial" articles of the entire Convention.[112] Because it explicitly creates a range of obligations for States Parties which entail far-reaching interference with the exercise of the right to freedom of expression (in particular), Article 4 presented "many difficulties in all stages of its drafting".[113] In that respect, it was no different to the corresponding article in the earlier UN Declaration on the Elimination of All Forms of Racial Discrimination (1963).[114] The complexity of the article is underscored by the varying nature of the obligations it creates.

The introductory paragraph to Article 4, ICERD, is condemnatory, but it also requires States to undertake to adopt certain "immediate and positive measures". It contains the all-important "due regard" clause which, in effect, clarifies that the objectives set out in Article 4 must be pursued consistently with a wider range of human rights. The use of the term "racial hatred" gave rise to the same kind of debates as those triggered by the term "hatred" in the context of the drafting of Article 20, ICCPR (*supra*). Again, the question of the feasibility of effectively addressing a mental or emotional state was central here, but as Natan Lerner points out, the question became much more acute in the context of the drafting of Article 4(a), where the term "hatred" was put forward as a crucial element of what would become a punishable offence.[115] The requirement that States "undertake to adopt immediate and positive measures designed to eradicate all incitement to, or acts of, such discrimination" are not objectionable as such, but Theodor Meron has perceptively drawn attention to the largely under-scrutinised potential of the words "*inter alia*" which precede the specifically enumerated measures to be adopted by

---

112 Natan Lerner, *The U.N. Convention on the Elimination of all Forms of Racial Discrimination* (2nd Edition) (Alphen aan den Rijn, The Netherlands, Sijthoff & Noordhoff, 1980), p. 43.

113 *Ibid.*, p. 47.

114 Article 9 of the Declaration reads:
"1. All propaganda and organizations based on ideas or theories of the superiority of one race or group of persons of one colour or ethnic origin with a view to justifying or promoting racial discrimination in any form shall be severely condemned.
2. All incitement to acts of violence, whether by individuals or organizations against any race or group of persons of another colour or ethnic origin shall be considered an offence against society and punishable under law.
3. In order to put into effect the purposes and principles of the present Declaration, all States shall take immediate and positive measures, including legislative and other measures, to prosecute and/or outlaw organizations which promote or incite to racial discrimination, or incite to or use violence for purposes of discrimination based on race, colour or ethnic origin."

115 Natan Lerner, *The U.N. Convention on the Elimination of all Forms of Racial Discrimination* (2nd Edition), *op. cit.*, p. 48.

States to the aforementioned end.[116] However, as he sardonically also points out, "even those measures which are enumerated pose problems".[117]

Before examining the enumerated measures, a few words on the "due regard" clause are in order. The clause was introduced by way of amendment by the Nigerian delegate in the Third Committee. The purpose of the amendment was to assuage widely-held fears among (especially Western) delegates that the envisaged State obligations would unduly encroach on the right to freedom of expression (and association). The generalised reference to the UDHR implicitly included Articles 19 (freedom of opinion and expression) and 20 (freedom of assembly and association), as well as Article 29 (limitations on the exercise of rights and freedoms), to which Articles 19 and 20 are subject. Article 29(2) is of particular relevance; it reads:

> In the exercise of his rights and freedoms, everyone shall be subject only to such limitations as are determined by law solely for the purpose of securing due recognition and respect for the rights and freedoms of others and of meeting the just requirements of morality, public order and the general welfare in a democratic society.

Thus, it is clear that the principles embodied in the UDHR include not only substantive rights, but also the permissibility of limitations on the exercise of those rights in certain circumstances.[118] Had the "due regard" clause not been so astutely inserted into Article 4's opening paragraph, most of the enumerated measures would have been deemed incompatible with the right to freedom of expression.

Article 4(a), the first of the Article's three operative paragraphs, enjoins States *inter alia* to declare a number of offences punishable by law. Given the abstruse style of writing throughout the Convention, especially in Article 4, it is useful to itemise the relevant offences, as follows:

– all dissemination of ideas based on racial superiority;
– all dissemination of ideas based on racial hatred;
– incitement to racial discrimination;
– all acts of violence against any race or group of persons of another colour or ethnic origin;

---

116 Theodor Meron, "The Meaning and Reach of the International Convention on the Elimination of All Forms of Racial Discrimination", 79 *The American Journal of International Law* (No. 2, April 1985), pp. 283–318, at 298.

117 *Ibid.*

118 For commentary, see: Torkel Opsahl, "Articles 29 and 30: The Other Side of the Coin", in Asbjorn Eide, Gudmundur Alfredsson, Göran Melander, Lars Adam Rehof and Allan Rosas with the collaboration of Theresa Swinehart, Eds., *The Universal Declaration of Human Rights: A Commentary* (Norway, Scandinavian University Press, 1992), pp. 449–470.

- incitement to such acts;
- the provision of any assistance to racist activities, including the financing thereof.

Questions about the nature and extent of State obligations under Article 4 are old, but recalcitrant. Differing interpretations of key terms and phrases have been advanced by various experts and the resultant confusion has been compounded by some astounding examples of drafting slippage by CERD itself. Whereas the individual offences which States are obliged to declare punishable by law have been unpacked here for the purposes of clarity, when CERD enumerated those offences in its General Recommendation XV ("Organized violence based on ethnic origin" (Art. 4)), it failed to mention "incitement to racial discrimination". Instead, it referred to "incitement to racial hatred" (para. 3), which simply does not figure in Article 4(a). Most unfortunately, this slippage was not a once-off occurrence. The mistake was repeated in General Recommendation XXXI on the prevention of racial discrimination in the administration and functioning of the criminal justice system (para. 4(a)).

Although this appears to be a simple editorial error, its consequences are potentially significant. The purpose of General Recommendations (GRs) is to elucidate the text of ICERD on the basis of CERD's accumulated experience of monitoring procedures. As such, GRs are increasingly relied upon as valuable points of reference by States Parties and indeed all other interested parties as well. For such an inaccuracy to slip into two separate GRs significantly increases the risk of misquotation (and therefore misunderstanding) of the actual obligation, as set out in the original text of the Convention. Indeed, this risk has already materialised: the EU Network of Independent Experts on Fundamental Rights has, for example, referred to the categories of misconduct that are to be penalized under Article 4(a), ICERD, by quoting (but without spotting) the inaccurate wording of GR XV[119] instead of the primary text of the Convention. Of course, typical disclaimers about GRs not being binding on States Parties and the primacy of the original text of the Convention do serve to mitigate the effect of these slippages, but they certainly do not help the general problem of uncertainty about the precise obligations created by Article 4.

One final point to be made in this connection concerns the substantive offences which are the at the centre of the drafting errors in GRs XV and XXXI: the actual offence of "incitement to racial discrimination" and the interloper offence of "incitement to racial hatred". The difference between these offences is by no means

119 E.U. Network of Independent Experts on Fundamental Rights, *Combating Racism and Xenophobia through Criminal Legislation: The Situation in the EU Member States*, Opinion No. 5–2005, 28 November 2005, p. 27.

cosmetic, which underscores the seriousness of the drafting errors. As the UN High Commissioner for Human Rights succinctly put it when discussing relevant interpretive questions in a different context:

> Unlike incitement to an act, it is almost impossible to prove whether hatred *per se* is or is not likely to result from the dissemination of certain statements. Regular evidentiary techniques may be employed to assess the risk of a particular illegal act occurring but these do not work well in assessing the risk of a purely psychological outcome. International courts have tended to avoid the issue and, instead, either simply conclude, perhaps after a cursory scan of the context, that the statements would be prone to have this result, or they focus on other factors, such as intent.[120]

One key difference between the ICCPR and leading European treaties and other instruments which include measures for combating racism, on the one hand, and ICERD on the other hand, is that the latter requires that States render the dissemination of ideas based on racial superiority or racial hatred – without further explicit qualification – offences punishable by law. There is no requirement of intent, nor is there any requirement that harm or other concrete consequences would flow from the dissemination of such ideas. This is in striking contrast to other leading conventions and other non-treaty reference points in international law. For instance, the Additional Protocol to the Convention on cybercrime, concerning the criminalisation of acts of a racist and xenophobic nature committed through computer systems provides for certain acts to be criminalised "when committed intentionally and without right" (eg. Article 3.1). Similarly, ECRI General Policy Recommendation No. 7 on national legislation to combat racism and racial discrimination also provides for the penalisation of certain acts "when committed intentionally", as well as repeatedly emphasising that to penalise acts, they have to be committed "with a racist aim" (para. 18). Further, the European Union's Council Framework Decision on combating certain forms and expressions of racism and xenophobia by means of criminal law provides for the criminalisation of certain "intentional conduct" (Article 1), but also considers issues relating to motivation and (likely) causation.[121] Such requirements are important safeguards for the protection of the right to freedom of expression. The absence of such safeguards could rule out the possibility of examining any contextual situations (which could have a determinative impact on the consequences to which the impugned speech could lead). For example:

---

120 UN High Commissioner for Human Rights, "Incitement to racial and religious hatred and the promotion of tolerance", Report pursuant to Implementation of General Assembly Resolution 60/251 of 15 March 2006 entitled "Human Rights Council", Doc. No. A/HHRC/2/6, 20 September 2006, para. 69.

121 All of these texts are properly contextualised and discussed in greater detail, *infra*.

- Public debate: arguments advanced in the heat of debate and which unintentionally cause offence should not – normally speaking – be punishable, otherwise the vigour of public debate would be seriously jeopardised.
- Satire: by definition, satire and cartoons, etc., are irreverent and seek to challenge and provoke. In the absence of hatred or incitement, such types of expression clearly fall within the legitimate exercise of the right to freedom of expression.
- Unintentionally harmful expression: there is a world of difference between misguided or thoughtless expression that is incidentally harmful and expression that is deliberately calculated to be abusvie or is fuelled by some kind of *animus*.

Nevertheless, in the context of ICERD, the relevance of qualifications such as intent and harmful consequences have been roundly dismissed, both by a major report on the implementation of Article 4,[122] and by CERD itself. As regards the former, José Inglés (the Rapporteur) stated that "the mere act of dissemination is penalized, despite lack of intention to commit an offence and irrespective of the consequences of the dissemination, whether it be grave or insignificant".[123] This has been borne out by CERD's review of States reports.[124] It is interesting to note that the original draft of Article 4(a) did include a consequentialist component, but that it was ultimately omitted from the final text after a divisive vote in the General Assembly.

As has been pointed out by the UN High Commissioner for Human Rights, the absence of any requirement of intent or impact "may seem a subtle difference but it is significant in determining the scope of the law"[125] and, crucially, the manner of its formulation at the national level. ICERD in general and Article 4 in particular are not self-executing.[126] The amount of discretion available to States for the transposition of ICERD's obligations into their domestic (legal) orders varies according to the specificity of the obligation. Thus, Article 2.1(d) confers some discretion on States as to the fulfilment of their general obligations under the Convention. It reads: "[e]ach State Party shall prohibit and bring to an end, by all appropriate means, including legislation as required by circumstances, racial discrimination by any persons, group or organization". The discretion – such as it is

122 José D. Inglés, CERD Special Rapporteur, Study on the Implementation of Article 4 of the International Convention on the Elimination of All Forms of Racial Discrimination, A/CONF.119/10, 18 May 1983.

123 Inglés, *op. cit.*, at para. 83. This is shored up by similar individual references to all dissemination of ideas based on racial superiority (para. 93) and to all dissemination of ideas based on racial hatred (para. 96).

124 See further: Patrick Thornberry, "Confronting Racial Discrimination: A CERD Perspective", 5 *Human Rights Law Review* (No. 2, 2005), pp. 239–269.

125 UN High Commissioner for Human Rights, "Incitement to racial and religious hatred and the promotion of tolerance", *op. cit.*, para. 39.

126 Michael Banton, *International Action Against Racial Discrimination* (Oxford, Clarendon Press, 1996), p. 196.

– stems from the import of the phrase "by all appropriate means" and from the clear suggestion that those means could include legislation "as required by circumstances". Thus, the manner of implementation is not exclusively legislative – other measures (which are often more effective for the attainment of specific goals in specific contexts) are also countenanced. Similarly, the adoption of new legislation is only required to the extent that existing legislation and other measures do not effectively fulfil relevant State obligations.

Nevertheless, Article 2.1(d) is only applicable to the extent that more specific obligations are not stipulated in individual articles, such as Article 4(a). Thus, the limited flexibility offered by Article 2.1(d) for the fulfillment of other State obligations is overridden by the explicit and more exacting requirement that States declare the acts enumerated in Article 4(a) "offences punishable by law". As already intimated by the foregoing discussion, the phrase "punishable by law" is generally interpreted as obliging States to penalize or criminalize the offences in question. Furthermore, as with Article 4 in its entirety, the obligations created by Article 4(a) are mandatory in character.[127] The CERD has stated that in order to satisfy these obligations, "States parties have not only to enact appropriate legislation but also to ensure that it is effectively enforced".[128] It reasons that because "threats and acts of racial violence easily lead to other such acts and generate an atmosphere of hostility, only immediate intervention can meet the obligations of effective response".[129]

According to Patrick Thornberry, the rationale behind the "strongly preventive or pro-active mode" of Article 4 "may be understood by reflecting on such phenomena as the discourses of dehumanisation that are characteristic elements of genocidal processes, or, less dramatically, on the climate of oppression that may flourish if unchecked against vulnerable minorities".[130] He further notes, perspicaciously, that "[v]ulnerable groups well appreciate that the lines between thought, public discourse and oppressive action can be very thin".[131]

The mandatory nature of this requirement that States criminalise the enumerated acts, coupled with the lack of discretion available to States to make the punishability of the acts conditional on considerations such as the intent of its perpetrator or their (likely) harm-producing effects, is clearly very problematic from the perspective of

127 See, for example: Legislation to eradicate racial discrimination (Art. 4), General Recommendation VII, Committee on the Elimination of Racial Discrimination, 23 August 2005, para. 1; Organized violence based on ethnic origin (Art. 4), General Recommendation XV, Committee on the Elimination of Racial Discrimination, 23 March 1993, para. 2.

128 CERD General Recommendation XV, *op. cit.*, para. 2.

129 *Ibid.*

130 (footnote omitted) Patrick Thornberry, "Confronting Racial Discrimination: A CERD Perspective", *op. cit.*, at 253.

131 *Ibid.*

freedom of expression. Even reliance on the "due regard" clause cannot resolve the potential frictions involved here as the utility of the clause lies in its reference to/invocation of prevailing standards of international law. However, the restrictions on freedom of expression provided for in Article 4(a), ICERD, go further than those countenanced in either the UDHR or the ICCPR.

In light of all the foregoing, Theodor Meron has concluded that in its interpretive approach to Article 4, CERD "appear[s] to endorse the notion that [Article 4] is based on absolute liability".[132] This conclusion is radical, but not without some validity. Whereas "strict liability" can be taken to mean "[l]iability for a crime that is imposed without the necessity of proving *mens rea* with respect to one or more of the elements of the crime",[133] Meron uses the term, "absolute liability", which in some jurisdictions goes even further than strict liability and implies that "the only defences available [to the crime] are the basic ones of insanity, automatism, or necessity".[134] Whether Article 4(a) does in fact rest on a notion of "strict" or "absolute" liability remains a moot question.

Article 4(a) also sits uneasily with certain other provisions in ICERD. The relationship between the limited flexibility as to the measures to be adopted by States under Article 2.1(d) and the strict requirement to declare certain acts "offences punishable by law" under Article 4(a) is not entirely coherent. One major incongruity is that "incitement to racial discrimination" is included under Article 4(a), meaning that it should be criminalized by States, whereas "racial discrimination" proper is covered by Article 2.1(d), meaning that it only has to be prohibited, but does not necessarily have to be criminalized, if other means are deemed more "appropriate" for bringing it to an end. Thus, provision is made for incitement to racial discrimination – an inchoate offence – to be more severely dealt with than racial discrimination – the principal offence being incited.[135]

Notwithstanding the foregoing, it is crucially important to stress that the fulfilment by States Parties of their obligations under Article 4 must be achieved while having "due regard" to the principles embodied in the Universal Declaration of Human Rights and the rights explicitly set out in Article 5, ICERD.[136] "The right to freedom

132 Theodor Meron, "The Meaning and Reach of the International Convention on the Elimination of All Forms of Racial Discrimination", *op. cit.*, at 303.

133 Elizabeth A. Martin, Ed., *A Dictionary of Law* (Fourth Edition) (Oxford, Oxford University Press, 1997).

134 Andrew Ashworth, *Principles of Criminal Law* (Second Edition), *op. cit.*, p. 159.

135 See further, Karl Josef Partsch, "Racial Speech and Human Rights: Article 4 of the Convention on the Elimination of All Forms of Racial Discrimination", *op. cit.*, at 27.

136 The list of rights set out in Article 5 is non-exhaustive: Non-discriminatory implementation of rights and freedoms (Art. 5), General Recommendation XX, CERD, 15 March 1996, para. 1.

of opinion and expression" is among those rights specifically enumerated at Article 5.[137]

CERD's Opinion in the case, *The Jewish Community of Oslo & others v. Norway*,[138] is highly revelatory of the Committee's current thinking on the relationship between Articles 4 and 5, ICERD. The factual background to the case involved a march and speech in Askim (near Oslo) to commemorate Rudolf Hess. It was organised by a group known as the "Bootboys". The applicants pointed to a number of instances of racist intolerance and racially-motivated attacks in the months subsequent to the march, which they attributed to the fact that the march had taken place at all. The conviction of the leader of the march (Mr. Sjolie) for violation of the Norwegian Penal Code (in particular the provision dealing with offences that may be summarised as "hate speech") was eventually overturned by the Norwegian Supreme Court. The applicants then turned to the CERD, claiming that as a result of the acquittal, "they were not afforded protection against the dissemination of ideas of racial discrimination and hatred, as well as incitement to such acts"[139] during the march and that they were not afforded a remedy against this conduct, as required by ICERD.

It fell to the Committee to decide whether the impugned statements by Mr. Sjolie would be protected by the "due regard" clause in Article 4. The Committee noted that "the principle of freedom of speech has been afforded a lower level of protection in cases of racist and hate speech dealt with by other international bodies, and that the Committee's own General recommendation No 15 clearly states that the prohibition of all ideas based upon racial superiority or hatred is compatible with the right to freedom of opinion and expression".[140] It further notes that:

> the 'due regard' clause relates generally to all principles embodied in the Universal Declaration of Human Rights, not only freedom of speech. Thus, to give the right to freedom of speech a more limited role in the context of article 4 does not deprive the due regard clause of significant meaning, all the more so since all international instruments that guarantee freedom of expression provide for the possibility, under certain circumstances, of limiting the exercise of this right.[141]

The Committee concluded that, given the "exceptionally/manifestly offensive character" of the impugned statements, they are not entitled to protection by the due regard clause and therefore Mr. Sjolie's acquittal by the Norwegian Supreme Court had given rise to a violation of Article 4, ICERD.

---

137 Article 5(d)(viii).

138 Communication No. 30/2003, CERD Opinion of 22 August 2005.

139 *Ibid.*, para. 3.1.

140 (footnote omitted) *Ibid.*, para. 10.5. It does not, however, refer to any specific examples.

141 *Ibid.*

In its General Recommendation XXX, "Discrimination Against Non Citizens",[142] the CERD sets out a number of general principles, on the basis of which it recommends that States Parties to ICERD, "as appropriate to their specific circumstances", adopt various measures, including:

> III. Protection against hate speech and racial violence
>
> 11. Take steps to address xenophobic attitudes and behaviour towards non-citizens, in particular hate speech and racial violence, and to promote a better understanding of the principle of non-discrimination in respect of the situation of non-citizens;
> 12. Take resolute action to counter any tendency to target, stigmatize, stereotype or profile, on the basis of race, colour, descent, and national or ethnic origin, members of "non-citizen" population groups, especially by politicians, officials, educators and the media, on the Internet and other electronic communications networks and in society at large;

Article 4, ICERD, clearly includes restrictions on the right to freedom of expression that are additional to – and more far-reaching than – those set out in Articles 19 and 20, ICCPR. This is particularly true of the requirement that States "declare an offence punishable by law all dissemination of ideas based on racial superiority". The CERD is of the opinion that that requirement "is compatible with the right to freedom of opinion and expression".[143] It seeks to ground its opinion in references to Article 29(2) of the Universal Declaration of Human Rights and Article 20, ICCPR. The reference to the former provision draws attention to the "duties and responsibilities" that right-holders must observe while exercising their rights and freedoms.[144] It is surprising, however, that no reference is made to Article 19(3), which contains an equivalent provision that is more specific to the rights to freedom of opinion and expression. The reference to Article 20, ICCPR, is specifically to the obligation on States to prohibit by law "[a]ny advocacy of national, racial or religious hatred that constitutes incitement to discrimination, hostility or violence". Regardless of how the Committee seeks to square this circle, the fact remains that Article 4, ICERD, is more restrictive of the right to freedom of opinion and expression than analogous provisions in the ICCPR.

---

142 Discrimination Against Non Citizens, General Recommendation XXX, CERD, 1 October 2004.
143 CERD General Recommendation XV, *op. cit.*, para. 4.
144 Article 29(2) of the Universal Declaration of Human Rights reads: "In the exercise of his rights and freedoms, everyone shall be subject only to such limitations as are determined by law solely for the purpose of securing due recognition and respect for the rights and freedoms of others and of meeting the just requirements of morality, public order and the general welfare in a democratic society."

On the basis of the brief foregoing analysis alone,[145] it seems difficult to speak of a universal approach to "hate speech".[146] This is not surprising: different treaties and bodies pursue different objectives, within the constraints of different mandates, and employing different strategies in the process. The absence of a *universal* approach is not nearly as grave as the absence of *approximate* coherence across treaties would be.

6.1.4 UNESCO standards

While not legally-binding on States, a number of international instruments adopted by UNESCO merit consideration, because of their general relevance to the freedom of expression/anti-racism interface and also their specific relevance to the role of the media in this area. For instance, Article 5.3 of the UNESCO Declaration on Race and Racial Prejudice (1978) reads:

> The mass media and those who control or serve them, as well as all organized groups within national communities, are urged – with due regard to the principles embodied in the Universal Declaration of Human Rights, particularly the principle of freedom of expression – to promote understanding, tolerance and friendship among individuals and groups and to contribute to the eradication of racism, racial discrimination and racial prejudice, in particular by refraining from presenting a stereotyped, partial, unilateral or tendentious picture of individuals and of various human groups. Communication between racial and ethnic groups must be a reciprocal process, enabling them to express themselves and to be fully heard without let or hindrance. The mass media should therefore be freely receptive to ideas of individuals and groups which facilitate such communication.

---

145 Constraints of space prevent a more detailed discussion, but see further: Natan Lerner, *The U.N. Convention on the Elimination of all Forms of Racial Discrimination* (Second Edition), *op. cit.*; Drew Mahalic & Joan Gambee Mahalic, "The Limitation Provisions of the International Convention on the Elimination of All Forms of Racial Discrimination", 9 *Human Rights Quarterly* (No. 1, February 1987), pp. 74–101; Theodor Meron, "The Meaning and Reach of the International Convention on the Elimination of All Forms of Racial Discrimination", *op. cit.*; Karl Josef Partsch, "Racial speech and human rights: Article 4 of the Convention on the Elimination of All Forms of Racial Discrimination", in Sandra Coliver, Ed., *Striking a Balance: Hate Speech, Freedom of Expression and Non-discrimination, op. cit.*; Egon Schwelb, "The International Convention on the Elimination of All Forms of Racial Discrimination", 15 *International and Comparative Law Quarterly* (October 1966), pp. 996–1068.

146 For further probing of this question, see: Toby Mendel, "Does International Law Provide for Sensible Rules on Hate Speech?", in Michael Herz & Peter Molnar, Eds., *The Content and Context of Hate Speech: Rethinking Regulation and Responses* (New York, Cambridge University Press, forthcoming, 2011).

This provision recognises the paradoxical potential of the media both to curb and to exacerbate racism and racial prejudice and it highlights relevant responsibilities of media professionals. The provision is further bolstered, in particular, by Article 6.2[147] and Article 7[148] of the Declaration.

Another example is provided by Article 3.2 of UNESCO's Declaration of Principles on Tolerance (1995), which reads:

> [...] The communication media are in a position to play a constructive role in facilitating free and open dialogue and discussion, disseminating the values of tolerance, and highlighting the dangers of indifference towards the rise in intolerant groups and ideologies.

Again, this is important recognition of the forum- and information-providing roles played by the media in pluralistic democratic society.

6.1.5 Other UN standards and mechanisms

6.1.5(i) World Conference against Racism and Review Conference

The World Conference against Racism, Racial Discrimination, Xenophobia and Related Intolerance was held in Durban, South Africa, from 31 August to 8 September 2001. The focus of the Declaration and Programme of Action of the World Conference[149] is broad and it reflects a diversity of thematic and regional priorities. The evident zeal of the language used in these documents augurs well for their effective implementation. While the stigmatisation and negative stereotyping of vulnerable individuals or groups of individuals are criticised in the Declaration (para. 89), it is simultaneously stressed that a possible antidote to such trends could

---

147 Article 6.2 reads: "So far as its competence extends and in accordance with its constitutional principles and procedures, the State should take all appropriate steps, inter alia by legislation, particularly in the spheres of education, culture and communication, to prevent, prohibit and eradicate racism – racist propaganda, racial segregation and apartheid and to encourage the dissemination of knowledge and the findings of appropriate research in natural and social sciences on the causes and prevention of racial prejudice and racist attitudes with due regard to the principles embodied in the Universal Declaration of Human Rights and in the International Covenant on Civil and Political Rights."

148 Article 7 reads: "In addition to political, economic and social measures, law is one of the principal means of ensuring equality in dignity and rights among individuals, and of curbing any propaganda, any form of organization or any practice which is based on ideas or theories referring to the alleged superiority of racial or ethnic groups or which seeks to justify or encourage racial hatred and discrimination in any form. States should adopt such legislation as is appropriate to this end and see that it is given effect and applied by all their services, with due regard to the principles embodied in the Universal Declaration of Human Rights [...]."

149 See: Report of the World Conference against Racism, Racial Discrimination, Xenophobia and Related Intolerance, Durban, 31 August – 8 September 2001, Doc. No. A/CONF.189/12.

lie in the robust exercise of the corrective powers of the media (para. 90). The promotion of multiculturalism by the media is a crucial ingredient of such an antidote (para. 88). These anxieties about the use and misuse of the media are equally applicable, if not moreso, to new technologies and in particular, the Internet (paras. 90–92). This is also borne out in the Declaration.[150]

The Programme of Action, for its part, revisits these themes, but in a manner that is mindful of their practical application. To this end, it calls for the promotion of voluntary ethical codes of conduct, self-regulatory mechanisms and policies and practices by all sectors and levels of the media in order to forward the struggle against racism (para. 144). It also advocates, within the parameters of international and regional standards on freedom of expression, greater (and where applicable, concerted) State action to counter racism in the media (para. 145). The dissemination of racist speech and the perpetration of similar racist acts over the Internet and via other forms of new information and communications technologies should merit particular attention (para. 147).[151] A list of suggested practical approaches to relevant problems is then enumerated.[152]

The Durban Review Conference, held in 2009,[153] continued to emphasise the importance of – and need to follow up on – a number of issues relating to freedom of expression that were identified at the 2001 Conference.[154] For instance, the Review Conference's Outcome Document reaffirms the positive role that freedom of expression and the media can play in countering racism (paras. 54–58) and the importance of promoting educational programmes and intercultural and interreligious dialogue as well (paras. 106–110).

The Review Conference's broader engagement with freedom of expression issues did, however, court controversy. The final text of the Conference addressed the polemical and politically prominent topic of the "defamation of religions" by stating that it:

---

150 These issues are dealt with most extensively in paras. 86–94 of the Declaration.

151 See further in this connection and in the context of follow-up activities to the Durban Declaration and Programme of Action: Yaman Akdeniz, "Stocktaking on efforts to combat racism on the Internet", Background Paper to High Level Seminar, UN Commission on Human Rights – Intergovernmental Working Group on the Effective Implementation of the Durban Declaration and Programme of Action, January 2006.

152 All of these issues are dealt with primarily in paras. 140–147 of the Programme of Action.

153 For a detailed overview and analysis, see: Corinne Lennox, "Reviewing Durban: Examining the Outputs and Review of the 2001 World Conference against Racism", 27 *Netherlands Quarterly of Human Rights Law Review* (No. 2, 2009), pp. 191–235.

154 Outcome document of the Durban Review Conference, 24 April 2009. For an overview and analysis that foreground certain freedom of expression issues, see: Dimitrina Petrova, "'Smoke and Mirrors': The Durban Review Conference and Human Rights Politics at the United Nations", 10 *Human Rights Law Review* (No. 1, 2009), pp. 129–150.

> *Deplores* the global rise and number of incidents of racial or religious intolerance and violence, including Islamophobia, anti-Semitism, Christianophobia and anti-Arabism manifested in particular by the derogatory stereotyping and stigmatization of persons based on their religion or belief [...].[155]

It has been noted that an earlier draft of the Outcome document referred to "derogatory stereotyping and stigmatization of religions" – instead of "[...] persons based on their religion or belief".[156] The final wording is consonant with extant international legal standards, whereas the draft text was not. The document further grounds this concern in the actual provisions of international human rights law when it subsequently reiterates relevant permissible restrictions on the right to freedom of expression, as set out in Article 20, ICCPR and Article 4, ICERD (but without naming them specifically).[157] Relatedly, the Outcome document also seeks to advance discussion and understanding of the relationship between Articles 19 and 20, ICCPR, by implicitly supporting an OHCHR proposal to organise regional expert workshops on conceptual and practical/implementation aspects of the prohibition of incitement to various offences.[158]

6.1.5(ii) Work of Special Rapporteurs on Freedom of Expression

It is important to advert to the relevance and value of the normative work being carried out by various Special Rapporteurs within the United Nations system to the issues presently under discussion. The Special Rapporteur on the promotion and protection of the right to freedom of opinion and expression and the Special Rapporteur on contemporary forms of racism, racial discrimination, xenophobia and related intolerance spring instantly to mind, but it would be remiss to disregard the work of the Special Rapporteur on freedom of religion and belief, and that of other specialised mandates, on the grounds of perceived irrelevance. However, a comprehensive overview of their relevant work is beyond the scope of this book.

By way of final focus in this section, in their Joint Statement on Racism and the Media in 2001,[159] the UN Special Rapporteur on Freedom of Opinion and Expression, the OSCE Representative on Freedom of the Media and the OAS Special Rapporteur on Freedom of Expression, insisted that:

---

155 (Emphasis per original) Outcome document of the Durban Review Conference, *op. cit.*, para. 12.

156 Dimitrina Petrova, "'Smoke and Mirrors': The Durban Review Conference and Human Rights Politics at the United Nations", *op. cit.*, at 148.

157 Outcome document of the Durban Review Conference, *op. cit.*, para. 13.

158 *Ibid.*, para. 134.

159 Joint Statement on Racism and the Media by the UN Special Rapporteur on Freedom of Opinion and Expression, the OSCE Representative on Freedom of the Media and the OAS Special Rapporteur on Freedom of Expression, 27 February 2001.

> Any civil, criminal or administrative law measures that constitute an interference with freedom of expression must be provided by law, serve a legitimate aim as set out in international law and be necessary to achieve that aim. This implies that any such measures are clearly and narrowly defined, are applied by a body which is independent of political, commercial or other unwarranted influences and in a manner which is neither arbitrary nor discriminatory, and are subject to adequate standards against abuse, including the right of access to an independent court or tribunal. If these safeguards are not in effect, there is a very real possibility of such measures being abused, particularly where respect for human rights and democracy is weak, and hate speech laws have in the past been used against those they should be protecting.
>
> In accordance with international and regional law, hate speech laws should, at a minimum, conform to the following:
> - no one should be penalised for statements that are true;
> - no one should be penalised for the dissemination of hate speech unless it has been shown that they did so with the intention of inciting discrimination, hostility or violence;
> - the right of journalists to decide how best to communicate information and ideas to the public should be respected, particularly when they are reporting on racism and intolerance;
> - no one should be subject to prior censorship; and
> - any imposition of sanctions by courts should be in strict conformity with the principle of proportionality.

The Joint Statement takes a multifaceted approach to the relationship between racism and the media and in addition to the civil, criminal and administrative measures detailed above, it emphasises the importance of freedom of information and of promoting tolerance (discussed in greater detail, *infra*). While not legally binding in any formal sense, the Joint Statement is of certain interpretive value, not least because it reveals current thinking by the (then) three IGO special mandates for protecting freedom of expression about relevant existing legal standards.

6.2 Council of Europe instruments: contrived consistency?[160]

6.2.1 European Convention on Human Rights[161]

The European Convention on Human Rights is the veritable centrepiece of human rights protection in Europe. Article 10, ECHR, reads as follows:

---

160 For an overview of the Council of Europe's activities in this domain, see: *Activities of the Council of Europe with Relevance to combating Racism and Intolerance*, European Commission against Racism and Intolerance, Doc. CRI (2004) 7, February 2004.

161 The analysis presented in this sub-section overlaps to an extent with a relevant section in Tarlach McGonagle, "A Survey and Critical Analysis of Council of Europe Strategies for Countering

1. Everyone has the right to freedom of expression. This right shall include freedom to hold opinions and to receive and impart information and ideas without interference by public authority and regardless of frontiers. This article shall not prevent States from requiring the licensing of broadcasting, television or cinema enterprises.
2. The exercise of these freedoms, since it carries with it duties and responsibilities, may be subject to such formalities, conditions, restrictions or penalties as are prescribed by law and are necessary in a democratic society, in the interests of national security, territorial integrity or public safety, for the prevention of disorder or crime, for the protection of health or morals, for the protection of the reputation or rights of others, for preventing the disclosure of information received in confidence, or for maintaining the authority and impartiality of the judiciary.

As with corresponding provisions in other international treaties, Article 10 sets out the right to freedom of expression, while recognising that its exercise involves duties and responsibilities and that it may be restricted on a number of enumerated grounds.

In its seminal ruling in *Handyside v. the United Kingdom*, the European Court of Human Rights affirmed that freedom of expression "is applicable not only to 'information' or 'ideas' that are favourably received or regarded as inoffensive or as a matter of indifference, but also to those that offend, shock or disturb the State or any sector of the population. Such are the demands of that pluralism, tolerance and broadmindedness without which there would be no democratic society".[162] That ruling served to open up the critical space between types of expression that are inoffensive and therefore uncontroversially protected by Article 10 and types of expression that are excluded from its protection by virtue of Article 17 (entitled "Prohibition of abuse of rights"; see *infra*).[163] The question of whether, or to what extent, "hate speech" should be protected is particularly contentious.

The European Court of Human Rights first examined the interaction between freedom of expression and relevant provisions of ICERD in *Jersild v. Denmark*.[164] In this case, also known as the "Greenjackets" case, the Court found that the

---

'Hate Speech'", in Michael Herz & Peter Molnar, Eds., *The Content and Context of Hate Speech: Rethinking Regulation and Responses*, *op. cit.*

162 *Handyside v. the United Kingdom*, Judgment of the European Court of Human Rights of 7 December 1976, Series A, No. 24, para. 49.

163 For extensive details of relevant case-law, see: Mario Oetheimer, "Protecting Freedom of Expression: The Challenge of Hate Speech in the European Court of Human Rights Case Law", 17 Cardozo J. Int'l & Comp. L. 427 (2009); Mario Oetheimer, "La Cour européenne des Droits de l'Homme face au discours de haine" (2007) 69 (1) *Rev trim d h* 63; Anne Weber, *Manual on hate speech* (Strasbourg, Council of Europe, 2009).

164 *Jersild v. Denmark*, Judgment of the European Court of Human Rights of 23 September 1994, Series A, No. 298.

conviction of a journalist – for aiding and abetting in the dissemination of racist views in a televised interview he had conducted with members of an extreme right-wing group ("the Greenjackets") – amounted to a violation of Article 10, ECHR. The Court's consideration of Article 10, ECHR, in light of ICERD (and in particular Article 4 thereof) was, however, regrettably summary and it failed to grapple with the substantive issues involved. It merely stated that it is not for the Court to interpret the "due regard" clause in Article 4, ICERD, but that "its interpretation of Article 10 of the European Convention in the present case is compatible with Denmark's obligations under the UN Convention".[165] The Court held that Jersild's conviction was not "necessary in a democratic society" and that it therefore violated his rights under Article 10, ECHR. This was largely due to considerations of context in (news) reporting and the importance of journalistic autonomy for the functioning of democracy. The positive obligations imposed on States Parties to ICERD by Article 4 were not deemed to have been contravened.[166]

The Grand Chamber of the European Court of Human Rights affirmed in its *Nachova* judgment that "the authorities must use all available means to combat racism and racist violence, thereby reinforcing democracy's vision of a society in which diversity is not perceived as a threat but as a source of its enrichment".[167] This is an important formulation of the robust stance consistently taken by the Court against racism in its manifold manifestations, including racist expression. In a long line of cases, the Court has consistently refused to grant any protection under Article 10 ECHR to racist speech[168] or to statements denying, disputing or minimising the Holocaust.[169]

In the *Seurot* case, for instance, a teacher was sanctioned for an article he wrote that was published in a school bulletin. In the article, he deplored – as he put it – the overrunning of France by "hordes of Muslims"[170] from North Africa. The European Court of Human Rights found that this sanction did not violate the applicant's rights

---

165 *Ibid.*, para. 30. See also, paras. 21, 28, 29, 31.

166 Also of note here is the divisiveness of the judgment: the Court found in favour of a violation of Article 10 by twelve votes to seven.

167 *Nachova and others v Bulgaria*, Judgment of the European Court of Human Rights (Grand Chamber) of 6 July 2005, para. 145. See also: *Timishev v Russia*, Judgment of the European Court of Human Rights (Second Section) of 13 December 2005, para. 56; *D.H. and Others v the Czech Republic*, Judgment of the European Court of Human Rights (Grand Chamber) of 13 November 2007, para. 176.

168 Recent examples include: *Seurot v. France*, Inadmissibility decision of the European Court of Human Rights (Second Section) of 18 May 2004, Appn. No. 57383/00; *Norwood v. United Kingdom*, Inadmissibility decision of the European Court of Human Rights of 16 November 2004, Appn. No. 23131/03, Reports 2004-XI.

169 Recent examples include: *Garaudy v. France*, Inadmissibility decision of the European Court of Human Rights (Fourth Section) of 24 June 2003, Appn. No. 65831/01, Reports 2003-IX. See further, Chapter 7.3.1.

170 Author's translation (the decision is only available in French), p. 2.

under Article 10, ECHR, because of the undeniably racist tone of the article and the duties and responsibilities of the applicant in his capacity as a teacher.

In the *Norwood* case, the applicant, a regional organiser for the British National Party (an extreme right-wing political party) displayed in the window of his flat a poster depicting the Twin Towers in flame, the words "Islam out of Britain – Protect the British People" and a symbol of a crescent and star in a prohibition sign. The applicant had been convicted of a public order offence by the domestic courts and the European Court of Human Rights agreed with the assessment of the domestic courts and concluded that his conviction did not breach Article 10, ECHR because:

> [...] the words and images on the poster amounted to a public expression of attack on all Muslims in the United Kingdom. Such a general, vehement attack against a religious group, linking the group as a whole with a grave act of terrorism, is incompatible with the values proclaimed and guaranteed by the Convention, notably tolerance, social peace and non-discrimination.

The Court followed this key finding in *Pavel Ivanov v. Russia*,[171] a case involving a conviction for incitement of hatred towards the Jewish people. The European Court of Human Rights agreed with the domestic courts' finding that the series of articles written and published by the applicant had a "markedly anti-Semitic tenor".[172]

Cases involving claims for freedom of expression for racist, xenophobic or anti-Semitic speech, Holocaust denial, or (neo-)Nazi ideas, are routinely held to be manifestly unfounded under Article 17 ('Prohibition of abuse of rights'), ECHR, and thus declared inadmissible. Article 17 was designed as an in-built safety mechanism to prevent the Convention from being subverted by those whose motivation is contrary to its letter and spirit.[173] It reads:

> Nothing in this Convention may be interpreted as implying for any State, group or person any right to engage in any activity or perform any act aimed at the destruction of any of the rights and freedoms set forth herein or at their limitation to a greater extent than is provided for in the Convention.

Elements of Nazi ideology or activities inspired by Nazism have figured strongly in the bulk of the aforementioned batch of inadmissibility decisions. The extent to which Nazism is incompatible with the ECHR can be gauged from the oft-quoted pronouncement of the European Commission of Human Rights in *H., W., P. and K.*

171 *Pavel Ivanov v. Russia*, Inadmissibility decision of the European Court of Human Rights (First Section) of 20 February 2007, Appn. No. 35222/04.

172 *Ibid.*, p. 4.

173 See further, Tarlach McGonagle, "Protection of Human Dignity, Distribution of Racist Content (Hate Speech)", in Susanne Nikoltchev, Ed., *Co-Regulation of the Media in Europe*, *IRIS Special* (European Audiovisual Observatory, Strasbourg, 2003), pp. 43–46, at 46.

v. Austria: "National Socialism is a totalitarian doctrine incompatible with democracy and human rights and [that] its adherents undoubtedly pursue aims of the kind referred to in Article 17".[174] The Court took its most trenchant stance against hate speech to date in the *Garaudy v. France* case,[175] which involved a challenge to the French Courts' conviction of the applicant for the denial of crimes against humanity, the publication of racially defamatory statements and incitement to racial hatred. The European Court of Human Rights held that:

> [...] There can be no doubt that denying the reality of clearly established historical facts, such as the Holocaust, as the applicant does in his book, does not constitute historical research akin to a quest for the truth. The aim and the result of that approach are completely different, the real purpose being to rehabilitate the National-Socialist regime and, as a consequence, accuse the victims themselves of falsifying history. Denying crimes against humanity is therefore one of the most serious forms of racial defamation of Jews and of incitement to hatred of them. The denial or rewriting of this type of historical fact undermines the values on which the fight against racism and anti-Semitism are based and constitutes a serious threat to public order. Such acts are incompatible with democracy and human rights because they infringe the rights of others. Its proponents indisputably have designs that fall into the category of aims prohibited by Article 17 of the Convention.
> The Court considers that the main content and general tenor of the applicant's book, and thus its aim, are markedly revisionist and therefore run counter to the fundamental values of the Convention, as expressed in its Preamble, namely justice and peace. [...][176]

A more problematic case, perhaps, as far as the boundaries of freedom of expression are concerned, was *Lehideux and Isorni v. France*.[177] The case concerned an advertisement in a national newspaper, *Le Monde*, as part of a campaign for the rehabilitation of the memory of General Philippe Pétain: the advertisement presented the General's life in a selective and positive manner, with certain dark chapters of the General's life being conspicuous by the absence of any reference thereto. In this case, the European Court again confirmed that protection would be withheld from remarks attacking the core of the Convention's values.[178] However, the impugned advertisement (as it did not amount to Holocaust denial or any other type of expression that would have prevented it from wriggling through the meshes

---

174 Inadmissibility decision of the European Commission of Human Rights, Appn. No. 12774/87, 62 DR (1989) 216, at pp. 220/1.

175 *Garaudy v. France*, Inadmissibility decision of the European Court of Human Rights (Fourth Section) of 24 June 2003, Application No. 65831/01.

176 *Ibid.*, p. 23 of the official English translation of excerpts from the decision.

177 *Lehideux & Isorni v. France*, 23 September 1998, Reports of Judgments and Decisions, 1998-VII.

178 *Ibid.*, para. 53. See also *Jersild v. Denmark*, *op. cit.*, para. 35.

of the Article 17 net) was held to be one of a class of polemical publications entitled to protection under Article 10.[179]

The above-cited judicial pronouncements have, both individually and collectively, usefully helped to clarify the status of performative speech[180] which is offensive, but does not necessarily amount to one of the various forms of advocacy or incitement defined in international human rights treaties.[181] As the relevant corpus of case-law from the European Court of Human Rights continues to grow, so too does the illumination of this rather grey area. *Gündüz v. Turkey*, for instance, also contributes to our understanding of where relevant lines are likely to be drawn by the Court. The case arose out of the participation of the applicant – the leader of an Islamic sect – in a live studio debate on topics such as women's clothing, Islam, secularism and democracy. The applicant was convicted by the Turkish Courts for incitement to hatred and hostility on the basis of a distinction founded on religion. However, the European Court of Human Rights held:

> [...] Admittedly, there is no doubt that, like any other remark directed against the Convention's underlying values, expressions that seek to spread, incite or justify hatred based on intolerance, including religious intolerance, do not enjoy the protection afforded by Article 10 of the Convention. However, the Court considers that the mere fact of defending sharia, without calling for violence to establish it, cannot be regarded as "hate speech". Moreover, the applicant's case should be seen in a very particular context. Firstly, as has already been noted [...], the aim of the programme in question was to present the sect of which the applicant was the leader; secondly, the applicant's extremist views were already known and had been discussed in the public arena and, in particular, were counterbalanced by the intervention of the other participants in the programme; and lastly, they were expressed in the course of a pluralistic debate in which the applicant was actively taking part. Accordingly, the Court considers that in the instant case the need for the restriction in issue has not been established convincingly.[182]

The case, *Féret v. Belgium*,[183] arose from the conviction of a Belgian politician for incitement to hatred, discrimination and violence due to the racist and xenophobic

---

179 *Ibid*., paras. 52, 55.

180 For a general exploration of "performative speech", see: J.L. Austin, *How to do things with words* (Oxford/New York/Toronto/Melbourne, Oxford University Press, Repr., 1980).

181 See, in particular, Article 20 of the International Covenant on Civil and Political Rights, which reads:
"1. Any propaganda for war shall be prohibited by law.
2. Any advocacy of national, racial or religious hatred that constitutes incitement to discrimination, hostility or violence shall be prohibited by law."

182 *Gündüz v. Turkey*, Judgment of the European Court of Human Rights (First Section) of 4 December 2003, para. 51.

183 *Féret v. Belgium*, Judgment of the European Court of Human Rights (Second Section) of 16 July 2009.

content of party political tracts distributed in the context of an electoral campaign. At the operative time, the applicant, Daniel Féret, was chairman of the far-right Belgian political party, *Front National*, editor-in-chief of the party's political publications, owner of the party's website (which was also used to distribute the impugned political tracts) and a member of the Belgian House of Representatives. Féret was sentenced to 250 hours of community service relating to the integration of foreign nationals in Belgium, together with a 10-month suspended prison sentence. Furthermore, he was ruled ineligible to stand for parliamentary elections for a 10-year period and ordered to pay a provisional sum of 1 Euro to each of the civil parties involved.

The European Court of Human Rights found that the applicant's right to freedom of expression had not been violated, *inter alia*, because of the volatility of racist or xenophobic expression during electoral periods[184] and the duty of politicians "to refrain from using or advocating racial discrimination and recourse to words or attitudes which are vexatious or humiliating because such behaviour risks fostering reactions among the public which are incompatible with a peaceful social climate and could erode confidence in democratic institutions".[185] In light of the civil nature of the sanctions and the suspended nature of the prison sentence, the Court found the sanctions not to be excessive.[186] The controversial nature of this judgment and the extent to which relevant questions persist can be gleaned from the Joint Dissenting Opinion to the judgment, in which, *inter alia*, the relationship between heated political invective and racist expression is examined, as well as the speculative nature of the link between the impugned expression and the potential harms it could cause.[187]

The foregoing analysis sketches the broad lines of the European Court of Human Rights' main principles governing (various kinds of) racist and hateful expression. At first glance, Article 17 appears to *prima facie* deny protection to a range of particularly abusive types of expression, but when the finer contours of relevant case-law are traced, it can be seen that substantive examinations are mounted by the Court. This points up that the Court's reliance on Article 17 is not always consistent in practice,[188] which is certainly a concern for future doctrinal development.

184 *Ibid.*, para. 76.

185 *Ibid.*, para. 77. Author's translation (as of this writing, the judgment is only available in French).

186 *Ibid.*, para. 80.

187 Dissenting Opinion of Judge Sajó, joined by Judges Zagrebelsky and Tsotsoria.

188 See further: David Keane, "Attacking hate speech under Article 17 of the European Convention on Human Rights", 25 *Netherlands Quarterly of Human Rights* (No. 4, 2007), pp. 641–663; Hannes Cannie & Dirk Voorhoof, "The Abuse Clause and Freedom of Expression in the European Human Rights Convention: An Added Value for Democracy and Human Rights Protection?", 29 *Netherlands Quarterly of Human Rights* (No. 1, 2011), pp. 54–83.

6.2.2 Other relevant Council of Europe treaties

Needless to say, a considerable number of Council of Europe treaties other than its flagship ECHR also contain important provisions designed to counter and prohibit racism. A few of the most relevant treaty provisions will now be considered.

6.2.2(i) Cybercrime Convention and its Additional Protocol

One of the fiercest criticisms of the Council of Europe's Convention on Cybercrime[189] in the latter stages of its drafting and subsequent to its opening for signature in November 2001 concerned its failure to address acts of racism and xenophobia committed through computer systems.[190] This *lacuna* was swiftly filled, however, by the drafting of an Additional Protocol to the Convention on Cybercrime, concerning the criminalisation of acts of a racist and xenophobic nature committed through computer systems.[191] The Additional Protocol concerns "acts", and not just "expression", although the latter is the type of act likely to receive the most attention. The Preamble to the Additional Protocol equates racist and xenophobic acts with "a violation of human rights and a threat to the rule of law and democratic stability". Also of importance for present purposes is the preambular recognition that the Protocol "is not intended to affect established principles relating to freedom of expression in national legal systems".

The goal of the Additional Protocol – to supplement the Convention as regards racist and xenophobic acts committed through computer systems (Article 1) – entails States Parties enacting appropriate legislation and ensuring that it is effectively enforced.[192] Article 2(1) of the Additional Protocol states that:

> "*racist and xenophobic material*" means any written material, any image or any other representation of ideas or theories, which advocates, promotes or incites hatred, discrimination or violence, against any individual or group of individuals, based on race, colour, descent or national or ethnic origin, as well as religion if used as a pretext for any of these factors.[193]

A major section of the Additional Protocol concerns measures to be taken at the national level. In this regard, States are obliged to "adopt such legislative and other

---

189 ETS No. 185, entry into force: 1 July 2004.

190 See, *inter alia*, Opinion No. 240 of the Parliamentary Assembly of the Council of Europe: "Draft additional protocol to the Convention on Cybercrime concerning the criminalisation of acts of a racist and xenophobic nature committed through computer systems", 27 September 2002.

191 ETS No. 189, entry into force: 1 March 2006.

192 See further, Explanatory Report to the Additional Protocol to the Convention on cybercrime, concerning the criminalisation of acts of a racist or xenophobic nature committed through computer systems, adopted on 7 November 2002, para. 9.

193 See further, *ibid.*, paras. 10–22.

measures as may be necessary to establish as criminal offences under its domestic law, when committed intentionally and without right, the following conduct: distributing, or otherwise making available, racist and xenophobic material to the public through a computer system" (Article 3(1)). Central to this definition is the presence of intent or *mens rea*, which is a basic requirement for the establishment of criminal offences generally. The corollary of this provision is that Internet Service Providers (ISPs) should not attract criminal liability for the dissemination of impugned material where it has merely acted as conduit, cache or host for such material.[194]

States are, however, given certain leeway not to criminalise relevant acts where the material "advocates, promotes or incites discrimination that is not associated with hatred or violence, *provided that other effective remedies are available*" (Article 3(2): emphasis added). This constitutes an important gesture towards – and endorsement of – the efficacy and value of, for example, self- and co-regulatory complaints and sanctioning mechanisms.

Article 4 requires States Parties to criminalise the following conduct when it is committed "intentionally and without right": "threatening, through a computer system, with the commission of a serious criminal offence as defined under its domestic law, (i) persons for the reason that they belong to a group, distinguished by race, colour, descent or national or ethnic origin, as well as religion, if used as a pretext for any of these factors, or (ii) a group of persons which is distinguished by any of these characteristics". This spans both public and private communications, unlike the target of the similarly-worded Article 5 ('Racist and xenophobic motivated insult'), which is only concerned with public communications. The conduct to be criminalised under Article 5 is: "insulting publicly, through a computer system, (i) persons for the reason that they belong to a group distinguished by race, colour, descent or national or ethnic origin, as well as religion, if used as a pretext for any of these factors; or (ii) a group of persons which is distinguished by any of these characteristics".

The decision to cast the utterance of insults as a criminal act could potentially grate with the established Article 10 case-law of the European Court of Human Rights. The cause of concern here is that the definitional threshold for "insult" could be deemed to be rather low and thus potentially open to abuse. As discussed, *supra*, according to the seminal principle laid down in the *Handyside* case (and consistently followed by the Court ever since), freedom of expression extends "not only to 'information' or 'ideas' that are favourably received or regarded as inoffensive or as

194 *Ibid.*, para. 25. Similarly, pursuant to Article 7 ('Aiding and abetting'), ISPs are also shielded from liability in the outlined circumstances: *ibid.*, para. 45.

a matter of indifference, but also to those that offend, shock or disturb the State or any sector of the population".

Article 6 of the Additional Protocol ('Denial, gross minimisation, approval or justification of genocide or crimes against humanity') introduces a novel focus into international human rights treaty law. For the first time, the scope of the offence has been extended to apply to genocides other than the Holocaust. Article 6 reads:

> 1 Each Party shall adopt such legislative measures as may be necessary to establish the following conduct as criminal offences under its domestic law, when committed intentionally and without right:
>
> distributing or otherwise making available, through a computer system to the public, material which denies, grossly minimises, approves or justifies acts constituting genocide or crimes against humanity, as defined by international law and recognised as such by final and binding decisions of the International Military Tribunal, established by the London Agreement of 8 August 1945, or of any other international court established by relevant international instruments and whose jurisdiction is recognised by that Party.
>
> 2 A Party may either
>
> a require that the denial or the gross minimisation referred to in paragraph 1 of this article is committed with the intent to incite hatred, discrimination or violence against any individual or group of individuals, based on race, colour, descent or national or ethnic origin, as well as religion if used as a pretext for any of these factors, or otherwise
>
> b reserve the right not to apply, in whole or in part, paragraph 1 of this article.

6.2.2(ii) European Convention on Transfrontier Television

Article 7(1) of the European Convention on Transfrontier Television[195] insists that broadcast material must (in its presentation and content) "respect the dignity of the human being and the fundamental rights of others". It also states that programmes shall not "give undue prominence to violence or be likely to incite to racial hatred".

6.2.2(iii) Framework Convention for the Protection of National Minorities

Despite its failure to specifically mention the term "hate speech", the Framework Convention for the Protection of National Minorities (FCNM)[196] has nevertheless

---

195 ETS No. 132 (entry into force: 1 May 1993), as amended by a Protocol thereto, ETS No. 171, entry into force: 1 March 2002.

196 ETS No. 157, entry into force: 1 February 1998.

elaborated a comprehensive strategy for tackling intolerance, hatred and (other) various contributory causes of hate speech. The strategy focuses on the twin goals of facilitating and creating expressive opportunities for minorities and of promoting intercultural dialogue, understanding and tolerance. The strategy derives from the interplay between Articles 6 and 9, FCNM, and is considered in detail in Chapter 8.2.1.

6.3 Other European standards: an ancillary normative dimension

6.3.1 European Union standards

6.3.1(i) General

The struggle against racism is informing public and judicial policy to an unprecedented extent in a European Union (EU) whose erstwhile goals were primarily economic cooperation and the consolidation of peace through trade. This has been particularly true since the entry into force of the Treaty of Lisbon, which has led, *inter alia*, to the Charter of Fundamental Rights of the European Union acquiring binding legal effect and an obligation on the EU to accede to the European Convention on Human Rights.

Article 1 of the Charter of Fundamental Rights of the European Union stresses the inviolability of human dignity. That the Charter should begin with a focus on human dignity is not merely of symbolic importance; it also lays down one of the document's main ideological cornerstones.[197] It has been argued that Article 1 constitutes not only a fundamental right in itself, but the "real basis" of other fundamental rights.[198] Following this line of argumentation, Article 1 necessarily informs other rights enshrined in the Charter, such as Article 11 (Freedom of expression and information), which reads as follows:

> 1. Everyone has the right to freedom of expression. This right shall include freedom to hold opinions and to receive and impart information and ideas without interference by public authority and regardless of frontiers.
> 2. The freedom and pluralism of the media shall be respected.

---

197 Article 1 reads: "Human dignity is inviolable. It must be respected and protected." See also the Charter's preambular reference to human dignity, which identifies it as one of the "indivisible, universal values" on which the European Union is founded (Recital 2).

198 Wolfgang Heyde, "Article 1 – Human Dignity", in The Commentary of the Charter of Fundamental Rights of the European Union, June 2006, at p. 25. See also: Note from the Praesidium, Draft Charter of Fundamental Rights of the European Union, Doc. No. CHARTE 4473/00, Brussels, 11 October 2000, p. 3.

In terms of interpretative clarity, it is important to note that Article 11 of the Charter has deliberately been very closely aligned with Article 10, ECHR. The alignment is usefully synopsised in the Commentary of the Charter of Fundamental Rights of the European Union, as follows:

> [...] according to the non-binding explanation of the Praesidium, pursuant to Article 52(3) of the Charter,[199] the meaning and scope of this right are the same as those guaranteed by the ECHR. Therefore the limitations which may be imposed on it, shall not exceed those provided for in Article 10(2) of the Convention, without any prejudice to any restrictions which Community law may impose on Member States' rights, for instance on the right to introduce the licensing arrangements referred to in Article 10(1) of the ECHR.[200]

Article 1 also informs Article 20 (Equality before the law), which is reinforced by Article 21 (Non-discrimination). It is also easy to detect its relevance to the Charter's in-built safety mechanism, i.e., its prohibition of abuse of rights clause (Article 54).[201]

In 1996, a Joint Action (96/443/JHA) concerning action to combat racism and xenophobia was adopted on the basis of Article K.3 of the Treaty on the European Union.[202] The Joint Action sought to ensure effective legal cooperation between Member States in combating racism and xenophobia. It aimed for Member States to make certain listed types of racist and xenophobic behaviour punishable as criminal offences, or to derogate from the principle of double criminality in respect of such behaviour. Following the first assessment of the Joint Action in 1998, the European Commission proceeded in 2001 to put forward a Proposal for a Council Framework Decision on combating racism and xenophobia.[203] Progress towards the adoption of the Proposal was stymied by deep-seated concerns among certain Member States about the implications of the Proposal for freedom of expression.[204]

---

199 Author's footnote: Article 52 of the Charter is entitled "Scope of guaranteed rights".

200 Gabor Halmai, "Article 11 – Freedom of expression and information", in The Commentary of the Charter of Fundamental Rights of the European Union, *op. cit.*, at p. 122.

201 It reads: "Nothing in this Charter shall be interpreted as implying any right to engage in any activity or to perform any act aimed at the destruction of any of the rights and freedoms recognised in this Charter or at their limitation to a greater extent than is provided for herein."

202 Joint Action of 15 July 1996 adopted by the Council on the basis of Article K.3 of the Treaty on European Union, concerning action to combat racism and xenophobia (96/443/JHA), OJ L 185 of 24 July 1996.

203 COM(2001) 664 final, Brussels, 28 November 2001. However, see also in this connection: Council of the European Union Interinstitutional File: 2001/0270 (CNS), Brussels, 27 May 2005.

204 "No agreement on the framework decision on combating racism and xenophobia at the Justice and Home Affairs Council", Press release of the Luxembourg Presidency of the Council of the European Union, 2 June 2005. See also, in this connection: the EU Annual Report on Human Rights – 2005, Doc. No. 12416/05, 28 September 2005, at p. 108; "The Need for a Unified Stance

These concerns persisted despite the Proposal's preambular assurance that "[T]his Framework Decision respects the fundamental rights and observes the principles recognised in particular by the European Convention on Human Rights, in particular Articles 10 and 11 thereof, and by the Charter of Fundamental Rights of the European Union, and notably Chapters II and VI thereof".[205] The impasse that resulted from certain Member States' concerns prompted the European Commission to request the EU Network of Independent Experts on Fundamental Rights "to submit an opinion on existing legislation on racism and xenophobia and in particular, on the issues surrounding the borderline between freedom of expression and the repression of racism and xenophobia",[206] which it duly did.

In 2006, Italy (which had strongly opposed the Commission's 2001 Proposal) withdrew its reservations to the text. That development enabled debate to be recommenced within the Council on the basis of a compromise proposal put forward during the Luxembourg Presidency in 2005.[207] Subsequently, in 2007, the Council reached a political agreement on the text and it was submitted to Parliament for renewed consultation.[208] The text was considered by the European Parliament in its legislative resolution of 29 November 2007.[209] Ultimately, in November 2008, the Council of the European Union adopted the Framework Decision, the title of which had by now changed to "on combating certain forms and expressions of racism and xenophobia by means of criminal law".[210]

---

in Combating Racism and Xenophobia", Speech by Vice-President of the European Commission Frattini, Vienna, 22 June 2006.

205 Recital 15, COM(2001) 664 final, *op. cit.*

206 Combating Racism and Xenophobia through Criminal Legislation: the Situation in the EU Member States, Opinion No. 5–2005, EU Network of Independent Experts on Fundamental Rights, 28 November 2005, p. 5.

207 For further details of the chronology of the Proposal, see: Explanatory Statement to Draft Report on the proposal for a Council Framework Decision on combating certain forms and expressions of racism and xenophobia by means of criminal law (11522/2007 – C6–0246/2007 – 2001/0270(CNS)), Committee on Civil Liberties, Justice and Home Affairs (Rapporteur: Martine Roure), 19 September 2007.

208 General Secretariat of the Council, Proposal for a Council Framework Decision on combating certain forms and expressions of racism and xenophobia by means of criminal law, Doc. No. 11522/07, n.d.

209 European Parliament legislative resolution of 29 November 2007 on the proposal for a Council Framework Decision on combating certain forms and expressions of racism and xenophobia by means of criminal law (11522/2007 – C6–0246/2007 – 2001/0270(CNS)), Doc. No. P6_TA-PROV(2007)0552.

210 Council of the European Union Framework Decision 2008/913/JHA of 28 November 2008 on combating certain forms and expressions of racism and xenophobia by means of criminal law, OJ L 328/55 of 6 December 2008.

The main purposes of the Framework Decision can be gleaned from selected Recitals in its Preamble.[211] For instance, it is styled as a response to the need to define a common criminal law approach to racism and xenophobia within the EU, "in order to ensure that the same behaviour constitutes an offence in all Member States and that effective, proportionate and dissuasive penalties are provided for natural and legal persons having committed or being liable for such offences" (Recital 5). However, its focus on criminal law "is limited to combating particularly serious forms of racism and xenophobia" and should be seen as one part of a broader framework of measures to counter racism and xenophobia (Recital 6). Furthermore, owing to extant differences between Member States' cultural and legal traditions, "full harmonisation of criminal laws is currently not possible" (Recital 6). In other words, only a limited level of harmonisation is envisaged. It claims that the "[a] pproximation of criminal law should lead to combating racist and xenophobic offences more effectively, by promoting a full and effective judicial cooperation between Member States" (Recital 12). Finally, in this connection, Recital 13 is also important:

> Since the objective of this Framework Decision, namely ensuring that racist and xenophobic offences are sanctioned in all Member States by at least a minimum level of effective, proportionate and dissuasive criminal penalties, cannot be sufficiently achieved by the Member States individually, since such rules have to be common and compatible and since this objective can therefore be better achieved at the level of the European Union, the Union may adopt measures, in accordance with the principle of subsidiarity as referred to in Article 2 of the Treaty on European Union and as set out in Article 5 of the Treaty establishing the European Community. In accordance with the principle of proportionality, as set out in the latter Article, this Framework Decision does not go beyond what is necessary in order to achieve that objective.

The terms "racism and xenophobia" are of pivotal importance to the Framework Decision. Nevertheless, neither term is defined in the text.[212] The Framework Decision's most important provisions are set out in Article 1, which is entitled "Offences concerning racism and xenophobia":

> 1. Each Member State shall take the measures necessary to ensure that the following intentional conduct is punishable:

211 The dual aims of the draft Framework Decision were stated more succinctly in Article 1 of the Commission's 2001 Proposal: to lay down "provisions for approximation of laws and regulations of the Member States and for closer co-operation between judicial and other authorities of the Member States regarding offences involving racism and xenophobia".

212 The terms were defined in draft Article 3 of the Commission's 2001 Proposal, as follows: "the belief in race, colour, descent, religion or belief, national or ethnic origin as a factor determining aversion to individuals or groups".

(a) publicly inciting to violence or hatred directed against a group of persons or a member of such a group defined by reference to race, colour, religion, descent or national or ethnic origin;
(b) the commission of an act referred to in point a) by public dissemination or distribution of tracts, pictures or other material;
(c) publicly condoning, denying or grossly trivialising crimes of genocide, crimes against humanity and war crimes as defined in Articles 6, 7 and 8 of the Statute of the International Criminal Court, directed against a group of persons or a member of such a group defined by reference to race, colour, religion, descent or national or ethnic origin when the conduct is carried out in a manner likely to incite to violence or hatred against such a group or a member of such a group;
(d) publicly condoning, denying or grossly trivialising the crimes defined in Article 6 of the Charter of the International Military Tribunal appended to the London Agreement of 8 August 1945, directed against a group of persons or a member of such a group defined by reference to race, colour, religion, descent or national or ethnic origin when the conduct is carried out in a manner likely to incite to violence or hatred against such a group or a member of such a group.

2. For the purpose of paragraph 1 Member States may choose to punish only conduct which is either carried out in a manner likely to disturb public order or which is threatening, abusive or insulting.

3. For the purpose of paragraph 1, the reference to religion is intended to cover, at least, conduct which is a pretext for directing acts against a group of persons or a member of such a group defined by reference to race, colour, descent, or national or ethnic origin.

4. Any Member State may, at the time of the adoption of this Framework Decision by the Council, make a statement that it will make punishable denying or grossly trivialising the crimes referred to in paragraph 1(c) and/or (d), only if the crimes referred to in these paragraphs have been established by a final decision of a national court of this Member State and/or an international court, or by a final decision of an international court only.

Article 2 enjoins Member States to take the measures necessary to ensure that the instigation of and aiding and abetting in the commission of, conduct covered by Article 1(1)(c) and (d), is punishable. Also of note is that Article 4 requires Member States to ensure that for offences other than those covered by Articles 1 and 2, racist and xenophobic motivation is considered an aggravating factor, or that such motivation may be taken into consideration by the courts in the determination of penalties for offences.

The text contains repeated statements of deference to the right to freedom of expression, as enshrined in the ECHR and the Charter of Fundamental Rights of the European Union, and as developed in the constitutional and legal systems of

Member States. Recitals 14 and 15 of the Preamble and Article 7 of the Framework Decision all profess this deference.[213] The clear repetition involved here can be explained as an endeavour to allay the fears of certain Member States that the Framework Decision would reduce the protection afforded to the right to freedom of expression, as discussed *supra*. A final provision meriting mention because of its direct implications for the right to freedom of expression is Article 9, entitled "Jurisdiction". Express consideration is given to relevant conduct committed through information systems. More specifically, Article 9(2) provides:

> When establishing jurisdiction in accordance with paragraph 1(a), each Member State shall take the necessary measures to ensure that its jurisdiction extends to cases where the conduct is committed through an information system and:
> (a) the offender commits the conduct when physically present in its territory, whether or not the conduct involves material hosted on an information system in its territory;
> (b) the conduct involves material hosted on an information system in its territory, whether or not the offender commits the conduct when physically present in its territory.

This provision is highly significant as it fills a gap left by older texts which did not anticipate the complex jurisdictional issues that would be raised by the subsequent advent of the Internet and Internet-based communicative techniques. As such, it reduces the possibility of offences committed through information systems remaining unpunished due to jurisdictional vacuums.

The Framework Decision is comprehensive in scope and will be the mainstay of future anti-racism action within the EU, not least because it has repealed and replaced Joint Action 96/443/JHA (discussed *supra*).[214]

6.3.1(ii) The Audiovisual Media Services Directive

The Audiovisual Media Services (AVMS) Directive devotes surprisingly little attention to measures to be taken to prevent the broadcasting of hateful content. The Directive's most relevant provision is Article 6, which reads:

---

213 Article 7, entitled "Constitutional rules and fundamental principles", reads:
"1. This Framework Decision shall not have the effect of modifying the obligation to respect fundamental rights and fundamental legal principles, including freedom of expression and association, as enshrined in Article 6 of the Treaty on European Union.
2. This Framework Decision shall not have the effect of requiring Member States to take measures in contradiction to fundamental principles relating to freedom of association and freedom of expression, in particular freedom of the press and the freedom of expression in other media as they result from constitutional traditions or rules governing the rights and responsibilities of, and the procedural guarantees for, the press or other media where these rules relate to the determination or limitation of liability."

214 Article 11, *ibid*. See also Recital 16.

> Member States shall ensure by appropriate means that audiovisual media services provided by media service providers under their jurisdiction do not contain any incitement to hatred based on race, sex, religion or nationality.

This article represents a slightly reworded version of the equivalent provision (Article 22a) in the AVMS Directive's forerunner, the "Television without Frontiers" (TWF) Directive, but it alters little in terms of the substance of the provision. However, it is noteworthy that it explicitly links the issues of "incitement to hatred" and "jurisdiction". The tightening-up and intended clarification of the provisions on jurisdiction[215] was one of the major impulses in the process leading to the proposed revision of the Directive. A number of cases involving the broadcasting by satellite of "hate speech" into Europe have also conditioned regulatory thinking on this issue. It is also interesting to note that the initial formal proposal from the European Commission to revise the TWF Directive would have expanded the scope of the reference to incitement to hatred. It targeted incitement to hatred based on "sex, racial or ethnic origin, religion or belief, disability, age or sexual orientation".[216] That proposed revision would have directly incorporated the impermissible grounds of discrimination set out in (then) Article 13 of the EC Treaty, but it would also have juxtaposed notions of "hatred" and "discrimination". The conceptual and practical implications of treating both notions in the same way have already been outlined in the context of ICERD, *supra*, and are also relevant here. The European Parliament proposed a number of amendments to the Commission's initial text, including the introduction of references to human dignity and integrity.[217] Those proposed amendments were ultimately not adopted in the final text.

---

215 See further: Berend Jan Drijber, "Jurisdictie in de Richtlijn audiovisuele mediadiensten", 20 *Mediaforum* (Themanummer Richtlijn Audiovisuele Mediadiensten, No. 2, February 2008), pp. 62–27; Egbert Dommering, "[TWF Directive] Article 2 (Country of Origin Principle)" and "[AVMS Directive] Article 2 (Country of Origin Principle)" in Oliver Castendyk, Egbert Dommering & Alexander Scheuer, Eds., *European Media Law* (Alphen a/d Rijn, Kluwer Law International, 2008), pp. 337–357 and 847–850, respectively; Tarlach McGonagle & Ad van Loon, *IRIS Special: Jurisdiction over Broadcasters in Europe – Report on a Round-table Discussion*, (Strasbourg, European Audiovisual Observatory, 2002); Thomas Gibbons, "Jurisdiction over (Television) Broadcasters: Criteria for Defining 'Broadcaster' and 'Content Service Provider'", in A. Rossnagel, Ed., *Die Zukunft der Fernsehrichtlinie/The Future of the 'Television without Frontiers' Directive* (Baden-Baden, Germany, Nomos, 2005), pp. 53–60; André Lange & Susanne Nikoltchev, "Transfrontier Television in the European Union: Market Impact and Selected Legal Aspects", Background Paper, Ministerial Conference on Broadcasting organised by the Irish Presidency of the European Union, Dublin and Drogheda, 1–3 March 2004.

216 Proposal for a Directive of the European Parliament and of the Council amending Council Directive 89/552/EEC on the coordination of certain provisions laid down by law, regulation or administrative action in Member States concerning the pursuit of television broadcasting activities (13 December 2005).

217 Amendment 44: Article 3e (Directive 89/552/EEC), Report on the proposal for a directive of the European Parliament and of the Council amending Council Directive 89/552/EEC on the coordination of certain provisions laid down by law, regulation or administrative action in

Whereas Article 6 focuses on audiovisual media services, Article 9 provides a complementary focus on audiovisual commercial communications. Article 9(1)(c), AVMS Directive, is an amended version of Article 12, TWF Directive; it reads:

> audiovisual commercial communications shall not:
> (i) prejudice respect for human dignity;
> (ii) include or promote any discrimination based on sex, racial or ethnic origin, nationality, religion or belief, disability, age or sexual orientation;
> [...]

Its first prong (human dignity) remains unchanged; its second prong is extended to read "include or promote" and the range of bases for impermissible discrimination is expanded along the lines[218] proposed by the European Parliament for audiovisual media services and audiovisual commercial communications alike. As was shown in the preceding paragraph, the proposed expansion of the range of bases for impermissible discrimination was not adopted in respect of audiovisual media services. Finally, the reference to offensiveness to religious or political beliefs, contained in the third prong to Article 12, TWF, has been dropped.[219] This is a significant omission, especially when considered in the contentious context of the (limits of) legal permissibility of offensive expression.

Article 3(1) of the AVMS Directive states that "Member States shall ensure freedom of reception and shall not restrict retransmissions on their territory of audiovisual media services from other Member States for reasons which fall within the fields coordinated by [the] Directive". It is possible for Member States to "provisionally derogate" from those obligations, *inter alia*, when "a *television broadcast* coming from another Member State manifestly, seriously and gravely infringes [...] Article 6".[220] "In respect of *on-demand audiovisual media services*", however, Member States "may take measures to derogate from those obligations when the measures in question are "necessary" for, *inter alia*, "public policy, in particular the prevention, investigation, detection and prosecution of criminal offences, including the protection of minors and the fight against any incitement to hatred on grounds of

---

Member States concerning the pursuit of television broadcasting activities, European Parliament Committee on Culture and Education, Rapporteur: Ruth Hieronymi, 22 November 2006, Doc. No. A6–0399/2006 (final); Amendment 107: Article 3e (Directive 89/552/EEC), European Parliament legislative resolution on the proposal for a directive of the European Parliament and of the Council amending Council Directive 89/552/EEC on the coordination of certain provisions laid down by law, regulation or administrative action in Member States concerning the pursuit of television broadcasting activities (COM(2005)0646-C6–0443/2005–2005/0260(COD)) (Codecision procedure – first reading), 13 December 2006 (Doc. No. P6_TA-PROV(2006)0559).

218 Note that the European Parliament did not include "nationality" in its list of bases for impermissible discrimination, but that it was included in Article 3e(c) (ii), AVMSD.

219 Article 12(c), TWF Directive, read: "be offensive to religious or political beliefs".

220 (emphasis added) Article 3(2), AVMS Directive.

race, sex, religion or nationality, and violations of human dignity concerning individual persons".[221]

The question of banning/blocking (particular kinds of) broadcasts from other countries is neither new nor unique.[222] It raises a number of questions which are ideologically and legally troublesome.[223] Interestingly, one viewpoint aired during the drafting of Article 19 of the Universal Declaration of Human Rights, was that the phrase, "regardless of frontiers" implied ideological barriers and geo-political ones.[224] In Europe, the search for appropriate answers to relevant questions has become pressing,[225] but the general preoccupation is less with ideological concerns (as the broadcasts in question are measured against the yardstick of the main international legal norms) than with the legalistic/jurisdictional and technological complexities involved.[226] This is reflected in the focuses of the ongoing attempts of European regulatory authorities to consolidate existing cooperation between them, specifically with a view to combating incitement to hatred disseminated by (satellite) broadcasting.[227] The catalyst for these consolidation initiatives was a growing

---

221 (emphasis added) Article 3(4), AVMS Directive.

222 See *supra* in the context of the discussion of the Genocide Convention. For a European perspective, see also: Arie Bloed and Pascale C.A.E. de Wouters d'Oplinter, "Jamming of Foreign Radio Broadcasts", in Arie Bloed and Pieter van Dijk, Eds., *Essays on Human Rights in the Helsinki Process* (Dordrecht, Martinus Nijhoff Publishers, 1985), pp. 163–180.

223 See further, David Goldberg, "Europe Bans Terrorist Media: What Sort of Antidote to Poisonous Voices?", 17 Cardozo J. Int. & Comp. L. 445 (2009).

224 The view was put forward by the Filipino delegate, Mr Aquino. For commentary, see: Albert Verdoodt, *Naissance et signification de la Déclaration des droits de l'homme* (Louvain, E. Warny, 1964), p. 190; Lauri Hannikainen and Kristian Myntti, "Article 19", in Asbjorn Eide *et al.*, Eds., *The Universal Declaration of Human Rights: A Commentary, op. cit.*, pp. 275–286, at pp. 277–278.

225 The issue has been described as "absolutely and urgently" requiring closer cooperation between relevant regulatory authorities throughout the EU, in candidate countries and in the European Economic Area. Conclusions of the High-level Group of Regulatory Authorities in the Field of Broadcasting – Incitement to hatred in broadcasts coming from outside of the European Union: European Broadcasting Regulators coordinate procedures to combat hate broadcasts in Europe, 17 March 2005.

226 In the post-World War II period, however, the political debate about banning/blocking broadcasts was overtly ideological. In the debate, States positioned themselves on predictable sides of the usual Cold-War battle-lines. Whereas Western States promoted the principle of a free flow of information with minimal restrictions, the Soviet Bloc advocated principles of State sovereignty and non-intervention. This led to what has been termed an "Electronic War between East and West": Arie Bloed and Pascale C.A.E. de Wouters d'Oplinter, "Jamming of Foreign Radio Broadcasts", *op. cit.*, at p. 165. The debate was firmly polarised and particularly bitter, as can be gauged from relevant discussions which took place in the CSCE context: see further the account provided in *ibid.*

227 Tarlach McGonagle, "European Commission: Broadcasting Regulators Fight Incitement to Hatred", *IRIS* 2005–5: 5; Mara Rossini, "European Commission: Broadcasting Regulators Encouraged to Reinforce Cross-border Cooperation under the Television without Frontiers Directive", *IRIS* 2006–5: 7.

concern about the difficulties in regulating content that incites to racial and religious hatred which is broadcast from non-EU countries, as exemplified by the cases in which the French authorities banned the channels, *Al Manar*[228] and *Sahar 1*.[229] The channels were prohibited on account of the (violent) anti-Semitic content of their programming. Although both channels were subsequently also banned in other countries, eg. the Netherlands, their programming has continued to be available online.[230]

It should also be noted in passing that an earlier precedent for such concerns was the *Med TV* saga.[231] In 1999, the former British Independent Television Commission (ITC) suspended and subsequently revoked the satellite television licence of *Med TV* (a service targeting a Kurdish audience) for repeated breaches of the terms of its licence agreement and the ITC Programme Code. More specifically, the ITC found that *Med TV* had broadcast material "likely to encourage or incite to crime or lead to disorder".[232] In another case involving a Kurdish television station, *ROJ TV*, the Turkish Embassy in Denmark (where *ROJ TV* was based) submitted a complaint to the Danish Radio and Television Board alleging that the station had links with illegal organisations and that some of its programming amounted to incitement to hatred. The Danish Radio and Television Board considered the complaint and concluded that the impugned elements of *ROJ TV*'s programming did not amount to incitement to hatred, as set out in relevant legislative provisions, and therefore was not in breach of the same provisions.[233]

The need for maximum coordination and cooperation between regulatory authorities is particularly evident concerning jurisdictional questions.[234] The case of *Extasi TV*

---

228 See further: Amélie Blocman, "FR – CSA Calls on Courts for Immediate Stop to Broadcasting by Unapproved Foreign Satellite Channel", *IRIS* 2004–9: 11; Amélie Blocman, "FR – *Al Manar* TV Soap Opera Continues", *IRIS* 2005–1: 12 and Amélie Blocman, "FR – Eutelsat Must Stop Broadcasting Al Manar TV", *IRIS* 2005–2: 12; Philippe Achilléas, "La diffusion par satellite de programmes illégaux – L'affaire *Al Manar*", *Communication – Commerce électronique* (Février 2005), pp. 39–42; "La régulation des chaînes extra-communautaires et la lutte contre le racisme et l'antisémitisme", *La Lettre du CSA* (No. 185, June 2005), p. 15.

229 See further: Amélie Blocman, "FR – CSA Serves another Formal Notice on Eutelsat", *IRIS* 2005–3: 11; Amélie Blocman, "FR – *Conseil d'Etat* Upholds the Formal Notice Served on Eutelsat", *IRIS* 2005–4: 9.

230 See further: Rosa Hamming, "NL – Satellite Broadcasts Disseminating Hatred Blocked", *IRIS* 2006–3: 17.

231 See further: Stefaan Verhulst, "United Kingdom: MED-TV Receives Suspension Order", *IRIS* 1999–4: 13; Tony Prosser, "United Kingdom: Regulator Revokes Licence of Satellite Broadcaster", *IRIS* 1999–7: 12.

232 ITC News Release of 22 March 1999.

233 For a full summary of the decision, see: Elisabeth Thuesen, "DK – Complaint of the Turkish Embassy against the Kurdish ROJ TV", *IRIS* 2005–7: 10.

234 See generally, Joan Botella I Corral and Emmanuelle Machet, "Co-ordination and Co-operation between Regulatory Authorities in the Field of Broadcasting" in Susanne Nikoltchev, Ed., *IRIS*

usefully illustrates the point.[235] The UK authorities banned the television service *Extasi TV* because it had been broadcasting violent pornography and had thereby "manifestly, seriously and gravely" infringed Article 22 of the TWF Directive.[236] The European Commission identified "uncertainty as to which Member State had jurisdiction over [Extasi TV]" as a complicating factor in the case.[237] It could therefore be suggested that enhanced coordination between relevant regulatory authorities might have served to dispel some of the uncertainty in question. One of the tangible consequences of the case was the inclusion of an identification requirement for audiovisual media service providers in Article 5 of the AVMS Directive.[238]

The need for coordination and cooperation between regulatory authorities is by no means limited to States within the "European audiovisual area"; recognition of the importance of intercultural dialogue has been a catalyst for the establishment of contact groups and meetings between European and non-European regulatory authorities.[239]

6.3.2 OSCE standards

The Organization for Security and Co-operation in Europe (OSCE) also boasts a range of politically-binding commitments dealing with human rights generally and the promotion of tolerance and non-discrimination in particular. The bulk of these commitments have emerged from the so-called "human dimension" of the OSCE's

---

Special: Audiovisual Media Services without Frontiers – Implementing the Rules (Strasbourg, European Audiovisual Observatory, 2006), pp. 13–20.

235 See: David Goldberg, "GB – Government and Media Regulator Act Against Unacceptable Satellite TV Services and Programming", *IRIS* 2005–3:12.

236 Fifth Report from the Commission to the Council, the European Parliament, the European Economic and Social Committee and the Committee of the Regions on the application of Directive 89/552/EEC "Television without Frontiers", COM(2006) 49 final, 10 February 2006, p. 5.

237 *Ibid.*

238 Article 5, AVMS Directive reads:
"Member States shall ensure that audiovisual media service providers under their jurisdiction shall make easily, directly and permanently accessible to the recipients of a service at least the following information:
(a) the name of the media service provider;
(b) the geographical address at which the media service provider is established;
(c) the details of the media service provider, including its electronic mail address or website, which allow it to be contacted rapidly in a direct and effective manner;
(d) where applicable, the competent regulatory or supervisory bodies."

239 See further, Karol Jakubowicz, "Implementation and Monitoring: Upholding Human Rights and Cultural Values" in Susanne Nikoltchev, Ed., *IRIS Special: Audiovisual Media Services without Frontiers – Implementing the Rules*, *op. cit.*, pp. 35–44.

work.[240] They have been developed at successive Summits of Heads of State or Government, beginning with the Helsinki Final Act (1975), through the Charter of Paris for a New Europe (1990), "The Challenges of Change" – Helsinki (1992), "Towards a Genuine Partnership in a New Era" – Budapest (1994), the Lisbon Document (1996) and the various documents of the Istanbul Summit (1999). Relevant declarations and documents have also resulted from other meetings.

Specialised institutions within the OSCE apparatus deserve particular mention, including: the Office for Democratic Institutions and Human Rights (ODIHR), the Office of the Representative on Freedom of the Media (RFOM), the Office of the High Commissioner on National Minorities (HCNM). Each of these offices has been responsible for important normative work concerning the interface between freedom of expression and anti-racism. In 2003, ODIHR was asked by the OSCE Ministerial Council to act as a collection point for information related to tolerance and non-discrimination on the basis of information received from Participating States, civil society and intergovernmental organisations.

Particular themes addressed in the context of the OSCE's work on tolerance and non-discrimination include: anti-Semitism, freedom of religion or belief, gender-based discrimination, hate crime, hate on the Internet, homophobia, intolerance against Muslims, racism and xenophobia, Roma, Sinti and Travellers.[241] Ample references to the importance of protecting and promoting the right to freedom of expression, as such, are also to be found throughout OSCE documents pertaining to human rights and democracy.

Conclusions

There has been much debate in recent years about the actual and desirable limits to freedom of expression. The former can be objectively determined whereas the latter tend to be subjective and sometimes speculative. There is a pressing need for law- and policy-makers to have a very clear understanding of the precise limitations on the right to freedom of expression that are permissible under international law, as well as the precise nature and extent of the State obligations which they engender. Any permissible limitations on the right to freedom of expression must be interpreted restrictively. Through meticulous analysis, this Chapter provides the necessary clarification in respect of limits concerning incitement, hatred, offence, etc.

---

240 There are three main "dimensions" to the OSCE's work: the politico-military dimension, the economic and environmental dimension and the human dimension.

241 See further, the OSCE/ODIHR Tolerance and Non-discrimination Information System: < http://tnd.odihr.pl/>.

Much of the confusion about relevant limitations originates in the primary texts, but is perpetuated from within by bodies charged with interpretation or monitoring of relevant treaties. As far as the ICCPR is concerned, the main interpretive standards are very outdated: the General Comments on Articles 19 and 20 were adopted in 1983. HRC Communications on relevant issues are not voluminous and only offer limited clarification of the frictional aspects of the relationship between the right to freedom of expression and the right to non-discrimination/equality. The confusion surrounding exact State obligations under (Article 4 of) ICERD is generally the result of poor drafting exacerbated by over-zealous and under-contextualised application of standards. More particularly, as this Chapter has shown, CERD has misquoted the Convention it is supposed to oversee in at least two of its General Recommendations. Although this glaring error does not appear to have been spotted by other commentators, it represents an embarrassing setback for the aim of enhancing clarity and awareness of the precise content of relevant State obligations under ICERD.

At the European level, the European Convention on Human Rights is the single most important legal instrument that has given shape to the right to freedom of expression. The parameters of the right have been determined by the European Court of Human Rights' interpretation of Articles 10 and 17, in particular. In short, a wide zone of protection has been created for various types of expression, especially when they contribute to public debate, even in terms that may offend, shock or disturb the State or any sector of the population. Only particularly egregious or abusive types of expression are beyond the pale of this protection: racist, xenophobic or anti-Semitic expression, Holocaust denial or (neo-)Nazi ideas, for example. The importance of the approach taken by the European Court of Human Rights is powerful and centrifugal. It forms the point of departure for all other Council of Europe treaties and other standard-setting initiatives. It also serves as a primary reference point for relevant EU initiatives.

A noteworthy trend in recent standard-setting by both the Council of Europe and the EU is the tentative extension of criminal sanctions for Holocaust denial to also apply to other genocides (as established by international law). The tentative nature of the extension is largely explained by the varying approaches taken across EU Member States and the historical and emotive ballast weighing down those approaches. It is important to consider this overt preference for a criminal law approach alongside the wide range of other, non-criminal (and often non-legal) approaches discussed in Chapter 8. Both types of approach complement each other in an overall "horses for courses" approach against "hate speech".

Chapter 7
"Hate speech" and intolerance targeting minorities

Introduction

The central argument of this chapter is that "hate speech" is more a term of art or convenience than a term of legal precision. It remains undefined, which leaves it open to over- or underinclusiveness. This is problematic from the perspective of legal foreseeability. This chapter unravels the term "hate speech" and shows that it is a catch-all term covering different types of speech which vary in the intensity of their message and in the harms they occasion. In order to better appreciate the nature of the harms involved, this exercise in conceptual unravelling draws on critical race theory perspectives on "hate speech". This ensures a victim-oriented approach to relevant legal standards.

The broadness of the term, "hate speech", is a major reason why anti-"hate speech" laws often prove ineffective in practice – another key focus of this chapter. The analysis then turns to particular types of expression that may or may not constitute "hate speech" and may or may not lead to the invocation of permissible restrictions on the right to freedom of expression under international law. Whereas racism and related forms of expression are generally and uncontroversially regarded as being beyond the purview of international legal protection, the focus here is on a murkier doctrinal interface: that of freedom of expression and freedom of religion or belief. After a general exploration of this interface, specific attention will be placed on three topical and controversial issues: Holocaust and genocide denial; the so-called "defamation" of religions, and the protection of founders of religions. These general and specific focuses are all of relevance for (religious) minorities.

7.1 Irruption of "hate speech" into international human rights law and discourse

The term, "hate speech", which enjoys widespread and largely uncontested currency nowadays, does not lend itself easily to legal definition. Intuitively, there can be no objection to Bhikhu Parekh's condemnation of "hate speech" as "objectionable for both intrinsic and instrumental reasons, for what it is and what it does".[1] However, it is important to be wary of the disarming and deceptive familiarity of the term,

1 Bhikhu Parekh, "Hate speech: Is there a case for banning?", 12 *Public Policy Research* (No. 4, December 2005-February 2006), pp. 213–223, at 217.

and of reflexive calls for the banning of "hate speech" because "hate speech" is a term which refers to a whole spectrum of negative discourse stretching from hate and incitement to hatred; to abuse, vilification, insults and offensive words and epithets; and arguably also to extreme examples of prejudice and bias.[2] In short, virtually all racist and related declensions of noxious, identity-assailing expression could be brought within the wide embrace of the term.

The shift from moral condemnation to legal regulation (or prohibition) inevitably calls for greater definitional refinement than has hitherto been provided by any international, legally-binding treaty or related adjudicative authority. As one commentator has put it:

> The multiple forms of anti-egalitarian expression that exist are neither equally harmful nor performative; we must not, therefore, lose sight of the link between the norm that the state is drafting and the broader public policies involved when identifing [sic] the specific forms of anti-egalitarian expressions to discourage.[3]

The *precise* term "hate speech" is not enshrined in any of the leading international legally-binding instruments. It is used by the European Court of Human Rights, but it is not organic to the European Convention on Human Rights. It is an imported product – and a fairly recent import at that. The *precise* term was never used by the Court (or the now-defunct European Commission of Human Rights) before 1999.[4] Prior to that, the vocabulary was different, even if the targeted mischiefs were pretty much the same.[5] The Court has not yet defined the term and in some judgments, it even uses it in inverted commas (scare quotes).[6] One cannot help but wonder whether this indicates a certain unease with the concept?

It should be noted that the Court does not use the term, "hate speech", systematically. It is perhaps still too early to say what added value or clarity the introduction of the

2 James Jacobs & Kimberley Potter, *Hate Crimes: Criminal Law and Identity Politics* (New York, Oxford University Press, 1998), p. 11.

3 Jean-François Gaudreault-DesBiens, "From Sisyphus's Dilemma to Sisyphus's Duty? A Meditation on the Regulation of Hate Propaganda in Relation to Hate Crimes and Genocide", (2000) 46 McGill L.J. 121, at 133. See also in this connection, Bhikhu Parekh, "Hate speech: Is there a case for banning?", *op. cit.*, at 222.

4 It would appear that the term was first used in four Judgments of the European Court of Human Rights, all of 8 July 1999: *Sürek v. Turkey (No. 1)*, para. 62; *Sürek & Özdemir v. Turkey*, para. 63; *Sürek v. Turkey (No. 4)*, para. 60 and *Erdogdu & Ince v. Turkey*, para. 54.

5 For details of relevant case-law, see: Mario Oetheimer, "Protecting Freedom of Expression: The Challenge of Hate Speech in the European Court of Human Rights Case Law", 17 Cardozo J. Int'l & Comp. L. 427 (2009); Mario Oetheimer, "La Cour européenne des Droits de l'Homme face au discours de haine" (2007) 69 (1) *Rev trim d h* 63; Anne Weber, *Manual on hate speech* (Strasbourg, Council of Europe, 2009).

6 See, for example, *Gündüz v. Turkey*, Judgment of the European Court of Human Rights (First Section) of 4 December 2003, para. 51.

term has brought to the Court's jurisprudence relating to Articles 10 and 17, ECHR – at least in the absence of its own definition of the term. The Court sometimes refers to the Council of Europe's Committee of Ministers' Recommendation (97) 20 on "Hate Speech", which *describes* the term (albeit for the purposes of the application of the principles set out in the Appendix to the Recommendation) as "covering all forms of expression which spread, incite, promote or justify racial hatred, xenophobia, antisemitism or other forms of hatred based on intolerance, including: intolerance expressed by aggressive nationalism and ethnocentrism, discrimination and hostility against minorities, migrants and people of immigrant origin".[7] This description is helpful, but only in a limited way, because the Recommendation is not legally-binding on States. Similarly, the gradual development and consolidation of relevant jurisprudence also help to further our understanding of the term, or at least of the Court's interpretation of the term. The Court's judgment in *Gündüz v. Turkey*, discussed in Chapter 6.2.1, illustrates the point.

"Hate speech" has already been described as an imported term. It was initially propelled to international prominence primarily by critical race scholarship originating in the United States (see further, *infra*). Critical race theory is (to put it very summarily) an approach to racism where the victim and the victim's perspective are given pride of place.[8] It seeks to ensure that law and policy are adequately informed by circumstances and experiences of victims of racism.

There are some important lessons to be learned from critical race theory. Prompted partly by its central theses, and partly by an integrated conceptualisation of human rights, a purposive definitional approach to hate speech is called for and not a restrictive one. The guiding question should be "what harms ought to be prevented?" To paraphrase Kevin Boyle and Anneliese Baldaccini, the focus should be on the "core mischiefs at which the struggle against racism is aimed".[9] Those "core mischiefs" are the various ways in which hate speech interferes with other rights or "operative public" values: dignity, non-discrimination and equality, (effective)

---

7 Recommendation No. R (97) 20 of the Committee of Ministers to Member States on "hate speech", 30 October 1997, Appendix.

8 See generally: Mari J. Matsuda, Charles R. Lawrence III, Richard Delgado & Kimberlè Williams Crenshaw, Eds., *Words That Wound: Critical Race Theory, Assaultive Speech, and the First Amendment* (Boulder, etc., Westview Press, 1993); Richard Delgado & Jean Stefancic, Eds., *Critical Race Theory: the cutting edge* (2nd Edition) (Philadelphia, PA, Temple University Press, 2000); Richard Delgado & Jean Stefancic, *Understanding Words That Wound* (Boulder, CO, Westview Press, 2004).

9 Kevin Boyle & Anneliese Baldaccini, "A Critical Evaluation of International Human Rights Approaches to Racism", in Sandra Fredman, Ed., *Discrimination and Human Rights: The Case of Racism* (New York, Oxford University Press, 2001), pp. 135–191, at 152.

participation in public life (including public discourse[10]), expression, association, religion, etc. The prevention of particular harms suffered by victims should also be considered: psychic harm, damage to self-esteem, inhibited self-fulfilment, etc.[11] All in all, the range of harms to be prevented is varied and complex. The challenge is therefore to identify "which criteria allow us to distinguish between harms that justify restrictions and those that do not".[12]

Partly in recognition of the complexity of relevant harms, different treaties and bodies have different approaches (conceptual and practical) to the question of legitimate restrictions on freedom of expression. The right to freedom of expression, as vouchsafed by international law, comprises the right to hold opinions and to seek, receive and impart information. As such, it covers extremely dynamic processes which typically involve not only speakers and listeners, but also, very often, third parties who are not directly targeted by particular instances of expression, but for whom that expression may nonetheless have implications. The importance of the consequences of expression should therefore be stressed, as well as the need to develop suitable methodological tools for the evaluation of such consequences. This prompts questions about negative reporting on and stereotyping of certain groups in society: what are their cumulative effects on the rest of society? Does their wider dissemination via mainstream media make them more influential of public opinion, more corrosive of societal values or more subliminally effective than full-blown extremism circulated in fringe fora?

Such questions cannot be answered *in abstracto*.[13] As Robert Post has noted, "[a]udiences always evaluate communication on the basis of their understanding of its social context".[14] When applying their normative principles to specific factual circumstances, adjudicative bodies should give sufficient weighting to factors such as the intent of the speaker and "contextual variables".[15] The latter could include the nature and impact of the medium used to convey the expression; audience-related considerations; socio-political factors; the nature and severity of the sanction imposed (when the adjudicative body is acting in a review capacity), etc.

Because so many rights and values are potentially affected by hate speech and because there are divergent legally-based interpretations of the legitimacy of limitations on freedom of expression, it is not enough to concentrate exclusively on

10 For a thorough analysis of this topic, see: Robert C. Post, "Racist Speech, Democracy, and the First Amendment", 32 Wm. & Mary L. Rev. 267 (1991).

11 See generally, Mari Matsuda *et al.*, *Words that Wound*, *op. cit.*

12 David Kretzmer, "Freedom of Speech and Racism", 8 Cardozo L. Rev. 445 (1987), at 478.

13 See further: *ibid.*, at 462.

14 Robert C. Post, "Racist Speech, Democracy, and the First Amendment", *op. cit.*, at 307.

15 Michel Rosenfeld, "Hate Speech in Constitutional Jurisprudence: A Comparative Analysis", 24 Cardozo L. Rev. 1523 (2003), at 1565.

negative State obligations for countering hate speech. It is not simply a case of drawing a line that would mark the *ne plus ultra* of permissible expression. Rather, a more comprehensive and nuanced approach is required. Such an approach would necessarily include the facilitation of expression and the promotion of pluralism and tolerance. The media are vital – in different ways – to the effectiveness of such an approach.

The role of the media as the Fourth Estate or democratic/public watchdog is well-documented (see further, Chapter 3), but their importance for democracy is by no means limited to their checking function *vis-à-vis* the organs of State. Of increasing importance is their contribution to public debate by providing fora for expression and communication. In an ever-changing technological context, the level of moderation of expressive fora is also highly relevant. By way of illustration, the moderation of online fora points to control of content, whereas the absence, or reduced levels, of moderation suggest a more open debate. The responsibility of media for content, especially in interactive communicative fora online, is becoming increasingly tied to these and related considerations. Responsibility also extends to the conditions of access to the media because of the gate-keeping function they perform.

In its current state of development, international law does not recognise a freedom of forum or an individual or group right of access to particular media (absent any mitigating circumstances such as monopoly ownership in the broadcast sector). However, the ability to exercise the right to freedom of expression in an effective manner is contingent on the availability and accessibility of viable expressive/communicative opportunities and fora. Expressive opportunities cannot be considered viable if discriminatory practices prevail in relation to access to the media or other expressive fora. Thus, the right to non-discrimination/equality and the right to effective participation in public life are implicated here, along with the right to freedom of expression. This means that a powerful triumvirate of rights are brought to bear on the issue of access to the media, thereby demonstrating the synergic interplay between different rights.

Under international human rights standards, it is possible to detect a significant emphasis on State obligations to facilitate expression, both for its own sake and also specifically because of its instrumental importance for promoting pluralism and tolerance. The Durban Declaration and Programme of Action[16] and the Framework Convention for the Protection of National Minorities, in particular, adopt root-and-branch approaches to combating "hate speech" and anti-egalitarian speech by

16 World Conference against Racism, Racial Discrimination, Xenophobia and Related Intolerance, Durban, 2001: Declaration and Programme of Action.

targeting the hatred and intolerance from which they spawn.[17] Central to their strategies is the promotion of counter-speech, or more accurately, increased/enhanced expressive opportunities, especially via the media. The promotion of tolerance and of intercultural understanding and dialogue is similarly prioritised. Measures advocated include specialised training for journalists on intercultural themes, ensuring access to media for minorities or other groups, funding of various initiatives promoting ethical journalism and programme production, etc. Crucially, a sense of deference to principles of media autonomy/editorial freedom is consistently advocated in respect of these measures. Encouragement, not prescription, is the strategy to be employed.[18]

Lee C. Bollinger brings tolerance and hate speech together in his tolerance principle of free speech, the starting-point of which is "an understood commitment to extraordinary self-restraint; coupled [...] with a willingness to be sensitive to context".[19] He states that the "strong presumption in favor of toleration [...] can be overcome only after it is determined that the society has little or nothing to gain" from exercising tolerance, "and, by comparison, a great deal to lose".[20] This is an allusion to the theory that hate speech – despite its moral repugnancy – *can* have some, limited, instrumental value to society.[21] Wojciech Sadurski, for instance, remarks that "hate speech" can, occasionally, sensitise the public to prevailing currents of racism in society, thus prompting a redoubling of efforts to eradicate it through educational and other initiatives.[22] He also notes that legal tolerance of such speech could allow us to challenge our closest-held convictions. Exposure to extremist view-points, the Mill-inspired argument runs, challenges us and forces us to re-examine our understandings, ideas and values by jolting us out of our unthinking complacency.[23] These liberal-minded, admittedly abstract theories, must not be lightly discounted. However, in the cut and thrust of policy formulation, they are often drowned out by clamouring for the prioritisation of consequentialist arguments.

---

17 See further, Tarlach McGonagle, "The international and European legal standards for combating racist expression", *op cit.*

18 See the Council of Europe's Committee of Ministers' Recommendation (97) 21 on the media and the promotion of a culture of tolerance.

19 Lee C. Bollinger, *The Tolerant Society* (New York, Oxford University Press, 1989), p. 197.

20 *Ibid.*

21 Ronald Dworkin, *Taking Rights Seriously* (London, Duckworth & Co. Ltd., 1977), p. 200.

22 Wojciech Sadurski, "Racial Vilification, Psychic Harm, and Affirmative Action", in Tom Campbell & Wojciech Sadurski, Eds., *Freedom of Communication* (England, Dartmouth Publishing Company, 1994), pp. 77–94, at 78.

23 Franklyn S. Haiman, *Speech and Law in a Free Society* (USA, University of Chicago Press, 1981), p. 99.

Such arguments often explore, as Richard Delgado has done,[24] the far-reaching effects of hate speech targeting (racial) minorities: including the internalisation of insults by victims (leading to a colouration of societal values and attitudes); negative psychological responses to stigmatisation (leading to humiliation, isolation and emotional distress); the reinforcement of social stratification, etc. And it *is* minorities who are the real victims of hate speech as it is generally thought that the privileges flowing from the entrenched, socially-advantageous position of the majority protect its members from hate speech. By analogy, Lilliputian arrows are unable to hurt a social Gulliver.

A purely abstract analysis of Bollinger's tolerance of free speech principle would likely fail to address many practical issues which would have to be scrupulously examined for the drafting of a legal framework to deal with hate speech. These would include: individual sensitivities to hate speech (in the event of the creation of a new tort for hate speech, should an egg-shell-skull rule or some other threshold apply?); group libel; whether a speech-action distinction should be recognised, or whether all expression (including symbolic speech) should be considered together, by virtue of its communicative impact.

7.1.1 The effectiveness of "hate speech" laws

Scepticism abounds concerning the effectiveness of so-called "hate speech" laws, so much so that it has even been suggested that blanket prohibitions on racially-motivated hate speech, far from being a "noble innovation", might amount to no more than a "quixotic tilt at windmills which belittles great principles of liberty".[25] This is due in no small measure to the infinite variety of forms, the "endlessly variegated shades of meaning",[26] of racist speech. The circumvention of laws prohibiting or restricting speech has never been a problem for those intent on doing so.[27] "All regulation encourages evasion, but the very ambiguity of speech that makes law such a crude response further facilitates evasion", Richard Abel avers.[28]

---

24 Richard Delgado, "Words that Wound: A Tort Action for Racial Insults, Epithets, and Name-Calling", 17 *Harvard Civil Rights-Civil Liberties Law Review* (1982), pp. 133–181.

25 Alexander Bickel, *The Morality of Consent* (New Haven, Yale University Press, 1975), p. 71, quoting Jackson J. in *Kunz v. New York* 340 U.S. 290 (1951).

26 Robert C. Post, "Racist Speech, Democracy, and the First Amendment", *op. cit.*, at 293.

27 In her examination of censorship from a historical perspective, Sue Curry Jansen shows this to have been the case throughout the ages: "The language of Aesop became the *lingua franca* of the new republic [Republic of Athens]... They used the slippery edges of language to comply with the letter of the law of Inquisition, while boldly defying its spirit." – Sue Curry Jansen, *Censorship: The Knot That Binds Power and Knowledge* (New York & Oxford, Oxford University Press, 1991), p. 69.

28 Richard Abel, *Speech and Respect* (London, Stevens & Sons/Sweet & Maxwell, 1994), p. 98.

He continues: "[r]acists translate hate into pseudo-science, substituting regression analyses for vulgarities".[29] It is relatively easy for a skilled polemicist to appropriate an entirely new lexicon in order to avoid legal prosecution for the dissemination of ideas deemed noxious to society. Codified terms become common currency. Gloves of velvet are worn on iron claws of hatred. The platitudes of political correctness are a mere smokescreen for more sinister intent. The nature of discourse is altered and it will be as esoteric or as exoteric as the level of complicity between speaker and listener will dictate. Talk of "cultural coherence", "traditional values", "the erosion of a core identity" and "preservation of national unity" are all loaded terms: they are the sheathed daggers of racist and xenophobic mentalities.[30]

The inventiveness of this verbal chameleonism cannot be matched by any legislation, as legislation, by definition, must be clear and precise. This fundamental imbalance in the conflict between law and racism goes a long way towards explaining the ineffectiveness of hate speech laws designed to promote equality and to eradicate discrimination in all of its many ugly guises. "If suppression is directed only at the crudest or most 'odious' messages, it will be dealing with the most superficial aspects of the problem of group prejudice and hatred, for the most odious are likely to be the least effective in accomplishing their purposes", according to Franklyn S. Haiman.[31] "[G]roup prejudice and hatred when packaged in subtle or sophisticated communication wrappings",[32] are therefore not usually susceptible to legal sanction.

It has been argued that laws seeking to counter or sanction "hate speech" are not only crude instruments for their intended purpose; they also fail to address the deep-rooted causes of "hate speech". As noted by Thomas Emerson:

> Conflicts between groups will never be settled in litigation over the question whether one group has been defamed. The tactics of arousing racial, religious or class hatred are too subtle to be bound by such controls. The effort to use the judicial process for this purpose merely diverts attention and energies from far more important measures essential to resolve the underlying grievances.[33]

---

29 *Ibid.*, p. 100.

30 These terms take "the place of outright appeals to racial prejudice; but although the language is softer and spoken more often than not by persons [...] innocent of consciously malign motives, it still serves racist ends in relation to which it stands as a code." – Stanley Fish, *There's No Such Thing as Free Speech and it's a Good Thing, Too* (New York, Oxford University Press, 1994), p. 13.

31 Franklyn S. Haiman, *Speech and Law in a Free Society, op. cit.*, p. 94.

32 *Ibid.*, p. 88.

33 Thomas I. Emerson, *The System of Freedom of Expression* (New York, Random House, 1970), p. 398.

Doubt may be cast over the effectiveness of hate speech laws for three reasons other than trends towards deceptively sanitised racist speech. First, it is very difficult to gauge the deterrent value of lending increased severity to legal sanctions when they involve an element of racial animus. Second, as Sandra Coliver argues on the basis of comprehensive evidence: administrative and other informal measures targeting prevention and redress are often better-suited than legal remedies for the promotion of tolerance and non-discrimination. This thesis is bolstered by the observation that "[T]he flagrant abuse of laws which restrict hate speech by the authorities at precisely those times when an even-handed approach to conflict is crucial provides the most troubling indictment of such laws".[34] Thus, she posits, "equality and dignity rights, as well as free speech rights, are best advanced by the narrowest of restrictions on hate speech" and "[t]he possible benefits to be gained by such laws simply do not seem to be justified by their high potential for abuse".[35] Third, litigation based on "hate speech" laws can have the unintended adverse consequence of generating publicity for the propagators of "hate speech" and their agenda.

Stereotyping, particularly in the media, has invidious and attritive effects on the groups it targets. The denigratory quotient of stereotyping is high: "press attacks on black people defy the very existence of a culture. At a minimum they redefine that culture in terms of deprivation, atrophy, and destruction".[36] Notwithstanding the tendency of stereotyping to perpetuate existing societal inequalities and reinforce prejudices, warnings against the dangers of censoring such practices are not misplaced.[37] Any legislative provisions seeking to address a concept as definitionally elusive as stereotyping would, by necessity, be grounded in vagueness. Dangers inhere in any policy that would seek to punish generally derogatory media portrayals of groups (in contradistinction to incitatory speech) or take action against overt and subliminal racism in the media.

The mainstream media – as well as the partisan, hateful organs of propaganda – are quite capable of peddling negative images of particular groups, or racist ideas. There can be no doubt whatever as to the incredible power wielded by the mass media. Spasmodic, and alas, systemic outpourings of racism have precipitated unprecedented media awareness of, and sensitivity to, the issue of

---

34 Sandra Coliver, "Hate Speech Laws: Do They Work?", in Sandra Coliver, Ed., *Striking a Balance: Hate Speech, Freedom of Expression and Non-discrimination* (United Kingdom, ARTICLE 19/University of Essex, 1992), pp. 363–373, at 373.

35 *Ibid.*, p. 363.

36 C. Ginsburg, "Destruction of Local Cultures Through Mass Communications", Kathleen Mahoney & Paul Mahoney, Eds., *Human Rights in the Twenty-first Century: A Global Challenge* (Part 2) (Netherlands, Kluwer Academic Publishers, 1993), pp. 777–781, at 780.

37 See further, Onora O'Neill, "Practices of toleration", in Judith Lichtenberg, Ed., *Democracy and the mass media* (USA, Cambridge University Press, 1990), pp. 155–185, p. 164.

race. This sensitivity, in its turn, has prompted the incorporation into journalistic codes of practice, ethics and house-style guides of principles and objectives aimed at ensuring a responsible treatment of subjects with potential for sparking social conflagrations.[38] The deleterious effects of negative stereotyping, prejudiced reporting and outright hatred have informed the drafting of these provisions. Heightened consciousness is equally being reflected in international norms.

It is incontestable that the power of the media can be used towards egregious ends. Rabid, racist rants targeting asylum-seekers and members of minority groups feature all-too-regularly in public life and in the media with varying degrees of prominence. Equally incontestable is the fact that the media *can* play a role in the dissemination of hate speech, with *Radio Mille Collines* in Rwanda being an example of just how devastatingly influential propaganda can be in fomenting incitement to hatred and genocide.[39] Indeed, three key media figures (two from *Radio Mille Collines* and one from the *Kangura* newspaper) were convicted for "genocide, incitement to genocide, conspiracy, and crimes against humanity, extermination and persecution" by the International Criminal Tribunal for Rwanda in December 2003.[40] It is no surprise that Article 20, ICCPR, and Article 3 of the Genocide Convention explicitly prohibit such incitement.

Policy preoccupations that are so manifest on the international scene are also replicated at the national level. Without seeking to diminish in any way the social imperative of eliminating racism, it must be stated that legislative intervention ought to be mindful of the potentially adverse effects any new and aggressive wording could have on the right to freedom of expression. The danger that the vigour of public debate could be asphyxiated by pandering excessively to societal sensitivities or exaggerated concerns for political correctness must be guarded

---

38 Typifying the approach of national journalistic codes of ethics, Article 10 of the NUJ's Code of Conduct reads as follows: "A journalist shall only mention a person's race, colour, creed, illegitimacy, marital status (or lack of it), gender or sexual orientation if this information is strictly relevant. A journalist shall neither originate nor process material which encourages discrimination, ridicule, prejudice or hatred on any of the above-mentioned grounds." A specific section of the International Federation of Journalists, International Media Working Group Against Racism and Xenophobia (IMRAX), is responsible for conducting most of its anti-racism work.

39 Aryeh Neier, "Clear and present danger", 27 *Index on Censorship* 57 (1/1998), at 59. See generally, *Broadcasting Genocide: Censorship, propaganda and state-sponsored violence in Rwanda, 1990–1994* (ARTICLE 19, England, 1996), *Deadly Marionettes: State-sponsored violence in Africa* (ARTICLE 19, England, 1997) and also M. Lenkova, Ed., *'Hate Speech' in the Balkans* (Athens, International Helsinki Federation for Human Rights, 1998).

40 *The Prosecutor v. Ferdinand Nahimana, Jean-Bosco Barayagwiza and Hassan Ngeze*, Case No. ICTR-99–52-T, Judgment of Trial Chamber 1 of the International Criminal Tribunal for Rwanda of 3 December 2003.

against.[41] The uninhibited exercise of the right to freedom of expression can allow it to play a crucial role in the furtherance of anti-racism strategies. This is widely recognised.[42] Only when there is a direct and incontrovertible nexus between particular forms of expression and actual harm or distress, should there be contemplation of curbing or, *a fortiori*, sanctioning, that expression.

Legislation requires a very clear exposition of the policy objectives which inform it, accompanied by lucid, thoughtful and watertight definitions of all relevant terminology. A connection between expression and harm or other alleged negative consequences cannot simply be presupposed. Rather, a very strong causal link between particular instances of expression and evident adverse, proximate consequences ought to be proved as a prerequisite for punishing expression by the law. Thus, a crucial consideration is often the "nature and imminence"[43] of the impugned expression, which will necessarily vary from case to case.

As argued *supra*, hate speech comprises an entire spectrum of negatively-motivated discourse. Its chameleon qualities afford it a flexibility which legislation cannot match. Thus, nuanced, subtle, subliminal racism is always likely to wriggle its way through the meshes of any legal definition. Given the increased sanitisation of racist language, its infinitely variegated hues and potential for sophisticated packaging, it is important to resist the obvious temptation to have recourse to the blanket-banning of racist speech (which could only be sure of sanctioning the crudest, vilest forms of racism in any case).

It is important to realise that one single statute simply cannot be a panacea for all the outpourings of hatred in a given society. One piece of legislation cannot simultaneously be the alpha and the omega of an entire nation's war against racism; nor should it entertain any ambition to fulfil such a role. Greater attention should be paid to the wider context in which key pieces of legislation operate; greater reliance should be placed on (complementary) non-legal measures which aspire to the realisation of the same broad aims. Education must top the list of non-legal measures, owing to its potential for stimulating greater public consciousness of racism and empathy towards its victims. Billowing black smoke does not warrant societal intolerance or legislative repression, for this is too little, too late. Rather, the focus should be on fire prevention.

---

41 See generally, Egbert Dommering, "Tolerantie, de vrijheid van meningsuiting en de Islam", in A.W. Hins and A.J. Nieuwenhuis, Eds., *Van zender naar ontvanger* (Amsterdam, Otto Cramwinckel, 2003), pp. 89–108.

42 This is recognised, *inter alia*, by the World Declaration (see, in particular, paras. 88, 90, discussed *supra*).

43 Ruth Gavison, "Incitement and the Limits of Law", in Robert C. Post, Ed., *Censorship and Silencing: Practices of Cultural Regulation* (Los Angeles, The Getty Research Institute for the History of Art and the Humanities, 1998), pp. 43–66, at 52.

7.1.2 Critical race theory

Chapter 6 explored the incompatibility of more virulent strains of "hate speech" with the most fundamental tenets of democracy and how international human rights law has consistently interpreted such speech to be unworthy of legal protection. The previous sub-sections in this chapter have explored various rationales for countering "hate speech", the vagueness of the term and the (related) problems of exclusive reliance on anti-"hate speech" laws to combat the phenomenon.

It is also very important to analyse "hate speech", or forms of expression tending towards "hate speech", in terms of the impact – both potential and real – which it has on the expressive and communicative opportunities of persons belonging to (racial) minorities at societal level. This is one of the central focuses of a growing body of interdisciplinary scholarship known as critical race theory.[44] In short, this scholarship derives from critical theory proper, which has been described as "a normative reflection that is historically and socially contextualized".[45] By way of further elucidation: "[c]ritical theory presumes that the normative ideals used to criticize a society are rooted in experience and reflection on that very society, and that norms can come from nowhere else".[46]

Critical race theory, then, pursues a more specific, subjective agenda. For instance, it "challenges ahistoricism and insists on a contextual/historical analysis of the law. Current inequalities and social/institutional practices are linked to earlier periods in which the intent and cultural meaning of such practices were clear".[47] Furthermore, it "insists on recognition of the experiential knowledge of people of color and our communities of origin in analyzing law and society".[48]

It is frequently asserted by critical race theorists – and indeed others who position themselves outside that branch of scholarship – that engrained prejudicial, discriminatory and hateful attitudes towards particular societal groups and the cumulation of institutional and societal practices reflecting those attitudes lead to the erosion of self-esteem of members of affected groups, thereby ultimately resulting in a foreclosure of their speech. In a social climate where discrimination

---

44 See generally: Mari J. Matsuda, Charles R. Lawrence III, Richard Delgado & Kimberlè Williams Crenshaw, Eds., *Words That Wound: Critical Race Theory, Assaultive Speech, and the First Amendment, op. cit.*; Richard Delgado & Jean Stefancic, Eds., *Critical Race Theory: the cutting edge* (2nd Edition), *op. cit.;* Richard Delgado & Jean Stefancic, *Understanding Words That Wound, op. cit.*

45 Iris Marion Young, *Justice and the Politics of Difference* (Princeton, Princeton University Press, 1990), p. 5.

46 *Ibid.*

47 Mari J. Matsuda *et al.*, *Words That Wound: Critical Race Theory, Assaultive Speech, and the First Amendment*, *op. cit.*, p. 6.

48 *Ibid.*

prevails, viewpoints of members of certain minority groups are regarded as being of inferior value in deliberative processes. The "silencing" argument – also frequently deployed by feminist scholars as an argument for the prohibition of pornography – is causal. Hate speech used by members of dominant societal groups becomes a tool of degradation and subordination. Hate speech does not simply result from that discriminatory climate – it actually contributes to its creation.

Two important penultimate observations about critical race theory must be made, both of which are prompted by the fact that the US has always been – and continues to be – the fountainhead of critical race theory and activism. This is important, first of all, because it points to a very particular cultural context and history of racism. It is important, secondly, because of its implicit acknowledgement that the development of critical race theory took place against the back-cloth of a particular constitutional ethos and system "in which free speech is given an especially exalted jurisprudential status [...]".[49] In other words, critical race theory was largely born out of a distinctive set of circumstances and then shaped by a distinctive constitutional tradition. These observations go a long way towards explaining the polarised, black-and-white character of debates concerning critical race theory.[50]

The approach to racist speech that predominates in European and international law is much more relativised.[51] Freedom of expression is less absolutist, less hubristic, less gung-ho and commensurately more receptive to the accommodation of other societal imperatives, in particular the elimination of racism. The express recognition that the exercise of the right to freedom of expression is subject to certain limitations and that it carries with it "(special) duties and responsibilities" greatly facilitates the task of reconciling critical race theory with freedom of expression values.

Nevertheless, despite the entrenched, opposing positions of proponents of critical race and First Amendment stalwarts, some commentators have sought to demonstrate that the two standpoints are not irredemiably polarised. Mari Matsuda, for instance, has argued that racist speech could be actionable without violating the essence of contemporary understanding of the First Amendment. She takes the view that "racist speech is best treated as a sui generis category, presenting an idea so historically untenable, so dangerous, and so tied to perpetuation of violence and degradation of the very classes of human beings who are least equipped to respond

---

49 Kenneth Lasson, "To Stimulate, Provoke, or Incite?: Hate Speech and the First Amendment", *op. cit.*, at 283.

50 See further: Frederick Schauer, "Media Law, Media Content and American Exceptionalism", in Susanne Nikoltchev, Ed., *IRIS Special – Political Debate and the Role of the Media: The Fragility of Free Speech* (Strasbourg, European Audiovisual Observatory, 2004), pp. 61–70.

51 See further: Kevin Boyle, "Hate Speech: The United States Versus the Rest of the World?", 53 Me. L. Rev. 487 (2001).

that it is properly treated as outside the realm of protected discourse".[52] She puts forward three characteristics that distinguish "the worst, paradigm example of racist hate messages from other forms of racist and nonracist speech",[53] which would allow for prosecution of the former. Those "identifying characteristics" are:

1. The message is of racial inferiority
2. The message is directed against a historically oppressed group
3. The message is persecutory, hateful, and degrading.[54]

Immediately after enumerating the characteristics, Matsuda insists that "[m]aking each element a prerequisite to prosecution prevents opening of the dreaded floodgates of censorship".[55] It is instructive to lift Matsuda's characteristics out of their immediate First Amendment context and to consider them in terms of prevailing international law. It is submitted here that the mere fact that a message is "persecutory, hateful, and degrading" would presumptively, i.e., absent any particular and unusual mitigating circumstances, be sufficient reason to deny that message protection under Article 10(2), ECHR, Article 19(3), ICCPR, or *a fortiori*, Article 4 *juncto* 5, ICERD. The communication of a message of "racial inferiority" would clearly contravene Article 4(a), ICERD. The targeting of a "historically oppressed group" is, of itself, clearly an insufficient reason to deny protection to a particular message, but its redolence of Article 27, ICCPR, could help to usefully bolster a claim based on either of the other two arguments.

Although it may at times appear that the values promoted by critical race theorists and First Amendment scholars are antipodal, Matsuda's attempt to reconcile the would-be opposites is but one example of how that myth could be debunked. There are surely others. The relationship between critical race theory and international law is fraught with discernibly less tension. Indeed, as will be outlined below, critical race theory is largely congruent with the essential thrust of generalist international human rights law. The main source of tension that could be identified is a source of tension that characterises the relationship between Articles 19 and 20, ICCPR, on the one hand, and ICERD (especially Articles 1, 4 and 5) on the other hand (see Chapter 6.1.2 and 6.1.3).

---

52 Mari J. Matsuda, "Public Response to Racist Speech: Considering the Victim's Story", in Mari J. Matsuda *et al.*, Eds., *Words That Wound: Critical Race Theory, Assaultive Speech, and the First Amendment*, *op. cit.*, pp. 17–51, at 35.

53 *Ibid.*, p. 36.

54 *Ibid.* It is interesting to note that in an earlier enumeration of these "identifying characteristics", the third characteristic was formulated differently: "The message endorses or implements persecution, hatred, or degradation of the group" – Mari J. Matsuda, "Outsider Jurisprudence: Toward a Victim's Analysis of Racial Hate Messages", in Monroe H. Freedman & Eric M. Freedman, Eds., *Group Defamation and Freedom of Speech: The Relationship Between Language and Violence*, (USA, Greenwood Press, 1995), pp. 87–120, at 101.

55 *Ibid.*

7.2 A square conceptual peg in a round normative hole?

There is no doubt that the myriad questions surrounding the regulation of "hate speech" collectively represent a very perplexing moral, legal and socio-political conundrum.[56] The apparent intractability of the whole often seems to be captured in T.S. Eliot's image of squeezing "the universe into a ball" and rolling it "towards some overwhelming question".[57] Yet, the conundrum need not be so intractable, actually. Just how overwhelming and intractable the question may seem will depend on the frame of enquiry in which it is placed: philosophical, political, legal or some combination or offshoot of the foregoing. The frame chosen here is international human rights law and necessarily its animating principles of democracy and justice. This will facilitate the mapping of particular types of "hate speech" onto particular provisions in international human rights law, thereby ameliorating the vagueness of the term.

Before pursuing this enquiry within the announced normative frame, a few cursory remarks plucked from a couple of time-honoured texts of political philosophy seem apposite for the purposes of contextualisation. It should be noted, for instance, that even seminal treatises such as Locke's *A Letter Concerning Toleration* and Mill's *On Liberty*, purposely fix principled boundaries for what is societally tolerable in terms of public expression. Locke sought to demarcate the zone of toleration by insisting that: "[n]o opinions contrary to human society, or to those moral rules which are necessary to the preservation of civil society, are to be tolerated by the magistrate".[58]

It is often overlooked that Mill, for his part, clearly countenanced the denial of legal protection to certain types of expression due to the moral repugnancy of their content.[59] Indeed, Mill's whole treatise is sprinkled with important recognitions of exceptions to the sanctity of his truth-championing rationale for freedom of expression. For instance, he acknowledges the legitimacy of restricting the principle of freedom of expression on the basis of considerations such as "harm to others"[60]

---

56 See further: Michael Herz & Peter Molnar, Eds., *The Content and Context of Hate Speech: Rethinking Regulation and Responses* (New York, Cambridge University Press, forthcoming 2011).

57 The full citation is: "To have squeezed the universe into a ball/To roll it towards some overwhelming question", T.S. Eliot, "The Love Song of J. Alfred Prufrock", in T.S. Eliot, *The Complete Poems and Plays* (England, Faber & Faber, 1969), pp. 13–17, at 15.

58 John Locke, *A Letter Concerning Toleration*, pp. 14–56, in John Horton & Susan Mendus, Eds., *John Locke A Letter Concerning Toleration in Focus* (London, Routledge, 1991).

59 See further, Frederick Schauer, "Social Epistemology, Holocaust Denial and the Post-Millian Calculus", in Michael Herz & Peter Molnar, Eds., *The Content and Context of Hate Speech: Rethinking Regulation and Responses*, *op. cit.*

60 John Stuart Mill, *On Liberty and other essays* (Oxford, Oxford University Press, 1998), p. 62.

and "injury to others".[61] He continues in a more explicit vein: "[w]henever, in short, there is a definite damage, or a definite risk of damage, either to an individual or to the public, the case is taken out of the province of liberty, and placed in that of morality or law".[62]

From the foregoing, it is clear that the need for regulation of "hate speech" – owing to its moral repugnancy and probable harm to others – is hardly in dispute. The preferred frame of enquiry here, *viz.* international human rights law, is even more dispositive of the question. By virtue of the – by now – well-entrenched "abuse of rights" doctrine in positive international human rights law, proponents of "hate speech" are, absent extraordinary mitigating factors, precluded from relying on international instruments in order to defend their putative right to freedom of speech. A detailed discussion of the operation of this doctrine in relation to "hate speech" under the European Convention on Human Rights has already been provided in Chapter 6.2.1. Here, it is sufficient to recall that the doctrine is regularly relied upon to prevent the proverbial hijacking of relevant instruments for purposes that are contrary to their letter and spirit.[63]

If the regulation or prohibition of the more virulent or abusive forms of "hate speech" is relatively uncontroversial from the perspective of international human rights law, the same cannot be said of the question of defining "hate speech", as has already been shown in the first section of this chapter. When international adjudicative bodies assess the necessity of measures deemed to constitute an interference with the right to freedom of expression, there should be systematic examination of a number of considerations, such as: intent of speaker, context (including form of expression), demonstrable harmful impact. The systematic examination of these considerations would necessarily have to show sensitivity to "contextual variables",[64] such as "the particular history and nature of discrimination, status as minority or majority group, customs, common linguistic practices, and the relative power or powerlessness of speakers and their targets within the society involved".[65]

61 *Ibid.*, p. 63.

62 *Ibid.*, p. 91.

63 By way of aside, though, it is interesting to note Frederick Schauer's philosophical challenge to the notion of "abuse" of the right to freedom of expression. He reasons that "the proper use of 'abuse' implies that the conduct referred to is within the scope of the right, and that is consistent with [the argument that] that conduct is outside that scope": Frederick Schauer, *Free speech: a philosophical enquiry* (Cambridge, etc., Cambridge University Press, 1982), p. 146. See also, *ibid.*, pp. 145 and 147.

64 Michel Rosenfeld, "Hate Speech in Constitutional Jurisprudence: A Comparative Analysis", 24 Cardozo L. Rev. 1523 (2003), at 1565.

65 *Ibid.* This list is not intended to be exhaustive.

If impugned speech does not amount to impermissible kinds of "hate speech" or is unlikely to lead to violence, there remains one futher angle of enquiry to be explored. This involves prising open the nature of the protection afforded "the reputation or rights of others" by Article 10(2). This leads to a particularly difficult – and subjective – judgment-call. The explicit protection of reputational and other rights of other persons (and the permissibility of certain restrictions on the exercise of the right to freedom of expression, when adequately based on those grounds) – is difficult to square with one of the central and constant principles of the European Court's jurisprudence, i.e., that protection of freedom of expression, as guaranteed by Article 10, ECHR, extends to information or ideas "that offend, shock or disturb the State or any sector of the population".

Freedom of expression is generally regarded as concerning "speakers, recipients (listeners, readers, and viewers), and of the general public",[66] and how the respective (and sometimes competing) rights and interests of each of the interested parties measure up to one another cannot be determined *in abstracto*, but only on a case-by-case basis.[67] The difficulty of reconciling the rights of others with the protection of offensive speech brings the third-listed (and often neglected) category – the general public – into analytical prominence. In certain cases, it is the rights of a particular sub-set of the general public, i.e., the non-target audience or bystanders,[68] that seem most jeopardised by offensive speech. T.M. Scanlon has posited that the interests of bystanders in restricting speech are in: (i) "avoiding the undesirable side effects of acts of expression" (eg. traffic jams, noise and litter, etc.), and more importantly, (ii) "the effect expression has on its audience", i.e., "harmful changes in audience belief and behavior" towards (particular) bystanders, eg. minorities.[69] Regulation of expression in order to meet the second objective is *prima facie* considerably more far-reaching than the "time, place and manner" restrictions that would typically be entailed by the former. That is because it requires the prevention of the "effective communication of an idea".[70]

The reconciliation exercise is much more complicated than pitting critical race theory against a hard-nosed version of individualistic liberalism. Critical race theory holds that offence directed at a participant in a public debate on account of his/her membership of a particular group can qualitatively affect his/her ability to

66 Eric Barendt, *Freedom of Speech* (2nd Edition) (Oxford, Oxford University Press, 2005), p. 6; see also, Frederick Schauer, *Free speech: a philosophical enquiry*, *op. cit.*, p. 49. Alternative configurations are, of course, possible: for instance, T.M. Scanlon refers to the interests of participants, audience and bystanders: T.M. Scanlon, "Freedom of expression and categories of expression", in T.M. Scanlon, *The Difficulty of Tolerance: Essays in Political Philosophy* (United Kingdom, Cambridge University Press, 2003), pp. 84–112, at 86–93.

67 See further, Frederick Schauer, *Free speech: a philosophical enquiry*, *op. cit.*, p. 105.

68 T.M. Scanlon, "Freedom of expression and categories of expression", *op. cit.*, at 92–93.

69 *Ibid.*, p. 92.

70 *Ibid.*, p. 93.

participate in that debate. This view has been vigorously contested in other quarters, however. Ronald Dworkin, for one, pays short shrift to the idea that individuals are (or even should be) entitled to be insulated from speech that would adversely affect their self-esteem (or self-respect) or the esteem (or respect) in which others hold them. He argues: "[p]eople of a thousand different convictions or shapes or tastes understandably feel ridiculed or insulted by every level of speech and publication in every decent democracy in the world".[71] He continues:

> A culture of independence almost guarantees that this will be so. Certainly, we should be decent to one another, and bigotry is despicable. But if we really came to think that we violated other people's rights whenever we reported sincere views that denigrated them in their own or others' eyes, we would have compromised our own sense of what it is to live honestly. We must find other, less suicidal, weapons against racism and sexism. We must, as always, put our faith in freedom, not repression.[72]

If there is no *general* right not to be offended – and it is resolutely submitted here that there is not – to what extent can the virtue of pluralistic tolerance be taken to cover the safeguarding of respectfulness towards members of other ethnicities, religious persuasions, etc.? The forthcoming analysis will reveal the existence of a circumspect right not to be offended in certain, particular circumstances – namely where racism and religious beliefs are directly concerned – and even then *only* when the offence attains a very high level of intensity or abuse. Racist expression and other more virulent types of "hate speech" have been amply dealt with in Chapter 6. The forthcoming analysis will therefore deal with the even greyer area of religious beliefs. This area is a heatedly disputed terrain between, on the one side, the pluralistic and tolerant zone carved out for robust public debate by *Handyside* and its jurisprudential progeny, and on the other side, racist and other types of abusive expression that do not enjoy legal protection.

As will now be demonstrated, the European Court of Human Rights has developed a set of roughly coherent principles to guide the resolution of boundary disputes in this area. Among the most important cases from which those principles have been gleaned are the cases, *Otto-Preminger-Institut v. Austria*,[73] and *Wingrove v. the United Kingdom*,[74] with new focuses being introduced by a later cluster of cases in which *Ginewski v. France*[75] (discussed below) is central.

---

71 Ronald Dworkin, *Freedom's Law* (Oxford University Press, New York, 1999), pp. 259–260.

72 (footnote omitted) *Ibid.*, p. 260.

73 *Otto-Preminger-Institut v. Austria*, Judgment of the European Court of Human Rights of 20 September 1994, Series A, no. 295-A.

74 *Wingrove v. United Kingdom*, Judgment of the European Court of Human Rights of 25 November 1996, Reports of Judgments and Decisions, 1996-V.

75 *Giniewski v. France*, Judgment of the European Court of Human Rights (Second Section) of 31 January 2006.

In *Otto-Preminger*, the applicant association (a private film-house) claimed (ultimately unsuccessfully) that its rights under Article 10, ECHR, had been violated by the seizure and forfeiture of a film (*Das Liebeskonzil*) it had planned to screen. The domestic Austrian courts found the characterisations of God, Jesus and Mary in the film to come within the definition of the criminal offence of disparaging religious precepts. Before it could actually be shown, the film was seized by the relevant national authorities in the context of criminal proceedings against the manager of the applicant association concerning the film.

At issue in the *Wingrove* case was the rejection by the British Board of Film Classification of an application for a classification certificate for the applicant's film, *Visions of Ecstasy*. The film, a short experimental video work, portrayed Saint Teresa engaging in acts of an overtly sexual nature, including with the body of the crucified Christ.[76]

These cases are, of course, supplemented by a raft of other cases, which will also duly be discussed. Broadly speaking, apart from one – potentially significant – discrepancy, there is little amiss with the Court's normative principles concerning permissible limits to freedom of expression when the exercise of the right interferes with the religious beliefs and convictions of others.

Where the Court's approach misfires, and has repeatedly misfired in the past, is in its application of those principles to specific factual situations. *İ.A. v. Turkey*,[77] a case centring on a conviction arising out of "an abusive attack on the Prophet of Islam" and in which the Court concluded that there had been no violation of Article 10, is a good example of such misfiring. The Court was split (by four votes to three)[78] and the joint dissenting opinion was unusually forthright in its suggestion that "the time has perhaps come to 'revisit'" the case-law on which the judgment was based (specifically *Otto-Preminger* and *Wingrove*), because it "seems to place too much emphasis on conformism or uniformity of thought and to reflect an overcautious and timid conception of freedom of the press".[79] This case will be subjected to critical examination in due course. First, however, the relevant principles of the Court will be set out.

---

76 Paras. 9, 61.

77 Judgment of the European Court of Human Rights (Second Section) of 13 September 2005.

78 Judges Baka, Turmen, Ugrekhelidze and Mularoni subscribed to the majority opinion, whereas Judges Costa (Section President), Cabral Barreto and Jungwiert issued a joint dissenting opinion.

79 Joint dissenting opinion, *ibid.*, para. 8.

7.2.1 Rough coherence of principles[80]

As explained in detail in Chapter 5, pluralism and tolerance are among the most powerful of the ECHR's animating principles. Time and again, the Court has averred in its case-law on freedom of religion that [societal] pluralism has been hard-won over the ages and that it is indissociable with democratic life. In the same vein, the Court has consistently held in its case-law on freedom of expression that pluralism, along with the adjacent concepts of tolerance and broadmindedness, constitutes one of the essential hallmarks of democratic society. Pluralism entails diversity and divergence, which in turn can often involve a certain amount of contention and even antagonism.[81] Thus, as famously stated in the *Handyside* case, information and ideas which "offend, shock or disturb the State or any sector of the population" must be allowed to circulate in order to safeguard the "pluralism, tolerance and broadmindedness" that underpin "democratic society".[82] In principle, this vigorous conception of freedom of expression applies to all matters of general public interest, including religious beliefs and affairs.[83]

Given the contiguous nature of the concepts of pluralism and tolerance, as developed by the European Court of Human Rights, Chapter 5 merges the concepts into one and speaks of (comprehensive) pluralistic tolerance,[84] a notion that implies a certain degree of reciprocal respect between the different constituent groups of any democratic society. Pluralistic tolerance can be well served by robust protection for freedom of expression, for example, when offensive expression advances discussions on matters of public interest. As posited by Robert Post: "[o]utrageous speech calls community identity into question, practically as well as cognitively, and thus it has unique power to focus attention, dislocate old assumptions, and shock its audience

---

80 This and the following subsections are a reworked version of Tarlach McGonagle, "An Ode to Contextualisation: *İ.A. v. Turkey*", [2010] 1 *Irish Human Rights Law Review*, pp. 237–251.

81 *Kokkinakis v. Greece*, Judgment of the European Court of Human Rights of 19 April 1993, para. 33; *Metropolitan Church of Bessarabia and others v. Moldova*, Judgment of the European Court of Human Rights of 13 December 2001, para. 123; *Hasan & Chaush v. Bulgaria*, Judgment of the European Court of Human Rights of 26 October 2000, para. 78; *Serif v. Greece*, Judgment of the European Court of Human Rights of 14 December 1999, para. 49; *Agga v. Greece*, Judgment of the European Court of Human Rights of 17 October 2002, paras. 53, 56; *Manoussakis v. Greece*, Judgment of the European Court of Human Rights of 29 August 1996, para. 44; *Supreme Holy Council of the Muslim Community v. Bulgaria*, Judgment of the European Court of Human Rights of 16 December 2004, para. 93.

82 *Handyside v. the United Kingdom*, Judgment of the European Court of Human Rights of 7 December 1976, Series A, No. 24, para. 49.

83 However, a crucial caveat to this general proposition will be entered *infra*.

84 Joseph Raz sometimes uses the term "pluralist toleration", which seems to have essentially the same meaning: Joseph Raz, "Free Expression and Personal Identification", 11 *Oxford Journal of Legal Studies* (No. 3, 1991), pp. 303–324, at 322.

into the recognition of unfamiliar forms of life".[85] However, the operative definition of "outrageous speech" is crucial here and it would have to be clarified. In any case, if the right to freedom of expression is to be interpreted consistently with the notion of pluralistic tolerance, the protection of the rights of others must be borne in mind.

In this respect, Article 10(2), ECHR, refers explicitly to the "duties and responsibilities" on which the exercise of the right to freedom of expression is contingent, and also the legitimacy of restricting the exercise of the right in order to protect the rights of others. As regards the application of these considerations to religious beliefs and affairs, the Court recognises the need to protect the deepest feelings and convictions of "others" from substantial or serious offence.[86] Similarly, it considers that the "respect for the religious feelings of believers as guaranteed in Article 9 [...] can legitimately be thought to have been violated by provocative portrayals of objects of religious veneration; and such portrayals can be regarded as malicious violation of the spirit of tolerance [...]".[87] This is because the beliefs in question are qualitatively different to other types of beliefs. David Edwards has explained that qualitative difference by observing that the "recognition of what is 'sacred' involves an affirmation of what is believed to be of ultimate value in experience, and of what is of deepest concern in life".[88] That is the transformative factor that legitimates the special consideration for earnestly and deeply held religious beliefs.

Having said that, it is imperative that the exceptional regard in which religious beliefs can be held not be used as a convenient excuse for stifling debate on matters of interest to the public.[89] Again, as Edwards has observed, the "determination of spiritual value is a matter of persuasion, of exposition, and (perhaps) argument, and in any such process there must be the possibility of contradiction, condemnation and offence".[90]

In the *Otto-Preminger-Institut* case, the European Court of Human Rights held that "in the context of religious opinions and beliefs", the duties and responsibilities which accompany the right to freedom of expression, may legitimately include:

> an obligation to avoid as far as possible expressions that are gratuitously offensive to others and thus an infringement of their rights, and which therefore do not contribute to any form of public debate capable of furthering progress in human affairs.[91]

---

85 Robert C. Post, *Constitutional Domains: Democracy, Community, Management* (Cambridge, Massachusetts, Harvard University Press, 1995), p. 139.

86 *Wingrove v. United Kingdom*, *op. cit.*, para. 58.

87 *Otto-Preminger-Institut v. Austria*, *op. cit.*, para. 47.

88 David Edwards, "Toleration and the English blasphemy law", in John Horton & Susan Mendus, Eds., *Aspects of Toleration* (London & New York, Methuen & Co., 1985), pp. 75–98, at 84.

89 See, in this respect, *Giniewski v. France*, *op. cit.*, paras. 50 & 51.

90 *Ibid.*, p. 82.

91 *Op. cit.*, para. 49; *Giniewski v. France*, *op. cit.*, para. 43.

Whether by accident or design, the reformulation of this principle in *Wingrove v. United Kingdom* and in *Murphy v. Ireland*[92] differs from its original articulation in *Otto-Preminger*. This is not a problem in itself; indeed, many principles are reworked and refined by the Court in the course of subsequent applications. In this case, however, some unexplained shifts of definitional emphasis appear to have been introduced. Instead of referring to expressions that are gratuitously offensive to others *and* an infringement of their rights *and* worthless from the perspective of public debate, the Court uses the more terse, alternative formula, "gratuitously offensive to others and profanatory".[93] No explanation is offered as to why the cumulative elements of the infringement of rights of others and the absence of any contribution to public debate were dropped. Nor is any attempt made to tease out the definitional scope of the notion of profanity, although it could be deduced from *Wingrove* that the "degree of profanation" would have to be "high" and the extent of insult to religious feelings "significant".[94] As a result of this inconsistent use of phraseology in the Court's approach to offensiveness in the context of religious opinions and beliefs, it is not possible to state with much confidence or precision what the official barometer actually is.

7.2.2 Contextual variables

Frederick Schauer has claimed that in previous and ongoing efforts to elucidate the scope of the right to freedom of expression, "there has been too much distillation and not enough dissection".[95] The *İ.A.* case illustrates Schauer's point perfectly. The essence of the Court's judgment in the case is a distillation of the main principles from its relevant case-law, but its application of those principles to the facts of the case is limited to one paragraph. In other words, what is missing is the dissection of key principles through their application to a set of specific factual circumstances.

In *İ.A. v. Turkey*, the Court applied its relevant general principles to the circumstances of the case as follows:

---

92 Judgment of the European Court of Human Rights (Third Section) of 10 July 2003. In this case, the applicant (a pastor affiliated to the Irish Faith Centre – "a bible based Christian ministry in Dublin" *ibid.*, para. 7) argued unsuccessfully that the refusal to broadcast an advertisement for the Irish Faith Centre, pursuant to a legislative prohibition on the broadcasting of religious advertising in Ireland, violated his rights under Articles 9 and 10, ECHR. Although the case was not *prima facie* about offence to the religious beliefs of others, the issue was considered in the Court's judgment.

93 *Wingrove v. United Kingdom*, *op. cit.*, para. 52. The formulation, "gratuitously offensive to others and profane", was used in *Murphy v. Ireland*, *op. cit.*, para. 65.

94 *Wingrove v. United Kingdom*, *op. cit.*, para. 60.

95 Frederick Schauer, *Free speech: a philosophical enquiry*, *op. cit.*, p. 85.

> However, the present case concerns not only comments that offend or shock, or a "provocative" opinion, but also an abusive attack on the Prophet of Islam. Notwithstanding the fact that there is a certain tolerance of criticism of religious doctrine within Turkish society, which is deeply attached to the principle of secularity, believers may legitimately feel themselves to be the object of unwarranted and offensive attacks through the following passages: "Some of these words were, moreover, inspired in a surge of exultation, in Aisha's arms... God's messenger broke his fast through sexual intercourse, after dinner and before prayer. Muhammad did not forbid sexual intercourse with a dead person or a live animal."[96]

It then found that the measures interfering with the applicant's freedom of expression aimed to offer protection against offensive attacks on matters regarded as sacred by Muslims and as such, corresponded to a "pressing social need".[97] It affirmed that the Turkish authorities had not overstepped their margin of appreciation and that the stated reasons for the impugned restrictions were "relevant and sufficient".[98] As regards the proportionality question, the Court referred to the fact that copies of the book had not been seized and also to the "insignificant" nature of the fine imposed.[99]

The strongly-worded joint dissenting opinion in the case begins by cautioning against being *blasé* about the Court's seminal pronouncement in *Handyside*, or using it in a merely sloganistic way.[100] It emphasises the "limited practical impact on society of the author's statements"[101] and points out that the likelihood that unorthodox religious views would "offend or shock the faith of the majority of the population" is an insufficient reason "in a democratic society to impose sanctions on the publisher of a book".[102] It readily acknowledges that the attacks on Muhammad contained in the passage from the book quoted *supra* "may cause deep offence to devout Muslims, whose convictions are eminently deserving of respect." In the same vein, it also refers to the "sacred" status of the Prophet in Islam.[103] Nonetheless, it rejects the idea that an entire book be condemned and its publisher criminally sanctioned on the basis of isolated passages in the book. It particularly rues the institution of criminal proceedings by the public prosecutor – and not by an offended member of the public – in the present case.[104] The dissenting judges also took issue with the perceived proportionality of the sanctions imposed on the applicant. They insist that any criminal conviction gives rise to a chilling effect and

96 *Ibid.*, para. 29.
97 *Ibid.*, para. 30.
98 *Ibid.*, para. 31.
99 *Ibid.*, para. 32.
100 Joint dissenting opinion, *ibid.*, para. 1.
101 Joint dissenting opinion, *ibid.*, para. 2.
102 Joint dissenting opinion, *ibid.*, para. 3.
103 Joint dissenting opinion, *ibid.*, para. 4.
104 Joint dissenting opinion, *ibid.*, para. 5.

leads to increased incidence of self-censorship.[105] As such, the dissenting opinion draws attention to the importance of "contextual variables"[106] in the Court's reasoning.

When the Court applies its normative principles to specific factual circumstances, it should systematically examine whether sufficient weighting has been given to factors such as: the intent of the speaker; "contextual variables", and the demonstrably harmful impact of the impugned expression. The Court has repeatedly stressed the importance of a context-sensitive approach, but as will presently be shown, it does not always practise what it preaches. The intent or motivation of the speaker is important as it can have significant bearing on how expression that is offensive to religious convictions is evaluated. There is a world of difference between misguided or thoughtless expression and that which is deliberately calculated to be offensive or which is fuelled by some kind of *animus*. Therefore, proof of an element of *scienter* (i.e., knowledge that the expression will or is likely to cause offence) should be required in order for liability to attach in civil proceedings,[107] and proof of *mens rea* in criminal proceedings.[108] Contextual variables could include the nature and impact of the medium used to convey the expression; audience-related considerations; socio-political factors; the nature and severity of the sanction imposed, etc. The requirement of "demonstrably harmful impact" is a safeguard measure that insists on the establishment of a clear causal link between the impugned expression and the alleged resultant harm to others (eg. gratuitous offence to their religious convictions). Some authors have employed different terminology (such as "appreciable"[109]) to create comparable safeguards, but those terms are suggestive of weaker forms of probabilism and are therefore liable to unduly restrict the right to freedom of expression.

---

105 Joint dissenting opinion, *ibid.*, para. 6.

106 Michel Rosenfeld, "Hate Speech in Constitutional Jurisprudence: A Comparative Analysis", *op. cit.*, at 1565.

107 By analogy, the *scienter* element is quite a common feature of (campus) hate speech codes: see further, Richard Delgado & Jean Stefancic, *Understanding Words That Wound*, *op. cit.*, p. 115.

108 It should however be noted in passing that the European Commission of Human Rights found the strict liability nature of the crime of blasphemous libel unobjectionable in the facts of *Gay News Ltd. & Lemon v. United Kingdom* (discussed further, below).

109 George Kateb writes: "[...] expression is harmful when its long-term tendency or indirect but appreciable result is the invasion of rights or fundamentally immoral conduct on a significant scale." – George Kateb, "The Freedom of Worthless and Harmful Speech", in Bernard Yack, Ed., *Liberalism without Illusions* (Chicago, University of Chicago Press, 1996), pp. 220–240, at p. 228.

7.2.2(i) Impact of publication

The joint dissenting opinion in *İ.A.* emphasises the likely impact of the publication. It had a limited,[110] once-off print-run, and the evidence before the Court did not indicate how many people actually read the book. The dissenting judges deduce from the fact that the book was not reprinted that the number of actual readers was small. Thus, one of the frequently-invoked rationales for regulating or restricting expression, *viz.* the impact/influence argument, offers a rather weak justification for interfering with the applicant's right to freedom of expression in the circumstances of the present case. Furthermore, as pointed out by the same Section of the Court just a few months before it returned its *İ.A.* judgment, the novel as a medium is "a form of artistic expression that appeals to a relatively narrow public compared to, for example, the mass media".[111] By counterpoising a novel with the "mass media",[112] the Court seeks (albeit with clumsy wording) to distinguish between different media on the basis of their circulation, and by extension, their potential reach and impact.[113] Such reasoning was explicated more clearly by the Court in *Lindon & others v. France*, when it describes the novel as "a form of artistic expression that, although potentially maintaining its readership for a longer period, appeals generally to a relatively narrow public compared with the print media".[114]

The specificity of a particular medium and its potential impact on the public are rightly considered by the Court to be relevant contextualising factors in many cases.[115] For instance, as the Court has repeatedly pointed out, "the audiovisual

---

110 Note that para. 5 of the Court's judgment refers to a print-run of 2,000 copies, whereas para. 2 of the joint dissenting opinion refers to 2,500. The correct figure would appear to be 2,000 copies, as the original French-language versions of the judgment and joint dissenting opinion both refer to 2,000 copies.

111 *Alinak v. Turkey*, Judgment of the European Court of Human Rights (Second Section) of 29 March 2005, para. 41. See also, *ibid.*, para. 45. The case arose out of the conviction of a former member of parliament, *inter alia* for incitement to hatred and hostility, for a novel (based on real events) he had written. The European Court of Human Rights found that there had been a violation of the applicant's right to freedom of expression because, notwithstanding the "very hostile" tone of some passages in the book, "their artistic nature and limited impact reduced them to an expression of deep distress in the face of tragic events, rather than a call to violence" – *ibid.*, para. 45.

112 One could, for instance, argue that a novel could be included in a definition of "mass media"; it is submitted here that the Court actually intended to distinguish between novels on the one hand, and newspapers and broadcasting on the other.

113 The Court has also taken this approach in other cases: see, for example, *Arslan v. Turkey*, Judgment of the European Court of Human Rights of 8 July 1999, para. 48.

114 Judgment of the European Court of Human Rights (Grand Chamber) of 22 October 2007, para. 47.

115 Eg. *Murphy v. Ireland*, *op. cit.*, para. 69.

media have often a much more immediate and powerful effect than the print media".[116]

For present purposes, it should additionally be noted that there can be no suggestion of a captive audience here, and that members of the public would have had to buy the book in order to be confronted with its content. However, arguments such as these have not had a particularly happy history before the adjudicative organs of the ECHR, or at least not in the context of offence to religious beliefs. They do not, for instance, correspond to the approach taken by the European Commission of Human Rights in the case of *Gay News Ltd. & Lemon v. United Kingdom*.[117] In that case, the Commission observed that the "issue of the applicants' journal containing the incriminated poem was on sale to the general public, *it happened to get known in some way or other* to the private prosecutor who was so deeply offended that she decided to take proceedings against the publication of this poem [...]".[118]

Although the case of *Müller & others v. Switzerland* involved (sexual) morals rather than offence to religious convictions,[119] it offers a useful analogy on the question of the public's exposure to potentially offensive material. In that case, a crucial consideration for the Court was that the impugned paintings were:

> painted on the spot – in accordance with the aims of the exhibition, which was meant to be spontaneous – and the general public had free access to them, as the organisers had not imposed any admission charge or any age-limit. Indeed, the paintings were displayed in an exhibition which was unrestrictedly open to – and sought to attract – the public at large.[120]

---

116 *Jersild v. Denmark*, Judgment of the European Court of Human Rights of 23 September 1994, Series A, no. 298, para. 31; *Murphy v. Ireland, op. cit.*, para. 69; *Radio France v. France*, Judgment of the European Court of Human Rights of 30 March 2004, para. 39, and (for very similar wording) *Purcell et al. v. Ireland*, Decision of inadmissibility of the European Commission of Human Rights of 16 April 1991, Application No. 15404/89.

117 *X. Ltd. & Y. v. United Kingdom*, Application No. 8710/79, Decision of inadmissibility of the European Commission of Human Rights of 7 May 1982, 28 D.R. 77 (November 1982). The case involved a conviction for blasphemy arising out of the publication of a poem, "The Love that Dares to Speak its Name" by Prof. James Kirkup, in a magazine called *Gay News*. According to the headnote of the House of Lords' decision in the case, the poem "purported to describe in explicit detail acts of sodomy and fellatio with the body of Christ immediately after his death and ascribed to Him during His lifetime promiscuous homosexual practices with the Apostles and other men." – cited in *ibid.*, para. 1.

118 (Emphasis added), *ibid.*, para. 12.

119 *Müller & others v. Switzerland*, Judgment of the European Court of Human Rights of 24 May 1988, Series A, No. 133. In this case, the applicant artists were convicted and their paintings confiscated on the grounds that the latter were obscene; the Court found that the measure served the legitimate aim of protecting public morals and held that Article 10 had not been violated.

120 *Ibid.*, para. 36.

Another – little-known – case, *S. v. Switzerland*,[121] also concerning the display of obscene material to the general public, is analogously useful as well. The European Commission of Human Rights concluded from the facts of the case that there was "no danger of adults being confronted with the film against or without their intention to see it" and that it was undisputed "that minors had no access to the film" either.[122] The Commission continued by stating that "since no adult was confronted unintentionally or against his will with the film [...] there must be particularly compelling reasons justifying the interference at issue".[123]

In its *Otto-Preminger* judgment, the Court observed that access to the (proposed) screening of the film was subject to an admission fee and an age-limit. As "the film was widely advertised", there was "sufficient public knowledge of the subject-matter and basic contents of the film to give a clear indication of its nature". The Court then offers a baffling *non sequitur*: "for these reasons, the proposed screening of the film must be considered to have been an expression sufficiently 'public' to cause offence".[124] This finding goes against the grain of the relevant reasoning relied upon in *Müller*, *supra*. The dissenting judges reached a very different conclusion, *viz*. that the advance publicity material issued by the applicant cinema: (i) aimed to warn the public about the critical way in which the film dealt with the Roman Catholic religion, and (ii) actually "did so sufficiently clearly to enable the religiously sensitive to make an informed decision to stay away". These conclusions prompted two further conclusions of note by the dissenting judges: (i) there was "little likelihood" of "anyone being confronted with objectionable material unwittingly", and (ii) the applicant association had acted "responsibly in such a way as to limit, as far as it could reasonably have been expected to, the possible harmful effects of showing the film".[125] It is submitted here that the dissenting opinion is more convincing than the majority opinion on this particular point.

In the *Wingrove* case, the European Commission had set considerable store by the probability that a short experimental video work would have a very limited reach and impact. The Delegate of the Commission submitted to the Court that the "risk that any Christian would unwittingly view the video was therefore substantially reduced and so was the need to impose restrictions on its distribution".[126] The possibility of further restricting distribution of the video to licensed sex shops was mooted and it was also pointed out that the boxes containing the video cassettes

---

121 *S. v. Switzerland*, Report of the European Commission of Human Rights of 14 January 1993, Application No. 17116/90, para. 62.

122 *Ibid.*, para. 62.

123 *Ibid.*, para. 65.

124 *Op. cit.*, para. 54.

125 *Ibid.*, Joint dissenting opinion of Judges Palm, Pekkanen and Makarczyk, para. 9.

126 *Ibid.*, para. 62.

would have included a description of its content.[127] The Court, however, responded by pointing out that once available, videos can be "copied, lent, rented, sold and viewed in different homes, thereby easily escaping any form of control by the authorities".[128] Thus, it found the consideration of the UK authorities that the film "could have reached a public to whom it would have caused offence" to be "not unreasonable" in the circumstances of the case.[129]

Whereas the majority of the Court in the *İ.A.* case accepted unquestioningly that Muslims would be insulted by certain passages in the novel and that the need to protect them "against offensive attacks" on matters they regarded as sacred, other case-law is less assuming. In *Tatlav*, for instance, where the applicant had been convicted for the defilement of religion, the Court found that the book that had prompted the conviction (entitled "The reality of Islam") contained sharp critism of religion from a socio-political perspective.[130] However, while distinguishing its judgment in the *İ.A.* case, it considered that the impugned statements did not have an insulting tone directly targeting believers, nor an abusive attack on sacred symbols, in particular those of Muslims, who on reading the book could nonetheless feel offended by the somewhat caustic commentary on their religion.[131]

Likewise, in a batch of other cases sharing key factual similarities, *viz.*, proselytism in the aftermath of an earthquake in Turkey,[132] the Court focused on the immediate and tragic context of the earthquake and described the impugned statements in each case as having a proselytic character and tending to foster superstition, intolerance and obscurantism by ascribing religious meaning to a natural disaster. Nevertheless, the Court held, however shocking or offensive the impugned statements may have been, they did not incite to violence in any way, nor did they promote hatred of non-members of the religious community in question.[133]

7.2.2(ii) Specificity of genre

A novel should ordinarily be "entitled to be judged by the criteria relevant to that genre including a considerable freedom of imaginative exploration".[134] The

127 *Ibid.*

128 *Ibid.*, para. 63.

129 *Ibid.*

130 *Aydin Tatlav v. Turkey*, *op. cit.*, para. 28.

131 *Ibid.*

132 *Nur Radyo Ve Televizyon Yayinciligi A.Ş v. Turkey*, Judgment of the European Court of Human Rights (Section 2) of 27 November 2007; *Kutlular v. Turkey*, Judgment of the European Court of Human Rights (Section 4) of 29 April 2008. C.f. *Mehmet Cevher Ilhan v. Turkey*, Judgment of the European Court of Human Rights (Section 2) of 13 January 2009.

133 *Nur Radyo v. Turkey*, *op. cit.*, para. 30; *Kutlular v. Turkey*, *op. cit.*, paras. 48 and 49.

134 Bhikhu Parekh, *Rethinking Multiculturalism: Cultural Diversity and Political Theory* (Second Edition) (New York, Palgrave Macmillan, 2006), p. 320. Parekh's supporting example relates

applicant in the *İ.A.* case had argued in domestic proceedings that the impugned novel should have been analysed by literary specialists. This argument does not appear to have been pursued by the applicant before the European Court, which limited itself to acknowledging that the author's views were conveyed in a "novelistic style", without probing the matter any further. The joint dissenting opinion, likewise, failed to adequately pick up on the argument. In its case-law, the Court has consistently held that Article 10 "protects not only the substance of the ideas and information expressed, but also the form in which they are conveyed".[135] It is submitted here that in order to adequately protect the substance of ideas and information expressed in a novel, the Court ought to give due consideration to stylistic and other specificities that are relevant to the genre. Indeed, this is the thrust of one of its main lines of reasoning in the aforementioned *Alinak* case.[136]

By selecting the passages in the book that were deemed to be the most offensive, isolating them and examining them out of context, the conclusion that they were unacceptably abusive was a foregone one. The same conclusion might very well have been reached if the passages had been examined in their original context (as intended by the author), but the conclusion would have been all the stronger for having been subjected to such an embedded analysis. As it stands, without the benefit of any insights that might have been generated by such an analysis, the Court's conclusion may be intuitively correct from a moral perspective, but it lacks methodological rigour. It should be noted, by way of contrast, that the Court's finding of a violation of Article 10 in its *Paturel* judgment was partly due to the fact that the French Courts had convicted the applicant on the basis of impugned extracts from a written work which had been assessed out of the context of the work as a whole and without acknowledging the documentary materials which had been provided in the work in support of the impugned passages.[137] The importance of reading impugned passages in their original context is recurrently emphasised in the Court's case-law,[138] which makes it all the more puzzling that its judgment in the *İ.A.* case deviated from that norm.

---

specifically to Salman Rushdie's novel, *The Satanic Verses*, but it is nevertheless illustrative of a broader range of possibilities: he points out that the "offensive passages occur within the dream of a demented man, and hence not in the same category as unambiguous expressions of abuse and ridicule by the author", *ibid.* Contrast, however, the approach taken by the European Court of Human Rights in *Lindon & others v. France*, where the juxtaposition of fact and fiction served to limit the novelist's freedom of expression: *op. cit.*, para. 55.

135 See, amongst other authorities, *De Haes & Gijsels v. Belgium*, Judgment of the European Court of Human Rights of 24 February 1997, Reports of Judgments and Decisions 1997-I, para. 48.

136 *Op. cit.*, paras. 41–45.

137 Case of *Paturel v. France*, Judgment of the European Court of Human Rights (First Section) of 22 December 2005, para. 50.

138 See, amongst other examples, *Abdullah Aydin v. Turkey (No. 2)*, Judgment of the European Court of Human Rights (Third Section) of 10 November 2005, para. 25.

7.2.2(iii) Proportionality of sanctions

The Court has frequently observed that "the nature and severity of the penalty imposed are factors to be taken into account when assessing the proportionality of the interference",[139] especially when the penalty in question risks creating a chilling effect on discussion of matters of public interest.

In the *İ.A.* case, the Court took cognisance, first of all, of the fact that the domestic authorities did not seize the book. Puzzlingly, this seems tantamount to praising the Turkish authorities merely for abstaining from a course of action that is generally regarded as anathema to freedom of expression. As a measure effectively constituting prior restraint, the seizure of the impugned novel would rightly have been regarded as a very far-reaching infringement of the applicant's freedom of expression. However, in the stream of case-law currently under discussion, prior restraint has encountered considerably less resistance than in other types of Article 10 cases. In *Otto-Preminger*, neither the seizure nor the forfeiture of the film was found to amount to a violation of Article 10. However, the dissenting judges in that case did warn that "[t]here is a danger that if applied to protect the perceived interests of a powerful group in society, such prior restraint could be detrimental to that tolerance on which pluralist democracy depends".[140] In *Wingrove*, the ban on the video was total, a fact which prompted the Court to acknowledge that the prior restraint involved in the case called for "special scrutiny".[141] In the heel of the hunt, the measure of "special scrutiny" required was arguably not forthcoming, as the Court professed its satisfaction at the "high threshold of profanation embodied in the definition of the offence of blasphemy under English law" and ceded a wide margin of appreciation to the national authorities in the matter.[142]

Secondly, in *İ.A.*, the Court also took cognisance of the [monetary] insignificance of the fine imposed. The joint dissenting opinion concedes that the fact that the prison sentence was commuted into a modest fine is significant, but the fears of the dissenting judges have not been completely allayed: "[f]reedom of the press relates to matters of principle, and any criminal conviction has what is known as a 'chilling effect' liable to discourage publishers from producing books that are not strictly conformist or 'politically (or religiously) correct'".[143] The same argument was also

---

139 *Sürek v. Turkey (No. 1)*, Judgment of the European Court of Human Rights of 8 July 1999, Reports of Judgments and Decisions, 1999-IV, para. 64.

140 *Op. cit.*, Joint dissenting opinion, para. 4.

141 *Ibid.*, para. 58, following its earlier findings in *Observer & Guardian v. United Kingdom*, Judgment of the European Court of Human Rights of 26 November 1991, Series A, no. 216, para. 60. See also in this connection the dissenting opinions of Judges De Meyer and Lohmus in the *Wingrove* case.

142 *Ibid.*, para. 61.

143 Joint dissenting opinion, *İ.A. v. Turkey*, *op. cit.*, para. 6.

applied by the Court in its unanimous finding of a violation of Article 10 in the *Tatlav* case.[144]

Generally-speaking, the Court's approach to the dissuasive impact of a criminal sanction tends to vary according to the circumstances of the case.[145]

7.2.2(iv) New doctrinal directions?

It is most unlikely that the Court will formally take the bold step of severing its own doctrinal chain, as it was urged to do by the dissenting judges in the *İ.A.* case.[146] But perhaps such a radical step, with all the political and face-losing consequences it would likely entail, is not entirely necessary in order to reshape relevant case-law in its future judgments. To the extent that the principle of *stare decisis* "creates a chain of cases, in which each decision is an interpretation of immediately prior decisions", it offers the flexibility of distinguishing between the application of relevant principles in previous and new sets of circumstances.[147] As has been argued throughout this section, the relevant principles are – by and large – sound; it is the application of those principles that has been a source of disappointment. As the principles are not objectionable, there is no pressing need to repudiate them; rather, the focus should be on ensuring that whenever the Court applies relevant principles in the future, it does so in a way that distinguishes unsatisfactory precedents set by the mis-application of principles in its earlier case-law.

The case of *Giniewski* provides useful relevant examples of how this can be done: it distinguishes, *inter alia*, certain contextualising elements of the *Otto-Preminger* and *İ.A.* cases, from the circumstances with which it was faced.[148] The case involved the conviction of a journalist (who was acquitted on appeal, but ordered to pay nominal damages and to foot the bill for the publication of the appellate decision in one national newspaper) for defamation in respect of an article he had written criticising a Papal Encyclical and exploring possible links between a particular

144 *Aydin Tatlav v. Turkey*, Judgment of the European Court of Human Rights (Second Section) of 2 May 2006, para. 30.

145 Contrast, for example, *Sürek v. Turkey (No. 1)*, *op. cit.*, paras. 63 and 64 and *Chauvy & Others v. France*, Judgment of the European Court of Human Rights (Second Section) of 29 June 2004, para. 78, with *Jersild v. Denmark*, *op. cit.*, para. 35 and *Giniewski v. France*, *op. cit.*, para. 55.

146 See generally in this connection: Robin C.A. White & Iris Boussiakou, "Separate opinions in the European Court of Human Rights", 9 *Human Rights Law Review* (No. 1, 2009), pp. 37–60; Robin C.A. White & Iris Boussiakou, "Voices from the European Court of Human Rights", 27 *Netherlands Quarterly of Human Rights* (No. 2, 2009), pp. 167–189; Alastair Mowbray, "An Examination of the European Court of Human Rights' Approach to Overruling its Previous Case Law", 9 *Human Rights Law Review* (No. 2, 2009), pp. 179–201.

147 Robert Post, "Theories of Constitutional Interpretation", in Robert Post, Ed., *Law and the Order of Culture* (California, University of California Press, 1991), pp. 13–41, at 20.

148 *Op. cit.*, para. 52.

doctrine and the origins of the Holocaust. The European Court of Human Rights found that the applicant's right to freedom of expression had been violated because his article did not set out to attack religious beliefs, but to contribute to an ongoing debate on topics of interest to the general public.

More specifically, the Court took the view that "although the applicant's article criticised a papal encyclical and hence the Pope's position, the analysis it contained could not be extended to Christianity as a whole, which was made up of various different strands, several of which rejected papal authority".[149] The Court considered the applicant's article to be a contribution to an important topic of public debate and that the article was neither "gratuitously offensive" nor "insulting and that it did not "incite to disrespect or hatred", or for that matter, "cast doubt in any way on clearly established historical facts".[150]

In other comparable case-law, the Court has also recognised the primacy of public debate on religious matters and has distinguished between (strong) criticism of religious officials on the one hand, and religious beliefs, on the other hand. The case, *Albert-Engelmann-Gesellschaft mbH v. Austria*,[151] for instance, involed statements expressed in a letter to the editor of a magazine "writing on church issues and related to a religious debate which was of considerable interest to the concerned religious community at the time of the events".[152] The statements in question gave an opinion on reform of the Catholic Church and suggested that a Mr. Paarhammer, who then held a number of positions, including Vicar General of the Salzburg Archdiocese, was a "'rebel' and 'critical of the Church' and that he had 'publicly criticised and disparaged the Pope in an extremely offensive manner'".[153] The Court found the impugned statements to be permissible value judgments and not a "gratuitous personal attack" on a particular individual who occupied a formal position within the church and had contributed to the religious debate in question.[154]

A similar approach was taken by the Court in the case of *Klein v. Slovakia*, the factual backdrop to which was the sharp criticism of an Archbishop who called for the film, *The People vs. Larry Flynt*, and its accompanying poster, to be withdrawn.[155] The applicant journalist was convicted of the offence of "Defamation of nation, race and belief".[156] In finding a violation of Article 10, the Court followed its *Giniewski* judgment and stated that the applicant's "strongly worded pejorative

---

149 *Ibid.*, para. 49.
150 *Ibid.*, para. 52.
151 Judgment of the European Court of Human Rights (First Section) of 19 January 2006.
152 *Ibid.*, para. 30.
153 *Ibid.*, para. 32.
154 *Ibid.*, paras. 32–33.
155 Judgment of the European Court of Human Rights (Fourth Section) of 31 October 2006.
156 Ibid., para. 50.

opinion related exclusively to the person of a High Representative of the Catholic Church in Slovakia"[157] and that the impugned article "neither unduly interfered with the right of believers to express and exercise their religion, nor did it denigrate the content of their religious faith".[158]

A recurrent problem in the relevant case-law of the Court is the inadequate attention it has tended to give to contextualising factors when assessing whether impugned practices measure up to its principles. Contextualising factors can often have a relativising (or occasionally, even a transformative) impact on the interpretation of the bare facts of a case, and the Court should pay increased attention to the importance of contextualising factors in the future.

The foregoing section details specific examples of contextualising factors that have been under-explored in the relevant case-law of the Court. Finally – to round off the foregoing critical dissection with further critical distillation – another lingering problem with *Otto Preminger* and its jurisprudential progeny must be addressed. The problem concerns the lax and seemingly unquestioning manner in which the Court has tended to apply the margin of appreciation doctrine in relevant cases.

It cannot be gainsaid that religious affairs have an immense inherent capacity for contentiousness. It is also generally true that States authorities are in the best position to take the measure of local religious sensitivities (but whether they can be trusted to do so fairly and objectively is another matter entirely). Nevertheless, the margin of appreciation doctrine must not be allowed to become a smoke-screen behind which States and the European Court can hide, instead of facing up to complex, divisive issues. In a number of the cases analysed in detail, *supra*, the Court has (too) readily endorsed States authorities' justifications of measures restricting the right to freedom of expression.

Those justifications have often included the preservation of religious peace and harmony and the avoidance of societal divisions – even when those goals do not seem to be particularly threatened by the impugned expression. For example, it seems both implausible and incongruous that the broadcasting of an informative, inoffensive advertisement for a particular minority religious group would lead to "unrest" in contemporary Ireland. That argument, however, was factored into the Court's reasoning in the *Murphy* case.[159] The question of religious advertising was made the subject of a public consultation conducted by the Irish Department of Communications, Marine and Natural Resources in 2003. The public consultation was concluded after the European Court had found that the existing statutory

157 *Ibid.*, para. 51.
158 *Ibid.*, para. 52.
159 *Murphy v. Ireland, op. cit.*, paras. 73 *et seq.*

prohibition on broadcasting religious advertising *as applied to the facts in the Murphy case* did not amount to a violation of Article 10. Upon the conclusion of the public consultation, it was announced at the beginning of 2004 that there would be no change to the *status quo*.[160] Interestingly, apart from acknowledging that the subject is "very emotive", the Minister did not rely on the argument of divisiveness which had struck such a loud chord with the European Court in the *Murphy* case. Rather, he stated his preoccupying concern to be the intrusiveness of religious advertisements when broadcast to captive audiences and the principle of equality of arms.[161]

Similarly, in *Leroy v. France*, a case involving a conviction for glorification of terrorism arising out of a cartoon published by way of reaction to the 11 September attack on the Twin Towers in New York,[162] the Court referred to the political volatility of the Basque region (where the cartoon was published) but failed to link the content of the cartoon to the immediate regional political situation.[163]

The outcome, in each case, has been in favour of majoritarian or orthodox or conventional religious beliefs. Quite simply, as David Richards has pointed out, "the measure of constitutional protection for conscientiously dissenting speech could not be the dominant orthodoxy that it challenged, for that would trivialize the protection of free speech to whatever massaged the prejudices of dominant majorities".[164] Greater critical engagement with the particular circumstances of individual cases is required in order to ensure that the Court's judgments in this area are realistic and convincing.

Context may not be everything (although an old platitude of literary criticism tells us otherwise), but if the European Court of Human Rights continues to ignore the importance of contextualising factors in its jurisprudence, it will surely do so at its peril.

---

160 "Dermot Ahern Retains Ban on Religious Advertising", Press Release of the Department of Communications, Marine and Natural Resources, 29 January 2004.

161 The Minister's press release stated: "Advertising on radio and television is significantly more intrusive than advertising in other media given the pervasive nature of the media. I don't believe that Irish people would want, on balance, that religious interests should be able to buy air-time to deliver an unchallenged message – one which other interests through lack of resources might not be able to match or counter".

162 *Leroy v. France*, Judgment of the European Court of Human Rights (Fifth Section) of 2 October 2008. The Court concluded that there had not been a violation of the applicant's right to freedom of expression.

163 *Ibid.*, para. 45.

164 David A.J. Richards, *Free Speech and the Politics of Identity* (New York, Oxford University Press, Inc., 1999), p. 197.

7.3 Specific current controversies as stress tests for the right to freedom of expression

Having analysed the relevant jurisprudence of the European Court of Human Rights at length, and before closing the discussion on the scope of the heavily qualified right not to be offended, three current controversies merit close attention: denial or trivialisation of genocide and other crimes against humanity; "defamation" of religions, and protection of founders of religions.

7.3.1 Denial or trivialisation of genocide and other crimes against humanity

Debates centring on whether or not free speech principles should afford any protection for the denial or trivialisation of genocide and other crimes against humanity remain topical and heated. Nevertheless, international human rights law has (until recently) consistently refused to extend protection to such types of expression, as will presently be demonstrated.

Holocaust denial is a *sui generis* type of hate speech. It is morally reprehensible for a number of reasons: it is a common and convenient vehicle for conveying anti-Semitic sentiments; it denies survivors recognition of the dignity-stripping devastation which defines the Holocaust; it minimises the suffering and ultimate fate of those who were murdered in pursuit of the Nazis' programme of elitarian-inspired hatred; it amounts to hatred directed against a group and against individual members of that group and it reinforces trends of discrimination and persecution. And this is true of every group that was subjected to systematic annihilation under the Nazi regime – Jews, Communists, Gypsies, the Mentally and Physically Disabled and others. In light of the harm caused by Holocaust denial, the case for legal prohibitions on such speech would appear to be socially imperative. The thesis that Holocaust denial should automatically be proscribed, irrespective of considerations such as intent, the time, place and manner of its delivery or its actual impact, is built on the premise that to allow Holocaust denial is, *ipso facto*, to confer a certain legitimacy on the content of this kind of speech.[165]

It is often the wont of so-called 'revisionist historians' and (extreme) right-wing politicians to seek to dress up their work or statements in the emperor's clothing of "academic freedom" and "freedom of speech". Neither claim is of immediate relevance, however. Myriad sound bites seek to strike high-minded chords: the truth is unattainable; our conceptions thereof are doomed to relativity; no facts should be immune to challenge, to vigorous questioning, as this is a vector for the advancement

165 Alexaner Bickel, *The Morality of Consent*, *op. cit.*, p. 73; Roger Eatwell, "The Holocaust Denial: a Study in Propaganda Technique", in L. Cheles, R. Ferguson & M. Vaughan, Eds., *Neo-Fascism in Europe* (New York, Longman Inc., 1991), pp. 120–146, at 123.

of society; no belief should be allowed to be sclerotised in accordance with the prevailing currents of any time or creed. The high road to self-righteousness is paved with such platitudes, perversely chosen in the hope that their rhetorical resonance will distract from the main issues involved.

But these are no more than empty sound bites and their echo *is* hollow, for not all disputes concerning the veracity of established facts are of a similar nature. Holocaust deniers are often quick to liken their contestations of orthodox accounts of the history of the Second World War to Galileo's dissent from the catholic, conventional wisdom of yesteryear which dictated that the sun revolved around the earth. However, the primordial difference between Holocaust denial and Galileo's celebrated refusal to recant ("*eppur si muove!*") is that the issue of hatred was not central to the debate in which the principles of modern astronomy finally triumphed. Doubting and questioning with a view to stimulating reflection and debate are laudable, but not when their propelling force is hatred.

Such is the emotive content of any expression merely evoking the Shoah,[166] that the delicate judicial balancing of seemingly antipodal interests will be necessarily deferential to the rights and reputations of those affected by the harmful tendencies of such speech. Stanley Fish concedes that "although we ourselves are certain that the Holocaust was a fact, facts are notoriously interpretable and disputable; therefore nothing is ever really settled, and we have no right to reject something just because we regard it as pernicious and false".[167] However, he continues, "when it happens that the present shape of truth is compelling beyond a reasonable doubt, it is our moral obligation to act on it and not defer action in the name of an interpretative future that may never arrive".[168] In aggregate, this is recognition that conceptions of truth can only ever be relative and that ideas *can* be suppressed on the basis of their harmful content. The upshot of Fish's assertion is that the memory of those who perished in the Holocaust should never be jettisoned in favour of a cargo of spuriously-motivated arguments about the fallibility of any so-called "truth".

There are discernible similarities in the material facts of most of the negationist cases to have been brought before the European Commission of Human Rights. The applicants all sang from the same heinous hymn-sheet. Holocaust denial was their common refrain, but there were slight variations in the specific cadenzas of this

166 See, for instance, the controversy (misplaced accusations of trivialisation of the Holocaust) which surrounded 'La vita è bella' (Italy, 1997), the Roberto Benigni film which won the Grand Prix at the Cannes Film Festival in 1998 and the Academy Award for Best Foreign Language Film in the same year. See further in this connection, Anne-Marie Bacon, *The Shoah on screen – Representing crimes against humanity* (Volume I) (Strasbourg, Council of Europe, 2006).

167 Stanley Fish, *There's No Such Thing as Free Speech and it's a Good Thing, Too* (New York, Oxford University Press, 1994), p. 113.

168 *Ibid.*

distasteful orchestra, including: allegations that the Holocaust was invented for the purposes of extorting monetary compensation from the German authorities; aggressive advocacy of the reinstitution of National Socialism and the racial discrimination inherent in its philosophy; various Nazi-inspired activities; the sinister, spurious questioning of the scientific feasibility of mass gassing.

In *X v. FRG*,[169] it was held that to prohibit an individual from displaying pamphlets alleging that the Holocaust was "a lie" and a "zionistic swindle" is a measure that is "necessary in a democratic society for the protection of the reputation of others". The Commission focused not only on the pamphlets' distortion of relevant historical facts, but also on the attack they contained on the "reputation of all those who were described as liars or swindlers, or at least as persons profiting from or interested in such lies or swindles".[170] The conviction of a journalist for the publication of pamphlets aggressively advocating the reinstitution of National Socialism and the racial discrimination inherent in its philosophy, was held, in *Kühnen v. FRG*,[171] to be necessary in democratic society "in interests of national security and public safety and for protection of rights of others".[172] Similarly, in *Rebhandl v. Austria*,[173] the Commission upheld the conviction of the applicant for, *inter alia*, distributing "publications denying in particular the existence of the gassing of Jews in the concentration camps under the Nazi regime" on the basis of the public interest in the prevention of crime and disorder and the protection of reputations and rights. This, too, was the logic applied by the European Court of Human Rights in *Witzsch v. Germany*,[174] a case involving a conviction for disparaging the dignity of the dead. In that case, the language employed was more open-ended, as it spoke of "the requirements of protecting the interests of the victims of the nazi regime".

H., W., P., and K. v. Austria[175] dealt with convictions for acts performed by the applicants in connection with their membership of and leadership in *Aktion Neue Rechte* (ANR). The Commission held that legal prohibitions on activities inspired by National Socialism *are* "necessary in a democratic society in the interests of national security and territorial integrity and for the prevention of crime".[176] It is perhaps noteworthy that the activities of the applicants involved the preparation and

169 Decision of inadmissibility of the European Commission of Human Rights, Appn. No. 9235/81, 29 DR 194 (1982).
170 *Ibid.*, p. 198.
171 Decision of inadmissibility of the European Commission of Human Rights, Appn. No. 12194/86, 56 DR 205 (1988).
172 *Ibid.*, p. 205.
173 Decision of inadmissibility of the European Commission of Human Rights of 16 January 1996, Appn. No. 24398/94.
174 Decision of inadmissibility of the European Court of Human Rights of 20 April 1999, Appn. No. 41448/98.
175 Decision of inadmissibility of the European Commission of Human Rights, Appn. No. 12774/87, 62 DR (1989) 216.
176 *Ibid.*, p. 216.

publication of pamphlets which described the Holocaust as a lie; propagated theories about alleged biological differences between races, principles of elitarianism and endorsements of *Lebensraum* and other National Socialist doctrines which constituted part of their own party's manifesto. The most significant feature of this case was the Commission's observation that "National Socialism is a totalitarian doctrine incompatible with democracy and human rights and that its adherents undoubtedly pursue aims of the kind referred to in Article 17".[177] This is a very candid and important recognition of the hateful ideology that forms the bedrock of Nazism. It is, in effect, the equation of membership of the National Socialist Party with an espousal of all of its ideals. *Ochensberger v. Austria*[178] was another case challenging a conviction for National Socialist activities and was declared inadmissible on much the same grounds.

The Commission's finding in *Honsik v. Austria*[179] is a carbon-copy of its finding in the *H., W., P. and K. v. Austria* application as exactly the same reasons are offered in attesting to the necessity of the conviction for social democracy. Furthermore, the incompatibility of National Socialism with democracy and human rights is reiterated. The conviction in the instant case was "pour avoir nié dans une publication la réalité du génocide perpetré dans les chambres à gaz des camps de concentration sous le régime national-socialiste".[180]

In *Walendy v. Germany*,[181] the Commission refused to admit a complaint by the applicant about a search and the seizure of an unlawful publication containing an article which amounted to a denial of the systematic annihilation of Jews under the Third Reich. This, the Commission held, "constituted an insult to the Jewish people and at the same time a continuation of the former discrimination against the Jewish people".[182] In *E.F.A. Remer v. Germany*,[183] the applicant's suggestions that "le sort des Juifs sous le régime national-socialiste avait été 'inventé' de toutes pièces à des

177 *Ibid.*, pp. 220/1. See p. 216 for almost identical language, and also *Nachtmann v. Austria*, Decision of inadmissibility of the European Commission of Human Rights of 9 September 1998, Appn. No. 36773/97. This unsuccessful application was taken by the head of editorial staff of a periodical that published an article which grossly denied and minimised National Socialist genocide and other National Socialist crimes. Nigh-identical language is also employed in *Schimanek v. Austria*, Appn. No. 32307/96.

178 Decision of inadmissibility of the European Commission of Human Rights, Appn. No. 21318/93, 18 EHRR-CD, pp. 170–172.

179 Decision of inadmissibility of the European Commission of Human Rights, Appn. No. 25062/94, 83-B DR 77 (1995).

180 "[F]or having denied in a publication the reality of the genocide perpetrated in the gas chambers of the concentration camps under the National-Socialist regime" (author's translation). *Ibid.*, p. 77.

181 Decision of inadmissibility of the European Commission of Human Rights, Appn. No.21128/92, 80-A DR 94.

182 *Ibid.*, p. 99.

183 Decision of inadmissibility of the European Commission of Human Rights, Appn. No. 25096/94, 82-A DR 117.

fins d'extorsion"[184] ensured that his attempt to challenge his conviction for incitement to hatred and to racial hatred was declared inadmissible.

Notwithstanding the Commission's repeated refusals even to countenance speech involving Holocaust denial, or by extension, speech used by proponents of National Socialism in furtherance of their stigmatised brand of politics, one case which did manage to slip through the net and was duly considered by the Court in 1998 was *Lehideux & Isorni v. France*, discussed in Chapter 6.[185] This judgment was a rare instance of freedom of expression outweighing the perceived harms of discourse which is colourably negationist, anti-Semitic or totalitarian, when these two potentially countervailing concerns were balanced on the judicial scales. Other highly-publicised cases centring on Holocaust denial have also originated in France.[186]

The application in *Marais v. France*,[187] declared manifestly unfounded by the Commission, arose out of an article entitled 'La chambre à gaz homicide du Struthof-Natzweiler, un cas particulier' ('The homicidal gas chamber of Struthof-Natzweiler, a particular case'; author's translation) written by the applicant for the periodical *Révision*. The Commission considered the content of the article to question "l'existence et l'usage de chambres à gaz pour une extermination humaine de masse".[188] The conviction of Marais was pursuant to "l'article 24*bis* de la loi du 29 juillet 1881" (otherwise known as "la loi Gayssot", 13 July 1990). A wave of anti-semitism swept through France in 1990, culminating in the desecration of tombs in a Jewish cemetry at Carpentras in August of that year. The Government's response to this surge in anti-Semitism was the enactment of the so-called Gayssot Act. Also the fulcrum of the case, *Faurisson v. France* (see Chapter 6.1.2), the Gayssot Act was intended to be a main plank in the French Government's programme against racism and anti-Semitism; a hefty legislative sandbag to counter the rising tide of intolerance.

The so-called "revisionist historian", David Irving, was mentioned in an application which was rejected by the European Commission – *Nationaldemokratische Partei*

184 "[T]he fate of the Jews under the National-Socialist regime had been 'invented' purely for the purposes of extortion" (author's translation). *Ibid.*, p. 122.

185 Reports, 1998-VII.

186 These include (albeit only in the national courts) the conviction of Jean-Marie Le Pen, leader of the extreme right-wing party, *Le Front national*, for describing the Nazi gas chambers as "un point de détail" in the history of the Second World War. He was found guilty by the Cour de cassation (the French equivalent of the Supreme Court) in 1989 for the banalisation of constitutive acts of crimes against humanity ("banalisation d'actes constitutifs de crimes contre l'humanité"). See further, J.-Y. Camus, *Le Front National* (Toulouse, Editions Milan, 1998), p. 41.

187 Decision of inadmissibility of the European Commission of Human Rights, Appn. No. 31159/96, 86-A DR 184 (1996).

188 "[T]he existence and use of gas chambers for mass human extermination" (author's translation). *Ibid.*, p. 190.

Deutschlands Bezirksverband Munchen-Oberbayern v Germany.[189] At issue in the case was an imposition on the organisers of a meeting (at which Irving was due to speak) of an obligation to take appropriate measures to ensure that the Nazi persecution of Jews would not be denied or called into question during the meeting.

If it is accepted that Holocaust Denial is a legitimate and proportionate, and indeed, necessary restriction on freedom of expression, this begs the question whether the same should be the case for speech seeking to minimise, trivialise or deny the occurrence of other genocides. This question is problematic as Article 3 of the Convention on the Prevention and Punishment of the Crime of Genocide (the Genocide Convention) does not include genocide-denial as one of its five enumerated "punishable" acts.[190] These acts are: "(a) genocide [as defined in Article 2]; (b) conspiracy to commit genocide; (c) direct and public incitement to commit genocide; (d) attempt to commit genocide; (e) complicity in genocide." As documented in Chapter 6.1, various aspects of the crime of incitement were the subject of protracted wrangling during the drafting of the Genocide Convention, but genocide-denial as such was not dwelt upon.[191]

It is certainly a question deserving further exploration whether the scope of the Genocide Convention could be extended to include genocide-denial. It is difficult to envisage different standards being applied to different genocides: international law would surely be above the egregious practice of hierarchising horror. In any event, the definition of genocide would have to be stringently applied, for as posited by William Schabas: there is no "magic threshold past which ethnically motivated killing becomes genocide. The real test lies in the intent of the perpetrator".[192] Genocide is defined by Article 2 of the Genocide Convention as:

> … any of the following acts committed with intent to destroy, in whole or in part, a national, ethnical, racial or religious group, as such:
> (a) Killing members of the group;
> (b) Causing serious bodily or mental harm to members of the group;
> (c) Deliberately inflicting on the group conditions of life calculated to bring about its physical destruction in whole or in part;
> (d) Imposing measures intended to prevent births within the group;
> (e) Forcibly transferring children of the group to another group.

---

189 Decision of inadmissibility of the European Commission of Human Rights, Appn. No. 25992/94, 84-A DR 149 (1996).

190 The Convention on the Prevention and Punishment of the Crime of Genocide, 1948, Article 3: "The following acts shall be punishable: (a) genocide [as defined in Article 2]; (b) conspiracy to commit genocide; (c) direct and public incitement to commit genocide; (d) attempt to commit genocide; (e) complicity in genocide."

191 See generally, William A. Schabas, "Hate Speech in Rwanda: The Road to Genocide", 46 *McGill Law Journal* 141 (2000), pp. 141–171.

192 *Ibid.*, p. 144.

Once the definitional criteria of "genocide" have been met, a further question comes a-begging: should temporal restrictions attach to a putative offence of genocide-denial? How recent would the genocide have to be in order to merit its classification as an offence punishable by law? Of course, the debate surrounding the criminalisation of genocide-denial need not be the sole preserve of the Genocide Convention. However, other international law instruments have been slow to meet the issue head on. In fact, the Additional Protocol to the Convention on Cybercrime, concerning the criminalisation of acts of a racist and xenophobic nature committed through computer systems (mentioned *supra*) is the only international treaty to date which seeks to tackle the issue of the denial of genocides other than/as well as the Holocaust (and it has yet to enter into force). The operative provision of the Additional Protocol reads as follows:

> **Article 6 – Denial, gross minimisation, approval or justification of genocide or crimes against humanity**
>
> 1 Each Party shall adopt such legislative measures as may be necessary to establish the following conduct as criminal offences under its domestic law, when committed intentionally and without right:
>
> distributing or otherwise making available, through a computer system to the public, material which denies, grossly minimises, approves or justifies acts constituting genocide or crimes against humanity, as defined by international law and recognised as such by final and binding decisions of the International Military Tribunal, established by the London Agreement of 8 August 1945, or of any other international court established by relevant international instruments and whose jurisdiction is recognised by that Party.
>
> 2 A Party may either
>
> a require that the denial or the gross minimisation referred to in paragraph 1 of this article is committed with the intent to incite hatred, discrimination or violence against any individual or group of individuals, based on race, colour, descent or national or ethnic origin, as well as religion if used as a pretext for any of these factors, or otherwise
>
> b reserve the right not to apply, in whole or in part, paragraph 1 of this article.

While the text of Article 6 is silent on possible temporal restrictions to the recognition of genocides for the purpose of penalising their denial, one can extrapolate from the Explanatory Report to the Additional Protocol that the focus is primarily on genocides perpetrated in the latter half of the twentieth century up to the present day. The basis of this reading of the text is the following passage:

> […] The drafters agreed that it was important to criminalize expressions which deny, grossly minimise, approve or justify acts constituting genocide or crimes against humanity, as defined by international law and recognised as such by final and binding decisions of the International Military Tribunal, established by the London Agreement of 8 April 1945. This owing to the fact that the most important and established conducts, which had given rise to genocide and crimes against humanity, occurred during the period 1940–1945. However, the drafters recognised that, since then, other cases of genocide and crimes against humanity occurred, which were strongly motivated by theories and ideas of a racist and xenophobic nature. Therefore, the drafters considered it necessary not to limit the scope of this provision only to the crimes committed by the Nazi regime during the 2nd World War and established as such by the Nuremberg Tribunal, but also to genocides and crimes against humanity established by other international courts set up since 1945 by relevant international legal instruments (such as UN Security Council Resolutions, multilateral treaties, etc.). Such courts may be, for instance, the International Criminal Tribunals for the former Yugoslavia, for Rwanda, the Permanent International Criminal Court. This Article allows to refer to final and binding decisions of future international courts, to the extent that the jurisdiction of such a court is recognised by the Party signatory to this Protocol.[193]

Where would this leave the French Bill on the calling into question of the Armenian Genocide?[194] The French Bill is a topical example of broader, recrudescent questions. For instance, to what extent (if any) is it legitimate for a State to use the coercive force of its laws to mandate particular interpretations of historical events?[195] The same question could be asked in relation to the objective of sustaining particular versions of a population's collective identity or memory. It is submitted here that States proposing such legislation would have to discharge a very heavy burden of proof to show that the proposed measures would not constitute an illegitimate interference with the exercise of the right to freedom of expression under prevailing international legal standards.

The European Court of Human Rights has considered questions such as these on a number of occasions. The case of *Odabasi and Koçak v. Turkey* concerned the conviction by the Turkish courts of an author and publisher for having defamed the memory of Atatürk.[196] The Court concluded that the convictions constituted a violation of Article 10, ECHR, and the key part of its reasoning reads as follows:

---

193 Explanatory Report to the Additional Protocol to the Convention on Cybercrime, *op. cit.*, para. 40.

194 A Bill to prohibit the calling into question of the Armenian genocide (Proposition de Loi tendant à réprimer la contestation de l'existence du génocide arménien), 12 October 2006. The Bill was passed at first reading by the French Assemblée Nationale.

195 For further discussion, see: Lawrence Douglas, "Policing the Past: Holocaust Denial and the Law", in Robert C. Post, Ed., *Censorship and Silencing: Practices of Cultural Regulation*, *op. cit.*, pp. 67–87; Eric Stein, "History Against Free Speech: The New German Law Against The 'Auschwitz' – And Other – 'Lies'", 85 Mich. L. Rev. 277 (1986).

196 Judgment of the European Court of Human Rights (Fourth Section) of 21 February 2006.

> En l'occurrence, la Cour ne peut négliger qu'Atatürk, père fondateur de la Turquie, est une figure emblématique de la Turquie moderne. En sanctionnant les requérants, les autorités turques ont voulu agir pour empêcher que la société turque, attachée à cette figure, ne se sente attaquée dans ses sentiments de manière injustifiée. Cependant, lorsque l'on examine les affirmations litigieuses dans leur ensemble, force est de constater qu'elles ne visaient pas directement et personellement Atatürk, mais l'idéologie <<kémaliste>>. Dès lors, la Cour observe que les requérants n'ont pas porté de jugement de valeur et se sont contentés de relater certains faits sous la forme introductive, invitant le lecteur, et plus précisement la gauche turque, à y répondre. [...][197]

The cited passage provides cause for concern. First, the Court points out that the impugned statements did not target Atatürk directly and personally. Instead they targeted Kemalist ideology. The cause for concern here is the apparent implication of the Court's remarks, namely that if the impugned statements had targeted Atatürk directly and personally that there may have been grounds to restrict the applicants' right to freedom of expression. Notwithstanding Atatürk's "emblematic" status "in modern Turkey", he was a political figure. Thus, any suggestion that he or his (posthumous) reputation should benefit from additional protection, is surely at odds with one of the most consistent lines in the Court's Article 10 case-law, namely that in democratic society, and especially in the context of public or political debate, politicians ought to withstand robust criticism. Second, the Court sets store by the fact that the applicants did not make value-judgments, but limited themselves to introducing certain facts and inviting the reader and more specifically, the political left, to respond to the same. Again, the cause for concern lies in what the remark could seem to imply, i.e., that if the applicants had made value-judgments that they might not have benefited from the same level of protection. This would clearly have been out of kilter with the Court's settled case-law on value-judgments, which are an integral part of public debate and journalistic activity. Protection for value-judgments can only be contested when they have no factual grounding and are made maliciously. This was patently not the case here. A third cause for concern lies in a statement by the Court in paragraph 24 of its judgment, which immediately follows the above-cited excerpt. It concludes that the impugned passages in the book do not incite to violence, armed resistance or uprising and that they do not amount to hate speech. However, further explanation of this conclusion is not forthcoming and in the absence of a firm definition of "hate speech", our understanding of relevant issues is not elucidated in any way.

A second example of the Court engaging with such issues concerns historical events and collective memory. In *Chauvy & Others v. France*, the Court took the view that, aside from "the category of clearly established historical facts – such as the

---

197 *Ibid.*, para. 23.

Holocaust – whose negation or revision is removed from the protection of Article 10 by Article 17":

> [...] it is an integral part of freedom of expression to seek historical truth and it is not the Court's role to arbitrate the underlying historical issue, which is part of a continuing debate between historians that shapes opinion as to the events which took place and their interpretation.[198]

The case required the balancing of two competing interests, *viz.*, the public interest in being informed of the circumstances in which Jean Moulin, a leading figure in the French Resistance against the Nazi occupation in the Second World War, was arrested, and the need to protect the reputation of Mr and Mrs Aubrac, two other important members of the Resistance. It had been suggested in a book that the latter had been in some way responsible for the arrest, suffering and death of Moulin. In exercising its supervisory function, the European Court of Human Rights found that the approach and reasoning in the French courts' decisions constituted "relevant and sufficient reasons" for the convictions imposed in the domestic legal system. It therefore concluded that Article 10 had not been violated.

The judgment did, however, contain a couple of other statements which potentially have relevance beyond the facts of the instant case. Most importantly, for present purposes, was the Court's acceptance of the French courts' finding that "the author had failed to respect *the fundamental rules of historical method* in the book and had made particularly grave insinuations".[199] The reference to the fundamental rules of historical method can be taken as a concrete example of the duties and responsibilities that accompany the exercise of the right to freedom of expression in the context of historical debate.

Prima facie, a judicial focus on Holocaust denial may seem slightly anachronistic, as World War II and its atrocities very gradually recede into the collective memory and younger generations succeed previous generations, whose lives were closer to the tragedies and suffering of those years. Such an observation would, however, be simplistic. The heyday of Nazism did indeed span a fixed and finite period. However, its spectre continues to haunt modern times and the supposed values, or more accurately, the counter-values, of Nazism are immutable. These are counter-values against which society must always guard vigilantly. As noted by the writer William Faulkner: "The past is never dead. It's not even past".[200]

---

198 *Chauvy & Others v. France*, Judgment of the European Court of Human Rights of 29 June 2004, para. 69.

199 (emphasis added). *Ibid.*, para. 77.

200 William Faulkner, *Requiem for a Nun* (New York, Vintage Books, 1975), Act I, Scene III, (Stevens), p. 80.

These perspectives resonate in one of the theses advanced by Lawrence Douglas, namely that "the problem that the Holocaust poses to the law today is less one of assigning responsibility than one of preserving responsible memory [...] The law has been enlisted in the project of safeguarding historical truth".[201] This is one rationale for the continued existence and enforcement of Holocaust-denial laws; the second is that consistently advanced by the French Government in defence of the Gayssot Act (considered *supra*). Defamation of the dead and insulting of survivors lies somewhere in-between these two rationales, given that it approximates towards the "intentional infliction of emotional distress".[202] Douglas' synthesis of these rationales is insightful:

> [...] criminalizing Holocaust denial anticipates a time when the event will no longer remain alive in the memory of survivors, as the group of plaintiffs who could claim emotional distress will have died off. The law thus prepares us for a rapidly approaching future in which the Holocaust will have become an artifact of history. [...] Why then do we need the law to secure the Holocaust in responsible memory, when we do not need a law to remind us that the earth revolves around the sun or that Napoleon's armies fought at Waterloo? Part of the answer seems to lie in a fear of the spread of the disbelief that Primo Levi notes first greeted news of the camps. The very extraordinary nature of Nazi genocide, it is argued, renders it vulnerable to a campaign of scepticism.[203]

He continues by extending the logic of his own analysis to a broader plane:

> Perhaps, then, it can be argued that Holocaust denial does not so much offend a particular group or history itself as it insults the very notions of meaning upon which the liberal concept of public discourse is predicated. This claim is far more foundational, for it does not insist that Holocaust denial can be silenced because it insults codes of civil behavior and speech; rather, it contends that because Holocaust denial makes a mockery of conventions of truth-testing and good faith conversation, it violates the most basic norms that make intelligible the concept of public discourse.[204]

This analysis would appear to underlie the European Commission's finding in *Rebhandl v. Austria* (discussed *supra*) that "the applicant's publications ran counter one of the basic ideas of the Convention, as expressed in its preamble, namely justice and peace, and further reflect racial and religious discrimination".[205]

---

201 Lawrence Douglas, "Policing the Past: Holocaust Denial and the Law", *op. cit.*, at 68.

202 *Ibid.*, p. 69, quoting Elie Wiesel.

203 *Ibid.*, p. 70.

204 *Ibid.*, p. 71.

205 The same reasoning and language were employed by the Commission in *D.I. v. Germany*, Appn. No. 26551/95; a case in which the applicant "historian"'s denial of the existence of gas chambers at Auschwitz had led to his conviction by the German courts under the relevant sections of the German Penal Code, for insult and for blackening the memory of the deceased.

According to this school of thought, Holocaust denial is but one, specific form of attack on justice, peace, equality, harmony and other venerated values of democracy. However, the case which offers the clearest elucidation yet of the rationales governing the Court's approach to Holocaust denial is the *Garaudy v. France* judgment.[206] The following extract from the judgment is revelatory of the Court's reasoning:

> [...] There can be no doubt that denying the reality of clearly established historical facts, such as the Holocaust, as the applicant does in his book, does not constitute historical research akin to a quest for the truth. The aim and the result of that approach are completely different, the real purpose being to rehabilitate the National-Socialist regime and, as a consequence, accuse the victims themselves of falsifying history. Denying crimes against humanity is therefore one of the most serious forms of racial defamation of Jews and of incitement to hatred of them. The denial or rewriting of this type of historical fact undermines the values on which the fight against racism and anti-Semitism are based and constitutes a serious threat to public order. Such acts are incompatible with democracy and human rights because they infringe the rights of others. Its proponents indisputably have designs that fall into the category of aims prohibited by Article 17 of the Convention.
> The Court considers that the main content and general tenor of the applicant's book, and thus its aim, are markedly revisionist and therefore run counter to the fundamental values of the Convention, as expressed in its Preamble, namely justice and peace. [...][207]

The various rationales for prohibiting negationism, as discussed in the preceding paragraphs, are broadly congruent. They focus on the protection of the rights of others, namely their dignity and good name, as well as non-discrimination and equality. Next to those rationales, however, other rationales have been advanced, but they do not fit easily into the aforementioned congruence. For instance, William Schabas has noted that negationism has been described "as a form of incitement to genocide".[208] It is respectfully submitted here that this suggestion appears to rest both on a *non sequitur* and on a misrepresentation. As to the former: it is difficult to conceive of circumstances in which negationist statements *per se* would readily be interpreted as inciting new genocidal offences. However egregious the minimalisation or trivialisation or denial of previous genocides, in particular the Holocaust, may be, in the absence of other determinant factors, negationism on its own, cannot be assumed to constitute the intensity of advocacy necessary to meet the definitional criteria of incitement to genocide (which, under Article III of the Genocide Convention, would have to be "direct and public" incitement anyway).

---

206 *Garaudy v. France*, Inadmissibility decision of the European Court of Human Rights (Fourth Section) of 24 June 2003, Application No. 65831/01.

207 *Ibid.*, p. 23 of the official English translation of excerpts from the decision.

208 William A. Schabas, *Genocide in International Law: The Crimes of Crimes* (Cambridge, Cambridge University Press, 2000), p. 280.

As to the misrepresentation: Schabas attributes the description of negationism as a form of incitement to genocide to Benjamin Whitaker, who was the Special Rapporteur to the UN Sub-Commission on Prevention of Discrimination and Protection of Minorities charged with the task of preparing a major report "on the question of the prevention and punishment of the crime of genocide" in the mid-1980s.[209] The alleged source of the description – para. 49 of Whitaker's report – does not make any reference to incitement, let alone incitement to genocide. Rather, the paragraph notes the plans of the German Government to criminalise attempts to deny or minimise the truth about Nazi crimes. It then acknowledges that different States have different views and policies on those questions, as well as the sincerity in the "differences of opinion [...] as to whether this problem is best dealt with by education and constant vigilance or by the influence of legislation". Nor is negationism described as incitement to genocide in either of the two preceding paragraphs that make up the relevant section ("Propaganda in favour of genocide") of the report. In para. 47, Whitaker notes the suggestion that "public propaganda aimed at promoting the commission of acts of genocide, *or* attempts to rewrite history so as either to falsify the truth about or to glorify its occurrence, of which there are examples in more than one country today, should be brought within the terms of the Convention",[210] but ultimately does not take a stand on the question. In para. 48, he writes that "it can be argued that propaganda for genocide should not be considered as any less grave than propaganda for war, prohibited by Article XX(1) of the Covenant on Civil and Political Rights, or propaganda in favour of racial superiority, prescribed by Article IV of the Convention on the Elimination of All Forms of Racial Discrimination". This is a reasonable argument, but again, it cannot be construed as bracketing together negationism and incitement to genocide. It is important to scotch the suggestion that Whitaker described negationism as a form of incitement to genocide because of the *de facto* or political imprimatur that could be perceived as attaching to such a description by virtue of the official capacity in which his report was written.

7.3.2 "Defamation" of religions

In the final years of the UN Commission on Human Rights' existence, the topic, "Combating defamation of religions", became a recurrent agenda item. Every year, since 1999, the Commission adopted a Resolution on the topic – sponsored by individual States (usually Pakistan) on behalf of the Organization of the Islamic

209 Revised and updated report on the question of the prevention and punishment of the crime of genocide prepared by Mr. B. Whitaker, 2 July 1985, UN Doc. No. E/CN.4/Sub.2/1985/6 (see also the Corrigendum thereto: UN Doc. No. E/CN.4/Sub.2/1985/6/Corr.1).

210 Emphasis added.

Conference.[211] In December 2005, the UN General Assembly followed suit by adopting an identically-titled Resolution.[212] It has continued to adopte identically-titled Resolutions on an annual basis since.[213] In March 2007, the UN Human Rights Council, which replaced the Commission, adopted an identically-titled Resolution too.[214] It did so again in 2008, 2009 and 2010.[215] These texts strongly resemble each other; any differences are minor, with one exception (see further, *infra*).

The UNGA Resolutions can be roughly divided into four main focuses: a preamble; provisions that identify and criticise particular practices that do or could plausibly relate to the alleged offence of "defamation" of religions (although the text makes no attempt to define the alleged offence); provisions that identify and criticise practices that do not appear to be even of penumbral relevance to the alleged offence, and suggested measures to be undertaken in order to combat "defamation" of religions. Of greatest interest here are the second and third categories.

The failure to define the term, "defamation of religions", leaves it open-ended and potentially very broad indeed.[216] Sejal Parmar writes that it "appears as a term of art to infer a distinct phenomenon that is 'a serious affront to human dignity' itself".[217] She correctly notes that the term "gains its meaning from the negative consequences to which it apparently gives rise".[218] Among the practices that would or could fall within the presumptive definitional ambit of "defamation" of religions are:

211 UN Human Rights Commission Resolutions 1999/82 of 30 April 1999, 2000/84 of 26 April 2000, 2001/4 of 18 April 2001, 2002/9 of 15 April 2002, 2003/4 of 14 April 2003, 2004/6 of 13 April 2004 and 2005/3 of 12 April 2005. See further, Kevin Boyle, "The Danish Cartoons", 24 *Netherlands Quarterly of Human Rights* (No. 2, 2006), pp. 185–191.

212 UNGA Resolution 60/150, "Combating defamation of religions", 16 December 2005.

213 UNGA Resolution 61/164, "Combating defamation of religions", 19 December 2006; UNGA Resolution 62/154, "Combating defamation of religions", 18 December 2007; UNGA Resolution 63/171, "Combating defamation of religions", 18 December 2008; UNGA Resolution 64/156, "Combating defamation of religions", 18 December 2009; UNGA Resolution 65/224, "Combating defamation of religions", 21 December 2010.

214 UN Human Rights Council Resolution 4/9, "Combating defamation of religions", 30 March 2007.

215 UN Human Rights Council Resolution 7/19, "Combating defamation of religions", 27 March 2008; UN Human Rights Council Resolution 10/22, "Combating defamation of religions", 26 March 2009; UN Human Rights Council Resolution 13/16, "Combating defamation of religions", 25 March 2010.

216 See further: John Cerone, "Inappropriate Renderings: The Danger of Reductionist Resolutions", 33 Brook. J. Int'l L. 357 (2008), at 375.

217 Sejal Parmar, "The Challenge of 'Defamation of Religions' to Freedom of Expression and the International Human Rights System", [2009] E.H.R.L.R. (No. 3), 353–375, at 359.

218 *Ibid.*

- "negative stereotyping of religions [...]";[219]
- "intensification of the [overall] campaign of defamation of religions";[220]
- "Islam is frequently and wrongly associated with human rights violations and terrorism";[221]
- "programmes and agendas pursued by extremist organizations and groups aimed at the defamation of religions, in particular when supported by Governments";[222]
- "in the context of the fight against terrorism and the reaction to counter-terrorism measures, defamation of religions becomes an aggravating factor that contributes to the denial of fundamental rights and freedoms of target groups, as well as their economic and social exclusion".[223]

Taken together, these provisions prompt a number of conceptual criticisms. The most fundamental of those criticisms is that religions do not have any "right", as such, to be protected from criticism, no matter what level of intensity that criticism may reach. One could, however, argue that the (special) duties and responsibilities that accompany the exercise of the right to freedom of expression require those exercising that right to abstain from engaging in criticism of religions that is abusive towards their adherents. But that is not at all the same thing as to imply the existence of a reputational right for religions. Nor does it imply a specific right for aggrieved adherents of those religions. One can only validly speak of an actual right not to have one's freedom of religion interfered with.

As already signalled, the Resolutions address a number of concerns that are only tangentially related to the alleged offence of "defamation" of religions (if at all):

219 Res. 60/150, para. 1; Res. 61/164, para. 1; Res. 62/154: para. 2; Res. 63/171, para. 2; Res. 64/156, para. 2; Res. 65/224, para. 2.

220 Res. 60/150, para. 3; Res. 61/164, para. 3; Res. 62/154, para. 6; Res. 63/171, para. 5; Res. 64/156, para. 5; Res. 65/224, para. 5.

221 Res. 60/150, para. 4; Res. 61/164, para. 4; Res. 62/154, para. 5; Res. 63/171, para. 7; Res. 64/156, para. 7; Res. 65/224, para. 7.

222 Res. 60/150, para. 5; Res. 61/164, para. 5; Res. 62/154, para. 4 (where "condoned" is used instead of "supported"); Res. 63/171, para. 4 ("[...] aimed at creating and perpetuating stereotypes about certain religions, in particular when condoned by Governments"); Res. 64/156, para. 4("[...] aimed at creating and perpetuating stereotypes about certain religions, in particular when condoned by Governments"); Res. 65/224, para. 4 ("[...] aimed at creating and perpetuating stereotypes about certain religions, in particular when condoned by Governments").

223 Res. 60/150, para. 7; Res. 61/164, para. 7; Res. 62/154, para. 7; Res. 63/171, para. 6 (where "incitement to religious hatred" is added as an aggravating factor); Res. 64/156, para. 6 (also mentioning "incitement to religious hatred"); Res. 65/224, para. 6 (also mentioning "incitement to religious hatred", but replacing "defamation" of religions with "vilification" of religions).

- "[...] manifestations of intolerance and discrimination in matters of religion or belief [...]";[224]
- "physical attacks and assaults on businesses, cultural centres and places of worship of all religions as well as targeting of religious symbols";[225]
- "the ethnic and religious profiling of Muslim minorities in the aftermath of the tragic events of 11 September 2001";[226]
- "the use of the print, audio-visual and electronic media, including the Internet, and any other means to incite acts of violence, xenophobia or related intolerance and discrimination against Islam or any other religion".[227]

Manifestations of intolerance and discrimination in matters of religion or belief are best dealt with under existing provisions against discrimination. Likewise, the problem of ethnic and religious profiling also falls squarely under existing provisions and mechanisms against discrimination.

The focus on attacks on premises is conceptually unsatisfying too. First, the conventional meaning of "assault" under criminal law is an attack (or imminent/impending attack) on a person (not on buildings or artefacts as suggested in the Resolutions). Second, attacks on, or the causation of damage to, property are best dealt with under standard criminal law provisions. It would be appropriate to recalibrate the Resolutions' relevant references by emphasising the motivation behind these acts, *viz.*, targeting persons based on their religious or other beliefs, or their membership of or association with particular religious groups.

Similar objections must be raised to the paragraph on the media. First, violence, xenophobia or related intolerance and discrimination can, by definition, only take place against persons – not doctrines. By extension, the same must apply to incitement to such actions. Furthermore, as an offence, incitement is very distinct from defamation. The former is undue inducement to commit certain (in this context, prohibited) acts; the latter concerns causation of damage to reputational interests.

---

224 Res. 60/150, para. 1; Res. 61/164, para. 1; Res. 62/154, para. 2; Res. 63/171, para. 2; Res. 64/156, para. 2; Res. 65/224, para. 2.

225 Res. 60/150, para. 2; Res. 61/164, para. 2; Res. 62/154, para. 3; Res. 63/171, para. 3; Res. 64/156, para. 3; Res. 65/224, para. 3. Note that the wording changes from Res. 63/171 onwards.

226 Res. 60/150, para. 3; Res. 61/164, para. 3; Res. 62/154, para. 6; Res. 63/171, para. 5; Res. 64/156, para. 5; Res. 65/224, para. 5 (where the wording is shortened to read: "the ethnic and religious profiling of religious minorities.").

227 Res. 60/150, para. 6; Res. 61/164, para. 6; Res. 62/154, para. 8; Res. 63/171, para. 9 (where the wording ends "against any religion, as well as targeting of religious symbols"); Res. 64/156, para. 9 (same wording as per Res. 63/171, para. 9); Res. 65/224, para. 9 (with the wording now ending as follows: "[...] as well as the targeting and desecration of holy books, holy sites, places of worship and religious symbols of all religions").

Looking beyond a purely textual analysis of the Resolutions, the ostensible aim of this initiative is clear: to curb (harsh) criticism of religions, particularly Islam. Its motivation is brazenly partisan: as reflected by the texts ("despite their titular neutrality"[228]), the concern is primarily for the protection of Islam, and extends only secondarily to other religions. Such partisanship and hierarchisation of religions are difficult to justify, especially in a text with aspirations to universal application. Absent convincing and pressing reasons for such a confessional hierarchisation, the practice should be avoided. Non-Muslim States might perhaps be less resistant to the aims of this initiative if it were to be calibrated in a more religion-neutral manner, eg. if it were to seek to curb the "defamation" of all religions in a more egalitarian way.[229] As demonstrated above, some specific references to Islam in earlier UNGA Resolutions have been replaced by references to "any religion" in later UNGA Resolutions.

The use of scare quotes in this study when referring to the "defamation" of religions is a deliberate ploy to alert the reader to the conceptual confusion engendered by the term. Defamation, traditionally and conventionally, is centrally about the protection of an individual's good name and reputation; the esteem in which s/he is held by other (right-thinking) members of society.[230] Definitions of defamation abound and the one followed here is taken from ARTICLE 19's *Defining Defamation: Principles on Freedom of Expression and Protection of Reputation*.[231] According to those principles:

> Defamation laws cannot be justified unless their genuine purpose and demonstrable effect is to protect the reputations of individuals – or of entities with the right to sue and be sued – against injury, including by tending to lower the esteem in which they are held within the community, by exposing them to public ridicule or hatred, or by causing them to be shunned or avoided.[232]

Another relevant definitional criterion for defamation, which is not expressly mentioned in the foregoing citation, but which is generally implicit in *Defining Defamation*, is that it consists of the wrongful publication of a *false* statement about

228 Sejal Parmar, "The Challenge of 'Defamation of Religions' to Freedom of Expression and the International Human Rights System", *op. cit.*, at 367.

229 See further, Kevin Boyle, "The Danish Cartoons", *op. cit.*

230 See generally, Marie McGonagle, *Media Law* (Second Edition) (Dublin, Thomson Round Hall, 2003), Chapter 4 – "Defamation", pp. 64–149; for the essential features of the offence and an historical overview of its development, see in particular, pp. 64–74.

231 London, ARTICLE 19, 2000. These Principles are part of ARTICLE 19's International Standards Series; they "are based on international law and standards, evolving state practice (as reflected, inter alia, in national laws and judgments of national courts), and the general principles of law recognised by the community of nations. [...]", "Introduction", *ibid.*, p. 1.

232 *Ibid.*, Principle 2: Legitimate Purpose of Defamation Laws: (a).

a person.[233] This explains the legitimacy of "proof of truth" as a defence in defamation actions. It also points up the unsuitability of defamation actions as a mechanism for seeking to legally restrict or punish expressions of opinion. By definition, the truth of statements of opinion (or "value-judgments") is not susceptible to proof, and as such, they must be distinguished from statements of fact, the truth of which can ordinarily be proven (to some level of satisfaction, at least).[234]

The regular scope of defamation is also subject to a couple of further delimitations, both of which are captured well by Defining Defamation. Principle 2(b) reads:

> Defamation laws cannot be justified if their purpose or effect is to protect individuals against harm to a reputation which they do not have or do not merit, or to protect the 'reputations' of entities other than those which have the right to sue and to be sued. In particular, defamation laws cannot be justified if their purpose or effect is to:
> [...]
> ii. protect the 'reputation' of objects, such as State or religious symbols, flags or national insignia;
> [...]
> v. allow individuals to sue on behalf of a group which does not, itself, have status to sue.

Because the notion of "reputation" is at the very core of defamation, its extension to "religions" is problematic. Religions *qua* belief systems do not have reputations in the same sense that individuals do. This distinction is implicitly recognised by the European Court of Human Rights: in the *Giniewski* case (see further, *supra*), the Court upheld the legitimacy of the aim of the challenged interference with the applicant's right to freedom of expression, which it summarised as being "to protect a group of persons from defamation *on account of their membership of a specific religion*".[235] The Court held that this aim corresponded to the protection of "the reputation or rights of others" (Article 10(2), ECHR). Crucially, the focus was on defamation of *(a group of) persons*, not *religions*, as such. It is more apt to speak of the (cognitive and affective) associations made by individuals in relation to religions, but it would involve considerable semantic stretch to characterise such associations as reputational. This particular analogy is therefore limited. The analogy of group defamation, on the other hand, is more viable, because it is concerned with a group – necessarily comprising a body of individuals – and not a creed or any other inanimate object.[236]

---

233 See, for example, Bryan McMahon & William Binchy, *Irish Law of Torts* (3rd Edition), (Dublin, Butterworths, 2000), p. 882.

234 *Lingens v. Austria*, Judgment of the European Court of Human Rights of 8 July 1986, Series A, No. 103, para. 46.

235 (emphasis added) *Giniewski v. France*, *op. cit.*, para. 40.

236 For comprehensive treatment of group defamation, see: Monroe H. Freedman & Eric M. Freedman, Eds., *Group Defamation and Freedom of Speech: The Relationship Between*

This conceptual reservation about the transferability of defamation leads into the second relevant delimitation of the scope of defamation, announced *supra*. Principle 2(c) of *Defining Defamation* reads:

> Defamation laws also cannot be justified on the basis that they serve to protect interests other than reputation, where those interests, even if they may justify certain restrictions on freedom of expression, are better served by laws specifically designed for that purpose. In particular, defamation laws cannot be justified on the grounds that they help maintain public order, national security, or friendly relations with foreign States or governments.

Clearly, therefore, defamation is not the malleable concept that some people would like to believe. A useful addendum to Principle 2(c) is that defamation is equally unsuited to protecting the very vague notion of "dignity", a concept with which reputation has a certain affinity.[237]

When these general principles are applied to the aforementioned initiative within the UN, "Combating defamation of religions", the conceptual premises of that initiative – just like its political motivation (see *infra*) – are revealed to be shaky. It represents an attempt to extend the scope of defamation to cover a subject for which it is ill-suited. If that subject is deserving of protection, alternative means to ensure that protection should be explored. While religions are not entitled to protection *per se*, persons who do hold religious beliefs are entitled not to have those beliefs abused or outraged. The distinction is perhaps a fine one, but it is not necessarily unworkable, for instance, if one were to endorse Jean-François Gaudreault-DesBiens' proposition that "offensive expression targets ideas, while abusive expression targets human beings".[238]

Furthermore, there are strong grounds for arguing that no new measures are required to safeguard such a right: adequate mechanisms are already at hand. The ECHR is well-poised to deal dispositively with the issue (see further, Chapter 6.2.1), as is the ICERD – at least to the extent that the abuse of religious beliefs could be considered a proxy for racial discrimination. In this connection, caution has been

---

Language and Violence (USA, Greenwood Press, 1995). See, in particular, Louis Henkin, "Group Defamation and International Law", *ibid.*, pp. 123–134. See also: Natan Lerner, *Group Rights and Discrimination in International Law* (2nd Edition) (The Hague, Martinus Nijhoff Publishers, 2003); Thomas David Jones, *Human Rights: Group Defamation, Freedom of Expression and the Law of Nations* (The Netherlands, Martinus Nijhoff Publishers, 1998).

237 See further: Marie McGonagle, *Media Law*, *op. cit.*, p. 64; Eric Barendt, "What is the point of Libel Law?", 52 *Current Legal Problems* (1999) 110, at 117.

238 Jean-François Gaudreault-DesBiens, "From Sisyphus's Dilemma to Sisyphus's Duty? A Meditation on the Regulation of Hate Propaganda in Relation to Hate Crimes and Genocide", *op. cit.*, at 135.

urged not to confuse "a racist statement and an act of defamation of religion",[239] but given the amount of conceptual confusion that inheres in the latter, it is plausible that certain types of abusive expression (in the sense set out by Gaudreault-DesBiens) could come within the scope of ICERD's attentions. As noted by Conor Gearty, some religions have a "powerful ethnic tinge" and "[i]n such situations, the concept of religious intolerance must stand or fall apart from ethnicity in a way that is not altogether unproblematic".[240]

If the true purpose of "defamation of religions" is the protection of religious sensitivities, then a different calculus necessarily applies. As stated by the UN Special Rapporteur on freedom of religion or belief and the UN Special Rapporteur on contemporary forms of racism, racial discrimination, xenophobia and related intolerance:

> The right to freedom of expression can legitimately be restricted for advocacy that incites to acts of violence or discrimination against individuals on the basis of their religion. Defamation of religions may offend people and hurt their religious feelings but it does not necessarily or at least directly result in a violation of their rights, including their right to freedom of religion. Freedom of religion primarily confers a right to act in accordance with one's religion but does not bestow a right for believers to have their religion protected from all adverse comment.[241]

Notwithstanding this clarification of the actual scope of relevant provisions of international law, two UNGA Resolutions on "Combating defamation of religions" (i.e., Res. 61/164 and Res. 62/154) and the Human Rights Council's Resolution 4/9, also entitled, "Combating defamation of religions", misrepresent the legal reality. The misrepresentation takes place in the following paragraph:

> *Emphasizes* that everyone has the right to freedom of expression, which should be exercised with responsibility and may therefore be subject to limitations as provided by law and necessary for respect of the rights or reputations of others, protection of national security or of public order, public health or morals and respect for religions and beliefs.[242]

---

239 Implementation of General Assembly Resolution 60/251 of 15 March 2006 entitled "Human Rights Council", Report of the Special Rapporteur on freedom of religion or belief, Asma Jahangir, and the Special Rapporteur on contemporary forms of racism, racial discrimination, xenophobia and related intolerance, Doudou Diène, further to Human Rights Council decision 1/107 on incitement to racial and religious hatred and the promotion of tolerance, 20 September 2006, A/HRC/2/3, para 49.

240 Conor A. Gearty, "The Internal and External 'Other' in the Union Legal Order: Racism, Religious Intolerance and Xenophobia in Europe", in Philip Alston *et al.*, Eds., *The EU and Human Rights* (New York, Oxford University Press, 1999), pp. 327–358, at 337.

241 Report further to Human Rights Council decision 1/107 on incitement to racial and religious hatred and the promotion of tolerance, *op. cit.*, para. 37.

242 (Italics per original text; underlining added by author for emphasis) UNGA Res. 61/164, para. 9 and UN Human Rights Council Resolution 4/9, para. 10. The equivalent paragraph in UNGA

The limitations on the right to freedom of expression listed in the cited paragraph are consistent with those explicitly enumerated in Article 19(3), ICCPR, except for the underlined limitation – "respect for religions and beliefs". That limitation is without *any* basis in international human rights law and it is hard to avoid the conclusion that it has been included in a deliberately stealthy manner in order to further the objectives of the Resolution as a whole. It is a serious misrepresentation, all the moreso because of its repetition: after its initial inclusion in UNGA Res. 61/164, it was again included in UNGA Res. 62/154 and UN Human Rights Council Res. 4/9.

As Jeroen Temperman has forcibly argued, this "Counter-Defamation Discourse" is "utterly unacceptable" because it: "(i) seeks to shift the emphasis from protection of the rights of individuals to protection of religions per se; (ii) introduces grounds for limitation of human rights, particularly of the right to freedom of expression, that are not – and should not become – recognised by international human rights law (for example, 'respect for religions', 'respect for people's religious feelings'); and (iii) seeks to reformulate the right to freedom of religion or belief so as to include a right to have one's religious feelings respected [...]".[243]

The misrepresentation of the actual scope of relevant limitations on the right to freedom of expression under international human rights law was not repeated in UNGA Resolutions 63/171, 64/156 or 65/224. Each of these Resolutions states accurately what the permissible limitations are, as does the Human Rights Council's Resolution 7/19. However, the subsequent two Resolutions adopted by the Human Rights Council – 10/22 (2009) and 13/16 (2010) both add a new limitation: "general welfare".[244] Again, this additional ground for limiting the right to freedom of expression has no basis in international human rights law. Furthermore, it is an undefined and potentially very broad term, which would render its application problematic and leave it open to abuse. The equivalent Human Rights Council Resolution (16/18) in 2011 (discussed in more detail, below), does not enumerate the permissible grounds for limiting freedom of expression.

A third and closely related objection to "defamation of religions" is that its chilling effect on the discussion of religious issues which are of public interest is potentially

Res. 62/154, para. 10, is worded slightly differently, but the misrepresentation remains the same. It reads: "*Emphasizes* that everyone has the right to hold opinions without interference and the right to freedom of expression, and that the exercise of these rights carries with it special duties and responsibilities and may therefore be subject to limitations as are provided for by law and are necessary for respect of the rights or reputations of others, protection of national security or of public order, public health or morals and respect for religions and beliefs" (Italics per original text; underlining added for emphasis).

243 Jeroen Temperman, "Blasphemy, Defamation of Religions and Human Rights Law", 26 *Netherlands Quarterly of Human Rights* (No. 4, 2008), pp. 517–545, at 533.

244 Paragraphs 10 and 11, respectively.

huge. It is important to be eternally vigilant against attempts to legally enshrine measures that would have the effect of cordoning off religious beliefs and preventing them from being a subject of debate, or of criticism, for that matter. In the absence of any explicit or ulterior racist or discriminatory motives, hatred or incitement, it is perfectly legitimate to criticise religions and religious beliefs – even in virulent terms. Such are the demands of pluralism, tolerance and broadmindedness without which there would be no democratic society, to use the formulae of the European Court of Human Rights.

The defilement of religions – a comparable notion, but one that does not carry the same baggage of conceptual confusion as defamation of religions – is also gradually beginning to make inroads into the case-law of the European Court of Human Rights. The Court considered the offence in *Aydin Tatlav v. Turkey*,[245] but held that the impugned book did not amount to a defilement of Islam, despite its strong criticism of that religion in the socio-political sphere. Crucial to the Court's reasoning was its finding that the tone of the book was not insulting and that it did not constitute an abusive attack against sacred symbols. It is not yet clear whether the offence of defilement of religions will develop over time into a type of protection that is qualitatively different from the existing, heavily qualified, protection afforded to the religious beliefs of others under the ECHR.

Having considered the conceptual shortcomings of "defamation of religions", attention can now be switched to the political ramifications of the campaign. As already noted, one of the major instigators and sponsors of the campaign is the Organization of the Islamic Conference. The campaign must be understood as an attempt to counter the undeniable intensification of Islamophobia in the wake of 11 September 2001.[246] However, notwithstanding whatever sympathy European States may have with the objective of combating Islamophobia, they have overwhelmingly opposed the campaign to combat "defamation" of religions in the General Assembly. This is evident from voting patterns in the GA on Resolutions 60/150, 61/164 and 62/154, all of which were approved by convincing majorities.[247] Of the (then) 55 Participating States of the OSCE, only nine voted in favour of the

245 Judgment of the European Court of Human Rights (Second Section) of 2 May 2006, Application No. 50692/99.

246 See for example, European Monitoring Centre on Racism and Xenophobia, "Muslims in the European Union: Discrimination and Islamophobia" (2006).

247 Resolution 60/150 was adopted by a recorded vote of 101 in favour to 53 against, with 20 abstentions (source: Official Records of UN General Assembly Sixtieth session, 64th plenary meeting, 16 December 2005, Doc. A/60/PV.64, p. 11); Resolution 61/164 was adopted by a recorded vote of 111 in favour to 54 against, with 18 abstentions (source: Official Records of UN General Assembly Sixty-first session, 81st plenary meeting, 19 December 2006, Doc. A/61/PV.81, p. 19).

first Resolution.[248] One State abstained[249] and the remainder[250] voted against the Resolution. Votes cast by European States in respect of the subsequent two Resolutions were exactly the same.[251] On each occasion, the nature of the vote was such that no prior debate took place in the GA plenary meeting. However, after the recorded vote, delegations were invited to give explanations of their votes. On neither occasion did any European State take the floor in its own right and interventions made on behalf of the European Union by delegates representing the States holding the EU Presidency at the operative time (i.e., the United Kingdom and Finland, respectively) focused on Resolutions other than 'Combating defamation of religions'. Given that the EU Member States voted *en bloc* against the Resolution, it is perhaps surprising that no formal statement was made outlining collective European concerns about the Resolution.

There is another very impelling reason why the conceptual shortcomings of "defamation of religions" must be assessed in political terms. This concerns "the principle of the ratchet", which has been developed elsewhere by Michael Banton.[252] According to that principle, when particular concepts or formulations are agreed upon in international fora and are consequently included in official texts, they can serve as a basis for the achievement of further political gains at a later stage. This is because they can be re-affirmed and strengthened in subsequent texts (such is the nature of progress in political discussions[253]). Conversely, though, it can prove very difficult to dislodge concepts and terminology once they become embedded in official texts. Depending on the nature of the texts in question, those concepts and terminology could form the basis of obligations for States. As regards General Assembly Resolutions such as those concerning "defamation of religions", the relevant obligations are political rather than legal in character, but that does not rule out the possibility that a future convention (which would be legally binding on all

248 Azerbaijan, Belarus, Kazakhstan, Kyrgyzstan, the Russian Federation, Tajikistan, Turkey, Turkmenistan and Uzbekistan.

249 Armenia. It should be noted that no European States were absent when the vote was taken.

250 The only OSCE Participating State which is not a member State of the United Nations is The Holy See. It does enjoy observer status at the UNGA, but it does not have voting rights.

251 The only difference was that whereas Serbia & Montenegro voted against the Resolution in 2005, only Serbia did so in 2006. Following the dissolution of Serbia & Montenegro as a unitary political entity and the establishment of Montenegro as an independent State, Montenegro was accepted as a UN Member State on 28 June 2006 by virtue of GA Resolution A/RES/60/264. However, there is no mention of Montenegro having participated in the relevant GA vote, or as having been absent at the operative time. In 2007, both Serbia and Montenegro voted against Res. 62/154.

252 Michael Banton, *The International Politics of Race*, *op. cit.*, pp. 77, 79–80.

253 He writes: "If a discussion leads to a conclusion such that the next discussion starts from the position reached on the previous occasion, then some progress has been made. At the UN such a conclusion is usually expressed in the form of a resolution, which can sometimes move on to a General Assembly declaration and eventually to a convention." – Michael Banton, *International Action Against Racial Discrimination*, *op. cit.*, at p. 48.

States acceding to it) would not draw on the language of such resolutions on the basis that they are the expression of agreement among a majority of States on a specific topic. The reference to the ratchet is explained by the ease with which particular formulations can move up a notch and the concomitant difficulties in brining them back down again. Banton illustrates the practical operation of the principle as follows:

> A group of states takes an initiative, secures agreement on a particular action, and then tries to use this as a foundation for a further step forward whenever an opportunity presents itself. Once a form of words has been accepted it can be used again or moved up a notch; this is the function of rhetoric in official conferences. It is difficult to disengage a ratchet and undo a previous agreement. Opportunities for tightening a ratchet and taking that further step may arise after a disaster when there is a feeling that 'something must be done', or when a special meeting – like a world conference – is convened to consider a particular problem.[254]

It is certainly plausible that highly volatile incidents such as the Danish Cartoons affair could further galvanise an already very potent political alliance within the UNGA, spearheaded by the OIC but with many fellow-travellers rightly riled at the intensification of Islamophobia in Western States and foreign military intervention in Iraq, Afghanistan and elsewhere. In such a scenario, it is most likely that the language of the existing Resolutions on "combating defamation of religions" would be built upon, ratchet-like, in order to further the campaign. Indeed, the ratchet has already been engaged, insofar as the follow-up measures envisaged by the Resolutions have required the High Commissioner on Human Rights and a number of the Special Rapporteurs to address the issue and report their findings to the Human Rights Council. The legitimacy conferred on the concept of "defamation of religions" by virtue of its inclusion in successive UNGA Resolutions has allowed it to seep into other branches of the UN and seek further legitimation there. This has the effect of familiarising and consolidating the concept through extra exposure.

The foregoing has exposed some of the fundamental legal and political shortcomings of the anti-defamation of religions campaign within the UN. Over the course of time, the exclusive focus on Islam has been broadened to include other religions. Some of the rhetoric has also been mollified. One of the far-reaching misstatements of international law has also been corrected (only to be replaced by another one). These developments are attributable in no small measure to vigorous awareness-raising, critical analysis and strategic engagement by the NGO community.[255] One can now speak of a discernible change of course in the anti-defamation of religions

254 Michael Banton, *The International Politics of Race*, *op. cit.*, pp. 79–80.

255 See generally, Sejal Parmar, "The Challenge of 'Defamation of Religions' to Freedom of Expression and the International Human Rights System", *op. cit.*

campaign. For instance, UNGA Resolution 65/224 refers only sporadically to the defamation of religions (including in its title), now preferring the "vilification" of religions instead. Whether this terminological shift is portentous remains to be seen. Another terminological shift is clearly significant. It concerns the title of the 2011 Human Rights Resolution on relevant issues. Resolution 16/18 is entitled "Combating intolerance, negative stereotyping and stigmatization of, and discrimination, incitement to violence and violence against, persons based on religion or belief".[256] While the shift of titular emphasis is significant, the substantive shift, evident in the text, is even moreso. The positive role of freedom of expression in countering the phenomena alluded to in the Resolution's title is underscored, as are the values of diversity and dialogue.

The prognosis for the anti-defamation of religions campaign – under whatever name it will take in the future – is uncertain. Despite terminological changes and certain conceptual and strategic adjustments, it would be premature to predict that the campaign is petering out. Heed for Michael Banton's ratchet principle and fears of the inflation of human rights (*in casu* religious rights) therefore remain in order.

7.3.3 Protection of founders of religions

On 30 September 2005 the Danish newspaper, *Jyllands-Posten*, published 12 cartoons depicting/caricaturing the Prophet Mohammed. The paper's intention was, it claimed, to draw attention to the prevalence of self-censorship in respect of Islam in general and in respect of pictorial representations of the Prophet Mohammed, in particular. The political, diplomatic and socio-economic fall-out from the original publication, the ensuing swirl of events, including republication of the cartoons and their further dissemination (accompanied, in some instances, by additional cartoons) by particular parties, was devastating. At the epicentre of the so-called Danish cartoons controversy was not only the *fact* of the depiction of the Prophet Mohammed, but also the *nature* of the depiction. Of course, in order for the controversy to "metastasize" as dramatically as it did,[257] a whole concatenation of extra dynamics had to be at play. As the circumstances of the controversy are well-known,[258] they will not be rehearsed again here.

---

256 Human Rights Council Resolution 16/18, "Combating intolerance, negative stereotyping and stigmatization of, and discrimination, incitement to violence and violence against, persons based on religion or belief", 24 March 2011.

257 Richard N. Winfield, "An Editorial Controversy Metastasizing: Denmark's Hate Speech Laws", 24 *Communications Lawyer* (Spring 2006), pp. 35–37.

258 See: David Keane, "Cartoon Violence and Freedom of Expression", 30 *Human Rights Quarterly* (No. 4, November 2008), pp. 845–875.

From a legal perspective,[259] the controversy prompts a range of pressing questions, the most obvious of which is whether there were grounds for considering the (re-) publication of the cartoons to be in contravention of international human rights standards. An ancillary question concerns the nature and extent of the (special) duties and responsibilities of those involved in different capacities in the separate acts of publication and re-publication. These questions have been analysed meticulously elsewhere by leading experts;[260] the intention here is to raise the broader question of whether it could or should be legitimate to restrict freedom of expression in order to protect founders of religions or religious deities. This broader question fits in with the overall enquiry of this chapter, in particular when considered from the perspective of minority religions.

The drafting process of the UN draft Convention on Freedom of Information (see further, Chapter 4.1.1(ii)) offers an intriguing dimension to the present discussion. It will be recalled that in 1959, the Third (Social, Humanitarian and Cultural) Committee of the UN General Assembly began a detailed discussion of a draft text of the proposed Convention. "Article 2, dealing with permissible restrictions on the exercise of the freedom of information, was widely regarded in the Third Committee as the heart of the draft Convention".[261] Relevant official documentation from the United Nations reveals that there was concern within the Third Committee that "if far-reaching limitations were made permissible, the Convention would be transformed into an instrument for restricting freedom of information".[262] On 2 December 1960, the Third Committee adopted Article 2 as a whole and as amended.[263] The adopted version of the Article read:

> **Article 2**
>
> 1. The exercise of the freedoms referred to in article 1 carries with it duties and responsibilities. It may, however, be subject only to such necessary restrictions as

---

259 An application concerning the cartoons was lodged at the European Court of Human Rights, but it was declared inadmissible owing to the absence of any jurisdictional connection between the applicants (who were resident in Morocco) and Denmark (the State against which the application was lodged): *Ben El Mahi & others v. Denmark*, Decision of inadmissibility of the European Court of Human Rights of 11 December 2006, Appn. No. 5853/06. The applicants had complained that the publication of the cartoons violated their rights under Article 9 *juncto* 14, ECHR. They had also sought to rely on Article 17 *juncto* 10, ECHR.

260 Kevin Boyle, "The Danish Cartoons", *op. cit.*; András Sajó, "Countervailing Duties as Applied to Danish Cheese and Danish Cartoons", in András Sajó, Ed., *Censorial Sensitivities: Free Speech and Religion in a Fundamentalist World* (Utrecht, Eleven International Publishing, 2007), pp. 273–307; Guy Haarscher, "Free Speech, Religion, and the Right to Caricature", in *ibid.*, pp. 309–328; Robert Post, "Religion and Freedom of Speech: Portraits of Muhammad", in *ibid.*, pp. 329–351.

261 *Yearbook of the United Nations 1960*, p. 335.

262 *Ibid.*

263 This involved a roll-call vote of 50 to 5, with 19 abstentions.

> are clearly defined by law and applied in accordance with the law in respect of: national security and public order (*ordre public*); systematic dissemination of false reports harmful to friendly relations among nations and of expressions inciting to war or to national, racial or religious hatred; attacks on founders of religions; incitement to violence and crime; public health and morals; the rights, honour and reputation of others; and the fair administration of justice.
> 2. The restrictions specified in the preceding paragraph shall not be deemed to justify the imposition by any State of prior censorship on news, comments and political opinions and may not be used as grounds for restricting the right to criticize the Government.

Of particular significance for present purposes is the uncommon inclusion of "attacks on founders of religions" as an explicit, permissible ground for restricting the right to freedom of expression. This limitation is distinguishable from the more common – and generic – limitation "expressions inciting to [...] national, racial or religious hatred". The inclusion of the limitation protecting the founders of religions was proposed by the Pakistani representative and it was accepted by the Third Committee by 22 votes to nine, with 47 abstentions.

As this draft Convention was ultimately never adopted, any assessment of its provisions will be, at best, speculative. Nevertheless, it is useful to dwell on the significance of the limitation on freedom of expression that had been envisaged for the founders of religions. It is perhaps facile to suggest that if the draft Convention had been adopted, the Danish cartoons controversy could have been resolved very summarily by international law. However, without the benefit of interpretative aids, it is difficult to say with any degree of precision how the terms "religions" and "founders" would have been defined. The stringency with which draft Article 2(2) would have been applied would also surely have been instructive.

The issue of protection for founders of religions has also been explored in ongoing discussions of recent controversies. For example, Egbert Dommering has drawn a distinction between the Church (as an institution) and Faith (as personified by a religious deity).[264] The former is a legitimate target of scrutiny, criticism and parody, he argues, whereas the latter is at least a more problematic, if not an illegitimate, target of such treatment. This distinction could be usefully considered alongside other contextualising factors[265] wherever relevant, or most topically, in the Danish cartoons affair. Such factors could include the:

264 E.J. Dommering, "De Deense beeldenstorm", 11 *NJB* (17 March 2006) 634–638.

265 For a more detailed analysis of the importance of contextualising factors generally, see further, *infra*. For an exploration of contextualising elements specifically in the Danish cartoons affair, see: Kevin Boyle, "The Danish cartoons", *op. cit.*

(i) motivation of the newspaper in deciding to publish the cartoons
(ii) context in which the cartoons were published
(iii) manner in which the cartoons were published (i.e., how they were presented)
(iv) subsequent behaviour of the newspaper
(v) subsequent behaviour of other newspapers
(vi) unrest and violence in *alleged* reaction to the publication of the cartoons

One problematic and inescapable question concerning any legally-enshrined protection for the founders of religion arises from the growing number of belief systems recognised as religions. The founders of some of those religious movements will inevitably continue to be responsible for the spiritual leadership and guidance of their congregations. Could the protection of founders of religions insulate such religious leaders from the kind of criticism to which politicians are expected to withstand by virtue of the public nature of their functions? The question is of great practical importance. There is a real danger danger that any would-be right to protection for such religious leaders, unless very carefully circumscribed, would serve as a shield against legitimate criticism.

Another conundrum that arises from the related question of whether religious deities generally (whether they are also recognised as the founders of religions or not) should be entitled to protection from severe criticism. It is submitted that the same reasoning outlined in the previous paragraph in respect of founders of religions should also be applied here. Religions which recognise multiple deities would require careful and particular consideration in this connection. It would, in any event, be inappropriate for States authorities to purport to distinguish between deities or rank them in terms of sacredness.[266]

These questions must be considered in the broader context of the discussion, *supra*, about the extent to which particular types of expression are actually capable of interfering with the religious rights of others. More specifically, attention should focus on the extent to which disparagement of, or insult to, religious leaders could actually interfere with ability of their followers to effectively hold or manifest their religious beliefs. In *Choudhury v. the United Kingdom*, the European Commission of Human Rights found that the causal link between the expression in question (Salman Rushdie's novel, *The Satanic Verses*) and an interference with the religious rights of others had not been established.[267] It found that in the circumstances of the case at hand, Article 9, ECHR, did not guarantee a right to institute criminal

---

266 For an enlightening discussion of these and related questions, see: David Edwards, "Toleration and the English blasphemy law", in John Horton & Susan Mendus, Eds., *Aspects of Toleration* (London & New York, Methuen & Co., 1985), pp. 75–98, esp. at 84 *et seq*.

267 *Choudhury v. the United Kingdom*, Decision of inadmissibility of the European Commission of Human Rights of 5 March 1991, Appn. No. 17439/90. The applicant "sought to have criminal proceedings brought against the author and publisher of "Satanic Verses" in order to vindicate

proceedings "against those who, by authorship or publication, offend the sensitivities of an individual or a group of individuals".[268] In its decision in *Dubowska & Skup v. Poland* (concerning "the distorted publication of sacred images" of worship of a particular religious group),[269] the Commission was more willing to countenance the possibility that expression could interfere with the religious rights of others and that States are accordingly obliged to ensure that means of legal redress are available to ensure that "an individual will not be disturbed in his worship by the activities of others".[270] However, in the specific circumstances of the case, the necessary link was not established to the satisfaction of the Commission. The reasoning behind the need to establish a clear link between offensive expression and the violation of religious rights must also apply, *mutatis mutandis*, to any would-be protection for the founders of religions.

Conclusions

This Chapter explains that the term, "hate speech", is capable of having multiple meanings. It is a catchy term and it appeals as a convenient short-hand term denoting various types of hateful expression. However, precisely because of the broadness of its scope, the term is of limited usefulness from a legal perspective. It tends to distract from extant international human rights standards rather than clarify them.

For instance, as demonstrated in this chapter, the term, "hate speech", is not organic to the ECHR and that it was first used by the Court in 1999, without any explanation of why it was being introduced into its jurisprudential lexicon or where its theoretical origins lay. In the absence of any attempt by the Court to define the term (which, certainly from the perspective of critical race theory emanating from the US, has a much broader meaning than is generally appreciated), it should be used with circumspection. While the importance of countering "hate speech" cannot be gainsaid, once the term is used in a legal sense, there is a greater need for conceptual and terminological precision to attach to the notion than in respect of non-legal measures.

The selected specific focuses of this chapter – the complex interplay between the rights to freedom of expression and freedom of religion; the denial or minimisation of genocide and other crimes against humanity; the so-called "defamation" of

---

his claim that the book amounted to a scurrilous attack on, inter alia, his religion" – *ibid.*, para. 1.

268 *Ibid.*, para. 1 (in section of decision entitled 'The Law').

269 *Dubowska & Skup v. Poland*, Decision of inadmissibility of the European Commission of Human Rights of 18 April 1997, Appn. Nos. 33490/96 and 34055/96.

270 *Ibid.*, para. 2 (in section of decision entitled 'The Law').

religions, and the protection of founders of religions – are all good examples of the politicisation of international human rights law. In each case, political pressures have sought to contest or re-set the boundaries of freedom of expression, as recognised under international human rights law. It is of paramount importance that international adjudicatory, standard-setting and monitoring bodies continue to clarify (as necessary) existing standards governing the right to freedom of expression and vigilantly guard against their inflation or dilution. In this regard, it is imperative that they ensure consistency in their application of key legal principles to the (often highly sensitive) contextual variables that shape specific cases. This pleads for the centrality of international standards and frontal engagement with the varying intensities and harms associated with different types of "hate speech".

Chapter 8
Integrated approaches to countering "hate speech"

Introduction

This chapter is situated at the confluence of Chapters 5, 6 and 7. It proposes the Council of Europe's Framework Convention for the Protection of National Minorities (FCNM) as a case study of an integrated approach to counter "hate speech". The approach taken by the Advisory Committee (AC) on the FCNM in its monitoring activities is integrated insofar as it combines legal and non-legal strategies against "hate speech". First, the AC's approach seeks to foster what has been termed "comprehensive pluralistic tolerance" in Chapter 5. Second, it is mindful of the over-arching international and European legal standards governing "hate speech" (detailed in Chapter 6) and operates within that framework. Third, the diversity of strategies it employs to combat "hate speech" testifies to an awareness of the diversity of types of expression potentially covered by the term (as explained in Chapter 7). This facilitates a tailoring of strategies to specific types of "hate speech" and specific contextual variables, leading to an overall approach that could be described as a "horses-for-courses" approach.

Whereas the chapter's central focus is the FCNM, it also considers other Council of Europe standards and international developments. In respect of the former, it seeks to demonstrate that the approach taken by the FCNM actually typifies the approach taken across the Council of Europe. In respect of the latter, it seeks to tentatively indicate that the FCNM's integrated approach against "hate speech" is broadly consistent with emergent (normative) trends at the international level as well.

8.1 Theoretical foundations for an integrated approach to countering "hate speech"

This section will examine and evaluate the theory – variously conceived – that a policy of "more speech" or "counter-speech" can be an effective means of combating hate speech. It is sometimes posited that effective opportunities to respond to hate speech – to meet it head-on – can help to reduce its impact or expose its frailties. However, this proposition is open to challenge, especially in the context of individual situations where the "inflammatory words [are] spit out nose-to-nose"[1] and the

1 Kenneth Lasson, "To Stimulate, Provoke, or Incite?: Hate Speech and the First Amendment", in Monroe H. Freedman & Eric M. Freedman, Eds., *Group Defamation and Freedom of Speech:*

target of hate speech is in a position of subjugation or intimidation *vis-à-vis* the speaker.

Critical race theorists are very dismissive of the alleged usefulness of "more speech" as a particularised remedy for hate speech, for a number of reasons. First, the utterance of hate speech in an individualised situation is frequently likened to a slap in the face rather than an invitation to engage in rational, reasonable discourse.[2] As explained by Charles R. Lawrence III:

> The injury is instantaneous. There is neither an opportunity for intermediary reflection on the idea conveyed nor an opportunity for responsive speech. [...] The racial invective is experienced as a blow, not a proffered idea, and once the blow is struck, it is unlikely that dialogue will follow. Racial insults are undeserving of [...] protection because the perpetrator's intention is not to discover truth or initiate dialogue, but to injure the victim.[3]

Thus styled, the speech act is much more performative than propositional. It clearly falls in the category of socially worthless epithets or personal abuse that are "not in any proper sense communication of information or opinion [...]" deserving of protection.[4] Its performative character is abusive and assaultive. Instead of eliciting a verbal response from the target, a more probable reaction would be "flight rather than fight".[5] Such a response is in itself problematic because "[t]argets choose to avoid racist encounters whenever possible, internalizing the harm rather than escalating the conflict".[6] The psychic effects of assaultive, racist speech can be far-reaching, especially when the harm they occasion tends to be internalised.[7] Furthermore, from the perspective of criminal law: "[l]ack of a fight and admirable self-restraint then defines the words as nonactionable".[8]

The Relationship Between Language and Violence (USA, Greenwood Press, 1995), pp. 267–306, at 267.

2 Richard Delgado & Jean Stefancic, *Understanding Words That Wound* (Boulder, CO, Westview Press, 2004), p. 207.

3 Charles R. Lawrence III, "If He Hollers Let Him Go: Regulating Racist Speech on Campus", in Mari J. Matsuda, Charles R. Lawrence III, Richard Delgado, and Kimberlè Williams Crenshaw, *Words That Wound: Critical Race Theory, Assaultive Speech, and the First Amendment* (Boulder, etc., Westview Press, 1993), pp. 53–88, at 68.

4 *Cantwell v. Connecticut*, 310 US 296 (1940), at 309–310; *Chaplinsky v. New Hampshire*, 315 US 568 (1942), at 572.

5 Mari J. Matsuda, "Public Response to Racist Speech: Considering the Victim's Story", in Mari J. Matsuda *et al.*, *Words That Wound, op. cit.*, pp. 17–51, at 35.

6 *Ibid.*

7 See further, Richard Delgado, "Words that Wound: A Tort Action for Racial Insults, Epithets, and Name-Calling", 17 *Harvard Civil Rights-Civil Liberties Law Review* (1982), pp. 133–181, and the more in-depth discussion of this topic in Chapter 7.

8 *Ibid.*

Its contribution to a discussion on matters of public interest or to an "unfettered interchange of ideas for the bringing about of political and social changes desired by the people" is nil.[9] In fact, given the intimidatory context in which it is uttered, it is pre-emptive of further discussion. The intimidatory element can be reinforced by broader contextual circumstances, such as the doctrine of historical inequities and their continuing effects (discussed in Chapter 1) or general "structural injustice". David Richards has defined this term as "a cultural pattern and practice that abridge the human rights of an entire class of persons on inadequate grounds of dehumanizing stereotypes of religion or race or gender or gendered sexuality".[10]

As posited by Lawrence: "[e]ach individual message gains its power because of the cumulative and reinforcing effect of countless similar messages that are conveyed in a society where racism is ubiquitous".[11] Other leading critical race theorists have also argued cogently that the "incessant and compounding" aspects of "hate speech" exacerbate its impact.[12] It seems highly plausible that in a society where racism or hostility towards (particular) minorities is deep-seated and prevalent, the sense of vulnerability ordinarily felt by persons belonging to minorities would be compounded. Patterns of discriminatory practices or persecution against specific groups are inevitably going to colour the personal experiences of their individual members, as well as their participation in public life.

The arguments of the foregoing paragraphs can also be merged into a more complex – but perhaps also more tenuous – argument, *viz.* that hate speech can also be performative of discrimination.[13] In other words, because of its perlocutionary effects,[14] an expression of hate speech could be considered an act of discrimination. An analogous argument has regularly been deployed in feminist literature claiming that pornography is an act of discrimination and subjugation and should not therefore be regarded as a category of expression that is entitled to any kind of constitutional protection. This argument has proved (highly) controversial in academic circles, not least because of the evidentiary difficulty involved: it can be

---

9 *Roth v. the United States*, 354 US 476 (1957), at 484.

10 David A.J. Richards, *Free Speech and the Politics of Identity* (New York, Oxford University Press, Inc., 1999), p. 240.

11 Charles R. Lawrence III, "If He Hollers Let Him Go", *op. cit.*, at 68–69.

12 Richard Delgado & Jean Stefancic, "Four Observations about Hate Speech", 44 Wake Forest L. Rev. 353 (2009), at 367–368.

13 See further, Wojciech Sadurski, "Racial Vilification, Psychic Harm, and Affirmative Action", in Tom Campbell & Wojciech Sadurski, Eds., *Freedom of Communication* (England, Dartmouth Publishing Company, 1994), pp. 77–94; Rae Langton, "Speech Acts and Unspeakable Acts", 22 *Philosophy & Public Affairs* 293; Wojciech Sadurski, "On 'Seeing Speech Through an Equality Lens': A Critique of Egalitarian Arguments for Suppression of Hate Speech and Pornography", 16 *Oxford Journal of Legal Studies* (No. 4, Winter 1996), pp. 713–723.

14 For an influential exploration of locutionary, illocutionary and perlocutionary acts, see: J.L. Austin, *How to do things with words* (Oxford, Oxford University Press, 1980 (reprint of second edition)), esp. Chapters VIII *et seq.*

very difficult to establish – to the satisfaction of a court of law – a causal relationship between a precise utterance and precise discriminatory consequences. Such a case is usually built on empirical evidence. Regardless of how far this argument can be pushed, it does provide a useful additional point of reference. Lee C. Bollinger has – without referring to the anti-pornography or analogous arguments – given a rather clear-worded formulation to one of their essential upshots: "[t]he general point is not only that free speech sometimes involves situations where minorities are being injured (by the speech), but also that the implementation of free speech protection may itself become implicated in that injury, thus reinforcing or stimulating other (non-speech) discrimination".[15]

Hitherto, the focus has been on the harm occasioned by hate speech on individuals and on the groups of which they are members. A further dimension also deserves mention: the broader public. Although society is not directly harmed (eg. in a psychic sense) by individual instances of hate speech, it is adversely affected.[16] Hate speech has broader repercussions than those visited on its immediate victims: prevailing societal attitudes could conceivably be affected by the prevalence of hate speech (particularly if such a phenomenon is met with official impunity or unchecked by societal resistance); community relations could deteriorate due to heightened tensions brought on by a hardening of public discourse; norms of civility and mutual respect could be damaged, etc. On the other hand, though, it is also conceivable that a rising spiral of hate speech in a given community could galvanise its members into taking concerted (informal) action against the phenomenon.

In conclusion, when elevated from the micro- to the macro-level,[17] however, the "counter-speech" theory against hate speech becomes more promising, although it does remain somewhat resistant to empirical verification. The institution of counter-speech at societal level prompts a reconceptualisation of counter-speech as not merely a reactionary force against hate speech (with limited effect), but as a pre-emptive force (with considerable potential) as well. As such, it is a longer-term strategy that places considerable faith in the empowering and identity-sustaining properties of speech. It also implicitly endorses the importance of egalitarian public debate and dialogical interaction as prerequisites for pluralistic tolerance.

---

15 Lee C. Bollinger, "Notes Toward an Idea: Freedom of Speech and Minorities in the United States", in Yoram Dinstein & Mala Tabory, Eds., *The Protection of Minorities and Human Rights* (Dordrecht, Martinus Nijhoff Publishers, 1992), pp. 171–185, at 180.

16 See further: Thomas David Jones, *Human Rights: Group Defamation, Freedom of Expression and the Law of Nations* (The Netherlands, Martinus Nijhoff Publishers, 1998), p. 89.

17 See generally in this connnection, Katharine Gelber, *Speaking Back: The free speech versus hate speech debate* (John Benjamins Publishing Company, Amsterdam, 2002).

8.2 An integrated approach in practice: case study of the Council of Europe

This section[18] will offer an analysis of how the twin goals of facilitating and creating expressive opportunities and of promoting intercultural dialogue and understanding are becoming increasingly prominent in the Council of Europe's approaches to the protection of minority rights. Article 10, ECHR, and relevant case-law of the European Court of Human Rights, as set out in Chapter 6.2.1, remain crucial reference points. The Council of Europe's flagship convention dealing with minority rights, the Framework Convention for the Protection of National Minorities (FCNM), contains provisions which provide for freedom of expression (including rights of access to various types of media) and for the promotion of tolerance. These provisions are expressly linked in the FCNM and their interaction to date has proved instructive. The coupling of freedom of expression and the promotion of tolerance has also been a feature of other Council of Europe standard-setting measures, with varying results.

8.2.1 Framework Convention for the Protection of National Minorities

What is instructive about the FCNM's approach to the protection of minorities against hate or discriminatory speech is the synergic interaction of Articles 6 and 9. For instance, Article 6(2) has been described as providing "negative reinforcement" for *inter alia* Article 9.[19] The synergies generated represent a particularly promising strategy for countering hate speech on a long-term basis. They seek to address the problem before it actually spawns, by emphasising the need to foster improved inter-ethnic and intercultural (the terms are used interchangeably in AC Opinions) understanding and tolerance through the development of dialogical relationships between communities. As will be seen below, a key role has been identified for the media in this preventive strategy: one which involves the harnessing of their communicative potential for the promotion of tolerance and intercultural understanding.

An important caveat ought to be entered at this juncture: the media should in no way be compelled to serve the goal of promoting tolerance and intercultural understanding. Such compulsion (as opposed to encouragement) – by legal or other

---

18 The analysis presented in this section overlaps in places with certain sections in Tarlach McGonagle, "A Survey and Critical Analysis of Council of Europe Strategies for Countering 'Hate Speech'", in Michael Herz & Peter Molnar, Eds., *The Content and Context of Hate Speech: Rethinking Regulation and Responses* (New York, Cambridge University Press, forthcoming 2011).

19 Geoff Gilbert, "Article 6", in Marc Weller, Ed., *The Rights of Minorities in Europe: A Commentary on the European Framework Convention for the Protection of National Minorities* (Oxford and New York, Oxford University Press, 2005), pp. 177–191, at 191.

means – would presumptively fall foul of the principle of media autonomy, which is protected under the more general right to freedom of expression. Any commitments by the media to pursue such objectives must therefore be undertaken voluntarily. As explained in a different, but not entirely dissimilar, context:

> As concerns the propagation of racism and intolerance there is, in principle, scope for imposing legally binding standards without violating freedom of expression and the principle of editorial independence. However, as concerns the promotion of a positive contribution by the media, great care needs to be taken so as not to interfere with these principles. This area calls for measures of encouragement rather than legal measures.[20]

As will be shown below, this caveat is consistently heeded in the FCNM monitoring process.

8.2.1(i) Studying the chemistry between Articles 6 and 9

Although there are two main prongs to the process of monitoring the implementation of the FCNM at national level, *viz.*, the adoption of Opinions by the AC and Resolutions by the Committee of Ministers, the emphasis in this section will be on the former. The reason is that the vastly superior level of detail in AC Opinions is more conducive to the formulation of an overall FCNM strategy against hate and discriminatory speech than the comparative terseness of corresponding Committee of Ministers' Resolutions. Moreover, it is easier to discern the contours of an overall strategy where issues and responses are most fully explored. The format of Committee of Ministers' Resolutions is (necessarily) summary and reflective of the follow-up functions for which such Resolutions are intended.

The AC's approach to the promotion of tolerance, intercultural dialogue, respect and understanding is comprehensive and considered. It recognises: (a) the media *can* play an influential role in shaping societal attitudes and behaviour (for better or for worse); (b) societal attitudes and behaviour are shaped by a multitude of factors (of which the media are only one), and (c) attitudinal and behavioural patterns in society are highly complex and composite in character (and they in turn influence the environment in which the media operate).

---

20 Explanatory Memorandum to Recommendation No. R (97) 20 on "Hate Speech", *op. cit.*, para. 12. This was the reasoning behind the decision for the Committee of Ministers to adopt two separate Recommendations on relevant issues, one dealing with the negative role which the media may play in the propagation of hate speech, and the other dealing with the positive contribution which the media can make to countering such speech (see further, *infra*).

(a) Media influence

Among the main preoccupations of the AC is the ability of the media to contribute to the promotion of tolerance and intercultural understanding, as well as to the elimination of negative stereotyping and negative portrayal of minorities. These objectives are clearly intertwined, both in theory and in practice. Unsurprisingly, they have consistently been flagged as issues of concern in the majority of AC Opinions.[21]

The agenda-setting role of the media can have great importance for the validation of the cultures, languages, lifestyles and other central concerns of minorities. In this context, the following questions gain in pertinence: Is coverage of minority issues quantitatively and qualitatively adequate? Is that coverage responsive to the informational, cultural, linguistic and other needs of its target minority audiences? Are representatives of minorities involved to a meaningful extent in the selection of the topics and the production of the programmes? Are such programmes broadcast in mainstream or minority media? To what extent are minority issues covered by the public service broadcasting system? Is coverage assured during primetime or merely during off-peak slots? These – and a gamut of other related – questions have occasionally surfaced in connection with Article 6, but they fall more squarely within the ambit of Article 9.[22]

Nevertheless, their relevance to the promotion of intercultural understanding, in particular, cannot be gainsaid. For instance, as stated by the AC: "In order to facilitate mutual understanding and dialogue and to increase public awareness about minorities, the public television service should find ways to provide more convenient time-slots for minority programmes".[23] The transmission of minority-centred programmes can expose wider *tranches* of society to minority perspectives and cultures, thereby raising the profile of minority cultures and their prestige outside of minority groups themselves (see further, Chapter 5). These are important arguments for the transmission and legitimisation of minority cultures. They give considerable credence to the argument that "more speech" can, in certain circumstances, amount to an effective, pre-emptive strategy against hate speech. The nature and extent of

---

21 Unless stated otherwise, references to specific AC "Opinions" designate Opinions adopted by the AC in the course of the First Monitoring Cycle. Opinions adopted in the course of the Second or Third Monitoring Cycles will be explicitly described as such.

22 See further Chapter 11 and also Tarlach McGonagle, "Commentary: Access to the media of persons belonging to national minorities", in *Filling the frame: Five years of monitoring the Framework Convention for the Protection of National Minorities* (Strasbourg, Council of Europe Publishing, 2004), pp. 144–159.

23 AC's Second Opinion on Romania, adopted on 24 November 2005, para. 120. See also the AC's Second Opinion on the Czech Republic, adopted on 24 February 2005, paras. 108 and 193.

media coverage are related to, but also logically prior to, the problem of negative reporting on, and stereotyping of, minorities.

Various responses have been proposed by the AC to the problem of negative reporting, many of which centre on the promotion of balanced and accurate reporting;[24] adherence to journalistic codes of ethics and standards, etc.[25] The AC has consistently placed heavy emphasis on the importance of special training initiatives and programmes for journalists on minority issues.[26] The goal is to familiarise journalists with minority issues and pertinent sensitivities that are likely to arise in the course of their coverage of those issues. Exchange programmes for journalists have also been considered, with the same goals in mind.[27] Related strategies also include the establishment of ethnically diverse training courses in journalism,[28] with a view to increasing the number of persons from different ethnic, religious and other groups entering the media sector in professional capacities.[29] These emphases are part of a rather comprehensive approach to counter negative reporting.[30]

The AC often calls for vigilance by State authorities towards negative reporting as a suitable counter-measure to the same. However, those calls are accompanied by standard reminders of the need to show deference to the principle of (editorial) independence of the media, and also, on occasion, by reminders of the need to observe overarching principles of freedom of expression as well.[31] For example:

> The Advisory Committee *finds* that in the field of media, certain widely read newspapers continue, when reporting on subjects concerning immigration and asylum, to adopt an approach which contributes to the feelings of hostility and rejection against immigrants, refugees and asylum seekers and to strengthening the stereotypes associated with Roma. The Advisory Committee *considers* that the Austrian authorities should pursue their efforts to impress on the media, without encroaching on their editorial independence, the need to report fairly on minorities.[32]

---

24 See, for example, AC's Opinion on Slovakia, adopted on 22 September 2000, Section: "In respect of Article 6".

25 Of particular importance in this connection is the practice of only mentioning the ethnic origin of subjects of reporting when strictly relevant: see, for example, AC's Opinion on the United Kingdom, adopted on 30 November 2001, para. 53.

26 See, for example, AC's Opinions on Albania, adopted on 12 September 2002 (para. 98), Lithuania, adopted on 21 February 2003 (para. 45), Spain, adopted on 27 November 2003 (para. 63), Sweden, adopted on 20 February 2003 (paras. 34, 78), Ukraine, adopted on 1 March 2002 (para. 39).

27 AC's Opinion on Slovakia, *op. cit.*, Section: "In respect of Article 6".

28 AC's Second Opinion on Denmark, adopted on 9 December 2004, para. 95.

29 *Ibid.*, para. 103.

30 AC's Opinion on the Russian Federation, adopted on 13 September 2002, para. 135.

31 AC's Second Opinion on Italy, adopted on 24 February 2005, para. 82.

32 (emphasis per original) AC's Opinion on Austria, adopted on 16 May 2002, para. 85. See also, AC's Opinion on "the former Yugoslav Republic of Macedonia", adopted on 27 May 2004, para. 55.

On a related tack, it is significant that the AC resists any temptation to endorse a hypodermic media model. Rather, it recognises – correctly – that while the media do *influence* public opinion, they do not simply *determine* it. While media coverage may perpetuate, reinforce[33] or exacerbate negative societal attitudes and prejudices towards minorities, they can only be charged with having generated those prejudices in the first place in very exceptional circumstances. This presumption can be brought under intense scrutiny when the culpability of the media in fomenting inter-ethnic tensions and unrest is blatant, for example in the much-publicised riots in Kosovo in March 2004.[34]

In the same vein, the AC recognises that the media are not the only actors involved in the influencing of public opinion. For instance, it frequently draws attention to the roles and special responsibilities of law enforcement agents and the judiciary in combating racism. The AC regularly brings politicians and public officials under scrutiny on account of racist views and utterances. Importantly, it does not do so in a blanket or mantra-like way: it tends to specify the levels at which, or sectors in which, the emergence of discrimination or racist views and practices are most acutely in evidence (eg. *local* public authorities[35] and politicians[36]).

(b) The shaping of societal attitudes and behaviour

The previous sub-section broached the issue of how the media can contribute to the shaping of societal attitudes and behaviour. Obviously, the media can usefully provide fora where diverse societal groups can build up awareness and understanding of one another, but by the same token, other non-media fora can also prove very effective for such purposes. The general importance of raising mutual cultural awareness among various groups in society is consistently prioritised in the AC's approach;[37] this applies not only to majority-minority relations (including between

---

33 AC's Second Opinion on Estonia, adopted on 24 February 2005, para. 73.

34 AC's Opinion on Kosovo, adopted on 25 November 2005, para. 58. This Opinion does not fall squarely within the regular monitoring work of the AC; rather, it was adopted pursuant to the Agreement between the Council of Europe and the United Nations Interim Administration Mission in Kosovo (UNMIK) on the Technical Arrangements Related to the Framework Convention for the Protection of National Minorities, concluded on 23 August 2004. See further, Tarlach McGonagle, "Advisory Committee on the Framework Convention for the Protection of National Minorities: Media-specific Provisions in Opinion on Kosovo", *IRIS* 2006–4: 3; Robert Gillette, "Kosovo: Media and the Riots of March 2004", in Susanne Nikoltchev, Ed., *IRIS Special – Political Debate and the Role of the Media: The Fragility of Free Speech* (Strasbourg, European Audiovisual Observatory, 2004), pp. 101–103.

35 AC's Second Opinion on the Czech Republic, *op. cit.*, para. 11.

36 AC's Second Opinion on Croatia, adopted on 1 October 2004, para. 80.

37 See, for example, AC's Opinions on Bosnia & Herzegovina, adopted on 27 May 2004 (para. 138), Ireland, adopted on 22 May 2003 (para. 67), Slovenia, adopted on 12 September 2002 (para. 91).

States authorities and relevant NGOs[38]), but also between various minorities.[39] Awareness is implicitly taken to be a stepping-stone to intercultural understanding. Recommended awareness-raising measures can be either general in character, or can relate to specific groups or events or issues (eg. the Holocaust[40]). Thus viewed, awareness helps to ground the dialogical processes that lead to the achievement of greater societal tolerance. The AC has tentatively teased out this philosophy on several occasions, such as in the following specific situation in the Slovak Republic:

> [...] the Advisory Committee is convinced that a fuller understanding of Roma culture by the public at large and by officials, which can only be gained if Roma themselves are willing to provide input, would help to counter discriminatory acts and attitudes. In this connection, the Advisory Committee also notes that studies suggest that the attitudes of the majority towards the Hungarian minority are most positive in the regions where Hungarians constitute a relatively high proportion of the population and where there is constant interaction between the majority and the said minority. [...][41]

The AC has also developed this philosophy in respect of the often inextricable nature of culture, language and identity. It has, for instance, warned that "[o]ver-insistence on the homogeneity of the Polish population may have an adverse effect on the rights of persons belonging to national minorities to assert their identity".[42] This implies a sense of concern that a level playing pitch would exist for minorities to define themselves on their own terms at the national level.

Communicative engagement is essential for the purpose of building inter-group awareness and understanding. This implies a need for opportunities for the sharing of information and perspectives. Opportunities for self-definition are crucial for minorities, especially given the corrective potential of such opportunities *vis-à-vis* dominant or prevalent societal attitudes regarding them. The AC has rightly recognised the centrality of prevalent, negative attitudes towards (discrete) minorities in the larger picture of societal tolerance and intercultural understanding. Such attitudes are often a product of ignorance, fear and long-held prejudices (eg. anti-Semitism and anti-Roma sentiment),[43] but they can also be coloured by specific

---

38 AC's Second Opinion on Moldova, adopted on 9 December 2004, para. 58.

39 See, for example, AC's Opinion on "the former Yugoslav Republic of Macedonia", *op. cit.*, para. 122.

40 AC's Second Opinion on Romania, *op. cit.*, para. 86.

41 AC's Opinion on Slovakia, *op. cit.*, para. 25.

42 AC's Opinion on Poland, adopted on 27 November 2003, para. 48.

43 Respectively: AC's Opinions on Switzerland, adopted on 20 February 2003, para. 40, and Ukraine, *op. cit.*, para. 91.

situations (eg. regional agitations – or overspill therefrom,[44] ongoing conflicts[45]) or happenings (eg. increased Islamophobia in the wake of the terrorist attacks of 11 September 2001[46]).

Various examples of societal attitudes hardening around specific religious and linguistic differences between discrete groups in society are also considered by the AC. A recurrent source of contention in different countries is the adequacy of facilities for religious minorities to worship. As noted by the AC, such disputes can escalate to the point of potentially "undermining intercultural dialogue with persons belonging to the Muslim faith"[47] (to give one concrete example). Disagreements about language-related matters have also been known to spawn intolerance.[48] Aside from confrontations over religious and linguistic differences, the latter can also form a purely practical obstacle to inter-group communication and understanding. This helps to explain the AC's finding in its First Opinion on Estonia that "further efforts are needed to counter excessive division in the media environment between the media consumed by the majority population and that followed by the minority population".[49] The "excessive division" referred to was largely along linguistic lines. The AC also advocated support for bilingual initiatives in the media sector, which "should be seen as a central element of integration efforts in Estonia, where many persons belonging to national minorities continue to follow to a large extent the media based in the Russian Federation".[50]

(c) The complex and composite character of societal attitudes and behaviour

The comprehensive approach of the AC to Article 6 facilitates an examination of the many influences that contribute to the shaping of societal attitudes. Prime examples of such influences include recent patterns of immigration and migration

44 AC's Second Opinion on Hungary, adopted on 9 December 2004, para. 61, which refers to certain consequences in Hungary of unrest in the Balkans.

45 Eg. Chechnya – AC's Opinion on the Russian Federation, *op. cit.*, paras. 57, 65, 138; Transnistria – AC's Second Opinion on Moldova, *op. cit.*, para. 60.

46 AC's Opinions on Norway, adopted on 12 September 2002 (para. 36), Sweden, *op. cit.* (para. 37), the United Kingdom, *op. cit.* (para. 51).

47 In this particular example, the dispute surrounded the absence of any "full-scale mosque in Denmark": AC's Second Opinion on Denmark, *op. cit.*, para. 88. For similar facts and assessment/prognosis, see also, AC's Second Opinion on Slovenia, adopted on 26 May 2005, para. 98.

48 AC's Opinions on Moldova, adopted on 1 March 2002 (paras. 45, 106, 107), Norway, *op. cit.* (para. 35) and Ukraine, *op. cit.* (paras. 35, 90); AC's Second Opinion on Moldova, *op. cit.* (paras. 17, 59).

49 AC's Second Opinion on Estonia, *op. cit.*, para. 70.

50 *Ibid.*, para. 19. See also, para. 72.

or other demographic shifts;[51] recent or ongoing armed conflict;[52] swells in racist sentiment and surges in racist crimes.[53] Sensitivities surrounding historical symbols can also cause tensions to flare up.[54] The AC is right to dwell on these factors as their explanatory power is considerable. When a general "climate of hostility" (eg. towards immigrants) prevails in a given society, or when a "strong seam of intolerance" can readily be detected, it is hardly surprising that such attitudes would be expressed in the media as well, thereby contributing to a vicious opinion-shaping circle.[55]

Mention of hostility towards immigrants prompts a very important aside. The protection afforded by the FCNM is, as its title suggests, restricted to "national minorities". Perplexingly, as noted in Chapter 2, this term is neither defined nor adequately explained in either the text of the FCNM or in its Explanatory Report. The precise meaning of the term is highly contestable.[56] Nevertheless, the AC has repeatedly insisted that Article 6 "has a wide personal scope of application, covering also asylum seekers, migrants and other persons belonging to groups that have not traditionally inhabited the country concerned".[57] While the language varies from Opinion to Opinion (eg. sometimes reference is made instead to "immigrants and refugees"[58] coming within its scope), the essential point remains the same: the objectives set out in Article 6 are to be strived for also in respect of new or non-traditional minorities, or in other words, "all persons living on the territory"[59] of a Contracting State.[60] In this sense, the personal scope of Article 6 is more far-

51 See, for example, AC's Opinions on Ireland, *op. cit.* (paras. 58, 115), Italy, adopted on 14 September 2001 (para. 40), "the former Yugoslav Republic of Macedonia", *op. cit.* (para. 57).

52 See, for example, AC's Opinions on Bosnia & Herzegovina, *op. cit.* (para. 135) and "the former Yugoslav Republic of Macedonia", *op. cit.* (para. 121).

53 See, for example, AC's Opinions on Hungary, *op. cit.* (Section: "In respect of Article 6"), the Russian Federation, *op. cit.* (para. 137), Slovakia, *op. cit.* (para. 27).

54 AC's Second Opinion on Italy, *op. cit.*, para. 75.

55 AC's Second Opinion on Denmark, *op. cit.*, paras. 20, 77, 80, 96.

56 For discussions of conflicting interpretations of the meaning of the term, see *inter alia*: Geoff Gilbert, "The Council of Europe and Minority Rights", 18 *Human Rights Quarterly* (1996) pp. 160–189, at 165–166 and 169–170; Heinrich Klebes, "The Council of Europe's Framework Convention on National Minorities", 16 *Human Rights Law Journal* (No. 1–3, 1995) pp. 92–98, at 93; Rosalyn Higgins, "Minority Rights: Discrepancies and Divergencies Between the International Covenant and the Council of Europe System", in Rick Lawson & Matthijs de Blois, Eds., *The Dynamics of the Protection of Human Rights in Europe: Essays in Honour of Henry G. Schermers (Vol. III)* (Dordrecht, Martinus Nijhoff Publishers, 1994), pp. 195–209, at 202.

57 AC's Opinion on Ireland, *op. cit.*, para. 61.

58 AC's Opinion on Spain, *op. cit.*, para. 49.

59 AC's Second Opinion on the Czech Republic, *op. cit.*, para. 87.

60 Another slight variant on the formulation crops up in the context of the AC's Second Opinion on Italy, adopted on 24 February 2005, where the scope of Article 6 is stated as applying to all persons living on the [national] territory, including "asylum-seekers, refugees and persons belonging to other groups that have not traditionally inhabited the country concerned": para. 77.

reaching than that of most other provisions of the FCNM.[61] This would suggest that whenever tolerance and intercultural understanding are threatened – as they would be by hate or discriminatory speech, persons belonging to *all* minorities would stand to benefit from the FCNM's provisions.

Attitudes that prevail in society inevitably seep into institutional frameworks too. The effects of embedded, institutionalised racism and discrimination are highly exclusionary. They foreclose opportunities for effective participation in deliberative processes. They erode trust and respect for the organs of the State. Systematic or routine police brutality against specific minorities illustrates the point most sharply. The AC has found that such practices "have disastrous psychological effects on the persons concerned and are bound to undermine the community's confidence in the police".[62] The AC has pointed firmly towards the role to be played by State authorities to curb such practices.

Next to institutional practices and culture, a State's constitutional and legislative culture is also of cardinal contextual importance. The AC has frequently homed in on the problem of inadequate enforcement of (legislative) provisions designed to curb racist activities. The problem has many facets. In the first place, there is the problem of under-reporting and -recording of racist incidents[63] and the inadequate availability of data on racist or ethnically-motivated crimes generally.[64] Second, there is the problem of lax enforcement of existing legislation, which results in few prosecutions being initiated and even fewer prosecutions being successfully concluded. Third, these factors combine to undermine the deterrent and symbolic value assigned to relevant legislation. The dangers for society accruing from a culture of lax enforcement or impunity are great, even if they are not obviously immediate and tangible. A kind of "slow-burn" principle can apply. As the AC has cautioned:

> Even though there are not always individually identifiable victims or economic interests at stake [...] the possible effects on the spirit of tolerance, mutual respect and understanding among all persons, irrespective of their ethnic, cultural or religious identity, must not be underestimated.[65]

The usefulness of this particular wording lies in its neatly suggested coverage for immigrants and migrants alike.

61 See also, in this connection, Article 4, FCNM, which concerns equality and non-discrimination.

62 AC's Opinion on Romania, adopted on 6 April 2001, para. 41. The causes that contribute to the erosion of confidence in State institutions such as the police and the courts are captured well in the AC's Second Opinion on the Czech Republic, *op. cit.*, para. 98.

63 AC's Opinion on the United Kingdom, *op. cit.*, para. 113.

64 AC's Opinion on Spain, *op. cit.*, para. 55.

65 AC's Opinion on Poland, *op. cit.*, para. 57.

8.2.1(ii) Affirmation of the AC's approach

At the beginning of the previous section, the importance of Committee of Ministers' Resolutions in shaping a distinct FCNM strategy against hate and discriminatory speech was somewhat relativised and downplayed. However, the intention was not to write the Committee of Ministers out of the script altogether. Although its Resolutions do not ordinarily provide extra elucidation of concepts or issues, the Committee of Ministers has meaningfully picked up on a number of the themes explored in the foregoing paragraphs. If nothing else, this has at least helped to affirm and consolidate the strategy pursued by the AC, particularly as regards the need for States Parties to encourage media engagement in the promotion of intercultural dialogue and in combating discrimination, negative stereotypes, intolerance and xenophobia.[66]

8.2.1(iii) Conclusions

The coupling of freedom of expression and the promotion of tolerance is a feature of various Council of Europe standard-setting measures, most notably the Committee of Ministers' twin Recommendations on "Hate Speech" and on the media and the promotion of a culture of tolerance.[67] What is distinctive about the FCNM is the extent to which its monitoring process has facilitated an exploration of the actual interplay between freedom of expression and the promotion of tolerance.

Crucially, that exploration highlights the interconnectedness of diverse factors which tend to engender circumstances in which hate and discriminatory speech can flourish. By insisting on the need to pre-emptively address those contributory causes of hate speech, the FCNM seeks to reduce the incidence of manifestations of intolerance and hatred (including hate speech).

The root-and-branch nature of the approach adopted in the FCNM monitoring process boasts two key strategic strengths: (i) it facilitates preventive, pre-emptive measures for combating hate speech; (ii) it does not preclude or even prejudice the possibility of ultimate recourse to tighter, punitive measures against hate speech (if and when dictated by the urgency of circumstances). As such, it is submitted here that the approach merits increased consideration by law- and policy-makers alike.

---

66 The terms used here have been cherry-picked from a number of country-specific Resolutions adopted by the Committee of Ministers, most specifically: Resolution ResCMN(2005)5 on the implementation of the FCNM by Croatia, 28 September 2005; Resolution ResCMN (2006)5 on the implementation of the FCNM by Italy, 14 June 2006; Resolution ResCMN(2005)8 on the implementation of the FCNM by Moldova, 7 December 2005, and Resolution ResCMN(2006)6 on the implementation of the FCNM by Slovenia, 14 June 2006. All of these Resolutions pertain to the Second Monitoring Cycle.

67 *Op. cit.*

8.2.2 Non-treaty-based approaches to hate speech

The Council of Europe actively engages in a wide range of standard-setting activities against hate speech which are not based on specific treaties.

8.2.2(i) Standard-setting by the Committee of Ministers

Resolution 68 (30)

The primary aim of Resolution 68 (30), entitled, "Measures to be taken against incitement to racial, national and religious hatred",[68] is to press Member States of the Council of Europe to sign, ratify and subsequently give domestic legal effect to ICERD.[69] It requests governments to affirm the importance of the schemes of human rights protection offered by both the Universal Declaration of Human Rights and the ECHR when depositing their instruments of ratification of ICERD.[70] It urges States authorities to bring their influence to bear on the United Nations to push for the successful completion of work on a draft convention for the elimination of all forms of intolerance and of discrimination based on religion or belief.[71] As can be seen from its first three substantive provisions, Resolution 68 (30) was very much a product of its time.[72] Under the Resolution's fourth substantive provision, governments are asked to "review their legislation in order to ensure that it provides for effective measures on the matter of prohibition of racial discrimination as well as on the related question of the elimination of all forms of intolerance and discrimination based on religion or belief".

Recommendations

One of the two main points in Recommendation (92) 19 on video games with a racist content is that States authorities should: "review the scope of their legislation in the fields of racial discrimination and hatred, violence and the protection of

68 Adopted on 31 October 1968.

69 *Ibid.*, para. A.1.

70 *Ibid.*, para. A.2.

71 *Ibid.*, para. A.3.

72 For example, the decision to prioritise the preparation of a UN Declaration on the Elimination of All Forms of Intolerance and of Discrimination Based on Religion or Belief (adopted in 1981) in effect eventually led to the (indefinite) abandonment of plans to elaborate an international convention on the same themes. See further: Kevin Boyle, "Religious Intolerance and the Incitement of Hatred", in Sandra Coliver, Ed., *Striking a Balance: Hate Speech, Freedom of Expression and Non-discrimination* (United Kingdom, ARTICLE 19/University of Essex, 1992), pp. 61–71, at 63–64; Natan Lerner, "The Nature and Minimum Standards of Freedom of Religion and Belief", 2000 B.Y.U.L. Rev. 905, at 918.

young people, in order to ensure that it applies without restriction to the production and distribution of video games with a racist content".[73]

Recommendation (97) 20 on "Hate Speech"[74] deserves special attention for the forthright manner in which it seeks to provide "elements which can help strike a proper balance [between fighting racism and intolerance and protecting freedom of expression], both by the legislature and by the administrative authorities as well as the courts in the member States".[75] The seriousness with which it was prepared is also noteworthy: this involved the instruction – by the Steering Committee on the Mass Media – of a Group of Specialists on media and intolerance "to examine, *inter alia*, the role which the media may play in propagating racism, xenophobia, anti-Semitism and intolerance, as well as the contribution they may make to combating these phenomena".[76] The Group examined existing international legal instruments, the domestic legislation of Member States of the Council of Europe and various relevant studies,[77] including a specially-commissioned study on codes of ethics dealing with media and intolerance.[78]

It is clear from the Preamble to the Recommendation that it is anchored in the prevailing standards of international law as regards both freedom of expression and anti-racism. It is not coy about the need to grapple with "all forms of expression which incite to racial hatred, xenophobia, antisemitism and all forms of intolerance, since they undermine democratic security, cultural cohesion and pluralism". It also recognises and draws attention to a number of the central paradoxes involved, eg. that the dissemination of such forms of expression via the media can lead to their having "a greater and more damaging impact", but that there is nevertheless a need to "respect fully the editorial independence and autonomy of the media". These are circles that are not easily squared in the abstract, hence the aim of the Recommendation to provide "elements" of guidance for application in specific cases.

---

73 Recommendation No. R (92) 19 of the Committee of Ministers to Member States on video games with a racist content, 19 October 1992, para. a.

74 Recommendation No. R (97) 20 of the Committee of Ministers to Member States on "Hate Speech", 30 October 1997.

75 Explanatory Memorandum to Recommendation No. R (97) 20 on "Hate Speech", para. 23.

76 *Ibid.*, para. 8.

77 Special mention is given to the study prepared for ECRI by the Swiss Institute of Comparative Law: *Legal measures to combat racism and intolerance in the member States of the Council of Europe*, Doc. CRI (95) 2 (Strasbourg, 2 March 1995). See further: *ibid.*, para. 9.

78 Doc. MM-S-IN (95) 21, also published as: Kolehmainen/Pietilainen, "Comparative Study on Codes of Ethics Dealing with Media and Intolerance" in Kaarle Nordenstreng, Ed., *Reports on Media Ethics in Europe* (University of Tampere, Finland, Series B 41, 1995). See further: *ibid.*, para. 10.

The operative part of the Recommendation calls on national governments to: take appropriate steps to implement the principles annexed to the Recommendation (see further, *infra*); "ensure that such steps form part of a comprehensive approach to the phenomenon, which also targets its social, economic, political, cultural and other root causes"; where States have not already done so, "sign, ratify and effectively implement" ICERD in their domestic legal orders, and "review their domestic legislation and practice in order to ensure that they comply with the principles" appended to the Recommendation.

The principles in question address a wide range of issues. Principle 1 points out that public officials are under a special responsibility to refrain from making statements – particularly to the media – which could be understood as, or have the effect of, hate speech.[79] Furthermore, it calls for such statements to be "prohibited and publicly disavowed whenever they occur". According to Principle 2, States authorities should "establish or maintain a sound legal framework consisting of civil, criminal and administrative law provisions on hate speech which enable administrative and judicial authorities to reconcile in each case respect for freedom of expression with respect for human dignity and the protection of the reputation or rights of others". It suggests detailed ways and means of achieving such ends. Principle 3 stresses that States authorities should ensure that within their legal frameworks, "interferences with freedom of expression are narrowly circumscribed and applied in a lawful and non-arbitrary manner on the basis of objective criteria".

Principle 4 affirms that some particularly virulent strains of hate speech might not warrant any protection whatsoever under Article 10, ECHR. This is a reference to the import of Article 17, ECHR, and to existing case-law on the interaction of Articles 10 and 17 (see further, Chapter 6.2.1). Principle 5 highlights the need for a guarantee of proportionality whenever criminal sanctions are imposed on persons convicted of hate speech offences.

Principle 6 harks back to the *Jersild* case, calling for national law and practice to clearly distinguish "between the responsibility of the author of expressions of hate speech on the one hand and any responsibility of the media and media professionals contributing to their dissemination as part of their mission to communicate information and ideas on matters of public interest on the other hand". The reasoning behind this Principle is that "it would unduly hamper the role of the media if the mere fact that they assisted in the dissemination of the statements engaged their

79 The Appendix to the Recommendation begins by clarifying the scope of "hate speech": "For the purposes of the application of these principles, the term 'hate speech' shall be understood as covering all forms of expression which spread, incite, promote or justify racial hatred, xenophobia, antisemitism or other forms of hatred based on intolerance, including: intolerance expressed by aggressive nationalism and ethnocentrism, discrimination and hostility against minorities, migrants and people of immigrant origin."

legal responsibility or that of the media professional concerned".[80] Principle 7 develops this reasoning by stating that national law and practice should be cognisant of the fact that:

- reporting on racism, xenophobia, anti-Semitism or other forms of intolerance is fully protected by Article 10(1), ECHR, and may only be restricted in accordance with Article 10(2);
- when examining the necessity of restrictions on freedom of expression, national authorities must have proper regard for relevant case-law of the European Court of Human Rights, including the consideration afforded therein to "the manner, contents, context and purpose of the reporting";
- "respect for journalistic freedoms also implies that it is not for the courts or the public authorities to impose their views on the media as to the types of reporting techniques to be adopted by journalists."

Whereas combating hate speech may be considered a defensive or reactionary battle, the promotion of tolerance – an objective to which it is intimately linked – is more pro-active.[81] Recommendation No. R (97) 21 on the media and the promotion of a culture of tolerance[82] was conceived of as the logical complement to the Recommendation on "Hate Speech". It was decided to prepare two separate Recommendations, one dealing with the negative role which the media may play in the propagation of hate speech, and the other dealing with the positive contribution which the media can make to countering such speech. The main reasoning behind this decision was explained as follows:

> As concerns the propagation of racism and intolerance there is, in principle, scope for imposing legally binding standards without violating freedom of expression and the principle of editorial independence. However, as concerns the promotion of a positive contribution by the media, great care needs to be taken so as not to interfere with these principles. This area calls for measures of encouragement rather than legal measures.[83]

The Recommendation urges governments of Member States to raise awareness of the media practices it promotes in all sections of the media and to remain open to supporting initiatives which would further the objectives of the Recommendation. The list of recommended professional practices is non-exhaustive. It is suggested

---

80 Explanatory Memorandum to Recommendation No. R (97) 20, *op. cit.*, para. 38.

81 It should also be mentioned that the European Commission against Racism and Intolerance frequently refers to the need to assure minority groups effective access to the media, *inter alia*, in order to counter negative stereotypes of their cultures and lifestyles, and more generally to promote inter-community understanding and tolerance.

82 Recommendation No. R (97) 21 of the Committee of Ministers to Member States on the media and the promotion of a culture of tolerance, 30 October 1997.

83 Explanatory Memorandum to Recommendation No. R (97) 20, *op. cit.*, para. 12.

that initial and further training programmes could do more to sensitise (future) media professionals to issues of multiculturalism, tolerance and intolerance. Reflection on such issues is called for among the general public, but crucially also within media enterprises themselves. It is also pointed out that it would be desirable for representative bodies of media professionals to undertake "action programmes or practical initiatives for the promotion of a culture of tolerance" and that such measures could viably be complemented by codes of conduct.

Broadcasters, especially those with public service mandates, are encouraged to "make adequate provision for programme services, also at popular viewing times, which help promote the integration of all individuals, groups and communities as well as proportionate amounts of airtime for the various ethnic, religious and other communities". They are also encouraged to promote the values of multiculturalism in their programming, especially in their programme offer targeting children. Finally, the Recommendation mentions the benefits of advertising codes of conduct which prohibit discrimination and negative stereotyping. It equally mentions the usefulness of engaging the media to actively disseminate advertising campaigns for the promotion of tolerance.

The purpose of Recommendation (2000) 4 on the education of Roma/Gypsy children in Europe[84] is to attempt to set right the entrenched disadvantages affecting Roma/Gypsy children in the education sector. The Recommendation therefore addresses structural and content-related matters; recruitment and training of teachers; quality control and review; consultation and coordination.

As its title suggests, Recommendation (2001) 6 on the prevention of racism, xenophobia and racial intolerance in sport,[85] aims to eradicate racism in sporting circles. Its point of departure is a broad definition of racism and it focuses on coordination and the sharing of responsibilities between relevant authorities and other parties. It proposes numerous legislative measures and pays particular attention to the possible mechanics of their implementation. It also countenances other, non-legislative measures to be taken in sports grounds, as well as at local and institutional levels.

While Recommendation (2001) 8 on self-regulation concerning cyber content[86] does not contain any provisions dealing specifically with racism or racist speech, its

---

84 Recommendation No. R (2000) 4 of the Committee of Ministers to member states on the education of Roma/Gypsy children in Europe, 3 February 2000.

85 Recommendation Rec (2001) 6 of the Committee of Ministers to member states on the prevention of racism, xenophobia and racial intolerance in sport, 18 July 2001.

86 Recommendation Rec (2001) 8 of the Committee of Ministers to member states on self-regulation concerning cyber content (self-regulation and user protection against illegal or harmful content on new communications and information services), 5 September 2001.

Preamble recalls the relevance of such issues to self-regulation of online content. It refers to, *inter alia*, Recommendation (92) 19 on video games with a racist content, Recommendation (97) 20 on "Hate Speech" and Article 4, ICERD.

For its part, Recommendation Rec(2003)9 on measures to promote the democratic and social contribution of digital broadcasting[87] emphasises in its preambular section "the need to safeguard essential public interest objectives in the digital environment, including freedom of expression and access to information, media pluralism, cultural diversity, the protection of [...] human dignity [...]". In the Appendix to the Recommendation, this emphasis is placed on a more substantive footing by a call for "[T]he protection of [...] human dignity, and non-incitement to hatred and violence, notably that of racial and religious origin" to "continue to receive particular attention in the digital convergence environment".[88] It is by no means superfluous to insist on the continued relevance of these fundamental values in the context of the digitisation of the media, as they tend to often be eclipsed by technology-related discussions.

Declarations

A number of the Committee of Ministers' (political) Declarations also contain provisions that deal with the perpetration of racist offences via various forms of mass media. For instance, its Declaration on a European policy for new information technologies calls on States:[89]

- to ensure respect for human rights and human dignity, notably freedom of expression, as well as the protection of minors, the protection of privacy and personal data, and the protection of the individual against all forms of racial discrimination in the use and development of new information technologies, through regulation and self-regulation, and through the development of technical standards and systems, codes of conduct and other measures;
- to adopt national and international measures for the effective investigation and punishment of information technology crimes and to combat the existence of safe havens for perpetrators of such crimes;

  [...]
- to enhance this framework of protection, including the development of codes of conduct embodying ethical principles for the use of the new information technologies.

---

87 Recommendation Rec(2003)9 of the Committee of Ministers to member states on measures to promote the democratic and social contribution of digital broadcasting, 28 May 2003.

88 Appendix to the Recommendation, para. 9.

89 Declaration on a European policy for new information technologies, 7 May 1999, Section (v), 'With respect to Protection of rights and freedoms'.

While the Declaration on freedom of communication on the Internet[90] does not zone in specifically on racism, its Preamble does refer to several principles and international instruments which treat relevant issues extensively. As such, it is a document which is of clear – but only indirect and general – relevance.

The Preamble to the Declaration on freedom of political debate in the media[91] recalls the Committee of Ministers' earlier Recommendation on hate speech and emphasises "that freedom of political debate does not include freedom to express racist opinions or opinions which are an incitement to hatred, xenophobia, antisemitism and all forms of intolerance". In the substantive part of the Declaration – under the heading 'Remedies against violations by the media' – it is stated that:

> […] Defamation or insult by the media should not lead to imprisonment, unless the seriousness of the violation of the rights or reputation of others makes it a strictly necessary and proportionate penalty, especially where other fundamental rights have been seriously violated through defamatory or insulting statements in the media, such as hate speech.

The Declaration on freedom of expression and information in the media in the context of the fight against terrorism[92] "invites" media professionals "to consider" suggestions such as:

- to bear in mind the significant role which they can play in preventing "hate speech" and incitement to violence, as well as in promoting mutual understanding;
- to be aware of the risk that the media and journalists can unintentionally serve as a vehicle for the expression of racist or xenophobic feelings or hatred;
- to bear in mind the importance of distinguishing between suspected or convicted terrorists and the group (national, ethnic, religious or ideological) to which they belong or to which they claim to subscribe;
- to set up training courses, in collaboration with their professional organisations, for journalists and other media professionals who report on terrorism, on their safety and the historical, cultural, religious and geopolitical context of the scenes they cover, and to invite journalists to follow these courses.

Terrorism is a highly flammable topic, both in terms of political policy and debate, as well as in media coverage of the same. Its flammability increases the risk of emotionally-fuelled treatment of relevant issues. Hence the importance of specific

---

90 Council of Europe Committee of Ministers Declaration on freedom of communication on the Internet, 28 May 2003.

91 Council of Europe Committee of Ministers Declaration on freedom of political debate in the media, 12 February 2004.

92 Declaration on freedom of expression and information in the media in the context of the fight against terrorism, 2 March 2005.

provisions aiming to ensure that the depiction of certain groups remain within the bounds of the temperate, despite the flammability of the subject matter. Responsible, value-sensitive journalism is the lodestar here, but the aim is followed in a non-coercive way, thereby respecting the principle of media autonomy. The Declaration's promotion of responsible journalism concerns professional practice and training programmes: this is evidence of a simultaneous commitment to the immediate and longer-term goals of countering hate speech.

The Declaration on human rights and the rule of law in the Information Society, adopted in May 2005,[93] was submitted as a Council of Europe contribution to the Tunis Phase of the World Summit on the Information Society (WSIS)[94] in November 2005.

The first section of the Declaration is entitled "Human rights in the Information Society". Its treatment of "the right to freedom of expression, information and communication" includes the assertion that existing standards of protection should apply in digital and non-digital environments alike and that any restrictions on the right should not exceed those provided for in Article 10 of the European Convention on Human Rights (ECHR). It calls for the prevention of state and private forms of censorship and for the scope of national measures combating illegal content (eg. racism, racial discrimination and child pornography) to include offences committed using information and communications technologies (ICTs). In this connection, greater compliance with the Additional Protocol to the Cybercrime Convention is also urged.

The second section of the Declaration sets out a "multi-stakeholder governance approach for building the information society". Of most relevance for present purposes is the following prescription:

> With regard to self- and co-regulatory measures which aim to uphold freedom of expression and communication, private sector actors are encouraged to address in a decisive manner the following issues:
> - hate speech, racism and xenophobia and incitation to violence in a digital environment such as the Internet;
>   […]
> - the difference between illegal comment and harmful comment.

93 Declaration of the Committee of Ministers on human rights and the rule of law in the Information Society, 13 May 2005.

94 The WSIS was an initiative organised by the International Telecommunication Union (ITU), a UN agency under the auspices of which "governments and the private sector coordinate global telecom networks and services". The Summit was held in two phases: the first took place in Geneva in 2003 and the second in Tunis in 2005.

8.2.2(ii) Standard-setting by the Parliamentary Assembly

The Parliamentary Assembly of the Council of Europe (PACE) – the organisation's deliberative organ – has, since 2005, adopted a range of texts focusing on specific issues that arise in the fraught relationship between the rights to freedom of expression and freedom of religion and "hate speech".[95] This sustained focus could be seen as a response to highly visible political controversies. In particular, it has coincided with the fallout from the controversial publication – initially by a Danish newspaper, *Jyllands-Posten*, on September 30, 2005 and subsequently elsewhere – of 12 cartoons that included caricatures of the Prophet Mohammed (see further, Chapter 7.3.3).

All of the texts in question are (explicitly) grounded in relevant provisions of the ECHR, and distil or draw on principles elaborated in case-law of the European Court of Human Rights. The basic message imparted by the PACE's across its relevant texts is that freedom of expression, as guaranteed by Article 10, ECHR, "should not be further restricted to meet increasing sensitivities of certain religious groups," but "hate speech against any religious group is not compatible with the fundamental rights and freedoms guaranteed by the Convention and the case law of the Court".[96] This statement seeks to prevent the dilution – based on subjective religious sensitivities – of existing legal protections of freedom of expression.[97] It posits that restrictions on expression may be justified when "hate speech" is at issue, but not merely on the basis of increasing religious sensitivities.

The PACE's strategies to counter "hate speech" mirror those of other bodies of the Council of Europe. As such, they entail preventive and prohibitive measures on the one hand, and promotional and facilitative measures on the other hand.

---

95 For example: Recommendation 1706 (2005) on media and terrorism, adopted on 20 June 2005; Resolution 1495 (2006) on combating the resurrection of nazi ideology; Resolution 1510 (2006) on freedom of expression and respect for religious beliefs, adopted on 28 June 2006; Recommendation 1768 (2006) on the image of asylum seekers, migrants and refugees in the media, adopted on 5 October 2006; Resolution 1563 (2007) on combating anti-Semitism in Europe, adopted on 27 June 2007; Recommendation 1804 (2007) on State, religion, secularity and human rights, adopted on 29 June 2007; Recommendation 1805 (2007) on blasphemy, religious insults and hate speech against persons on grounds of their religion, adopted on 29 June 2007.

96 *Ibid.*, para. 12. See also, PACE Recommendation 1768 (2006), *op. cit.*, PACE Recommendation 1804 (2007), *op. cit.*, and PACE Recommendation 1805 (2007), *op. cit.*

97 This position has been further explicated as follows: "While we have an acknowledged duty to respect others and must discourage gratuitous insults, freedom of expression cannot, needless to say, be restricted out of deference to certain dogmas or the beliefs of a particular religio us community": "State, religion, secularity and human rights", PACE Recommendation 1804 (2007), *op. cit.*, para. 19.

Relevant PACE texts clearly emphasise the importance of effective enforcement of national legislation prohibiting incitement to hatred, violence, or discrimination (and to first adopt such legislation where it does not already exist). Member States are also invited to "adopt and implement penal legislation against, *inter alia*, the public dissemination or public distribution, or the production or storage of material with a racist content or purpose".[98] The PACE similarly prioritises the effective enforcement of (national) legislation "criminalising anti-Semitic and other hate speech"; the prosecution of political parties which promote anti-Semitic ideas; the criminalization of racially-motivated public denials of crimes of genocide, crimes against humanity, or war crimes; and the strengthening of legislative provisions making anti-Semitic motivation an aggravating factor in criminal cases.[99] In its Resolution, 'Towards decriminalisation of defamation', the PACE takes its cue from General Policy Recommendation No. 7 of the European Commission against Racism and Intolerance (ECRI, see further *infra*) and calls on Member States to "make it a criminal offence to publicly incite to violence, hatred or discrimination, or to threaten an individual or group of persons, for reasons of race, colour, language, religion, nationality or national or ethnic origin where those acts are deliberate".[100] It then calls for "only incitement to violence, hate speech and promotion of negationism" to be made "punishable by imprisonment".[101]

These calls to criminalise hate speech are very worrying, given the potentially wide scope of "hate speech". In the absence of a clear and authoritative legal definition of the term at the level of the Council of Europe, Member States are likely to determine its scope as they see fit. It is not implausible that this call could legitimate national provisions for prison sentences for "lesser" forms of "hate speech". The call also sits uneasily with other passages in the Resolution, "Towards decriminalisation of defamation", which alert to the dangers of abusive restrictions on freedom of expression.[102]

Relevant PACE texts also emphasise the importance of a range of non-prescriptive measures, in particular those aimed at fostering (structured) communicative opportunities. The promotion of dialogical interaction between religious groups is routinely encouraged and a specific role for the media in furtherance of such

---

98 PACE Recommendation 1768 (2006), *op. cit.* In the same Recommendation, PACE also invites Member States to "adopt and implement legislation penalising leaders of groups promoting racism, and suppress public financing of organisations carrying out or supporting such activities".

99 PACE Resolution 1563 (2007), *op. cit.*

100 "Towards decriminalisation of defamation", PACE Resolution 1577 (2007), adopted on 4 October 2007, para. 17.4.

101 *Ibid.*, para. 17.5.

102 *Ibid.*, paras. 12–15. See also in this connection, "Towards decriminalisation of defamation", PACE Recommendation 1814 (2007), adopted on 4 October 2007, para. 1.

interaction has been identified.[103] Repeated references are made to the need for media codes of conduct/ethics to include specific guidelines for tackling stereotyping and intolerance.[104] In this regard, the PACE advocates responsible reporting which generally protects vulnerable minorities, migrants, and refugees from negative stereotyping and promotes positive media representations of such groups, as well as their participation in media activities.[105] Several capacity-building measures have been put forward in connection with the latter: training, funding, and other promotional measures concerning the production and broadcasting of programs featuring minorities, including in mainstream television programs and at peak viewing times.

In the context of media reporting on terrorism, the PACE "invites media professionals" *inter alia* to "avoid aggravating, through their news and comments, the societal tensions underlying terrorism, and in particular to refrain from disseminating any kind of hate speech".[106] The PACE has also regularly called for media complaints bodies to be adequately equipped to deal effectively with instances of "offences to religious persuasions";[107] "intolerant, racist or xenophobic attitudes towards migrants, asylum seekers or refugees";[108] and "anti-Semitism and other forms of hate speech".[109]

8.2.2(iii) European Ministerial Conferences on Mass Media Policy

European Ministerial Conferences on Mass Media Policy have been held periodically since the mid-1980s. These conferences involve the participation of Ministers (or their delegates) with relevant portfolios at the national level. As such, the Ministerial Conferences can be distinguished from the day-to-day activities of the Council of Europe. Their relevance stems from their purpose to map out future European media policy, supplemented by action plans for its implementation.

The first three European Ministerial Conferences on Mass Media Policy and the sixth such Conference did not examine the issues of hate speech or tolerance and

---

103 PACE Resolution 1510 (2006), *op. cit.*, paras. 14 & 16 (which refers to the role of the media); PACE Resolution 1563 (2007), *op. cit.*, and PACE Recommendation 1804 (2007), *op. cit.*

104 PACE Resolution 1510 (2006), *op. cit.*, para. 15, PACE Recommendation 1768 (2006), *op. cit.*, and PACE Recommendation 1563 (specifically in respect of anti-Semitic stereotypes and prejudices), *op. cit.*

105 PACE Recommendation 1768 (2006), *op. cit.*

106 PACE Recommendation 1706 (2005), Media and terrorism, *op. cit.*, para. 8(vi).

107 PACE Resolution 1510 (2006), *op. cit.*, para. 15.

108 PACE Recommendation 1768 (2007), *op. cit.*

109 PACE Resolution 1563 (2007), *op. cit.*, para. 12.14.

intolerance in the media sector in any direct or meaningful way. Their thematic preoccupations lay elsewhere.[110]

During the 4th European Ministerial Conference on Mass Media Policy,[111] however, these issues were broached in two of the texts adopted during the Conference. In Resolution No. 2: Journalistic Freedoms and Human Rights, Principle 7(f) sets out generally that the "practice of journalism in a genuine democracy" implies "avoiding the promotion of any violence, hatred, intolerance or discrimination based, in particular, on race, sex, sexual orientation, language, religion, politics or other opinions, national or regional origin, or social origin." In the Declaration on media in a democratic society, the Ministers of participating States condemn, "in line with the Vienna Declaration, all forms of expression which incite to racial hatred, xenophobia, anti-Semitism and all forms of intolerance, since they undermine democratic security, cultural cohesion and pluralism".[112] They also affirm "that the media can assist in building mutual understanding and tolerance among persons, groups and countries and in the attainment of the objectives of democratic, social and cultural cohesion announced in the Vienna Declaration".[113] These two principles again reflect the conceptual bifurcation between curbing hate speech and promoting understanding and tolerance – a distinction that has (by and large) consistently been adhered to throughout relevant Council of Europe instruments. Relatedly, in the Action Plan adopted at the Conference, it was proposed that the Committee of Ministers of the Council of Europe "**Study**, in close consultation with media professionals and regulatory authorities, possible guidelines which could assist media professionals in addressing intolerance in all its forms".[114]

It was the 5th European Ministerial Conference on Mass Media Policy[115] that paid the greatest attention to relevant issues to date. Paras. 11 and 12 of the Political Declaration adopted at that Conference refer in general terms to the potential offered and risks posed by new communications and information services for freedom of expression and other rights and values. In a similar vein, Resolution No. 1: The impact of new communication technologies on human rights and democratic

110 1st European Ministerial Conference on Mass Media Policy (Vienna, 9–10 December 1986): *The future of television in Europe*; 2nd European Ministerial Conference on Mass Media Policy (Stockholm, 23–24 November 1988): *European Mass Media Policy in an international context*; 3rd European Conference on Mass Media Policy (Nicosia, 9–10 October 1991): *Which way forward for Europe's media in the 1990s?*; 6th European Ministerial Conference on Mass Media Policy (Cracow, 15–16 June 2000): *A media policy for tomorrow.*

111 Prague, 7–8 December 1994: *The media in a democratic society.*

112 Principle 7.

113 Principle 8.

114 (emphasis per original) Action Plan setting out strategies for the promotion of media in a democratic society addressed to the Committee of Ministers of the Council of Europe (Point 6 – "Media and intolerance").

115 Thessaloniki, 11–12 December 1997: *The Information Society: a challenge for Europe.*

values, emphasises the Ministers' condemnation of the use of new technologies and services "for spreading any ideology, or carrying out any activity, which is contrary to human rights, human dignity, and democratic values", as well as their resolve to "combat such use".[116]

Resolution No. 2: Rethinking the regulatory framework for the media, calls on participating States to give domestic effect to the principles enshrined in the Committee of Ministers' Recommendations on, *inter alia*, "hate speech" and on the media and the promotion of a culture of tolerance.[117] It also calls on States authorities "to ensure that measures for combating the dissemination of opinions and ideas which incite to racial hatred, xenophobia, anti-Semitism and all forms of intolerance through the new communications and information services duly respect freedom of expression and, where applicable, the secrecy of correspondence".[118] The reinforcement of cooperation within the Council of Europe, while liaising with other IGOs and "interested professional organisations", is also advocated.[119] Such cooperation should have standard-setting aspirations, initially for Europe and later for further afield too. The suggested focus is on "problems of delimiting public and private forms of communication, liability, jurisdiction and conflict of laws in regard to hate speech disseminated through the new communications and information services".[120]

The Conference's Action Plan calls for study of "the practical and legal difficulties in combating the dissemination of hate speech, violence and pornography via the new communications and information services, with a view to taking appropriate initiatives in a common pan-European framework". As already mentioned *supra*, it also calls for the "periodical evaluation" of Member States' "follow-up" to the Committee of Ministers' Recommendations on, *inter alia*, "hate speech" and on the media and the promotion of a culture of tolerance. In addition, it seeks a periodical evaluation of the implementation of Article 7 of the European Convention on Transfrontier Television (ECTT) by Member States, particularly as regards the "responsibilities of broadcasters with regard to the content and presentation of their programme services". Finally, it provides for an examination – "as appropriate" – of the "advisability of preparing in addition other binding or non-binding instruments".

The 7th European Ministerial Conference on Mass Media Policy, entitled, *Integration and diversity: the new frontiers of European media and communication policy*, was held in Kyiv, Ukraine, in March 2005. At the conference, the ministers

116 Para. 9. See also, para. 19(i), where these points are reiterated in very similar language.

117 Para. 8(i).

118 Para. 8(ii).

119 Para. 8(iii).

120 Para. 8(iii).

of participating States undertook, *inter alia*, to: "step up their efforts to combat the use of the new communication services for disseminating content prohibited by the Cybercrime Convention and its additional Protocol concerning the criminalisation of acts of a racist and xenophobic nature committed through computer systems".[121]

In order to reflect changing notions of the media, the most recent European ministerial conference was calibrated differently – as the "1st Council of Europe Conference of Ministers responsible for Media and New Communication Services", entitled *A new notion of media?*[122] The political texts adopted at the Conference pay scant attention to "hate speech". This is difficult to explain, given that: (i) there is a real resurgence of "hate speech" in a new media context, which poses considerable regulatory challenges, and (ii) the purpose of the Conference was to map out priorities in European media policy to be addressed by the Council of Europe in the coming years.[123]

8.2.2(iv) The European Commission against Racism and Intolerance (ECRI)

The European Commission against Racism and Intolerance (ECRI) was established in 1993, and it was under its auspices that the preparations in Europe for the World Conference against Racism, Racial Discrimination, Xenophobia and Related Intolerance (2001) were largely coordinated.

ECRI's work has three main focuses: its so-called "country-by-country" approach (which involves the ongoing monitoring of relevant issues in Member States[124]) and work on general themes (which includes the elaboration of general policy recommendations, as well as the collection and promotion of examples of "good practice" in the struggle against racism), and engagement with civil society. More specifically, its objectives have been listed as follows:

- to review member states' legislation, policies and other measures to combat racism, xenophobia, antisemitism and intolerance, and their effectiveness;
- to propose further action at local, national and European level;
- to formulate general policy recommendations to member states;
- to study international legal instruments applicable in the matter with a view to their reinforcement where appropriate.[125]

---

121 Resolution No. 3, "Human rights and regulation of the media and new communication services in the Information Society", para. 18. See further, Tarlach McGonagle, "Ministerial Conference on Mass Media Policy", *IRIS* 2005–7: 2.

122 *A new notion of media?*, 28–29 May 2009, Reykjavik, Iceland.

123 See further: Tarlach McGonagle & Kim de Beer,, "*A brave new media world?* Een kritische blik op het nieuwe mediabeleid van de Raad van Europa", 22 *Mediaforum* 2010–5, pp. 146–156.

124 This is a report-based system.

125 Article 1, Appendix to Resolution (2002)8, Statute of the European Commission against Racism and Intolerance (ECRI).

The challenge of combating racism and intolerance in a way that is duly respectful of the right to freedom of expression is a recurrent issue in both ECRI's country-monitoring work and its work on general themes.[126] In order to take stock of and evaluate appropriate legal and policy measures for the realisation of this aim, ECRI has actively engaged with civil society, most notably by organising a multi-party expert seminar on the topic at the end of 2006.[127] While it is too early yet to assess (or even predict) the impact of that seminar on ECRI's strategies for meeting the challenge, it can be observed that its engagement with relevant issues to date has produced mixed results.

The different focuses of ECRI's work cast it in different roles which entail different responsibilities. In its country-monitoring work, ECRI's role is essentially that of a watchdog. It monitors and analyses ongoing developments and periodically issues specific recommendations tailored to specific problems. The exercise presents and processes information about (especially problematic) developments with a view to facilitating their ultimate resolution. In its work on general themes, on the other hand, ECRI assumes a more explicit and general standard-setting role. By virtue of its normative intentions in this respect, its responsibilities are greater. The elaboration of recommendations designed for general application by all States requires greater care and precision than the formulation of specific problem-solving recommendations focusing on specific issues in specific States. This is not to downplay the importance of the latter task; rather, it seeks to make an epistemological relativisation, the importance of which will become apparent in the following analysis. The relativisation in question is this: in light of their purported wider applicability and (presumably) longer durability, the ability of general policy recommendations to withstand strict scrutiny in terms of their conceptual and terminological precision is more important than in the case of issue-/situation-specific recommendations. As will be demonstrated, occasional lapses in conceptual and terminological precision could have an adverse effect on the credibility of ECRI's standard-setting role in respect of certain key issues.

The following analysis will analyse how the challenge of combating racism and intolerance in a way that is duly respectful of the right to freedom of expression has been dealt with, first in ECRI's most recent country-monitoring work and then in its work on general themes.

---

126 Explanatory Note to ECRI Expert Seminar on combating racism while respecting freedom of expression, Strasbourg, 16–17 November 2006, p. 1.

127 The proceedings of the expert seminar have been published as: ECRI, *Combating racism while respecting freedom of expression* (Strasbourg, Council of Europe, 2007).

Country-monitoring work

On the basis of the third round of ECRI's country-monitoring work,[128] there is clear evidence that ECRI espouses a root-and-branch approach, similar to that pursued by the Advisory Committee on the FCNM, to the imperative of countering racist expression and intolerance. There is also clear evidence that ECRI's approach, again like that of the AC, is mindful of the importance of the right to freedom of expression and the differential roles of the media in this context. As such, the overall pattern that emerges from the country reports surveyed includes recommendations for both punitive and preventive measures, the most salient of which will now be discussed.

In terms of punitive measures, a recurrent general recommendation is that States authorities strengthen existing legislative provisions prohibiting incitement to hatred,[129] or ensure that existing provisions are vigorously implemented.[130] Similarly, ECRI regularly recommends particular vigilance in identifying and prosecuting cases of incitement to or dissemination of hatred by media professionals.[131] In cases where racist articles have been published, ECRI often calls for the perpetrators to be prosecuted and punished.[132] Curiously, in the reports surveyed, ECRI has focused on the *publication* of racist *articles* and made few comparable recommendations about the dissemination of racist expression via the broadcast media. Some of the recommendations for punitive measures specifically concern racist and xenophobic material on the Internet, however.[133] The specificity of such a focus demonstrates the growing nature of the problem, yet such recommendations are by no means systematic in ECRI's country reports. This begs the question of whether the problem is equally pressing in all States.

Alongside its recommendations for prosecution and punishment in a system built around legislation and the courts, other recommendations call for the adoption[134]

128 At the time of writing, the fourth round of monitoring was ongoing. This analysis is based on the third round because it is the most recent *concluded* round of monitoring. References to States in this subsection therefore implicitly refer to ECRI Reports on those States adopted in the course of its third monitoring cycle.

129 Denmark, para. 92; Norway, para. 101; Former Yugoslav Republic of Macedonia, para. 95.

130 Lithuania, para. 62.

131 Czech Republic, para. 65; Luxembourg, para. 77; Romania, para. 113; Russia, para. 120; Sweden, para. 9.

132 Bulgaria, para. 63; Croatia, para. 82; Estonia, para. 115 (the phrase, "duly prosecuted", is used here instead of the reference to "prosecute and punish"); Greece, para. 98; Poland, para. 79; Turkey, para. 100.

133 Finland, para. 91; France, para. 107; Germany, para. 111; Lithuania, para. 64; Portugal, para. 92; Sweden, para. 83.

134 Albania, para. 70; Austria, para. 73; Czech Republic, para. 65; Germany, para. 78; Turkey, para. 100.

and/or implementation[135] by the media sector of self-regulatory codes which would include provisions on racism, discrimination and responsible reporting on minorities. The frequency with which this kind of recommendation is made is indicative of ECRI's awareness of, and deference to, the principle of media autonomy which is a central principle of the Council of Europe's approach to freedom of expression. ECRI's commitment to this principle is even more obvious in its regular encouragement of the State authorities to: "impress on the media, without encroaching on their editorial independence, the need to ensure that reporting does not contribute to creating an atmosphere of hostility and rejection towards members of any minority groups".[136] Slight, mainly negligible, variations in wording occur,[137] but a more significant variation involves instances in which particular minority groups are specified.[138] In the report on the United Kingdom, the authorities are furthermore encouraged to impress on the media (without encroaching on their editorial indepence) "the need to play a proactive role in countering such an atmosphere".[139]

In respect of certain countries, the wording does change in ways that (possibly/ presumably) reflect certain contextual specificities of those countries. In the case of Ireland, for instance, "ECRI recommends that, while fully respecting the principle of freedom of expression and editorial independence, the authorities encourage fairness when issues pertaining to ethnic minority groups, asylum seekers, refugees and immigrant communities are discussed by the media".[140] In the report on Germany, the focus of attention is on "the need to ensure that reporting does not perpetuate racist prejudice and stereotypes".[141] These emphases on fairness and on racist prejudice/stereotypes are more particularised than the more open-ended formula, "atmosphere of hostility and rejection", thus suggesting a more pointed,

---

135 Austria, para. 73; Belgium, para. 59; Germany, para. 78; Hungary, para. 85; Norway, para. 80; Former Yugoslav Republic of Macedonia, para. 94.

136 See, for example, Cyprus, para. 90; Finland, para. 90.

137 See, for example, Austria, para. 73; Portugal, para. 87.

138 For example, in the report on Iceland, members of "immigrant, Muslim or Jewish communities" are singled out for attention (para. 80); in the report on Italy, the "minority groups" are explicitly considered to include "non-EU citizens, Roma, Sinti and Muslims" (para. 79); in the report on Lithuania, members of the "Jewish, Roma and Chechen communities" are expressly mentioned (para. 63); in the report on Portugal, the specification involves "immigrants and Gypsies" (para. 87); in the report on the Russian Federation, "visible minority groups" (the formula that is used instead of "any minority groups") are stated as "including Roma, Chechens and other Caucasians, as well as citizens from CIS countries" (para. 121); in the report on Spain, particular reference is made to "the Roma, Muslims and immigrants" (para. 86); in respect of the United Kingdom, the atmosphere of hostitility and rejection to be avoided is described as being "towards asylum seekers, refugees and immigrants or members of any minority group, including Roma/ Gypsies, Travellers and Muslims" (para. 79).

139 United Kingdom, para. 79; see also, Germany, para. 78.

140 Ireland, para. 112.

141 Germany, para. 78.

situation-specific approach by ECRI (as opposed to a sound, but vague, recommendation that could uncontroversially be applied to any country situation). Another, somewhat blander, variant on the general theme is that States authorities alert the media (i.e., professionals and organisations) to "the dangers of racism and intolerance".[142] It is unclear why this less demanding recommendation is preferred to the more robust formula discussed in the current and previous paragraphs for some countries.

It is significant to note that this particular recommendation is systematically accompanied by the further recommendation that States authorities should: "engage in a debate with the media and members of other relevant civil society groups on how this could best be achieved".[143] An exception is found in the report on the Russian Federation and it is submitted that that was a missed opportunity to underscore the importance of civil society participation in media policy formulation in a country where weak traditions of such participation need to be strengthened.[144] Again, slight, mainly negligible variations in wording arise in this respect,[145] but in the report on the United Kingdom, ECRI recommends that "any successful initiatives developed at local level in this field, be reproduced on a broader scale at national level".[146] In the report on Spain, the need for measures at the local and national levels is also adverted to.[147] In the report on Portugal, the authorities are encouraged to "hold discussions with the media and other relevant civil society players [...]"[148] and it is submitted that the reference to discussions is preferable to the more consistently used reference to "debate", which has the connotation of a more confrontational encounter.

As already mentioned, ECRI has also shown its awareness of the potential role that freedom of expression can play in countering racist speech. It has sought to harness that potential by encouraging (rather than prescribing, again out of deference to the principle of media autonomy) more and better media coverage of minority issues,[149] a goal which could be advanced in a number of ways. For example, it recommends more State support for training schemes for media professionals on issues such as

---

142 Bulgaria, para. 63; Croatia, para. 82; Greece, para. 98; Hungary, para. 85 (here, the reference is to "the danger of negative reporting"); Poland, para. 79; Switzerland, para. 60 (here, the point is styled as furher sensitisation to the need to report on asylum-seekers and refugees in a more balanced fashion, "without resorting to language and propaganda which are likely to exacerbate public prejudice and hostility"); Turkey, para. 100.

143 Cyprus, para. 90; Finland, para. 90; Iceland, para. 80; Italy, para. 79; Lithuania, para. 63; Slovenia, para. 87.

144 Russian Federation, para. 121.

145 See, for example, Portugal, para. 87.

146 United Kingdom, para. 79.

147 Spain, para. 86.

148 Portugal, para. 87.

149 Albania, para. 71; Austria, para. 74; Former Yugoslav Republic of Macedonia, para. 137.

reporting in a diverse society;[150] human rights, racism, racial discrimination[151] and anti-Semitism.[152] Another way of advancing the goal of more and better media coverage of minority issues is by seeking to ensure greater representation of persons from immigrant backgrounds in the media profession.[153] This approach is explicitly based on the assumption that the enhanced representation of immigrants in media structures will have a positive impact on the representation of immigrants in media output.

ECRI also underscores the importance of access to electronic and print media for persons belonging to minorities, generally,[154] as well as the specific importance of ensuring the "adequate availability of electronic media in the language of national minorities".[155] The promotion via the media of minority identities[156] and of "an atmosphere of appreciation of diversity"[157] are also recommended, as is the creation of a shared forum in which separate linguistic communities can receive the same information, with a view to strengthening inter-group relations.[158]

The striking similarities between the approaches taken by ECRI and the AC on the FCNM augur well for the further development and consolidation of a broadly consistent approach by the various bodies of the Council of Europe to the perennial problem of effectively combating racist and discriminatory speech without circumscribing the right to freedom of expression beyond the legitimate restrictions on the right which are recognised under international law.

Work on general themes

ECRI's General Policy Recommendations (GPRs) are the mainstay of its work on general themes. They are as follows:

1. Combating racism, xenophobia, antisemitism and intolerance (1996)
2. Specialised bodies to combat racism, xenophobia, antisemitism and intolerance at national level (1997)

---

150 Austria, para. 73; Germany, para. 78;.

151 Denmark, para. 108; Estonia, para. 115; Romania, para. 112 ("national and local media training courses on combating discrimination"); Slovakia, para. 91 (this provision is directed at "professionals", presumably including, although without specifying, "media" professionals).

152 Luxembourg, para. 77.

153 Austria, para. 73; Belgium, para. 60; France, para. 105 (and see also para. 104 for details of a positive initiative in this connection); Germany, para. 78; Norway, para. 80. In these examples, references to "the press" are presumably expansive, i.e., to the press as an institution. It is submitted here that "the media" would have been a more suitable term.

154 Albania, para. 72.

155 Austria, para. 74.

156 Slovenia, paras. 73–74.

157 Albania, para. 70.

158 Estonia, para. 114.

3. Combating racism and intolerance against Roma/Gypsies (1998)
4. National surveys on the experience and perception of discrimination and racism from the point of view of potential victims (1998)
5. Combating intolerance and discrimination against Muslims (2000)
6. Combating the dissemination of racist, xenophobic and antisemitic material via the Internet (2000)
7. On national legislation to combat racism and racial discrimination (2002)
8. On combating racism while fighting terrorism (2004)
9. On the fight against antisemitism (2004)
10. On combating racism and racial discrimination in and through school education (2006)
11. On combating racism and racial discrimination in policing (2007)
12. On combating racism and racial discrimination in the field of sport (2008)

The first and most self-evident *forte* of ECRI's thematic approach is the opportunity it affords to ring-fence particular issues and grapple with their specifics in much more detail and with much more rigour than would be possible in general texts. Its focuses on the Internet and on the fight against terrorism are illustrative of such detailed treatment. However, its handling of these issues is not without flaws.

In GPR No. 6,[159] the credibility of ECRI's single-minded pursuit of the goal of eliminating racist and xenophobic content online is compromised somewhat by its failure at any stage to acknowledge and weigh up relevant freedom of expression interests. In the preambular section, reference is made to GPR No. 1, and a supporting citation is provided, as follows:

> Recalling that, in its general policy recommendation No 1, ECRI called on the governments of Council of Europe member States to ensure that national criminal, civil and administrative law expressly and specifically counters racism, xenophobia, antisemitism and intolerance
>
> Stressing that, in the same recommendation, ECRI asked for the aforementioned law to provide in particular that oral, written, audio-visual expressions and other forms of expression, including the electronic media, inciting to hatred, discrimination or violence against racial, ethnic, national or religious groups or against their members on the grounds that they belong to such a group are legally categorised as a criminal offence, which should also cover the production, the distribution and the storage for distribution of the material in question.

This citation of GPR No. 1 in GPR No. 6 is, however, abridged, although no indication is given that this is the case. The omitted section of the full, original text

159 ECRI general policy recommendation no. 6, "Combating the dissemination of racist, xenophobic and anti-Semitic material via the Internet", adopted on 15 December 2000.

is italicised below; in the relevant part of GPR No. 1, ECRI recommends States governments to:

> Ensure that national criminal, civil and administrative law expressly and specifically counter racism, xenophobia, anti-semitism and intolerance, inter alia by providing:
>
> [...]
>
> – that, *in conformity with the obligations assumed by States under relevant international instruments and in particular with Articles 10 and 11 of the European Convention on Human Rights,*
>
> oral, written, audio-visual expressions and other forms of expression, including the electronic media, inciting to hatred, discrimination or violence against racial, ethnic, national or religious groups or against their members on the grounds that they belong to such a group are legally categorised as a criminal offence, which should also cover the production, the distribution and the storage for distribution of the material in question.

This omission pushes the language employed in GPR No. 6 away from the wording of existing international law standards. And it does so to a significant extent. Articles 10 (Freedom of expression) and 11 (Freedom of assembly and association), ECHR, both contain limiting – or so-called "claw-back" – clauses (which could easily be invoked, and are in practice, to counter racist expression and activities); similar limitations govern the exercise of the rights to freedom of expression and association as guaranteed by the International Covenant on Civil and Political Rights; ICERD contains a crucial "due regard" clause, which requires a balancing of anti-racist objectives with other fundamental human rights. It is therefore very remiss of ECRI to fail to consider its own immediate objectives in the context of existing human rights as provided for by international law, especially the right to freedom of opinion, expression and information. This failure to square up to the potential interaction (and incidental friction) between rights is apparent in ECRI's other GPRs too.

While GPR No. 6 does acknowledge the Internet's potential for combating racism, *inter alia*, through self-regulatory measures, the transfrontier sharing of information concerning "human rights issues related to anti-discrimination", and the (further) development of educational and awareness-raising networks, the absence of references to freedom of expression and other pertinent rights conveys the impression of a document that is somewhat skewed in terms of the range of its sources of inspiration.

GPR No. 8,[160] which examines how anti-racism could be integrated into the fight against terrorism, also departs from the tried and trusted formulae of "hard" international law, albeit to a lesser extent. In its Preamble, it stresses that "the response to the threat of terrorism should not itself encroach upon the very values of freedom, democracy, justice, the rule of law, human rights and humanitarian law that it aims to safeguard, nor should it in any way weaken the protection and promotion of these values". This recognition of relativism is welcome. However, it could also be submitted that this statement would have been all the more forceful if it had been more firmly rooted in international human rights treaties. The verbal phrase, "encroach upon", is vague and invites subjective interpretation. If the statement had been aligned more closely to the language employed in specific provisions of, for example, the ECHR, or if it had clearly referred to such provisions, the degree of subjectivity would have been reduced. Closer conceptual and linguistic alignment with the ECHR would automatically point to a body of relevant judicial pronouncements, thereby offering authoritative interpretative clarity.

Furthermore, GPR No. 8 refers to "certain visible minorities", a term which is not used in any (well-known) international (legal or political) instruments.[161] The problems of defining and categorising minorities have proved vexed enough under international law,[162] without muddying the waters further by introducing novel terms of uncertain scope. Indeed, no multi-lateral European-, or global-level, treaty contains a definition of "minority". For their part, the drafters of the FCNM conceded the impossibility of forging "a definition capable of mustering general support of all Council of Europe member States".[163] It would appear that the appeal of the term "certain visible minorities" lies in the alleged flexibility it offers ECRI in the course of its work.[164] However, that argument, as well as the claim that the notion of visibility can cover linguistic and religious minorities,[165] is unconvincing.

To suggest that linguistic and religious minorities are categories of "visible minorities" seems to confuse visibility with identifiability. Visibility refers to

---

160 ECRI general policy recommendation no. 8 on combating racism while fighting terrorism, adopted on 17 March 2004.

161 The term is, however, used by some commentators (eg. Ted R. Gurr, *Peoples versus States: Minorities at Risk in the New Century* (Washington, United States Institute of Peace, 2000), at p. 165) and in conventional political discourse in some countries (eg. Canada).

162 See generally: Francesco Capotorti, *Study on the rights of persons belonging to ethnic, religious and linguistic minorities* (E/CN.4/Sub.2/384/Rev.1) (New York, United Nations, 1979), esp. p. 96, para. 568; John Packer, "Problems in Defining Minorities", in Deirdre Fottrell and Bill Bowring, Eds., *Minority and Group Rights in the New Millennium* (The Netherlands, Kluwer Law International, 1999), pp. 223–273; Geoff Gilbert, "The Council of Europe and Minority Rights", 18 *Human Rights Quarterly* (1996), pp. 160–189.

163 Explanatory Report to the Framework Convention for the Protection of National Minorities, para. 12.

164 The author has heard this suggestion made informally.

165 The author has also heard this suggestion made informally.

features that can be seen, i.e., physical and superficial details, and it is only by serious doctoring (if not corruption) of the ordinary meaning of visibility that it could be extended to linguistic and religious characteristics. Granted, the outward manifestation of religious beliefs can often be visible (eg. particular types of clothing, symbols or other details of self-presentation), but not always. Furthermore, the argument that linguistic specificity can also be visible is, at best, somewhat strained. In short, it is reductionist to seek to describe (the expression of) identity-related specificities as visible; the reality of their existence and expression is much more complex and multi-dimensional. Finally, in this connection, the term "certain visible minorities" has considerable exclusionary potential. Whatever protection is intended by the term would appear to be limited by the cumulative qualifiers, "certain" and "visible". On the basis of such wording, "certain other" visible minorities, as well as "invisible" minorities, are implicitly excluded from the protection on offer.[166] For this reason, use of the term has been discouraged in certain circles, eg. the English judiciary.[167] Given the problematic nature of the focus on "certain visible minorities", it is difficult to agree with the suggestion that it boasts superior flexibility to alternative formulations of equivalent notions that are more ingrained in international legal and political discourse.

A second *forte* of ECRI's thematic approach is that it enables more generous attention to be given to specific groups, for example those groups which have traditionally suffered – and continue to suffer – from racism and racist discrimination. This is illustrated by the GPRs focusing specifically on the Roma/ Gypsies, Muslims and anti-Semitism. These policy recommendations are very important as they address the root causes of racism and not merely its concrete manifestations. As such, they look at situational and systemic discrimination and explore ways of countering and eliminating the same.

These three GPRs were not cast in the same mould: differences in prioritisation and language are easily detectable. Of itself, this is not a problem. Indeed, it is perfectly understandable that different groups could be best served by different emphases and approaches. However, one can also witness here a recurrence of the previously mentioned tendencies to resort to language that is inconsistent with that of codified international law and the failure to adequately capture the underlying concepts of international law. In particular, insufficient consideration has been given to relevant interlinkage with other rights guaranteed by international law,[168] meaning that a

166 I am grateful to Prof. Geoff Gilbert for suggesting this point to me.

167 Lord Chief Justice Woolf, *Equal Treatment Benchbook* (May 2004); for commentary, see: 'In the News', *Index on Censorship* 3/2004, p. 6.

168 GPR No. 3 does not explicitly refer to any specific provisions of the ECHR; GPR No. 5 mentions Articles 9 and 14, ECHR, but not, for example, Article 10; GPR No. 9 mentions Article 14, ECHR, Protocol No. 12 to the ECHR, and Article 10, ECHR (but this reference is not so much an affirmation of the right to freedom of expression as a reiteration of the fact that certain types of expression do not enjoy Article 10 protection).

hugely important and hugely relevant source of legal and philosophical inspiration has not been fully tapped into.

Another instance of digression from the terms of conventional international law again involves minorities. In GPR No. 5, which focuses on Muslims, ECRI makes certain recommendations to "the governments of member States, where Muslim communities *are settled and live in a minority situation* in their countries" (emphasis added). Again, "in a minority situation", is a turn of phrase that is unfamiliar to leading international texts dealing with minority rights. However, the words, "are settled", are much more problematic. Such a verbal construction would appear to limit the beneficiaries of the recommended measures to non-nomadic Muslim groups, a limitation which is arbitrary, potentially discriminatory and – it must be hoped – unintended by its drafters.

The third *forte* of the thematic approach to combating racism is that it has provided ECRI with a very useful means to address policy, institutional and methodological/procedural questions. In terms of policy, GPR Nos. 1 and 7 are the most important. GPR No. 1, entitled "Combating racism, xenophobia, antisemitism and intolerance",[169] stands out among other GPRs for its ability to see the proverbial bigger picture. It recognises that international law is the backdrop to the struggle against racism and that the obligations imposed on States by international law must remain salient. GPR No. 7 – on national legislation to combat racism and racial discrimination[170] – is somewhat weaker in that regard, but its shortcomings are offset to some extent by its accompanying Explanatory Memorandum. This is one of only three GPRs to have such an appendix, and the explanatory detail it provides on the recommendations concerning constitutional, civil and administrative, and criminal law, is to be welcomed.[171]

As regards institutional questions, GPR No. 2 calls for the establishment of specialised bodies to combat racism at the national level and makes recommendations concerning the functions, responsibilities and working methods of such bodies.[172] Finally, as regards methodological/procedural questions, GPR No. 4 is based on the premise that attitudinal information and experiential information are very important

---

169 ECRI general policy recommendation no. 1: Combating racism, xenophobia, antisemitism and intolerance, adopted on 4 October 1996.

170 ECRI general policy recommendation no. 7 on national legislation to combat racism and racial discrimination, adopted on 13 December 2002.

171 For further commentary, see: Giancarlo Cardinale, "The Preparation of ECRI General Policy Recommendation No 7 on National Legislation to Combat Racism and Racial Discrimination", in Jan Niessen and Isabelle Chopin, Eds., *The Development of Legal Instruments to Combat Racism in a Diverse Europe*, *op. cit.*, pp. 81–92. The other GPRs with explanatory memoranda are Nos. 11 and 12.

172 ECRI general policy recommendation no. 2, "Specialised bodies to combat racism, xenophobia, anti-Semitism and intolerance at national level", adopted on 13 June 1997.

complements to statistical information.[173] It therefore focuses on the need to gather and process information about how (potential) victims experience and perceive racism. This approach is consistent with the key tenets of critical race theory (see further Chapter 7.1.2).

When assessing ECRI's thematic work at the macro level, two main points should be made. The first is gleaned from, or more accurately, is a summation of, the earlier critique: the GPRs do not always reflect the letter and spirit of international law provisions. Nor do they always manage to achieve the desirable, and indeed necessary, linkage with other fundamental rights. The second point is that the thematic approach pursued by ECRI very importantly allows it to be responsive to changing agendas of racism and racial discrimination. By setting its own thematic agenda, ECRI has also managed to be pro-active in its decisions to pursue certain topics. This is conducive to fostering dynamic working methods.

By way of conclusion to this analysis of ECRI's thematic work, another document should also be briefly discussed: its Declaration on the use of racist, antisemitic and xenophobic elements in political discourse.[174] The Declaration begins by stating that tolerance and pluralism are cornerstones of democracy and that diversity "considerably enriches" democratic societies. Any affirmation of the right to freedom of expression is once again conspicuous by its absence. Given the thematic focus, this omission is regrettable: the counterbalancing and promotional qualities of free expression could usefully have been emphasised in the context of removing racist expression from political discussion.[175]

When stressing that "political parties can play an essential role in combating racism, by shaping and guiding public opinion in a positive fashion", the Declaration appears to have missed a useful opportunity to pick up on, and thereby consolidate, precedents in ECRI's earlier thematic work. For instance, it could have explicitly referred to "the particular responsibility of political parties, opinion leaders and the media not to resort to racist or racially discriminatory activities or expressions" in contexts where terrorism fans racist flames.[176]

---

173 ECRI general policy recommendation no. 4, "National surveys on the experience and perception of discrimination and racism from the point of view of potential victims", adopted on 6 March 1998.

174 Adopted on 17 March 2005.

175 See, in particular, Recommendation No. R (97) 21 of the Committee of Ministers to Member States on the media and the promotion of a culture of tolerance (discussed further, *infra*).

176 For a consideration of the responsibilities of parliamentarians in combating hate speech, see: Summary and Recommendations presented by the Rapporteur of the Seminar, Mr. Emile Guirieoulou, Seminar for Chairpersons and Members of Parliamentary Human Rights Bodies on Freedom of Expression, Parliament and the Promotion of Tolerant Societies, Organized jointly by the Inter-Parliamentary Union and ARTICLE 19, Geneva, 25–27 May 2005.

The above criticisms are intended to be constructive. Particularly when dealing with legal issues, ECRI's public statements have, on occasion, been lacking in conceptual depth, balance and consistency, as well as linguistic precision. Unless checked, such tendencies could adversely affect ECRI's credibility, which would be most unfortunate, given all of the very important work that ECRI has carried out to date in this very difficult and demanding field. It is submitted here that a more considered and more expansive conceptualisation of ECRI's work would do much to offset any scepticism about the adequacy of its treatment of legal issues. Increased attention to legal contextualisation would be very useful in this regard too. It would also help to refute suggestions that ECRI operates in a kind of echo chamber because of the limited range and self-reinforcing nature of the sources of inspiration referred to in much of its work.

8.3 Evaluation of integrated approaches to countering "hate speech"

Racism will never be driven away by a resolute alliance of prohibitive measures and (threats of) criminal sanctions. Long, hard experience has taught that the only way of effectively combating racism is to address its root causes as well as its various manifestations. What is required is a comprehensive approach, comprising educational, cultural, social, legal, political, economic and other initiatives. The validity and viability of such a multi-faceted approach to countering racism apply equally at international, national and sub-national levels.

Different limbs of the Council of Europe tackle the problem of racism in different ways. Although the relevant strategies are not formally coordinated by any central figure or body, their collective impact in recent years has been commendable, especially in terms of awareness-raising among States authorities and the mainstreaming of the anti-racist agenda in the Council's own activities. Needless to say, this enhanced attention and support for anti-racist goals at the intergovernmental level consequently reverberates in civil society at the national level too. All of this is to the credit of the Council of Europe, and particularly to ECRI, its specialised anti-racist body.

However, the centripetal tendencies in the Council of Europe's anti-racism policies and practices do not always yield positive results. What is gained in flexibility of approach is sometimes lost in coherence and consistency of result. The main message of the latter half of this chapter is that the Council of Europe's anti-racism activities would be rendered more effective if they were to be better focused and coordinated. Whatever its shortcomings, the ECHR offers a definite conceptual and legal framework within which the democratic imperative of combating racism can be pursued. It is therefore very important to retain the ECHR as a central reference point; for it to continue to be the touchstone for the Council's anti-racist strategies. The body of case-law built up by the Strasbourg court over the years situates the elimination of racism at the heart of the Convention's aspirations, but without allowing it to unquestioningly override other fundamental rights.

The point made in the tail-end of the preceding sentence is crucial. However laudable the zealous pursuit of anti-racist objectives may be, it should not take place in a closed ideological vault. It should remain open to, and be part of, the swirling interplay of other fundamental human rights guaranteed by international law. It follows from the analysis in the second half of this chapter that a number of the Council of Europe's anti-racist initiatives (especially policy statements) would gain in political credibility if their conceptual and legal underpinnings were to be firmed up. This could be achieved, *inter alia*, by meeting head-on the potential tension generated by interaction with other human rights, rather than shying away from it, and by recognising such potential as creative rather than destructive.

This is perhaps best illustrated by exploring the relationship between the right to freedom of expression and the right not to be subjected to racism or racist discrimination. This relationship is often – erroneously – presumed to be conflictual, because of "excessive focus on the negative, rather than the positive, impact of freedom of expression on racial equality".[177] Freedom of expression is not only a constitutive right, but an instrumental one. As such, it can serve specific ends, like facilitating the expression of those who oppose racism.[178] The media, in particular, can play a powerful corrective and promotional role against racism.[179]

It is also often assumed that when the right to freedom of expression and the right not to be subjected to racism or racist discrimination are applied to the same factual situation, one of the "competing" sets of objectives will triumph over the other. However, such an assumption over-simplifies matters. The relationship between the right to freedom of expression and the right to be free from racism is not necessarily confrontational and interaction between the two rights/objectives rarely involves one simply triumphing over the other. According to the European Court of Human Rights, protecting freedom of expression on the one hand, and fighting racism and

177 ARTICLE 19 – Global Campaign for Free Expression, Memorandum on Freedom of Expression and Racism for The World Conference against Racism, Racial Discrimination, Xenophobia and Related Intolerance, London, 2001, p. 4.

178 It can even be argued that given the inherent limitations on the exercise of the right to freedom of expression, and the resultant legal restrictions on racist expression, anti-racists are in a position to enjoy the benefits of the right more consummately than their racist counterparts.

179 See further: Recommendation (97) 21 on the media and the promotion of a culture of tolerance, *op. cit.*; Joint Statement on Racism and the Media by the UN Special Rapporteur on Freedom of Opinion and Expression, the OSCE Representative on Freedom of the Media and the OAS Special Rapporteur on Freedom of Expression, 27 February 2001.

intolerance on the other, are reconcilable goals.[180] Moreover, both are imperatives for democratic society, which prompts the conclusion that "it would be unacceptable to give, in a general fashion, precedence to either one at the expense of the other".[181] Instead of a blanket or general rule preferring one set of objectives to the other, what is required is "highly contextualized analysis"[182] on a case-by-case basis. This would facilitate the search for equitable accommodations of divergent interests and – ultimately – for "those circumstances and conditions in which one right should be preferred over the other", as well as "coherent justifications for which right is preferred in particular circumstances".[183]

In conclusion, other branches of the Council of Europe, especially ECRI, would do well to seek to emulate the Court's tendency to contextualise the fight against racism in the catalogue of rights vouchsafed not only by the ECHR, but also by other relevant instruments of international law, such as ICERD. Proper legal contextualisation would provide a solid basis for optimising the enormous potential of diversified anti-racism strategies.

Whereas Chapter 8.2 considered the Council of Europe's anti-racism strategies, in particular those pursued under the FCNM, as an example of an integrated approach to combating hate speech and promoting tolerance, the question of the existence or feasibility of a similarly coherent model at the global level, was not specifically addressed. A case could perhaps be made for the suitability of ICERD as a basis for such a model. The main drawback of such an approach would be that both ICERD and CERD place much heavier emphasis on prohibitive and punitive measures than on promotional ones, so much so that some academic commentators have deplored the neglect suffered by Article 7, ICERD,[184] which reads:

> States Parties undertake to adopt immediate and effective measures, particularly in the fields of teaching, education, culture and information, with a view to combating prejudices which lead to racial discrimination and to promoting understanding, tolerance and friendship among nations and racial or ethnical groups, as well as to propagating the purposes and principles of the Charter of the United Nations, the

---

180 See the discussion of the *Jersild* case, *supra*.

181 Explanatory Memorandum to Recommendation No. R (97) 20 on "Hate Speech", *op. cit.*, para. 23.

182 Mari J. Matsuda, "Public Response to Racist Speech: Considering the Victim's Story", in Mari J. Matsuda *et al.*, Eds., *Words That Wound: Critical Race Theory, Assaultive Speech, and the First Amendment*, *op. cit.*, pp. 17–51, at 46.

183 Kevin Boyle, "Overview of a Dilemma: Censorship versus Racism", in Sandra Coliver, Ed., *Striking a Balance: Hate Speech, Freedom of Expression and Non-discrimination*, *op. cit.*, pp. 1–8, at 1.

184 See, for example: Stephanie Farrior, "The Neglected Pillar: The "Teaching Tolerance" Provision of the International Convention on the Elimination of All Forms of Racial Discrimination", 5 ILSA J. Int'l & Comp. L. 291 (1999), pp. 291–299.

> Universal Declaration of Human Rights, the United Nations Declaration on the Elimination of All Forms of Racial Discrimination, and this Convention.

Irrespective of the feasibility of replicating the "model" of the FCNM for combating hate speech and promoting tolerance at the global level, it is important to note that the essence of the approach that characterises the FCNM "model" is regularly advocated at the global level. Examples include recent CERD General Recommendations (as discussed in Chapter 6.1.3), the Programme of Action adopted at the Durban World Conference against Racism in 2001 (see Chapter 6.1.5(i)) and a number of the annual joint declarations issued by the various IGOs' specialised mandates on the right to freedom of expression.[185] Of particular relevance here are the specialised mandates' Joint Statement on Racism and the Media of 2001 and their (untitled) Joint Declaration of 2006. The following excerpt is from the former:

> Promoting Tolerance
>
> Media organisations, media enterprises and media workers – particularly public service broadcasters – have a moral and social obligation to make a positive contribution to the fight against racism, discrimination, xenophobia and intolerance. There are many ways in which these bodies and individuals can make such a contribution, including by:
>
> - designing and delivering media training programmes which promote a better understanding of issues relating to racism and discrimination, and which foster a sense of the moral and social obligations of the media to promote tolerance and knowledge of the practical means by which this may be done;
> - ensuring that effective ethical and self-regulatory codes of conduct prohibit the use of racist terms and prejudicial or derogatory stereotypes, and unnecessary references to race, religion and related attributes;
> - taking measures to ensure that their workforce is diverse and reasonably representative of society as a whole;
> - taking care to report factually and in a sensitive manner on acts of racism or discrimination, while at the same time ensuring that they are brought to the attention of the public;
> - ensuring that reporting in relation to specific communities promotes a better understanding of difference and at the same time reflects the perspectives of those communities and gives members of those communities a chance to be heard; and
> - promoting a culture of tolerance and a better understanding of the evils of racism and discrimination.

185 Annual Joint Declarations by the Special Rapporteurs on freedom of expression/media have been adopted since 1999.

The following excerpt is from their 2006 Joint Declaration:

Freedom of Expression and Cultural/Religious Tensions

- The exercise of freedom of expression and a free and diverse media play a very important role in promoting tolerance, diffusing tensions and providing a forum for the peaceful resolution of differences. High profile instances of the media and others exacerbating social tensions tend to obscure this fact.
- Governments should refrain from introducing legislation which makes it an offence simply to exacerbate social tensions. Although it is legitimate to sanction advocacy that constitutes incitement to hatred, it is not legitimate to prohibit merely offensive speech. Most countries already have excessive or at least sufficient 'hate speech' legislation. In many countries, overbroad rules in this area are abused by the powerful to limit non-traditional, dissenting, critical, or minority voices, or discussion about challenging social issues. Furthermore, resolution of tensions based on genuine cultural or religious differences cannot be achieved by suppressing the expression of differences but rather by debating them openly. Free speech is therefore a requirement for, and not an impediment to, tolerance.
- Professional and self-regulatory bodies have played an important role in fostering greater awareness about how to report on diversity and to address difficult and sometimes controversial subjects, including intercultural dialogue and contentious issues of a moral, artistic, religious or other nature. An enabling environment should be provided to facilitate the voluntary development of self-regulatory mechanisms such as press councils, professional ethical associations and media ombudspersons.

  The mandates of public service broadcasters should explicitly require them to treat matters of controversy in a sensitive and balanced fashion, and to carry programming which is aimed at promoting tolerance and understanding of difference.

Conclusions

The central challenge for IGOs when countering "hate speech" is to devise standards that effectively curb or eliminate such speech in practice, but do not emasculate the right to freedom of expression in the process. For instance, negative stereotyping and biased portrayals of minorities do not meet internationally-recognised grounds for restricting the right to freedom of expression, but nevertheless, they are certainly capable of having harmful consequences, not just for persons targeted by them, but for society in general. This apparent dilemma does not, however, leave States powerless to deal with such practices. Not only is it possible for States to resort to a range of non-legal remedies and pro-active policies to counter such practices, they are under a duty to do so. The precise nature of those duties must be informed at all times by the public operative value of comprehensive pluralistic tolerance.

It is important to resist political pressures which would water down or limit existing guarantees of freedom of expression *and* protection from racist/"hate" speech. It is imperative that a genuinely, fully integrated approach to human rights be pursued. Because hate speech adversely affects many other rights and occasions a range of different types of harms, a root-and-branch approach is required to counter its effects. Abusive speech can unproblematically be restricted by legal measures, but for other types of speech not meeting the threshold required by internationally-recognised restrictions, a coherent and systematic approach to contextualising factors is necessary. The imperative of combating "hate speech" creates a range of different obligations for States authorities, which are discharged through different types of action. The advocated root-and-branch approach should comprise an appropriately equilibrated set of legal and non-legal measures.

The Council of Europe's anti-racism strategies, in particular those pursued under the FCNM and by ECRI, provide an example of an integrated approach to combating "hate speech" and promoting pluralistic tolerance, which has successfully led to the development of an important body of best practices for States authorities and third parties such as the media. The feasibility of replicating a similarly coherent model at the global level is more difficult, owing to the divergence of treaties involved, each with its own particular objectives, standards and emphases. No single existing treaty at UN-level would be an obvious choice as a basis for such a model. As regards ICERD, for example, both the text of the Convention and CERD place much heavier emphasis on prohibitive and punitive measures than on promotional ones, thereby resulting in a failure to fully reflect the necessary interplay between relevant human rights and the stabilising role of pluralistic tolerance.

Irrespective of the feasibility of replicating the "model" of the FCNM for combating hate speech and promoting tolerance at the global level, it is important to note that the essence of the approach that characterises the FCNM "model" is regularly advocated at the global level. Examples include *recent* CERD General Recommendations, the Programme of Action adopted at the Durban World Conference against Racism in 2001 and a number of the annual joint declarations issued by the various IGOs' specialised mandates on the right to freedom of expression.

Part IV

Regulation and facilitation of expression to promote minority rights

Chapter 9
Media-related pluralism

Introduction

This chapter picks up on the theme of pluralistic tolerance, addressed earlier in Chapter 5. It presents a specific application of the generic principle: media-related pluralism, whereas another specific application, cultural and linguistic diversity, is explored in Chapter 10. Meaningful analysis requires a certain amount of unpacking of the concept of media-related pluralism. The unpacking that takes place here distinguishes between structural and substantive aspects of media-related pluralism. The attempt at conceptual clarification is followed by an assessment of relevant legal standards at the international and European levels.

9.1 Connecting pluralistic tolerance to media-related pluralism

The general principle of pluralistic tolerance outlined in Chapter 5 has many offshoots which give rise to specific, idiosyncratic applications of the principle. These specific applications remain connected to the general principle, however, and in the case of freedom of expression, the nodal connection is particularly strong. This is because pluralistic tolerance is only possible when a dialogical relationship exists between various societal groups. The existence of such a relationship depends in turn on the existence of an adequate number of appropriate fora in which inter-group dialogue can take place. As Peter Dahlgren has pointed out, "pluralistic society should contain many different forms of public discourse, with many registers and inflections".[1]

Groups require expressive opportunities for political and cultural reasons and the existence of such opportunities can prove determinative of whether the right to freedom of expression is real or merely illusory in particular circumstances. These expressive opportunities facilitate participation in political affairs and public life; the articulation and advancement of cultural values and identities and thereby lifestyle validation and cultural and linguistic transmission. However, pluralistic tolerance is not uni-, but multi-directional. A number of corollaries follow from

---

1 Peter Dahlgren, "Enhancing the Civic Ideal in Television Journalism", in Kees Brants, Joke Hermes & Liesbet van Zoonen, Eds., *The Media in Question: Popular Cultures and Public Interests* (London, SAGE Publications Ltd., 1998), pp. 89–100, at 92.

these premises: first of all, that expressive opportunities must be nurtured for all (democracy-beholden) groups, including minorities.

Second, the importance of the right to receive information, especially about other groups, is reinforced. Inter-group or intercultural dialogue and understanding require the presence of communicative intent and the realisation of that intent. Such reasoning underscores "the assumption that the widest possible dissemination of information from diverse and antagonistic sources is essential to the welfare of the public".[2] This quotation has admittedly been lifted out of its original context here, but justifiably so, because its pairing of "diverse and antagonistic sources" is very instructive for present purposes. In the interest of promoting pluralistic tolerance, it is not enough to merely insist on the availability of a diversity of sources of information – as is the wont of most pertinent international standard-setting documents; the further requirement that at least some of those sources be discordant with one another is also crucial. This argument holds equal validity in the contexts of inter-cultural relations and of public deliberation on matters of general interest. Prejudice, ignorance and Mill's "dead dogma" are the dangers to be averted here.

Denis McQuail has enumerated the "[m]ain public benefits of diversity" as follows:

- Opening the way for social and cultural change, especially where it takes the form of giving access to new, powerless or marginal voices
- Providing a check on the misuse of freedom (for instance, where the free market leads to concentration of ownership)
- Enabling minorities to maintain their separate existence in a larger society
- Limiting social conflicts by increasing the chances of understanding between potentially opposed groups and interests
- Adding generally to the richness and variety of cultural and social life[3]

McQuail's insightful list prompts a number of general remarks. First, taken together, these identified benefits constitute a persuasive argument supporting the view that diversity is a public good. Second, it is clear that minorities stand to benefit significantly from the existence of media-related diversity. Third, the list convincingly demonstrates the umbilical nature of the link between media-related pluralism and access to the media.

In more specific terms, though, the benefit of "[l]imiting social conflicts by increasing the chances of understanding between potentially opposed groups and

2 Black, J. (delivering the opinion of the Court), *Associated Press v. United States*, 326 US 1 (1945), at 20.

3 Denis McQuail, *McQuail's Mass Communication Theory* (5th Edition) (Great Britain, SAGE Publications Ltd., 2005), p. 197.

interests" is of greatest immediate interest. This point rests on the intuitive logic that greater dialogical interaction between societal groups is likely to breed greater familiarity between them (see further, Chapter 5.2.1). In developing a parallel line of thought, Joseph Raz has argued that the expression and portrayal in public of different lifestyles serve the dual functions of validation and familiarisation. He refers to contemporary society's high dependence "on public communication to establish a common understanding of the ways of life, range of experiences, attitudes, and thinking which are common and acceptable in their society".[4]

9.2 Media-related pluralism: structural and substantive considerations

In any consideration of pluralism in the realm of freedom of expression, questions concerning the purpose, design and impact of media pluralism are likely to predominate. These questions arise logically and legitimately from the particularly influential role played by the media in modern democratic society (see further, Chapter 3). As Thomas Gibbons has put it: "pluralism requires that programming should be distributed so that no particular point of view gains a disproportionate advantage from use of a medium which is pervasive and relatively limited in the variety of channels that it can provide".[5] This view is couched in terms of distributive or procedural fairness, depending on where the emphasis is laid. The fundamental public-interest rationale being applied here is that no vested interest – whether State, politically-partisan, or sectional third-party (especially of a corporate or religious nature) – should be allowed to dictate or distort the range of available information. It is necessary to foreclose the possibility that political and cultural narratives be unduly controlled by factional or majoritarian interests. The range of available information is, after all, the raw material which human cognitive and emotional faculties process into opinions.

Structural pluralism and substantive or content pluralism are intimately linked. However, as David Ward has stressed, "[a]lthough the protection of structural pluralism remains a key policy objective in the media sector its impact on content pluralism in a comparative context has been a neglected field of research".[6] Here, the linkage between both types of pluralism is viewed as essential.

---

4 Joseph Raz, "Free Expression and Personal Identification", 11 *Oxford Journal of Legal Studies* (No. 3, 1991), pp. 303–324, at 312.

5 Thomas Gibbons, *Regulating the Media* (Second Edition) (London, Sweet & Maxwell, 1998), p. 98.

6 David Ward, Final report on the study on "the assessment of content diversity in newspapers and television in the context of increasing trends towards concentration of media markets", Group of Specialists on Media Diversity (MC-S-MD), Media Division, Directorate General of Human Rights, Council of Europe, 27 February 2006, Doc. No. MC-S-MD (2006) 001, p. 5.

9.2.1 Conceptual confusion

In one of his most famous treatises, the legal theorist Wesley Newcomb Hohfeld remarked that "in any closely reasoned problem, whether legal or non-legal, chameleon-hued words are a peril both to clear thought and to lucid expression".[7] Pluralism in respect of the media could certainly be considered to be such a "chameleon-hued" word. As already noted in Chapter 5.2, the use of the term is bedevilled by a lack of definitional precision and consistency across international instruments and academic literature.

The (perceived) interchangeability of the terms "pluralism" and "diversity" often lies at the source of the inconsistencies of usage. Some authors and bodies have clear preferences for one term or the other, whereas some use both terms seemingly indiscriminately.[8] The absence of any widely-recognised definition of either term in international legal instruments merely exacerbates the conceptual messiness. Some commentators have attempted to painstakingly establish clear distinctions between the two, but their efforts are ultimately unconvincing. In light of the conceptual circularity involved, the approach to definitions and terminology pursued here is purely pragmatic. It does not claim to set out an authoritative, hard-and-fast distinction between "pluralism" and "diversity", but merely to provide a reasoned frame for further analysis. Thus, pluralism is generally taken to refer to issues of media ownership; of choices available to the public between providers of services. Diversity, for its part, is most often taken to refer to the range of programmes and services available to the public. The legal and semantic overlap between pluralism and diversity is unclear, and the terms are frequently used interchangeably, not only by the Court itself, but also by expert commentators.

This tentative distinction between pluralism and diversity will now be pruned in order to allow for further analytical growth. Earlier, general references to pluralism relating to the media have tended to be couched as "media-related pluralism". This term has been chosen advisedly: the usefulness of the qualifier, "media-related", is that it encapsulates both media pluralism and media diversity. Its usefulness is truly borne out when discussing texts that use both terms interchangeably.

---

7 Wesley Newcomb Hohfeld, *Fundamental Legal Conceptions* (Ed. Walter Wheeler Cook) (USA, Yale University Press, 1919), p. 35. This book comprises Hohfeld's two seminal articles, "Some Fundamental Legal Conceptions as Applied in Judicial Reasoning [I]", (1913) 23 *Yale Law Journal*, 16, and "Fundamental Legal Conceptions as Applied in Judicial Reasoning [II]", (1917) 26 *Yale Law Journal*, 710, and other materials.

8 See, by way of example: Media diversity in Europe – report prepared by the AP-MD (Advisory Panel to the CDMM on media concentrations, pluralism and diversity questions), Doc. No. H/APMD (2003) 1, December 2002. This report is discussed further, *infra*.

A number of commentators have pointed out the unhelpful but continuing tendency to elide the terms, "media ownership" and "media pluralism".[9] It has correctly been suggested that ownership does not convey the same meaning or conceptual complexity as pluralism, but that the terms' continued elision is due, at least in part, to the predominance of European Union policy developments in this area, which emphasise competition issues and single market objectives.[10]

9.2.2 Structural considerations

The thrust of the observations and arguments of the preceding paragraph are rather general in their inclination. They strongly suggest that media pluralism is merely instrumental (to the goal of informational pluralism), but upon closer examination this initial suggestion is broken down and the lines of argumentation are finessed. Gibbons, again, has usefully distinguished between three distinct levels of media-related pluralism: content, source and outlet.[11] Of these three levels, content is the most substantive in character and therefore the ultimate end-goal. It is concerned with variety in political and cultural media output, both as regards information and opinion. Source and outlet, by contrast, are instrumental. They are useful means by which the ultimate end-goal may be achieved. However, they are not entirely dispositive as they cannot, of themselves, guarantee the achievement of the ultimate end-goal.

Other analyses also attempt to disaggregate the different levels of "media pluralism", such as the following example from the Council of Europe's Committee of Ministers, which states that the notion "should be understood as diversity of media supply, reflected, for example, in the existence of a *plurality of independent and autonomous media* (generally called structural pluralism) as well as a *diversity of media types and contents (views and opinions) made available to the public*".[12]

---

9 David Ward, Final report on the study on "the assessment of content diversity in newspapers and television in the context of increasing trends towards concentration of media markets", *op. cit.*, p. 5.

10 Dietrich Westphal, "Media Pluralism and European Regulation", [2002] EBLR 459–487, at 487.

11 Thomas Gibbons, "Concentrations of Ownership and Control in a Converging Media Industry", in Chris Marsden & Stefaan Verhulst, Eds., *Convergence in European Digital TV Regulation* (London, Blackstone Press Ltd., 1999), pp. 155–173, at 157. This distinction is replicated in the Joint Declaration on Diversity in Broadcasting, adopted by the UN Special Rapporteur on Freedom of Opinion and Expression, the OSCE RFOM, the OAS Special Rapporteur on Freedom of Expression and the ACHPR Special Rapporteur on Freedom of Expression and Access to Information, 12 December 2007.

12 (emphasis per original) Explanatory Memorandum to Recommendation No. R (99)1 of the Committee of Ministers to member states on measures to promote media pluralism, adopted on 19 January 1999, para. 3. Note, however, that CM Recommendation No. R (99)1 has since been superseded by CM Recommendation CM/Rec(2007)2 on media pluralism and diversity of media content and the 2007 CM Declaration on protecting the role of the media in democracy in the context of media concentration (for a more detailed discussion, see Chapter 9.3.2(iii)).

Again, pride of place is given to media "supply" (or output or content, depending on the preferred terminology). The need to stress the interrelationship between substantive and structural considerations when determining pluralism is also replicated. However, the distinction between the "plurality of independent and autonomous media" and "diversity of media types" is not drawn as a bright shining line. To what extent do these formulations correspond to Gibbons' neater categories of "source" and "outlet", respectively? It is also puzzling that instead of bracketing two instrumental aspects of pluralism together and recognising the separateness of the substantive aspect, as rationalised in the previous paragraph, the Committee of Ministers opted instead to consider a "diversity of media types" as more substantive than structural and therefore shack it up with "media contents".

In light of these puzzles, it is submitted here that the disaggregation carved out by Gibbons is cleaner. One possible shortcoming of his disaggregation, however, is that it is likely to become increasingly difficult to sustain in light of continued trends towards technological convergence and vertical integration (of programme and content production and distribution). These developments tend to blur distinctions between substantive and structural aspects of the media that have been more obvious in the traditional broadcasting sphere.

9.2.2(i) Source/Ownership

Although it was written over 50 years ago, the seminal publication of the Commission on Freedom of the Press, *A Free and Responsible Press*, contains much wisdom that has managed to retain its relevance in modern times. The Commission warned, in micro terms, that "the first danger to free expression will always be the danger at the source, the timidity of the issuer, or his purchasability".[13] The danger, of course, is considerably amplified when considered in macro terms. Thus, the Commission posited that "[T]hrough concentration of ownership the flow of news and opinion is shaped at the sources; its variety is limited",[14] and that this "[C] oncentration of power substitutes one controlling policy for many independent policies, lessens the number of major competitors, and renders less operative the claims of potential issuers who have no press".[15]

The entrenchment of the mass media oligopoly dominated by the corporations referred to by Ben Bagdikian – descriptively rather than admiratively – as "the Big Five"[16] is frequently used as an example of how the concentration of media

13 The [Hutchins] Commission on Freedom of the Press, *A Free and Responsible Press* (University of Chicago Press, Chicago, 1947), pp. 113–114.

14 *Ibid.*, p. 124.

15 *Ibid.*, p. 130.

16 Ben H. Bagdikian, *The New Media Monopoly* (Boston, Beacon Press, 2004). The five conglomerates in question are: Time Warner, the Walt Disney Company, Rupert Murdoch's News Corporation, Viacom and Bertelsmann – pp. 3 *et seq.*

ownership can determine the fundamental course of news and cultural production. Edward S. Herman and Noam Chomsky consider the mass media of the US to be "effective and powerful ideological institutions that carry out a system-supportive propaganda function".[17] Indeed, their propaganda model:

> sees the media as serving a "societal purpose," but not that of enabling the public to assert meaningful control over the political process by providing them with the information needed for the intelligent discharge of political responsibilities. On the contrary, a propaganda model suggests that the "societal purpose" of the media is to inculcate and defend the economic, social, and political agenda of privileged groups that dominate the domestic society and the state. The media serve this purpose in many ways: through selection of topics, distribution of concerns, framing of issues, filtering of information, emphasis and tone, and by keeping debate within the bounds of acceptable premises.[18]

At least three caveats should be entered here. First, Herman and Chomsky are not known for the timidity of their political opinions. Second, their analysis and criticisms focus on the US media, and third, their analysis is now somewhat dated, having been based on trends up to the late 1980s. Nevertheless, these caveats should not detract unduly from the underlying validity and force of the criticisms made. The meticulous study undertaken by the authors does raise very serious questions about the lack of independence and impartiality of the mass media, which is also significantly compromised by the cosiness of relationships between leading figures in the political and journalistic establishments.[19] Moreover, and this is an enduring point that certainly has not been eroded by the passage of time: the mass media dispose of immense power to create and shape news and cultural content. In the quotation above, Herman and Chomsky very usefully disaggregate a number of the different stages in the production chain, each of which presents new opportunities for shaping the informational product before it is finally offered to the public.

The ability of the media to influence the collection, production and presentation of information allows them to exert considerable influence over the formation of public opinion. When media ownership becomes concentrated in the hands of a small elite, the ability to steer public debate and ultimately public opinion becomes similarly concentrated. The danger that arises in such a scenario is evident from the observation that "smoothest road to control of political conduct is by control of opinion".[20] Granted, ability to influence should not automatically be equated with "control", but the potential danger for the former to grow into the latter is patent.

---

17 Edward S. Herman & Noam Chomsky, *Manufacturing Consent: The Political Economy of the Mass Media* (Great Britain, Vintage, 1994), p. 306.

18 *Ibid.*, p. 298.

19 See generally: Anthony Lewis, "Law and the Press: A Deadly Embrace?", 33 *The Irish Jurist* (1998), pp. 34–46.

20 John Dewey, *The Public and its Problems* (Chicago, The Swallow Press, Inc., 1954), p. 182.

The US does not have a monopoly on extreme concentrations of media ownership. The most infamous home-grown European example of media ownership concentration is Italy, which has drawn intense scrutiny and stern criticism from a number of international organisations, including the Council of Europe (Parliamentary Assembly (PACE),[21] Venice Commission[22]), European Union (Parliament[23]) and the OSCE Representative on Freedom of the Media.[24]

The precise concern, as stated in the PACE Resolution on the so-called "Italian anomaly", is that "concentration of political, commercial and media power" in the hands of the (then) Italian Prime Minister, Silvio Berlusconi, is jeopardising media pluralism, as guaranteed by Article 10 of the European Convention on Human Rights. This state of affairs has resulted from the collective failure of successive Italian governments to effectively grapple with persistent conflicts between political and media (ownership) interests – by legislative or other means. The nature of the concentration of power when the PACE Resolution was adopted was as follows: the Italian television market has in effect become a duopoly as Mediaset, a company owned by the Prime Minister, along with RAI, the public service broadcaster, "command together about 90% of the television audience and over three quarters of resources in the sector"; a situation which gives rise to anti-trust concerns.[25] The much-publicised conflict of interests involving the Prime Minister is democratically problematic,[26] especially in light of documented political interference with the

21 Monopolisation of the electronic media and possible abuse of power in Italy, Resolution 1387 (2004) (Provisional Edition), Parliamentary Assembly of the Council of Europe, 24 June 2004 and Monopolisation of the electronic media and possible abuse of power in Italy, Report of the Committee on Culture, Science and Education (Rapporteur: Mr. Paschal Mooney), Parliamentary Assembly of the Council of Europe, 3 June 2004, Doc. 10195 (see also the Opinion of the Committee on Legal Affairs and Human Rights, (Rapporteur: Mr. Abdülkadir Ates), 22 June 2004, Doc. 10228). See further: Tarlach McGonagle, "Parliamentary Assembly: New Resolution Critical of Media Concentration in Italy", *IRIS* 2004–7: 3.

22 Opinion on the compatibility of the Laws "Gasparri" and "Frattini" of Italy with the Council of Europe standards in the field of freedom of expression and pluralism of the media (Opinion No. 309/2004), European Commission for Democracy through Law (Venice Commission), 13 June 2005, Doc. No. CDL-AD (2005) 017. See further: Tarlach McGonagle, "Venice Commission: Opinion on Freedom of Expression and Media Pluralism in Italy", *IRIS* 2005–8: 5.

23 Report on the risks of violation, in the EU and especially in Italy, of freedom of expression and information (Article 11(2) of the Charter of Fundamental Rights) (2003/2237/(INI)), Committee on Citizens' Freedoms and Rights, Justice and Home Affairs (Rapporteur: Johanna L.A. Boogerd-Quaak), 5 April 2004, Doc. A5–0230/2004 (Final). See further: Tarlach McGonagle, "European Parliament: Adoption of Report on Media Independence and Pluralism", *IRIS* 2004–6: 6.

24 "Visit to Italy – The Gasparri Law: Observations and Recommendations", OSCE Representative on Freedom of the Media, 7 June 2005.

25 Further details of how this duopoly is compounded are provided in para. 5 of the Resolution and in the extensive, identically-titled report on which the Resolution is based: both, *op. cit.*

26 As stated in the OSCE RFOM's report: "Italy has an ongoing record of control over public-service television by political parties and governments. As the Prime Minister is also the country's main media entrepreneur, co-owning *Mediaset*, the 'traditional' fears of governmental

operations of the RAI. Furthermore, the situation was likely to be exacerbated by the adoption of the Gasparri and Frattini Laws (see further, *infra*).

The entire case for plurality of sources and ownership rests on the premise that there is an assumptive – or perhaps even probabilistic – relationship between source/ownership and content. As noted, for instance, by the Recommendation No. R (99) 1 of the Committee of Ministers of the Council of Europe on measures to promote media pluralism, "the existence of a multiplicity of autonomous and independent media outlets at the national, regional and local levels *generally enhances* pluralism and democracy".[27] The foregoing discussion of US and Italian examples weighs very heavily in support of that crucial premise, but that does not mean that its veracity can be taken for granted (hence the italicisation of "generally enhances" in the foregoing citation). According to Toby Mendel:

> A highly concentrated media market may offer enormous choice in terms of number of broadcast channels and even of topics and styles. However, it is also susceptible of political and/or owner interference with the result that the coverage of certain important political issues may be suppressed or limited, undermining the quality of information made available to the public.[28]

On a similar tack, many scholars have cautioned against equating plurality of source/ownership or indeed outlets with diversity of media content. The former is primarily quantitative, whereas the latter, which is best gauged by media performance, is primarily qualitative. As Jan van Cuilenburg has put it: "highly competitive media markets may still result in excessive sameness of media contents, whereas one should at least theoretically not exclude the possibility of media oligopolies or even monopolies to produce a highly diverse supply of media content".[29] Indeed, such caution is not just theoretical: some empircial data suggests that there is not always a "a strong link between concentration of markets and the diversity of content" and that even "[M]arkets that are strongly concentrated can demonstrate similar levels of content diversity as markets that are less concentrated".[30]

---

control of *RAI* are aggravated by worries of a general governmental control of the nation's most important information source, television" –*op. cit*., p. 14.

27 (emphasis added). Recital 4, Recommendation No. R (99) 1 of the Committee of Ministers to Member States on measures to promote media pluralism, 19 January 1999.

28 Toby Mendel, "Restrictions on Political Expression", in Susanne Nikoltchev, Ed., *Political Debate and the Role of the Media: The Fragility of Free Speech, IRIS Special* (Strasbourg, European Audiovisual Observatory, 2004), pp. 41–50, at 44.

29 Jan van Cuilenburg, "Diversity Revisited: Towards a Critical Rational Model of Media Diversity", in Kees Brants, Joke Hermes & Liesbet van Zoonen, Eds., *The Media in Question: Popular Cultures and Public Interests*, *op. cit*., pp. 38–49, at 41.

30 David Ward, Final report on the study on "the assessment of content diversity in newspapers and television in the context of increasing trends towards concentration of media markets", *op. cit*., p. 2.

Relevant assumptions about linkage between ownership and content also apply, *mutatis mutandis*, to minority ownership and minority content. In the US, for example, it has been a longstanding view of the Federal Communications Commission (FCC) that "ownership is a prime determinant of the range of programming available".[31] Consistent with that view, it has further concluded that there is an "empirical nexus between minority ownership and greater diversity".[32] The well-known *Metro Broadcasting* case provides detailed judicial treatment of that empirical nexus and merits some consideration here.[33] Importantly, the FCC and Congress conceded that the empirical assumption in question could not be clinically proven, but they did insist on the careful and protracted enquiry, study and reflection that preceded the conclusion that such linkage did in fact exist. The following passage from the Supreme Court's judgment reveals the thinking behind the FCC's minority ownership provisions:

> Neither Congress nor the FCC assumes that in every case minority ownership and management will lead to more minority-oriented programming or to the expression of a discrete "minority viewpoint" on the airwaves. Nor do they pretend that all programming that appeals to minorities can be labeled "minority" or that programming that might be so described does not appeal to nonminorities. Rather, they maintain simply that expanded minority ownership of broadcast outlets will, in the aggregate, result in greater broadcast diversity. This judgment is corroborated by a host of empirical evidence suggesting that an owner's minority status influences the selection of topics for news coverage and the presentation of editorial viewpoint, especially on matters of particular concern to minorities, and has a special impact on the way in which images of minorities are presented. In addition, studies show that a minority owner is more likely to employ minorities in managerial and other important roles where they can have an impact on station policies. [...][34]

9.2.2(ii) Outlet

The existence of a range of media outlets is similarly an important, but of itself, insufficient safeguard for the preservation of media-related pluralism. More specifically, it plays an assumptively instrumental role in ensuring diversity of

---

31 *Metro Broadcasting, Inc., v. Federal Communications Commission, et al.*, 497 US 547, at 549.

32 *Ibid.*

33 The Supreme Court's judgment in *Metro Broadcasting* was later overturned by its subsequent judgment in *Adarand Constructors, Inc. v. Pena*, 515 US 200, on the grounds that the wrong standard of scrutiny had been applied by the Court in the former case. In short, the Court in Metro Broadcasting had held that congressionally mandated "benign" racial classifications only had to satisfy "intermediate scrutiny". As such, it departed from earlier judicial precedents to which the Court returned in *Adarand*, *viz.* that strict scrutiny of governmental racial classifications is essential due to the difficulty of determining whether such a classification is in fact "benign". This, however, should not detract from the interest/relevance of the FCC's rationales for its minority ownership provisions, as quoted.

34 *Ibid.*, pp. 549; 579–582.

media output. Having said that, the primary freedom of expression interest in maintaining a plurality of media outlets in society is that such plurality implies at least the potential for more extensive access to expressive opportunities. In a roundabout way, extensive access for diverse groups in society should enhance the availability of diverse media output.

The argument from pluralism is not the strongest argument that could be furnished for the importance of maintaining a wide range of media outlets in society. A more persuasive argument is that a variety of outlets should, on the balance of probabilities or law of averages, lead to the possibility of individuals and groups having more effective expressive opportunities. As is evident from the discussion of media functionality in Chapter 3.2.1, different types of media outlet are more suitable than others for the dissemination of particular types of media content. Thus, the more plurality in available media outlets, the greater the likelihood that there will be suitable channels for various kinds of content to be transmitted by the media. Moreover, the plurality of outlets should also extend to geographical reach, linguistic competences, technological capacities, etc. To illustrate the point: the contribution of a wide selection of national newspapers to overall diversity in media output may be limited, if the newspaper titles are not distributed throughout the country. Similarly, if all broadcasting stations transmit content exclusively in the State language, that will also be to the detriment of overall diversity in media output. An abundance of diverse content on digital television may be irrelevant to minorities due to the prohibitive cost of acquiring the technology needed to view that content. These practical examples all demonstrate the need for a range of distinctive media outlets to be fostered if media-related pluralism is to be guaranteed at all geographical levels and for all sections of society.

A further, consumer-oriented, argument is that a pluralistic offer of media outlets enables individuals to choose the means by which they receive their information and ideas in accordance with their own consumption preferences and habits. This argument could also be described as autonomy-based, or even as a variant sub-element of the democratic-participation theory (eg. to the extent that one is more receptive to information and ideas communicated in a way or format with which one is familiar, thereby increasing the ease of intelligibility and ultimate effectiveness of the communication). The argument gains in significance in the context of increasingly converged and multifunctional media. In this technological context, access to a wide range of media platforms is an essential (but not necessarily sufficient) requirement for access to truly diverse content and services. It is therefore important that different types of content-providers, especially (different types of) broadcasters have equitable access, to and are able to operate on, different distribution platforms.[35] In this connection, it has been urged that the digital dividend (i.e., the "radio spectrum freed as a result of the switchover from analogue to digital broadcasting"[36]) be used for the advancement of diversity in broadcasting.[37]

Opinions are divided on how external pluralism (i.e., pluralism across the entire media sector),[38] can best be achieved. Some scholars hold out that the objective is best-served by (State-induced) encouragement of "a multiplicity of outlets, rather than compelling a few outlets to represent everybody, seems a far preferable course of action".[39] The latter model is that of internal pluralism, which is usually reserved for public service broadcasters. This proposition is, however, sometimes regarded as inadequate, as "the mere increase in the number of channels which will be brought about by digital television is not sufficient in itself to guarantee media pluralism".[40] Other additional criteria, such as the determination of relevant markets and shares of relevant markets, remain important for assessing whether sufficient pluralism can be achieved.

9.2.3 Substantive considerations

The interrelationship and interdependence between structure and substance in respect of media-related pluralism has already been underscored. Structural factors are often perceived primarily in instrumentalist terms, in view of their impact on substantive matters. The focus of this subsection will be on media content/output/production and it will accordingly draw on the instrumentalist perception of structural considerations. It will therefore lean in the direction of constructivist or post-critical theories concerning the generation and acquisition of knowledge. Thus, in contradistinction to objectivist theories, it will be assumed that information (and,

---

35 This point is made, *inter alia*, in the Joint Declaration on Diversity in Broadcasting, adopted by the UN Special Rapporteur on Freedom of Opinion and Expression, the OSCE RFOM, the OAS Special Rapporteur on Freedom of Expression and the ACHPR Special Rapporteur on Freedom of Expression and Access to Information, 12 December 2007.

36 Declaration of the Committee of Ministers on the allocation and management of the digital dividend and the public interest, 20 February 2008.

37 *Ibid.*; Joint Declaration on Diversity in Broadcasting, *op. cit.* See further: David Korteweg & Tarlach McGonagle, "The Digital Dividend: Opportunities and Obstacles", in Susanne Nikoltchev, Ed., *Switchover to the Digital Dividend, IRIS plus 2010–6,* pp. 7–26.

38 See further, Eric Barendt, *Broadcasting Law: A Comparative Study* (Oxford, Clarendon Press, 1993), pp. 96–97.

39 Thomas I. Emerson, *The System of Freedom of Expression* (New York, Random House, 1970), p. 671.

40 European Commission for Democracy through Law (Venice Commission), Opinion on the compatibility of the Laws "Gasparri" and "Frattini" of Italy in the field of freedom of expression and pluralism of the media, June 2005, Opinion No. 309/2004, para. 264; see also, PACE: discussion of Italian Gasparri Law, *op. cit.*

a fortiori, ideas) presented by the media is always refracted through a miscellany of vested interests. Moreover, information-gathering processes also affect the manner in which information is finally presented to the public. In epistemological terms, then, information is invariably relativised by a range of contextualities and contingencies. Sue Curry Jansen has developed this point, stating *inter alia* that "the new sociology or anthropology of knowledge assumes that knowledge, truth, and facts are social constructions, artifacts of communication, community, and culture".[41] How information is then processed into knowledge depends on other, subjective epistemological criteria, such as "perceptual and interactional strategies";[42] again, as Curry Jansen has claimed, "we *always* approach knowledge through the portals of our interests".[43]

The ability to access a wide range of media content is crucial for persons belonging to minorities for a number of reasons. The existence of diverse media content has a direct bearing on their informational and expressive rights, as well as their cultural and linguistic rights. Consequently, it affects their ability to participate effectively in public life. The particular relevance for minorities of theories relating to these substantive matters is explored throughout Chapters 10 and 11.

9.2.4 Gauging media-related pluralism

When it comes to gauging media-related pluralism, important distinctions have to be drawn between State obligations and media responsibilities. Here, perceived conceptual differences between pluralism and diversity acquire a practical significance which can often be glossed over in other analytical frameworks. On the one hand, State obligations tend towards pluralism of source and outlet, and owing to the complex juridical nature of the State obligations in this respect, a separate analytical framework will be proposed. On the other hand, media responsibilities essentially concern diversity of content and are thus evaluated on the basis of performative criteria. Each will now be considered in turn.

9.2.4(i) State obligations

The importance of States' positive obligations to safeguard pluralism and access has already been adumbrated in Chapter 4.1.2. In order to attempt to properly ascertain the nature and extent of State obligations to uphold media-related pluralism, the relationship between the right to freedom of expression and media-

41 Sue Curry Jansen, *Censorship: The Knot That Binds Power and Knowledge* (New York, Oxford University Press, 1991), p. 182.

42 *Ibid.*, p. 182.

43 (Emphasis per original) *ibid.*, p. 183.

related pluralism must first be explored. Various conceptions of that relationship have been advanced.

According to one conception, pluralism is a prerequisite for true freedom of expression. For instance, it has been submitted that "a free and pluralist media is an essential requirement for the full respect of the right of freedom of expression and information [...]".[44] In other words, media-related pluralism is set out as being logically prior to freedom of expression and as an enabling condition for the exercise of that right.

An opposing conception of the relationship between freedom of expression and media-related pluralism casts the former as being instrumental to the achievement of the latter. In other words, the right to freedom of expression is viewed, not as a constitutive right, but as a functionalist one. One of its main purposes is therefore to advance the objective of media-related pluralism.

A third conception, favoured by Eric Barendt, wisely avoids being drawn on the above "chicken-and-egg" debate.[45] It stresses that freedom of expression both "reflects and reinforces pluralism'[46] and its "values of diversity and variety".[47] Barendt has neatly described media-related pluralism as "the objective of ensuring the access of citizens to a wide variety of opinion and sources of information".[48]

As discussed in greater detail, *infra*, the European Court of Human Rights has held that the States is the "ultimate guarantor" of pluralism, especially "in relation to audio-visual media, whose programmes are often broadcast very widely".[49] This places the State under a positive obligation to uphold pluralism, in particular in the broadcasting sector. Again, as will be shown below, the Court has not fully explicated what this positive State obligation entails. In order to try to fill this theoretical lacuna in the Court's jurisprudence, consideration will now be given to the meaning and implications of that obligation.

---

44 European Parliament Resolution on the risks of violation, in the EU and especially in Italy, of freedom of expression and information (Article 11(2) of the Charter of Fundamental Rights), *op. cit.*, p. 7.

45 However, he does consider media freedom (as a particular subset of freedom of expression) to be an instrumental freedom, "rather than a primary or fundamental human right". He continues: "Press claims to special privileges and immunities should only be recognized insofar as they promote the values of freedom of speech, in particular the public interest in pluralism in its sources of information.": Eric Barendt, *Freedom of Speech* (2nd Edition) (Oxford, Oxford University Press, 2005), p. 422. See also in this connection, *ibid.*, p. 430.

46 *Ibid.*, p. 34.

47 *Ibid.*, p. 35.

48 *Ibid.*, p. 430.

49 *Informationsverein Lentia & Others v. Austria*, Judgment of the European Court of Human Rights of 28 October 1993, para. 38.

A pertinent point of departure to this discussion is provided by Onora O'Neill, who has convincingly argued that the "communicative obligations of any democratic society" entail both perfect and imperfect obligations.[50] She cites non-coercion and non-deception as examples of "perfect communicative obligations". Media-related pluralism and access to expressive opportunities, on the other hand, would more aptly be considered to be imperfect communicative obligations. The essence of such obligations is that they "are not owed to specified others so have no correlative rights, yet must be met if public communication in a democracy is to be possible".[51]

This is certainly an interesting articulation of media-related pluralism, but *prima facie*, it sits somewhat uneasily with Hohfeld's schematization of jural relations as opposites and correlatives.[52] One of the essential elements of the Hohfeldian scheme is that "a duty is the invariable correlative of that legal relation which is most properly called a right or claim".[53] This begs the question whether the existence of a right to media-related pluralism can legitimately be asserted (at least on a Hohfeldian model of rights). Perhaps one way to give an affirmative answer to the question, without rejecting O'Neill's consideration of "imperfect communicative obligations", would be to invoke the notion of collective rights, already discussed in Chapter 1.

According to Joseph Raz, three conditions must be satisfied before the existence of a collective right can be recognised:

> First, it exists because an aspect of the interest of human beings justifies holding some person(s) to be subject to a duty. Second, the interests in question are the interests of individuals as members of a group in a public good and the right is a right to that public good because it serves their interest as members of the group. Thirdly, the interest of no single member of that group in that public good is sufficient by itself to justify holding another person to be subject to a duty.[54]

To summarise the foregoing, then: the European Court of Human Rights has repeatedly held that the State is the ultimate guarantor of pluralism, particularly in the audiovisual sector. However, neither the theoretical underpinnings of this finding, nor its likely implications, have been fully spelt out by the Court. As such, a State obligation to guarantee media-related pluralism has been identified, without expressly stating that that obligation flows from a specific right to media-related pluralism. Assuming, *pace* Hohfeld, that the existence of an obligation is predicated on the existence of a correlative right, the nature of that right must be inferred.

---

50 Onora O'Neill, "Practices of toleration", in Judith Lichtenberg, Ed., *Democracy and the mass media* (USA, Cambridge University Press, 1990), pp. 155–185, at 170.

51 *Ibid.*, at 171. See also, *ibid.*, at 173.

52 Wesley Newcomb Hohfeld, *Fundamental Legal Conceptions*, *op. cit.*, pp. 36 *et seq.*

53 *Ibid.*, p. 39.

54 Joseph Raz, *The Morality of Freedom* (New York, Oxford University Press, 1986), p. 208.

Given that media-related pluralism can uncontroversially be regarded as a public good, it appears largely unproblematic to consider the right in question, if it does indeed exist, to be collective in nature. This postulation is further supported by the view that the State obligation to guarantee media-related pluralism can at best be considered an imperfect communicative obligation as it lacks a specific object.

The next question to be addressed concerns how to measure the discharge of State obligations to guarantee media-related pluralism in less theoretical and more concrete terms.

It is useful to recall at this stage that the right to freedom of expression is doubly amalgative: first, it amalgamates the right to freedom of opinion, expression and information, and second, it amalgamates the rights and interests of speakers, listeners and the public in general. A restriction on any of these constituent conceptual elements of the right to freedom of expression can ordinarily be considered to be a restriction on the right proper. However self-evident this point may seem, it is imperative that it be reiterated here because doctrinal patterns tend to emphasise an apparent primacy of the right to impart information, or, in other words, the *expressive* rights of *speakers*. However, no relevant provision of international law seeks to establish any kind of hierarchy between the amalgamated rights involved. Indeed, in the *travaux préparatoires* of the ICCPR, it is explicitly recorded that "no definite understanding appeared to have been established" in respect of the question "whether freedom to seek and freedom to receive information should be subject to the same restrictions as freedom to impart information, and whether they should be subject to any restrictions at all".[55]

In order for a State to effectively guarantee media-related pluralism and (thereby enhance freedom of expression), it is most likely that protective *and* promotional measures will be required. Toby Mendel advances several examples of the latter: rules requiring "broadcasters to carry minimum quotas of local content"; broadcast licensing "to ensure orderly use of frequencies in the public interest"; "Rules designed to prevent undue concentration of media ownership", and "rules limiting private political advertising during election periods".[56] However, he rejects the appelation, "positive measures", as "both inappropriate and inadequate".[57] He reasons that: "such a classification fails to capture the rationale for these measures", which "are not designed to promote more expression, however that may be defined, but rather to enhance the quality of the expression that is available".[58] On initial consideration, this observation may seem a little too hasty. The ultimate, longer-

55 Marc Bossuyt, *Guide to the "Travaux Préparatoires" of the International Covenant on Civil and Political Rights*, (Dordrecht, etc., Martinus Nijhoff Publishers, 1987), p. 393.

56 Toby Mendel, "Restrictions on Political Expression", *op. cit.*, at 43.

57 *Ibid.*

58 *Ibid.*, at 44.

term objective of such measures is usually to promote the free flow of certain kinds of expression. There is, as Mendel points out, concern for the quality of the expression that is available, but also for the quality and quantity of types of expression that are not (sufficiently) available. Even if the measures listed above have the immediate aim and impact of restricting certain types of expression, that aim is instrumental (and secondary) to the achievement of their more fundamental aim, *viz.* the promotion of certain types of expression on the grounds that they will enhance the quality of public discussion. These quibbles aside, the subsequent development of Mendel's reasoning is highly instructive:

> It is submitted that the measures noted above, rather than being positive in nature, are better understood as promoting the right to receive, rather than to impart, information and ideas. It may be noted that, in many cases, these measures actually limit the right to impart information and ideas. As such, they pit the speaker against the listener, a private rights model of freedom of expression against one which seeks to preserve public expressive space, a traditional, non-interference, paradigm against one which calls for regulation to protect the right to receive.
>
> In most cases, restrictions on freedom of expression are specifically designed to promote other social interests, such as privacy, public order or the administration of justice. The measures noted above, in contrast, are designed to promote freedom of expression, albeit one aspect, perhaps one conception, of this right and frequently at the expense of another. This does not mean that such measures may not, if they do also restrict another aspect, or perhaps another conception of, freedom of expression, be deemed to be in breach of this right.[59]

Mendel then continues by pondering how courts should assess the legitimacy of these measures and determine whether they are consistent with or in conflict with freedom of expression, thereby following through on the likely practical implications of his theoretical distinctions. He argues that the three-part test traditionally applied under international law (i.e., that restrictions on the right must be prescribed by law; serve a legitimate purpose, and be necessary to secure that purpose) usually turns on the necessity criterion, which entails a "presumption in favour of protecting the right to freedom of expression".[60] Such a presumption is not appropriate, however, "when the legitimate interest being served is actually a human right and particularly when that right is freedom of expression", he contends.[61] "In other words", he argues, "it is not appropriate to apply an analysis that automatically accords one conception of freedom of expression priority over another".[62] A more satisfying approach, both philosophically and practically, he argues, would be for courts "to start by assessing whether, taking all of the circumstances into account, the

59 *Ibid.*
60 *Ibid.*
61 *Ibid.*
62 *Ibid.*

impugned measures do, on balance, restrict freedom of expression".[63] The idea that the overall "enrichment of public debate"[64] should be the "touchstone"[65] for judicial analysis has also met with approval in other contexts (eg. the permissibility of State regulation of expression under the First Amendment of the US Constitution[66] and the resolution of conflicts within a media organisation[67]). Intuitively, such an approach would seem to pave the way for a consequentialist assessment of the impugned measures, their impact on the different sets of values underlying different stake-holder interests in freedom of expression and the comparative restrictiveness of alternative measures.[68]

Needless to say, the foregoing discussion does not plead for an outright *volte-face* from the predominance of speaker-oriented balancing exercises by the judiciary. It is, for example, equally difficult to accept Justice White's famous dictum in the *Red Lion* case, "[i]t is the right of the viewers and listeners, not the right of the broadcasters, which is paramount".[69] Justice White's assertion is simply too sweeping, too cut-and-dry. What *is* recommended is a judicial approach that is more sensitive to the various and often competing interests of speakers, listeners/viewers and the wider public, than is currently the case. As already noted, the key evaluative criterion should be the overall impact of an impugned measure on (the quality of) public debate.

To conclude, concerns for media-related pluralism (and specifically for diversity in media content) and the quality of public debate are primarily concerns that relate to the right to receive information. This holds true under various justificatory theories of freedom of expression, especially the truth-finding theory and the democratic-participation theory. In trends towards homogeneity and conventionalism, the first casualties are always minority and unorthodox perspectives. Despite an apparent hesitancy on the part of courts to weigh different constitutive elements, or competing conceptions, of freedom of expression, it is likely that in the future, they will

---

63 *Ibid.*

64 Owen M. Fiss, "Free Speech and Social Structure", 71 *Iowa Law Review* 1405 (1986), at 1416.

65 *Ibid.*

66 *Ibid.*

67 Barendt has argued that: "Hard cases concerning the resolution of free speech conflicts within a media organization can most satisfactorily be resolved by the court determining which result enhances the values of freedom of expression, in particular, the public interest in the dissemination of information of political or social significance and the values of pluralism – the diversity of sources of information and the range of opinion available to the public" – Eric Barendt, *Freedom of Speech* (2nd Edition), *op. cit.*, p. 444.

68 T.M. Scanlon, "Content regulation reconsidered", in T.M. Scanlon, *The Difficulty of Tolerance: Essays in Political Philosophy* (United Kingdom, Cambridge University Press, 2003), pp. 151–168, at 166–167.

69 *Red Lion Broadcasting Co., Inc. v. Federal Communications Commission*, 395 US 367 (1969), at 390.

increasingly be confronted with the challenge of doing so.[70] The reluctance of courts to engage with and judicially enforce media-related pluralism, especially as regards diversity of content, is perhaps understandable. Rachael Craufurd Smith has suggested that "[t]here are so many different ways of achieving pluralism, and so many different gradations of achievement, that the strong subjective element in programme policy is likely, and not without good reason, to deter judicial evaluation in all but the clearest cases of failure".[71] Her remarks are indeed borne out in practice, as will become apparent from the discussion of the jurisprudence of the European Court of Human Rights in Chapter 9.3.3.

For the moment, though, a further reason why pluralism does not easily lend itself to justiciability needs to be examined. It is widely accepted that the State is under a duty to ensure that the media "provide a wide variety of programmes and present all relevant strands of political and social opinion"[72] – without encroaching unduly on their autonomy, of course. The State usually seeks to discharge this duty by means of legislative impositions on broadcasters requiring them to provide a balanced range of programming and to uphold certain qualitative standards such as impartiality, objectivity, etc. Such obligations usually bind public service broadcasters in a more stringent way than their private-sector counterparts. Although such impositions have the *de facto* effect of trammelling the editorial autonomy of broadcasters, the measures are designed to ultimately enrich the quality of broadcasting output, to the benefit of the (viewing or listening) public. Whatever the reach of this principle, or how far its motivation will travel in practice, it does not in any sense confer a right on viewers or listeners "to determine what is contained in the broadcasting schedules".[73] Nor can it ordinarily be construed as founding a right for individuals to receive particular types of content.[74] At a theoretical level, it does not stretch beyond the basis for a claim for diversity of political and cultural content; more specific entailments can only be established at the regulatory level (and not as part of the general, abstract right). These points reinforce the observation made earlier that pluralism is an essentially imprescriptible obligation.

9.2.4(ii) Media responsibilities

Media sociology offers a choice of methodological approaches to measuring the diversity of media content. First, though, it is useful to identify the main features of such content diversity. Denis McQuail has prioritised the following:

---

70 Toby Mendel, "Restrictions on Political Expression", *op. cit.*, at 44–45.

71 Rachael Craufurd Smith, *Broadcasting Law and Fundamental Rights* (Oxford, Clarendon Press, 1997), pp. 169–170.

72 Eric Barendt, *Broadcasting Law*, *op. cit.*, p. 105.

73 *Ibid.*, p. 42.

74 For a more detailed discussion of these questions – based on emergent international and European case-law, see Chapters 1.4.1, 10.1.1 and 10.3.1.

- a wide range of choice for audiences, on all conceivable dimensions of interest and preference;
- many and different opportunities for access by voices and sources in society;
- a true or sufficient reflection in media of the varied reality of experience in society.[75]

Second, given the difficulty of measuring these features in the abstract, suitable external standards have to be selected, against which specific media output can be measured. As McQuail has observed, "[l]ack of diversity can be established only by identifying sources, references, events, types of content, and so on, which are missing or under-represented".[76] The diversity of media content should therefore be seen as relative and not absolute. Furthermore, it is clear from McQuail's prioritisation of characteristic features of content diversity that he does not regard the notion as self-contained or hermetic. Instead, its relationship of qualified dependence on "many and different opportunities for access [...]" for a broadly representative cross-section of society is emphasised. Audiences are implicitly differentiated and the element of choice regarding interests and preferences is also foregrounded.

According to Jan van Cuilenburg, the diversity of media content has traditionally been measured under two main normative frameworks (or variants or combinations thereof). These frameworks prioritise "reflection" (of diversity in society) and "openness" (striving for *perfect* equality of access for all persons and ideas in society). Both have their drawbacks: the former tends to favour conventionalism and homogeneity; the latter can lead to disproportionate distribution of expressive opportunities and informational offers (to the advantage of unrepresentative factions). Van Cuilenburg takes the view that in the future, a framework combining contextual and procedural aspects will prevail when it comes to measuring the diversity of media content. As to the contextual aspects: a suitable "enabling environment"[77] must first exist to secure media freedom. As to the procedural: governmental regulation is countenanced in order to ensure and enhance certain process values relating to freedom of expression. Such a model would therefore attribute greater weighting to "openness" (in Van Cuilenburg's sense of the term) than to "reflection" or representativeness (in media output). While he is certainly correct to insist on the interdependence of contextual and procedural considerations, some elements of his arguments remain open to challenge.

---

75 Denis McQuail, *McQuail's Mass Communication Theory* (5th Edition), *op. cit.*, p. 355.

76 *Ibid.*

77 See generally: Monroe Price & Peter Krug, *The Enabling Environment for Free and Independent Media: Contribution to Transparent and Accountable Governance*, Office of Democracy and Governance, Bureau for Democracy, Conflict, and Humanitarian Assistance, US Agency for International Development (Occasional Papers Series, January 2002).

For instance, he writes: "[f]rom the perspective of democratic truth-finding and political and cultural innovation it is particularly the confrontation of ideas that is important, aside from whether social support is large or small. Mainstream should have no more opportunity to manifest itself than the unorthodox minority".[78] These postulations are problematic. First, societal support for ideas *does* matter – much more than Van Cuilenburg seems prepared to acknowledge. Non-propositional elements of ideas are important because they are often very good indicators of the intensity with which ideas are endorsed or rejected and they also contribute to the prioritisation of ideas in public debate. Aside from "democratic truth-finding" (an unusual formulation) and "political and cultural innovation", the ability to gauge levels of support for particular ideas (as reflected, *inter alia*, by the exposure they are given in the media) is of crucial importance for participation in democratic politics and society. It is not enough to be aware of the existence of an idea: it must also be possible to test its theoretical mettle in the arena of public opinion.

Second, the demand that mainstream and minority elements of society should have perfectly equal opportunities to express themselves is also contestable, at least insofar as it could lead to a corruption of some of the most basic precepts of democracy. It has been argued in previous chapters that society should continually guard against tyranny of the majority, but that minority diktat is also a menace to democratic society. Both are distortions of what democracy is most fundamentally about: majority rule that provides adequate accommodation for the effective participation of non-majority factions. Under such a model of democracy, results cannot and must not be pre-ordained. Rather, the emphasis must be on procedural values and the facilitation of opportunities to achieve results. Moreover, to pre-determine that all ideas should be given equal airing in public (regardless of their representativeness) could lead to contrived focuses for debate and also damage the agenda-setting autonomy of majority and minority sections of society alike. Both of these arguments are of particular relevance for the media.

9.3 Interrelationship of international legal standards

Given the conceptual salience of pluralistic tolerance and media-related pluralism to various theories of freedom of expression, outlined above, it is perhaps puzzling that relevant notions (however styled) have not found more direct expression in positive international law. Most international texts refer only to the right to freedom of information and ideas in whatever form. Arguably, such references do encompass the notion of pluralism, but the absence of explicit references means that such arguments are not fully conclusive. Indeed, the drafting histories of many leading

78 Jan van Cuilenburg, "Diversity Revisited: Towards a Critical Rational Model of Media Diversity", *op. cit.*, at 48.

international human rights treaties reveal that pluralism has tended to play a surprisingly low-key role.

Another plausible explanation for the apparent muffling of pluralism in international law-making is that it can be readily subsumed into other, broader, more traditional rationales for the protection of freedom of expression. On such a theoretical level, Frederick Schauer aligns his (independent) "argument from diversity" very closely with the more time-honoured "argument from truth".[79] Similarly, Eric Barendt, who consistently emphasises the special importance of pluralism in terms of freedom of expression, also adverts to the congruent features of pluralism and free expression theories based on the discovery of truth and democratic participation.[80] The converse to the main argument of this paragraph is that the dangers posed by the absence of media-related pluralism could also be countered by a variety of specific (consequentialist) measures that would impose certain limitations on the media (in particular).

9.3.1 United Nations standards

Pluralism, as a value, can be said (at best) to be implicitly recognised by Article 19, ICCPR. The drafting history of that article shows an acute awareness on the part of the drafters that freedom of expression is simultaneously a "precious heritage" and a "dangerous instrument".[81] Although the drafters conceded that the free flow of information could be obstructed by licensing,[82] governmental interference[83] and other factors,[84] the focus of their proposed limitations to the exercise of the right to freedom of expression was primarily negative. They do not appear to have given any serious consideration to more positive and pre-emptive measures such as the safeguarding of media-related pluralism. Thus, the point that small, poor countries, with underdeveloped media systems would be at a competitive disadvantage transnationally, although raised,[85] failed to generate sufficient concern for media-related pluralism to be prioritised in a meaningful textual or other manner.

This apparent oversight is, however, corrected to some extent by a succinct, but significant statement in the UN Human Rights Committee's new draft General

---

79 Frederick Schauer, *Free speech: a philosophical enquiry* (Cambridge, etc., Cambridge University Press, 1982), pp. 66–67.

80 Eric Barendt, *Freedom of Speech* (2nd Edition), *op. cit.*, p. 25.

81 Marc Bossuyt, *Guide to the "Travaux Préparatoires" of the International Covenant on Civil and Political Rights*, *op. cit.*, p. 386.

82 *Ibid.*, p. 383.

83 *Ibid.*, p. 385.

84 *Ibid.*, p. 396/7.

85 *Ibid.*, p. 393.

Comment No. 34 on Article 19, ICCPR.[86] It affirms that: "[a]s a means to protect the rights of media users, including members of ethnic and linguistic minorities, to receive a wide range of information and ideas, States parties should take particular care to encourage an independent and diverse media".[87] The explicit mention of ethnic and linguistic minorities is a clear recognition of the specificity of their expressive and informational rights and needs.

Even in the thematically more specific and detailed UN Draft Convention on Freedom of Information, notions of pluralism were neither prevalent nor prominent (see further, Chapter 4.1.1). The first early and significant draft contained no express reference whatever to either pluralism or diversity.[88] Nor did it stress any congruent notions into which pluralism or diversity could plausibly be subsumed. By 1959, however, tentative efforts had been made to bring pluralism in from the conceptual cold. The Preamble to the draft Convention included some references that touched on pluralism:

> *Considering* that the free interchange of accurate, objective and comprehensive information and of opinions, both in the national and in the international spheres, is essential to the cause of democracy and peace and for the achievement of political, social, cultural and economic progress,
> *Considering* that freedom of information implies respect for the right of everyone to form an opinion through the fullest possible knowledge of the facts,
> [...]
> *Recognizing* that in order to achieve these aims the media of information should be free from pressure or dictation, but that these media, by virtue of their power for influencing public opinion, bear to the peoples of the world a great responsibility, and have the duty to respect the truth and to promote understanding among nations [...][89]

Much more importantly, though, one aspect of media-related pluralism was significantly upgraded in the substantive part of the draft Convention. Article 1(a) read as follows: "Each Contracting State undertakes to respect and protect the right of every person to have at his disposal diverse sources of information".[90] The introduction of this provision was made at the behest of France, which is perhaps unsurprising, given the importance attached to the value of pluralism in the French Constitution.[91]

86 Draft General Comment No. 34 (Upon completion of the first reading by the Human Rights Committee), Doc. No. CCPR/C/GC/34/CRP.6, 3 May 2011.

87 *Ibid.*, para. 13.

88 *Yearbook of the United Nations*, 1947–1948, p. 593.

89 *Yearbook of the United Nations*, 1959, pp. 213–214.

90 Article 1 (as a whole and as amended) was adopted by the Third Committee on 7 December 1959, by 41 votes to 4, with 21 abstentions: *ibid.*, p. 214.

91 Article 11, Déclaration des droits de l'homme et du citoyen, 1789, as discussed in Rachael Craufurd-Smith, *Broadcasting Law and Fundamental Rights*, *op. cit.*, pp. 162 *et seq.*

The Convention on the Rights of the Child (CRC) represents a high water-mark of sorts in terms of the explicit recognition of media-related pluralism in UN treaties. Article 17, CRC, emphatically underscores the conceptual centrality of pluralism (or at least the plurality of sources) in respect of freedom of expression:

> States Parties recognize the important function performed by the mass media and shall ensure that the child has access to information and material from a diversity of national and international sources, especially those aimed at the promotion of his or her social, spiritual and moral well-being and physical and mental health.

The remainder of Article 17, comprising five subsections, addresses how those objectives should be realised, i.e., by encouraging: (a) "the mass media to disseminate information and material of social and cultural benefit to the child [...]"; (b) "international co-operation in the production, exchange and dissemination of such information and material from a diversity of cultural, national and international sources"; (c) "the production and dissemination of children's books"; (d) "the mass media to have particular regard to the linguistic needs of the child who belongs to a minority group or who is indigenous"; (e) "the development of appropriate guidelines for the protection of the child from information and material injurious to his or her well-being [...]". Thus, it can be concluded that Article 17 is concerned with pluralism as regards content/output ("information and material of social and cultural benefit" – s-s. (a); language – s-s. (d)); sources (s-s. (b)); genres within the mass media (eg. the emphasis on books in s-s. (c)). These concerns correspond to Gibbons' triumvirate categories of content, source and outlet, discussed *supra*. They are also reflected in the normative approach taken in the UNESCO Convention on the Protection and Promotion of the Diversity of Cultural Expressions, as detailed in Chapter 10.2.2.

9.3.2 Council of Europe standards

9.3.2(i) European Court of Human Rights

Deep concerns for the maintenance of pluralism in the media sector inform debates on whether States should pro-actively support the media in financial and logistical terms. The European Court of Human Rights has offered some interpretative guidance concerning States' obligations specifically to promote pluralism in terms of freedom of expression. This guidance – such as it is – is gleaned primarily from a cluster of cases involving disputes arising out of the allocation of broadcasting licences.

In *Groppera Radio AG & others v. Switzerland*,[92] the Court subjected the third sentence of Article 10(1)[93] – and relevant discussions recorded in the *travaux préparatoires* of the ECHR[94] – to careful scrutiny. On the basis of this scrutiny, the Court concluded that "States are permitted to control by a licensing system the way in which broadcasting is operated in their territories, particularly in its technical aspects", subject to the requirements of Article 10(2).[95] The Court later expanded the scope of that finding in the *Informationsverein Lentia & Others v. Austria* case, when it made the seminal pronouncement:

> Technical aspects are undeniably important, but the grant or refusal of a licence may also be made conditional on other considerations, including such matters as the nature and objectives of a proposed station, its potential audience at national, regional or local level, the rights and needs of a specific audience and the obligations deriving from international legal instruments.
>
> This may lead to interferences whose aims will be legitimate under the third sentence of paragraph 1, even though they do not correspond to any of the aims set out in paragraph 2. The compatibility of such interferences with the Convention must nevertheless be assessed in the light of the other requirements of paragraph 2.[96]

This reasoning paved the way for the next crucial pronouncement made by the Court in the *Lentia* case, i.e., that in a democratic society, freedom of expression allows the press to impart information and ideas which the public is moreover entitled to receive and:

> Such an undertaking cannot be successfully accomplished unless it is grounded in the principle of pluralism, of which the State is the ultimate guarantor. This observation is especially valid in relation to audio-visual media, whose programmes are often broadcast very widely.[97]

This was hitherto the clearest statement in the jurisprudence of the European Court of Human Rights concerning the obligation on States to uphold pluralism in the

---

92 Judgment of the European Court of Human Rights of 28 March 1990.

93 "This Article shall not prevent States from requiring the licensing of broadcasting, television or cinema enterprises."

94 *Groppera Radio AG & others v. Switzerland*, *op. cit.*, paras. 60–61. In the latter paragraph of the judgment, Article 19, ICCPR, and the drafting process from which it emerged were similarly scrutinised.

95 *Ibid.*, para. 61. See also, *Autronic AG v. Switzerland*, Judgment of the European Court of Human Rights of 24 April 1990, para. 52 of which affirmed that the final sentence of Article 10(1) is subject to Article 10(2), as well as *Informationsverein Lentia & Others v. Austria,* Judgment of the European Court of Human Rights of 28 October 1993, para. 29.

96 Para. 32.

97 *Ibid.*, para. 38; *VgT Verein gegen Tierfabriken v. Switzerland*, Judgment of the European Court of Human Rights (Second Section) of 28 June 2001, para. 73.

context of freedom of expression. Although the principle seems rather unequivocal, fault has been found with the choice of wording used by the Court on account of its terseness. Rachael Craufurd Smith, for instance, notes that "the Court in *Lentia* did not hold that the state, as 'guarantor' of the communication of information and ideas to the public, was also under a legal obligation to ensure its provision".[98] However, the Court designates the State as the ultimate guarantor of the principle of pluralism – not of "the communication of information and ideas to the public". To dwell on the distinction between both formulations is not to split hairs. Without further qualification, the responsibility of a State to guarantee "the communication of information and ideas to the public" is simply too vague to be meaningful. Granted, pluralism is also a rather vague notion, but not in the same order. Moreover, in legal terms, to be the guarantor of something plainly creates a legal obligation to uphold it and ensure its existence.

The essence of Craufurd Smith's observation prompts further reflection on the Court's intentions. Neither in *Lentia*, nor for a long time afterwards, did the Court endeavour to develop criteria or indicators for measuring the extent to which States effectively discharge their responsibility to safeguard pluralism. While the Court's failure to develop such criteria was regrettable from the point of view of predicting future doctrinal development, it is perhaps unsurprising for two main reasons. First, as the Court has repeatedly held, it is not its task "to indicate which means a State should utilise in order to perform its obligations under the Convention".[99] Indeed, this inherent restriction on judicial powers is by no means unique to the European Court of Human Rights. The tenet has general validity and applicability. As posited by Jack Balkin:

> Where affirmative liberties are at stake, the most that courts can do is define a range of alternatives for the political branches to pick from, or direct the political branches to propose their own alternatives and then accept them if they appear reasonably calculated to succeed. In other words, the effective protection of affirmative liberties requires considerably more judicial restraint than the protection of negative liberties.[100]

It should also be borne in mind that the margin of appreciation doctrine exerts a further restraining influence on the Court in respect of the level of activism it may legitimately pursue. In consequence, the Court has always been very reluctant to usurp in any way the fact-finding or evaluative functions of the national courts – sometimes, it must be said, with unfortunate conservatism.

---

98 Rachael Craufurd Smith, *Broadcasting Law and Fundamental Rights*, *op. cit.*, p. 182.

99 *VgT Verein gegen Tierfabriken v. Switzerland*, *op. cit.*, para. 78.

100 J.M. Balkin, "Some Realism about Pluralism: Legal Realist Approaches to the First Amendment", 1990 Duke L.J. 375, at 413.

A second possible explanation as to why the Court's jurisprudence on media-related pluralism is somewhat lacking in explanatory power can be found by scrutinising and relativising the broader doctrinal picture. As has been argued in a different context, it is only over the stretch of time and experience, with the repetition of patterns and the accumulation of case-law that suitable evaluative criteria are developed by the judiciary.[101] In keeping with this logic, the development of a clearer understanding of the nature of positive State obligations in this regard will be gradual.

Nevertheless, some fragmentary elements of this understanding had actually been put in place in the *Lentia* case itself. The Court accepted then that the "monopoly system operated in Austria is capable of contributing to the quality and balance of programmes, through the supervisory powers over the media thereby conferred on the authorities".[102] However, it cautioned that of all the means of ensuring respect for pluralism:

> a public monopoly is the one which imposes the greatest restrictions on the freedom of expression, namely the total impossibility of broadcasting otherwise than through a national station and, in some cases, to a very limited extent through a local cable station. The far-reaching character of such restrictions means that they can only be justified where they correspond to a pressing need.[103]

Technological progress, the development of transfrontier broadcasting and comparative practices in other States have all contributed to divesting the so-called "scarcity argument" for maintaining State broadcasting monopolies of its earlier persuasiveness. In consequence, notwithstanding the potential for internal pluralism within State monopoly structures, such structures are presumptively deemed to be contrary to the safeguarding of pluralism. This line of reasoning has consistently been applied by the Court in relevant cases since *Lentia*, such as *Radio ABC v. Austria*[104] and *Tele 1 Privatfernsehgesellschaft Mbh v. Austria*.[105]

In *Demuth v. Switzerland*,[106] the Court reiterated that the pursuit of pluralism in broadcasting is a legitimate public policy goal for States, subject to the proportionality of the measure used for that purpose.[107] The Court balanced "the

---

101 Tarlach McGonagle, "Workshop Report: The Changing Hues of Political Expression in the Media", in Susanne Nikoltchev, Ed., *IRIS Special: Political Debate and the Role of the Media – The Fragility of Free Speech* (Strasbourg, European Audiovisual Observatory, 2004), pp. 1–30, at 29.

102 *Informationsverein Lentia & Others v. Austria*, *op. cit.*, para. 33.

103 *Ibid*, para. 39.

104 Judgment of the European Court of Human Rights of 20 October 1997.

105 Judgment of the European Court of Human Rights of 21 September 2000.

106 Judgment of the European Court of Human Rights (Second Section) of 5 November 2002.

107 *Ibid.*, paras. 43 and 44.

legitimate need for the quality and balance of programs in general" and the applicant's right to impart information and ideas. It referred to the potential of audiovisual media for wide diffusion and concluded that "[i]n view of their strong impact on the public, domestic authorities may aim at preventing a one-sided range of commercial television programs on offer".[108] On the facts of the instant case, this reasoning was unsatisfactory. First of all, the impact of the partisan television output would have been limited by the proposed duration of the broadcast – "two hours, to be repeated during 24 hours and to be renewed once a week" (although it was planned to extend its duration "later"). Secondly, notwithstanding the Court's reluctance to interfere with the respondent State's margin of appreciation in broadcasting matters, it could usefully have dwelt further on the likelihood that CAR TV's broadcasts would jeopardise the overall pluralism of the Swiss broadcasting sector.

In *Manole and others v. Moldova*, a case involving governmental interference in the operations of the public service broadcaster, the Court finally cut the Gordian knot: it spelt out in detail what the State's role as the ultimate guarantor of pluralism in the audiovisual sector entails, including relevant positive obligations (particularly in respect of public service broadcasting).[109] The Court considered that, "in the field of audiovisual broadcasting", the State is under a duty "to ensure":

> first, that the public has access through television and radio to impartial and accurate information and a range of opinion and comment, reflecting *inter alia* the diversity of political outlook within the country and, secondly, that journalists and other professionals working in the audiovisual media are not prevented from imparting this information and comment.[110]

It added that the choice of the means by which to achieve these aims "must vary according to local conditions and, therefore, falls within the State's margin of appreciation".[111] It then recalled its previous case-law (eg., the *Lentia* and *Tele 1* cases) which recognised the ability of a public service broadcasting system to contribute "to the quality and balance of programmes", but noted at the same time that "there is no obligation under Article 10 to put in place such a service, provided that some other means are used to the same end".[112] Furthermore, according to the Court:

> Where a State does decide to create a public broadcasting system, it follows from the principles outlined above that domestic law and practice must guarantee that the system provides a pluralistic service. Particularly where private stations are still too

108 *Ibid.*, para. 43.
109 Judgment of the European Court of Human Rights (Fourth Section) of 17 September 2009.
110 *Ibid.*, para. 100.
111 *Ibid.*
112 *Ibid.*

> weak to offer a genuine alternative and the public or State organisation is therefore the sole or the dominant broadcaster within a country or region, it is indispensable for the proper functioning of democracy that it transmits impartial, independent and balanced news, information and comment and in addition provides a forum for public discussion in which as broad a spectrum as possible of views and opinions can be expressed.[113]

The Court subsequently went on to style these implications of the State's role as the ultimate guarantor of pluralism in the audiovisual sector as positive obligations.[114] It also stated in that respect that "the standards relating to public service broadcasting which have been agreed by the Contracting States through the Committee of Ministers of the Council of Europe provide guidance as to the approach which should be taken to interpreting Article 10 in this field".[115]

Generally speaking, the Court's deliberations on safeguarding pluralism in the media have been informed by the need to make efficient use of scarce frequencies.[116] However, with the proliferation of new technological possibilities for broadcasting, the persuasiveness of the scarcity argument has been in steady decline. Despite an obvious tendency for the synchronous deployment of arguments from scarcity and for pluralism, rumours of the demise of the latter have been greatly exaggerated. Rather, technological advances have given rise to new types of concerns for pluralism in the media, eg. the implications of: cross-media ownership; the prominence of (minority) channels in electronic programme guides (EPGs); digital switch-over strategies, and the reservation of multiplex capacity for particular public-interest purposes.[117]

9.3.2(ii) European Convention on Transfrontier Television

Despite the relative paucity of case-law dealing specifically with pluralism and freedom of expression, its importance cannot be gainsaid. The symbiotic relationship between the two is examined in a number of texts adopted, *inter alia*, by the Committee of Ministers of the Council of Europe (see further, *infra*). First and foremost among those texts is the Declaration on the freedom of expression and information (1982), which provides that States "should adopt policies designed to foster as much as possible a variety of media and a plurality of information sources, thereby allowing a plurality of ideas and opinions".[118] To this end, the Declaration

113 *Ibid.*, para. 101.

114 *Ibid.*, para. 107.

115 *Ibid.*

116 See, for example, *Hins & Hugenholtz v. the Netherlands*, Application No. 25987/94, Decision of inadmissibility of the European Commission of Human Rights of 7 March 1996.

117 See further, Chapter 3.3 and Chapter 11.

118 Committee of Ministers' Declaration on the Freedom of Expression and Information, 29 April 1982, para. 6.

sets for States the objective of achieving "the existence of a wide variety of independent and autonomous media, permitting the reflection of diversity of ideas and opinions".[119]

The importance attached to this objective in the 1982 Declaration achieved an elevated status when a new provision, "Media pluralism", was incorporated into the European Convention on Transfrontier Television (ECTT) by its Amending Protocol in 1997.[120] It reads:

> **Article 10*bis* – Media pluralism**
>
> The Parties, in the spirit of co-operation and mutual assistance which underlies this Convention, shall endeavour to avoid that programme services transmitted or retransmitted by a broadcaster or any other legal or natural persons within their jurisdiction, within the meaning of Article 3, endanger media pluralism.

However, this provision – despite the symbolic importance of its inclusion – disappoints in many respects. It is little more than a perfunctory genuflection towards media pluralism. It does not impose any specific obligations on States and it is devoid of explanatory value. Furthermore, the terse corresponding entry in the Explanatory Report to the ECTT is also sorely wanting in terms of its ability to elucidate the notion or the full significance of its inclusion in the Convention.[121]

Article 10*bis*, ECTT, also seems to be viewed with a certain amount of dissatisfaction within the Council of Europe, including in the Standing Committee on Transfrontier Television and the CDMC. Against the background of the proposed modernisation of the EU's "Television without Frontiers" Directive (which ultimately became the Audiovisual Media Services (AVMS) Directive), the Standing Committee on the ECTT and the Council of Europe's Steering Committee on the Media and New Communication Services (CDMC) considered that the best option for any re-assessment of the ECTT's future development would be "modernising the ECTT in close alignment with the new [AVMS] Directive, and possibly adding some new issues".[122] Subsequently, the Secretariat submitted a number of proposals for new human rights-related issues to be introduced into the ECTT – including media pluralism – to the Standing Committee for its consideration. The proposals were not accepted, *inter alia*, because some members of the Standing Committee were of the

---

119 *Ibid.*, Section II, *d.*

120 ETS No. 171, entry into force: 1 March 2002.

121 Explanatory Report to the European Convention on Transfrontier Television, as amended by the provisions of the Protocol (ETS No. 171) which entered into force, on 1 March 2002, para. 204.

122 Karol Jakubowicz, "Implementation and Monitoring: Upholding Human Rights and Cultural Values", in Susanne Nikoltchev, Ed., *IRIS Special: Audiovisual Media Services without Frontiers – Implementing the Rules* (Strasbourg, European Audiovisual Observatory, 2006), pp. 35–44, at 42.

view that media pluralism would be better regulated at the national (as opposed to the international) level.

Notwithstanding the foregoing, it would appear that *if* the inclusion of particular new issues or focuses in the ECTT would indeed distinguish its scope from that of the new Directive, a possible adjustment of the ECTT might be examined more concretely. One question in respect of media pluralism that was considered by the Standing Committee, concerned "the potential extension of Article 10*bis*, so as to distinguish clearly between the question of diversity of content and that of media concentration, each concerned with the very general concept of media pluralism".[123] Such a clarifying amendment would have been welcome. However, on the basis of the theoretical discussion in Chapter 9.2, it is clear that a proposed amendment to explain the interlinkage between important discrete components of the notion of media pluralism could and should go much further than simply distinguishing between diversity of content and concentration of media ownership. In any event, the discussion has now become largely redundant, in light of the formal discontinuation of the revision of the ECTT.[124]

9.3.2(iii) Non-treaty-based standard-setting

A more serious attempt by the Council of Europe to engage with the details and difficulties – conceptual and practical – involved in (media) pluralism, came in the form of a Recommendation addressed by the Committee of Ministers to Member States: Recommendation No. R (99) 1 on measures to promote media pluralism. That text has, however, since been superseded by the very detailed and expansive approach taken by Recommendation CM/Rec(2007)2 on media pluralism and diversity of media content[125] and Declaration on protecting the role of the media in democracy in the context of media concentration.[126] CM Rec(2007)2 recognises the importance of distinguishing between structural pluralism and diversity of content and addresses both in a way that reflects the specificities of new technologies. It also shows keen awareness of the importance of relevant capacity-building measures to ensure the effective use of media technologies and singles out the particular needs of minorities and other groups in this connection.

Other Committee of Ministers' Recommendations link pluralism to other democracy-inspired objectives, like the promotion of public debate and the duty of the media to inform. One of the central premises of Recommendation (2004) 16 on

123 *Ibid.*, at 44.
124 See: Council of Europe Press Release, "Transfrontier television: the revision of the Convention discontinued", 4 February 2011.
125 Adopted by the Committee of Ministers on 31 January 2007.
126 Adopted by the Committee of Ministers on 31 January 2007.

the right of reply in the new media environment[127] is that the corrective potential of such a right helps to further "the interest of the public to receive information from different sources, thereby guaranteeing that they receive complete information".[128] This thinking underscores the important role of the media in providing information to the public – a critical step in the opinion-formation process of members of the public. Similar ideals and visions are promoted, specifically as regards political affairs, in the Declaration on freedom of political debate in the media (2004).[129] In the even more specific context of media coverage of electoral campaigns, "regulatory frameworks should encourage and facilitate the pluralistic expression of opinions via the broadcast media".[130] Issues of balance and impartiality are very much to the fore in media coverage of elections, and again, policies and practices aiming to ensure balanced coverage can safeguard diverse opinions.

The objective of ensuring that the media keep the public adequately informed on matters of general interest has also been stated to apply in cyberspace. For example, the Preamble to the Declaration on freedom of communication on the Internet (2003),[131] refers to the need to guarantee "the right of users to access pluralistic content from a variety of domestic and foreign sources".

It should be noted as well that a veritable *leitmotif* of the Committee of Ministers' texts is the belief that public service broadcasting has a very special role to play in the advancement of cultural and linguistic diversity. This role is dealt with in greatest detail in Recommendation (96) 10 on the guarantee of the independence of public service broadcasting;[132] Recommendation (99) 1 on measures to promote media pluralism; Recommendation (2003) 9 on measures to promote the democratic and social contribution of digital broadcasting;[133] Recommendation CM/Rec(2007)3 on the remit of public service media in the information society,[134] and Recommendation CM/Rec(2007)16 on measures to promote the public service value of the Internet.[135] However, it is also emphasised in numerous other Recommendations and Declarations by the Committee of Ministers and in numerous texts adopted by the Parliamentary Assembly of the Council of Europe.

---

127 Adopted by the Committee of Ministers on 15 December 2004.

128 Preamble to the Recommendation.

129 Adopted by the Committee of Ministers on 12 February 2004.

130 Recommendation CM/Rec(2007)15 on measures concerning media coverage of election campaigns, 7 November 2007, Section II.1.

131 Adopted by the Committee of Ministers on 28 May 2003.

132 Adopted by the Committee of Ministers on 11 September 1996.

133 Adopted by the Committee of Ministers on 28 May 2003.

134 Adopted by the Committee of Ministers on 31 January 2007.

135 Adopted by the Committee of Ministers on 7 November 2007.

9.3.2(iv) Framework Convention for the Protection of National Minorities

Article 9(4), FCNM, requires States "to adopt adequate measures in order to facilitate access to the media for persons belonging to national minorities and in order to promote tolerance and permit cultural pluralism". The use of the conjunction "and" makes it clear that the requirement to facilitate access for minorities to the media is distinct from, and in no sense conditional on, the other stated objectives of promoting tolerance and permitting cultural pluralism. Nevertheless, the fact that they have been positioned alongside each other, in the same paragraph, is suggestive of a perceived underlying connection between them. It is submitted here, reasonably (the *travaux préparatoires* of the FCNM do not offer any helpful guidance on this point), that these three objectives have been bracketed together on account of the inherent connection between the more general principle of pluralistic tolerance and its specific media-related pluralism, as developed at the very outset of this chapter.

Be that as it may, media-related pluralism has a similar "poor-relation" status under the FCNM to the status it has under many other international human rights treaties (see further, *supra*). It is not mentioned *per se* in Article 9, or anywhere else in the text of the FCNM, either as an objective or even *in passim*. On the whole, Article 9 is preoccupied with the expressive rights (and conditions for the exercise of those rights) of minorities – to the partial neglect of recipient-oriented rights and liberties. The defining, driving logic of the FCNM is that the position of national minorities in society is best protected through the enshrinement and enforcement of a catalogue of negative and positive rights. According to that logic, it may appear that there is nothing untoward about prioritising the advancement of rights that specifically benefit minorities over broader (and perhaps vaguer) societal concerns for media pluralism. However, this line of argument overlooks the essential role played by media pluralism in the furtherance of "a spirit of tolerance and intercultural dialogue" and "mutual respect and understanding and co-operation" at societal level (it will be recalled that these objectives are among those set out in Article 6(1), FCNM) (see further, Chapter 8.2.1). In light of these considerations, it must be concluded that the negligible attention paid to media-related pluralism in the text of the FCNM and in its monitoring process is a regrettable shortcoming of the overall approach. A more rounded assessment of minorities' freedom of expression rights and interests, i.e., sending *and receiving* information and ideas (and also as third parties affected by the same) would likely have yielded a different, more balanced sense of priorities.

The right of persons belonging to national minorities to receive information and ideas has, however, been the focus of attention in two distinct contexts. The first concerns transfrontier broadcasting and the second, geographical/technical obstacles impeding the reception of broadcasting signals. Consideration of the latter will be delayed until Chapter 11 as the Advisory Committee has tended to class such issues as coming under the rubric of "access". As will be argued in Chapter 11, this tests the elasticity of access as a concept, and is only really meaningful if a distinction is made between "passive" and "active" access.

9.3.2(v) European Charter for Regional or Minority Languages

A key observation made in the previous section in respect of Article 9, FCNM, *viz.* that the Advisory Committee's monitoring work has an indirect but indisputable impact on diversity/pluralism in the media, also holds true in respect of Article 11, ECRML. However, the impact is also direct as Article 11(3) reads:

> The Parties undertake to ensure that the interests of the users of regional or minority languages are represented or taken into account within such bodies as may be established in accordance with the law with responsibility for guaranteeing the freedom and pluralism of the media.

Although not all States Parties to the ECRML have committed themselves to this undertaking, a significant number have done so[136] and the Committee of Experts' monitoring of this provision has produced some useful interpretive results. This provision seeks to promote participatory inclusive deliberation, even if it does fall short of guaranteeing actual representation. The clause, "or taken into account" could dilute the impact of the provision as a whole if it were to be interpreted without sufficient rigour. In practice, the Committee of Experts has paid attention to the *effectiveness* of the mechanisms used to ensure that the interests of speakers of regional or minority languages are heard within relevant bodies:

> While the implementation of this article does not require that each individual Part III language should have its own representative on the bodies in question, it does require that adequate systems or processes exist to ensure that the interests of speakers of each Part III language are in fact represented or taken into account.[137]

It is clear that this goal could be realised by structural or procedural means, but preferably through the "active participation" of speakers of regional or minority languages.[138] It is also clear that the onus is on States Parties which have committed themselves to Article 11(3) to demonstrate the effectiveness of the manner in which the interests of speakers of designated languages are represented or taken into account. For example, the UK committed itself to apply Article 11(3) to the Welsh language, but the Committee of Experts noted in its First Report on the UK that it had not been made aware of any intention to include a representative of regional or minority languages on the board of OFCOM, nor had it been informed of any

136 Armenia, Bosnia and Herzegovina, Croatia, Finland, Hungary, Montenegro, Poland, Romania, Serbia, Slovakia, Slovenia, Spain, Switzerland, Ukraine, United Kingdom.

137 Second Report on Croatia, 26 November 2004, para. 180.

138 First Report on Croatia, 2 December 2000, Boxed Comment after para. 100.

alternative means by which the objectives of Article 11(3) would be realised.[139] This suggests flexibility as to the means, but firmness as to the goals.

The reference to "bodies [...] with responsibility for guaranteeing the freedom and pluralism of the media" is instinctively suggestive of regulatory authorities in the media sector. On at least one occasion, however, the Committee of Experts takes a more expansive understanding of the provision, i.e., when it appeared to apply the provision to the administrative structures of a public service broadcaster (PSB). In its Second Report on Finland, the Committee stated that it had not received any information "as to how the interests of the Sami are taken into account in the administration of the Finnish Broadcasting Company or in other bodies as may be established with the responsibility to ensure the freedom and pluralism of the media".[140] The wording used is not, of itself, conclusive as to whether it was indeed the intention of the Committee to extend the application of Article 11(3) in this manner. Moreover, on another occasion when it commented on representation in decision-making structures and bodies responsible for guaranteeing freedom and pluralism of the media in the same paragraph, it did distinguish between them.[141] In any case, even if this extension of Article 11(3) proves to be a once-off occurrence, it must nevertheless be considered presumptively invalid to take this approach because to have responsibility for guaranteeing freedom and pluralism of the media, a body would have to be vested with powers of oversight and sanction. By virtue of its mandate, a PSB may be (and more often than not is) required *to contribute to or promote* pluralism *in* the media. As held by the European Court of Human Rights in the *Lentia* case, the ultimate responsibility for guaranteeing pluralism in the media rests with States or its (regulatory) organs. Moreover, unless a PSB is in a complete monopoly position, it could at best only guarantee pluralism in respect of its own services, in other words in the PSB sector and not "of" the media generally. The distinction between internal and external pluralism is relevant here.[142]

9.3.3 European Union standards[143]

9.3.3(i) Charter of Fundamental Rights of the European Union

The symbiosis between freedom of expression and media pluralism has also been enshrined as a central concept in Article 11 (Freedom of expression and information)

139 First Report on the UK, 29 August 2003, para. 171. It is noteworthy that in its Second Report on the UK, the Committee of Experts reported that OFCOM had established an office in Wales "with a Welsh representative on the Content Board" and that it had also created an advisory committee for Wales: Second Report on the UK, 14 September 2006, para. 249.

140 Second Report on Finland, 24 March 2004, para. 152.

141 First Report on Switzerland, 1 June 2001, para. 149.

142 Second Report on Switzerland, 24 March 2004, paras. 131–132.

143 Please note that Treaty articles cited in this section generally correspond to actual numbering at operative times, which is not necessarily the same as current numbering.

of the Charter of Fundamental Rights of the European Union (hereinafter, the Nice Charter), which reads:

1. Everyone has the right to freedom of expression. This right shall include freedom to hold opinions and to receive and impart information and ideas without interference by public authority and regardless of frontiers.
2. The freedom and pluralism of the media shall be respected.

The direct and succinct formulation leaves no doubt that the drafters plainly sought to attach importance to media pluralism. This is attested to by the Explanatory Note, which explains that Article 11(2) "spells out the consequences of paragraph 1 regarding freedom of the media".[144] However, notwithstanding the (now) legally-binding character of the Nice Charter, there are good grounds for fearing that the importance of the explicit reference to media pluralism is primarily symbolic. The actual impact of Article 11(2) remains to be seen, first of all because "respected" is a significantly weaker formulation than, for example, "guaranteed" or "secured" (even if it is preceded by "shall"). As such, it involves a considerably lighter commitment for States. Second, the Explanatory Note does not spell out the essence or scope of media pluralism, which suggests a non-committal attitude to – or wariness of – its actual or potential implications. Such attitudes could plausibly be explained by the political contentiousness of the issue of media pluralism within the EU institutions (see further, Chapter 9.3.3(iii)).

Article 11 of the Nice Charter has a dual objective. First, it seeks to provide a modernised articulation of Article 10 ECHR, which would implicitly crystallise and incorporate the body of case-law developed by the European Court of Human Rights over the years.[145] It is also intended to reflect – or at least not depart from – the central principles of the relevant case-law of the Court of Justice of the European Communities (ECJ). The Explanatory Note confirms that Article 11(2) is indeed based on relevant ECJ case-law regarding television – especially the case *Stichting Gouda*, discussed *infra*, as well as the Protocol on the system of public broadcasting in the Member States annexed to the EC Treaty and the Television without Frontiers Directive – especially its Recital No. 17.[146] That Recital reads as follows:

> Whereas this Directive, being confined specifically to television broadcasting rules, is without prejudice to existing or future Community acts of harmonization, in

144 Note from the Praesidium, Draft Charter of Fundamental Rights of the European Union – Text of the explanations relating to the complete text of the Charter as set out in CHARTE 4487/00 CONVENT 50, 11 October 2000, CHARTE 4473/00, p. 14.

145 See further: Paul Mahoney, "The Charter of Fundamental Rights of the European Union and the European Convention on Human Rights from the Perspective of the European Convention", 23 *Human Rights Law Journal* 300–303 (2002).

146 Note from the Praesidium, *op. cit.*, p. 14.

> particular to satisfy mandatory requirements concerning the protection of consumers and the fairness of commercial transactions and competition.

It seems odd, however, that the (Explanatory) Note from the Praesidium should refer to Recital No. 17 in this connection, but not to Recital No. 16, which appears to be of even greater relevance:

> Whereas it is essential for the Member States to ensure the prevention of any acts which may prove detrimental to freedom of movement and trade in television programmes or which may promote the creation of dominant positions which would lead to restrictions on pluralism and freedom of televised information and of the information sector as a whole.

9.3.3(ii) European Court of Justice

The issue of media pluralism arises in several ECJ cases, but again, the judicial interpretation offered generally fails to provide much additional elucidation of the precise scope of the principle.

One of the ECJ's earliest cases dealing with media-related pluralism was *Bond van Adverteerders & others v. The Netherlands*.[147] The background to the case involved the statutory advertising monopoly that existed in the Netherlands at the operative time. Under that monopoly, only one organisation – the STER – was allowed to broadcast advertisements.[148] The STER's task was to organise the transmission of advertising prepared by third parties, to which it sold airtime.[149] The STER was bound by statute to transfer its receipts to the State, which used them to subsidise national broadcasters and the press.[150] Pursuant to relevant statutory provisions, there was a prohibition on the distribution by cable of programmes transmitted by broadcasters established in other Member States that contained advertising intended specifically for the Netherlands. The Dutch authorities explained that the use of revenues generated by the STER for the purpose of funding national broadcasters and the press was to enable them to preserve their non-commercial character. They maintained, additionally, that "a pluralistic broadcasting system is conceivable only if the *Omroeporganisaties* [i.e., broadcasters] are non-commercial in character".[151]

---

147 Case 352/85, Judgment of the Court of Justice of the European Communities of 26 April 1988, ECR 1988, p. 2085. It should be noted that this judgment predated the adoption of the Television without Frontiers Directive.

148 *Ibid.*, para. 3.

149 *Ibid.*, para. 25.

150 *Ibid.*, paras. 3 & 35.

151 *Ibid.*, para. 35. At the relevant time, the Dutch broadcasting system was characterised by its "pillarised" structure, under which each pillar was expected to contribute to the overall pluralism of the system.

The Court found that the distribution by cable of programmes transmitted by broadcasters established in other Member States did constitute a transfrontier service under Articles 59 and 60 of the Treaty.[152] It also found the Dutch statutory prohibition on the same to be discriminatory as national broadcasters were not subject to the same restriction on their right to freedom to provide services.[153] It pointed out that the only permissible derogation in a case such as this would be one grounded in a justification of public policy.[154] However, it insisted that "economic aims, such as that of securing for a national public foundation all the revenue from advertising intended especially for the public of the member state in question, cannot constitute grounds of public policy within the meaning of Article 56 of the Treaty".[155] The Dutch authorities, for their part, argued that "in the final analysis, the prohibitions of advertising and subtitling have a non-economic objective, namely that of maintaining the non-commercial and, thereby, pluralistic nature of the Netherlands broadcasting system".[156] Ultimately, the Court found the impugned measures to be disproportionate and contrary to relevant Treaty provisions. In reaching its decision, it adverted to the fact that the Dutch authorities themselves had conceded that less restrictive, non-discriminatory measures could have been adopted in order to achieve the intended objectives.[157]

A very interesting question, raised formally by the Dutch national court in the *Bond van Adverteerders* case but left unanswered by the Court, read as follows:

> Can the generally accepted principles of Community law (in particular the principle of proportionality) and the fundamental rights enshrined in Community law (in particular the freedom of expression and freedom to receive information) impose directly applicable obligations on the Member States in the light of which national rules such as those concerned here must be assessed, regardless of whether or not any written provisions of Community law are applicable thereto?[158]

The Court interpreted this question as referring to the principle of proportionality and the scope of Article 10, ECHR.[159] However, it ultimately regarded the question as redundant, stating that the answers it had given to the earlier questions would enable the national court to "resolve the dispute before it in light of those answers alone".[160] To this day, neither the ECJ nor the European Court of Human Rights has squared up fully to this question and answered it in a detailed and definitive way.

152 *Ibid.*, paras. 12–17.
153 *Ibid.*, paras. 26–27; 29–30.
154 *Ibid.*, paras. 32–33.
155 *Ibid.*, para. 34.
156 *Ibid.*, para. 35.
157 *Ibid.*, para. 37. See also para. 36.
158 *Ibid.*, para. 10.
159 *Ibid.*, para. 40.
160 *Ibid.*, para. 41.

In *Stichting Gouda v. CVDM*,[161] the ECJ accepted that a cultural policy aimed at safeguarding freedom of expression for diverse societal groups "may indeed constitute an overriding requirement relating to the general interest which justifies a restriction on the freedom to provide services".[162] It also pointed out, however, that there is no necessary connection between such national cultural policies and conditions relating to the structures of foreign broadcasters; nor did it see any need for national cultural policies to concern itself with the latter.[163] The same cultural policy was also examined in *Commission v. The Netherlands*.[164] In that case, the ECJ pointed out the connection between pluralism and the guarantee of freedom of expression enshrined in Article 10, ECHR,[165] but also found that the goal of pluralism in the audiovisual sector did not require a prohibition on national broadcasters from using production services of broadcasters in other jurisdictions.[166]

The Court upheld these findings concerning the preservation of pluralism in the media in *Commission v. Belgium*,[167] a case in which Belgium was found to be in breach of its obligations under Article 2 of the Television without Frontiers (TWF) Directive, on account of a system of prior authorisation for the retransmission by cable of television broadcasts emanating from other Member States. On the facts of the case at hand, the Court held that the Belgian authorities had failed to satisfactorily demonstrate the necessity and proportionality of the contested system of prior authorisation for the protection of "pluralism in the audiovisual field or in the media generally".[168] The Court also rejected the Belgian Government's submission that the impugned system was intended to serve certain cultural objectives and was therefore justified "inasmuch as Directive 89/552, and in particular Articles 4 and 5, must be construed in the light of Article 128 of the Treaty [...]".[169] The Court recalled that the cultural objectives of the TWF Directive

161 Case C-288/89, *Stichting Collectieve Antennevoorziening Gouda and others v. Commissariaat voor de media* [1991], Judgment of the Court of Justice of the European Communities of 25 July 1991, ECR I-4007.

162 *Ibid.*, para. 23. See also paras. 22, 24.

163 *Ibid.*, para. 24.

164 Case C-353/89, *Commission of the European Communities v. Kingdom of the Netherlands* [1991], Judgment of the Court of Justice of the European Communities of 25 July 1991, ECR I-4069.

165 *Ibid.*, para. 30. See also *Stichting Gouda, op. cit.*, para. 23; Case C-260/89, *Ellinki Radiophonia Tiléorassi AE and Panellinia Omospondia Syllogon Prossopikou v. Dimotiki Etairia Pliroforissis and Sotirios Kouvelas and Nicolaos Avdellas and others* [1991], Judgment of the Court of Justice of the European Communities of 18 June 1991, ECR I-2925, para. 45; *TV10 SA v. Commissariaat voor de media* [1994], Judgment of the Court of Justice of the European Communities (Fifth Chamber) of 5 October 1994, ECR I-4795, para. 25.

166 *Commission v. the Netherlands, op. cit.*, para. 31.

167 Case C-11/95, *Commission v. Belgium* [1996], Judgment of the Court of Justice of the European Communities of 10 September 1996, ECR I-4115, para. 54.

168 *Ibid.*, para. 55.

169 *Ibid.*, paras. 46, 47. The reference here is to (former) Article 128 of the Treaty establishing the European Community. That Article, concerning the promotion of cultural diversity, has since

are encapsulated in Recitals 17 and 18 of its Preamble and also in its Articles 4 and 5, before stating that Article 128 of the Treaty "does not in any way authorize the receiving State, by way of derogation from the system established by Directive 89/552, to make programmes emanating from another Member State subject to further controls".[170]

In an abstrusely worded sentence in *Vereniging Veronica Omroep v. CVDM*,[171] the ECJ authorises Member States to use legislative means to prohibit broadcasting organisations under its jurisdiction from investing in foreign broadcasting organisations or from providing other forms of assistance to the latter "where those activities are directed towards the establishment of a commercial television station whose broadcasts are intended to be received, in particular, in the territory of the first Member State and those prohibitions are necessary in order to ensure the pluralistic and non-commercial character of the audio-visual system introduced by that legislation".[172]

The factual background to the *Familiapress* case[173] involved the distribution in Austria of a German publication offering prizes for crossword competitions; this practice fell foul of a statutory prohibition in Austria on publishers of periodicals inviting consumers to take part in draws. The Austrian Government submitted that the aim of the relevant national legislation was to preserve press diversity, and that such a justification could be considered an overriding requirement for the purposes of Article 30. The ECJ, following its earlier judgments in *Commission v. Netherlands* and *Veronica v. CVDM*, re-affirmed that the "[M]aintenance of press diversity may constitute an overriding requirement justifying a restriction on free movement of goods" as "[S]uch diversity helps to safeguard freedom of expression [...]".[174] It reiterated that such overriding requirements must be interpreted "in the light of the general principles of law and in particular of fundamental rights",[175] including freedom of expression.[176] The Court found that "[A] prohibition on selling publications which offer the chance to take part in prize games competitions may detract from freedom of expression".[177] However, basing its remarks on the *Lentia* judgment of the European Court of Human Rights (see Chapter 9.3.2(i)), the ECJ

moulted into Article 167 of the Treaty on the Functioning of the European Union (see further, Chapter 10.3.2).

170 *Ibid.*, para. 50.

171 Case C-148/91, *Veronica Omroep Organisatie v. Commissariaat voor de Media* [1993], Judgment of 3 February 1993, ECR I-487.

172 *Ibid.*, para. 15.

173 Case C-368/95, *Vereinigte Familiapress Zeitungsverlags- und vertriebs GmbH v. Heinrich Bauer Verlag* [1997], Judgment of 26 June 1997, ECR I-3689.

174 *Ibid.*, para. 18.

175 *Ibid.*, para. 24.

176 *Ibid.*, para. 25.

177 *Ibid.*, para. 26.

stated that derogations from freedom of expression for the purpose of maintaining press diversity are permissible, as long as they are prescribed by law and necessary in a democratic society.[178]

The essential question to be considered by the Court, therefore, was "whether a national prohibition such as that in issue [...] is proportionate to the aim of maintaining press diversity and whether that objective might not be attained by measures less restrictive of both intra-Community trade and freedom of expression".[179] It continued:

> To that end, it should be determined, first, whether newspapers which offer the chance of winning a prize in games, puzzles or competitions are in competition with those small press publishers who are deemed to be unable to offer comparable prizes and whom the contested legislation is intended to protect and, second, whether such a prospect of winning constitutes an incentive to purchase capable of bringing about a shift in demand.

The Court thereby opted to frame its enquiry in terms of the impact of unfair competition; considerations relating directly to freedom of expression simply did not figure. Even the suggestions that "blacking out or removing the page on which the prize competition appears in copies intended for Austria or a statement that readers in Austria do not qualify for the chance to win a prize" were considered uniquely as measures that would be "less restrictive of free movement of goods" than the contested outright prohibition. The fact that such measures would also be less restrictive on freedom of expression is not even adverted to. The competition-centric reasoning employed by the Court is therefore regrettably lop-sided.[180] Thus, it concluded that Article 30 of the Treaty would not preclude legislation such as that which was the focus of the *Familiapress* case, as long as it is "proportionate to maintenance of press diversity and that that objective cannot be achieved by less restrictive means", and that the above-mentioned assumptions hold true. It added that "the national prohibition must not constitute an obstacle to the marketing of newspapers which, albeit containing prize games, puzzles or competitions, do not give readers residing in the Member State concerned the opportunity to win a prize", before concluding that the national court should determine whether the

---

178 *Ibid.*, para. 26.

179 *Ibid.*, para. 27.

180 It could be mentioned in passing that this down-playing of freedom of expression interests by the ECJ is consistent with its broader doctrinal patterns. The economic objectives of the EU have unsurprisingly played a determinative role in shaping *its* development of freedom of expression interests. The right to freedom of expression has therefore traditionally been relativised in terms of values associated with the goal of achieving free trade in the context of European economic integration. Attempts by the European Court of Human Rights to balance freedom of expression and public policy objectives such as the prevention of unfair competition and false/misleading advertising have also led to unsatisfactory results.

relevant conditions "are satisfied on the basis of a study of the national press market concerned".[181]

In *TV10 SA*, the purpose of safeguarding pluralism was spelt out by the ECJ, drawing explicitly on its earlier *ERT* and *Commission v. Netherlands* judgments, as being "to preserve the diversity of opinions, and hence freedom of expression [...]".[182] In short, TV 10 was a broadcasting company whose activities (especially the transmission of programming by cable) were directed primarily at the Netherlands, but which had – according to the *Commissariaat voor de media* (the Dutch media regulatory authority) and upheld by the *Raad van State* (Dutch Council of State) – established itself in Luxembourg in order to circumvent national legislation applying to domestic [Dutch] broadcasters. One of the objectives of the legislation in question was to safeguard "the pluralist and non-commercial content of programmes".[183] The ECJ concluded that "the Treaty provisions on freedom to provide services are to be interpreted as not precluding a Member State from treating as a domestic broadcaster a broadcasting body constituted under the law of another Member State and established in that State but whose activities are wholly or principally directed towards the territory of the first Member State, if that broadcasting body was established there in order to enable it to avoid the rules which would be applicable to it if it were established within the first State".[184]

By way of conclusion, it can be seen from the brief foregoing overview that the ECJ has recognised the value of pluralism and its potential role in guaranteeing expressive opportunities for discrete societal groups and thereby helping to ensure that diverse opinions remain in circulation. Yet, there is something unsatisfactory about this distillation: its explanatory power as regards the importance of media pluralism for democracy is weak. The ECJ has shown little interest in elaborating a comprehensive theoretical basis for its standpoints on these matters. The largely inconclusive nature of its doctrine to date could be taken as supporting Thomas Gibbons' suggestion that "media pluralism was not promoted for the purpose of supporting a more democratic role for the media, as might be supposed from its content", but that "[I]nstead, the idea was adopted as a transitional concept that conveniently assisted a shift from public service dominance to a market approach".[185]

181 *Familiapress*, *op. cit.*, para. 34.

182 Case C-23/93, *TV 10 SA v. Commissariaat voor de Media*, *op. cit.*, para. 25.

183 *Ibid.*, para. 21.

184 *Ibid.*, para. 26.

185 Thomas Gibbons, "Pluralism, guidance and the new media", in Christopher T. Marsden, Ed., *Regulating the Global Information Society* (London & New York, Routledge, 2000), pp. 304–315, at 307.

9.3.3(iii) Other regulatory measures

Although "the protection of media pluralism is primarily a task for the Member States",[186] a number of relevant references and provisions do exist at the EU-level. A major instrument in the EU's regulatory approach to media pluralism is the Merger Regulation.[187] Under Article 21(4) of the Merger Regulation, Member States are allowed to "take appropriate measures to protect legitimate interests" (i.e., public security, plurality of the media and prudential rules", thereby putting them beyond the ordinary purview of the Regulation. Any "appropriate measures" thus adopted must be "compatible with the general principles and other provisions of Community law".

Furthermore, Article 8.1 of the EU's Framework Directive,[188] states that "National regulatory authorities may contribute within their competencies to ensuring the implementation of policies aimed at the promotion of cultural and linguistic diversity, as well as media pluralism". Similarly, its Radio Spectrum Decision[189] establishes procedures in order to, *inter alia*:

> facilitate policy making with regard to the strategic planning and harmonisation of the use of radio spectrum in the Community taking into consideration *inter alia* economic, safety, health, public interest, freedom of expression, cultural, scientific, social and technical aspects of Community policies as well as the various interests of radio spectrum user communities with the aim of optimising the use of radio spectrum and of avoiding harmful interference.[190]

9.3.3(iv) European Commission

In January 2007, then Information Society and Media Commissioner Viviane Reding and Commission Vice-President Margot Wallstrom, presented their joint,

186 Commission of the European Communities, Green Paper on Services of General Interest, COM(2003) 270 final, 21 May 2003, para. 74; Communication from the Commission to the Council, the European Parliament, the European Economic and Social Committee and the Committee of the Regions The Future of a European Regulatory Audiovisual Policy, COM(2003) 784 final, 15 December 2003, p. 8. See also: European Commission Staff Working Document, Media pluralism in the Member States of the European Union, SEC(2007) 32, 16 January 2007.

187 Council Regulation (EC) No 139/2004 of 20 January 2004 on the control of concentrations between undertakings (the EC Merger Regulation), OJ L 24/1, 29 January 2004.

188 Directive 2002/21/EC of the European Parliament and of the Council of 7 March 2002 on a common regulatory framework for electronic communications networks and services (Framework Directive), OJ L 108/33, 24 April 2002.

189 Decision No. 676/2002/EC of the European Parliament and of the Council of 7 March 2002 on a regulatory framework for radio spectrum policy in the European Community (Radio Spectrum Decision), OJ L 108/1, 24 April 2002.

190 Article 2(a), *ibid.*; see also, in the same connection, Recitals 3 and 8 of the Decision.

three-step, approach to media pluralism.[191] The first step was the preparation of a Commission Staff Working Document on the topic, providing an initial sense of the terrain. The second step was to commission an independent study on media pluralism in EU Member States "to define and test concrete and objective indicators for assessing media pluralism in EU Member States". The third step was to have been the preparation of a Communication by the Commission on the indicators for media pluralism in the EU Member States. The Communication was initially envisaged for 2008, but it has since been removed (without acknowledgement or explanation) from the website. It is therefore unclear whether the Commission has any intention of pursuing its engagement with media pluralism issues, for instance by way of follow-up to the *Independent Study on Indicators for Media Pluralism in the Member States*.[192]

The study constructs a risk-analysis theory of media pluralism and maps relevant laws and practice across EU Member States. It comprises legal, socio-demographic and economic components and the "risk domains" it identifies are:

- Pluralism of media ownership and control
- Media types and genres
- Political pluralism in the media
- Cultural pluralism in the media
- Geographical pluralism in the media

9.3.3(v) European Parliament

It should also be mentioned that throughout the 1990s, various initiatives to develop formal regulatory instruments (i.e., directives) to deal specifically with media pluralism were taken, but ultimately shelved, due *inter alia* to their political contentiousness and failures to reach necessary inter-institutional agreement within the EU. Although those various initiatives did not culminate in the adoption of a relevant directive, they were politically very significant for the development of policy approaches to issues relating to media pluralism. However, given that relevant details and debates are only of tangential interest to minority rights, they will only be signalled here, but not explored any further.

---

191 "Media pluralism: Commission stresses need for transparency, freedom and diversity in Europe's media landscape", European Commission Press Release, IP/07/52, 16 January 2007.

192 ICRI *et al.*, *Independent Study on Indicators for Media Pluralism in the Member States – Towards a Risk-Based Approach*, July 2009 (rendered public in October 2009). For an overview of the study, see: Peggy Valcke, Robert Picard, Miklos Sukosd, Beata Klimkiewicz, Brankica Petkovic, Cinzia dal Zotto and Robin Kerremans, "The European Media Pluralism Monitor: Bridging Law, Economics and Media Studies as a First Step towards Risk-Based Regulation in Media Markets", 2 *Journal of Media Law* (No. 1, 2010), pp. 85–113.

As already mentioned, plans to develop regulation in this field have merely been shelved – not binned – and they tend to intermittently re-appear on political agendas. In 2004, for example, the European Parliament adopted a Resolution on the risks of violation, in the EU and especially in Italy, of freedom of expression and information (Article 11(2) of the Charter of Fundamental Rights).[193]

The Resolution stresses that media independence and pluralism are crucial for guaranteeing the right to freedom of expression and information. Relevant issues are subjected to a detailed examination, particularly from the angles of audiovisual policy; public service broadcasting and the commercial media (but not other media types: see further, Chapter 3.2.2). Due emphasis is laid on the individual and collective impact of arguments from democracy; technological advances and constitutional and competition law considerations.

Attention is drawn to specific problems pertaining in a number of EU Member States: France; Germany; Ireland; the Netherlands; Poland; Spain; Sweden and the United Kingdom. The greatest scrutiny, however, is reserved for Italy, due to persistent concerns over high levels of concentration of ownership in the audiovisual market there, coupled with the prominence of political involvement in the same.

The proposed recommendations were distilled from concerns identified and explored in the body of the Resolution. For instance, it is stated that EU competence in policy and regulatory matters affecting the media, especially new technological features relating to digital television, should be used for furthering media pluralism and combating "horizontal and vertical media concentration in traditional as well as in new media markets" (para. 73).

The Resolution calls for specific lines of action on the part of the European Commission, including the submission of a communication on the state of media pluralism in the EU as soon as possible (para. 75). The envisaged scope of such a communication is broad, including a *compte rendu* of current measures and practice at the national and EU levels alike; explorations of possible and recommended courses of action, and the relevant mechanics of such action and any consultation procedures that would be involved. The Resolution also calls for the submission of "a proposal for a directive to safeguard media pluralism in Europe in order to complete the regulatory framework [...]" (para. 76). As noted in the previous subsection, it is unclear whether the Commission has any intention of pursuing these suggested lines of action.

---

193 Resolution on the risks of violation, in the EU and especially in Italy, of freedom of expression and information (Article 11(2) of the Charter of Fundamental Rights) (2003/2237/(INI)), 22 April 2004.

Another key recommendation is that "legislation should be adopted at European level to prohibit political figures or candidates from having major economic interests in the media [...] legal instruments should be introduced to prevent any conflict of interest [...]", and that the Commission should "submit proposals to ensure that members of government are not able to use their media interests for political purposes". The Commission is also called upon to devise an action plan on measures to promote pluralism in all EU sectors of activity. Twenty points are suggested for inclusion in such an action plan (para. 79). The substantive recommendations conclude with an invitation to the Italian Parliament to address the aforementioned concentration of media ownership and related problems in Italy (para. 87).

In 2007, the Parliament again engaged very extensively with media pluralism issues in its Resolution, 'Concentration and pluralism in the media in the European Union'.[194] It engages with the various dimensions of media pluralism – regulatory, technical, economic, social, etc. It examines the different contributions to media pluralism that are made by different media types (public service, commercial and community). It calls, *inter alia*, on the Commission to "commit itself to promoting a stable legal framework with a guaranteed high standard of protection of pluralism in all the Member States" (para. 7). It also asserts that the "main objectives of public authorities should be to create conditions that ensure a high level of media quality (including in the public media), secure media diversity and guarantee the full independence of journalists" (para. 9).

The Resolution "[r]eminds the Commission that on several occasions, it has been asked to draw up a directive that would aim to ensure pluralism, encourage and preserve cultural diversity as defined in the Unesco Declaration on cultural diversity, as well as to safeguard access for all media companies to the technical elements that can enable them to reach the public in its entirety" (para. 31). Other relevant and increasingly topical issues are also explored, such as the role of media literacy in supporting media pluralism and the implications for pluralism of how the digital dividend (i.e., the radio spectrum freed up by the switch-over from analogue to digital broadcasting) is allocated.

Conclusions

The bridging of Chapter 6 with Chapters 9–11 is crucial for the structure and substance of this book. By recognising that the promotion of pluralistic tolerance is logically complementary to the prohibition of abusive speech, a link is

---

194 European Parliament Resolution of 25 September 2008 on concentration and pluralism in the media in the European Union (2007/2253(INI)).

established between what are routinely termed "negative" and "positive" State obligations.

The importance of media- and information-related pluralism can be explained in two main ways: its ability to facilitate or strengthen pluralistic tolerance in democratic society (by ensuring that diverse information about different groups in society is transmitted through different outlets); its ability to strengthen a broad range of democratic values and goals (by ensuring that diverse information of all kinds is transmitted through different outlets). The reference to "media- and information-related pluralism" captures the importance of both structures (i.e., conduits and discursive fora) and content (ideas, opinions and information).

This Chapter endorses the description of the State obligation to guarantee pluralism in the media sector as an imperfect communicative obligation as the obligation is not due to specific individuals and it is not correlative to a particular right in the Hohfeldian sense. Nevertheless, it is a vital aspect of the right to freedom of expression and of democratic communication. Thus styled, media- and information-related pluralism is difficult to define, quantify or operationalise.

This Chapter therefore disaggregates the concept and explains its importance at various levels, in particular source/ownership, outlet and content. These levels span structures, processes and output; each of which offers opportunities for participation and discrimination/exclusion. The distinction between different levels allows for the meaningful application of considerations of media functionality in respect of the communicative needs and interests of persons belonging to minorities. International human rights treaties and other legally-binding texts regulating broadcasting at the global and European levels inadequately reflect this conceptual disaggregation and its practical advantages. A number of standard-setting initiatives that are not legally-binding on States do, however, recognise the theoretical and strategic benefits of such a differentiated approach to the safeguarding and promotion of media- and information-related pluralism. If relevant treaty monitoring processes were to be increasingly characterised by disaggregated approaches along the lines outlined above, it would greatly enhance progress towards the realisation of an objective that all-too-often remains out of reach due to the perceived vagueness of its essential features and its status as an imperfect obligation.

Chapter 10
Cultural and linguistic diversity

Introduction[1]

Having considered various aspects of media-related pluralism, the topics of cultural and linguistic diversity will be treated at this juncture, as they are specific applications of more general principles of pluralism and diversity. Cultural and linguistic diversity are major components of overall diversity of media content, but in keeping with the discussion in the previous chapter, some structural modalities can prove very influential in determining the level of cultural and linguistic diversity that is assured at the content-level. For instance, the UNESCO Convention on the Protection and Promotion of the Diversity of Cultural Expressions, discussed in Chapter 10.2.2, contains a number of provisions that reflect this realisation. As the media are important vectors of culture and language, their ability to contribute to the promotion of cultural and linguistic diversity, especially in terms of media output, should not be underestimated.

10.1 Connecting pluralistic tolerance and media-related pluralism to cultural and linguistic diversity

Culture has been described as "an overworked concept with little semantic precision",[2] and cultural rights as "the Cinderella of the human rights family".[3] To continue in the same metaphorical vein, the objective of promoting cultural diversity

---

1 The analysis in this Chapter draws, in places, on earlier work by the author, including "Promoting cultural diversity in the Irish broadcasting sector: an assessment of international standards and best practices with a view to their operationalisation in an Irish context", Study funded by a Broadcasting Authority of Ireland research grant, April 2010 and "The Promotion of Cultural Diversity via New Media Technologies: An Introduction to the Challenges of Operationalisation", *IRIS plus* (Supplement to *IRIS – Legal Observations of the European Audiovisual Observatory*, 2008–6).

2 Asbjorn Eide, "Cultural Rights as Individual Human Rights", in Asbjorn Eide *et al.*, Eds., *Economic, Social and Cultural Rights* (2nd Edition) (The Netherlands, Kluwer Law International, 2001), pp. 289–301, at 290.

3 G. Filibek, as cited in Halina Niec, "Casting the foundation for the implementation of cultural rights", in Halina Niec, Ed., *Cultural Rights and Wrongs: A collection of essays in commemoration of the 50th anniversary of the Universal Declaration of Human Rights* (United Kingdom, UNESCO, 1998), pp. 176–189, at 176. See also in this connection, Yvonne Donders, *Towards a Right to Cultural Identity?* (Antwerp/Oxford/New York, Intersentia, 2002), pp. 65 *et seq.*

could be considered a jaded ideal, worn-out by unfulfilled ambition and under-appreciation. Preambular provisions of treaties and non-binding standard-setting texts routinely refer to the objective of promoting cultural diversity, but only intermittently attempt to prise open the notion or provide for its concrete application. In recent years, however, the substantive sections of a variety of normative texts at European and international levels have begun to explore the content and scope of cultural diversity, as well as its relationship with "traditional" and "new" media technologies alike. The purpose of this Chapter is to explore the relationship between cultural rights and cultural diversity; examine what cultural diversity actually entails; explain why it ought to be promoted, and assess the important role of the media (traditional and new) in advancing that aim.

10.1.1 Defining culture and cultural rights

Culture is, as has already been suggested, a very nebulous concept, which explains why international instruments rarely seek to define its content or scope. One notable exception to this general reluctance is the UNESCO Universal Declaration on Cultural Diversity (2001),[4] the Preamble of which reaffirms that culture should be regarded as:

> the set of distinctive spiritual, material, intellectual and emotional features of society or a social group, and that it encompasses, in addition to art and literature, lifestyles, ways of living together, value systems, traditions and beliefs.

Even if they are in short supply in international instruments, attempted definitions of "culture" are important because they can serve as a basis for defining and determining the scope of cultural rights.[5] In the past, cultural rights have suffered from relative neglect and their development has proved somewhat stunted as a result. This relative neglect can be attributed to a number of factors, all of which concern perceptions about the status of cultural rights. For example, for as long as the view was entertained that a dichotomy existed between so-called first and second generations of human rights, i.e., civil and political rights on the one hand and economic, social and cultural rights on the other hand, cultural rights tended to be located in the latter category. Nowadays, the dominant view is that all human rights are interdependent and interrelated[6] and purported qualitative distinctions

---

4 Adopted unanimously by the UNESCO General Conference at its 31st session on 2 November 2001. For a detailed overview of UNESCO's other standard-setting and activities in the realm of culture, see generally: Yvonne Donders, "The History of the UNESCO Convention on the Protection and Promotion of the Diversity of Cultural Expressions" in Hildegard Schneider & Peter van den Bossche, Eds., *Protection of Cultural Diversity from a European and International Perspective* (Antwerp, Intersentia, 2008), pp. 1–30.

5 See generally: Adam Kuper, *Culture: The Anthropologists' Account* (Cambridge, Massachusetts/London, England, Harvard University Press, 1999).

6 World Conference on Human Rights – The Vienna Declaration, 1993 (esp. Article 5).

between both sets of rights (e.g. the assumption that economic, social and cultural rights do not give rise to firm State obligations) are consequently dismissed.[7] In any case, cultural rights would be best understood as spanning both categories, as will be demonstrated, *infra*. Whether cultural rights should be classed as individual or collective rights has also tended to be a perennial subject of debate.[8] A balanced view has been proposed which styles cultural rights as individual rights with a powerful collective dimension. Very often, cultural rights are primarily regarded as minority rights. While it cannot be gainsaid that cultural rights are indeed of vital importance for persons belonging to minorities who wish to protect and develop their cultures, it is inaccurate to claim that cultural rights are the preserve of minorities: dominant societal groups also have very valid and vested interests in maintaining their cultures.[9] It is therefore more correct to speak of the enhanced value of cultural rights for persons belonging to minorities than to claim exclusivity of relevance.

Next to the UNESCO Declaration – with its specific focus on cultural *diversity* – other more general international human rights instruments also contain occasional references to various rights associated with the enjoyment of culture, but without attempting to provide a comprehensive definition of the concept. For instance, Article 27(1) of the Universal Declaration of Human Rights reads: "Everyone has the right freely to participate in the cultural life of the community, to enjoy the arts and to share in scientific advancement and its benefits".[10]

Pursuant to Article 27 of the International Covenant on Civil and Political Rights (ICCPR), persons belonging to ethnic, religious or linguistic minorities shall not be

---

7 See further: Christian Tomuschat, *Human Rights: Between Idealism and Realism* (Second Edition) (Oxford, Oxford University Press, 2008), Chapter 3; Cees Flinterman, "Three Generations of Human Rights", in Jan Berting *et al.*, Eds., *Human Rights in a Pluralist World: Individuals and Collectivities* (Westport & London, Netherlands Commission for UNESCO/ Roosevelt Study Center/Meckler, 1990), pp. 75–81.

8 For a representative view of both sides of the debate, see, respectively: Asbjorn Eide, "Cultural Rights as Individual Human Rights", *op. cit.*; Lyndel V. Prott, "Cultural Rights as Peoples' Rights in International Law", in James Crawford, Ed., *The Rights of Peoples* (Oxford, Clarendon Press, 1988), pp. 93–106.

9 See generally: Asbjorn Eide, "Cultural Rights and Minorities: Essay in Honour of Erica-Irene Daes", in Gudmundur Alfredsson & Maria Stavropoulou, Eds., *Justice Pending: Indigenous Peoples and Other Good Causes* (The Hague, Martinus Nijhoff Publishing, 2002), pp. 83–97; Wolf Mannens, "The International Status of Cultural Rights for National Minorities", in Peter Cumper & Steven Wheatley, Eds., *Minority Rights in the 'New' Europe* (Great Britain, Kluwer Law International, 1999), pp. 185–196.

10 For commentary on Article 27, UDHR, and its drafting history, see, Albert Verdoodt, *Naissance et signification de la Déclaration des droits de l'homme* (Louvain, E. Warny, 1964), pp. 252–257; Yvonne Donders, *Towards a Right to Cultural Identity?*, *op. cit.*, pp. 139–144; Elsa Stamatopoulou, *Cultural Rights in International Law: Article 27 of the Universal Declaration and Beyond* (Leiden/Boston, Martinus Nijhoff Publishers, 2007).

denied the right *inter alia* "to enjoy their own culture". In order to uphold this right, "positive measures of protection" are required "not only against the acts of the State party itself, whether through its legislative, judicial or administrative authorities, but also against the acts of other persons within the State party".[11] Thus, Article 27, ICCPR, not only sets out positive obligations for States, it also envisages the horizontal application of those obligations to other actors. Furthermore, "ensuring the survival and continued development" of minority identities is linked to the enrichment of "the fabric of society as a whole" – an important argument for cultural diversity.[12]

The UN Human Rights Committee generally tends to find that Article 27 has been violated when an impugned measure has an impact so substantial that it in effect denies the complainant the right to enjoy his/her cultural rights.[13] More specifically, where "the use of a minority language press as means of airing issues of significance and importance" to a particular minority community, "by both editors and readers", is deemed to be "an essential element" of the minority's culture, an interference with the use of the minority language press can lead to a violation of Article 27.[14] This reasoning is applicable *mutatis mutandis* to broadcasting and other types of media.

For its part, Article 15 of the International Covenant on Economic, Social and Cultural Rights (ICESCR), formulates the right of everyone to participate in cultural life, to benefit from scientific progress and its applications and to enjoy intellectual property rights.[15]

For present purposes, cultural rights will be understood as a cluster of rights, and as including distinct cultural rights as well as cultural dimensions to a range of other human rights.[16] The exercise of cultural rights therefore entails the right to maintain and develop one's cultural identity, lead particular lifestyles, participate in cultural life and assemble, associate and organise for cultural purposes. The right to participate in cultural life implies the ability to access and exploit cultural heritage (including as recorded in audiovisual formats). Cultural heritage has been described as "a group of resources inherited from the past which people identify, independently

---

11 United Nations Human Rights Committee, General Comment No. 23: The rights of minorities (Art. 27), Doc. No. CCPR/C/21/Rev.1/Add.5, adopted on 8 April 1994, para. 6.1.

12 *Ibid.*, para. 9.

13 *Länsman et al. v. Finland*, Communication No. 511/1992, Views adopted on 26 October 1994, para. 9.5.

14 *Mavlonov & Sa'di v. Uzbekistan*, Communication No. 1334/2004, Views adopted on 19 March 2009, para. 8.7.

15 For commentary on Article 15, ICESCR, its drafting history and application, see, Yvonne Donders, *Towards a Right to Cultural Identity?*, *op. cit.*, pp. 144–162.

16 *Ibid.*, p. 73.

of ownership, as a reflection and expression of their constantly evolving values, beliefs, knowledge and traditions. It includes all aspects of the environment resulting from the interaction between people and places through time".[17]

10.1.2 Defining cultural diversity

When examining the notion of cultural diversity, it is important to avoid terminological entrapment. It is not sufficient to monitor the frequency with which the precise term, "cultural diversity", appears in normative human rights texts at the international level. One must instead look beyond the term and ensure that terminological variants and adjacent notions are also identified and examined. Thus, "cultural pluralism", will often be relevant, given its semantic congruence with "cultural diversity". Furthermore, "cultural heritage" and "cultural rights" can also usually lay claim to relevance, due to their relationship with "cultural diversity", as set out, *supra*. The same is true of "linguistic diversity" and "media pluralism".[18]

Cultural diversity is not a right, as such, or at least not a right that is straightforwardly justiciable. Rather, it can usefully be treated as an operative public value, in the sense developed by Bhikhu Parekh. He labels "operative public values" those values "that a society cherishes as part of its collective identity and in terms of which it regulates the relations between its members", and which "constitute the moral structure of its public life and give it coherence and stability".[19] To describe cultural diversity as an operative public value is therefore to insist that it is more than just a guiding interpretive principle for law- and policy-making. It is to point to the need to operationalise the notion; to incorporate it into regulatory, policy-making and institutional structures and practices and thereby ensure that it is meaningfully applied. Although the term, "operative public value" is academic in origin, the approach it implies is broadly consistent with that envisaged by a number of standard-setting texts at the international level, which employ different terminology. For instance, cultural diversity is described as an "essential public interest objective" in CM Recommendation Rec(2003)9 to member states on measures to promote the democratic and social contribution of digital broadcasting. Irrespective of the precise terminology used, the challenges of operationalisation remain the same.

---

17 Article 2a, Council of Europe Framework Convention on the Value of Cultural Heritage for Society, CETS No. 199, 27 October 2005.

18 The multivalent character of the notion of cultural diversity is captured in Article 6 of the UNESCO Declaration on Cultural Diversity.

19 Bhikhu Parekh, *Rethinking Multiculturalism: Cultural Diversity and Political Theory* (2nd Edition) (New York, Palgrave Macmillan, 2006), p. 363.

10.1.3 Rationales for the promotion of cultural diversity

Various rationales are advanced for promoting cultural diversity in normative texts at the European and international levels.[20] For present purposes, they will be loosely grouped as follows: the intrinsic argument; the identity argument; the non-discrimination/equality argument; the democratic argument; the societal argument, and the economic argument. Each of these rationales will now be briefly considered in turn.

Intrinsic Argument

Simply stated, this argument holds that cultural diversity is valuable in and of itself. It is intrinsically beneficial. The argument derives from the view that every culture is an inherent source of wealth and that their co-existence ultimately leads to their mutual enrichment.[21]

Identity Argument

This argument is premised on the view that cultural diversity arises from the co-existence of a multiplicity of cultural identities and practices. As such, the identity argument can be grounded in concerns for individual and group dignity. If individuals and groups are denied the freedom to maintain and develop their identities, including through exercising their rights to freedom of expression, association, etc., their dignity can be adversely affected.

Non-discrimination/Equality Argument

This argument draws on the transversal effects of the right not to be subjected to discrimination: the right necessarily extends to cultural rights. If the principles of non-discrimination and equality were not applied in respect of cultural rights, the prospect of achieving cultural diversity in society would be seriously curtailed.

Democratic Argument

The non-discrimination/equality argument also feeds into the democratic argument, which prioritises participation in public life, including cultural life[22] and public

---

20 For a concise, but representative overview, see *ibid.*, pp. 165–178.

21 The intrinsic argument is approximated in Article 1, UNESCO Declaration on Cultural Diversity, the Preamble to the UNESCO Convention on the Protection and Promotion of Cultural Expressions, and in a Eurocentric way in Article 167 TEC.

22 Article 15, FCNM.

debate.[23] As reasoned by Ed Baker, "[v]oice, more than vote, creates public opinion and provides the possibility of deliberation".[24] As the media are "the central *institution* of a democratic public sphere",[25] their role is crucial in promoting participation and cultural diversity. Access to cultural heritage is of considerable practical importance for democratic participation.[26]

Societal Argument

The societal argument holds that cultural diversity is "a source and factor, not of division, but of enrichment for each society".[27] It also holds that "a climate of tolerance and dialogue" is necessary for the realisation of this aim.[28] In other words, pluralistic tolerance is a precondition for cultural diversity, which in turn enhances societal cohesion and stability.

Economic Argument

This argument acknowledges the economic importance of the culture industries.[29] Creativity and diversity (cultural and linguistic) can stimulate economies and (labour) markets. Such acknowledgements complement a strictly human rights-based approach and make for a more multi-faceted approach to cultural diversity. Another dimension to this argument implicates cultural heritage, the active protection of which has been identified as "a central factor in the mutually supporting objectives of sustainable development, cultural diversity and contemporary creativity".[30]

The applicability of each of the above rationales is potentially subject to a common limitation: the question of whether the promotion of cultural diversity should entail the promotion of intolerant or repressive cultures. As noted by Davina Cooper: "in its enthusiasm to challenge disadvantage and to celebrate variety, diversity politics

---

23 European Commission, White Paper on a European Communication Policy, COM(2006) 35 final, Brussels, 1 February 2006, pp. 5–6.

24 C. Edwin Baker, "Viewpoint Diversity and Media Ownership", 60 *Federal Communications Law Journal* (No. 3, 2009), p. 651–671, at 654.

25 (emphasis per original), *ibid.*

26 Article 12, Council of Europe Framework Convention on the Value of Cultural Heritage for Society.

27 Recital 8, Preamble to FCNM.

28 *Ibid.*

29 This argument features strongly in relevant EU texts, but its relevance is also readily acknowledged in other texts, such as those emanating from the Council of Europe (e.g. CM Declaration on cultural diversity, para. 2.2) and the UNESCO Convention on the Protection and Promotion of the Diversity of Cultural Expressions.

30 Article 5, Council of Europe Framework Convention on the Value of Cultural Heritage for Society, *op. cit.*

comes unstuck when it is confronted with less attractive ways of living and being".[31] The question is vexed and it has generated extensive academic discussion, in particular in political science, cultural and legal studies.[32] Whereas a proper exploration of this discussion is beyond the scope of the present study, it remains important to acknowledge this potential limitation on the scope of cultural diversity. It can, for instance, assume great practical importance when the details of resource allocation or distributive policies are being worked out by policy-makers.

10.2 Universal standards: centrality of UNESCO instruments

10.2.1 UNESCO Declaration on Cultural Diversity[33]

As well as attempting to give shape to the notion of cultural diversity, the Preamble to the Declaration seeks to explicate the societal importance of the notion. It notes, for instance, that "culture is at the heart of contemporary debates about identity, social cohesion, and the development of a knowledge-based economy". It affirms that "respect for the diversity of cultures, tolerance, dialogue and cooperation, in a climate of mutual trust and understanding, are among the best guarantees of international peace and security". It also considers that "the process of globalization, facilitated by the rapid development of new information and communication technologies, though representing a challenge for cultural diversity, creates the conditions for renewed dialogue among cultures and civilizations". These preambular emphases already point towards the relevance of the substantive provisions of the Declaration to the cultural rights, needs and interests of persons belonging to minorities. On a general level, they can be said to collectively address overarching and often overbearing public policy questions, the successful resolution of which necessarily requires the effective participation of persons belonging to minorities. Importantly, the quoted preambular statements also recognise the complex ability of modern media to influence the formal and informal processes involved.

---

31 Davina Cooper, *Challenging Diversity: Rethinking Equality and the Value of Difference* (Cambridge, Cambridge University Press, 2004), p. 40.

32 For example, see generally: Will Kymlicka, *Multicultural Citizenship: A Liberal Theory of Minority Rights* (New York, Oxford University Press, 1995); Bhikhu Parekh, *Rethinking Multiculturalism: Cultural Diversity and Political Theory* (Second Edition) *op. cit.*; Dominic McGoldrick, "Multiculturalism and its Discontents", 5 *Human Rights Law Review* (No. 1, 2005), pp. 27–56.

33 Adopted unanimously by the UNESCO General Conference at its 31st session on 2 November 2001. For a detailed overview of UNESCO's other standard-setting and activities in the realm of culture, see generally: Yvonne Donders, "The History of the UNESCO Convention on the Protection and Promotion of the Diversity of Cultural Expressions", *op. cit.*

As an instrument devoted entirely to cultural diversity, the UNESCO Universal Declaration provides plenty of scope for in-depth exploration of its various component elements. Article 1 of the Declaration recognises that culture is not static and that its development is influenced by temporal and spatial considerations. It describes cultural diversity as "a source of exchange, innovation and creativity" and thus "the common heritage of humanity" which "should be recognized and affirmed for the benefit of present and future generations". This description, consistent with prevailing international standards, argues against any fly-in-amber style of preserving cultures, including minority cultures. In other words, cultures are organic and diverse and should be celebrated as such. The intergenerational transmission of cultural heritage in viable formats is of particular importance for ailing or endangered cultures.

Article 2, entitled "From cultural diversity to cultural pluralism", fails to elucidate the conceptual distinction between its two main focuses, but its underlying message is of particular relevance:

> In our increasingly diverse societies, it is essential to ensure harmonious interaction among people and groups with plural, varied and dynamic cultural identities as well as their willingness to live together. Policies for the inclusion and participation of all citizens are guarantees of social cohesion, the vitality of civil society and peace. Thus defined, cultural pluralism gives policy expression to the reality of cultural diversity. Indissociable from a democratic framework, cultural pluralism is conducive to cultural exchange and to the flourishing of creative capacities that sustain public life.

Article 3 mentions the contribution of cultural diversity to the development of economic and wholistic human capacities, all of which are of relevance for the purposes of personal self-fulfilment/realisation. Article 4 is easily recognisable as an abuse of rights clause: it states that cultural diversity may not be invoked to infringe upon or limit the scope of human rights, as guaranteed by international law. It emphasises that cultural diversity, human dignity and human rights and fundamental freedoms, "in particular the rights of persons belonging to minorities and those of indigenous peoples", are all bound together.

In the logic of the universality, indivisibility and interdependence of human rights, Article 5, entitled "Cultural rights as an enabling environment for cultural diversity", states that the full realisation of cultural rights is a prerequisite of cultural diversity. After referring to Article 27, UDHR, and Articles 13 and 15, ICESCR, it states that, "subject to respect for human rights and fundamental freedoms", all persons have the right to:

- "express themselves and to create and disseminate their work in the language of their choice, and particularly in their mother tongue";

- [enjoy] "quality education and training that fully respect their cultural identity";
- "participate in the cultural life of their choice and conduct their own cultural practices".

Article 6 articulates the importance of access to cultural diversity. It underscores the instrumental role of the media (traditional and new) in this regard: "Freedom of expression, media pluralism, multilingualism, equal access to art and to scientific and technological knowledge, including in digital form, and the possibility for all cultures to have access to the means of expression and dissemination are the guarantees of cultural diversity".

Subsequent Articles draw attention to the potential of cultural heritage for stimulating creativity and furthering intercultural dialogue (Article 7); "the specificity of cultural goods and services which, as vectors of identity, values and meaning, must not be treated as mere commodities or consumer goods" (Article 8); the importance of cultural policies for the creation of "conditions conducive to the production and dissemination of diversified cultural goods and services through cultural industries that have the means to assert themselves at the local and global level" and the prerogative of States to define and develop their own cultural policies (with due regard for their international obligations) (Article 9). Articles 10 and 11 focus respectively on "Strengthening capacities for creation and dissemination worldwide" and "Building partnerships between the public sector, the private sector and civil society". Finally, Article 12 outlines the role of UNESCO in respect of the Declaration and its responsibilities arising therefrom.

10.2.2 UNESCO Convention on the Protection and Promotion of the Diversity of Cultural Expressions

A new high water-mark was arguably reached on 20 October 2005, when the General Conference of UNESCO adopted a Convention on the Protection and Promotion of the Diversity of Cultural Expressions by 148 votes to two, with four abstentions.[34] The Convention represents a new terminological departure and an

---

34 Israel and the USA voted against the Convention and Australia, Honduras, Liberia and Nicaragua abstained. For a more comprehensive overview of the Convention's scope and provisions, see: Tarlach McGonagle, "UNESCO: New Convention on Diversity of Cultural Expressions", *IRIS – Legal Observations of the European Audiovisual Observatory*, 2005–10: 2; Rostam J. Neuwirth, "'United in Divergency?': A Commentary on the UNESCO Convention on the Protection and Promotion of the Diversity of Cultural Expressions", ZaöRV 66 (2006), 819–862. For details of the background to the adoption of the Convention and a critical analysis of its provisions, see: Hélène Ruiz Fabri, "Jeux dans la fragmentation: la Convention sur la promotion et la protection de la diversité des expressions culturelles", R.G.D.I.P. 2007–1, 43–87; Yvonne Donders, "The History of the UNESCO Convention on the Protection and Promotion of the Diversity of Cultural Expressions", *op. cit.*

adjusted conceptual positioning. The shift in terminology – from cultural diversity (as in the eponymous UNESCO Declaration) to the diversity of cultural expressions – is not merely semantic. It was a deliberate ploy by States, adopted at the very outset of the drafting process, to seek to narrow the focus of the proposed Convention.[35] The shift has been noted with a measure of trepidation by some commentators, who feel that it breaks continuity with a term that had been achieving a certain anchorage in relevant standard-setting and discussions on the international plane.[36] The conceptual repositioning involves greater attention for means than for ends and for the conviction that cultural diversity is instrumental in securing a range of cultural freedoms and exchange, including the free flow of cultural activities, goods and services.[37]

The Convention seeks to protect and promote the diversity of cultural expressions and to create an appropriate climate in which cultures can thrive. Other key goals are to strengthen awareness of and respect for such diversity at all levels and to encourage intercultural interaction and dialogue. The Convention also aims to stress the linkage "between culture and development for all countries, particularly for developing countries" and to "give recognition to the distinctive nature of cultural activities, goods and services as vehicles of identity, values and meaning". Of particular importance is its reaffirmation of "the sovereign rights of States to maintain, adopt and implement policies and measures that they deem appropriate for the protection and promotion of the diversity of cultural expressions on their territory". This objective clearly seeks to ensure that States retain control over their own cultural policies in the face of interventionist proclivities exhibited by various IGOs (not least concerning trade agreements). It is revisited in Article 5 of the Convention, where its reaffirmation has been referred to as the "normative heart" of the Convention.[38] As an objective, State sovereignty in cultural matters is an important precondition for the ability to adopt the programmatic measures envisaged under Articles 7 and 8 of the Convention to promote and protect cultural expressions (see further, *infra*). The Convention also aims to strengthen international cooperation and solidarity, especially by "enhancing the capacities of developing countries in order to protect and promote the diversity of cultural expressions".

It is useful at this juncture, after having explained the emphasis on State sovereignty and before examining the stated "Guiding Principles" of the Convention, to recall

---

35 Yvonne Donders, "The History of the UNESCO Convention on the Protection and Promotion of the Diversity of Cultural Expressions", *op. cit.*

36 See, for example, Rostam J. Neuwirth, "'United in Divergency?': A Commentary on the UNESCO Convention on the Protection and Promotion of the Diversity of Cultural Expressions", *op. cit.*, at 831.

37 Hélène Ruiz Fabri, "Jeux dans la fragmentation: la Convention sur la promotion et la protection de la diversité des expressions culturelles", *op. cit.*, at 53.

38 "Le coeur normative de la convention": *ibid.*, at 71.

Yvonne Donders' cautionary observation that the Convention is not and was never intended to be a human rights instrument, *proprement dit*.[39] It focuses on States' prerogatives (in particular to "introduce culturally motivated measures"[40]) as opposed to individual human rights, although the latter are listed among the Convention's "Guiding Principles".

Article 2 sets out those "Guiding Principles": respect for human rights and fundamental freedoms; [State] sovereignty; equal dignity and respect for all cultures; international solidarity and cooperation; the complementarity of economic and cultural aspects of development; sustainable development; equitable access, and openness and balance. It should be noted in passing that the principle of equal dignity and respect for all cultures, as outlined, includes a specific reference to the cultures of persons belonging to minorities and indigenous peoples. It is also noteworthy that the principle of equitable access to a "rich and diversified range of cultural expressions from all over the world and access of cultures to the means of expressions and dissemination" is considered an important factor for "enhancing cultural diversity and encouraging mutual understanding". Here, as in an increasing number of international treaties, the interlinkage between freedom of expression (i.e., to receive and impart ideas and information), cultural diversity and understanding/tolerance, is set out in explicit fashion.

The definitional framework for the Convention is provided in Article 4, which states that cultural diversity "refers to the manifold ways in which the cultures of groups and societies find expression" – both within and among groups and societies. It further points to the possibility that such expression can take place through a variety of activities, means and technologies. This recognition is important in respect of media regulation and is considered in more detail in Chapter 3. "Cultural expressions" are described as "those expressions that result from the creativity of individuals, groups and societies, and that have cultural content". The significance of the focus on cultural activities, goods and services has already been adverted to, *supra*. They are taken to be "activities, goods and services, which at the time they are considered as a specific attribute, use or purpose, embody or convey cultural expressions, irrespective of the commercial value they may have". By highlighting that activities, goods and services can have inherent cultural features, notwithstanding the co-existence of commercial features, this definitional provision provides support for the claim that a main purpose of the Convention is political delineation. Hélène Ruiz Fabri, for instance, has argued that the Convention

39 Yvonne Donders, "The History of the UNESCO Convention on the Protection and Promotion of the Diversity of Cultural Expressions", *op. cit.*

40 Rachael Craufurd Smith, "The UNESCO Convention on the Protection and Promotion of the Diversity of Cultural Expressions: Building a New World Information and Communication Order?", 1 *International Journal of Communication* (2007), pp. 24–55.

constitutes a basis for mounting a challenge to an exclusively commercial approach to relevant issues.[41]

Article 5 reiterates the sovereign rights of States in respect of cultural matters and Article 6 proceeds to explore a range of measures that States Parties may adopt with a view to protecting and promoting the diversity of cultural expressions. A list of illustrative examples of appropriate measures is preferred to a general definition of the same. The indicative list of measures includes: regulation; public financing; provision of opportunities for the "creation, production, dissemination, distribution and enjoyment of such domestic cultural activities, goods and services, including provisions relating to the language used for such activities, goods and services"; ensuring effective access for "domestic independent cultural industries and activities in the informal sector" to "the means of production, dissemination and distribution of cultural activities, goods and services"; encouragement of [efforts of] non-profit organisations, public and private institutions, artists and other cultural professionals; establishment and support of public institutions, "as appropriate". Last, but certainly not least, "measures aimed at enhancing diversity of the media, including through public service broadcasting", are also contemplated.

The promotion and protection of cultural expressions are each given separate consideration in the context of States Parties' relevant rights and obligations (Articles 7 and 8, respectively). No explanation is offered for the curious inversion of "promotion" and "protection": protection is logically prior to promotion and such an ordering is reflected in the title of the Convention itself, as well as elsewhere in international human rights law. Whereas earlier drafts of the Convention had proposed the imposition of substantive obligations on States Parties for the realisation of the aims of the Convention, they were progressively watered down and were not retained in the adopted text. This is perhaps explainable by a concern to make the Convention palatable to a larger number of States, including those with weak economies which would be apprehensive about the financial implications of (additional and specific) positive obligations.

Under Article 7 ('Measures to promote cultural expressions'), States Parties "shall endeavour to create in their territory an environment which encourages individuals and social groups" to carry out a number of activities. Reliance on weak wording like "endeavour" and vague aims like the creation of an environment which encourages certain action, does not augur well for the effective attainment of the aims in question. The shortcomings of this kind of language have already been exposed in some detail in respect of the FCNM, where such formulations are recurrent. In the first place, individuals and social groups should be encouraged:

41 Hélène Ruiz Fabri, "Jeux dans la fragmentation: la Convention sur la promotion et la protection de la diversité des expressions culturelles", *op. cit.*, at 55.

> to create, produce, disseminate, distribute and have access to their own cultural expressions, paying due attention to the special circumstances and needs of women as well as various social groups, including persons belonging to minorities and indigenous peoples.

This reference to creation, production, dissemination, distribution and access to cultural expressions, like other similarly itemised references elsewhere in the Convention, is important as it implicates a range of actors at different stages of the generation and transmission of cultural expressions.[42] The explicit call for attention for the situational specificities of persons belonging to minorities is also welcome. Both of these references are meaningful considerations when it comes to the actual realisation of the right to freedom of expression for persons belonging to minorities.

Secondly, individuals and groups should be encouraged "to have access to diverse cultural expressions from within their territory as well as from other countries of the world". The importance of the transnational dimension has traditionally suffered from relative neglect in discussions about "cultural diversity" (to revert to more familiar parlance). However, the requirement that States endeavour to create an environment which encourages its subjects to have access to diverse cultural expressions is lofty and does not give rise to any justiciable or even quantifiable legal obligation. Alternative wording could have required States to endeavour to facilitate effective access to diverse cultural expressions of domestic and foreign origin. Such wording does not give rise to easily assessable legal obligations either, but it would signal a more serious sense of moral commitment than the present wording. Finally, the wording employed in Article 7(2)[43] saps the provision of all vigour and helps to compound the criticism that the Convention's objectives are poorly served by its "substantive" provisions.[44] It requires States to "endeavour to recognize" the important contribution and roles of artists, communities and organisations involved in cultural creativity to the fostering of the diversity of cultural expressions.

Article 8 is entitled 'Measures to protect cultural expressions'. More specifically, it concerns the ability of a State Party "to determine the existence of special situations where cultural expressions on its territory are at risk of extinction, under serious threat, or otherwise in need of urgent safeguarding". Even in such situations of real

---

42 See also: Hélène Ruiz Fabri, "Jeux dans la fragmentation: la Convention sur la promotion et la protection de la diversité des expressions culturelles", *op. cit.*, at 73.

43 Article 7(2) reads: "Parties shall also endeavour to recognize the important contribution of artists, others involved in the creative process, cultural communities, and organizations that support their work, and their central role in nurturing the diversity of cultural expressions".

44 For a different version of this criticism, see: Rostam J. Neuwirth, "'United in Divergency?': A Commentary on the UNESCO Convention on the Protection and Promotion of the Diversity of Cultural Expressions", *op. cit.*, at 861.

peril for cultural expressions (overlooking the awkwardness of the reference to a risk of extinction of cultural expressions (which are by nature inanimate), instead of cultures (which are organic)), a State Party is not obliged to take action, but "may" do so. The failure to prescribe concrete action by States in such scenarios and only to allow it provides further evidence of the Convention's overall weakness.[45] Article 17 provides for 'International cooperation in situations of serious threat to cultural expressions', i.e., situations determined in accordance with Article 8.

A number of procedural priorities are identified as being important for the pursuit of the Convention's goals: information-sharing and transparency; education and public awareness; participation of civil society, and promotion of international cooperation (Articles 9–12, respectively). Article 9(a) requires States Parties to "provide appropriate information in their reports to UNESCO every four years on measures taken to protect and promote the diversity of cultural expressions within their territory and at the international level". Rachael Craufurd Smith has lambasted this provision for its inherent weaknesses: no obligation on States Parties to report on their countries' state of cultural diversity in general terms; no obligation to report on measures or factors adversely affecting cultural diversity in their countries; no provision for sanctions for failure to file reports; no provision for effective monitoring and follow-up by an independent body.[46] As such, the promise of more robust proposals on the table during the drafting process failed to materialise.[47]

Article 12(d) explicitly recognises the potential of new technologies to contribute to the attainment of these aims and accordingly calls for the promotion of their use. The Convention also underscores the importance of States Parties' commitment to the integration of culture in their development policies at all levels with a view to maintaining and enhancing the diversity of cultural expressions (Article 13), as well as to "cooperation for sustainable development and poverty reduction, especially in relation to the specific needs of developing countries, in order to foster the emergence of a dynamic cultural sector" (Article 14).

Article 18 of the Convention provides for the establishment of an "International Fund for Cultural Diversity" which is to be financed by, *inter alia*, voluntary contributions by States Parties, "funds appropriated for this purpose by the General Conference of UNESCO", contributions from miscellaneous sources and "any interest due on resources of the Fund". A voluntary basis for financing the Fund can hardly be regarded as a secure basis, so until practice proves otherwise, the

45 See also, Hélène Ruiz Fabri, "Jeux dans la fragmentation: la Convention sur la promotion et la protection de la diversité des expressions culturelles", *op. cit.*, at 72.

46 Rachael Craufurd Smith, "The UNESCO Convention on the Protection and Promotion of the Diversity of Cultural Expressions: Building a New World Information and Communication Order?", *op. cit.*, at 38.

47 *Ibid.*

existence of the Fund can only be viewed as precarious.[48] The administration of the Fund is one of the tasks to be carried out by an Intergovernmental Committee for the Protection and Promotion of the Diversity of Cultural Expressions, set up pursuant to Article 23 of the Convention.

Article 20 is entitled "Relationship to other treaties: mutual supportiveness, complementarity and non-subordination"; as such, it addresses a key preoccupation of States from the very beginning of the drafting process.[49] The compromise wording which prevailed strives to promote complementarity between the Convention and other international treaties; thereby avoiding controversial confrontations or hierarchisations.[50]

The provisions for the settlement of disputes (Article 25 and the Annex entitled 'Conciliation Procedure') are also deficient for their failure to mandate parties involved in the proposed conciliation procedure to accept the findings of the purpose-created Conciliation Commission. The Commission is only empowered to make proposals for the resolution of disputes and the Parties involved are not obliged to accept the same proposals, merely to consider them in good faith. Again, in the absence of provision for possible sanctions for ignoring or rejecting the proposal of the Commission, the dispute-resolution apparatus is rendered potentially toothless.[51]

In accordance with Article 29, having been ratified by the requisite 30 States, the Convention entered into force on 18 March 2007. The accession of the European Community to the Convention on 18 December 2006 proved a crucial catalyst for its entry into force. However, the importance of the Convention had already been recognised by other IGOs, in particular the Council of Europe. The Committee of Ministers of the Council of Europe adopted a Recommendation calling on Member States to ratify, accept, approve or accede to the UNESCO Convention at the earliest opportunity. The Recommendation was prompted by the recognition of "the commonality between the objectives and guiding principles" set out in the Convention and "a number of Council of Europe instruments concerning culture as

48 See further on this point, Rachael Craufurd Smith, "The UNESCO Convention on the Protection and Promotion of the Diversity of Cultural Expressions: Building a New World Information and Communication Order?", *op. cit.*, at 38 and 53.

49 See further: Yvonne Donders, "The History of the UNESCO Convention on the Protection and Promotion of the Diversity of Cultural Expressions", *op. cit.*

50 See further, *ibid.*

51 For further critique, see: Rachael Craufurd Smith, "The UNESCO Convention on the Protection and Promotion of the Diversity of Cultural Expressions: Building a New World Information and Communication Order?", *op. cit.*, at 39.

well as the media".[52] The Recommendation also declared that "in the context of its work, the Council of Europe will have due regard to the provisions of the UNESCO Convention and will contribute to their implementation".

It is, as of yet, too early to evaluate the real (initial) impact of the Convention. Much will depend, as Ruiz Fabri correctly points out, on the establishment and effectiveness of the Convention's organs;[53] State practice relating to the Convention, and the engagement of civil society.[54] She is also right, however, to insist that political and symbolic importance of the adoption and entry-into-force of the Convention should not be understated. The Convention constitutes a significant statement of principle that State sovereignty should apply to cultural matters and thereby a counterweight to forcefully commercial approaches to cultural activities, goods and services.[55] As detailed in the foregoing analysis, certain discrete emphases in the text of the Convention (eg. the link between diversity of cultural expressions and intercultural dialogue and understanding (Article 2); the need to pay due attention to the specific circumstances of persons belonging to minorities (Article 7(1)(a)); threats to cultural expressions (Article 8) and the potential of new technologies to enhance the diversity of cultural expressions) hold considerable promise. Repeated references to the different stages and processes involved in the production, transmission and reception of cultural expressions are also valuable insofar as they prompt a disaggregated approach to the realisation of the right to freedom of expression. This also facilitates the task of addressing bottle-necks in the different stages of cultural activity. However, in practical terms, the programmatic character of envisaged State obligations and the general absence of operationalising criteria that would facilitate their realisation are major hurdles to be cleared.[56] The enduring impact of the Convention is likely to be best measured in terms of symbolism and awareness-raising; its consistent resort to non-committal language, although somewhat offset by intermittently more specific, programmatic provisions, means that it is unlikely to lead to meaningful legal achievements.[57]

---

52 Recommendation Rec(2006)3 of the Committee of Ministers to member states on the UNESCO Convention on the protection and promotion of the diversity of cultural expressions, adopted on 1 February 2006.

53 Hélène Ruiz Fabri, "Jeux dans la fragmentation: la Convention sur la promotion et la protection de la diversité des expressions culturelles", *op. cit.*, at 84.

54 *Ibid*, at 85.

55 *Ibid*, at 55 and 83.

56 Rostam J. Neuwirth, "'United in Divergency?': A Commentary on the UNESCO Convention on the Protection and Promotion of the Diversity of Cultural Expressions", *op. cit.*, at 860; Hélène Ruiz Fabri, "Jeux dans la fragmentation: la Convention sur la promotion et la protection de la diversité des expressions culturelles", *op. cit.*, at 72.

57 C.f. Rachael Craufurd Smith, "The UNESCO Convention on the Protection and Promotion of the Diversity of Cultural Expressions: Building a New World Information and Communication Order?", *op. cit.*, at 53.

10.2.3 World Summit on the Information Society (WSIS)

The Declaration of Principles adopted at the Geneva Phase of WSIS brackets cultural diversity and identity with linguistic diversity and local content.[58] Its approach to the promotion of cultural diversity is content-oriented and technologically-informed. Like the UNESCO Convention on the Protection and Promotion of the Diversity of Cultural Expressions, WSIS explicitly links the wider goal of promoting cultural diversity to the discrete goals of promoting the production of, and accessibility to, different types of content in diverse languages and formats.[59] These goals are, in turn, linked to the goal of promoting wide and inclusive participation in the Information Society.[60] It also emphasises the instrumental role that technology can play in presesrving cultural heritage, which it recognises as "a crucial component of identity and self-understanding of individuals that links a community to its past".[61]

At the Tunis Phase of WSIS, signatory States committed themselves to "promote the inclusion of all peoples in the Information Society through the development and use of local and/or indigenous languages in ICTs" and to generally continue to "protect and promote cultural diversity, as well as cultural identities, within the Information Society".[62] Although the specific interests of persons belonging to minorities are not mentioned in connection with the general goal of promoting cultural diversity, "particular attention" will be paid to the "special needs of marginalized and vulnerable groups of society, including [...] minorities [...]" in building the Information Society.[63]

58 "Building the Information Society: a global challenge in the new Millennium", Declaration of Principles, World Summit on the Information Society, Geneva, 12 December 2003, Doc. WSIS-03/GENEVA/DOC/4-E, Section 8, paras. 52–54.

59 *Ibid.*, para. 53, which reads: "[t]he creation, dissemination and preservation of content in diverse languages and formats must be accorded high priority in building an inclusive Information Society, paying particular attention to the diversity of supply of creative work and due recognition of the rights of authors and artists. It is essential to promote the production of and accessibility to all content – educational, scientific, cultural or recreational – in diverse languages and formats. The development of local content suited to domestic or regional needs will encourage social and economic development and will stimulate participation of all stakeholders, including people living in rural, remote and marginal areas."

60 *Ibid.*

61 *Ibid.*, para. 54.

62 Tunis Commitment, World Summit on the Information Society, Tunis, 18 November 2005, Doc. No. WSIS-05/TUNIS/DOC/7-E, para. 32.

63 WSIS (Geneva Declaration of Principles) "Building the Information Society: a global challenge in the new Millennium", *op. cit.*, para. 13, and reiterated in the Tunis Commitment, *op. cit.*, para. 20.

10.2.4 Joint IGO Special Mandates' Declaration on Diversity in Broadcasting

A final international initiative, which is not legally-binding, is also worthy of note on account of its thematic relevance and political significance: the Joint Declaration on Diversity in Broadcasting, adopted by the IGO specialised mechanisms for freedom of expression and/or the media, in 2007.[64] The United Nations Special Rapporteur on Freedom of Opinion and Expression, the Organization for Security and Co-operation in Europe Representative on Freedom of the Media, the Organization of American States Special Rapporteur on Freedom of Expression and the African Commission on Human and Peoples' Rights Special Rapporteur on Freedom of Expression and Access to Information adopt annual joint declarations on selected themes relating to freedom of expression. Their 2007 Joint Declaration examines general considerations such as regulatory principles and media governance, education and media literacy, transparency, and technological issues. It then prises open the notion of diversity as it applies to broadcasting, by examining, in turn, diversity of outlet, source and content.

10.3 European-level measures concerning cultural diversity

Attention will now turn to a selection of regulatory provisions at the European level which are implicitly, associatively or explicitly styled as promoting cultural diversity. As a result of the pronounced efforts undertaken by the Council of Europe and the European Union to synchronise their respective standard-setting measures pertaining to the audiovisual sector,[65] much of the content of the two IGOs' flagship instruments dealing with transfrontier broadcasting is strikingly similar.[66] Thus, there has traditionally been a degree of overlap between the Council of Europe's European Convention on Transfrontier Television (ECTT)[67] and the EU's Television

---

64 Joint Declaration on Diversity in Broadcasting, adopted by the UN Special Rapporteur on Freedom of Opinion and Expression, the OSCE RFOM, the OAS Special Rapporteur on Freedom of Expression and the ACHPR Special Rapporteur on Freedom of Expression and Access to Information, 12 December 2007. See further, Chapter 9.

65 Explanatory Report to the European Convention on Transfrontier Television, paras. 39, 40. See further: Daniel Krebber, *Europeanisation of Regulatory Television Policy: The Decision-making Process of the Television without Frontiers Directives from 1989 & 1997* (Nomos Verlagsgesellschaft, Baden-Baden, 2002), esp. Chaps. 4, 5 & 6.

66 See further: Tarlach McGonagle, "Workshop Report", in Susanne Nikoltchev, Ed., *IRIS Special: Audiovisual Media Services without Frontiers – Implementing the Rules* (Strasbourg, European Audiovisual Observatory, 2006), pp. 47–59, at 47–49; Pierre Goerens, "Interplay Between Relevant European Legal Instruments – ECTT and TVwF Directive: Competition or Complementarity?", in *ibid.*, pp. 1–11.

67 Council of Europe (1989), *European Convention on Transfrontier Television (1989), ETS No. 132, as amended by its Amending Protocol* (1998), ETS No. 171, which entered into force on 1 March 2002.

without Frontiers Directive (TWF),[68] not least in how they purportedly set out to promote cultural diversity. However, the extent of this overlap has been reduced by the adoption of the EU's Audiovisual Media Services Directive in 2007 and the subsequent discontinuation of the revision of the Council of Europe's ECTT in 2011.

10.3.1 Council of Europe standards

10.3.1(i) Treaty-based standards

Various Council of Europe treaties serve to promote cultural diversity, either directly or indirectly. The European Convention on Human Rights (ECHR) does not explicitly provide for the protection of cultural rights and an initiative proposing to draft an additional protocol to the Convention on cultural rights in the 1990s never came to fruition.[69] However, given that cultural rights include a range of different rights, as outlined, *supra*, it is clear that the ECHR does, in practice, afford cultural rights a considerable degree of protection. Indeed, the growing recognition of cultural rights by the European Court of Human Rights accounts in large measure for what has been termed the Court's "burgeoning minority rights jurisprudence".[70] This case-law focuses on issues such as non-discrimination/equality, enjoyment of a particular way of life, association, religion, education and expression. The present analysis will sketch the interface between this case-law and Article 10, ECHR.

As noted above, pluralism and diversity are contiguous concepts. The European Court of Human Rights has considered the nature of pluralism on numerous occasions (see further, Chapter 5.3). It has repeatedly found that pluralism demands a certain balancing of majority/minority interests and the democratic accommodation of the latter.[71] This finding is firmly anchored in the principle of pluralism, for which freedom of expression is a prerequisite.[72]

---

68 Council Directive 89/552/EEC of 3 October 1989 on the coordination of certain provisions laid down by law, regulation or administrative action in Member States concerning the pursuit of television broadcasting activities, OJ L 298/23, 17 October 1989, and amended by Directive 97/36/EC of the European Parliament and of the Council of 30 June 1997, OJ L 202/60, 30 July 1997.

69 For an overview of the process, see: Patrick Thornberry & Maria Amor Martin Estebanez, *Minority Rights in Europe* (Germany, Council of Europe, 2004), p. 205.

70 Geoff Gilbert, "The Burgeoning Minority Rights Jurisprudence of the European Court of Human Rights", 24 *Human Rights Quarterly* (No. 3, 2002), pp. 736–780.

71 *Young, James & Webster v. United Kingdom*, Judgment of the European Court of Human Rights of 13 August 1981, Series A No. 44 p. 25, para. 63; *Chassagnou & Others v. France*, Judgment of the European Court of Human Rights of 29 April 1999, para. 112; *Gorzelik & Others v. Poland*, Judgment of the European Court of Human Rights (Grand Chamber) of 17 February 2004, para. 90.

72 *Gorzelik & Others v. Poland*, *op. cit.*, paras. 91 and 92.

The Court has also consistently held that the State is the "ultimate guarantor" of the principle of pluralism, especially "in relation to audio-visual media, whose programmes are often broadcast very widely".[73] This important finding points to positive obligations on the part of States authorities in order to uphold pluralism in the (audiovisual) media sector. It is best explained by the democratic argument discussed above. As the Court has also held: "groups and individuals outside the mainstream [must be able] to contribute to the public debate by disseminating information and ideas on matters of general public interest [...]".[74]

Similarly, the Court has found that all sections of the public must be able to receive a wide range of information and ideas. This principle is nicely illustrated in the case, *Khurshid Mustafa & Tarzibachi v. Sweden*.[75] The Court acknowledged that it was of "particular importance" for the applicants, as an immigrant family from Iraq living in Sweden, to be able to receive a wide range of information (i.e., not just political and social news, but also "cultural expressions and pure entertainment") from their country of origin in order to be able to maintain contact with their native culture and language.[76]

The judgment is also noteworthy for the Court's readiness to focus not only on "the substance of the ideas and information expressed, but also the form in which they are conveyed".[77] It found that the applicants:

> might have been able to obtain certain news through foreign newspapers and radio programmes, but these sources of information only cover parts of what is available via television broadcasts and cannot in any way be equated with the latter.[78]

As such, the Court recognises that the mere existence of other expressive or informational opportunities is not sufficient: they must also be viable opportunities in the sense that they are suited to the expressive or informational purpose of the individual or group concerned. One of the upshots of this finding by the Court is that the availability of culturally diverse content in other media does not remove the need for culturally diverse content in the audiovisual sector.

---

73 *Informationsverein Lentia & Others v. Austria*, Judgment of the European Court of Human Rights of 24 November 1993, Series A No. 276, para. 38.

74 *Steel & Morris v. United Kingdom*, Judgment of the European Court of Human Rights (Fourth Section) of 15 February 2005, para. 89.

75 Judgment of the European Court of Human Rights (Third Section) of 16 December 2008. For a short case-note, see: "Eviction: Satellite Dish", E.H.R.L.R. 2009, 2, 268–270.

76 *Ibid.*, para. 44.

77 See, *inter alia*, *Oberschlick v. Austria*, Judgment of the European Court of Human Rights of 23 May 1991, Series A no. 204, para. 57; *Jersild v. Denmark*, Judgment of the European Court of Human Rights of 23 September 1994, Series A no. 298, para. 31.

78 *Khurshid Mustafa & Tarzibachi v. Sweden*, *op. cit.*, para. 45.

Besides the European Convention on Human Rights, the relationship between freedom of expression and cultural and linguistic diversity is palpable in other Council of Europe treaties. One of the early treaties elaborated by the Council of Europe was the European Cultural Convention. It is deliberately general in character and was designed to "foster [...] the study of the languages, history and civilisation of the others and of the civilisation which is common to [all nationals of States Parties to the Convention]".[79] It is an important point of general reference, but it does not specifically address the potential contribution of the media to the promotion of cultural diversity (or, needless to say, that of new media technologies).

Article 10 of the European Convention on Transfrontier Television (ECTT), is entitled "Cultural objectives", but its focus is very Eurocentric and does not explicitly embrace the promotion of cultural diversity *per se*. Rather, it seeks to promote European works/production by requiring broadcasters to devote the majority proportion of their transmission time to European works (Article 10(1)) and to get States to "look together for the most appropriate instruments and procedures to support, without discrimination between broadcasters, the activity and development of European production, particularly in countries with a low audiovisual production capacity or restricted language area" (Article 10(3)). As such, its contribution to the promotion of cultural diversity is limited and specific.

The importance of protecting and promoting cultural heritage and audiovisual heritage for ensuring a favourable enabling environment for the promotion of cultural diversity has already been explained, *supra*. Two Council of Europe treaties dealing specifically with those issues are the Framework Convention on the Value of Cultural Heritage for Society[80] and the European Convention for the Protection of the Audiovisual Heritage.[81]

The Framework Convention on the Value of Cultural Heritage for Society includes useful measures for promoting the protection of cultural heritage, like the requirement that States develop laws and policies for that purpose.[82] Specific emphases within the Framework Convention couple "access to cultural heritage" with "democratic participation" (Article 12) and "cultural heritage" with "knowledge". Such couplings underscore the importance of rendering cultural heritage accessible for the realisation of cultural rights and cultural diversity. A further coupling is of particular relevance for the promotion of cultural diversity by new media technologies: Article 14, entitled "Cultural heritage and the information society". It requires States Parties to "develop the use of digital technology to

---

79 European Cultural Convention, ETS No. 18, 19 December 1954 (entry into force: 5 May 1955), Preamble (Recital 5).

80 *Op. cit.*

81 ETS No. 183, 8 November 2001 (entry into force: 1 January 2008).

82 Article 5, Framework Convention on the Value of Cultural Heritage for Society.

enhance access to cultural heritage and the benefits which derive from it", *inter alia*, by "encouraging initiatives which promote the quality of contents and endeavour to secure diversity of languages and cultures in the information society".[83]

The Convention for the Protection of the Audiovisual Heritage, as its name suggests, focuses on audiovisual material recording and expressing cultural heritage.[84] Its central aim is to:

> ensure the protection of the European audiovisual heritage and its appreciation both as an art form and as a record of our past by means of its collection, its preservation and the availability of moving image material for cultural, scientific and research purposes, in the public interest.[85]

This aim is informed by the realisation that "Europe's heritage reflects the cultural identity and diversity of its peoples"[86] and the recognition that "moving image material",[87] as "a form of cultural expression reflecting contemporary society" and "an excellent means of recording everyday events [...]",[88] is a valuable cultural resource meriting concerted protection by States. Importantly, the Convention anticipates the potential of future technological developments for enhancing the preservation of audiovisual heritage. Article 18 explicitly provides for the conclusion of new Protocols "dealing with moving image material other than cinematographic works [...] with a view to developing, in specific fields, the principles contained in this Convention".

Two examples of treaties which contribute to the promotion of cultural diversity, without that objective necessarily being their central concern, are the European Charter for Regional or Minority Languages (ECRML)[89] and the Framework

---

83 Article 14.a, *ibid.* Undertakings listed in subsequent sub-sections of Article 14 are as follows: "b. supporting internationally compatible standards for the study, conservation, enhancement and security of cultural heritage, whilst combating illicit trafficking in cultural property;
c. seeking to resolve obstacles to access to information relating to cultural heritage, particularly for educational purposes, whilst protecting intellectual property rights;
d. recognising that the creation of digital contents related to the heritage should not prejudice the conservation of the existing heritage".

84 For an overview of the Convention, see: Sabina Gorini, "The Protection of Cinematographic Heritage in Europe", *IRIS plus* (Supplement to *IRIS – Legal Observations of the European Audiovisual Observatory*), 2004–8.

85 Article 1, Convention for the Protection of the Audiovisual Heritage.

86 Recital 3, Preamble, *ibid.*

87 "[M]oving image material" is defined in Article 2a of the Convention as "any set of moving images recorded by whatever means and on whatever medium, whether or not accompanied by sound, capable of conveying an impression of movement".

88 Recital 5, Preamble, *ibid.*

89 ETS No. 148, 5 November 1992 (entry into force: 1 March 1998).

Convention for the Protection of National Minorities (FCNM). In both treaties, the connection between freedom of expression, minority rights and cultural and linguistic diversity is clearly discernible. The Preamble to the ECRML acknowledges that:

> the protection and promotion of regional or minority languages in the different countries and regions of Europe represent an important contribution to the building of a Europe based on the principles of democracy and cultural diversity within the framework of national sovereignty and territorial integrity.[90]

Article 11, ECRML, entitled "Media", sets out a range of specific undertakings to which States can commit in order to promote the use of regional or minority languages in different types of media. The undertakings involve varying degrees of onerousness and the choice between them offers States a lot of flexibility to determine the precise focus and extent of their commitments in respect of the media. Article 11(3) is noteworthy for addressing an often underappreciated factor in the promotion of cultural diversity in the media sector. It offers States the possibility to:

> undertake to ensure that the interests of the users of regional or minority languages are represented or taken into account within such bodies as may be established in accordance with the law with responsibility for guaranteeing the freedom and pluralism of the media.

Article 12, ECRML, is entitled, "Cultural activities and facilities" and comprises a list of possible measures to be taken by States Parties with a view to enhancing cultural activities and facilities in regional or minority languages. The activities and facilities include "especially libraries, video libraries, cultural centres, museums, archives, academies, theatres and cinemas, as well as literary work and film production, vernacular forms of cultural expression, festivals and the culture industries, including **inter alia** the use of new technologies".[91] Thus, the exploitation of new media technologies is expressly envisaged for the development of cultural activities and facilities.[92]

Whereas the title of the FCNM may suggest a certain narrowness of focus, it actually addresses many issues concerning society as a whole, and not only persons belonging to national minorities. It pursues its central objective – the protection of national minorities – in a complex, majority-minority dialectic. In other words, it

90 Recital 7, ECRML. See also, Explanatory Report to the ECRML, para. 11.

91 Bold text per original.

92 For detailed commentary, see: Tom Moring & Robert Dunbar, *The European Charter for Regional or Minority Languages and the media* (Strasbourg, Council of Europe Publishing, 2008).

strives to assure the protection of national minorities within the broader context of pluralist society.[93] The importance of the FCNM has already been referred to in the context of the so-called "societal" argument for promoting cultural diversity. Other provisions of the FCNM provide further evidence of the strong linkage between the goals of promoting tolerance, intergroup understanding and cultural diversity, and in particular, the instrumental importance of the media in respect of each goal:

> The Parties shall encourage a spirit of tolerance and intercultural dialogue and take effective measures to promote mutual respect and understanding and co-operation among all persons living on their territory, irrespective of those persons' ethnic, cultural, linguistic or religious identity, in particular in the fields of education, culture and the media. (Article 6(1), FCNM)

> In the framework of their legal systems, the Parties shall adopt adequate measures in order to facilitate access to the media for persons belonging to national minorities and in order to promote tolerance and permit cultural pluralism. (Article 9(4), FCNM).

In practice, the monitoring of the FCNM involves examination of behavioural and structural media regulation at national and sub-national levels. It also takes account of functional differences between different types of media, eg. public-service, community and commercial, each of which can contribute to the goal of promoting cultural diversity in different ways (see further, Chapter 11.3.1).

10.3.1(ii) Non-treaty-based standards

Alongside the treaty-based standard-setting work of the Council of Europe concerning the promotion of cultural diversity via (new) media, a host of relevant standard-setting texts has also been adopted by its Committee of Ministers (CM). These texts are not legally-binding on the Member States of the Council of Europe, but they are of political importance. They often map out ongoing or anticipated developments in relation to freedom of expression and the media at European and national levels. As such, they are regarded as an important means of ensuring the effective realisation of the right to freedom of expression throughout Europe.[94] The most important of the CM's standard-setting texts for present purposes will now be presented in tabular form:

---

93 This is evident from various preambular provisions and, more substantively, Article 6(1), FCNM.

94 Declaration of the Committee of Ministers on measures to promote the respect of Article 10 of the European Convention on Human Rights, 13 January 2010.

Text	Topic
Declaration (2009)	Role of community media in promoting social cohesion and intercultural dialogue
Declaration (2008)	Allocation & management of the digital dividend & the public interest
Rec (2007) 16	Promotion of public service value of the Internet
Rec (2007) 3	Remit of public service media in the information society
Rec (2007) 2	Media pluralism and diversity of media content
Declaration (2007)	Protecting role of media in democracy & in context of media concentration
Declaration (2006)	Guarantee of the independence of PSB in the member states
Declaration (2005)	Human rights and the rule of law in the Information Society
Rec. No. R (2003) 9	Promotion of democratic and social contribution of digital broadcasting
Political Message (2003)	Political Message to the World Summit on the Information Society
Declaration (2000)	Cultural diversity
Declaration (1999)	A European policy for new information technologies
Rec. No. R (99) 1	Measures to promote media pluralism
Rec. No. R (99) 14	Universal community service concerning new communication and information services
Rec. No. R (96) 10	Guarantee of independence of public service broadcasting
Declaration (1982)	Freedom of expression and information

Instead of conducting an itemised analysis of these CM texts, their essence will be examined in the context of public service broadcasting/media and, more generally, public service values. Beforehand, though, it is necessary to briefly signal the importance of relevant texts emanating from other limbs of the Council of Europe.

The promotion of cultural diversity via the media has regularly appeared on the agenda of European Ministerial Conferences on Mass Media Policy.[95] These Conferences, involving the participation of Ministers (or their delegates) with relevant portfolios at national level, have been held periodically since the mid-1980s. As such, the Ministerial Conferences can be distinguished from the day-to-day activities of the Council of Europe. Their relevance stems from their purpose to map out future European media policy, supplemented by action plans for its implementation. In total, seven such conferences were convened under the auspices of the Council of Europe. The preparation of these Conferences and the implementation of resultant Action Plans are overseen by the Council of Europe's Steering Committee on Media and New Communication Services (CDMC) – an

95 See generally, *European Ministerial Conferences on Mass Media Policy: Texts Adopted*, Media Division, Directorate General of Human Rights, Doc. No. DH-MM (2006) 4 (Strasbourg, 2006).

expert body comprising members nominated by Member States of the Council of Europe.[96] In order to reflect changing notions of the media, the most recent conference, held in Reykjavik in 2009, was calibrated differently – as the "1st Council of Europe Conference of Ministers responsible for Media and New Communication Services".[97]

The prioritisation of the objective of promoting cultural diversity in the digital environment, including the potential role of public service broadcasting, was emphatic in the Ministerial Conference held in Kyiv in 2005, especially in Resolution No. 2, adopted at the Conference: "Cultural diversity and media pluralism in times of globalisation". The Ministerial Conference held in Reykjavik in 2009 picked up on relevant themes, especially in respect of the potential role of public service media. The thrust of the approach taken in the texts adopted at the Reykjavik Conference is to consolidate and continue earlier and ongoing Council of Europe policy-making and standard-setting work in this area.

The Parliamentary Assembly of the Council of Europe has also adopted texts dealing with these issues, most pertinently its Recommendation 1848 and Resolution 1636, both dating from 2008 and both entitled, "Indicators for media in a democracy". Relevant themes also feature in a range of other texts, to varying degrees, including, Recommendation 1878 (2009), "Funding of public service broadcasting"; Recommendation 1855 (2009), "The regulation of audio-visual media services; Recommendation 1067 (1987) on the cultural dimension of broadcasting in Europe; Resolution 1313 (2003), "Cultural co-operation between Europe and the south Mediterranean countries"; Recommendation 1641 (2004), "Public service broadcasting", and Recommendation 1674 (2004), "Challenges facing the European audiovisual sector".

Public service broadcasting/media

By virtue of its philosophy and mandate, public service broadcasting (or public service media, as they are increasingly being called in deference to the diversification of technological forms across which they (may) operate) is simultaneously an ideal agent to, and an ideal forum in which to, promote cultural diversity.[98] The promotion of cultural diversity is widely regarded as a general objective of PSB,[99] but it can

---

96 Terms of reference of the Steering Committee on Media and New Communication Services (CDMC), n.d., para. 4(iv).

97 *A new notion of media?*, 28–29 May 2009, Reykjavik, Iceland.

98 For further analysis, see: Irini Katsirea, "Cultural Diversity in Broadcasting", in David Goldberg, Gavin Sutter & Ian Walden, Eds., *Media Law and Practice* (Oxford, Oxford University Press, 2009), pp. 463–499, at pp. 483–496.

99 Preamble, Declaration on the guarantee of the independence of public service broadcasting in the member states, 27 September 2006; Preamble, Recommendation Rec(2003)9 on measures to

also feature in a more detailed fashion among the more specific objectives of PSB.[100] For example, the CM's Recommendation on the remit of public service media in the information society emphasises that:

> In their programming and content, public service media should reflect the increasingly multi-ethnic and multicultural societies in which they operate, protecting the cultural heritage of different minorities and communities, providing possibilities for cultural expression and exchange, and promoting closer integration, without obliterating cultural diversity at the national level.[101]

It should be noted that the Recommendation understands cultural diversity in an open, inclusive way – there is no question of the notion being restricted to European cultural diversity, as in the aforementioned regulatory measures prescribing the transmission of European audiovisual works. This is clear from para. 24 of the Recommendation, which states: "[p]ublic service media should promote respect for cultural diversity, while simultaneously introducing the audience to the cultures of other peoples around the world".

PSB is currently in a state of transition, but as Karol Jakubowicz has observed, "there was hardly a time in the eight decades of PSB's existence when it was not 'in transition'".[102] He describes the challenges constantly faced by PSB as being "at once conceptual and contextual": different understandings of the role of PSB and the fact that "changing contexts of PSB operation have always affected the shape, nature and objectives of that media institution and positioned it in society and on the media scene in a variety of ways".[103] The current state of transition has been triggered by technological, market-related and socio-cultural trends.[104] How PSB engages with these new trends will largely determine its future, but its engagement must also remain within relevant parameters set by EU law, e.g. rules and guidelines governing State funding for PSB and the relationship between such funding and PSB mandates (see Chapter 10.3.2). Broadcasting technologies are becoming inexorably digitised and converged. If PSB is to retain its previous (or even current)

---

promote the democratic and social contribution of digital broadcasting; Declaration on Cultural Diversity, 7 December 2000, para. 2.5.

100 For an overview of relevant Council of Europe standards in this area, see: Susanne Nikoltchev, "European Backing for Public Service Broadcasting: Council of Europe Rules and Standards", in Susanne Nikoltchev, Ed., *IRIS Special: The Public Service Broadcasting Culture* (Strasbourg, European Audiovisual Observatory, 2007), pp. 7–15. For extensive examples in a range of European States, see the country overviews in *ibid.*

101 *Ibid.*, para. 23.

102 Karol Jakubowicz, "Public Service Broadcasting: A Pawn on an Ideological Chessboard", in Els De Bens, Ed., *Media Between Culture and Commerce* (Bristol, UK & Chicago, USA, Intellect, 2007), pp. 115–141, at 116.

103 *Ibid.*

104 See, *ibid.*, at 120.

level of influence in this new technological environment, it is imperative that it develops into an effective player across diverse media types and formats.

Calls for increased general PSB exploitation of new technological opportunities are also increasingly being linked to the specific goal of promoting cultural diversity. For example, again in its Recommendation on the remit of public service media in the information society, the CM stated:

> Public service media should play a particular role in the promotion of cultural diversity and identity, including through new communication services and platforms. To this end, public service media should continue to invest in new, original content production, made in formats suitable for the new communication services. They should support the creation and production of domestic audiovisual works reflecting as well local and regional characteristics.[105]

Public service values

The CM's Recommendation on measures to promote the public service value of the Internet,[106] picks up on this theme. Its central objective is to prompt States authorities, where appropriate in cooperation with all interested parties, to take all necessary measures to promote the public service value of the Internet, *inter alia* by "upholding human rights, democracy and the rule of law [...] and promoting social cohesion, respect for cultural diversity and trust" in respect of the Internet and other ICTs. States authorities are expected to draw on the guidelines appended to the Recommendation in their efforts to realise its central objective. The guidelines have five main focuses: human rights and democracy; access; openness; diversity, and security. The guidelines' focus on diversity strives for equitable and universal involvement in the development of Internet and ICT content. As such, they encourage, *inter alia*:

- the development of a cultural dimension to digital content production, including by public service media;
- strategies and policies geared towards the preservation of digital heritage;
- participation in "the creation, modification and remixing of interactive content";
- measures for the production and distribution of user- and community-generated content;
- capacity-building for local and indigenous content on the Internet;
- multilingualism on the Internet.

---

105 CM Recommendation Rec(2007)3 on the remit of public service media in the information society, *op. cit.*, para. 19.

106 Recommendation CM/Rec(2007)16 of the Committee of Ministers to member states on measures to promote the public service value of the Internet, 7 November 2007.

The CM's Declaration on a European Policy for New Information Technologies also engages in a detailed way with the specific potential of new media technologies for stimulating cultural diversity. The most relevant section of the Declaration, section (iv) concerning diversity of content and language, includes the following aims:

- to encourage the development of a wide range of communication and information networks, as well as the diversity of content and language, so as to foster political pluralism, cultural diversity and sustainable development;
- to promote the full use by all, including minorities, of the opportunities for exchange of opinion and self-expression offered by the new information technologies;
- to acknowledge the usefulness of these technologies in enabling all European countries and regions to express their cultural identities;
- to encourage the provision of cultural, educational and other products and services in an appropriate variety of languages and to promote the greatest possible diversity of these products and services;
- [...][107]

These engagements with the specificities of new media technologies and their identification of how they can serve the goal of promoting cultural diversity are welcome. They represent a significant step forward from numerous generalised affirmations of the potential of new media technologies for promoting cultural diversity (which, while welcome in their own right, offered little practical guidance as to how they actually promoted the goal).[108]

10.3.2 European Union standards

Under the Treaty of Lisbon, the European Union's commitments to human rights are strengthened considerably (see further, Chapter 2.2.5), including in ways which have implications for the promotion of cultural diversity. For instance, Article 3(3) of the Treaty on European Union (TEU), states that the Union "shall respect its rich cultural and linguistic diversity, and shall ensure that Europe's cultural heritage is safeguarded and enhanced".

One of the most important legal bases for the protection of cultural heritage and diversity (including languages) has heretofore been Article 151 of the Treaty establishing the European Community (TEC), which, post-Lisbon, has become Article 167 of the Treaty on the Functioning of the European Union.[109] Article

---

107 CM Declaration on a European policy for new information technologies, 7 May 1999.

108 CM Declaration on cultural diversity, Preamble & para. 2.3; CM Declaration on human rights and the rule of law in the Information Society, Section 3; CM Declaration on a European Policy for New Information Technologies, 7 May 1999, Preamble.

109 Consolidated version, as published in the *Official Journal of the European Communities* of 9 May 2008, C 115/47.

167(1) states: "The Union shall contribute to the flowering of the cultures of the Member States, while respecting their national and regional diversity and at the same time bringing the common cultural heritage to the fore".[110] Article 167(4) follows up on that commitment: "The Union shall take cultural aspects into account in its action under other provisions of the Treaties, in particular in order to respect and to promote the diversity of its cultures".

Article 22 of the Charter of Fundamental Rights of the European Union[111] is entitled 'Cultural, religious and linguistic diversity'; it reads: "The Union shall respect cultural, religious and linguistic diversity". It is based on (former) Article 6, TEU, and Article 151(1) and (4) of the TEC.[112] Although the explicit reference to cultural diversity is welcome, 'shall respect' is a significantly weaker formulation than, for example, "guarantee", "secure" or "promote". As such, it involves a considerably lighter commitment for States. Second, the Explanatory Note does not spell out the essence or scope of cultural diversity, which suggests a non-committal attitude to – or wariness of – its actual or potential implications.

The commentary on Article 22 provided by the EU Network of Independent Experts on Fundamental Rights is very brief and does not meaningfully engage with the treatment of relevant legal issues under international (human rights) treaties, including the ECHR.[113] The commentary does, however, usefully refer to the link between cultural diversity and broadcasting. It describes the "Television without Frontiers" Directive as being the text that is probably the closest to Article 22 of the Charter because of the instrumentality of its quota system for European works for preserving cultural creation and therefore diversity.

10.3.2(i) Audiovisual Media Services Directive

Television broadcasters in Europe are subject to a quota system for European, and independent European, works, as traditionally set out under Articles 4 and 5 of the

110 See also in this connection, the subsequent paras. of Article 167, and Rachael Craufurd Smith, "From heritage conservation to European identity: Article 151 EC and the multi-faceted nature of Community cultural policy", 32 E.L. Rev. (February 2007), pp. 48–69.

111 Charter of Fundamental Rights of the European Union, Nice, 7 December 2000, as published in the *Official Journal of the European Communities* of 18 December 2000, C 364/1, and revised and published in the Official Journal of the European Communities of 14 December 2007, C 303/01.

112 Explanations relating to the Charter of Fundamental Rights, OJEC of 16 December 2004, OJ C 303/17 *et seq.*, and for Article 22 of the Charter, *ibid.*, at p. 25.

113 Florence Benoît-Rohmer, "Article 22 – Cultural, religious and linguistic diversity", in EU Network of Independent Experts on Fundamental Rights, *The Commentary of the Charter of Fundamental Rights of the European Union* (2006), pp. 197–199.

Television without Frontiers Directive.[114] The system was based on a rather convoluted definition of European works set out in Article 6, Television without Frontiers Directive.

The following analysis focuses initially on experience based on the Television without Frontiers Directive before examining the current regime set out by the Audiovisual Media Services Directive. The first focus is highly relevant for the second as relevant provisions have been retained (and supplemented) in the latter Directive. Key excerpts from Articles 4 and 5, Television without Frontiers Directive, are as follows:

> Article 4
>
> 1. Member States shall ensure where practicable and by appropriate means, that broadcasters reserve for European works, within the meaning of Article 6, a majority proportion of their transmission time, excluding the time appointed to news, sports events, games, advertising, teletext services and teleshopping. This proportion, having regard to the broadcaster's informational, educational, cultural and entertainment responsibilities to its viewing public, should be achieved progressively, on the basis of suitable criteria.
>
> Article 5
>
> Member States shall ensure, where practicable and by appropriate means, that broadcasters reserve at least 10% of their transmission time, excluding the time appointed to news, sports events, games, advertising, teletext services and teleshopping, or alternately, at the discretion of the Member State, at least 10% of their programming budget, for European works created by producers who are independent of broadcasters. This proportion, having regard to broadcasters' informational, educational, cultural and entertainment responsibilities to its viewing public, should be achieved progressively, on the basis of suitable criteria; it must be achieved by earmarking an adequate proportion for recent works, that is to say works transmitted within five years of their production.

The cited Articles tend to be regarded as the main provisions in the Television without Frontiers Directive which, by design or in effect, served the goal of promoting cultural diversity in broadcasting.[115] As no other Article in the Directive dealt with cultural diversity *per se*, it is perhaps predictable that the Articles

---

114 The Television without Frontiers Directive was the forerunner of the Audiovisual Media Services Directive.

115 Note, for example, their thematic coupling during the latest formal process of revision of the Television without Frontiers Directive: European Commission, *Cultural Diversity and the Promotion of European and Independent Audiovisual Production*, Issues Paper for the Liverpool Conference, July 2005.

promoting European, and independent European, works might, by default, be considered to be the most relevant. However, upon closer scrutiny, the perceived relevance of Articles 4 and 5 turns out to be somewhat specious as the (intended and actual) contribution of these Articles to the goal of promoting cultural diversity in broadcasting is actually quite limited.

Articles 4 and 5 have been roundly criticised by many commentators for being little more than EU cultural protectionism unconvincingly dressed up as promoting creativity and cultural diversity.[116] In reality, they pursue dual economic and cultural objectives, but those objectives are not evenly weighted. The actual wording of relevant preambular Recitals and of the Articles themselves, as well as the *Realpolitik* of their drafting history, all suggest that Articles 4 and 5 were really conceived of as protective economic measures, designed to support the European audiovisual industry in the face of US dominance of global audiovisual markets. Conversely, the cultural credentials of Articles 4 and 5 appeared questionable. They constituted particularly blunt instruments as regards their purported cultural objectives for a number of reasons: they lacked any qualitative criteria; they lacked any stipulations about time-scheduling and they lacked any requirement to reinvest percentages of *profits* in new, independent European production. Such shortcomings increased the likelihood of mere *pro forma* compliance with Articles 4 and 5 by cost-conscious broadcasters who might have preferred to meet their obligations by transmitting cheap, low-quality programming at off-peak hours. The reporting system concerning Articles 4 and 5 was primarily statistical, which made it very difficult to gauge the qualitative impact of the provisions. Furthermore, in the absence of what have been termed "public, precise and transparent indicators", it was often a problematic exercise to determine the exact extent to which States were actually discharging their relevant obligations.[117]

In light of the foregoing comments about the architectural design of Articles 4 and 5 being primarily quantitative, those Articles could appear to have been predicated on a deterministic understanding of television broadcasting. A proper evaluation of the effectiveness of the provisions would necessitate due consideration of attitudinal complexities in viewing processes/reception analysis. It would also need to be

---

116 See further: Tarlach McGonagle, "The Quota Quandary: An Assessment of Articles 4–6 of the Television without Frontiers Directive", in David Ward, Ed., *The European Union and the Culture Industries: Regulation and the Public Interest* (Aldershot, Ashgate Publishing Limited, 2008); Irini Katsirea, "Why the European broadcasting quota should be abolished", 28 *European Law Review* (No. 2, 2003), pp. 190–209; Jackie Harrison & Lorna Woods, "Television Quotas: Protecting European Culture?", 12 *Entertainment Law Review* (No. 1, 2001), pp. 5–14.

117 *Report on the application of Articles 4 and 5 of Directive 89/552/EEC (the "TV without Frontiers" Directive), as amended by Directive 97/36/EC, for the period 2001–2002 (2004/2236(INI))*, European Parliament Committee on Culture and Education, Rapporteur: H. Weber, Doc. No. A6–0202/2005, 21 June 2005, para. 7.

informed by awareness of changing patterns of media usage (eg. the emergence of new participatory paradigms in broadcasting; increasing audience preferences for user-generated content, etc.).

The myth that Articles 4 and 5 constituted important vectors for cultural diversity can also be exposed by referring to the Articles' Eurocentric focus. If they had been properly concerned about the promotion of cultural diversity, they would have had to embrace the belief that cultural diversity is valuable in and of itself and thus a source of societal enrichment. Based on the assumption that audiovisual content is capable of expressing cultural identities, traditions and aspirations, the prescription of measures protecting/promoting *European* audiovisual content, as opposed to *extra-* or *non-European* audiovisual content, would be difficult to reconcile with such a profession of faith in the inherent value of cultures. On such a reading, the Articles could be perceived as having implied a disconcerting hierarchisation of cultures and a *de facto* relegation of non-European cultures to a status of inferiority. However, given that the motivation for the protective/promotional measures for European audiovisual works was primarily economic – and not to promote cultural diversity as such, this criticism can hardly be sustained. To hold otherwise would be to fault Articles 4 and 5 for failing to fulfil goals imputed to them, but which they did not actually hold. The foregoing conceptual contradictions highlight the dangers involved in considering Articles 4 and 5 to be default measures for the promotion of cultural diversity.

The development of EU policy in audiovisual matters generally, and the negotiation, drafting and first formal revision of the Television without Frontiers Directive, in particular, have been described as struggles between different, or rather, opposing, philosophies of broadcasting. Interventionist (*dirigiste*) and liberal perspectives clashed repeatedly, and often acrimoniously, during the deliberative process. Articles 4 and 5 were a common site for those clashes. States espousing an interventionist approach to broadcasting, eg. France, insisted on the inclusion of the provisions and lobbied strongly for high prescriptions of European audiovisual content. Other States, such as Germany and the United Kingdom, which pursued more liberal philosophies as regards broadcasting, opposed the provisions and favoured limiting their scope.

Against this background of contention and political positioning, it is surprising that the previous debates were not re-ignited to any significant extent during the formal revision (and modernisation) of the Directive which culminated in its replacement by the Audiovisual Media Services (AVMS) Directive.[118] Articles 4 and 5 have

118 Directive 2007/65/EC of the European Parliament and of the Council of 11 December 2007 amending Council Directive 89/552/EEC on the coordination of certain provisions laid down by law, regulation or administrative action in Member States concerning the pursuit of television broadcasting activities, OJ L 332/27 of 18 December 2007.

remained essentially unchanged in the new text – as Articles 16 and 17, AVMS Directive. For its part, Article 6, Television without Frontiers Directive, has been repositioned, also substantively unchanged, within Article 1, AVMS Directive. Article 9, Television without Frontiers Directive – an exemption for "television broadcasts that are intended for local audiences and do not form part of a national network", remains unchanged too, but it has been renumbered as Article 18, AVMS Directive.

One of the most important novel features introduced by the AVMS Directive is the distinction between linear and non-linear audiovisual media services, described in the Directive as "television broadcasting" and "on-demand audiovisual media service[s]", respectively. The former are defined as services "provided by a media service provider for simultaneous viewing of programmes on the basis of a programme schedule" (Article 1(1)(e)). In other words, these are so-called "push" technologies (because content is "pushed" to viewers), such as traditional television broadcasting or other forms of scheduled broadcasting via the Internet or mobile phones. Non-linear audiovisual services, on the other hand, are defined as services "provided by a media service provider for the viewing of programmes at the moment chosen by the user and at his individual request on the basis of a catalogue of programmes selected by the media service provider" (Article 1(1)(g)). These are also known as "pull" technologies (because viewers "pull" content from networks) or on-demand services.

The AVMS Directive has introduced a form of tiered regulation, with different tiers of obligations and responsibilities applying to media service providers, depending on whether they provide linear or non-linear audiovisual media services. A basic, minimum level of content regulation applies to all audiovisual media services (Chapter III), whereas certain regulatory provisions apply only to non-linear audiovisual media services (Chapter IV). The distinction between the two is likely to be of capital importance in respect of the future realisation of the objective of promoting the distribution and production of European audiovisual content, as will be shown below.

The preamble to the AVMS Directive is sprinkled with references to the goal of promoting cultural diversity in the European audiovisual sector: most saliently, Recitals 4–7, 12, 63–75. These Recitals re-affirm the importance of cultural (and linguistic) diversity; reference relevant EU and other standards; set out various ways in which technology could advance the goal of promoting cultural and linguistic diversity, and explain the purported role the Directive could play in furthering the same aim. Recital 69 is highly pertinent; it engages directly and extensively with the goal of promoting cultural diversity specifically in respect of on-demand audiovisual media services. It reads:

> On-demand audiovisual media services have the potential to partially replace television broadcasting. Accordingly, they should, where practicable, promote the production and distribution of European works and thus contribute actively to the promotion of cultural diversity. Such support for European works might, for example, take the form of financial contributions by such services to the production of and acquisition of rights in European works, a minimum share of European works in video-on-demand catalogues, or the attractive presentation of European works in electronic programme guides. It is important to re-examine regularly the application of the provisions relating to the promotion of European works by audiovisual media services. Within the framework of the reports provided for under this Directive, Member States should also take into account, in particular, the financial contribution by such services to the production and rights acquisition of European works, the share of European works in the catalogue of audiovisual media services and the actual consumption of European works offered by such services.

The observations and objectives outlined in Recital 69 are shored up in more concrete terms in the substantive part of the Directive. Article 13 is the operative provision and it reads:

> 1. Member States shall ensure that on-demand audiovisual media services provided by media service providers under their jurisdiction promote, where practicable and by appropriate means, the production of and access to European works. Such promotion could relate, *inter alia*, to the financial contribution made by such services to the production and rights acquisition of European works or to the share and/or prominence of European works in the catalogue of programmes offered by the on-demand audiovisual media service.
> 2. Member States shall report to the Commission no later than 19 December 2011 and every four years thereafter on the implementation of paragraph 1.
> 3. The Commission shall, on the basis of the information provided by Member States and of an independent study, report to the European Parliament and the Council on the application of paragraph 1, taking into account the market and technological developments and the objective of cultural diversity.

Article 13's all-important first paragraph clearly steers a middle course between the two most opposing positions that could have been taken, i.e., to extend the application of Articles 4–5, Television without Frontiers Directive, fully to on-demand audiovisual media services, or not at all.[119] It is relevant to note in this connection that the Court of Justice of the European Communities (ECJ) had already held in the *Mediakabel* case that Articles 4 and 5 of the Television without

---

119 For a short overview of the different positions considered during the review of the Television without Frontiers Directive with a view to its modernisation, see: European Commission, *Cultural Diversity and the Promotion of European and Independent Audiovisual Production*, Issues Paper for the Liverpool Conference, July 2005, pp. 2–3; European Commission Expert Group, *Cultural Diversity and the Promotion of European and Independent Audiovisual Production*, May 2005, p. 5.

Frontiers Directive *do* apply to near-video-on-demand services.[120] The new obligation in Article 13 can more accurately be described as promotional rather than prescriptive. Member States are obliged to "ensure that on-demand audiovisual media services provided by media service providers under their jurisdiction promote [...] the production of and access to European works", but only "where practicable and by appropriate means". Such a qualification could easily render the obligation ineffective. It would be all too easy for States seeking to shirk this obligation to argue that the pursuit of the objective of promoting the production of and access to European works is not practicable in a complex and ever-changing technological environment.

Having said that, the qualification "where practicable and by appropriate means" does not sap the obligation of all its vitality. The fact that Article 13(1) (and Recital 69) sets out illustrative examples of what any "appropriate measures" could conceivably entail is helpful insofar as it offers some guidance as to how the obligation could be discharged in practice. It is also relevant that Article 13(2) creates new reporting obligations for Member States concerning the promotion, by on-demand services provided by audiovisual media service providers, of the production of and access to European works. These reporting obligations are additional to those already established pursuant to Articles 4 and 5 of the Television without Frontiers Directive. Another relevant consideration is that Article 13(3) envisages a double-barrelled evaluation exercise on the part of the European Commission (i.e., on the basis of information provided by Member States, on the one hand, and an independent study on the other). It is to be expected that in the fullness of time, the reporting and evaluation processes will facilitate the development of indicators and bench-marking criteria, as well as the identification of best practices, all of which will contribute to the realisation of the potential of Article 13.

Whatever the precise depth of potential that Article 13 does hold for contributing to the goal of promoting the production of and access to European works, its usefulness for the advancement of cultural diversity generally suffers from the same inherent conceptual constraints as Articles 4 and 5, Television without Frontiers Directive, as discussed, *supra*. It fails to articulate the goal of promoting cultural diversity in an inclusive way that would give due recognition to the importance of non-European audiovisual works (which, in practice, are often expressive of non-European cultures). It thereby fails to encourage, or even acknowledge the value of, audiovisual works emanating from non-European countries or their expression of the vitality and importance of cultural identities and imaginations which transcend, or are simply located beyond, Europe's political borders.

---

120 Case C-89/04, *Mediakabel BV v. Commissariaat voor de Media*, Judgment of the Court of Justice of the European Communities (Third Chamber) of 2 June 2005, ECR I-4891, esp. para. 51.

Finally, Recital 72, AVMS Directive, should be noted for an important limitation it places on the scope of Articles 16 and 17. It states that Articles 16 and 17 do not apply to "[c]hannels broadcasting entirely in a language other than those of the Member States". It adds: "[n]evertheless, where such a language or languages represent a substantial part but not all of the channel's transmission time, Articles 16 and 17 should not apply to that part of transmission time". The importance of this exemption lies in its relevance to channels targeting, either exclusively or primarily, linguistic minorities which are not "national" minorities. As already noted in Chapters 1 and 2, the rights and interests of non-national minorities often slip through regulatory cracks due to a European normative preoccupation with "national" minorities. This pre-empts the risk of a blanket-application of the European programming quota to the detriment of particular linguistic groups whose reliance on their own broadcasters is mainly for intra-group communicative purposes.

In light of the highlighted shortcomings of relevant provisions of the AVMS Directive, it is necessary to explore the suitability of other mechanisms for advancing cultural diversity in the broadcasting sector. Particular attention will be paid in the next sub-sections to the relevant potential of public service broadcasting/media (PSB/M), community broadcasting/media and must-carry provisions.[121]

10.3.2(ii) Public service broadcasting/media

The Protocol to the Treaty of Amsterdam on the system of public broadcasting in the Member States recognises that it is largely for each Member State to confer, design and organise the remit for PSB in their own countries.[122] It also sets out that State funding for PSB must be tied to the fulfilment of the broadcasters' public service remit. Further guidance on the question of State funding for PSB is provided by the European Commission's Communication on the application of State aid rules to public service broadcasting[123] and the criteria established by the ECJ in its *Altmark* judgment.[124] In 2008, the Commission launched a public consultation on the future framework for State funding of PSB.[125] The development of the public

---

121 For a more detailed analysis of public service and community media, see Chapter 3.2.2.

122 Protocol to the Treaty of Amsterdam amending the Treaty on European Union, the Treaties establishing the European Communities and certain related acts, signed at Amsterdam, 2 October 1997, OJ C 340/109 of 10 November 1997.

123 Communication from the Commission on the application of State aid rules to public service broadcasting (2001/C 320/04).

124 Case C-280/00, *Altmark Trans GmbH, Regierungspräsidium Magdeburg v. Nahverkehrsgesellschaft Altmark GmbH*, Judgment of the Court of Justice of the European Communities of 24 July 2003, Rec.2003, p.I-7747, esp. paras. (87, 88), 89–94.

125 As announced in the European Commission's press release, "State aid: Commission launches public consultation on the future framework for State funding of public service broadcasting", IP/08/24, 10 January 2008. See also: Review of the Communication from the Commission on the

service remit in the new media environment was identified as one of the important focuses of the consultation exercise.[126] In 2009, the Commission adopted: (i) a new Communication on its State aid assessment criteria for cinematographic and audiovisual works,[127] and (ii) a Communication on the application of State aid rules to public service broadcasting.[128] The latter Communication replaces the previous, identically-titled Communication adopted in 2001.

10.3.2(iii) Community broadcasting

The status of community broadcasting has been considerably enhanced by two Resolutions adopted by the European Parliament in 2008. The Resolution entitled 'Community media in Europe' provides extensive analysis of the objectives, features and importance of community media.[129] Some of the Resolution's provisions deal specifically with community media's contribution to cultural diversity. For instance, the first substantive provision of the Resolution "[s]tresses that community media are an effective means of strengthening cultural and linguistic diversity, social inclusion and local identity, which explains the diversity of the sector". Subsequent provisions continue in the same vein, linking the role of community media to some of the rationales for promoting cultural diversity outlined earlier in this chapter.

The Resolution, 'Concentration and pluralism in the media in the European Union', for its part, also extends recognition to community media as a distinct media type.[130] It recognises the importance of community media for ensuring overall pluralism in the European media landscape.

10.3.2(iv) Must-carry regulation

Must-carry provisions will be considered at this juncture, instead of under access rights in Chapter 11 because, as explained by Natali Helberger, "the must-carry principle is about the universal and equal accessibility of public interest

application of State aid rules to public service broadcasting (n.d.), available at: <http://ec.europa.eu/comm/competition/state_aid/reform/broadcasting_comm_questionnaire_en.pdf>.

126 *Ibid.* See, in particular, s.2.2.1 of the second-named document in the previous footnote.

127 Communication from the Commission concerning the State aid assessment criteria of the Commission communication on certain legal aspects relating to cinematographic and other audiovisual works (Cinema Communication) of 26 September 2001 (2009/C 31/01).

128 Communication from the Commission on the application of State aid rules to public service broadcasting of 2 July 2009 (2009/C 257/01).

129 European Parliament Resolution of 25 September 2008 on Community Media in Europe (2008/2011(INI)).

130 European Parliament Resolution of 25 September 2008 on concentration and pluralism in the media in the European Union (2007/2253(INI)).

programming" and "not about the individual consumer's access to a certain platform".[131]

So-called "must-carry" obligations,[132] i.e., (regulatory) provisions mandating access to electronic communications networks for certain parties, subject to certain conditions, have considerable potential for ensuring access for minority groups to structural means of audiovisual transmission. However, the exploitation of that potential – to the extent that it is actually realised in practice – tends to occur at the national and sub-national levels. The most important supra-national regulatory provisions governing must-carry are based on notions of "general interest objectives", which are left for determination by States authorities. The extent to which cultural diversity is inferred into such general interest objectives therefore depends on how well-disposed States authorities are towards the goal of promoting cultural diversity. More specifically, the extent to which minorities would feature in, or be catered for in, States' policies on cultural diversity is similarly wedded to the goodwill of States authorities.

Public service broadcasters are typical – but by no means the only – beneficiaries of must-carry regimes. Must-carry provisions can also apply to other types of broadcaster or content, including (as will be seen *infra*), commercial broadcasters which have public service obligations.

Must-carry obligations can prove of enormous importance to public service broadcasting, especially by helping to ensure its universal availability. The importance of must-carry provisions for ensuring the continued availability of PSB is heightening considerably in an increasingly digitised broadcasting environment. This realisation has prompted the Council of Europe's CM to urge that must-carry regulations continue to be "applied for the benefit of public service broadcasters as far as reasonably possible in order to guarantee the accessibility of their services and programmes" via diverse digital platforms.[133] The CM's concern would appear

131 Natali Helberger, *Controlling Access to Content: Regulating Conditional Access in Digital Broadcasting* (The Netherlands, Kluwer Law International, 2005), p. 112.

132 For an overview of current issues affecting "must-carry" obligations, see, generally, Susanne Nikoltchev, Ed., *IRIS Special: To Have or not to Have Must-carry Rules* (Strasbourg, European Audiovisual Observatory, 2005), and in particular, Sabina Gorini & Nico van Eijk, "Workshop on Must-Carry Obligations: Summary of the Discussion", in *ibid.*, pp. 1–5. See also: Mike Feintuck & Mike Varney, Media Regulation, *Public Interest and the Law* (Second Edition) (Edinburgh, Edinburgh University Press, 2006), pp. 227–229; Natali Helberger, *Controlling Access to Content: Regulating Conditional Access in Digital Broadcasting, op. cit.*, pp. 111–114, 202; Mike Varney, "Must-carry Obligations in the New European Regulatory Framework for Communications: A True Guardian of Pluralism and Diversity?", 14 *Utilities Law Review* (2004/2005), p. 68.

133 Recommendation Rec(2003)9 of the Committee of Ministers to member states on measures to promote the democratic and social contribution of digital broadcasting, 28 May 2003, Appendix, para. 21.

to have escalated since then. In its Recommendation on media pluralism and diversity of media content, adopted at the beginning of 2007, it stated:

> Member states should envisage, where necessary, adopting must carry rules for other distribution means and delivery platforms than cable networks. Moreover, in the light of the digitisation process – especially the increased capacity of networks and proliferation of different networks, member states should periodically review their must carry rules in order to ensure that they continue to meet well-defined general interest objectives. Member states should explore the relevance of a must offer obligation in parallel to the must carry rules so as to encourage public service media and principal commercial media companies to make their channels available to network operators that wish to carry them. [...][134]

At the EU level, the main regulatory provisions governing must-carry obligations are to be found in the EU's Universal Services Directive.[135] The key provisions are set out in Article 31, which is devoted exclusively to the topic. Article 31(1)[136] reads:

> Member States may impose reasonable 'must carry' obligations, for the transmission of specified radio and television broadcast channels and services, on undertakings under their jurisdiction providing electronic communications networks used for the distribution of radio or television broadcasts to the public where a significant number of end-users of such networks use them as their principal means to receive radio and television broadcasts. Such obligations shall only be imposed where they are necessary to meet clearly defined general interest objectives and shall be proportionate and transparent. The obligations shall be subject to periodical review.

The types of networks envisaged by this provision include cable, satellite and terrestrial broadcasting networks, but could also include other networks "to the extent that a significant number of end-users use such networks as their principal means to receive radio and television broadcasts".[137] It has been pointed out that

---

134 Recommendation Rec(2007)2 of the Committee of Ministers to member states on media pluralism and diversity of media content, 31 January 2007, para. 3.3.

135 Directive 2002/22/EC of the European Parliament and of the Council of 7 March 2002 on universal service and users' rights relating to electronic communications networks and services (Universal Services Directive). For commentary, see: Nico van Eijk, "New European Rules for the Communications Sector", *IRIS plus – Supplement to IRIS – Legal Observations of the European Audiovisual Observatory*, 2003–2, at 5–6.

136 Article 31(2) recognises the ability of States to determine appropriate remuneration (if any) in respect of measures taken in accordance with Article 31, provided that all network providers are treated in a non-discriminatory manner and that procedures governing remuneration (where it is provided for) are proportionate and transparent.

137 *Ibid.*, Recital 44. Also of relevance in this connection is Recital 45, which states: "Services providing content such as the offer for sale of a package of sound or television broadcasting content are not covered by the common regulatory framework for electronic communications networks and services". It further holds that "Providers of such services should not be subject to

this qualification concerning usage of a network by "a significant number of end-users" sits uneasily under the overarching theme of the Directive – *universal* access.[138] If the Directive is to remain true to its own internal logic, its concern should be to ensure access for all users to "a (minimum) must carry package because of the relevance of the programmes within the package".[139] Without further elaboration or refinement, this qualification concerning "a significant number of end-users" fails to acknowledge geographical specificity. This is potentially problematic as whether the existence of a "significant number" of end-users is calculated at the national, regional or local level will have very different implications for locally-concentrated minority groups.

Significantly, Article 31 does not require Member States to impose must-carry obligations on network providers – it merely allows them to do so. As the Directive recognises that the practice of imposing must-carry obligations already exists in various Member States,[140] the importance of Article 31 resides in the fact that it sets out the parameters which should govern any measures undertaken by Member States in respect of must-carry regimes. Recital 43 further clarifies the regulatory thinking behind Article 31 and the parameters it establishes: "Member States should be able to lay down proportionate obligations on undertakings under their jurisdiction, in the interest of legitimate public policy considerations, but such obligations should only be imposed where they are necessary to meet general interest objectives clearly defined by Member States in conformity with Community law and should be proportionate, transparent and subject to periodical review".

As it is left to States to formulate their own "public policy" and define their own "general interest objectives", the Directive does not enumerate – even for illustrative purposes – what kinds of general interest objectives could be involved.[141] In the absence of further specifications, one commentator has submitted that such general interest objectives would presumptively include pluralism and cultural diversity, but – following ECJ case-law – not objectives of an economic nature.[142] Thus, as

---

universal service obligations in respect of these activities" and that the Directive "is without prejudice to measures taken at national level, in compliance with Community law, in respect of such services".

138 Nico van Eijk, "Directive 2002/22/EC 'Universal Services Directive': 'Must Carry Obligations'", in Oliver Castendyk, Egbert Dommering & Alexander Scheuer, Eds., *European Media Law* (Alphen a/d Rijn, Kluwer Law International, 2008), pp. 1163–1174, at 1173.

139 *Ibid.*

140 *Ibid.*, Recital 43.

141 The only example specifically mentioned is "the transmission of services specifically designed to enable appropriate access by disabled users": *ibid.*, Recital 43.

142 Thomas Roukens, "What Are We Carrying Across the EU these Days?: Comments on the Interpretation and Practical Implementation of Article 31 of the Universal Services Directive", in Susanne Nikoltchev, Ed., *IRIS Special: To Have or not to Have Must-carry Rules*, *op. cit.*, pp. 7–19, at pp. 11–12.

already mentioned, Article 31 creates ample scope for the development of must-carry obligations pertaining to minorities.

The potential of must-carry provisions for PSB and for the promotion of cultural diversity was adverted to, albeit somewhat indirectly, in the leading ECJ case to date dealing with must-carry obligations, *United Pan-Europe Communications Belgium SA v. Belgium*.[143] Article 31 could not be considered in the case as the Universal Service Directive was not in force at the time of the adoption of the regulatory provisions under scrutiny in the case.[144] At issue in the case were national measures obliging cable operators to broadcast programmes transmitted by certain private broadcasters. The Belgian Conseil d'Etat referred four main questions to the ECJ for a preliminary ruling under Article 234 EC. Put broadly, those questions were designed to elicit interpretive clarification of, *inter alia*, Article 49 EC – freedom to provide services, and whether the national legislation at issue would constitute a prohibited interference with that freedom.

Aside from its consideration of various aspects of European law, eg. the general legitimacy of policies geared towards the maintenance of pluralism due to its connection to the right to freedom of expression, the ECJ also made a number of pronouncements concerning the goal of upholding pluralism in the specific factual circumstances of the case. Those pronouncements are significant, first because of their contribution to existing doctrine dealing with pluralism in the audiovisual sector, and second, because of their obvious bearing on the ability of discrete groups in society to access pluralistic audiovisual content and by extension audiovisual content which corresponds to their cultural and linguistic needs and preferences. For instance, the Court accepted that the national legislation at issue in the case "pursues an aim in the general interest, since it seeks to preserve the pluralist nature of the range of television programmes available in the bilingual region of Brussels-Capital and thus forms part of a cultural policy the aim of which is to safeguard, in the audiovisual sector, the freedom of expression of the different social, cultural, religious, philosophical or linguistic components which exist in that region".[145] The Court proceeds to state that such legislation "guarantees to television viewers in that region that they will not be deprived of access, in their own language, to local and national news as well as to programmes which are representative of their culture".[146] Although not explicitly referred to as "the promotion of cultural diversity in the broadcasting sector", that is actually what was at issue in the case at hand. The Court's key conclusions in its judgment read as follows:

---

143 Case C-250/06, Judgment of the Court of Justice of the European Communities (Third Chamber) of 13 December 2007.

144 *Ibid.*, paras. 25 and 26.

145 *Ibid.*, para. 42.

146 *Ibid.*, para. 43.

> [...] Article 49 EC is to be interpreted as meaning that it does not preclude legislation, such as the legislation at issue in the main proceedings, which requires, by virtue of a must-carry obligation, cable operators providing services on the relevant territory of that State to broadcast television programmes transmitted by private broadcasters falling under the public powers of that State and designated by the latter, where such legislation:
>
> – pursues an aim in the general interest, such as the retention, pursuant to the cultural policy of that Member State, of the pluralist character of the television programmes available in that territory, and
> – is not disproportionate in relation to that objective, which means that the manner in which it is applied must be subject to a transparent procedure based on objective non-discriminatory criteria known in advance.
>
> It is for the national court to determine whether those conditions are satisfied.[147]

The Court was also instructive on the point that a transparent procedure, based on objective non-discriminatory criteria known in advance, is a necessary safeguard against the arbitrary exercise by Member States of the discretion vested in them.[148] It specifies, for example, that:

> [...] each broadcaster must be able to determine in advance the nature and scope of the precise conditions to be satisfied and, where relevant, the public service obligations it is required to observe if it is to apply for that status. In that regard, the mere setting out, in the statement of reasons for the national legislation, of declarations of principle and general policy objectives cannot be considered sufficient.[149]

The standards of scrutiny envisaged here are very rigorous and specific and do much to foreclose the possibility of arbitrariness. The same rigour and specificity is evident again when the Court scrupulously tailors the basis of the must-carry status to the objective of securing pluralism by allowing certain access-oriented public service obligations. It states that:

> [...] such status should not automatically be awarded to all television channels transmitted by a private broadcaster, but must be strictly limited to those channels having an overall content which is appropriate for the purpose of attaining such an objective. In addition, the number of channels reserved to private broadcasters having that status must not manifestly exceed what is necessary in order to attain that objective.[150]

---

147 *Ibid.*, para. 51. See also, para. 52.

148 *Ibid.*, para. 46.

149 *Ibid.*

150 *Ibid.*, para. 47.

Finally, it should also be signalled that owing to the focus of "must-carry" obligations on access to networks and technical facilities, some commentators have advocated, perhaps controversially, the development of (complementary) "must-offer" regimes, which would aim to enhance access to specific content.[151] Such proposals style "must-carry" and "must-offer" obligations as constitutive elements of a concept of "universal service obligations with regard to content".[152] Additional measures supporting access to specific content – again, presumably determined on the basis of defined general interest objectives – could also have considerable potential for minorities. Much would depend on the extent to which minority perspectives, needs and interests would inform the determination of general interest objectives.

10.3.3 OSCE standards

The Guidelines on the use of Minority Languages in the Broadcast Media, elaborated under the auspices of the OSCE High Commissioner on National Minorities in 2003, are also relevant for the promotion of cultural and linguistic diversity.[153] The conceptual linkage between cultural and linguistic diversity and the contribution of minority rights protection to the promotion of cultural diversity are both evident in the Guidelines. The General Principles that inform the Guidelines are listed as: Freedom of Expression, Cultural and Linguistic Diversity, Protection of Identity and Equality and Non-Discrimination. The principle, "Cultural and Linguistic Diversity" is fleshed out as follows: "States should guarantee the freedom of choice by creating an environment in which a variety of ideas and information can flourish as communicated in various languages".

Conclusions

This chapter unravels the concept, "cultural diversity", and positions it in the broader context of culture and cultural rights, before examining standard-setting endeavours to promote cultural and linguistic diversity at the international and European levels. The obligation on States to uphold cultural and linguistic diversity could be described as an imperfect obligation that is closely connected with the right to freedom of expression, including for persons belonging to minorities. Cultural diversity entails the existence and expression of multiple cultural identities.

---

151 Peggy Valcke (in cooperation with David Stevens and Eva Lievens), "The Future of Must-Carry: From Must-Carry to a Concept of Universal Service in the Info-Communications Sector", in Susanne Nikoltchev, Ed., *IRIS Special: To Have or not to Have Must-carry Rules*, *op. cit.*, pp. 31–40, esp. at 32, 34, 35 & 39.

152 *Ibid.*, at 39.

153 Guidelines on the use of Minority Languages in the Broadcast Media OSCE High Commissioner on National Minorities, October 2003. For an overview and analysis, see Chapter 4.

Cultural diversity is enabled by a societal climate of pluralistic tolerance and by the transmission of cultural expressions via diverse media and in diverse fora. These aspects are foregrounded in the analysis.

The international treaty that embraces the foregoing considerations most extensively is the UNESCO Convention on the Protection and Promotion of the Diversity of Cultural Expressions. The adoption of the Convention was a symbolic milestone, but it is eviscerated by ineffectual language that gives rise to very weak legal obligations. Its usefulness lies rather in its disaggregation of strategies and issues alike. It helps to embed intercultural dialogue or understanding and it recognises the important contribution of minority cultures to the attainment of the more general goal of cultural diversity.

At the European level, the main regulatory instruments governing broadcasting do not make any earnest attempt to promote cultural diversity. Provisions for the protection and promotion of European and independent European works are often regarded as default measures to promote cultural diversity but several design-faults (Eurocentricity, exclusionary character, economic and quantitative preoccupations) prevent them from being properly considered as addressing cultural diversity, let alone promoting it. Nevertheless, the goal of promoting cultural and linguistic diversity via the media is advanced through various other (mainly non-binding) instruments (esp. Recommendations by the Council of Europe's CM) and regulatory measures at the national level (esp. concerning PSB and PSM, which is particularly suitable for the promotion of cultural and linguistic diversity by virtue of its ethos and mandate, and must-carry provisions). The advancement of cultural and linguistic diversity by media is also assured in no small measure by media- and information-related pluralism (as discussed in Chapter 9).

Chapter 11
Access rights

Introduction

As intimated in Chapter 5 and at various junctures in Chapter 7, media-related pluralism and access can be described as an essential double-helix of (positive) State obligations to uphold the right to freedom of expression. A clear complementarity exists between both: whereas audience interests tend to prioritise having "access to 'enough' expression [...] and that the expression to which they have access should not be distorted", participant interests are more likely to be concerned with "having "enough" opportunities for expression and the value of having these opportunities not be unfairly distributed".[1] While these sets of complementary interests are not "exactly coincident"[2] with one another, there are occasions on which their relationship can become one of intersection. Certain modalities of access to expressive opportunities can have direct implications for media-related pluralism, for instance (eg. "must-carry" provisions,[3] etc.).

It is not necessary for present purposes to fully explore all of the possible relational permutations and combinations involving media-related pluralism and access. The essential observation to be made is that there exists considerable conceptual proximity between the notions, but that the incidence and extent of overlap between them can only meaningfully be established when they are applied in concrete situations. The focus in this chapter will be on access, which is located at the confluence of the rights to freedom of expression, participation, non-discrimination and equality.

11.1 Rights-based theories of access to the media

This section will seek to position (putative) rights of access to expressive opportunities, and in particular the media, in the broader context of positive

---

1 T.M. Scanlon, "Content regulation reconsidered", in T.M. Scanlon, *The Difficulty of Tolerance: Essays in Political Philosophy* (United Kingdom, Cambridge University Press, 2003), pp. 151–168, at 163–164.

2 *Ibid.*

3 See generally, Susanne Nikoltchev, Ed., *IRIS Special – To Have or not to Have Must-carry Rules* (Strasbourg, European Audiovisual Observatory, 2005). See also the discussion in Chapter 10.3, *supra*.

international law provisions guaranteeing the right to freedom of expression. In this regard, Article 19(2), ICCPR, is of primary importance. It reads:

> Everyone shall have the right to freedom of expression; this right shall include freedom to seek, receive and impart information and ideas of all kinds, regardless of frontiers, either orally, in writing or in print, in the form of art, or through any other media of his choice.

This provision clarifies that in the exercise of their right to freedom of expression, individuals are entitled to choose the medium that they would like to use to convey information and ideas. Although this "freedom" is subject to certain restrictions, most pertinently those set out in Article 19(3), the potential import of Article 19(2) is far-reaching, but as yet somewhat understated and underdeveloped. The wording of Article 13(1), CRC,[4] is almost identical to that of Article 19(2), ICCPR, but there is no equivalent provision in Article 10, ECHR. The absence of such a provision in Article 10, ECHR, has certainly influenced relevant doctrinal development, as will now be demonstrated.

11.1.1 Freedom of expression and access rights

"[N]otwithstanding the acknowledged importance of freedom of expression", Article 10, ECHR, does not, in its current state of development, "bestow any freedom of forum for the exercise of that right".[5] That being so in a broader context, the same holds true in more specific contexts and the right to freedom of expression therefore does not include an individual or group right of access to *particular* means of expression or to *particular* media. The question has been considered on several occasions in relation to access to the broadcast media, but has consistently been dismissed. As stated by the European Commission of Human Rights in the *Haider v. Austria* case,[6] Article 10, ECHR: "cannot be taken to include a general and unfettered right for any private citizen or organisation to have access to broadcasting time on radio or television in order to forward his opinion, save under exceptional circumstances, for instance if one political party is excluded from broadcasting facilities at election time while other parties are given broadcasting time".[7] A right

4 It reads: "The child shall have the right to freedom of expression; this right shall include freedom to seek, receive and impart information and ideas of all kinds, regardless of frontiers, either orally, in writing or in print, in the form of art, or through any other media of the child's choice."

5 *Appleby and Others v. the United Kingdom*, Judgment of the European Court of Human Rights of 6 May 2003, para. 47.

6 Decision of inadmissibility of the European Commission of Human Rights (First Chamber) of 18 October 1995, Application No. 25060/94.

7 *Ibid.*, para. 3 (in section of decision entitled 'The Law').

of access must therefore be regarded as being highly contingent on specific circumstances.

Before exploring relevant case-law by the European Court of Human Rights, the notion of access needs to be unpacked. It is important to distinguish in the first place, whether access is conceived of as structural, procedural or substantive. In other words, does the sought-after access relate to a forum or medium, decision-making or production processes (within relevant structures), or content/output? Unless the notion is unpacked in this way (and indeed in even greater detail), its analytical usefulness is seriously curtailed.

Relevant statements of principle by the European Court of Human Rights can be summarised as follows:

- States are allowed – under the third sentence of Article 10(1) – to regulate broadcasting by a licensing system based on such criteria as the nature and objectives of the proposed station and its potential audience;
- States enjoy a certain margin of appreciation in this area, but it is subject to strict supervision due to the importance of the right to freedom of expression;
- Broadcasting enterprises have no guarantee of any right to a licence;
- The rejection by a State of an application for a broadcasting licence must not be manifestly arbitrary or discriminatory.

When assessing whether the rejection of an application for a broadcasting licence amounts to a breach of Article 10, the Court places arguably undue store by the availability of other means for applicants to exercise their right to freedom of expression. The appeal of this approach is, however, merely superficial. At its centre lies the assumption that the refusal to grant a licence for a particular bandwidth or geographical area is not necessarily disproportionate if there is no impediment to the broadcasting enterprise applying for a licence on another bandwidth or another geographical area. The Court relied heavily on this argument in *Brook v. The United Kingdom*,[8] a case in which the exclusion of short-wave frequncies from the licensing regime was contested. The Court pointed out that the applicant could have applied for, *inter alia*, "national or local radio licences on either AM or FM frequencies, or for satellite radio licences".[9] Similarly, in *United Christian Broadcasters Ltd. v. The United Kingdom*,[10] a case in which the applicant challenged its ineligibility, as a religious organisation, to even apply for a national broadcasting licence, the Court held:

8 *Brook v. the United Kingdom*, Application No. 38218/97, Decision of inadmissibility of the European Court of Human Rights (Third Section) of 11 July 2000.

9 *Ibid.*, p. 5.

10 *United Christian Broadcasters Ltd. v. the United Kingdom*, Application No. 44802/98, Decision of inadmissibility of the European Court of Human Rights (Third Section) of 7 November 2000.

> It is, moreover, significant that the limitation on the applicant's right to freedom of expression through radio broadcasting is far from being absolute, since there is no restriction on religious bodies applying for and being granted licences for local radio broadcasting.[11]

This line of reasoning is flawed. Instead of scrutinising the effect of the limitation on the applicant's right to freedom of expression and enquiring whether less restrictive measures might have been more proportionate, the Court focused on the fact that the restriction was not absolute. The Court was therefore measuring from the wrong end of the spectrum. Limitations on rights should be narrowly drawn and restrictively interpreted. They should be measured against less restrictive limitations, not more restrictive ones.

The approach taken by the Court in *Brook* and *United Christian Broadcasters* runs the risk of overlooking or at least downplaying the qualitative consequences that flow from the ability to broadcast on a particular frequency or to a particular target area. Different media initiatives have different needs and objectives (see Chapter 3, generally) and the availability of alternative broadcasting opportunities may be manifestly unsuited to specific broadcasting ambitions, thereby making the "alternative" more theoretical than real. In the *United Christian Broadcasters* case, the applicant association's target audience was geographically dispersed, which explains why it would find a national licence vastly more attractive than local broadcasting licences. The specific facts of this case point up a more general problem for minorities whose membership is not concentrated into localised pockets: the availability of alternative frequencies simply may not be a viable option. Purposive and media functionality considerations therefore merit greater judicial attention than they have hitherto received (see further, Chapter 3.2.1).

The Court adopted a variant on the above approach in the *Demuth v. Switzerland* case.[12] The applicant was refused a licence for CAR TV, a "segmented television program", which he intended to set up to cover "all aspects of car mobility and private road traffic, including news on cars, car accessories, traffic and energy policies, traffic security, tourism, automobile sport, relations between railways and road traffic and environmental issues". The programme offer would have been broadcast by cable in German and French. The applicant was refused a broadcasting licence because CAR TV's proposed programme offer was found not to meet the stipulated licensing requirements concerning cultural content and diversity. The European Court of Human Rights noted that the Federal Council's decision to turn down the application for a licence for CAR TV "was not categorical and did not exclude a broadcasting licence for once and for all".[13] It continued:

---

11 *Ibid.*, p. 6.

12 Judgment of the European Court of Human Rights of 5 November 2002, Reports 2002-IX.

13 *Ibid.*, para. 47.

> On the contrary, the Federal Council disclosed flexibility by stating that a segmented program such as Car Tv AG could obtain a licence if the content of its program further contributed to the "instructions" listed in Section 3 §1 of the RTA. In this context, the Court takes note of the Government's assurance before the Court that a licence would indeed be granted to Car Tv AG if it included cultural elements in its program.

The majority of the Court styled the possibility to adapt CAR TV's programme offer as a factor that mitigated the severity of the interference with the applicant's freedom of expression. However, the Court was wrong to describe this possibility as an example of "flexibility" on the part of the Federal Council. It would be more accurate to describe it as an example of "flexibility" being imposed on CAR TV. The specialised nature of the proposed television service would be diluted – and perhaps seriously compromised – by alterations to its programme offer. As pointed out in the dissenting opinion of Judge Jorundson, "this could not amount to a valid alternative for the applicant since the purpose of his program, as the name CAR TV AG suggested, was to deal exclusively with matters pertaining to automobiles".

Drawing on the discussion in Chapter 3.1.1, it is clear that requirements such as these would go against the ideological grain of several types of minority broadcasting, especially those with intra-community communicative objectives. The argument could also be made that this amounts to (in)direct interference with the principle of editorial autonomy.

It can be concluded that the existing case-law of the European Court of Human Rights offers little grounds for optimism as far as the future development of more robust access rights is concerned. However, the perspective is not necessarily as bleak as the foregoing overview of jurisprudence might initially suggest. Some measure of potential can be detected in the Court's judgment in the *Appleby* case. In that case, the applicants argued that the shopping centre to which they sought to gain access should be regarded as a "quasi-public" space because it was *de facto* a forum for communication. The Court held that:

> [Article 10, ECHR], notwithstanding the acknowledged importance of freedom of expression, does not bestow any freedom of forum for the exercise of that right. While it is true that demographic, social, economic and technological developments are changing the ways in which people move around and come into contact with each other, the Court is not persuaded that this requires the automatic creation of rights of entry to private property, or even, necessarily, to all publicly-owned property (Government offices and ministries, for instance). *Where however the bar on access to property has the effect of preventing any effective exercise of freedom of expression or it can be said that the essence of the right has been destroyed, the*

> *Court would not exclude that a positive obligation could arise for the State to protect the enjoyment of Convention rights by regulating property rights.*[14]

A crucially important factual feature of the *Appleby* case is that access was sought to privately-owned property *for communicative purposes*. This strengthens its analogous relevance to access to media, which often implicates the property and expressive rights of various parties.

Any prognosis for the future development of access rights must take cognizance of a number of relevant factors that can also provide impetus and direction for their growth. First, there is the inevitable interplay with, in particular, the rights to non-discrimination/equality and effective participation in public life. Second, without prejudice to any State obligations to take positive measures in order to ensure non-discrimination/equality in respect of freedom of expression (and including access to means of expression), States are under certain additional obligations by virtue of their commitment to render the right to freedom of expression effective in practice. Third, there is a dynamic quality that inheres in all rights and which implies that our understanding of rights is not static, but evolutive. These three growth-enhancing factors will now be considered in turn.

11.1.2 Interplay between rights

The inter-related and interdependent character of all human rights and the synergies generated by the interplay between freedom of expression and a range of other rights, such as the right to non-discrimination/equality, effective participation in public life, religious, cultural, linguistic and educational rights, has already been carried out in Chapter 4.4, so it will suffice to briefly re-emphasise a few central principles here. The focus will be on their relevance for access-related issues.

States Parties to the ICCPR are required in certain circumstances to "take affirmative action in order to diminish or eliminate conditions which cause or help to perpetuate discrimination prohibited by the Covenant".[15] Thus, the UN Human Rights Committee has held, "in a State where the general conditions of a certain part of the population prevent or impair their enjoyment of human rights, the State should take specific action to correct those conditions".[16] Measures constituting such affirmative State action are legitimised by their corrective, specific and temporary nature. Another crucial principle is that the prohibition of discrimination not only covers all rights enshrined in the ICCPR, but also has an autonomous

14 (emphasis added) *Appleby and Others v. the United Kingdom*, *op. cit.*, para. 47.

15 United Nations Human Rights Committee, General Comment 18, Non-discrimination, 10 November 1989, para. 10.

16 *Ibid.*

existence, thereby stretching to prohibit "discrimination in law or in fact in any field regulated and protected by public authorities".[17]

When applied to the right to freedom of expression, the upshot of these principles, taken together, is that it is incumbent on States authorities to actively seek to eliminate discriminatory regulations, structures and practices that prevent members of minority groups from effectively exercising their right to freedom of expression. This reading of general State obligations to combat discrimination and promote equality under the ICCPR gains in force when considered in conjunction with State obligations towards minorities. Under Article 27, ICCPR, "positive measures by States may also be necessary to protect the identity of a minority and the rights of its members to enjoy and develop their culture and language and to practise their religion, in community with the other members of the group"; such measures must be in accordance with Articles 2.1 and 26, ICCPR, and seek to correct "conditions which prevent or impair the enjoyment of the rights guaranteed under article 27".[18]

Insofar as the advancement of cultural, linguistic and religious objectives of minorities is partly dependent on the right to freedom of expression, positive State action is clearly required to eliminate discrimination and disadvantage in the system of freedom of expression. Moreover, the envisaged positive measures of protection are "required not only against the acts of the State party itself, whether through its legislative, judicial or administrative authorities, but also against the acts of other persons within the State party". Given the huge power of private media interests to shape the system of freedom of expression and influence its workings, this candid statement by the UN Human Rights Committee has potentially far-reaching implications. It essentially recognises that in order to be effective, positive State measures cannot be limited to State bodies, but should also be horizontally applicable. It thereby mandates States to take measures limiting the power of media, but any such measures would implicitly have to be guided by principles of media sovereignty and independence.

The scope of the right to effective participation in public life necessarily includes participation in public debate. To the extent that the media and other fora serve as sites in which public debate is conducted, access rights are crucially important. Linguistic rights are also crucially important in respect of access to the media and other expressive fora: an individual's linguistic ability or the *lingua franca* of a particular medium or forum can prove largely determinative of whether s/he can

---

17 *Ibid.*, para. 12.

18 United Nations Human Rights Committee, General Comment 23, The rights of minorities (Article 27), 8 April 1994, para. 6.2.

exercise his/her right to freedom of expression via that medium or forum in an effective and meaningful manner.[19]

Having briefly sketched the relevance of synergic interplay between selected rights for access-related issues, the enquiry will now turn to the question of the extent of relevant State obligations to render different kinds of access effective in practice. Building on the analysis carried out in Chapter 4.1.2, it is submitted that different types of obligations are implicated in different situations, and different levels of intervention may therefore be required to discharge them. Debate about the extent of State obligations in respect of the press (i.e., whether or not the State should be abstentionist or interventionist), was triggered by a proposal submitted in the earlier stages of the drafting process of the ICCPR. The proposal set out:

> In order to ensure the right of the free expression of opinion for large sections of the peoples and for their organizations, State assistance and co-operation shall be given in providing the material resources (premises, printing presses, paper, and the like) necessary for the publication of democratic organs of the press.[20]

This proposal was put forward by the USSR and it was very much in keeping with its Socialist credo. That it ultimately failed to prevail is of little surprise, given its in-built potential for arbitrary application and abuse by States Parties, not to mention the friction its adoption would have caused with principles of media autonomy. While the issue was uncontroversially removed from the ICCPR agenda, it re-appeared later on the UNESCO agenda in the context of the New World Information and Communication Order (NWICO) debate.[21] The NWICO agenda sought to promote a more equitable international communication order and free, multi-directional (as opposed to vertical or linear) information flows at the global level. To those ends, it sought to advance the concept of a "right" to communication, socially responsible journalism and other mechanisms for the circulation of information and ideas; it favoured the democratisation of (international) communications structures and processes (*inter alia* by making them more participatory in character) and strongly linked communicative rights to the whole development agenda. Its vision was very much shaped by the contemporary geo-political cleavages between North and South and East and West, which were perpetuated in culture, communications and commerce. The pursuit of the NWICO's objectives proved highly polemical and led to bitter political rifts within

---

19 See further in this connection: Seán MacBride *et al.*, *Many Voices One World: Towards a new more just and more efficient world information and communication order* (Great Britain, UNESCO, 1980), p. 51.

20 Marc Bossuyt, *Guide to the "Travaux Préparatoires" of the International Covenant on Civil and Political Rights* (Dordrecht, etc., Martinus Nijhoff Publishers, 1987), p. 374.

21 See: Seán MacBride *et al.*, *Many Voices One World: Towards a new more just and more efficient world information and communication order*, *op. cit.*

UNESCO, with long-term consequences, such as the withdrawal of the US and the UK from the organisation.

Such proposals were also discussed in the drafting of Article 9, FCNM, for example, the so-called FUEN draft for an additional protocol to the ECHR.[22] The draft included the provision that persons "belonging to ethnic groups" "shall have the right to equal access to the State's or to other public mass media, as well as the right to their own means of communication and adequate public subsidies for this purpose".[23] Ultimately, no explicit provision along these lines was retained in the final text of Article 9(3) specifically (or in any other part of Article 9 either). According to the Explanatory Report to the FCNM, "[N]o express reference has been made to the right of persons belonging to a national minority to seek funds for the establishment of media, as this right was considered self-evident".[24] This explanation is somewhat inadequate, however. There is a considerable gap between guaranteeing that adequate public subsidies are available (or a provision to that effect) and merely allowing minorities to *seek* funds. Asking costs nothing, as the old adage goes, but a firm undertaking by States to ensure that relevant funds are freed up for specific purposes such as the establishment of minority media outlets, has clear and potentially far-reaching financial consequences. It will be recalled that this issue had also proved controversial during the drafting of the Universal Declaration of Human Rights.[25]

The promotion of access to the media, including through regulatory, licensing and subsidising measures are recurrent priorities in, but are usually confined to, the non-legally binding media-related work of the Council of Europe.[26] This can be explained by the fact that the genuine sense of priority that is placed on such objectives, in principle, would meet much resistance in practice if commitments demanding considerable budgetary follow-up were to be legally enshrined. The politically-binding (and even then, often non-prescriptive) character of Committee of Ministers' Recommendations and other soft-law instruments

---

22 FUEN, Fundamental Rights of Persons Belonging to Ethnic Groups in Europe, Draft for an Additional Protocol to the ECHR (Revised FUEN Draft), 1994.

23 Article 10(2), *ibid.*

24 Explanatory Report to the FCNM, para. 61.

25 As explained in Chapter 2.1.3, René Cassin removed the reference to the ear-marking of public funds for minority educational and other institutions when he reworked John Humphrey's initial draft text.

26 See, for example, the following texts adopted by the Council of Europe's Committee of Ministers: Recommendation CM/Rec (2007)11 on promoting freedom of expression and information in the new information and communications environment, 26 September 2007; Declaration on human rights and the rule of law in the Information Society, 13 May 2005; Recommendation Rec (2003) 9 on measures to promote the democratic and social contribution of digital broadcasting, 28 May 2003; Recommendation No. R (99) 14 on universal community service concerning new communication and information services, 9 September 1999.

allows States to occupy an increasingly crowded comfort zone between conscience and cost.

11.1.3 Dynamism of rights

It is important to note that access rights are constantly developing. This "dynamic aspect" of rights is wholly consistent with the prevalent conception of human rights instruments as being living documents. The ability of rights to create new duties has also been described as "fundamental to any understanding of their nature and function in practical thought".[27] As any list of duties corresponding to a right can never be exhaustive, the full implications of a right cannot be predicted in advance – at least not always and not necessarily with any degree of certainty. As Joseph Raz has pointed out, "[T]he existence of a right often leads to holding another to have a duty because of the existence of certain facts peculiar to the parties or general to the society in which they live".[28] It is therefore conceivable that new (unforeseen) circumstances could very well give rise to a new duty being grounded in the previously recognised right.[29]

This theory of the dynamic character of rights can be explicated in a variety of ways. T.M. Scanlon, for instance, embeds it in his own analysis of rights, which maintains that a right has three essential components:

> (1) ends – the goals or values relative to which the consequences of unfettered discretion are judged to be unacceptable and the constraints proposed are held to be justified;
> (2) means – the particular constraints that the right in question is taken to involve; and
> (3) linking empirical beliefs about the consequences of unfettered discretion and about how these consequences would be altered by the constraints the right proposes. These include beliefs about the motivation of the relevant actors, about the opportunities to act that are already available to them, and about the collective results of the decisions that are likely to make. Also relevant here are facts about the institutional background that determine whether a given constraint is "in force".[30]

Under this theoretical model, Scanlon maintains that rights possess a "creative instability"[31] because of the susceptibility of our empirical beliefs to change and the unlikelihood that our understanding of a right's ends, means and empirical beliefs

---

27 Joseph Raz, *The Morality of Freedom* (New York, Oxford University Press, 1986), p. 171.
28 *Ibid.*
29 *Ibid.*, pp. 171, 185, 186.
30 T.M. Scanlon, "Content regulation reconsidered", *op. cit.*, at 152.
31 *Ibid.*, p. 154.

will, at any given time, make up a coherent whole. He argues that new or altered situations, or changes in our empirical beliefs, can prompt us to reappraise the adequacy of existing constraints, or even the sets of values "in terms of which existing constraints are justified".[32] The tension released by this fluctuating, three-way relationship "gives rights a dynamic quality that can lead to an almost constant process of revision", he concludes.[33]

In keeping with the foregoing comments by Raz and Scanlon, far-reaching technological developments could be classed as the kind of societal or factual changes that could give rise to the recognition of new duties flowing from an existing right, *in casu*, the right to freedom of expression. Successive waves of technological developments, especially and most recently, the advent of the Internet, have profoundly altered informational and communicative realities throughout the world. Those changes could not have been anticipated when leading human rights treaties with generic provisions safeguarding the right to freedom of expression were drafted and adopted. Consequently, prior understandings of the scope of the right to freedom of expression require urgent updating, adaptation and expansion in order to take account of, and accurately reflect, the complexities of the new communicative dispensation. The ICCPR is a case in point: it was opened for signature and ratification in 1966 and the General Comment on Article 19 dating from 1983 was the leading interpretive text for the Article until 2011.[34] Calls for the UN Human Rights Committee to adopt a new General Comment on Article 19, ICCPR, were therefore well-justified.[35]

The above observations were made in relation to the right to freedom of expression generally, but they are particularly true in relation to access to modern communications technologies. As Jack Balkin has opined:

> Where the exercise of a liberty depends upon technology, access to that technology largely determines the substantive liberty of the actor. Sometimes this is because the liberty in question cannot be enjoyed in any form without a general level of technology.[36]

---

32 *Ibid.*, p. 154.

33 *Ibid.*, p. 154.

34 General Comment No. 10 – Freedom of expression (Article 19), 29 July 1983. This General Comment is due to be replaced by General Comment No. 34. See further: Draft General Comment No. 34 (Upon completion of the first reading by the Human Rights Committee), Doc. No. CCPR/C/GC/34/CRP.6, 3 May 2011, para. 1.

35 Such calls have come from various quarters; see, *inter alia*, Jamie F. Metzl, "Information Technology and Human Rights", 18 *Human Rights Quarterly* (No. 4, 1996), pp. 705–746, at 743–744; Kevin Boyle & Cherian George, Final Report of the 8th Informal Asia-Europe Meeting (ASEM), Seminar on Human Rights – "Freedom of Expression", Siem Reap, Cambodia, 26–28 Cambodia, p. 7 (Recommendation No. 2).

36 J.M. Balkin, "Some Realism about Pluralism: Legal Realist Approaches to the First Amendment", 1990 Duke L.J. 375, at 406.

The future development of access rights will also inevitably give rise to a number of corresponding duties[37] – usually on the part of States authorities. An example of such an obligation is provided by the 2005 Joint Declaration adopted by the [then] three IGO special rapporteurs on freedom of expression, which states:

> The right to freedom of expression imposes an obligation on all States to devote adequate resources to promote universal access to the Internet, including via public access points. The international community should make it a priority within assistance programmes to assist poorer States in fulfilling this obligation.[38]

The IGO special rapporteurs expanded on relevant issues in their 2010 Joint Declaration, under the headings, "Freedom of Expression on the Internet" and "Access to Information and Communications Technologies".[39]

The identification of apposite State duties should be guided by realistic considerations of what is necessary to ensure the effective exercise of all component parts of the right to freedom of expression in practice. Increasingly, in this connection, emphasis is being placed on the availability and accessibility of new media technologies for everyone. This is a key strategy employed in efforts to bridge the digital divide and it accordingly involves the promotion of media and technological literacy.[40] The World Summit on the Information Society (WSIS) Principles and Commitment reveal a keen awareness of the impact of new technologies on contemporary communicative practices. As such, they seek to promote not access to particular media, but to "information and communication infrastructure and technologies" and "information and knowledge".[41] In respect of the former, the WSIS Geneva Principles state that "[U]niversal, ubiquitous, equitable and affordable access to ICT infrastructure and services, constitutes one

---

37 This is particularly what Joseph Raz had in mind when he referred to the "dynamic aspect of rights", cited *supra*.

38 Joint Declaration by the UN Special Rapporteur on Freedom of Opinion and Expression, the OSCE Representative on Freedom of the Media and the OAS Special Rapporteur on Freedom of Expression, 21 December 2005.

39 Tenth Anniversary Joint Declaration: Ten New Challenges to Freedom of Expression in the Next Decade, adopted by the UN Special Rapporteur on Freedom of Opinion and Expression, the OSCE RFOM, the OAS Special Rapporteur on Freedom of Expression and the ACHPR Special Rapporteur on Freedom of Expression and Access to Information, 2 February 2010, paras. 9 and 10, respectively.

40 See, for example, the Special Rapporteurs' Joint Declaration on Diversity in Broadcasting, *op. cit.*

41 Tunis Commitment, World Summit on the Information Society, Tunis, Doc. No. WSIS-05/TUNIS/DOC/7-E, 18 November 2005, para. 9, which summarises the key principles of the Geneva Declaration of Principles (in which paras. 21–23 deal with access to information and communication infrastructure and paras. 24–28 deal with access to information and knowledge): "Building the Information Society: a global challenge in the new Millennium", Declaration of Principles, World Summit on the Information Society, Geneva, Doc. No. WSIS-03/GENEVA/DOC/4-E, 12 December 2003.

of the challenges of the Information Society and should be an objective of all stakeholders involved in building it".[42] Its underlying reasoning is that "[C] onnectivity is a central enabling agent in building the Information Society".[43] In respect of the latter, the WSIS Geneva Principles state that:

> Information in the public domain should be easily accessible to support the Information Society, and protected from misappropriation. Public institutions such as libraries and archives, museums, cultural collections and other community-based access points should be strengthened so as to promote the preservation of documentary records and free and equiable access to information.[44]

The separate attention paid to the accessibility of structures and substance stems from an awareness of the technology-enhanced diversity of sources and vectors for information and ideas. The WSIS Principles and Commitments also recognise that the communicative effectiveness of relevant technologies relies heavily on ancillary factors, like capacity-building measures, the realisation of which may implicate certain State obligations.[45] In this connection, emphasis is also placed on the need to develop digital content in local languages.[46]

The impact of technology can also result in the identification of new State obligations in respect of the synergic interplay between the right to freedom of expression and other rights. The right to effective participation applies across an ever-expanding range of areas of public life. This is a logical consequence of continuous societal progress and attendant adjustments and extensions of democratic practices. With the increasing importance of the Internet and other online means of communication in governance as well as in everyday life, access to the Internet will become determinative for individuals' ability to participate effectively in public life. It must therefore surely only be a matter of time before international standard-setting bodies begin to push for a meaningful concatenation of expressive, participatory and access rights, especially in the realm of online communications.[47]

Other angles of approach to the intersection of rights of participation and access also boast validity and deserve further exploration. The question has, for instance, been framed in terms of "the right to participate fully as consumers and producers in the stream of media and telecommunications".[48] Some commentators have

42 WSIS Geneva Declaration of Principles, *op. cit.*, para. 21; see also, WSIS Tunis Commitment, *op. cit.*, para. 18.

43 *Ibid.*, para. 21.

44 *Ibid.*, para. 26.

45 WSIS Geneva Principles, section 4, paras. 29–34.

46 WSIS Tunis Commitment, para. 14.

47 See also, in this connection: David Honig, "What Kind of Future for Television?", 32 *Intermedia* (No. 4, November 2004), pp. 10–15, at 15.

48 *Ibid.*, at 14.

departed from the notion of rights of universal access to take the underlying concept a step further. Nico van Eijk, for instance, has referred in this context to a "contiguous" right to easily access information.[49] The subtext here is that the right is contiguous *to the right to freedom of expression*. Similarly, Owen Fiss has argued that a "proper regard for democratic values requires *easy access to all ideas*, for without such exposure the public is not likely to know its options or the costs of the present arrangements under which it lives".[50]

The validity of such a right of easy access to information and ideas has not gone unchallenged. So far, relevant issues have only been given rather scant consideration by the European Court of Human Rights. In *Appleby*, for instance, the applicants submitted that notwithstanding the existence of other expressive outlets, they had een denied "the easiest and most effective method of reaching people".[51] The Court dealt with this argument by focusing on the particular facts of the case at hand instead of seeking to elaborate any findings of more general applicability. Thus, the Court found that the applicants could not claim that they had been "effectively prevented from communicating their views to their fellow citizens"[52] as a result of the refusal by the property-owners to admit them onto their property. The Court would not be drawn on the question of whether the applicants' right to freedom of expression could otherwise be exercised in a meaningful manner.[53] It is still premature to speculate whether *Appleby* will become a controlling precedent for this question, but the Court's reliance on the central criterion of the effectiveness of the enjoyment of the right to freedom of expression seems both prudent and consistent with its settled case-law.[54] The ease with which information and ideas can be accessed is therefore perhaps best understood as a measure of the effectiveness with which the right to seek and receive information and ideas is exercised in practice.

11.1.4 Prognosis for the future development of access rights

The various contributions by the above-named factors to the ongoing and likely future development of access rights are highly synergic. Indeed, all of those factors converge in the following observations by T.M. Scanlon:

---

49 Nico van Eijk, "Search Engines: Seek and Ye Shall Find? The Position of Search Engines in Law", *IRIS plus* – Supplement to IRIS – Legal Observations of the European Audiovisual Observatory, 2006–2, pp. 5 and 7.

50 (emphasis added) Owen M. Fiss, "Silence on the Street Corner", XXVI *Suffolk University Law Review* (No. 1, Spring 1992), pp. 1–20, at 19.

51 *Appleby and Others v. the United Kingdom*, *op. cit.*, para. 48.

52 *Ibid.*

53 *Ibid.*

54 The European Court of Human Rights has consistently held that it seeks to guarantee not rights that are theoretical or illusory, but rights that are practical and effective. See further, Chapter 4.1.2.

> One aim of freedom of expression is to provide opportunities for the kind of public discussion that is an essential precondition for fair democratic politics. If the political system is to be fair, however, a significantly widespread equality of opportunity to engage in this discussion is required. [...] But in a society like ours, one cannot achieve a significant degree of equality of access to effective means of expression simply through the strategies that freedom of expression has traditionally involved (i.e. simply by constraining the power to regulate expression).[55]

Scanlon follows up on this observation by suggesting that the imperative of achieving a significant degree of equality of access to effective means of expression triggers positive State obligations to find new strategies for the same. Viewed from another angle, we witness a dove-tailing of the right to equality and the right to effective participation in public life. These rights join each other at the right to freedom of expression and glide further by virtue of their inherent dynamism.

A crucial notion in Scanlon's observation is that of access to "*effective* means of expression" (emphasis added). It is commonly – and correctly – believed that the right to freedom of expression does not include the right (or any other kind of entitlement, for that matter) for one's expression to achieve its desired perlocutionary effects or to lead to the achievement of particular results/consequences. Conversely, it cannot be accepted that freedom of expression is a purely self-regarding activity either. Otherwise, it would simply have no claim to special constitutional protection. In recent times, there has been much lively academic and political debate in the context of WSIS about whether or not the right to freedom of expression could usefully be restyled as a right to freedom of communication. One of the arguments that has featured in that debate suggests that such a step would be logical in light of the (implicit) communicative dimension already present in prevailing conceptions of freedom of expression and protected accordingly. A full discussion of the desirability of granting legal recognition to the right to freedom of communiation is beyond the scope of this book. Nevertheless, it is important to acknowledge the existence of that communicative dimension within the right to freedom of expression. The right to freedom of expression stretches to cover the free, multidirectional flow of information and ideas. The other-regarding aspect of expressive activity is therefore not in doubt.

On the basis of these observations, it is legitimate to hold that a speaker must be able to communicate his/her message to others. It is not enough – on any theory of freedom of expression, or under positive international law – for him/her to be able to utter his/her message in private and only in private. It is the variously designated public, interactional, communicative nature of the expressive act that is the essence of the right. This is not to presume or even infer that speakers enjoy any kind of

55 T.M. Scanlon, "Content regulation reconsidered", *op. cit.*, at 158–159.

entitlement to compel a reluctant audience.[56] Properly understood, it is the right to realise the communicative potential of expression (which is not the same as predetermining the outcome of expression). What matters, therefore is that expression would have a fair or reasonable chance of being effectively communicated. It is submitted here that that is how Scanlon's reference to "effective means of expression" should be construed.

Closely related to the notion of "effectiveness" of means of expression is the notion of equivalence of means of expression. As shown in the discussion on media functionality (Chapter 3.2.1), all media do not share the same objectives or *modus operandi* and their different outlooks and approaches can have significant bearing on the assessment of their actual effectiveness. Equality of expressive opportunity is only possible if the premise of comparable, or roughly equivalent, viability between media is upheld. As posited by Owen Fiss:

> to rely exclusively, or even primarily, on parading or picketing [...] would leave to the less powerful elements in society only the least effective modes of political persuasion. Compare one day's work of distributing pamphlets at a local shopping center with a half hour on TV. Effective speech in the modern age is not cheap.[57]

Such considerations can be determinative when the access of a would-be speaker to a particular medium is denied and the only alternative fora available are qualitatively different in character to the would-be speaker's first choice of medium. This proposition is obviously highly contingent on relevant circumstantial factors. The basic point, though, is that the effectiveness and equivalence of particular media can legitimately be taken into consideration when seeking to ascertain whether the right to freedom of expression has been infringed.

Given the quasi-public character of certain institutions, outlets or locations – a broad public interest in access can militate against narrow private interests, such as proprietary rights.[58] It may well prove necessary for the State to secure access for third parties to such places in order to ensure that the right to feedom of expression is not merely theoretical or illusory. That is the essence of the public forum doctrine, which could arguably be extended to means of expression such as the media (eg. insofar as they provide a public forum for debate). If opportunities to participate in public debate are stymied, there is little chance that the debate itself will be "uninhibited, robust and wide-open".[59]

---

56 Although on some versions of the theory of freedom of expression, such unsolicited exposure could be included. See further, T.M. Scanlon, "Content regulation reconsidered", *op. cit.*, at 154.

57 Owen M. Fiss, "Why the state?", in Judith Lichtenberg, Ed., *Democracy and the mass media* (USA, Cambridge University Press, 1990), pp. 136–154, at 150–151.

58 See: *Steel & Morris v. UK*, Judgment of the European Court of Human Rights (Fourth Section) of 15 February 2005; *Appleby v. UK, op. cit.*

59 *New York Times v. Sullivan*, 376 US 254 (1964), at 270.

Notwithstanding the fact that access rights are of a qualified nature, a violation of the right to impart information and ideas could arise if the denial of access were to be found to be arbitrary or discriminatory. This is further evidence of the cross-cutting nature of the right to non-discrimination and equality.

11.2 General "taxonomy" of access rights

The notion of access to the media is as crucial as it is amorphous. Any meaningful assessment of its importance for minorities must proceed from a clear delineation of its many applied meanings. In other words, what is required is – to borrow Monroe Price's catchy phrase – "a taxonomy of access".[60]

A preliminary distinction between possible types of access is self-explanatory and can be dealt with in a perfunctory manner. It is the distinction between the concepts implied by the somewhat uncouth terms, passive and active access.[61] The former term refers to end-users' ability to receive information/media output; it is consonant with the idea of universal service (to use conventional technical jargon). It is very important in terms of the right to receive information and ideas without restriction that physical, technological, linguistic, or indeed socio-economic factors should not impede the exercise of this right. Active access to the media suggests involvement in the creation of media output (especially by participation in managerial, editorial and production processes and representation in relevant structures) and this will be the main focus in our taxonomy of access proper.

Yet even the reference to "active access to the media" is deceptively self-contained: in reality, what is involved is varying degrees of access to different types of media. If the media are conceived of as complex processes with necessarily inter-related institutional, individual and group dynamics, it becomes important to identify and distinguish between the different degrees of access. First and foremost, the notion of active access implies, according to Karol Jakubowicz, "the ability of minorities to be actively involved in the work of the mainstream media in a variety of capacities, or to own and operate their own minority media".[62] It should also involve their "access to decision-making and the work of bodies involved in legislation,

60 Monroe E. Price, *Television The Public Sphere and National Identity* (New York, Clarendon Press, 1995), p. 194. See also: Monroe E. Price, "An Access Taxonomy", in Andras Sajo, Ed., *Rights of Access to the Media* (The Netherlands, Kluwer Law International, 1996), pp. 1–28.

61 See further: Karol Jakubowicz, "Report: A critical evaluation of the first results of the monitoring of the Framework Convention on the issue of persons belonging to national minorities and the media (1998–2003)", in *Filling the frame: Five years of monitoring the Framework Convention for the Protection of National Minorities* (Strasbourg, Council of Europe Publishing, 2004), pp. 113–138, at 133.

62 *Ibid.*

regulation and oversight of the media".[63] These different layers of access will be discussed in more concrete terms in Chapter 11.3, but for the moment, it suffices to link them back to earlier discussions about the promotion of pluralistic tolerance and intercultural dialogue in various institutional structures in the media sector (Chapter 5), as well as the potential of co-regulatory measures for enhancing the participatory rights of persons belonging to minorities in the media sector (see Chapter 3.3).

A plethora of different types of access can be recognised, both voluntary and mandated. Some are designed to enhance freedom of expression and its underlying value of pluralism; others seek to empower groups and individuals politically and culturally. Others still are designed to stimulate independence and creativity of output or uphold qualitative standards in output. Different types of access and factors affecting minorities' access to the media will be discussed in s. 11.3, *infra*. Beforehand, a classic form of access – the right of reply[64] – will be described in terms of the protection it is accorded under international law and its usefulness for minorities discussed. Public access channels will also be discussed.

11.2.1 Right of reply as a form of access

The putative right of reply is not provided for *expressis verbis* in the relevant articles of leading UN conventions or in the ECHR. The absence of a provision is by no means accidental.

The desirability of such a provision was debated on several occasions during the drafting of the ICCPR. A text submitted by the UN Conference on Freedom of Information contemplated the institution of such a right, which it formulated as follows: "A State may establish on reasonable terms a right to reply or a similar corrective remedy".[65] The usefulness of the right to reply was stressed – along with that of "subsequent criminal liability" – as a preferable means of correcting misinformation to prior censorship.[66] In the heel of the hunt, a provision enshrining the right of reply was omitted not for reasons of principle, but due to technical considerations. There was general consensus among the drafters that such a provision would be more at home in "special conventions in the field of freedom of information" than in the more generalist ICCPR.[67]

---

63 *Ibid.*, at 133–134.

64 See generally, Marie McGonagle, "A Right to Reply", in Manfred Wichmann & Wolfgang Heinz, Eds., *Freedom of Expression and Human Rights Protection* (Brussels, Friedrich Naumann Stiftung, 1998), pp. 271–292.

65 Drafting Committee, 2nd Session (1948), cited in Marc Bossuyt, *Guide to the "Travaux Préparatoires" of the International Covenant on Civil and Political Rights*, *op. cit.*, p. 374.

66 Marc Bossuyt, *Guide to the "Travaux Préparatoires" of the International Covenant on Civil and Political Rights*, *op. cit.*, p. 399.

67 *Ibid.*, p. 400.

For its part, the title of the UN Convention on the International Right of Correction[68] is at first glance slightly misleading. It could be taken to suggest a right of correction that is internationally available. The international dimension is present, but it is really concerned with a right of correction that is inter-national, or, more accurately, inter-State. This convention has long been regarded as ineffectual and irrelevant.

A right of reply is not expressly provided for in Article 10, ECHR, and relevant case-law from the adjudicatory organs in Strasbourg has accordingly been meagre. Nevertheless, the European Court of Human Rights has held that "as an important element of freedom of expression", the right of reply does fall within the scope of Article 10.[69] The Court puts this down to "the need to be able to contest untruthful information, but also to ensure a plurality of opinions, especially in matters of general interest such as literary and political debate".[70] Thus conceived, the dual purpose of recognising a right of reply under Article 10 can be described as to protect the rights of others (in accordance with Article 10(2)) and to act as a safeguard for the much-prized pluralism of information and opinions.[71]

In the case, *Ediciones Tiempo S.A. v. Spain*, the Commission refuted the suggestion that the judicially-enforced insertion of the aggrieved individual's reply was a disproportionate interference with the publication's right to freedom of expression. The Commission pointed out that the publishing house was not obliged to modify the content of the impugned article and moreover, it was allowed to republish its version of the facts alongside the aggrieved individual's reply.

In the case, *Melnychuk v. Ukraine*, the Court engaged more thoroughly with key aspects of the nature, scope and importance of the right to reply. The case involved a newspaper's refusal to publish the applicant's reply to a critical review of a book written by the applicant. The newspaper maintained that it had refused to publish the reply on the basis that it contained "obscene and abusive remarks" about the reviewer; that its reasoning had been communicated to the applicant and that he had declined the invitation to edit his reply accordingly.[72] The Court declared the application inadmissible and recalled once more that the right to freedom of expression does not confer on individuals or organisations "an unfettered right [...] to have access to the media in order to put forward opinions".[73] It then noted that "as a general principle, newspapers and other privately-owned media must be free

68 435 UNTS 191, entry into force: 1962.

69 *Melnychuk v. Ukraine*, Decision of inadmissibility of the European Court of Human Rights (Second Section) of 5 July 2005, para. 1 (p. 6 of decision).

70 *Ibid.*, para. 1 (pp. 6–7 of decision).

71 See also in this respect: *Ediciones Tempo S.A. v. Spain*, Decision of inadmissibility of the European Commission of Human Rights of 18 June 1987, Application No. 13010/87.

72 *Melnychuk v. Ukraine*, *op. cit.*, p. 2 of decision.

73 *Ibid.*, para. 1, p. 7 of decision.

to exercise editorial discretion in deciding whether to publish articles, comments and letters submitted by private individuals".[74] It acknowledged that, against this background, "exceptional circumstances" may nevertheless arise "in which a newspaper may legitimately be required to publish, for example, a retraction, an apology or a judgment in a defamation case".[75] Situations such as these may create a positive obligation "for the State to ensure an individual's freedom of expression in such media".[76] The Court concluded by reiterating that a general, base-line obligation of the State is to ensure, in any event, that "a denial of access to the media is not an arbitrary and disproportionate interference with an individual's freedom of expression, and that any such denial can be challenged before the competent domestic authorities".[77]

Article 8 of the European Convention on Tranfrontier Television also provides for a right of reply in the following terms:

> 1. Each transmitting Party shall ensure that every natural or legal person, regardless of nationality or place of residence, shall have the opportunity to exercise a right of reply or to seek other comparable legal or administrative remedies relating to programmes transmitted by a broadcaster within its jurisdiction, within the meaning of Article 5. In particular, it shall ensure that timing and other arrangements for the exercise of the right of reply are such that this right can be effectively exercised. The effective exercise of this right or other comparable legal or administrative remedies shall be ensured both as regards the timing and the modalities.
>
> 2. For this purpose, the name of the programme service or of the broadcaster responsible for this programme service shall be identified in the programme service itself, at regular intervals by appropriate means.

This provision can be relied upon by any "natural or legal person in order to correct inaccurate facts or information, in cases where such facts or information concern him/her or constitute an attack on his/her legitimate rights (especially in regards to his/her dignity, honour or reputation)".[78] As such, it can certainly be invoked by individual members of all minority groups, irrespective of the nature of those groups, as long as they are democratic.[79]

One of two documents cited as having influenced the text of Article 8,[80] the Committee of Ministers' Resolution (74) 26 on the right of reply – position of the

---

74 *Ibid.*
75 *Ibid.*
76 *Ibid.*
77 *Ibid.*
78 Explanatory Report to the European Convention on Transfrontier Television, as amended, para. 168.
79 *Ibid.*, para. 170.
80 *Ibid.*, para. 167.

individual in relation to the press, also dealt with the issue, but it has been thoroughly revised in order to take account of major technological developments in the media sector (eg. the existence and widespread use of electronic archives[81]). As a result, it has effectively been replaced by Recommendation Rec (2004) 16 of the Committee of Ministers to member states on the right of reply in the new media environment.[82] The Preamble to the Recommendation links the right of reply to, *inter alia*, the public's interest in receiving "information from different sources, thereby guaranteeing that they receive complete information". While this statement panders to the goal of pluralism, the right to reply, as configured in the Recommendation, is only of limited value in attaining that goal.

It is concerned with correcting specific, individual inaccuracies and is not designed to be a platform for countering broader patterns of stereotyping or negative reporting. According to the Recommendation, a reply must be limited to a correction of the facts challenged.[83] Moreover, it only applies to "factual inaccuracies and not opinions",[84] thereby adhering to the conceptual distinction consistently underlined by the European Court of Human Rights, *viz.* that the latter are not susceptible of proof. Again, the limited focus of the right *ratione materiae* points up its unsuitability for use as a foil for negative reporting. The basic point being made here is that the right of reply can be a valuable tool at the micro level, for dealing with specific instances of inaccurate reporting of facts, but it clearly cannot be taken as a central prong in a more ambitious, pro-active strategy of correction at the macro level.

As already mentioned, there have been pronounced efforts to synchronise the standard-setting measures of the Council of Europe and the European Union in the audiovisual sector.[85] It is therefore unsurprising that the EU's Audiovisual Media Services Directive should contain provisions guaranteeing a right to reply in almost identical terms to the ECTT. Article 28 of the Directive reads as follows:

> 1. Without prejudice to other provisions adopted by the Member States under civil, administrative or criminal law, any natural or legal person, regardless of nationality, whose legitimate interests, in particular reputation and good name, have been damaged by an assertion of incorrect facts in a television programme must have a right of reply or equivalent remedies. *Member States shall ensure that the actual*

81 Para. 7 of Recommendation Rec (2004) 16 and corresponding text in Explanatory Note.

82 Adopted by the Committee of Ministers on 15 December 2004.

83 Principle 5 – Exceptions.

84 Explanatory Memorandum to the draft Recommendation on the right of reply in the new media environment, CM(2004)206 addendum, 17 November 2004, para. 12.

85 Explanatory Report to the ECTT, paras. 39, 40. See further: Daniel Krebber, *Europeanisation of Regulatory Television Policy: The Decision-making Process of the Television without Frontiers Directives from 1989 & 1997* (Nomos Verlagsgesellschaft, Baden-Baden, 2002), esp. Chaps. 4, 5 & 6.

exercise of the right of reply or equivalent remedies is not hindered by the imposition of unreasonable terms or conditions. The reply shall be transmitted within a reasonable time subsequent to the request being substantiated and at a time and in a manner appropriate to the broadcast to which the request refers.

2. A right of reply or equivalent remedies shall exist in relation to all broadcasters under the jurisdiction of a Member State.

[...]

The italicised text was introduced by the amendment to the original Television without Frontiers Directive in 1997 and it seeks to vouchsafe the fairness and proportionality of modalities implementing the right of reply. As with its ECTT equivalent, the overriding concern is for the correction of inaccuracies that would adversely affect the legitimate (especially reputational) interests of natural or legal persons. The kind of access it offers is therefore subject to the same limitations of reaction and responsiveness. In a Recommendation on the protection of minors and human dignity and on the right of reply, adopted by the European Parliament and the Council of the European Union in 2006, EU Member States are called on to introduce measures regarding the right of reply (or "equivalent remedies") in relation to online media, taking into account the "particularities of each type of medium".[86]

The American Convention on Human Rights uniquely sets out the right of reply as an autonomous human right and should therefore be mentioned in passing.[87] It is not conceived of as a limitation on the right to freedom of expression or conditionalised in any other reductionist manner. The operative article reads:

Article 14 Right of reply

1. Anyone injured by inaccurate or offensive statements or ideas disseminated to the public in general by a legally regulated medium of communication has the right to reply or make a correction using the same communications outlet, under such conditions as the law may establish.
2. The correction or reply shall not in any case remit other legal liabilities that may have been incurred.

---

86 Recommendation of the European Parliament and of the Council of 20 December 2006 on the protection of minors and human dignity and on the right of reply in relation to the competitiveness of the European audiovisual and on-line information services industry (2006/952/EC), *Official Journal of the European Communities*, L378/72 of 27 December 2006, Section I, para. 1. See also, *ibid.*, Preambular para. 15 and Annex I.

87 American Convention on Human Rights, 22 November 1969, Organization of American States Treaty Series No. 36 (entry into force: 18 July 1978).

3. For the effective protection of honor and reputation, every publisher, and every newspaper, motion picture, radio, and television company, shall have a person responsible, who is not protected by immunities or special privileges.

One of the arguments of predilection of opponents of the right of reply is that by mandating such replies, pluralism is actually dimished as the reply takes up limited space (or airtime), thereby reducing further the available opportunities for the expression of yet other views.

To the extent that the right of reply is corrective in nature, it is an important but insufficient form of access for persons belonging to minority groups. It is a reactive mechanism which affords a valuable opportunity to set facts straight, counter individual prejudicial attacks and challenge specific instances of stereotyping. But its potential for advancing identity and culture is inherently (and severely) limited. It does not set its own terms; it responds to terms set by others. There is no provision for pre-emptive thrusts. It merely allows for ripostes within imposed strictures of substance and form. Defensive and parrying, it cannot be a basis for sustaining more positive images of minorities precisely because it is reactionary.

11.2.2 Public access channels

Public access channels on cable or satellite networks are channels that have been reserved for non-commercial purposes. Typically, such purposes would include various kinds of public interest broadcasting – in the realms of education, community matters, civic affairs, etc. Whereas must-carry obligations tend to concentrate on particular channels, obligations on cable or satellite operators to free up a portion of available capacity for public interest broadcasting can be open to a wider range of potential participants. The concept of public access channels is well-established in Germany, where they are known as *Öffene Kanale* (trans. "Open Channels").[88] This name captures the essential openness of the channels; indeed, the channels are in principle open to all parties who do not or cannot operate their own broadcasting station. They are designed to be accessible and inexpensive and in practice they are often State-subsidised. As such, public access channels offer considerable potential for ensuring minority access to programme transmission facilities. In practice, airtime is often offered on a first-come, first-served basis.

88 See further: Natali Helberger, "Germany", in Tarlach McGonagle, Bethany Davis Noll & Monroe Price, Eds., *Minority-Language Related Broadcasting and Legislation in the OSCE*, Study commissioned by the OSCE High Commissioner on National Minorities (Programme in Comparative Media Law and Policy (PCMLP), University of Oxford & the Institute for Information Law (IViR), University of Amsterdam, 2003), pp. 217–229, at 219; John Keane, *The Media and Democracy* (UK, Polity Press, 1991), p. 159; Donald R. Browne, *Ethnic Minorities, Electronic Media and the Public Sphere* (Cresskill, New Jersey, Hampton Press, Inc., 2005), p. 59.

In respect of minority use of public access channels, a noteworthy development is the emergence, particularly in urban contexts, of so-called "rainbow" stations. The name derives from the diversity of (ethnic) minorities using them. "Rainbow" stations have been defined by one commentator as "those stations (usually community radio) with a wide diversity in program content, divided into generally small segments of airtime".[89] An obvious attraction of rainbow stations (and public access channels generally) is the large measure of editorial autonomy enjoyed by minority groups availing of the opportunity presented. In light of the autonomously segmented broadcasting model involved, there is not necessarily much contact between representatives of the different groups. However, even if it does depend largely on the particular personalities involved on all sides, the potential for interaction and cooperation between the various groups does exist.

Conversely, one of the typical drawbacks of so-called "rainbow" community stations is the limited amount of airtime available to each minority group. Temporal restrictions impose editorial prioritisation, which more often than not result in preference being given to (local) news, chat shows, items on culture, religion, language (depending on the predominant interests of the group) and music.[90] Given the (predictable) prioritisation of what is perceived as staple content, there is little scope for more creative programming or diversity of genres and formats. Another conceivable drawback of such stations is the likelihood that the communicative process will not reach beyond members of the group itself. The wider public will not, for instance, gain exposure to the broadcasts by virtue of their transmission on a mainstream channel, thereby limiting the potential for inter-cultural communication.

Another version of public access stations worth mentioning is the *närradio* ("nearby radio"), developed in Denmark, Norway and Sweden.[91] Under these schemes (which appear to work well in practice), any group or association may apply to use low-power transmitters (located throughout the countries in question) to broadcast their own programmes.[92] A couple of practical problems associated with the system ought to be mentioned. First, the limited reach of the signals emitted by the transmitters means that the service is only suitable for groups whose members live within a narrow radius of the transmitter, eg. in urban or local rural areas. Second, "the program schedule for any given transmitter may be full in the more popular broadcast hours, so newcomers might have to settle for the early morning hours".[93] The potential of public access channels has also been recognised in relevant

89 Donald R. Browne, *Ethnic Minorities, Electronic Media and the Public Sphere*, *op. cit.*, p. 66 (fn. 36).

90 See *ibid.*, p. 167.

91 See further *ibid.*, pp. 58 and 60.

92 *Ibid.*

93 *Ibid.*, p. 58.

standard-setting texts. The 2003 Guidelines on the use of Minority Languages in the Broadcast Media, for instance, suggest that:

> States should consider providing "open channels" – i.e. program transmission facilities, which use the same frequency, shared by a number of linguistic groups within the service area – where there are technical limitations on the number of frequencies available and/or groups that do not have sufficient resources to sustain their own services.[94]

11.3 Development of rights of access to the media for minorities under international law

11.3.1 FCNM: factors affecting minorities' access to the media

A number of factors tend to influence minorities' access to the media, particularly in their own languages,[95] including:[96]

- Linguistic topography
- Official recognition of minorities/languages
- Market sustainability
- Licensing of broadcasters (*)
- Regulation of broadcasting output (*)
- Transfrontier dimension
- Temporal and qualitative criteria (*)
- Facilitative measures

In practice, these factors tend to ebb and flow into one another through tentatively-drawn definitional demarcations, and thereby defy neat categorisation. Nevertheless,

94 Section IV. Promotion of Minority Languages – A. Frequencies.

95 This subsection reworks and updates sections of: Tarlach McGonagle, "Commentary: Access of persons belonging to national minorities to the media" in *Filling the frame: Five years of monitoring the Framework Convention for the Protection of National Minorities*, *op. cit.*, pp. 144–159. For a more detailed analysis, see: Tarlach McGonagle, Bethany Davis Noll & Monroe Price, Eds., *Minority-language related broadcasting and legislation in the OSCE*, Study commissioned by the OSCE High Commissioner on National Minorities (Programme in Comparative Media Law and Policy (PCMLP), University of Oxford & the Institute for Information Law (IViR), University of Amsterdam, 2003), especially the section entitled 'Overview', pp. 1–31. The Overview points out which factors are of relevance in which countries.

96 Some of the factors listed here apply exclusively or almost exclusively to the broadcast media – they are denoted by asterisks. The discussion of the enumerated factors is consciously weighted in favour of the broadcast – as opposed to print – media as the former tend to have to operate in an environment that is comparatively more complicated in terms of regulatory permutations and combinations and technological considerations.

it is useful to examine the influence they can wield over access to the various stages of the printing/broadcasting process. As will now be discussed in greater detail, the Advisory Committee on the FCNM has been alert to the importance of these factors in its Opinions.[97] These factors have implications for how the right to freedom of expression is exercised in practice because they connect in different ways with the fundamental characteristics or situational specificities of persons belonging to minorities, both of which are, as explained in Chapter 3, of direct relevance for their ability to exercise their right to freedom of expression in an effective manner.

11.3.1(i) Linguistic topography

The linguistic topography of a State is as it is. It has inevitably been shaped by myriad historical, geographical, demographic, political, economic, sociological, cultural, religious and other influences. So, it is easiest simply to concede that "it is what it is" and deal with the reality at hand. More often than not, States are multilingual rather than monolingual, but this term, "multilingualism", is – of course – capable of having endless shades of meaning. It is how a State chooses to deal with its linguistic make-up that is crucial.

11.3.1(ii) Official recognition of minorities/languages

The recognition of some minorities/languages, but not of others, either by constitutional or legislative means, or even as a general principle of public policy, can have very practical and concrete consequences, for instance, for the distribution of the allocative resources of the State. To what extent should issues such as the numerical strength,[98] the geographical concentration, the internal organisational structures or the lobbying initiatives of minorities or linguistic minorities influence the distribution of a State's available financial resources? Express recognition does not necessarily have to be more effective than tacit, assumed or *de facto* recognition. Nor does recognition (of any kind) offer any guarantee of preferable or even adequate measures to further the use of minority languages in broadcasting. Conversely, though, non-recognition does not – of itself – preclude the adoption of effective measures in this regard. The Advisory Committee has homed in on the need for equality in the distribution of available resources, as exemplified by the following pronouncement:

---

97 For stylistic reasons, and especially to ease the task of the reader, a selection of examples of the Advisory Committee's consideration of these factors intersperse the more general analysis of the same. Unless otherwise stated, cited Advisory Committee Opinions relate to the first monitoring cycle of the FCNM.

98 This is one key aspect of a broader question which has been referred to as "Problems of Numbers": see John Packer, "Problems in Defining Minorities", in Deirdre Fottrell & Bill Bowring, Eds., *Minority and Group Rights in the New Millennium* (The Hague, Martinus Nijhoff Publishers, 1999), pp. 223–273, at 260.

> The Advisory Committee is concerned, however, at the uneven distribution of resources, concerning both television and radio programmes, among the various minorities. It considers the present situation problematic, since one of the main minorities, the Roma community, seems to have far less airtime than the others, particularly for programmes in its own language. Some programmes for Roma also appear to have been dropped. It is therefore important that the authorities look into this matter, and try to revise the balance – but without cutting airtime for other minorities.[99]

The Advisory Committee's concern for the fair distribution of resources is not limited to airtime: it has also called for available funding for minority programmes to be allocated on an "equitable" basis,[100] or to be reviewed/increased, paying particular attention to numerically-smaller minorities.[101]

11.3.1(iii) Market sustainability

This topic requires little elaboration. Nowadays, the media have to operate in an increasingly competitive and commercialised environment. This is especially true of the broadcasting sector. In consequence, the need to boost audience shares is growing steadily as a driver of broadcasting policy. Public service broadcasters (PSBs) are also willy-nilly caught up in this vortex, despite the specificity of their mandate. The stark reality is that minority-interest programmes (and especially minority-interest programmes in "less prevalent (national or regional) languages"[102]) almost never command large audience shares. This can have adverse effects on advertising revenues, which in turn can lead to a general reluctance to broadcast minority-language programmes, particularly at peak viewing/listening times. In such an inhospitable climate, a persuasive case can be made for contemplating prescriptive regulation; financial stimulation; administrative relaxation (see further, 'Facilitative measures', *infra*), all with a view to adequately catering for the needs and interests of persons belonging to national minorities. As noted by the Advisory Committee:

> [...] In so far as the national minorities encounter difficulties in financing their publications, the Advisory Committee urges the authorities to increase the relevant State support and to pay particular attention to the numerically smaller minorities, who do not have sufficient resources to sustain their publications.[103]

---

99 Advisory Committee Opinion on Romania, 6 April 2001, para. 46.

100 Advisory Committee Third Opinion on Croatia, 27 May 2010, para. 130.

101 Advisory Committee Third Opinion on Finland, 14 October 2010, para. 106.

102 Bruno de Witte, "Surviving in Babel? Language Rights and European Integration", in Yoram Dinstein & Mala Tabory, Eds., *The Protection of Minorities and Human Rights* (Dordrecht, Martinus Nijhoff, 1992), pp. 277–300, at 299.

103 Advisory Committee Opinion on Lithuania, 21 February 2003, para. 52.

When the situation of a particular minority group and/or its language is precarious, financial stimuli may prove necessary to ensure its survival. Similarly, some minority(-language) media are financially more robust than others: due to general trends of waning readerships, the traditional printed press is experiencing acute difficulties and is therefore also more reliant on public monies than more lucrative media. The Advisory Committee often addresses these issues, including jointly,[104] and has also recognised the importance of financial support for ensuring the online availability of information in minority languages.[105]

11.3.1(iv) Licensing of broadcasters

Licensing is a classic regulatory tool and sometimes a licensing/regulatory authority can be expressly ascribed the task of upholding freedom of expression, diversity, pluralism, the public interest and other key values in broadcasting. The principles of licensing may have to reflect these preoccupations, or even to stimulate programming for minorities. Such goals can be pursued by adopting and implementing distinct licensing policies for different types of broadcasting.

Responsiveness to the needs and interests of the target community is a standard feature of the licensing regime in many States. An ability to add to existing diversity in the broadcasting sphere can be a criterion affecting the licensing process. The likely benefits for the development of cultures of ethnic and other minorities can also be considered.[106]

Insofar as it is employed as a licensing criterion, preference for the use of a particular language can be an advance specification for a public tender. Otherwise, linguistic commitments can be agreed upon and formalised in an individualised manner, and later become binding, for example, by their incorporation into a broadcaster's *cahier des charges*.

It should also be noted that the promotion of the official/State language is often encountered as one of the stated goals of the licensing process. Again, the Advisory Committee has shown keen awareness of the interplay between such a goal and other relevant issues:

> [...] While recognising that the Russian Federation can legitimately demand broadcasting licensing of broadcasting enterprises and that the need to promote the state language can be one of the factors to be taken into account in that context, the said article appears to be overly restrictive as it implies an overall exclusion of the

104 Advisory Committee Second Opinion on Switzerland, 29 February 2008, para. 110, which calls for support for print media in the Romanche and Italian languages.

105 Advisory Committee Second Opinion on Sweden, 8 November 2007, para. 94.

106 See, for example, Advisory Committee Third Opinion on Croatia, *op. cit.*, para. 132.

> use of the languages of national minorities in federal radio and TV broadcasting. The Advisory Committee considers that such an *a priori* exclusion is not compatible with Article 9 of the Framework Convention, bearing in mind, *inter alia,* the size of the population concerned and the fact that a large number of persons belonging to national minorities are dispersed and reside within several subjects of the federation.[107]

A quick addendum to this consideration of licensing would do well to focus on the *prima facie* neutrality of the licensing system. Groups using less prevalent/dominant languages typically lack the financial and technological resources which would allow them to meet the – seemingly neutral and egalitarian – licensing specifications. Always of relevance, this gap between theoretical equality and effective equality is more acute in some States than in others.

11.3.1(v) Regulation of broadcasting output

11.3.1(v)(a) Broadcasting in general

Promotion of official/State language(s)

A recurrent feature of language regulation in broadcasting is the goal of promoting the official/State language. The legitimacy of such a goal (often to promote national identity, or intergroup communication and thereby social cohesion) is unlikely to be challenged (*inter alia* because it is widely considered to fall under the margin of appreciation doctrine), as long as it is tempered, proportionate and non-discriminatory in its design or effects. However, sometimes the goal of promoting a particular language is pursued with such zeal that the relevant provisions insist upon the mandatory use of the official/State language, or its nigh-mandatory use. Such zealous approaches are a cause of grave concern.

In most of the States where provision is made for the mandatory use/promotion of the official/State language, limited exceptions are countenanced by relevant legislation, thus mitigating the effect such provisions would otherwise have. Commonly, such exceptions include: programmes intended for minorities; educational or foreign-language programmes; musical programmes; live broadcasts from abroad, and translation requirements.[108]

---

107 Advisory Committee Opinion on the Russian Federation, 13 September 2002, para. 76. The Advisory Committee has also called for minority broadcasters to be exempt from State-language requirements for fixed percentages of airtime: see, for example, its Second Opinion on Serbia, 19 March 2009, para. 156.

108 See further, the 'Overview' in *Minority-language related broadcasting and legislation in the OSCE*, *op. cit.*, pp. 14–17.

It is obviously a constant concern that translation requirements (i) do not entail excessive financial, administrative or practical burdens for broadcasters operating in minority languages, and (ii) can be implemented in a flexible manner (i.e., choice of technique). This concern has not escaped the attention of the Advisory Committee either:

> […] The Advisory Committee agrees that it is often advisable, and fully in the spirit of the Framework Convention, to accompany minority language broadcasting with sub-titles in the state language. However, the Advisory Committee considers that, as far as private broadcasting is concerned, this goal should be principally pursued through incentive-based, voluntary methods, and that the imposition of a rigid translation requirement mars the implementation of Article 9 of the Framework Convention by causing undue difficulties for persons belonging to a national minority in their efforts to create their own media […].[109]

While translation requirements are often perceived in a negative light, they need not necessarily be a limiting factor. For example, subtitling practices, coupled with the use of modern technology, can facilitate the simultaneous reception of programmes in several languages.

General prescriptions requiring that a "reasonable", "significant" or "main part" or "considerable proportion" of programmes be in a given language are commonplace. More specific (i.e., percentaged) provisions or quotas are also frequently encountered and these can vary greatly from country to country.[110] Of course, the key concern here is to determine – in light of all relevant circumstances – the cut-off point at which a prescription favouring the use of one language begins to become a restriction on the use of others. This is quite an instrumentalist approach to the question of language-choice. As has been cogently argued by one commentator: "[r]estricting the use of certain languages simply cuts off potential audiences or makes it more difficult to reach them, and that harms one of the core interests underlying freedom of expression on any plausible account".[111] The Advisory Committee is again clearly attuned to such concerns:

> […] The Advisory Committee considers that, bearing in mind its implications for persons belonging to national minorities and the fact that excessive quotas may impair the implementation of the rights contained in Article 9 of Framework Convention, this practice needs to be implemented with caution. Furthermore, it

---

109 Advisory Committee Opinion on Estonia, 14 September 2001, para. 38.

110 For a more detailed analysis, the reader is referred once again to the 'Overview' in *Minority-language related broadcasting and legislation in the OSCE*, *op. cit.*: see, in particular, pp. 13–14.

111 Leslie Green, "Freedom of Expression and Choice of Language", in W.J. Waluchow, Ed., *Free Expression: Essays in Law and Philosophy* (Oxford, Clarendon Press, 1994), pp. 135–152, at 144.

> would need to be rooted in a more precise legislative basis than what is contained in the above-quoted provision [...].[112]

Promotion of minority languages

In a number of States, provisions for the use of minority languages in broadcasting are styled as the obverse of provisions for official/State languages. Where specific obligations concerning minority languages do not exist, another frequently-exploited way of pursuing the same goal is the existence of provisions for the promotion of minority cultures or (general) interests. Although some States lack statutory provisions for the use of minority languages in broadcasting which are applicable across the board, it can be deceptive not to examine other contextual considerations thoroughly. Legislative provisions may only apply to certain designated broadcasters (PSBs, for instance) or at certain (geographical) levels. Furthermore, legislative provisions may serve to affirm opportunities rather than stipulate prescriptions in concrete terms. Having said all that, legislation in a number of States does require broadcasters in general to provide for minority-language broadcasting (or at least for the languages of certain minorities (as defined by law)), or minority-oriented broadcasting.

11.3.1(v)(b) Public service broadcasting

The playwright Arthur Miller once remarked that a good newspaper is a nation talking to itself. By analogy, so too is a good PSB, which is arguably a more obvious vehicle for the advancement of socio-cultural and linguistic objectives than other types of broadcasters. This argument grows from traditional perceptions and expectations of PSBs, including that they would: deliver quality of services and output; boast general geographical availability; provide a wide range and variety of programmes and show concern for national *and* minority identities and cultures (see further, Chapter 3.2.2(ii)). The last-listed expectation is crucial. It demonstrates very clearly that PSBs have to tread a very fine line by trying to satisfy majority and minority sections of the population simultaneously. This is also true of the linguistic demands and preferences of any population. The challenge is therefore to provide general programming in mutually comprehensible languages so that inter-community communication can be safeguarded, while also catering for the extant linguistic specificities in society to the greatest extent possible.

As with the regulation of broadcasting in general, the language obligations on PSBs are also twofold: the official/State language and other languages. The focus here will be on the latter. General PSB obligations to ensure programming in various languages exist in some States, while elsewhere, the practice has been developed to

112 Advisory Committee Opinion on Ukraine, 1 March 2002, para. 46.

a limited degree without it actually being required by law. Specific prescriptions exist in a number of States too. Also of relevance are general requirements that PSBs must devote specified amounts or percentages of their broadcast time to minority groups, without any linguistic stipulations being applicable. While this approach does not preclude some of the available time being used for programming in minority languages, it has the advantage of showing greater deference to the editorial autonomy of those making use of the slots. It also recognises that minority interests are not necessarily tied to linguistic preferences.

11.3.1(vi) Transfrontier dimension

For reasons of geographical proximity; cultural affinity; ethnic dispersity; the hard facts of recent history or economic realities (if not to say vulnerabilities), or any combination of the above, bilateral agreements and cooperative initiatives can play a hugely significant role in securing access to the media, especially in relevant languages. Examples of bilateral agreements which are general in character and contain sections on broadcasting are numerous. Aside from such general treaties, States also adopt bilateral treaties specifically on broadcasting. In a number of countries, according to available means, technology is being harnessed in order to enhance transfrontier broadcasting targeting minorities.

All of this is built on the premise that the ability to receive broadcasting from abroad should not obviate the need or responsibility for States to keep their own houses in order as regards the fostering of domestic (minority-language) broadcasting and/or locally-produced programmes.[113] The Advisory Committee has repeatedly acknowledged the relevance and importance of broadcasts from neighbouring or kin-States for minorities.[114] Concern must therefore attach to any attempts by States to impose restrictions on the reception of broadcasts from other States (either from specific States or generally). In the words of the Advisory Committee:

> [...] The Advisory Committee [...] considers that availability of such programmes from neighbouring states does not obviate the necessity for ensuring programming on domestic issues concerning national minorities and programming in minority languages.[115]

---

113 See, for example, *ibid.*, para. 89 and Advisory Committee Second Opinion on Albania, 29 May 2008, para. 136.

114 See, for example, Advisory Committee Second Opinion on the United Kingdom, 6 June 2007, para. 167 and Advisory Committee Second Opinion on Germany, 1 March 2006, para. 92.

115 Advisory Committee Opinion on Albania, 12 September 2002, para. 50. See also: "[...] the Advisory Committee underlines that the availability of foreign broadcasting in Estonia in a language of a national minority does not eradicate the need for, and importance of, domestically produced broadcasting in that language." – Advisory Committee Opinion on Estonia, *op. cit.*, para. 37.

11.3.1(vii) Temporal and qualitative criteria

What is crucial here is ensuring a satisfactory response to the "needs and interests" of the target audience. Some States have made legislative provision for programming (i) catering for the needs and interests of persons belonging to national minorities, and (ii) in the languages of persons belonging to national minorities, to be broadcast at certain times. Less specific provisions have been adopted elsewhere, but share the same aim: for example, where a "fair balance" has to be struck between minority groups/languages, including in the allocation of broadcasting slots. The Advisory Committee has been highly critical of the practice of broadcasting minority programmes at inappropriate/off-peak times, thereby making it difficult for them to reach their full target audience.[116]

11.3.1(viii) Facilitative measures

A consideration of measures that promote access to, and the use of minority languages in, broadcasting is a problem-solving exercise; an invitation to think outside the box. Put briefly, it is the search for best practices, forwarding-looking and often experimental initiatives.

The representation of minorities in general and linguistic minorities in particular, on relevant authorities and decision-making bodies greatly enhances the development of policies and norms which cater for their needs and interests. Active, or better still, pro-active consultation with such groups by the relevant authorities and decision-making bodies is another way of pursuing the same goal. As such, these practices can be perceived as outgrowths of more general democratic principles. Perhaps the best relevant paradigm is that elaborated by Karol Jakubowicz: "representative participatory communicative democracy".[117] This involves the application of principles of participatory democracy to broadcasting (structures). The basic idea is that while not every individual member of a group can actually broadcast, the organisational structures of the broadcasting entity should strive to facilitate maximum participation by all members in influencing policies and fixing goals.

There are only very sporadic examples of broadcasting authorities incorporating concern for minority language interests into their structures (eg. by means of the appointment of a minority language officer or committee); more common are provisions guaranteeing general representation for persons belonging to national

116 See, for example, Advisory Committee Third Opinion on Hungary, 18 March 2010, paras. 89–95.

117 Karol Jakubowicz, "Access to the Media and Democratic Communication: Theory and Practice in Central and Eastern Europe", in András Sajó, Ed., *Rights of Access to the Media*, *op. cit.*, pp. 139–163, at 145.

minorities in their composition. Ensuring the meaningful involvement of persons belonging to national minorities in the various stages of the legislative process[118] is also a priority concern:

> [...] the Advisory Committee encourages the authorities to take account of the needs of persons belonging to national minorities when preparing and adopting this legislation. In its view, the Government should consult with national minority representatives in order to ensure that any support it provides will be sufficient to meet the needs and to strike an appropriate balance among the various national minorities in terms of media access and presence [...].[119]

In some States, language advisory councils have been established within PSB structures. In others, PSB audience councils, programming councils and advisory committees perform more general advisory roles, often as regards regional or local programming or programme schedules. It is interesting to compare the variety of approaches adopted by such advisory organs in different countries and to consider the extent to which they actively liaise with relevant audiences, including national minorities. The Advisory Committee has also considered relevant issues:

> [...] It notes that the absence of such programmes is explained by the fact that no request to that effect was ever made, but points out that a formal request to that effect is not a legal precondition for considering the implementation of such a facility [...].[120]

Notions of social and special-interest broadcasting can, when properly calibrated and applied, play an instrumental role in the promotion of minority languages in broadcasting. This concept is recognised in a number of countries and it leads to particular regimes applying to types of broadcasting dedicated to fulfilling specific societal missions or meeting stated niche interests (including those of linguistic minorities).

Another variant on this theme concerns special treatment for particular genres of broadcasters in terms of access to infrastructure and technology that would ordinarily be beyond their financial reach. It is fairly typical for such practices to involve the sharing of channels and frequencies between broadcasters in order to defray start-up and operational costs. They can also involve the hosting of minority-interest broadcast output by established broadcasters. A rich mine of potential could be tapped into here:

---

118 A number of definitions for co-regulation exist. Loosely put, it is a practice which involves both traditional law-makers and interested parties/representatives of civil society in the regulatory process. See further, Susanne Nikoltchev, Ed., *IRIS Special – Co-Regulation of the Media in Europe* (Strasbourg, the European Audiovisual Observatory, 2003).

119 Advisory Committee Opinion on Armenia, 16 May 2002, para. 54.

120 Advisory Committee Opinion on Denmark, 22 September 2000, para. 30.

> [...] The Advisory Committee also notes that digital, cable and satellite broadcasting will bring with it new and further possibilities for meeting demands. Encouragement should be given to opening up broadcasting further to national minorities, using for example opportunities offered by the implementation of new technologies.[121]

The aforementioned study, *Minority-language related broadcasting and legislation in the OSCE*, also documents the vast array of other measures that could broadly be categorised as facilitative of (i) improving access to broadcasting for persons belonging to national minorities, and (ii) the use of minority languages in broadcasting. These include flexible and favourable financing schemes and fiscal regimes and the placing of firm emphasis on capacity-building; a notion of wide embrace which could include ensuring greater support for the education and training – in their own languages – of (i) students of journalism and (ii) media professionals. The promotion of programme production and distribution can also make an important contribution to the creation of a healthier climate in which the goal of (qualitatively and quantitatively) increased broadcasting by and for persons belonging to national minorities, including in minority languages, can be achieved. Needless to say, the above all rings true for publications which share the same objectives as their audiovisual counterparts.

Finally, it should also be noted in passing that language policy documents are becoming increasingly commonplace; plotting future courses of action; devising development strategies; pursuing progress... or not. This observation is of relevance to the extent that States' language policies help to shape the matrix in which broadcasting and publishing in minority languages takes place, even when the theory and practice are out of sync with one another.

As discussed in Chapter 11.2, one cannot but help feeling that "access to the media" has become something of a stock phrase, the utility of which matches the vagueness that encompasses a number of specific concerns and contexts. Whatever benefits are likely to be gained by frequently relying on a sloganistic phrase of such broad compass, there is a danger that longer-term analytical aims will be compromised. This danger could be averted or reduced if the term were to be systematically linked back to more probing and contextualised analysis by the Advisory Committee.

11.3.2 ECRML: factors affecting minorities' access to the media

11.3.2(i) Official recognition of languages

The official recognition of languages can be of both practical and symbolic importance and the Committee of Experts has, on a number of occasions, been

121 Advisory Committee Opinion on the United Kingdom, 30 November 2001, para. 69.

confronted with uncertainties as to the status of languages/dialects and the nature of their recognition by States authorities. The status of the Kven language in Norway is a case in point. The Committee called for clarification of its status because, as it put it: the "Norwegian authorities seem, on the one hand, to acknowledge the Kven as a national minority, but on the other hand, not to take a stand as to whether the Kven language is a separate language from Finnish".[122] The acknowledgement of Kven as a separate language would, in the Committee's opinion, "probably facilitate the formulation of structured proposals for concrete measures".[123]

Without wishing to detract from the validity of the probabilistic assumption made by the Committee of Experts in respect of the benefits that would accrue from official recognition of the Kven language, the importance of official recognition for minority groups as groups should not be downplayed. Such recognition can constitute a constitutional or legislative basis for a range of participatory and other rights and entitlements. For example, it can lead to guarantees of representation in national councils for minorities, which must be consulted on all law- and policy-making initiatives that are of relevance to persons belonging to minorities.

Uncertainty about the status of a language can arise from its degree of distinctiveness, both in relation to other languages or in relation to dialects. In this vein, the Committee of Experts notes, but does not adopt a position on, a curious anomaly concerning the application of the Charter in the Netherlands. Whereas the Dutch authorities have recognised the position of Limburgish as a language under the Charter, the Dutch Language Union (*Taalunie*) recognises Limburgish only as a dialect and not as a language, as such.[124] As noted *supra*, different benefits tend to flow from different statuses, but the criteria for distinguishing between languages and dialects are generally political as well as socio-linguistic. As one commentator famously quipped, a language "is a dialect that has an army and navy".[125] The Committee of Experts has shown itself to be acutely aware of relevant complexities:

> Where there exists a linguistic continuum with persons in adjacent territories speaking variants similar to one another, the distinction between a language and a dialect can be a difficult question. It involves not only the linguistic criterion, but also often political, social, cultural and historical criteria.[126]

---

122 First Report on Norway, 1 June 2001, Finding D.

123 *Ibid.*

124 First Report on the Netherlands, 9 February 2001, para. 45.

125 Max Weinreich, cited in John Edwards, *Multilingualism* (London and New York, Routledge, 1994), p. 24.

126 First Report on Sweden, 6 December 2002, para. 31.

A final relevant consideration is the extent to which particular languages are moribund. The importance of the distinction between living and dead languages is self-evident, but nevertheless contentious.[127]

11.3.2 (ii) Active access to media

In respect of Croatia, the Committee found that a "major drawback to the application of the Charter" in respect of media and culture is the "lack of participation by the users or representatives of the regional or minority languages in the organization, planning and funding of activities in this field".[128] This finding is perspicacious because the distinct references to the organisational, planning and funding levels reflect an awareness of the different kinds of impact that participation can have at each of those levels. The strength of this finding therefore lies in its differentiation.

On other occasions, the Committee has focused on particular forms of participation and access. For instance, in respect of Cyprus, it has welcomed as a "form of *direct* participation" (emphasis added), the presentation of Armenian and Maronite programmes by members of the respective communities and the negotiation of the content of the programmes with CyBC.[129]

The importance of linguistic representation on PSB boards has also been acknowledged in the context of existing provisions for the same in several countries.[130]

The foregoing examples reveal that the ECRML does contain considerable potential for promoting the participatory rights of speakers of regional or minority languages in the media sector. However, this potential is subject to the inherent limitations of the Charter itself. As noted by the Committee of Experts in the analogous context of using regional or minority languages in dealings with States authorities:

> [...] Although the Charter can help regional or minority language speakers who have difficulty in communicating with authorities, its principal objective is to give regional or minority languages themselves a public dimension through their use in official situations, which confers an increased legitimacy on these languages. [...][131]

---

127 For example, the Committee of Experts noted that the extent to which Skolt Sami is still a living language is unclear: Third Report on Norway, 16 May 2007, para. 12.

128 First Report on Croatia, 2 December 2000, Finding E; see also: Second Report on Croatia, 26 November 2004, Recommendation 3.

129 First Report on Cyprus, 24 March 2006, para. 77.

130 First Report on Slovenia, 21 November 2003, paras. 144, 219; Second Report on Croatia, *op. cit.*, para. 180; Second Report on Finland, 24 March 2004, para. 152.

131 First Report on Denmark, 21 November 2003, Finding J.

11.3.2(iii) Market sustainability

The Committee of Experts has urged States authorities to make greater use of existing financial support schemes and legal regulations that allow for promoting the use of regional or minority languages in the media. It considers that such measures do not constitute "undue interference with editorial freedom" and that they should be relied on more extensively.[132] The Committee has also pointed out that although "Frisian radio and television are put on an equal footing with the Dutch language radio and television in other regions of the Netherlands", the "extra cost of broadcasting in Frisian is not therefore taken into account in the allocation of subsidies".[133]

11.3.2(iv) Facilitative measures

On a number of occasions, the Committee has recommended training for journalists in regional or minority languages,[134] which can be seen as a long-term strategy for producing (news) content in regional or minority languages.

Given that the ECRML is centrally concerned with the preservation of regional or minority languages, many of which are in situations of considerable precarity, it is not surprising that factors influencing linguistic survival are regularly assessed. This is more explicit than under the FCNM. For instance, public perceptions of regional or minority languages and the social prestige which they enjoy are a recurrent concern of the Committee of Experts. Prominent usage in the media, especially television, can "enhance considerably" the "social prestige" of a regional or minority language and thereby be "a crucial factor" for its protection and promotion.[135] More specifically, the Committee has pointed out that the use of a regional or minority language in the media can contribute to "making it a modern language and [encouraging] young people to learn and speak it".[136] The Committee has also noted other ways for improving the prestige of regional or minority languages, such as their inclusion in the cultural component of national foreign

---

132 See, for example, First Report on Germany, 5 July 2002, Finding N.

133 First Report on the Netherlands, 9 February 2001, Finding B. It should be noted, however, that in their Comments on the Report, the Dutch authorities subsequently pointed out that this situation had been addressed by an amendment of the Media Act in September 2000 which makes regional broadcasters as well as national public brodcasting eligible for funding to promote Dutch cultural radio and television broadcasting productions (Appendix II to Report).

134 See, for example: Report on Switzerland, 1 June 2001, Finding E.

135 Second Report on Switzerland, 24 March 2004, para. 118. The Committee of Experts follows up on this point in its Findings in the same report, reiterating that "the presence of a regional or minority language on television is of the utmost importance for its maintenance in modern societies" – Finding G.

136 Second Report on the Netherlands, 17 June 2004, Finding H.

policies. Thus, the Committee was critical of the omission of Frisian language and culture from the "Dutch cultural policy abroad".[137]

Role of the Committee of Ministers

The Committee of Ministers (CM) plays a similarly important role in the monitoring of the ECRML to the role it plays in the monitoring of the FCNM, detailed *supra*. Its country-specific Recommendations certainly have the potential to give the findings of the Committee of Experts a valuable political imprimatur. In practice, this potential has not been optimally exploited. As noted in respect of the CM's country-specific Resolutions concerning the application of the FCNM, the texts adopted by the CM are by their nature much more summary the ECRML's and essentialist than the more detailed, discursive reports drafted by the Advisory Committee on the FCNM or the ECRML's Committee of Experts. Their function is not to provide explanatory detail but to emphasise priorities in a way that purports to be politically meaningful.

Notwithstanding these qualifications, the overall impact of the CM's Recommendations has been disappointing. They are, in general, even less detailed than the CM's Resolutions concerning the FCNM and not infrequently lack media-specific recommendations (see further, Chapter 4.3.2). In those Recommendations in which media-specific measures were urged, they were often vague or sloganistic or reworded versions of obligations to which the State Party in question had already committed itself. As such, they have done little to raise general levels of understanding of the nature of States' obligations regarding the media under the Charter, let alone advance their implementation.

By way of illustration, the recommendations have tended to focus on "measures" (or even "concrete measures"[138]) "to improve the presence of" specific languages on radio and television, without specifying what type of [concrete] measures or what types of broadcasting.[139] The CM has also, on other occasions, called on States authorities to "take a more active approach towards promoting the presence of the regional or minority languages in the media" and to adopt a "structured approach"[140] or a "more structured policy"[141] for protecting and promoting the use of specific regional or minority languages in the media. Again, due to their generalistic

137 *Ibid.*, Finding I.

138 CM Recommendation on Finland (on basis of first report), 19 September 2001, para. 2. This recommendation was directed at increasing the presence of Sami within the media and called for "concrete measures" for "the creation of newspapers and the broadcasting of regular television programmes".

139 CM Recommendation on Armenia (on basis of first report), 14 June 2006, para. 3.

140 CM Recommendation on Spain (on basis of first report), 21 September 2005, para. 4.

141 CM Recommendation on Denmark (on basis of first report), 19 May 2004, para. 1.

formulation, such recommendations are of limited practical value. Similarly, the CM has recommended that State authorities "increase" radio and television broadcasting in specific languages, again without clarifying crucial aspects of its recommendation.[142] Granted, the CM cannot be too directional in its recommendations for fear of overstepping its mandate and leaving itself open to accusations of interventionism. However, the trouble with recommendations such as these is that they are too open-ended to press States towards targeted action to remedy the identified shortcomings in the way they have been discharging relevant obligations under the Charter. Calls for "resolute action", for instance, on the Swiss authorities "to improve the provision for Romansh on television and radio in the private sector",[143] are an improvement on the lame phrases adverted to *supra*, but only by virtue of their ability to convey a sense of urgency as to the need for State action.

Having said all that, there have been several examples of the CM rising above platitudes and hollow-sounding rhetoric to make more purposive recommendations. For instance, it recommended that the Croatian authorities:

> create institutional mechanisms that encourage direct participation of the users of regional or minority languages in planning, funding and organising cultural activities and in the field of the mass media.[144]

In respect of the Netherlands, the CM has urged the relevant national authorities to "take into account the special needs of broadcasting in Frisian and consider increasing its financial support".[145]

11.3.3 New technology-driven challenges for the FCNM and ECRML

As societies come to depend increasingly on new technologies for expressive and communicative purposes, the need for the public to have non-discriminatory, effective access to those technologies rises accordingly. Following this logic, it seems reasonable to countenance situations where the inability to access relevant technologies could impair the enjoyment of the right to receive and impart information and ideas. The digital divide is a major concern for many minority groups because such groups are regularly disadvantaged in socio-economic and political terms. Concerns relate to the use of relevant technologies both to receive and to impart information and ideas. When such disadvantages are suffered by persons belonging to national minorities, they can tend to compound their political

142 CM Recommendation on Austria (on basis of first report), 19 January 2005, para. 6.
143 CM Recommendation on Switzerland (on basis of second report), 22 September 2004, para. 4.
144 CM Recommendation on Croatia (on basis of first report), 19 September 2001, para. 3.
145 CM Recommendation on The Netherlands (on basis of first report), 19 September 2001, para. 3.

disenfranchisement, social exclusion and inability to effectively exercise their right to freedom of expression. This explains relevant drives for universal access and the general facilitation of access to communications technologies at IGO and State levels.

A further, important aspect of burgeoning technologies concerns the requisite knowledge and skills to use them. This concern is often explored under the headings of media or Internet literacy.[146] One definition of media literacy is "the ability to access, understand and create communications in a variety of contexts".[147] Again, there is good reason to fear that many members of minority groups will lack familiarity and know-how when it comes to the latest communications technologies. However, this need not always be the case: an OFCOM study revealed, *inter alia*, that "[o]verall in terms of usage and general competence, minority ethnic groups have somewhat higher levels of media literacy compared to the UK as a whole across the digital platforms".[148]

More substantively, though, technological advances are ushering in some truly transformative changes to the media sector: increased reliance on "pull" (as opposed to "push") technologies and the concomitant increase in audience choice; proliferation of opportunities to engage in unmediated mass communication; virtual elimination of traditional constraints on communication of temporal and spatial factors, etc. The growth of niche markets, the waning of public reliance on general interest intermediaries and the growing incidence of advance individual selection of news sources are all serving to insulate citizens from broader influences and ideas. These individualising trends in new forms of broadcasting also engender social fragmentation, by eroding the potential for shared experience through broadcasting. As Cass R. Sunstein has argued, "[W]ithout shared experiences, a heterogeneous society will have a much more difficult time in addressing social problems".[149]

These issues are currently being examined by the Council of Europe's Committee of Experts on Issues Relating to the Protection of National Minorities (DH-MIN).

---

146 See, for example, the Council of Europe's *Internet Literacy Handbook* (2004).

147 This is the definition elaborated by the UK's converged regulatory authority, OFCOM, after formal consultation with stakeholders. For an exploration of the prevalent academic, regulatory and policy definitions of "media literacy", see: Tarlach McGonagle, "Media Literacy: No Longer the Shrinking Violet of European Audiovisual Media Regulation?", in Susanne Nikoltchev, Ed., *Media Literacy, IRIS plus 2011–3* (Strasbourg, European Audiovisual Observatory, 2011), pp. 7–27.

148 OFCOM, "Media Literacy Audit: Report on media literacy amongst adults from minority ethnic groups", 3 April 2006, p. 5.

149 Cass R. Sunstein, *Republic.com* (USA, Princeton University Press, 2001), p. 9. See further: Tarlach McGonagle, "Changing Aspects of Broadcasting: New Territory and New Challenges", *IRIS plus*, Supplement to *IRIS – Legal Observations of the European Audiovisual Observatory*, 2001–10.

The Report which forms the basis of this examination,[150] as well as its accompanying Comments,[151] provide valuable overviews of the nature of many of the technological advances that are prompting reconfigurations of relevant paradigms in broadcasting regulation and practice. As such, they provide a very useful basis for further analysis of the precise implications of such changes for minorities' access to the media. Such further analysis would certainly be timely. Although originally uttered a number of years ago (already), Beth Simone Noveck's remark, "[t]hough the future is digital, our thinking about regulation is analogue",[152] retains a large degree of validity today, especially in the applied sphere of minority broadcasting regulation and practice.

Notwithstanding significant new technological opportunities, many of the familiar characteristics of existing media and regulatory and other factors influencing media activities, continue to be *de rigueur*. Moreover, the overarching framework of human rights and fundamental values remains unaltered. However, this should not in any way downplay the importance of technology-driven changes. Such changes merit careful examination in their own right, but also in terms of the adaptive strategies which they often engender in the more traditional media.[153] Thus, the continued relevance of many regulatory and other factors to minorities' access to the media may themselves undergo qualitative changes and acquire new focuses of application. Participatory concerns, for example, are likely to shift to the elaboration of digital switch-over strategies, and concerns for visibility of media services are likely to shift to electronic programme guides (EPGs).

Conclusions

The ability to exercise the right to freedom of expression effectively is very often contingent on having equitable access to viable expressive opportunities/fora. Nevertheless, the protection of the right to freedom of expression under international law does not, in its current state of development, guarantee any freedom of forum as

150 Tom Moring, "Access of national minorities to the media: new challenges", Report for the Committee of Experts on Issues Relating to the Protection of National Minorities (DH-MIN), Council of Europe, Doc. No. DH-MIN(2006)015.

151 Tarlach McGonagle, "Comments on the report on 'Access of minorities to the media: new challenges'", Committee of Experts on Issues Relating to the Protection of National Minorities (DH-MIN), Council of Europe, Doc. No. DH-MIN(2006)016; Karol Jakubowicz, "Comments on the report on 'Access of minorities to the media: new challenges'", Committee of Experts on Issues Relating to the Protection of National Minorities (DH-MIN), Council of Europe, Doc. No. DH-MIN(2006)017.

152 Beth Simone Noveck, "Thinking Analogue About Digital Television? Bringing European Content Regulation Into The Information Age", in Chris Marsden & Stefaan Verhulst, Eds., *Convergence in European Digital TV Regulation* (London, Blackstone Press Ltd., 1999), pp. 37–63, at 38.

153 See further, Tom Moring, "Access of national minorities to the media: new challenges", *op. cit.*

such. Nor does it ordinarily extend to include an individual or group right of access to a particular means of expression or to particular media. Such a right could only be construed in specific and exceptional circumstances, eg. monopoly situations in the broadcasting sector or systemic, discriminatory obstacles to access.

Although access to the media primarily concerns the right to freedom of expression, its other key concerns include the right to non-discrimination/equality and the right to effective participation in public life. This means that an extremely powerful coalition of rights is brought to bear on the question of access to the media. Moreover, this is an area in which it is imperative that the interpretive approach to relevant rights is dynamic. Provisions in international law promoting access to the media, such as they are, were drafted in an earlier era and have been left in the slipstream of technological and societal developments since. As those texts were intended to be evolutive and bases for the further development of human rights, they must be interpreted so as to reflect the profound changes that communicative practices have undergone in the intervening period. Authoritative interpretive texts should urgently be updated in order to engage with these new communicative realities in a way that anticipates further development and change.

At this juncture, the analysis again insists on the usefulness of the concept of media functionality: in light of the technology-driven changes to communicative practices, it is timely to assess the functionality of traditional and new media/communications technologies, specifically from the perspective of persons belonging to minorities. Again, the unpacking of the media into different types of media is a necessary analytical step: new technological capacities have enabled the explosion – in terms of volume and diversity – of media types and formats. Each offers a different level of functionality to its users.

The notion of access must also be broken down into its possible component parts: it, too, has been rendered more complex and layered due to technological developments. Access can denote access to regulatory mechanisms, institutional structures of the media, editorial and management processes, production facilities, software codes, transmission facilities, airtime, column inches or screen spaces or (in a more passive sense) to content. These distinctions largely mirror the emphasis in Chapter 9 on the distinct importance of gauging media- and information-related pluralism/diversity at the levels of source/ownership, outlet and content. Differentiation between qualitatively different types of access is therefore essential for evaluating their effectiveness in relation to the right of freedom of expression of persons belonging to minorities.

This Chapter's survey of jurisprudence emanating from the European Court of Human Rights, in particular, reveals that the Court appears to under-appreciate the instrumentality of access rights in rendering the right to freedom of expression effective in practice. In specific cases in which access to particular media has been denied, the Court has accepted far too unquestioningly that the mere availability of alternative means of expression meant that there had been no infringement of Article 10, ECHR. The critical questions that the Court should have asked – and should always ask – are whether the alternative means of expression are truly accessible to relevant parties, and whether they constitute viable alternatives. In this latter connection, an assessment of the functionality of the alternative means of expression is necessary: to what extent do the specific characteristics of the medium correspond to the specific communicative needs of the person seeking to exercise his/her right to freedom of expression? The alternative means of expression do not have to be identical to the means of expression to which access has been denied, but they should offer rough equivalence in terms of purpose, functionality and reach. Owing to the fundamental, compositional and situational characteristics of minority groups, it is harder to match the purposive features, functionality and reach of particular means of expression with groups' specific communicative needs. The above considerations should therefore be integrated more systematically into the monitoring of treaties such as the FCNM and the ECRML.

To date, the monitoring of both treaties has led to improved understandings of the importance of access to the media for persons belonging to minorities. It has done so by linking access to the advancement of cultural objectives, the promotion of pluralistic tolerance and a number of other goals. It has also done so by identifying a number of issues that tend to hinder access to the media in various ways. However, the different ramifications of access to the media – traditional and new – remain under-explored (although the general trend is gradually improving). The monitoring bodies' engagement with differentiated forms of access to various means of expression needs to become more thorough and more systematic than is presently the case. One of the commendable achievements of the monitoring of the FCNM and ECRML to date has been the elucidation of the content of the right to freedom of expression for persons belonging to minorities/speakers of regional or minority languages. This has also led to the elaboration of a valuable body of best practices. A more detailed and coherent approach to questions of media purpose, functionality and reach would greatly enhance the quality and accuracy of evaluations of whether the right to freedom of expression of persons belonging to minorities is effective in practice.

Summary and conclusions

Addressing the problématique

To recapitulate, the main objectives of this study have been to: (i) identify and group; contextualise and describe, and (iii) critically evaluate prevailing international legal standards concerning the dynamic interface between the right to freedom of expression and the rights of persons belonging to minorities. The critical evaluation was concerned, above all, with the effectiveness of the right to freedom of expression of persons belonging to minorities in practice. The central research question pursued was therefore formulated as follows: are the conceptualisation and calibration of relevant international legal standards sufficiently nuanced and robust to ensure that persons belonging to minorities are able to exercise their right to freedom of expression in an effective manner?

The third, and most challenging, prong to the central research question – the critical evaluation of standards – is all-important and will be the primary focus of these conclusions. Nevertheless, the importance of the first two components to the central research question should not be underestimated, owing to: (i) the disparate provisions of international standards that deal with relevant issues and the fact that they are binding on States to varying degrees; (ii) the multiplicity of contextualising factors that affect the framing and assessment of relevant international standards and how they are/ought to be interpreted – the interrelated character of all human rights; operative public values which shape the interpretive matrix; the relevance of media functionality and technological possibilities for the exercise of the right to freedom of expression in practice. This study has expressly sought to be theoretically informed and politically aware – an aim that necessarily leads to two further layers of contextualisation. All of these contextualising foci will feature recurrently in these conclusions.

Rights of persons belonging to minorities

Chapter 1 of this book begins by grouping and surveying the main rationales for the focus in international law on the protection of minority rights. In the interests of critical evaluation, it is important to consider the extent to which these rationales have informed the drafting and final wording of relevant international texts. The chapter examines the legal and political difficulties that explain why, to this day, no hard-and-fast definition of a "minority" has been enshrined in international law. Chapter 2 then charts the development of the international protection of minority rights through focuses on the emergence of key texts and institutional developments. Drawing on each of these elements, it assesses the *status quo* and makes a number of recommendations for future progress in respect of the protection of minority rights.

As argued in Chapter 1, the specificity of minority rights is not that they are conceptually distinct from or additional to universal human rights; rather, their realisation implicates different, and often more extensive, State obligations. The specificity of minority rights is worth dwelling on – also here in the conclusions – because it is conceptually fundamental to this book.

One of the premises on which the concept of minority rights rests is that an overly individualistic approach to human rights protection can, in various respects, prove inadequate for guaranteeing the effective realisation of the human rights of persons belonging to minorities. The limitations of a system of protection of human rights that is exclusively focused on individual rights are revealed by an examination of the most commonly invoked rationales for minority rights.

First, the most basic objective of minority rights is to ensure the existence and survival of minority groups *qua* groups (as opposed to their individual members). Second, minority rights are often regarded as an important mechanism for ensuring that the application of non-discrimination and equality provisions to persons belonging to minorities guarantee equality that is not merely formal but effective. This may necessitate specific measures in order to counteract "historical inequities" from which minority groups often suffer. Such trends of injustice, traditional or established patterns of persecution and discrimination, engrained societal prejudice, and other socio-cultural, economic and political factors stemming from membership of a minority group can be more or less determinative of how a group is structured and situated *vis-à-vis* other groups in society. In turn, these structural considerations can affect the substance of rights and strategies for their protection. On such a reading, minority rights aim to approximate for persons belonging to minorities the circumstances enjoyed by majority sections of the population. Thirdly and similarly, situational considerations arising from group membership can adversely affect the ability of members of a group to fully realise their individual right to cultural identity. The thickness of individual identity is a crucial notion for these purposes. This notion portrays identity not as simply innate, but as being shaped by a range of external influences, which often flow from group or societal associations.

A fourth principal rationale for minority rights recognises the importance of the group dimension to a range of individual rights. That recognition in no way presumes to affect the inalienability of individual human rights. Rather, it serves to stress the dual nature of minority rights or, in other words, their individual and collective dimensions. The symbiotic relationship between the individual and collective dimensions of minority rights is usefully illustrated by the example of linguistic rights. While the need for a right may be individual (eg. the right to use one's mother tongue), the exercise of the right can conceivably be collective and therefore dependent on interaction with others (eg. the ability to *effectively* use one's mother tongue). Cultural, participatory and associative rights also illustrate the inherent duality of minority rights. As a result of that duality, different strategies are required for the realisation of minority rights.

Despite these justifications for the protection of minority rights, the "fate of minorities" has suffered from congenital politicisation and prevarication. The consistent failure of international law-makers to forge a legally-recognised and -binding definition of a "minority" has merely exacerbated these congenital dispositions. The absence of a legally authoritative definition at the international level leaves the door open for subjective interpretations of the term at the national level. The erroneous – but prevalent – assumption that the official recognition of minority groups leads *ipso facto* to an obligation to guarantee a broad *corpus* of additional rights, or even to fuel the (latent) secessionist ambitions of minority groups, also explains the reluctance of many States to pursue the issue in international law-making fora. This fear is encapsulated in the perceived "spiral 'cultural autonomy, administrative autonomy, secession'".[1] As a general objection to minority rights, the presumption of a (direct) causal connection between the recognition of minority groups by States and their ultimate secession from the States that recognise them, is flawed. Minority rights are in no way contingent on the prior recognition of discrete minority groups by State authorities. It has long been held under international law that the existence of a minority is not a matter of law, but of fact.[2] Nor can it be a matter of political discretion either.

For the purposes of international law, the term, "minority", is not simply a description of a group that is numerically inferior to the majority population in a given society and whose members share certain characteristics or interests. Rather, it is understood as a group which is numerically inferior and distinguished on the basis of certain shared, specified – i.e., ethnic, cultural, religious or linguistic – characteristics. Furthermore, members of the group must harbour a sense of solidarity directed towards the preservation of their culture, traditions, religion or language. This is the general thrust of approximate definitions of a minority in intergovernmental circles, but slight variations in the formula do tend to come to

1 Heinrich Klebes, "The Council of Europe's Framework Convention for the Protection of National Minorities", 16 *Human Rights Law Journal* (No. 1–3, 1995), pp. 92–98, at 96.

2 Advisory Opinion of the Permanent Court of International Justice (PCIJ) in the *Greco-Bulgarian "Communities"* case: Advisory Opinion No. 17, July 31, 1930, Series B, No. 17, pp. 4 – 46, at 22. See also the corroborating statement at p. 27: "it is incorrect to regard the "community" as a legal fiction existing solely by the operation of the laws of the country".

the fore from time to time. Although a definition has never been formally adopted in a legally-binding multilateral treaty, the so-called "Capotorti definition" remains a central reference point in relevant debates. Under this approach, a combination of objective and subjective criteria is applied for the recognition of minority groups. The relevance of this approximate definition is relatively unchallenged at the European level, although regional and national (European) approaches do place heavier insistence on "national" minorities.

An important upshot of the foregoing is that relevant discussions at the highest level are (implicitly) framed in terms of a relatively narrow range of (supposedly) constitutive characteristics of minorities. In this connection, it is important to resist any implicit suggestion that collective identities are largely static. Characteristics that are constitutive *are* fundamental, but they are not necessarily fixed and they are capable of undergoing natural evolution or concerted development. Emphasis on the salient shared characteristics ascribed to all group members must not overlook the internal differentiation within the group. Rich literature exists in sociology and in political science demonstrating the thickness of identities and how they are shaped by myriad influences, including those relating to group membership. Definitional approaches to minorities should explicitly embrace the richness of that literature and reflect the importance of fluidity in notions of identity (i.e., the ability of individual identity to respond (and adapt) to changing personal and societal circumstances), which is of increasing relevance as networking and globalising trends in contemporary society continue unabated.

A more disconcerting problem with the definitional approach sketched above is the inclusion of a nationality criterion. This definitional element requires the prior presence (of unspecified duration) of a minority in a State in order for it to be recognised as a minority. The position taken in Chapters 1 and 2 is that it is inappropriate for the recognition of minority rights to be made contingent on such unspecified temporal considerations. As long as a minority group satisfies the other definitional requirements, its minority status should be recognised accordingly. The length of time a minority has been present in a State could, however, be a relevant consideration when assessing the extent of State obligations towards the realisation of a particular minority group's specific needs. The question of classification of minorities (for the purpose of ascertaining their needs and the extent of State duties towards them) is a separate and subsequent question to the questions of definition and recognition. "New" minorities should therefore be included under relevant international standards of protection. This is the line that has been taken by the UN Human Rights Committee, but the question has proved divisive in numerous international fora. The highly politicised nature of the question should not detract from the imperative of securing human rights for everyone. The importance of an effective right to freedom of expression is very often most acute for "new" minorities, migrant workers, recent immigrants, refugees and non-citizens, who are otherwise politically disenfranchised and are generally excluded from expressive fora and participatory structures and processes in public life. These arguments explain this study's insistence on the inclusion of "new" minorities under relevant international standards of protection.

Freedom of expression

The right to freedom of expression rests on different theoretical bases with varying levels of complementarity. Chapter 3 demonstrates that each of the traditionally-invoked rationales for freedom of expression has clear relevance for minorities – both in terms of their individual members and of their viability as collectivities. The rationale of self-fulfilment is particularly important for minorities which are distinguishable from other sections of the population by virtue of their linguistic and/or cultural identity. Their individual and collective self-fulfilment is contingent on their ability to fully exercise their right to freedom of expression in their own language(s) in public and in private and also to articulate and thereby develop and shape their cultural identity. As such, freedom of expression is vital for the protection, consolidation, (inter-generational) transmission, development and promotion of minority languages and cultures. The other main rationales for freedom of expression can be loosely grouped together as advancing: (i) the quest for truth/avoidance of error, and (ii) participation in democratic society. Again, the ability to receive and impart information and ideas in minority languages can determine the effectiveness of minority participation in public life. Moreover, communicative interaction is imperative in (pluralistic) democratic society, for example, for the preservation and cultivation of inter-group understanding and tolerance. In light of the foregoing, it is necessary to explore the theories and practical modalities of achieving such inter-group harmony in some detail. Pluralistic tolerance in society is undergirded by information- and media-related pluralism.

The ability of persons belonging to minorities to exercise their right to freedom of expression in an effective manner is largely determined by the availability and suitability of expressive fora and media. In this connection, it is necessary to disaggregate the concept of mass media and to conduct specific analyses of particular media philosophies/practices (eg. public service, community, commercial and transnational media) and their level of functionality for minorities. Different types of media correspond to varying degrees to the various but specific communicative needs and preferences of different minority groups in different situations. Degrees of media functionality are therefore crucial considerations in any assessment of whether the right to freedom of expression of persons belonging to minorities is exercised effectively by them in practice. This observation explains the centrality of media functionality to Chapter 3 in particular, but also to the book as a whole.

This analysis takes place against the background of the broader enabling environment for media freedom. In other words, the impact of regulation and regulatory policy on discrete media sectors, with particular emphasis on minorities, is evaluated. The analysis necessarily reckons with the advent of new media technologies (eg. increased convergence of media and increased reliance on user-generated content and the demise of general interest intermediaries) and new regulatory paradigms (eg. co-regulation), both of which have far-reaching implications for practices of communication and participation, including for persons belonging to minorities.

Mapping relevant international standards

The right to freedom of expression, as vouchsafed by international law, comprises a number of key components: the right to hold opinions and to seek, receive and impart information of all kinds regardless of frontiers. The full realisation of the right to freedom of expression necessarily involves different emphases on those individual components. Taken together, those components amount to more than the mere sum of their parts. They cover extremely dynamic processes which typically involve not only speakers and listeners, but also, very often, third parties who are not directly targeted by particular instances of expression, but for whom that expression may nonetheless have implications. The rights – and interests – of persons seeking, imparting and receiving information and opinions, as well as those who are indirectly affected by the same, do not always coincide. While it is important to distinguish between these sometimes divergent and sometimes even conflicting rights and interests ordinarily, the need to do so increases when parties in question are persons belonging to minorities. The reason is that certain group-specific characteristics or situational realities can heavily influence whether or not the rights in question can be exercised effectively by members of the group and the nature and extent of State obligations to ensure that the rights are fully realisable for members of the group.

The range of State obligations to guarantee the right to freedom of expression for persons belonging to minorities implies both preventive and promotional strategies for the full realisation of the different components of the right. It is argued in Chapter 4 that it is important to eschew a binary analytical framework dividing State obligations into the categories of "positive" and "negative", as the distinction between both categories is often fuzzy. It is tidier, conceptually, to view differing State obligations as points along the continuum of so-called "negative" and "positive" State obligations. Chapter 4 identifies a number of programmatic measures that could/should readily be adopted by States authorities in order to guarantee the effective exercise of the right to freedom of expression by persons belonging to minorities. The requirement that States adopt such measures flows from their generic duty to secure human rights for everyone and also specific obligations entered into under specialised minority treaties such as the FCNM.

Whereas the modern international human rights regime is primarily individualistic in character, pertinent treaties and their enforcement/monitoring mechanisms also have the wherewithal to engage with the specific implications of membership of particular, discrete groups in society for the exercise of human rights by members of such groups. The engagement in question can be based on treaties or treaty provisions explicitly focusing on minorities, or derived from other treaties or treaty provisions that are more general in their orientation. Explicit treaties or treaty provisions do not necessarily guarantee more effective engagement with minority rights than the engagement provided for by treaties or treaty provisions that are more general in focus. Very often, the "minority-sensitivity" of the interpretation of relevant norms and the nature of the mechanisms for their implementation are determinant.

The great challenge for international adjudicative bodies is to develop doctrine exploring and elucidating minority rights, while one of the challenges for international treaty-monitoring bodies is to identify and map out best relevant standards at the national and sub-national levels with a view to bringing them to prominence and replicating them at the level of international standard-setting. These distinct roles should not be confused; court decisions are essentially declaratory and courts should not ordinarily be in the business of making policy recommendations.

Although standard-setting exercises by competent bodies can usefully fill the interstices of international treaty law and seek to spell out in greater detail the implications of a right for a variety of parties and in a variety of concrete situations, such exercises need to be conducted with greater circumspection than is often the case at present. When standards pertaining to a particular treaty are elaborated by a competent court or a designated monitoring body, those standards must respect their anchorage in precise treaty provisions. Any standard-setting that does not follow the procedures germane to formal treaty drafting and amendment is subject to inherent limitations. When standards are elaborated extraneously to (specific) treaties, they must nevertheless be mindful of the legal standards enshrined in relevant specific treaties, otherwise it is likely that a problematic hiatus will result between actual legal standards and popular (mis-)understandings of the same.

These concerns have already been raised in Chapter 6 in respect of departures from legally-recognised limitations on the right to freedom of expression. ICERD sits somewhat uneasily with other leading international human rights treaties as regards its engagement with the right to freedom of expression. The operative article in ICERD, Article 4, provides for restrictions on the right to freedom of expression that go beyond those set out in any other comparable treaty. Article 4 is a composite and convoluted article and is widely regarded as having been poorly drafted. Nevertheless, the mitigating influence of Article 5, ICERD, could make the situation workable, but only if CERD would relinquish its hitherto overly strict interpretation of State obligations under Article 4. Its "strict liability" approach to expression is unnuanced and in conflict with prevailing international standards on freedom of expression. It refuses *ab initio* to contextualise expression or to assess or quantify its (likely) harmful impact. Furthermore, CERD is also guilty of mis-applying the standards enshrined in ICERD, thereby further compounding uncertainty as to the precise scope of those standards. As revealed in Chapter 6, two of CERD's key General Recommendations misquote the offences created under Article 4 and thereby misrepresent the nature of the State obligation(s) in question. The consequences of these errors were quick to ripple into other influential fora, as other bodies did not notice the mistake and quoted it in their own texts (eg. the EU Network of Independent Experts on Fundamental Rights). ECRI, too, has not always been rigorous enough in its standard-setting work. It has also misquoted its own standard-setting work and thereby downplayed the importance of freedom of expression.

Pluralistic tolerance and relational aspects of rights

The co-existence of minorities with other societal groups means that their rights must be recognised and realised in a manner that reflects the realities of pluralistic society. As the terms "pluralism" and "tolerance" tend to be invoked in the preambular provisions of international treaties (as opposed to their operative provisions), the fullness of their respective meanings is under-appreciated. The exploration of the theoretical ramifications of pluralism and tolerance elucidates the content of each. Chapter 5 merges the complex concepts of pluralism and tolerance and develops the concept of "pluralistic tolerance", which it styles as an operative public value, *pace* Bhikhu Parekh. To style "pluralistic tolerance" as an operative public value is to insist that it is more than a guiding interpretive principle for human rights generally and minority rights in particular. It is to point to the need to operationalise the value of "pluralistic tolerance"; to incorporate it in regulatory, policy and institutional practice so that it is meaningfully applied. This approach logically implies the facilitation of expressive and dialogical fora. A key purpose of "pluralistic tolerance" is to protect the vigour of public debate and uphold the importance for democratic society of contestation and criticism that takes place within the limits of appropriate legal standards.

This book takes as its conceptual point of departure the universality, indivisibility, interdependence and inter-relatedness of human rights as affirmed, *inter alia*, in the 1993 Vienna Declaration. Such an approach allows for the key focuses of the book – minority rights and freedom of expression – to be analysed not only in terms of their own intersectional aspects, but also in the broader context of their respective relationships with other human rights. This is important because it is more conducive to rounded and coherent reflection than an approach based on separate, particularised lines of enquiry. It allows for closer scrutiny of the abrasive and synergic aspects of the relationship between the right to freedom of expression, the rights of persons belonging to minorities and other rights, eg. non-discrimination/equality, participation, education, culture, religion and language. The right to freedom of expression clearly intersects with the added value of the minority-specific dimension to each of these rights. The presumptive coherence of all human rights does not preclude the possibility that their actual interplay, in specific circumstances, could involve varying degrees of friction. This explains the importance of pluralistic tolerance as an operative public value and as a guiding interpretive principle. Pluralistic tolerance can be considered "comprehensive" when it is meaningfully applied across the whole spectrum of human rights, and protects the space for frictional interaction between rights without vitiating the rights of their content.

Restricting expression in order to protect minorities

Under international law, the most fundamental obligation on States in respect of freedom of expression and the protection of minorities is to prohibit expression that incites to genocidal acts, racism or hatred against them. The types of incitement follow a general pattern, but their definitional contours are sketched differently in different treaties. Those contours tend to curve in the same direction, with the exception of ICERD, which encroaches further on the right to freedom of expression than any other international treaty with a comparable number of ratifications. There are several reasons for this, including: the difficulty of reaching political compromise on substantive issues (most notably squaring the prevention of racial discrimination with the rights to freedom of expression and association); the imperfect drafting which sought to express those compromises; the over-zealous interpretation of the treaty's provisions and the confusion resulting from their mis-application.

Discussions centring on the outer limits of protected expression are further complicated by the increasing tendency of international adjudicative and monitoring bodies, law- and policy-makers to take "hate speech" as the conceptual focus of their discourse. The term, as such, is not defined in any legally-binding international instrument, which means that its precise scope is somewhat speculative. At its core, "hate speech" is clearly about expression that is motivated by some kind of racial or kindred animus. However, the determination of its definitional perimeter is not straightforward. As explicated at length in Chapter 7 in the context of the jurisprudence of the European Court of Human Rights, because the term is not organic to the ECHR, it has not undergone the same natural interpretive growth as other terms that do figure in the original text of the Convention. Instead, the term was imported into the case-law of the Court in 1999 and has been invoked – sometimes nervously – on a regular basis since. In the absence of a definition of the term, the Court is quite right to be nervous about its application. The Court sometimes refers to the Committee of Ministers' Recommendation (97) 20 on "Hate Speech", which *describes* the term (albeit for the purposes of the application of the principles set out in the Appendix to the Recommendation) as "covering all forms of expression which spread, incite, promote or justify racial hatred, xenophobia, antisemitism or other forms of hatred based on intolerance, including: intolerance expressed by aggressive nationalism and ethnocentrism, discrimination and hostility against minorities, migrants and people of immigrant origin".[3]

An authoritative articulation of what exactly is meant by the term "hate speech" will necessarily have to precede its usage in a more confident way by the Court. The sudden, unexplained introduction of the term, without setting out its definitional parameters, is puzzling, given that the case-law of the Court prior to 1999 had already engaged – effectively – with the same kind of issues. That earlier case-law was grounded in more familiar and patiently developed terminology.

As demonstrated in Chapter 7, the need for caution is underscored by the origin of the term in the United States, and how critical race scholarship has developed prevalent understandings of the term. Critical race theory is (to put it very summarily) an approach to racism where the victim and the victim's perspective are given pride of place. It seeks to ensure that law and policy are adequately informed by circumstances and experiences of victims of racism. This suggests that the term "hate speech" has traditionally had a wider meaning than is commonly recognised; it cannot be assumed that it is straightforwardly synonymous with prevailing international legal standards on the restriction/prohibition of racist and other kinds of hateful expression. Critical race theory draws attention to the variety and complexity of harms suffered by victims of "hate speech": psychic harm, damage to self-esteem, inhibited self-fulfilment, etc.

Partly in recognition of the complexity of relevant harms, different treaties and bodies have different approaches (conceptual and practical) to the question of legitimate restrictions on freedom of expression. The challenge is therefore to identify "which criteria allow us to distinguish between harms that justify restrictions and those that do not".[4] The notion of "abusive speech"[5] could prove useful in this connection: it allows for a distinction to be made between expression

3 Appendix to Recommendation No. R (97) 20, adopted on 30 October 1997.

4 David Kretzmer, "Freedom of Speech and Racism", 8 Cardozo L. Rev. 445 (1987), at 478.

5 Jean-François Gaudreault-DesBiens, "From Sisyphus's Dilemma to Sisyphus's Duty? A Meditation on the Regulation of Hate Propaganda in Relation to Hate Crimes and Genocide", 46 McGill L.J. 121 (2000), at 133.

that offends human dignity and should be prohibited and expression that "offends, shocks or disturbs" certain sections of the population and should be tolerated in the spirit of broadmindedness that is a prerequisite to democratic society. The importance of the consequences of expression should also be stressed, as well as the need to develop suitable methodological tools for the evaluation of such consequences.

When applying their normative principles to specific factual circumstances, adjudicative bodies should give sufficient weighting to factors such as the intent of the speaker and "contextual variables".[6] The latter could include the nature and impact of the medium used to convey the expression; audience-related considerations; socio-political factors; the nature, necessity and proportionality of the measure(s) employed to restrict the perceived harm involved; the triviality/ seriousness of the perceived harm and the probability that it would in fact result from the impugned expression. Depending on the findings of such an assessment, it could become clear that a variety of policy measures and practical strategies could be relied upon to restrict the dissemination of objectionable expression. Whereas legal prohibitions are justified in respect of "abusive speech" (as defined *supra*), alternative, i.e., non-legal, measures can prove particularly effective in curbing the dissemination of expression which would not fall foul of existing restrictions on freedom of expression, but which is nevertheless harmful. Again, these conclusions plead for the concerted application of negative and positive measures in a comprehensive, but differentiated, approach to legally-based limitations on freedom of expression.

A significant emphasis on *positive* State obligations can be detected in international human rights law. The Durban Declaration and Programme of Action and the Framework Convention for the Protection of National Minorities, in particular, adopt root-and-branch approaches to combating hate speech by targeting the hatred and intolerance from which it spawns. Their strategies include the promotion of expressive opportunities, especially via the media, for persons belonging to minorities. The promotion of tolerance and of intercultural understanding and dialogue is similarly prioritised. Measures advocated include specialised training for journalists on intercultural themes, ensuring access to media for minorities or other groups, funding of various initiatives promoting ethical journalism and programme production, etc., as detailed in Chapter 8.

Another topical source of considerable confusion about the delineation of the outer limits of free expression concerns the protection of religious beliefs. Freedom of religion – as guaranteed by international law – does not include the right not to be

6 Michel Rosenfeld, "Hate Speech in Constitutional Jurisprudence: A Comparative Analysis", 24 Cardozo L. Rev. 1523 (2003), at 1565.

offended in one's religious beliefs or sensibilities. Instead, the main components of the operative right are to hold or change one's religion or belief and to manifest one's religion or belief, "in worship, teaching, practice and observance".[7] As such, it would require a high level of abusive expression to prevent or restrict the exercise of any of the constituent parts of the right to freedom of religion. Despite significant political gains achieved by the concerted international campaign against the so-called "defamation of religions", relevant legal standards do not protect religions *qua* belief systems from "defamation" or virulent criticism. Nor are spiritual leaders beyond the reach of criticism, legally-speaking, although the drafting history of an ultimately unfinished and unadopted draft UN Treaty on Freedom of Information favoured the inclusion of such protection for religious leaders as a permissible restriction on the right to freedom of expression.

A more promising angle of approach to the question therefore lies within the right to freedom of expression itself. The exercise of the right is governed by respect for certain duties and responsibilities and the right can also be limited, where necessary, in order to protect the rights of others. Hence, the European Court of Human Rights has elaborated a line of jurisprudence that seeks to stress that the gratuitous offence of religious beliefs and symbols that does not contribute to public debate cannot be justified by appealing to the right to freedom of expression. As Chapter 6 shows, this line of jurisprudence is not always consistent and it falters in places. Nevertheless, its general message is clear, even if greater refinement and consistency is required in the methodology it applies to the balancing of relevant rights and interests.

Whereas a legalistic analysis of these flash-points in the penumbral regions of freedom of expression can prove dispositive of certain controversies, the same can hardly be said of socio-political perspectives. In any given society, different groups may have different understandings and expectations of the real and symbolic functions of the law. The *causes célèbres* of *The Satanic Verses* and the "Mohammed Cartoons" are examples of *inter alia*, different, or rather, opposing perspectives on the limits of freedom of expression. Fora for expression and communication (i.e., exchange of information and opinions) have great potential for fomenting societal cohesion. This explains why increased attention for the role of different types of dialogical fora in the building of inter-ethnic knowledge, understanding and respect needs to be emphasised. Support for, and the development of, such fora are a necessary measure for giving effect to the "operative public value" of comprehensive pluralistic tolerance.

7 Article 9(1), ECHR.

Facilitating expression of minorities

Under international law, the most important obligations on States to facilitate the expressive rights of persons belonging to minorities are the promotion of information- and media-related pluralism and access to expressive fora, especially various media. Both pluralism and access are vitally important for linguistic and cultural identity – their preservation, transmission and development, but also for rights relating to effective participation in public life, religion and education. The different components of the right to freedom of expression are also relevant for the discharge of positive State obligations: pluralism is important mainly for the right to seek and receive information and ideas, whereas access is primarily geared towards the right to impart information.

It is a well-established principle of international human rights law that States are ultimately responsible for upholding pluralism in society generally and in the media sector in particular. Societal pluralism and media pluralism are not identical, but they are related in some important respects. The concept of comprehensive pluralistic tolerance is developed to describe the relationship between more generic notions of pluralistic tolerance and the more applied meaning of media pluralism. Information- and media-related pluralism is best gauged by integratively assessing substantive and structural features of a given mediascape and by having due regard for media functionality. Different media types and formats are differently suited to the fulfilment of individual informational, communicative, cultural and linguistic needs and preferences. These considerations apply, *mutatis mutandis*, to minorities.

The right to freedom of expression can only be fully realised when there is widespread access to a diverse range of expressive opportunities and sources of information and opinions. Quantitative and qualitative considerations are determinative here. Chapter 9 usefully disaggregates the concept of information- and media-related pluralism and explains its importance at various levels, in particular source/ownership, outlet and content. These levels span structures, processes and output, each of which offers different opportunities for the participation of persons belonging to minorities. As argued in Chapter 3 in respect of the usefulness of a disaggregated analytical approach to the media, the disaggregated analysis of information- and media-related pluralism conducted here allows for probing evaluation. As such, the systematic application of this disaggregated analytical approach to the monitoring of relevant provisions of relevant treaties would facilitate assessments of the effectiveness of operative treaty provisions in practice.

Chapter 10 advocates a disaggregated approach to cultural and linguistic diversity, along the lines of the UNESCO Convention on the Protection and Promotion of the Diversity of Cultural Expressions and various standard-setting texts from the

Council of Europe. Cultural diversity entails the existence and expression of multiple cultural identities. Cultural diversity is therefore enabled by a societal climate of pluralistic tolerance and by the transmission of cultural expressions via diverse media and in diverse fora. The disaggregated approach pursued here allows for greater analytical precision as regards the effectiveness of relevant instruments in the fulfilment of their objectives. The weak wording throughout the UNESCO Convention has had debilitating effects on the nature and extent of the legal obligations to which it creates/recognises for States Parties. As such, its main worth lies in the disaggregation of measures that could be used to advance its central goal. This is also the prime value of the Council of Europe's relevant standard-setting texts. Such disaggregation facilitates the identification and compilation of best practices for States which are amenable to the objective of protecting and promoting cultural diversity. Other legally-binding regulations, particularly those governing the European broadcasting sector do precious little to promote cultural diversity. The political rhetoric simply does not match the regulatory reality; relevant regulatory provisions are often overtly Eurocentric in their conceptualisation and calibration and do not view cultural diversity either as an expansive notion or as intrinsically valuable. This failure to engage with relevant objectives is disappointing as the media in general, and broadcasting in particular can have a huge impact on the vitality of a culture and its dissemination. This is particularly true of the cultures of persons belonging to minorities.

As well as guaranteeing media pluralism, the other main obligation on States to facilitate the expressive rights of persons belonging to minorities is to ensure access rights. This obligation is an obvious complement to its obligation to safeguard information- and media-related pluralism. The right to freedom of expression would not be effective if discriminatory practices were to prevail in relation to access to the media, or influential media. The right to effective participation in public life is obviously also implicated here. This means that a powerful triumvirate of rights (expression, non-discrimination and participation) are brought to bear on the issue of access to the media. This is without prejudice to the relevance of the possible cultural, linguistic and religious goals that might be pursued after having secured access.

Whereas there is no right to freedom of expression via a particular medium of one's choice, as such, adequate access to expressive opportunities and discursive fora requires the development and enforcement of certain procedural safeguards (at least). This is especially true for persons belonging to minorities; because of situational factors, established patterns of discrimination and persecution, etc., additional measures may often be required to ensure that their access to expressive fora are also real and effective. A "taxonomy of access"[8] – enumerating the many

---

8 Monroe Price, "An Access Taxonomy", in Andras Sajó, Ed., *Rights of Access to the Media* (The Hague, Kluwer Law International, 1996), pp. 1–28.

different forms that access could take – indicates that measures such as the right of reply and public-access channels, have different types and levels of potential for persons belonging to minorities.

Ownership, licensing and miscellaneous regulatory provisions can affect access in a variety of ways. The proportionality of regulation should always be assessed in light of a wide range of factors, including the existing political, social, religious, cultural and linguistic environment; the number, variety, geographical reach, character, function and languages of available broadcasting services, and the rights, needs, expressed desires and nature of the audience(s) affected.

Human rights are inherently dynamic and it is unsurprising that the advent of new information and communications technologies would have implications for rights and give rise to new applications of existing rights. It can at least be argued that the effective exercise of the right to freedom of expression (especially the right to seek and receive information) in the digital age is increasingly contingent on access to new technologies, the acquisition of relevant technological skills and fluency in media literacy, etc. These factors which increasingly determine the quality or effectiveness of access need to be consistently emphasised in policy- and law-making, and applied by adjudicative and monitoring bodies. They are precisely the kind of measures required to render principles of and provisions for freedom of expression operative and effective; to bridge the gap between theory and practice.

Media functionality, including a focus on the impact of new media techologies on communicative practices and regulatory approaches, is not merely of theoretical interest. The systematic inclusion of such considerations would be of enormous benefit for the analytical and insightful quality of the monitoring of international human rights treaties containing provisions concerning the right to freedom of expression. The organic vitality of those treaties and the rights they safeguard is not always reflected in authoritative interpretations of the same. For instance, for nearly 30 years, the most important texts elucidating the content and scope of Articles 19 and 20, ICCPR were the UN Human Rights Committee's General Comments Nos. 10 and 11 (respectively) – both of which were adopted in 1983.[9] Since then, staggering technological and societal changes have taken place with far-reaching implications for how information and ideas are sought, received and imparted. Technology is very often a crucial determinant of the effectiveness of the right to freedom of expression in concrete situations. It is therefore imperative that relevant legal provisions reflect contemporary realities; this necessarily involves engaging with the (varying levels of) functionality of old and new media technologies.

---

9 As this book was being finalised, the UN Human Rights Committee was on the verge of adopting a new General Comment No. 34 on Article 19, ICCPR – Freedom of opinion and expression.

Final remarks

In recent times, progress has steadily been made in terms of the reduction of conceptual and political resistance to minority rights' protection at IGO-level. An increasing number of standard-setting texts provide a largely consistent framework for the protection of minorities. Not all of those texts are legally-binding on States and those that are designed to be legally binding have not necessarily been signed or ratified by States with poor track-records in minority rights' protection. Another problem is that far-reaching reservations can effectively lead to the emasculation of States' substantive obligations under relevant treaties. Nevertheless, all of the relevant texts contribute in their own way to broadly consistent goals centring on the advancement of minority rights.

Progress can also be measured in terms of the extent to which minority rights have been mainstreamed within international human rights law and within key bodies involved in the protection and promotion of human rights standards. The growing number of agencies devoted to the cause is further evidence of the raised profile enjoyed by minority rights of late. Having largely achieved acceptance in international and regional European standards, the next challenge facing minority rights is their consolidation at the national and sub-national levels. In the spirit of the universality, indivisibility, interdependence and inter-relatedness of human rights, it is necessary to examine in a meticulous manner how all human rights relate in their respective ways to minority rights. This book has sought to do so in respect of the right to freedom of expression, a multi-layered, high-valency right. The resulting analysis has demonstrated that the interface between the two is extremely dynamic. The interplay between minority rights and the right to freedom of expression is occasionally frictional, but mostly generative of powerful synergies.

It is simply not possible to meaningfully condense an evaluation of the enormous complexities and extensive dimensions involved in the *problématique* of this book into a couple of paragraphs. These conclusions have condensed the analysis and arguments of the book. They have explained a number of strengths of the current set of international standards protecting and promoting the right to freedom of expression of persons belonging to minorities. They have also identified and criticised a long list of its shortcomings. Throughout the book, including in its conclusions, the effectiveness of the right to freedom of expression is consistently contextualised by references to (the importance of):

- Specific rationales for freedom of expression and minority rights;
- Assessments of the particular communicative needs of minorities, based on salient group characteristics and situational specificities;
- Comprehensive pluralistic tolerance as an operative public value;

- The interrelatedness and interdependence of all human rights;
- The interplay between freedom of expression, minority rights and other human rights;
- A favourable enabling environment and broader societal considerations;
- Media functionality (including its technological dimensions);
- The inherent dynamism of human rights;
- Qualitative and hierarchical distinctions between applicable legal and other standards, coupled with an understanding of their purpose, potential and limitations.

The systematic integration of these considerations, along the detailed lines drawn in this book, into interpretive and monitoring exercises of relevant international standards, would greatly enhance their consistency and clarity.

By critically evaluating all of these issues throughout the book, the journey undertaken ultimately also became its destination.

List of academic works consulted

Books

Abel, Richard, *Speech and Respect* (London, Stevens & Sons/Sweet & Maxwell, 1994).

Abel, Richard L., *Speaking Respect, Respecting Speech* (Chicago, University of Chicago Press, 1998).

Alcock, Antony, *A history of the protection of regional cultural minorities in Europe: from the Edict of Nantes to the present day* (Basingstoke, Macmillan, 2000).

Alexander, Larry, *Is There a Right of Freedom of Expression?* (New York, Cambridge University Press, 2005).

Alfredsson, Gudmundur & Stavropoulou, Maria, Eds., *Justice Pending: Indigenous Peoples and Other Good Causes – Essays in Honour of Erica-Irene A. Daes* (The Hague, Martinus Nijhoff Publishers, 2002).

Alfredsson, Gudmundur, *et al.*, Eds., *International Human Rights Monitoring Mechanisms: Essays in honour of Jakob Th. Möller* (The Hague/Boston/London, Martinus Nijhoff Publishers, 2001).

Alfredsson, Gudmundur & Macalister-Smith, Peter, Eds., *The Living Law of Nations: Essays on refugees, minorities, indigenous peoples and the human rights of other vulnerable groups in memory of Atle Grahl-Madsen* (Kehl, N.P. Engel, 1996).

Alston, Philip & De Schutter, Olivier, Eds., *Monitoring Fundamental Rights in the EU: The Contribution of the Fundamental Rights Agency* (Oxford & Portland Oregon, Hart Publishing, 2005).

Alston, Philip, Ed., *Peoples' Rights* (Oxford, Oxford University Press, 2001).

Alston, Philip, *et al.*, Eds., *The EU and Human Rights* (New York, Oxford University Press, Inc., 1999).

Alston, Philip, Ed., *The United Nations and Human Rights: A Critical Appraisal* (Oxford, Clarendon Press, 1992).

Anderson, Benedict, *Imagined Communities: Reflections on the Origin and Spread of Nationalism* (Revised Edition) (London & New York, Verso, 1991).

Appiah, Kwame Anthony, *The Ethics of Identity* (Princeton and Oxford, Princeton University Press, 2005).

Appiah, K. Anthony & Gutmann, Amy, *Color Conscious: The Political Morality of Race* (Princeton, New Jersey, Princeton University Press, 1996).

Appignanesi, Lisa, Ed., *Free Expression is No Offence* (London, Penguin Books, 2005).

Arendt, Hannah, *The origins of totalitarianism* (3rd Edition) (London, Allen & Unswin, 1966).

Arendt, Hannah, *The human condition* (Chicago, University of Chicago Press, 1958).

Arnull, Anthony & Wincott, Daniel, Eds., *Accountability and Legitimacy in the European Union* (Oxford, Oxford University Press, 2002).
Arzoz, Xabier, Ed., *Respecting Linguistic Diversity in the European Union* (Amsterdam & Philadelphia, John Benjamins Publishing Co., 2008).
Ashworth, Andrew, *Principles of Criminal Law* (Second Edition), (Oxford, Clarendon Press, 1995).
Atton, Chris, *Alternative Media* (London, Sage Publications, 2002).
Aurescu, Bogdan, Ed., *Kin-State Involvement in Minority Protection: Lessons Learned* (Bucharest, Romanian Association for International Law and International Relations, 2004).
Austin, J. L. *How to do things with words* (Oxford/New York/Toronto/Melbourne, Oxford University Press, Repr., 1980).
Bacon, Anne-Marie, *The Shoah on screen – Representing crimes against humanity* (Volume I) (Strasbourg, Council of Europe, 2006).
Bagdikian, Ben H., *The New Media Monopoly* (Boston, Beacon Press, 2004).
Baker, C. Edwin, *Media, Markets and Democracy* (USA, Cambridge University Press, 2002).
Baker, C. Edwin, *Human Liberty and Freedom of Speech* (New York, Oxford University Press Inc., 1989).
Banton, Michael, *The International Politics of Race* (Great Britain, Polity Press, 2002).
Banton, Michael, *Racial Theories* (Second Edition) (Cambridge, Cambridge University Press, 1998).
Banton, Michael, *International Action Against Racial Discrimination* (Oxford, Clarendon Press, 1996).
Barendt, Eric, *Freedom of Speech* (2nd Edition) (Oxford, Oxford University Press, 2005).
Barendt, Eric, *Broadcasting Law: A Comparative Study* (Oxford, Clarendon Press, 1993).
Barker, Paul, Ed., *Living as Equals* (Oxford, Oxford University Press, 1996).
Barrington, Mrs. Russell, Ed., *The Works and Life of Walter Bagehot* (Vol. VI) (London, Longmans, Green & Co., 1915).
Barron, Jerome A., *Public Rights and the Private Press* (Toronto, Butterworth & Co., 1981).
Bauman, Zygmunt, *Liquid Modernity* (Cambridge, Polity Press, 2000).
Bauman, Zygmunt, *Modernity and the Holocaust* (Cambridge, Polity Press, 2000).
Bauman, Zygmunt, *Globalisation: the Human Consequences* (Cambridge, Polity Press, 1998).
Beatson, Jack & Cripps, Yvonne, Eds., *Freedom of Expression and Freedom of Information: Essays in Honour of Sir David Williams* (New York, Oxford University Press, 2000).
Beck, Ulrich, *Risk Society: Towards a New Modernity* (trans. Mark Ritter) (London/Newbury Park/New Delhi, Sage Publications, 1992 (repr. 2002)).
Bell, Daniel, *The Coming of Post-Industrial Society: A Venture in Social Forecasting* (USA, Basic Books, 1999).
Bell, Daniel, *The End of Ideology: On the Exhaustion of Political Ideas in the Fifties* (Revised Edition) (New York, The Free Press, 1962).

Bell, Mark, *Anti-Discrimination Law and the European Union* (Oxford, Oxford University Press, 2002).

Benoît-Rohmer, Florence, *The minority question in Europe: towards a coherent system of protection for national minorities* (Germany, Council of Europe Publishing, 1996).

Bens, Els de, Ed., *Media Between Culture and Commerce* (Bristol & Chicago, Intellect Books, 2007).

Bergsmo, Morten, Ed., *Human Rights and Criminal Justice for the Downtrodden: Essays in Honour of Asbjorn Eide* (Leiden/Boston, Martinus Nijhoff Publishers, 2003).

Berlin, Isaiah, *Liberty* (Oxford, Oxford University Press, 2005) (Ed. Henry Hardy).

Berting, Jan, *et al.*, Eds., *Human Rights in a Pluralist World: Individuals and Collectivities* (Westport & London, Netherlands Commission for UNESCO/Roosevelt Study Center/ Meckler, 1990).

Bertrand, Claude-Jean, Ed., *An Arsenal for Democracy: Media Accountability Systems* (Cresskill, New Jersey, Hampton Press, Inc., 2003).

Bertrand, Claude-Jean, *Media Ethics & Accountability Systems* (New Brunswick & London, Transaction Publishers, 2000).

Bertrand, Claude-Jean, *L'Arsenal de la démocratie: Médias, déontologie et M*A*R*S* (Paris, Ed. Economica, 1999).

Bickel, Alexander, *The Morality of Consent* (New Haven, Yale University Press, 1975).

Blackburn, Robert & Polakiewicz, Jörg, Eds., *Fundamental Rights in Europe: The European Convention on Human Rights and its Member States, 1950–2000* (Oxford, Oxford University Press, 2001).

Bloed, Arie, Ed., *The Conference on Security and Co-operation in Europe: basic documents, 1993–1995* (The Hague, Martinus Nijhoff, 1997).

Bloed, Arie, Ed., *The challenges of change: the Helsinki Summit of the CSCE and its aftermath* (Dordrecht, Martinus Nijhoff, 1994).

Bloed, Arie, Ed., *The Conference on Cooperation and Security in Europe: Analysis and Basic Documents, 1972–1993* (Dordrecht, Martinus Nijhoff Publishers, 1993).

Bloed, Arie & Dijk, Pieter van, Eds., *Protection of Minority Rights through Bilateral Treaties: the Case of Central and Eastern Europe* (Dordrecht, Kluwer Law International, 1999).

Bloed, Arie & Dijk, Pieter van, Eds., *The Human Dimension of the Helsinki Process: the Vienna Follow-up Meeting and its Aftermath* (Dordrecht, Martinus Nijhoff Publishers, 1991).

Bloed Arie & Dijk, Pieter van, Eds., *Essays on Human Rights in the Helsinki Process* (Dordrecht, Martinus Nijhoff Publishers, 1985).

Blumler, Jay G., Ed., *Television and the Public Interest: Vulnerable Values in West European Broadcasting* (Great Britain, SAGE Publications Ltd., 1992).

Bollinger, Lee C., *Uninhibited, Robust, and Wide-Open: A Free Press for a New Century* (New York, etc., Oxford University Press, 2010).

Bollinger, Lee C. & Stone, Geoffrey R., Eds., *Eternally Vigilant: Free Speech in the Modern Era* (Chicago & London, University of Chicago Press, 2002).

Bollinger, Lee C., *The Tolerant Society – Freedom of Speech and Extremist Speech in America* (New York, Oxford University Press, 1989).
Bossuyt, Marc J., *Guide to the "Travaux Préparatoires" of the International Covenant on Civil and Political Rights* (Dordrecht, etc., Martinus Nijhoff Publishers, 1987).
Bourdieu, Pierre/Johnson, Randal, Ed., *The Field of Cultural Production: Essays on Art and Literature* (Cambridge, Polity Press, 1993).
Bourdieu, Pierre, *Language and Symbolic Power* (Cambridge, Polity Press, 1991).
Boyle, Kevin, Ed., *New Institutions for Human Rights Protection* (Oxford, Oxford University Press, 2009).
Boyle, Kevin, Ed., *Mary Robinson, A Voice for Human Rights* (Philadelphia, University of Pennsylvania Press, 2006).
Boyle, Kevin & Sheen, Juliet, Eds., *Freedom of Religion and Belief: A World Report* (London, Routledge, 1997).
Brants, Kees, Hermes, Joke & van Zoonen, Liesbet, Eds., *The Media in Question: Popular Cultures and Public Interests* (London, SAGE Publications Ltd., 1998).
Brölmann, Catherine, Lefeber, René & Zieck, Marjoleine, Eds., *Peoples and Minorities in International Law* (Dordrecht, Martinus Nijhoff, 1993).
Browne, Donald R., *Ethnic Minorities, Electronic Media and the Public Sphere* (Cresskill, New Jersey, Hampton Press, Inc., 2005).
Browne, Donald R. *Electronic Media and Indigenous Peoples: A Voice of Our Own?* (Ames, Iowa State University Press, 1996).
Buckley, Steve, Duer, Kreszentia, Mendel, Toby & Ó Siochrú, Seán, *Broadcasting, Voice, and Accountability: A Public Interest Approach to Policy, Law, and Regulation* (Ann Arbor, The University of Michigan Press/The World Bank, 2008).
Búrca, Gráinne de & Scott, Joanne, Eds., *The EU and the WTO: Legal and Constitutional Issues* (Oxford & Portland Oregon, Hart Publishing, 2001).
Butler, Judith & Spivak, Gayatri Chakravorty, *Who Sings the Nation State? language, politics, belonging* (London/New York/Calcutta, Seagull Books, 2007).
Butler, Judith, *Excitable Speech: A Politics of the Performative* (New York & London, Routledge, 1997).
Calabrese, Andrew & Sparks, Colin, Eds., *Toward a Political Economy of Culture: Capitalism and Communication in the Twenty-First Century* (Lanham, etc., Rowman & Littlefield Publishers, Inc., 2004).
Calhoun, Craig, LiPuma, Edward & Postone, Moishe, Eds., *Bourdieu: Critical Perspectives* (United Kingdom, Polity Press, 1993).
Calvino, Italo, *Six Memos for the Next Millennium* (Cambridge, Massachusetts, Harvard University Press, 1988) (Trans. Patrick Creagh).
Campbell, Tom & Sadurski, Wojciech, Eds., *Freedom of Communication* (England, Dartmouth Publishing Co. Ltd., 1994).
Campbell, Tom, Ewing, Keith & Tomkins, Adam, Eds., *Sceptical Essays on Human Rights* (Oxford, Oxford University Press, 2001).
Camus, Jean-Yves, *Le Front National* (Toulouse, Editions Milan, 1998).

Camus, Jean-Yves, Ed., *Les extrémismes en Europe: état des lieux en 1998* (France, Centre européen de recherche et d'action sur le racisme et l'antisémitisme / Éditions de l'aube, 1998).
Camus, Jean-Yves, *L'Extrême Droite Aujourd'hui* (Toulouse, Éditions Milan, 1996).
Cassese, Antonio, *International Law in a Divided World* (Oxford, Clarendon Press, 1986).
Cassidy, Eoin & McGrady, Andrew G., Eds., *Media and the Marketplace – Ethical Perspectives* (Dublin, Institute of Public Administration, 2001).
Castendyk, Oliver, Dommering, Egbert & Scheuer, Alexander, Eds., *European Media Law* (Alphen a/d Rijn, Kluwer Law International, 2008).
Castermans-Holleman, Monique, Van Hoof, Fried & Smith, Jacqueline, Eds., *The Role of the Nation-State in the 21st Century: Human Rights, International Organisations and Foreign Policy – Essays in Honour of Peter Baehr* (The Hague/Boston/London, Kluwer Law International, 1998).
Castiglione, Dario & Longman, Chris, Eds., *The Language Question in Europe and Diverse Societies: Political, Legal and Social Perspectives* (Oxford & Portland Oregon, Hart Publishing, 2007).
Chafee, Zechariah, Jr., *Free Speech in the United States* (Cambridge, Massachusetts, Harvard University Press, 1964).
Chalaby, Jean K., Ed., *Transnational Television Worldwide: Towards a New Media Order* (London/New York, I.B. Tauris, 2005).
Chapman, John W. & Shapiro, Ian, Eds., *Democratic Community* (New York, New York University Press, 1993).
Chapman, John W. & Wertheimer, Alan, Eds., *Majorities and Minorities* (New York, New York University Press, 1990).
Cheles, Luciano, Ferguson, Ronnie & Vaughan, Michalina, Eds., *Neo-Fascism in Europe* (New York, Longman Inc., 1991).
Christians, Clifford & Traber, Michael, Eds., *Communication Ethics and Universal Values* (Thousand Oaks/London/New Delhi, SAGE Publications, 1997).
Clapham, Andrew, *Human Rights Obligations of Non-State Actors* (Oxford, Oxford University Press, 2006).
Clapham, Andrew, *Human Rights in the Private Sphere* (Oxford, Clarendon Press, 1993).
Cohen, Marshall, Nagel, Thomas & Scanlon, Thomas, Eds., *Equality and Preferential Treatment* (Princeton, Princeton University Press, 1977).
Coliver, Sandra, Hoffman, Paul, Fitzpatrick, Joan & Bowen, Stephen, Eds., *Secrecy and Liberty: National Security, Freedom of Expression, and Access to Information* (The Hague, Martinus Nijhoff Publishers, 1999).
Coliver, Sandra, Ed., *Striking a Balance: Hate Speech, Freedom of Expression and Non-discrimination* (United Kingdom, ARTICLE 19/University of Essex, 1992).
The [Hutchins] Commission on Freedom of the Press, *A Free and Responsible Press* (Chicago, University of Chicago Press, 1947).
Condé, H. Victor, *A Handbook of International Human Rights Terminology* (Lincoln, NE, University of Nebraska Press, 1999).

Cooper, Davina, *Challenging Diversity: Rethinking Equality and the Value of Difference* (Cambridge, Cambridge University Press, 2004).
Cormack, Mike & Hourigan, Niamh, Eds., *Minority Language Media: Concepts, Critiques and Case Studies* (Clevedon, Multilingual Matters Ltd., 2007).
Costello, Cathryn & Barry, Eilis, Eds., *Equality in Diversity: The New Equality Directives* (Dublin, Irish Centre for European Law, 2003).
Cottle, Simon, Ed., *Ethnic Minorities and the Media: Changing Cultural Boundaries* (Buckingham & Philadelphia, Open University Press, 2000).
Council of Europe, *Filling the frame: Five years of monitoring the Framework Convention for the Protection of National Minorities* (Strasbourg, Council of Europe Publishing, 2004).
Council of Europe, *Mechanisms for the implementation of minority rights* (Germany, Council of Europe Publishing/European Centre for Minority Issues, 2004).
Council of Europe, *Freedom of conscience* (Strasbourg, Council of Europe Press, 1993).
Craufurd Smith, Rachael, Ed., *Culture and European Union Law* (Oxford, Oxford University Press, 2004).
Craufurd Smith, Rachael, *Broadcasting Law and Fundamental Rights* (Oxford, Clarendon Press, 1997).
Crawford, James, Ed., *The Rights of Peoples* (Oxford, Clarendon Press, 1988).
Crystal, David, *Language and the Internet* (Cambridge, Cambridge University Press, 2001).
Crystal, David, *Language Death* (Cambridge, Cambridge University Press, 2000).
Cuilenburg, Jan van & Wurff, Richard van der, Eds., *Media and Open Societies: Cultural, Economic and Policy Foundations for Media Openness and Diversity in East and West* (Amsterdam, Het Spinhuis, 2000).
Cumper, Peter & Wheatley, Steven, Eds., *Minority Rights in the 'New' Europe* (Great Britain, Kluwer Law International, 1999).
Curran, James & Morley, David, Eds., *Media and Cultural Theory* (London & New York, Routledge, 2006).
Curran, James & Seaton, Jean, *Power without Responsibility: The press, broadcasting, and new media in Britain* (Sixth Edition) (London and New York, Routledge, 2003).
Curran, James & Gurevitch, Michael, Eds., *Mass Media and Society* (Third Edition) (Great Britain, Arnold Publishers, 2000).
Dahlgren, Peter *Television and the Public Sphere: Citizenship, Democracy and the Media* (London, SAGE Publications, 1995).
Dahlgren, Peter & Sparks, Colin, Eds., *Communication and citizenship: journalism and the public sphere* (London, Routledge, 1997).
Danieli, Yael, Stamatopoulou, Elsa & Dias, Clarence J., Eds., *The Universal Declaration of Human Rights: Fifty years and beyond* (New York, United Nations Publishing, 1999).
Deibert, Ronald *et al.*, Eds., *Access Denied: The Practice and Policy of Global Internet Filtering* (Cambridge, Massachusetts & London, England, The MIT Press, 2008).
Delgado, Richard & Stefancic, Jean, *Understanding Words That Wound* (Boulder, CO, Westview Press, 2004).

Delgado, Richard & Stefancic, Jean, Eds., *Critical Race Theory: the cutting edge* (2nd Edition) (Philadelphia, PA, Temple University Press, 2000).

Detrick, Sharon, Doek, Jaap & Cantwell, Nigel, Eds., *The United Nations Convention on the Rights of the Child: A Guide to the "Travaux Préparatoires"* (Dordrecht/Boston/London, Martinus Nijhoff Publishers, 1992).

Dewey, John, *The Public and its Problems* (Chicago, The Swallow Press, Inc., 1954).

Dijk, Pieter van, Hoof, Fried van, Rijn, Arjen van & Zwaak, Leo, Eds., *Theory and Practice of the European Convention on Human Rights* (Fourth Edition) (Antwerpen/Oxford, Intersentia, 2006).

Dijk, P. van & Hoof, G.J.H. van, *Theory and Practice of the European Convention on Human Rights* (3rd Edition) (The Hague, Kluwer Law International, 1998).

Dijk, Teun A. van, *Racism and the Press* (London, Routledge, 1991).

Dinstein, Yoram & Tabory, Mala, Eds., *The Protection of Minorities and Human Rights* (Dordrecht, Martinus Nijhoff Publishers, 1992).

Dommering, Egbert, *De achtervolging van Prometheus: over vrijheid en bezit van informatie* (Amsterdam, Otto Cramwinckel Uitgever, 2008).

Donders, Yvonne, *Towards a Right to Cultural Identity?* (Antwerpen/Oxford/New York, Intersentia, 2002).

Downing, John & Husband, Charles, *Representing 'Race': Racisms, Ethnicities and Media* (London/Thousand Oaks/New Delhi, SAGE Publications, 2005).

Downing, John D.H., *et al.*, *Radical Media: Rebellious Communication and Social Movements* (Thousand Oaks/London/New Delhi, SAGE Publications Ltd., 2001).

Downing, John, *Radical Media: the Political Experience of Alternative Communication* (Boston, MA, South End Press, 1984).

Doyle, Gillian, *Media Ownership: The economics and politics of convergence and concentration in the UK and European media* (London/Thousand Oaks/New Delhi, SAGE Publications, 2002).

Drzemczewski, Andrew, *European Human Rights Convention in Domestic Law: A Comparative Study* (United Kingdom, Clarendon Press, 1985).

Dumont, Hugues, Mandoux, Patrick, Strowel, Alain et Tulkens, François, Eds., *Pas de liberté pour les ennemis de la liberté? Groupements liberticides et droit* (Brussels, Bruylant, 2000).

Dunbar, Robert, Parry, Gwynedd & Klinge, Simone, Eds., *The European Charter or Regional or Minority Languages: Legal Challenges and Opportunities* (Regional or Minority Languages, No. 5) (Strasbourg, Council of Europe Publishing, 2008).

Dworkin, Ronald, *Taking Rights Seriously* (London, Duckworth & Co. Ltd., 1977).

Dworkin, Ronald, *Freedom's Law* (New York, Oxford University Press, 1999).

Eco, Umberto, *Serendipities: Language and Lunacy* (Great Britain, Phoenix, 2000) (trans. William Weaver).

Edwards, John, *Multilingualism* (London and New York, Routledge, 1994).

Eide, Asbjorn, *et al.*, Eds., *Economic, Social and Cultural Rights* (2nd Edition) (The Netherlands, Kluwer Law International, 2001).

Eide, Asbjorn, Alfredsson, Gudmundur, Melander, Göran, Rehof, Lars Adam & Rosas, Allan, with the collaboration of Swinehart, Theresa, Eds., *The Universal Declaration of Human Rights: A Commentary* (Norway, Scandinavian University Press, 1992).

Eliot, T.S., *The Complete Poems and Plays* (England, Faber & Faber, 1969).

Elkin-Koren, Niva. & Netanel, Neil W., Eds., *The Commodification of Information* (The Hague, Kluwer Law International, 2002).

Emerson, Thomas I., *The System of Freedom of Expression* (New York, Random House, 1970).

Emerson, Thomas I., *Toward a General Theory of the First Amendment* (New York, Random House, 1966).

Eppstein, John, *Ten Years' Life of the League of Nations* (London, May Fair Press, 1929).

Essed, Philomena & Goldberg, David Theo, Eds., *Race Critical Theories* (UK/USA, Blackwell Publishers Ltd., 2002).

European Commission against Racism and Intolerance (ECRI), *Combating racism while respecting freedom of expression* (Strasbourg, Council of Europe, 2007).

European Institute for the Media (EIM), *Towards a European Common Market for Television: Contribution to the Debate* (Manchester, EIM, 1987).

Evans, Malcolm D., *Religious liberty and international law in Europe* (Cambridge, Cambridge University Press, 1997).

Extra, Guus & Gorter, Durk, Eds., *The Other Languages of Europe: Demographic, Sociolinguistic and Educational Perspectives* (Clevedon/Buffalo/Toronto/Sydney, Multilingual Matters Ltd., 2001).

Faulkner, William, *Requiem for a Nun* (New York, Vintage Books, 1975).

Feinberg, Joel, *Freedom and fulfillment: philosophical essays* (Princeton, Princeton University Press, 1992).

Feinberg, Joel, *Rights, justice, and the bounds of liberty: essays in social philosophy* (Princeton, Princeton University Press, 1980).

Feinberg, Joel & Gross, Hyman, Eds., *Philosophy of law* (4th Edition) (California, Wadsworth, 1991).

Feintuck, Mike & Varney, Mike, *Media Regulation, Public Interest and the Law* (Second Edition) (Edinburgh, Edinburgh University Press, 2006).

Fenwick, Helen & Phillipson, Gavin, *Media Freedom under the Human Rights Act* (Oxford, Oxford University Press, 2006).

Ferrell Lowe, Gregory & Nissen, Christian S., Eds., *Small Among Giants: Television Broadcasting in Smaller Countries* (Gothenburg, Sweden, Nordicom, 2011).

Finkielkraut, Alain, *L'humanité perdue – essai sur le XXe siècle* (France, Éditions du Seuil, 1996).

Finkielkraut, Alain, *La mémoire vaine – Du crime contre l'humanité* (France, Éditions Gallimard, 1989).

Fish, Stanley, *There's No Such Thing as Free Speech and it's a Good Thing, Too* (New York, Oxford University Press, 1994).

Fishman, Joshua A., Ed., *Handbook of Language & Ethnic Identity* (New York, Oxford University Press, 1999).

Fiss, Owen M., *The Irony of Free Speech* (Cambridge & London, Harvard University Press, 1996).

Firmage, G.J., Ed., *E.E. CUMMINGS COMPLETE POEMS 1904–1962* (New York, Liveright, 1994).

Fossum, John Erik & Schlesinger, Philip, Eds., *The European Union and the Public Sphere: A communicative space in the making?* (London & New York, Routledge, 2007).

Fottrell, Deirdre & Bowring, Bill, Eds., *Minority and Group Rights in the New Millennium* (The Netherlands, Kluwer Law International, 1999).

Fredman, Sandra, Ed., *Discrimination and Human Rights: The Case of Racism* (New York, Oxford University Press, 2001).

Freedman, Monroe H. & Freedman, Eric M., Eds., *Group Defamation and Freedom of Speech: The Relationship Between Language and Violence* (USA, Greenwood Press, 1995).

Freedman, Des, *The Politics of Media Policy* (Cambridge, Polity, 2008).

Friedman, Thomas L., *Longitudes and Attitudes: Exploring the World after September 11* (New York, Farar, Straus & Giroux, 2002).

Galenkamp, Marlies, *Individualism Versus Collectivism: The Concept of Collective Rights* (Rotterdam, Sanders Instituut, 1998).

Gawthrop, Louis C., *Public Service and Democracy: Ethical Imperatives for the 21st Century* (New York, Seven Bridges Press, LLC, 1998).

Gearty, Conor, *Can Human Rights Survive?* (Cambridge, Cambridge University Press, 2006).

Gelber, Katharine, *Speaking Back: The Free Speech Versus Hate Speech Debate* (Amsterdam/Philadelphia, John Benjamins Publishing Company, 2002).

Gellner, Ernest, *Thought and Change* (Repr.) (Chicago, University of Chicago Press, 1974).

Gellner, Ernest, *Nationalism* (London, Weidenfeld & Nicolson, 1997).

Gellner, Ernest, *Encounters with Nationalism* (Oxford, Blackwell, 1994).

Gellner, Ernest, *Nations and Nationalism* (Oxford, Blackwell, 1983).

Georgiou, Myria, *Diaspora, Identity and the Media: Diasporic Transnationalism and Mediated Spatialities* (Cresskill, New Jersey, Hampton Press, Inc., 2006).

Ghanea, Nazila & Xanthaki, Alexandra, Eds., *Minorities, Peoples and Self-Determination: Essays in Honour of Patrick Thornberry* (Leiden/Boston, Martinus Nijhoff Publishers, 2005).

Ghanea, Nazila, Ed., *The Challenge of Religious Discrimination at the Dawn of the New Millennium* (Leiden/Boston, Martinus Nijhoff Publishers, 2003).

Gibbons, Thomas, *Regulating the Media* (2nd Edition) (London, Sweet & Maxwell, 1998).

Glendon, Mary Ann, *A World Made New: Eleanor Roosevelt and the Universal Declaration of Human Rights* (New York, Random House, Inc., 2001).

Goldberg, David, Sutter, Gavin & Walden, Ian, Eds., *Media Law and Practice* (Oxford, Oxford University Press, 2009).

Goldberg, David, Prosser, Tony & Verhulst, Stefaan, *Regulating the Changing Media: A Comparative Study* (Oxford, Clarendon Press, 1998).

Goldberg, David, Prosser, Tony & Verhulst, Stefaan, *EC Media Law and Policy* (Addison Wesley Longman Ltd., Malaysia, 1998).
Gomien, Donna, Ed., *Broadening the Frontiers of Human Rights: Essays in Honour of Asbjorn Eide* (Norway, Scandinavian University Press, 1993).
Greenawalt, Kent, *Fighting Words: Individuals, Communities, and Liberties of Speech* (Princeton, New Jersey, Princeton University Press, 1995).
Greer, Steven, *The European Convention on Human Rights: Achievements, Problems and Prospects* (Cambridge, Cambridge University Press, 2006).
Grin, François, *Language policy evaluation and the European Charter for Regional or Minority Languages* (New York, Palgrave Macmillan, 2003).
Gudykunst, William B. & Kim, Young Yun, *Communicating with Strangers: An Approach to Intercultural Communication* (3rd Edition) (USA, McGraw-Hill Companies, Inc., 1997).
Gurr, Ted R., *Minorities at Risk: A Global View of Ethnopolitical Conflict* (Washington, United States Institute of Peace, 1993).
Gutmann, Amy & Thompson, Dennis, *Why Deliberative Democracy?* (Princeton & Oxford, Princeton University Press, 2004).
Haeck, Yves & Vande Lanotte, Johan, Eds., *Handboek EVRM: Deel 1 en 2* (Antwerp, etc., Intersentia, 2004/2005).
Haiman, Franklyn S., *Speech and Law in a Free Society* (USA, University of Chicago Press, 1981).
Hamelink, Cees J., *The Politics of World Communication: A Human Rights Perspective* (London/Thousand Oaks/New Delhi, SAGE Publications, 1994).
Hamilton, Hugo, *The Speckled People* (London, Fourth Estate, 2003).
Hannum, Hurst, *Autonomy, Sovereignty and Self-determination: The Accommodation of Conflicting Rights* (Philadelphia, University of Pennsylvania Press, 1996).
Hannum, Hurst, Ed., *Documents on autonomy and minority rights* (Dordrecht, M. Nijhoff, 1993).
Harcourt, Alison, *The European Union and the regulation of media markets* (Manchester, Manchester University Press, 2005).
Hardy, Christiane & Möller, Christian, Eds., *Spreading the Word on the Internet: 16 Answers to 4 Questions* (Vienna, OSCE Representative on Freedom of the Media, 2003).
Hare, Ivan & Weinstein, James, Eds., *Extreme Speech and Democracy* (Oxford, Oxford University Press, 2009).
Harris, David J., O'Boyle, Michael & Warbrick, Chris, *Law of the European Convention on Human Rights* (Second edition) (Oxford, Oxford University Press, 2009).
Harris, David J., O'Boyle, Michael & Warbrick, Chris, *Law of the European Convention on Human Rights* (London/Dublin/Edinburgh, Butterworths, 1995).
Harrison, Jackie & Woods, Lorna, *European Broadcasting Law and Policy* (Cambridge, Cambridge University Press, 2007).
Hastrup, Kirsten & Ulrich, George, Eds., *Discrimination and Toleration: New Perspectives* (The Hague/London/New York, Martinus Nijhoff Publishers, 2002).

Hazelcorn, Ellen & Smyth, Patrick, Eds., *Let in the Light: Censorship, secrecy and democracy* (Dingle, Ireland, Brandon Book Publishers Ltd., 1993).

Heaney, Séamus, *Electric Light* (London, Faber & Faber Ltd., 2001).

Heerikhuizen, Annemarie van, *et al.*, Eds., *Het Babylonische Europa: opstellen over veeltaligheid* (Amsterdam, Amsterdam University Press/Salome, 2004).

Hegarty, Angela & Leonard, Siobhan, Eds., *Human Rights: An Agenda for the 21st Century* (London & Sydney, Cavendish Publishing Ltd., 1999).

Helberger, Natali, *Controlling Access to Content: Regulating Conditional Access in Digital Broadcasting* (The Netherlands, Kluwer Law International, 2005).

Held, David, Ed., *Prospects for Democracy: North, South, East, West* (United Kingdom, Polity Press, 1993).

Henkin, Louis, Ed., *The International Bill of Rights* (New York, Columbia University Press, 1981).

Henrard, Kristin, Ed., *Double Standards Pertaining to Minority Protection* (Leiden/Boston, Martinus Nijhoff Publishers, 2010).

Henrard, Kristin, *Devising an Adequate System of Minority Protection: Individual Human Rights, Minority Rights and the Right to Self-Determination* (The Hague, Martinus Nijhoff Publishers, 2000).

Henrard, Kristin & Dunbar, Robert, Eds., *Synergies in Minority Protection: European and International Law Perspectives* (Cambridge, Cambridge University Press, 2008).

Herman, Edward S. & Chomsky, Noam, *Manufacturing Consent: The Political Economy of the Mass Media* (New York & London, Vintage, 1994).

Heyd, David, Ed., *Toleration: An Elusive Virtue* (Princeton, New Jersey, Princeton University Press, 1996).

Heyman, Steven J., *Free Speech & Human Dignity* (New Haven & London, Yale University Press, 2008).

Heyman, Steven J., Ed., *Hate Speech and the Constitution* (Garland Pub. Inc., New York, 1996).

Higgins, Rosalyn, *Problems and Process: International Law and How We Use it* (New York, Oxford University Press, 1994).

Hitchens, Lesley, *Broadcasting Pluralism and Diversity: A Comparative Study of Policy and Regulation* (Oxford and Portland, Oregon, Hart Publishing, 2006).

Hjarvard, Stig, Ed., *Media in a Globalized Society* (Denmark, Museum Tusculanum Press/ University of Copenhagen, 2003).

Hobsbawm, Eric J., *Age of Extremes: The Short Twentieth Century, 1914–1991* (London, Abacus, 1995).

Hobsbawm, Eric J., *Nations and nationalism since 1780: programme, myth, reality (2nd Edition)* (Cambridge, Cambridge University Press, 1992).

Hogan-Brun, Gabrielle and Wolff, Stefan, Eds., *Minority Languages in Europe: Frameworks, Status, Prospects* (Hampshire, England & New York, Palgrave Macmillan, 2003).

Hohfeld, Wesley Newcomb, *Fundamental Legal Conceptions* (New Haven & London, Yale University Press, 1919) (Ed. Walter Wheeler Cook).

Hollo, Lanna, *The European Commission against Racism and Intolerance (ECRI): Its first 15 years* (Strasbourg, Council of Europe Publishing, 2009).

Holzgrefe, J.L. & Keohane, Robert O., Eds., *Humanitarian intervention: ethical, legal and political dilemmas* (Cambridge, Cambridge University Press, 2003).

Horn, Frank, Ed., *Minorities and their Right of Political Participation* (Rovaniemi, University of Lapland/Lapland University Press, 1996).

Horton, John & Mendus, Susan, Eds., *Aspects of Toleration* (London & New York, Methuen & Co., 1985).

Horton, John & Mendus, Susan, Eds., *John Locke A Letter Concerning Toleration in Focus* (London, Routledge, 1991).

Hourigan, Niamh, *Escaping the Global Village: Media, Language & Protest* (Lanham, etc., Lexington Books, 2003).

Humphrey, John P., *Human Rights & the United Nations: a great adventure* (New York, Transnational Publishers, Inc., 1984).

Humphreys, P.J., *Mass Media and Media Policy in Western Europe* (Manchester, Manchester University Press, 1996).

Huntington, Samuel P., *The Clash of Civilizations and the Remaking of World Order* (London, New York, etc., Touchstone Books, 1998).

Ignatieff, Michael, *The Lesser Evil: Political Ethics in an Age of Terror* (Princeton, New Jersey, Princeton University Press, 2004).

Ignatieff, Michael, *et al.*, *Human Rights as Politics and Idolatry* (Princeton, New Jersey, Princeton University Press, 2001).

Imbleau, Martin, *La négation du génocide nazi, liberté d'expression ou crime raciste? Le négationnisme de la Shoah en droit international comparé* (Paris, L'Harmattan, 2003).

Israel, Jonathan I., *Radical Enlightenment: Philosophy and the Making of Modernity 1650–1750* (Oxford & New York, Oxford University Press, 2001).

Jacobs, James B. & Potter, Kimberly, *Hate Crimes: Criminal Law and Identity Rights* (New York, Oxford University Press, 1998).

Jakubowicz, Karol, *A new notion of media?: Media and media-like content and activities on new communications services* (Strasbourg, Council of Europe, April 2009).

Jakubowicz, Karol, *Rude Awakening: Social and Media Change in Central and Eastern Europe* (New Jersey, Hampton Press, Inc., 2007).

Jankowski, Nicholas W., Ed., *Community Media in the Information Age: Perspectives and Prospects* (Cresskill, New Jersey, Hampton Press, Inc., 2002).

Jankowski, Nick, Ole Prehn, Ole & Stappers, James, Eds., *The People's Voice: Local radio and television in Europe* (London, John Libbey & Co. Ltd., 1992).

Jansen, Sue Curry, *Censorship: The Knot That Binds Power and Knowledge* (New York & Oxford, Oxford University Press, 1991).

Jones, Thomas David, *Human Rights: Group Defamation, Freedom of Expression and the Law of Nations* (The Hague, Martinus Nijhoff Publishers, 1998).

Joseph, John E. & Taylor, Talbot J., Eds., *Ideologies of Language* (London & New York, Routledge, 1990).

Kalven, Harry Jr., *A Worthy Tradition: Freedom of Speech in America* (New York, Harper & Row Publishers, 1988).

Karlsreiter, Ana, Ed., *Media in Multilingual Societies: Freedom and Responsibility* (Vienna, OSCE Representative on Freedom of the Media, 2003).

Katsirea, Irini, *Public Broadcasting and European Law: A Comparative Examination of Public Service Obligations in Six Member States* (Alphen a/d Rijn, Kluwer Law International, 2008).

Keane, John, *The Media and Democracy* (United Kingdom, Polity Press, 1991).

Kedzia, Zdzislaw, Korula, Anna & Nowak, Manfred, Eds., *Perspectives of an All-European System of Human Rights Protection – The Role of the Council of Europe, the CSCE and the European Communities* (Germany, N.P. Engel, Publisher, 1991).

Kelly, Paul, Ed., *Multicultralism Reconsidered: Culture and Equality and its Critics* (United Kingdom, Polity Press, 2002).

Kemp, Walter A., Ed., *Quiet Diplomacy in Action: The OSCE High Commissioner on National Minorities* (The Hague/London/Boston, Kluwer Law International, 2001).

Kennedy, Michael and O'Halpin, Eunan, *Ireland and the Council of Europe: from isolation towards integration* (Strasbourg, Council of Europe Publishing, 2000).

Kieran, Matthew, *Media Ethics: A Philosophical Approach* (Westport, Connecticut & London, Praeger, 1997).

Kirk, John M. & Ó Baoill, Dónall P., Eds., *Towards our Goals in Broadcasting, the Press, the Performing Arts and the Economy: Minority Languages in Northern Ireland, the Republic of Ireland, and Scotland* (Belfast, Cló Ollscoil na Banríona, 2003).

Koopmans, Ruud & Statham, Paul, Eds., *Challenging immigration and ethnic relations politics* (Oxford, Oxford University Press, 2000).

Krebber, Daniel, *Europeanisation of Regulatory Television Policy: The Decision-making Process of the Television without Frontiers Directives from 1989 & 1997* (Baden-Baden, Nomos Verlagsgesellschaft, 2002).

Kretzmer, David & Kershman Hazan, Francine, Eds., *Freedom of Speech and Incitement against Democracy* (The Hague, Kluwer Law International, 2000).

Krishnaswami, Arcot, Special Rapporteur of the Sub-Commission on Prevention of Discrimination and Protection of Minorities, *Study of Discrimination in the Matter of Religious Rights and Practices* (New York, United Nations, 1960).

Kuper, Adam, *Culture: The Anthropologists' Account* (Cambridge, Massachusetts/London, England, Harvard University Press, 1999).

Kymlicka, Will, *Multicultural Odysseys: Navigating the New International Politics of Diversity* (Oxford, Oxford University Press, 2007).

Kymlicka, Will & Patten, Alan, Eds., *Language Rights and Political Theory* (New York, Oxford University Press, 2003).

Kymlicka, Will, *Contemporary Political Philosophy: An Introduction* (Second Edition) (New York, Oxford University Press, 2002).

Kymlicka, Will, *Multicultural Citizenship: A Liberal Theory of Minority Rights* (New York, Oxford University Press, 1995).

Kymlicka, Will, Ed., *The Rights of Minority Cultures* (New York, Oxford University Press, 1995).

Landau, Jacob M. & Kellner-Heinkele, Barbara, *Politics of Language in the ex-Soviet Muslim States* (London, Hurst & Co., 2001).

Lawson, Rick & de Blois, Matthijs, Eds., *The Dynamics of the Protection of Human Rights in Europe: Essays in Honour of Henry G. Schermers* (Vol. III) (Dordrecht, Martinus Nijhoff Publishers, 1994).

Lederer, Laura & Delgado, Richard, Eds., *The Price We Pay: The Case Against Racist Speech, Hate Propaganda And Pornography* (New York, Hill & Wang, 1995).

Lenkova, Mariana, Ed., *'Hate Speech' in the Balkans* (Athens, International Helsinki Federation for Human Rights, 1998).

Lerner, Natan, *Group Rights and Discrimination in International Law* (2nd Edition) (The Hague, Martinus Nijhoff Publishers, 2003).

Lerner, Natan, *The U.N. Convention on the Elimination of all Forms of Racial Discrimination* (Alphen aan den Rijn, The Netherlands/USA, Sijthoff & Noordhoff, 1980).

Lessig, Lawrence, *Code and Other Laws of Cyberspace* (New York, Basic Books, 1999).

Letschert, Rianne M., *The Impact of Minority Rights Mechanisms* (The Hague, T.M.C. Asser Press, 2005).

Levy, David A.L., *Europe's Digital Revolution: Broadcasting regulation, the EU and the nation state* (London & New York, Routledge, 1999).

Levy, Jacob T., *The Multiculturalism of Fear* (New York, Oxford University Press, 2000)

Lewis, Anthony, *Freedom for the Thought That We Hate: A Biography of the First Amendment* (New York, Basic Books, 2009).

Lichtenberg, Judith, Ed., *Democracy and the mass media* (Cambridge & New York, Cambridge University Press, 1990).

Lipstadt, Deborah, *Denying the Holocaust: The Growing Assault on Truth and Memory* (London, Penguin, 2003).

Loc Hong, Quoc, *The Legal Inclusion of Extremist Speech* (Nijmegen, Wolf Legal Publishers, 2005).

Longley, Michael, Ed., *Louis MacNeice Poems* (London, Faber & Faber Ltd., 2001).

Loveland, Ian, Ed., *Importing the First Amendment – Freedom of Expression in American, English and European Law* (Oxford, Hart Publishing, 1998).

MacBride, Seán, *et al.*, *Many Voices One World: Towards a new more just and more efficient world information and communication order* (Great Britain, UNESCO, 1980).

MacDonald, Ronald Saint John, Matscher, Franz and Petzold, H., Eds., *The European System for the Protection of Human Rights* (Dordrecht/Boston/London, Martinus Nijhoff Publishers, 1993).

MacKinnon, Catharine A., *Only Words* (London, Harper Collins Publishers, 1994).

Machet, Emmanuelle, *A Decade of EU Broadcasting Regulation: The Directive "Television without Frontiers"* (Germany, The European Institute for the Media, 1999).

Mahoney, Kathleen & Mahoney, Paul, Eds., *Human Rights in the Twenty-first Century: A Global Challenge* (Part 2) (Netherlands, Kluwer Academic Publishers, 1993).

Majone, Giandomenico, Ed., *Regulating Europe* (London & New York, Routledge, 1996).
Marsden, Christopher T., Ed., *Regulating the Global Information Society* (London & New York, Routledge, 2000).
Marsden, Chris & Verhulst, Stefaan, Eds., *Convergence in European Digital TV Regulation* (London, Blackstone Press Ltd., 1999).
Martin, Elizabeth A., Ed., *A Dictionary of Law* (Fourth Edition) (Oxford, Oxford University Press, 1997).
Matas, David, *Bloody Words: hate and free speech* (Winnipeg, Canada, Bain & Cox Publishers, 2000).
Matscher, Franz & Petzold, Herbert, Eds., *Protecting Human Rights: The European Dimension Essays in Honour of Gerard J. Wiarda* (2nd Edition) (Germany, Carl Heymanns Verlag KG, 1990).
Matsuda, Mari J., Lawrence, Charles R., III, Delgado, Richard & Williams Crenshaw, Kimberlè, Eds., *Words That Wound: Critical Race Theory, Assaultive Speech, and the First Amendment* (Boulder/San Francisco/Oxford, Westview Press, 1993).
May, Stephen, *Language and Minority Rights: Ethnicity, Nationalism and the Politics of Language* (England, Pearson Education Ltd., 2001).
McAdam, Doug, Tarrow, Sidney & Tilly, Charles, *Dynamics of Contention* (USA, Cambridge University Press, 2001);
McAdam, Doug, McCarthy, John D., Zald, Mayer N., Eds., *Comparative perspectives on social movements: Political opportunities, mobilizing structures, and cultural framings* (USA, Cambridge University Press, 1996).
McGoldrick, Dominic, *Human Rights and Religion: The Islamic Headscarf Debate in Europe* (Oxford and Portland, Oregon, Hart Publishing, 2006).
McGoldrick, Dominic, *The Human Rights Committee: Its Role in the Development of the International Covenant on Civil and Political Rights* (Second Edition) (Oxford, Clarendon Press, 1994).
McGonagle, Marie, *Media Law* (Second Edition) (Dublin, Thomson Round Hall, 2003)
McKinnon, Catriona & Castiglione, Dario, Eds., *The culture of toleration in diverse societies: Reasonable tolerance* (Manchester University Press, Manchester & New York, 2003).
McLuhan, Marshall & Fiore, Quentin, *The Medium is the Massage* (Great Britain, Penguin Books, 1967) (Co-ordinated by Jerome Agel).
McLuhan, Marshall, *Understanding Media* (Great Britain, Abacus, 1964).
McMahon, Bryan & Binchy, William, *Irish Law of Torts* (3rd Edition), (Dublin, Butterworths, 2000).
McNair, Brian, Hibberd, Matthew & Schlesinger, Philip, *Mediated Access: Broadcasting and Democratic Participation* (Luton, University of Luton Press, 2003).
McQuail, Denis, *McQuail's Mass Communication Theory* (5th Edition) (Great Britain, SAGE Publications Ltd., 2005).
McQuail, Denis, *Media Accountability and Freedom of Publication* (Oxford & New York, Oxford University Press, 2003).

Meerts, Paul, Ed., *Culture and International Law* (The Hague, Hague Academic Press, 2008).
Meijknecht, Anna K., *Towards International Personality: The Position of Minorities and Indigenous Peoples in International Law* (Antwerpen/Groningen/Oxford, Intersentia/Hart, 2001).
Meiklejohn, Alexander, *Free Speech And Its Relation to Self-Government* (New York, Harper & Bros., 1948).
Meiklejohn, Alexander, *Political Freedom: the constitutional powers of the people* (USA, Harper & Row, Publishers, Inc., 1965).
Melucci, Alberto, *Challenging codes: Collective action in the information age* (UK, Cambridge University Press, 1996).
Mendel, Toby, *Public Service Broadcasting: A Comparative Legal Survey* (Second Edition) (France, UNESCO, 2011).
Mendus, Susan, Ed., *The Politics of Toleration: Tolerance and Intolerance in Modern Life* (Edinburgh, Edinburgh University Press, 1999).
Mendus, Susan, Ed., *Justifying Toleration* (Cambridge, Cambridge University Press, 1988).
Meuris, Jacques, *Magritte* (Cologne, Taschen GmbH, 2004).
Miall, Hugh, Ed., *Minority Rights in Europe: The Scope for a Transnational Regime* (London, The Royal Institute of International Affairs/Pinter Publishers, 1994).
Miel, P. *et al.*, *Media Re:public: News and Information as Digital Media Come of Age* (Harvard, Berkmann Center for Internet & Society, Harvard University, 2008).
Mill, John Stuart, *On Liberty and other essays* (Oxford, Oxford University Press, 1998).
Milton, John, *Areopagitica and other Political Writings of John Milton* (Indianapolis, Liberty Fund, 1999).
Minow, Newton N., *Equal Time: The Private Broadcaster and the Public Interest* (New York, Atheneum, 1964) (Lawrence Laurent, Ed.).
Möller, Christian & Amouroux, Arnaud, Eds., *Governing the Internet: Freedom and Regulation in the OSCE Region* (Vienna, OSCE Representative on Freedom of the Media, 2007).
Moring, Tom & Dunbar, Robert, *The European Charter for Regional or Minority Languages and the media* (Strasbourg, Council of Europe Publishing, 2008).
Morley, David & Robins, Kevin, *Spaces of Identity: Global Media, Electronic Landscapes and Cultural Boundaries* (London, Routledge, 1995).
Morsink, Johannes, *The Universal Declaration of Human Rights: Origins, Drafting & Intent* (Philadelphia, PA, University of Pennsylvania Press, 1999).
Mosco, Vincent, *The Digital Sublime: Myth, Power, and Cyberspace* (Massachusetts, MIT Press, 2004).
Murphy, Tim, Ed., *Western Jurisprudence* (Dublin, Thomson Roundhall, 2004).
Musgrave, Thomas D., *Self-determination and National Minorities* (Oxford, Oxford University Press, 2000).
Nagel, Thomas, *Equality and Partiality* (New York & Oxford, Oxford University Press, 1991).

Napoli, Philip M., Ed., *Media Diversity and Localism: Meaning and Metrics* (Mahwah, New Jersey & London, Lawrence Erlbaum, 2007).

Neuwahl, Nanette A. & Rosas, Allan, Eds., *The European Union and Human Rights* (The Hague, Kluwer Law International, 1995).

Nic Shuibhne, Niamh, *EC Law and Minority Language Policy: Culture, Citizenship and Fundamental Rights* (The Netherlands, Kluwer Law International, 2002).

Niec, Halina, Ed., *Cultural Rights and Wrongs: A collection of essays in commemoration of the 50th anniversary of the Universal Declaration of Human Rights* (United Kingdom, UNESCO, 1998)

Niessen, Jan & Chopin, Isabelle, Eds., *The Development of Legal Instruments to Combat Racism in a Diverse Europe* (Leiden/Boston, Martinus Nijhoff Publishers, 2004).

Nieuwenhuis, Aernout J., *Over de grens van de vrijheid van meningsuiting: theorie, rechtsvergelijking, discriminatie, pornografie* (2e herz. dr.) (Nijmegen, Ars Aequi Libri, 2006).

Nieuwenhuis, Aernout and Hins, Wouter, Eds., *Van ontvanger naar zender: opstellen aangeboden aan prof. mr. J.M. de Meij* (Amsterdam, Cramwinckel, 2003).

Nikoltchev, Susanne, Ed., *Media Literacy, IRIS plus* 2011–3 (Strasbourg, European Audiovisual Observatory, 2011).

Nikoltchev, Susanne, Ed., *Switchover to the Digital Dividend, IRIS plus 2010–6* (Strasbourg, European Audiovisual Observatory, 2010).

Nikoltchev, Susanne, Ed., *IRIS Special: Audiovisual Media Services without Frontiers – Implementing the Rules* (Strasbourg, European Audiovisual Observatory, 2006).

Nikoltchev, Susanne, Ed., *IRIS Special – To Have or not to Have Must-carry Rules* (Strasbourg, European Audiovisual Observatory, 2005).

Nikoltchev, Susanne, Ed., *IRIS Special – Political Debate and the Role of the Media: The Fragility of Free Speech* (Strasbourg, European Audiovisual Observatory, 2004).

Nikoltchev, Susanne, Ed., *IRIS Special – Co-Regulation of the Media in Europe*, (Strasbourg, European Audiovisual Observatory, 2003).

Nikoltchev, Susanne, Ed., *IRIS Special: Jurisdiction over Broadcasters in Europe – Report on a Round-table Discussion*, (Strasbourg, European Audiovisual Observatory, 2002).

Nimmer, Melville B., *Nimmer on Freedom of Speech: A Treatise on the Theory of the First Amendment* (USA, Matthew Bender & Co. Inc., 1987).

Nissen, Christian S., Ed., *Making a Difference: Public Service Broadcasting in the European Media Landscape* (Eastleigh, John Libbey Publishing, 2006).

Noam, Eli, *Television in Europe* (Oxford University Press, New York, 1991).

Noll, Roger G. & Price, Monroe E., Eds., *A Communications Cornucopia: Markle Foundation Essays on Information Policy* (Washington, D.C., Brookings Institution Press, 1998).

Nordenstreng, Kaarle, Ed., *Reports on Media Ethics in Europe* (Finland, University of Tampere, 1995).

Nowak, Manfred, *U.N. Covenant on Civil and Political Rights – CCPR Commentary* (2nd revised edition) (Kehl, N.P. Engel, 2005).

Nowak, Manfred, *UN Covenant on Civil and Political Rights CCPR Commentary* (Kehl am Rhein, Germany, N.P. Engel, 1993).

Oetheimer, Mario, Ed., *Freedom of Expression in Europe: Case-law concerning Article 10 of the European Convention on Human Rights*, Human rights files, No. 18 (Strasbourg, Council of Europe, 2007).

Oetheimer, Mario, *L'Harmonisation de la liberté d'expression en Europe: contribution à l'étude de l'article 10 de la convention européenne des droits de l'homme et de son application en Autriche et au Royaume-Uni* (Paris, Éditions A. Pedone, 2001).

O'Flaherty, Michael, *Human Rights and the UN: Practice before the Treaty Bodies* (London, Sweet & Maxwell, 1996).

O'Neill, Onora, *Rethinking freedom of the press* (Dublin, Royal Irish Academy, 2004).

O'Reilly, Camille C., Ed., *Language, Ethnicity and the State* (Vols I & II) (Hampshire, England & New York, Palgrave, 2001).

OSCE Representative on Freedom of the Media, Ed., *From Quill to Cursor: Freedom of the Media in the Digital Era* (Vienna, OSCE RFOM, 2003).

Ovey, Clare & White, Robin, *Jacobs and White, The European Convention on Human Rights* (Fourth Edition) (Oxford, Oxford University Press, 2006).

Packer, John & Myntti, Kristian, Eds., *The Protection of Ethnic and Linguistic Minorities in Europe* (Finland, Abo Akademi University Institute for Human Rights, 1993).

Paletz, David L. & Jakubowicz, Karol, Eds., *Business as Usual: Continuity and Change in Central and Eastern European Media* (New Jersey, Hampton Press, Inc., 2003).

Parekh, Bhikhu, *Rethinking Multiculturalism: Cultural Diversity and Political Theory* (Second Edition) (New York, Palgrave Macmillan, 2006).

Peers, Steve & Ward, Angela, Eds., *The European Union Charter of Fundamental Rights* (Oxford and Portland Oregon, Hart Publishing, 2004).

Pennock, Roland J. & Chapman, John W., Eds., *Liberal Democracy: Nomos XXV* (New York, New York University Press, 1983).

Phillips, Alan, *The Framework Convention for the Protection of National Minorities: A Policy Analysis* (London, Minority Rights Group International, 2002).

Phillips, Alan and Rosas, Allan, Eds., *Universal Minority Rights* (Turku/Abo and London, Abo Akademi University Institute for Human Rights/Minority Rights Group (International), 1995).

Phillipson, Robert, Ed., *Rights to Language: Equity, Power, and Education* (Mahwah, New Jersey & London, Lawrence Erlbaum Associates, Publishers, 2000).

Pogany, Istvan, Ed., *Human Rights in Eastern Europe* (Aldershot, etc., Edward Elgar, 1995).

Popper, Karl, *The Open Society and Its Enemies (Volume I: The Spell of Plato)* (New York & London, Routledge, 2005).

Post, Robert C., Ed., *Censorship and Silencing: Practices of Cultural Regulation* (Los Angeles, The Getty Institute for the History of Art and the Humanities, 1998).

Post, Robert C., *Constitutional Domains: Democracy, Community, Management* (Cambridge, Massachusetts, Harvard University Press, 1995).

Post, Robert C., Ed., *Law and the Order of Culture* (California, University of California Press, 1991).
Postman, Neil, *Amusing Ourselves to Death: Public Discourse in the Age of Show Business* (Great Britain, Methuen, 1985).
Powe, Lucas A., Jr., *The Fourth Estate and the Constitution: Freedom of the Press in America* (California, University of California Press, 1991).
Price, Monroe E., *Media and Sovereignty – The Global Information Revolution and Its Challenge to State Power* (Massachusetts, MIT Press, 2002).
Price, Monroe E., Rozumilowicz, Beata and Verhulst, Stefaan G., Eds., *Media Reform: Democratizing the media, democratizing the state* (London, Routledge, 2002).
Price, Monroe E. & Thompson, Mark, Eds., *Forging Peace: Intervention, Human Rights and the Management of Media Space* (Edinburgh, Edinburgh University Press, 2002).
Price, Monroe E., *Television, The Public Sphere, and National Identity* (Oxford, Clarendon Press, 1995).
Prosser, Tony, *The Limits of Competition Law: Markets and Public Services* (Oxford, Oxford University Press, 2005).
Putnam, Robert D., *Bowling Alone: The Collapse and Revival of American Community* (New York, Simon & Schuster, 2000).
Raboy, Marc, Ed., *Global Media Policy in the New Millennium* (Luton, University of Luton Press, 2002).
Raboy, Marc, Ed., *Public Broadcasting for the 21st Century* (Academia Monograph 17) (Luton, University of Luton Press, 1996).
Räikkä, Juha, Ed., *Do We Need Minority Rights? Conceptual Issues* (The Hague, Martinus Nijhoff Publishers, 1996).
Rawls, John, *Political Liberalism* (Expanded Edition) (New York, Columbia University Press, 2005).
Rawls, John, *The Law of Peoples* (Cambridge, Massachusetts/London, England, Harvard University Press, 2002).
Rawls, John, *A Theory of Justice* (Revised Edition) (Cambridge, Massachusetts, Harvard University Press, 1999).
Raz, Joseph, *The Morality of Freedom* (New York, Oxford University Press, 1986).
Rehman, Javaid, *The Weaknesses in the International Protection of Minority Rights* (The Hague/London/Boston, Kluwer Law International, 2000).
Richards, David A.J., *Free Speech and the Politics of Identity* (New York, Oxford University Press, Inc., 1999).
Richter, Andrei, *Post-Soviet perspective on censorship and freedom of the media* (Moscow, UNESCO, 2007).
Riggins, Stephen Harold, Ed., *Ethnic Minority Media: An International Perspective* (USA, SAGE Publications, 1992).
Robertson, A.H., Ed., *Collected edition of the 'Travaux Préparatoires' of the European Convention on Human Rights* (The Hague, etc., Martinus Nijhoff, 1975–1985).
Robins, Kevin *et al.*, *The challenge of transcultural diversities: Cultural policy and cultural diversity* (Strasbourg, Council of Europe Publishing, 2006).

Rosenblum, Nancy L., Ed., *Liberalism and the Moral Life* (Massachusetts, Harvard University Press, 1989).

Rosas, Allan & Helgesen, Jan, Eds. (with the collaboration of Diane Goodman), *The Strength of Diversity: Human Rights and Pluralist Democracy* (Dordrecht/Boston/London, Martinus Nijhoff Publishers, 1992).

Rossnagel, A., Ed., *Die Zukunft der Fernsehrichtlinie/The Future of the 'Television without Frontiers' Directive* (Baden-Baden, Germany, Nomos, 2005).

Rousseau, Jean-Jacques, *The Social Contract* (London, Penguin, 2004) (Trans. Maurice Cranston).

Rousseau, Jean-Jacques, *Essai sur l'origine des langues* (Bibliothèque du graphe, texte intégral d'après l'édition A. Belin de 1817).

Rushdie, Salman, *Step across this line: collected non-fiction 1992–2002* (London, Vintage, 2002).

Sadurski, Wojciech, Ed., *Political Rights under Stress in 21st Century Europe* (New York, Oxford University Press Inc., 2006).

Sadurski, Wojciech, *Freedom of Speech and Its Limits* (Dordrecht/Boston/London, Kluwer Academic Publishers, 1999).

Sajó, András, Ed., *Censorial Sensitivities: Free Speech and Religion in a Fundamentalist World* (Utrecht, Eleven International Publishing, 2007).

Sajó, Andras, Ed., *Rights of Access to the Media* (The Hague, Kluwer Law International, 1996).

Sarat, Austin, Ed., *Race, Law & Culture* (New York, Oxford University Press, 1997).

Scanlon, T.M., *The Difficulty of Tolerance: Essays in Political Philosophy* (Cambridge, Cambridge University Press, 2003).

Schabas, William A., *Genocide in International Law* (Cambridge, Cambridge University Press, 2000).

Schauer, Frederick, *Free speech: a philosophical enquiry* (Cambridge, etc., Cambridge University Press, 1982).

Scheinin, Martin & Toivanen, Reetta, Eds., *Rethinking Non-Discrimination and Minority Rights* (Turku/Berlin, Institute for Human Rights, Abo Akademi University/German Institute for Human Rights, 2004).

Schlesinger, Philip, *Media, State and Nation: Political Violence and Collective Identities* (London/Newbury Park/New Delhi, SAGE Publications, 1991).

Schneider, Hildegard & Van den Bossche, Peter, Eds., *Protection of Cultural Diversity from a European and International Perspective* (Antwerp, Intersentia, 2008).

Schultz, Julianne, *Reviving the Fourth Estate: Democracy, Accountability and the Media* (Australia, Cambridge University Press, 1998).

Shapiro, Andrew L., *The Control Revolution* (New York, Public Affairs, 1999).

Shapiro, Ian & Kymlicka, Will, Eds., *Ethnicity and Group Rights* (NOMOS XXXIX) (New York & London, New York University Press, 1997),

Shue, Henry, *Basic Rights: Subsistence, Affluence, and U.S. Foreign Policy* (Princeton, New Jersey, Princeton University Press, 1980).

Siapera, Eugenia, *Cultural Diversity and Global Media: The Mediation of Difference* (United Kingdom, Wiley-Blackwell, 2010).

Sigler, Jay, *Minority Rights: a comparative analysis* (Connecticut, Greenwood Press, 1983).

Silverstone, Roger, *Why Study the Media?* (London/Thousand Oaks, CA/New Delhi, SAGE Publications, 1999).

Sinclair, John, Jacka, Elizabeth & Cunningham, Stuart, *New Patterns in Global Television* (Great Britain, Oxford University Press, 1996).

Skurbaty, Zelim, *As if Peoples Mattered* (The Hague, Martinus Nijhoff Publishers, 2000).

Skutnabb-Kangas, Tove, *Linguistic Genocide in Education – Or Worldwide Diversity and Human Rights?* (Mahwah, New Jersey & London, Lawrence Erlbaum Associates, Publishers, 2000).

Skutnabb-Kangas, Tove & Phillipson, Robert (in collaboration with Rannut, Mart), Eds., *Linguistic Human Rights: Overcoming Linguistic Discrimination* (Germany, Mouton de Gruyter, 1994).

Smolla, Rodney A., *Free Speech in an Open Society* (New York, Vintage Books, 1993).

Sohn, Louis B., Ed., *The CSCE and the Turbulent New Europe* (Washington D.C., Friedrich-Naumann-Stiftung, 1993).

Sola Pool, Ithiel de, *Technologies of Freedom* (Cambridge, Massachusetts and London, England, The Belknap Press of Harvard University Press, 1983).

Spiliopoulou Akermark, Athanasia, *Justifications of Minority Protection in International Law* (London/The Hague/Boston, Kluwer International Law, 1997).

Splichal, Slavko, Calabrese, Andrew & Sparks, Colin, *Information Society and Civil Society: Contemporary Perspectives on the Changing World Order* (Lafayette, Purdue University, 1994).

Splichal, Slavko & Wasko, Janet, Eds., *Communication and Democracy* (New Jersey, Ablex Publishing Corporation, 1993).

Stamatopoulou, Elsa, *Cultural Rights in International Law: Article 27 of the Universal Declaration and Beyond* (Leiden/Boston, Martinus Nijhoff Publishers, 2007).

Steiner, George, *After Babel – Aspects of language and translation* (3rd Edition) (Oxford, Oxford University Press, 1998).

Steiner, Henry J., Alston, Philip & Goodman, Ryan, *International Human Rights in Context* (3rd Edition) (Oxford & New York, Oxford University Press, 2008).

Steiner, Henry J. & Alston, Philip, *International Human Rights in Context* (2nd Edition) (Oxford & New York, Oxford University Press, 2000).

Stone, Geoffrey R., *Perilous Times: Free Speech in Wartime* (New York & London, W.W. Norton & Co., 2004).

Sumner, L. W., *The Hateful and the Obscene: Studies in the Limits of Free Expression* (Toronto/Buffalo/London, University of Toronto Press, 2004).

Sunstein, Cass R., *Republic.com 2.0* (Princeton NJ, Princeton University Press, 2007).

Suksi, Markku, Ed., *Autonomy: Applications and Implications* (The Hague, Kluwer Law International, 1998).

Tahzib, Bahiyyih G., *Freedom of Religion or Belief: Ensuring Effective International Legal Protection* (The Hague, Martinus Nijhoff, 1996).

Tambini, Damian & Cowling, Jamie, Eds., *New News? Impartial Broadcasting in the Digital Age* (London, Institute for Public Policy Research, 2002).

Taylor, Charles *et al.*, *Multiculturalism: Examining the Politics of Recognition* (Princeton, New Jersey, Princeton University Press, 1994).

Thompson, Allan, Ed., *The Media and the Rwanda Genocide* (London & Ann Arbor, Michigan, Pluto Press, 2007).

Thornberry, Patrick and Martín Estébanez, María Amor, *Minority Rights in Europe* (Strasbourg, Council of Europe, 2004).

Thornberry, Patrick, *International Law and the Rights of Minorities* (Oxford, Clarendon Press, 1991).

Tilly, Charles, *Durable Inequality* (Berkeley, University of California Press, 1998).

Toggenburg, Gabriel N., Ed., *Minority Protection and the Enlarged European Union: The Way Forward* (Budapest, Local Government and Public Service Reform Initiative/ Open Society Institute, 2004).

Tomasevski, Katarina, *Education Denied: Costs and Remedies* (London, Zed Books Ltd., 2003).

Tomuschat, C., *Human Rights: Between Idealism and Realism* (Second Edition) (Oxford, Oxford University Press, 2008).

Tracey, Michael, *The Decline and Fall of Public Service Broadcasting* (Oxford & New York, Oxford University Press, 1998).

Trifunovska, Snezana, Ed., *Minority Rights in Europe: European Minorities and Languages* (The Hague, T.M.C. Asser Press, 2001).

Tsesis, Alexander, *Destructive Messages: How Hate Speech Paves the Way for Harmful Social Movements* (New York, New York University Press, 2002).

Tunstall, Jeremy & Machin, David, *The Anglo-American Media Connection* (New York, Oxford University Press, 1999).

Valcke, Peggy, *Digitale Diversiteit: Convergentie van Media-, Telecommunicatie- & Mededingingsrecht* (Ghent, Larcier, 2004).

Van Dyke, Vernon, *Human Rights, Ethnicity, and Discrimination* (Westport, Connecticut/ London, England, Greenwood Press, 1985).

Varennes, Fernand de, *Language, minorities and human rights* (The Hague, Martinus Nijhoff, 1996).

Vedder, Anton, Ed., *Ethics and the Internet* (Antwerpen/Groningen, Intersentia, 2001).

Verdoodt, Albert, *Naissance et signification de la Déclaration des droits de l'homme* (Louvain, E. Warny, 1964).

Verstichel, Annelies, Alen, Andre, De Witte, Bruno & Lemmens, Paul, Eds., *The Framework Convention for the Protection of National Minorities: A Useful Pan-European Instrument?* (Antwerp/Oxford/Portland, Intersentia, 2008).

Walker, Samuel, *Hate Speech: The History of an American Controversy* (Lincoln & London, University of Nebraska Press, 1994).

Waluchow, W.J., Ed., *Free Expression: Essays in Law and Philosophy* (Oxford, Clarendon Press, 1994).

Walzer, Michael, *On Toleration* (New Haven & London, Yale University Press, 1997).

Walzer, Michael, *Politics and Passion: Toward a More Egalitarian Liberalism* (New Haven & London, Yale University Press, 2005).

Ward, David, Ed., *The European Union and the Culture Industries: Regulation and the Public Interest* (Hampshire, England, Ashgate Publishing Limited, 2008).

Ward, David, *The European Union Democratic Deficit and the Public Sphere: An Evaluation of EU Media Policy* (Amsterdam, etc., IOS Press, 2004).

Watson, Iarfhlaith, *Broadcasting in Irish: Minority language, radio, television and identity* (Dublin, Four Courts Press, 2003).

Weber, Anne, *Manual on hate speech* (Strasbourg, Council of Europe, 2009).

Weinstein, James, *Hate Speech, Pornography, and the Radical Attack on Free Speech Doctrine* (Boulder, CO, Westview Press, 1999).

Weller, Marc, Ed., *Universal Minority Rights: A Commentary on the Jurisprudence of International Courts and Treaty Bodies* (New York, Oxford University Press, 2007).

Weller, Marc, Ed., *The Rights of Minorities in Europe: A Commentary on the European Framework Convention for the Protection of National Minorities* (Oxford and New York, Oxford University Press, 2005).

White, Aidan, *To Tell You the Truth: The Ethical Journalism Initiative* (Brussels, International Federation of Journalists, 2008).

Wichmann, Manfred & Heinz, Wolfgang, Eds., *Freedom of Expression and Human Rights Protection* (Brussels, Friedrich Naumann Stiftung, 1998).

Wieten, Jan, Murdock, Graham & Dahlgren, Peter, Eds., *Television Across Europe: A Comparative Introduction* London, SAGE Publications Ltd., 2000).

Williams, Melissa S. and Macedo, Stephen, Eds., *Political Exclusion and Domination* (New York & London, New York University Press, 2005).

Williams, Raymond, *Television: Technology and cultural form* (London and New York, Routledge, 2003).

Witte, John, Jr., & Vyver, Johan D. van der, Eds., *Religious Human Rights in Global Perspective* (Vols. I & II) (The Hague, Martinus Nijhoff, 1996).

Woehrling, Jean-Marie, *The European Charter for Regional or Minority Languages: A critical commentary* (Strasbourg, Council of Europe Publishing, 2005).

Wolff, Robert Paul, Moore, Barrington, Jr. & Marcuse, Herbert, *A Critique of Pure Tolerance* (Boston, Beacon Press, 1969).

Wolff, Tim, *Multiculturalisme en neutraliteit* (Amsterdam, Vossiuspers/Universiteit van Amsterdam Press, 2005).

Wolfrum, Rüdiger, Ed., *United Nations: Laws, Policies and Practice* (Dordrecht, Martinus Nijhoff, 1995).

Wolfson, Nicholas, *Hate Speech, Sex Speech, Free Speech* (USA, Praeger, 1997).

Yack, Bernard, Ed., *Liberalism without Illusions* (Chicago, University of Chicago Press, 1996).

Young, Iris Marion, *Inclusion and Democracy* (New York, Oxford University Press Inc., 2000).

Young, Iris Marion, *Justice and the Politics of Difference* (Princeton, Princeton University Press, 1990).

Zellner, Wolfgang and Lange, Falk, Eds., *Peace and Stability through Human and Minority Rights: Speeches by the OSCE High Commissioner on National Minorities* (Baden-Baden, Nomos, 1999).
Zielonka, Jan, Ed., *Europe Unbound: Enlarging and reshaping the boundaries of the European Union* (London & New York, Routledge, 2002).
Zittrain, Jonathan, *The Future of the Internet And How to Stop It* (London, Penguin Books Ltd., 2009).
Zoonen, Liesbet van, *Entertaining the Citizen: When Politics and Popular Culture Converge* (USA, Rowman & Littlefield Publishers, Inc., 2005).

Journal articles & academic papers

Achilléas, Philippe, "La diffusion par satellite de programmes illégaux – L'affaire *Al Manar*", *Communication – Commerce électronique* (Février 2005), pp. 39–42.
Addis, Adeno, "Cultural Integrity and Political Unity: The Politics of Language in Multilingual States", 33 *Arizona State Law Journal* (Fall 2001), pp. 719–789.
Ader, Thorsten, "Cultural and Regional Remits in Broadcasting", *IRIS plus* (Supplement to *IRIS – Legal Observations of the European Audiovisual Observatory*), 2006–8.
Ader, Thorsten & Schoenthal, Max, "Access to Information on Government Action, especially from the Media Point of View", *IRIS plus* (Supplement to *IRIS – Legal Observations of the European Audiovisual Observatory*), 2005–2.
Aksoy, Asu & Robins, Kevin, "*Gecekondu*-style broadcasting in Turkey: a confrontation of cultural values", 21 *Intermedia* (No. 3, June-July 1993), pp. 15–17.
Alfredsson, Gudmundur, "A Frame an Incomplete Painting: Comparison of the Framework Convention for the Protection of National Minorities with International Standards and Monitoring Procedures", 7 *International Journal on Minority and Group Rights* (2000), pp. 291–304.
Alfredsson, Gudmundur & Zayas, Alfred de, "Minority Rights: Protection by the United Nations," 14 *Human Rights Law Journal* 1993, pp. 1–9.
Allott, Philip, "The Concept of International Law", EJIL 10 (1999), pp. 31–50.
Alston, Philip, "Conjuring up New Human Rights: A Proposal for Quality Control", 78 *American Journal of International Law* 607–621 (1984).
Arino, Mónica, "Digital War and Peace: Regulation and Competition in European Digital Broadcasting", 10 *European Public Law* (No. 1, 2004), pp. 135–160.
Bader, Veit, "Religious Diversity and Democratic Institutional Pluralism", 31 *Political Theory* (No. 2, April 2003), pp. 265–294.
Baker, C. Edwin, "Viewpoint Diversity and Media Ownership", 60 *Federal Communications Law Journal* (No. 3, 2009), pp. 651–671.
Baker, C. Edwin, "Genocide, Press Freedom, and the Case of Hassan Ngeze", Public Law and Legal Theory Research Paper Series, Research Paper No. 46 (SSRN, 31 January 2003).
Baker, C. Edwin, "Media Concentration: Giving up on Democracy", 54 Fla. L. Rev. 839 (December 2002), pp. 839–919.

Balkin, J.M., "Some Realism about Pluralism: Legal Realist Approaches to the First Amendment", 1990 Duke L.J. 375–430.
Barber, Benjamin R., "Which Technology for which Democracy? Which Democracy for which Technology?", *International Journal of Communiations Law and Policy* (No. 6, Winter 2000/2001).
Barendt, Eric, "What is the point of Libel Law?", 52 *Current Legal Problems* (1999) 110–128.
Barron, Jerome A., "Access to the Media – A Contemporary Appraisal", 35 Hofstra L. Rev. 937 (2006–2007).
Barron, Jerome A., "Rights of Access and Reply to the Media in the United States Today", *Communications and the Law* (April 2003), pp. 1–12.
Barron, Jerome A., "Access to the Press – A New First Amendment Right", 80 Harv. L. Rev. 1641–1678 (June 1967).
Baudis, Dominique, "Interdire l'incitation à la haine à la télévision: un défi européen", no. 177 *CSA La Lettre*, octobre 2004, p. 1.
Bavasso, Antonio F., "Electronic communications: a new paradigm for European regulation", 41 *Common Market Law Review* (2004), pp. 87–118.
Bavasso, Antonio F., "Public service broadcasting and State aid rules: between a rock and a hard place", 27 E.L.Rev. (June 2002), pp. 340–350.
Bellamy, Richard, "Toleration, Liberalism and Democracy: A Comment on Leader and Garzón Valdés, 10 *Ratio Juris* (No. 2, June 1997), pp. 177–186.
Bertoni, Eduardo Andres, "The Inter-American Court of Human Rights and the European Court of Human Rights: A Dialogue on Freedom of Expression Standards", [2009] E.H.R.L.R. (No. 3), 332–352.
Betzel, Marcel & Ward, David, "The Regulation of Public Service Broadcasters in Western Europe", 12 *Trends in Communication* (No. 1, 2004), pp. 47–62.
Bhabha, Jacqueline, "'Get Back to Where You Once Belonged': Identity, Citizenship, and Exclusion in Europe", 20 *Human Rights Quarterly* (1998), pp. 592–627.
Biltereyst, Daniël, "Language and Culture as Ultimate Barriers? An Analysis of the Circulation, Consumption and Popularity of Fiction in Small European Countries", 7 *European Journal of Communication* (1992), pp. 517–540.
Biltereyst, Daniel, "Resisting American Hegemony: A Comparative Analysis of the Reception of Domestic and US Fiction", 6 *European Journal of Communication* (1991), pp. 469–497.
Block, David, "Globalization, Transnational Communication and the Internet", 6 *International Journal on Multicultural Societies* (No. 1, 2004), pp. 13–28.
Bohman, James, "Deliberative Toleration", 31 *Political Theory* (No. 6, December 2003), pp. 757–779.
Bollinger, Lee C., "Free Speech and Intellectual Values", 92 *Yale Law Journal* 438 (January, 1983) (pp. 438–473).
Bollinger, Lee C., Jr., "Freedom of the Press and Public Access: Toward a Theory of Partial Regulation of the Mass Media", 75 *Michigan Law Review* (November 1976), pp. 1–42.

Born, G. & Prosser, T., "Culture and Consumerism: Citizenship, Public Service Broadcasting and the BBC's Fair Trading Obligations", 64 *The Modern Law Review* (Issue No. 5, September 2001), pp. 657–687.

Boven, Theo van, "Combating Racial Discrimination in the World and in Europe", 2 *Netherlands Quarterly of Human Rights* (1993), pp. 163–172.

Bovens, Mark, "Information Rights: Citizenship in the Information Society", 10 *The Journal of Political Philosophy* (No. 3, 2002), pp. 317–341.

Boyle, Kevin, "The Danish Cartoons", 24 *Netherlands Quarterly of Human Rights* (No. 2, 2006), pp. 185–191.

Boyle, Kevin, "Human Rights, Religion and Democracy: The Refah Partisi Case", 1 *Essex Human Rights Review* (No. 1, 2004), pp. 1–16.

Boyle, Kevin, "Hate Speech: The United States Versus the Rest of the World?", 53 Me. L. Rev. 487 (2001) (487–502).

Braddon-Mitchell, David & West, Caroline, "What is Free Speech?", 12 *The Journal of Political Philosophy* (No. 4, 2004), pp. 437–460.

Breitenmoser, Stephan and Richter, Dagmar, "Proposal for an Additional Protocol to the European Convention on Human Rights Concerning the Protection of Minorities in the Participating States of the CSCE", 12 *Human Rights Law Journal* (No. 6–7, 1991), pp. 262–265.

Brennan, Sir Gerard, "The Third Branch and the Fourth Estate", 32 *Irish Jurist* (1997), pp. 62–76.

Brennan, William J., "The Supreme Court and the Meiklejohnian Interpretation of the First Amendment", 79 Harv. L. Rev. 1–20 (November 1965).

Breton, Raymond, "Institutional Completeness of Ethnic Communities and the Personal Relations of Immigrants", Vol. LXX *The American Journal of Sociology* (No. 2, 1964), pp. 193–205.

Bribosia, Emmannuelle & Rorive, Isabelle, "Le voile à l'école: une Europe divisée", *Revue trimestrielle des droits de l'homme*, 2004, pp. 951–983.

Brison, Susan J., "The Autonomy Defense of Free Speech", 108 *Ethics* (January 1998), 312–339.

Brugger, Winfried, "The Treatment of Hate Speech in German Constitutional Law (Part I)", 3 *German Law Journal* (No. 12, December 2002).

Brugger, Winfried, "The Treatment of Hate Speech in German Constitutional Law (Part II)", 4 *German Law Journal* (No. 1, January 2003).

Buchanan, Allen, "Political Legitimacy and Democracy", 112 *Ethics* (July 2002), pp. 689–719.

Buchanan, Allen, "Recognitional Legitimacy and the State System", 28 *Philosophy & Public Affairs* (No. 1, 1999), pp. 46–78.

Búrca, Gráinne de, "Beyond the Charter: How Enlargement has Enlarged the Human Rights Policy of the European Union", 27 Fordham Int'l L.J. 679 (January 2004), pp. 679–714.

Callamard, Agnès, "Combating Discrimination and Intolerance with a Free Speech Framework", 5 *Religion and Human Rights* (2010), pp. 153–169.

Cannie, Hannes & Voorhoof, Dirk, "The Abuse Clause and Freedom of Expression in the European Human Rights Convention: An Added Value for Democracy and Human Rights Protection?", 29 *Netherlands Quarterly of Human Rights* (No. 1, 2011), pp. 54–83.

Carpentier, Nico & Scifo, Salvatore, "Introduction: Community media's long march", 27 *Telematics and Informatics* (2010), pp. 115–118.

Castendyk, Oliver, "Quotas in favour of independent producers: Article 5 of the 'Television without frontiers' Directive", 11 *Communications Law* (No. 3, 2006), pp. 88–96.

Cerone, John, "Inappropriate Renderings: The Danger of Reductionist Resolutions", 33 Brook. J. Int'l L. 357 (2008).

Chalaby, Jean K., "Deconstructing the transnational: a typology of cross-border television channels in Europe", 7 *New Media & Society* (No. 2, 2005), pp. 155–175.

Chalaby, Jean K., "Television for a New Global Order: Transnational Television Networks and the Formation of Global Systems", 65 *International Communication Gazette* (No. 6, 2003), pp. 457–472.

Chinkin, C.M., "The Challenge of Soft Law: Development and Change in International Law", 38 ICLQ (1989) pp. 850–866.

Coase, R.H., "The Federal Communications Commission", *The Journal of Law & Economics* (Vol. II, October 1959), pp. 1–40.

Cocker, Lawrence, "Hate Crime Statutes: Just? Constitutional? Wise?", 1992/1993 *Annual Survey of American Law*, 485–531.

Cohen, Jonathan, "More Censorship or Less Discrimination? Sexual Orientation Hate Propaganda in Multiple Perspectives", 46 *McGill Law Journal* [2000] 69–104.

Cohen, Andrew Jason, "What Toleration Is", 115 *Ethics* (October 2004), 68–95.

Coliver, Sandra, "Commentary to: The Johannesburg Principles on National Security, Freedom of Expression and Access to Information", 20 *Human Rights Quarterly* (1998), pp. 12–80.

Collins, Richard, "Unity in Diversity? The European Single Market in Broadcasting and the Audiovisual, 1982–92", 32 *Journal of Common Market Studies* (No. 1, March 1994), pp. 89–102.

Comanducci, Paolo, "Some Comments on Toleration", 10 *Ratio Juris* (No. 2, June 1997), pp. 187–192.

Connelly, Alpha, "The European Convention on Human Rights and the Protection of Linguistic Minorities", 2 *Irish Journal of European Law* (1993), pp. 277–293.

Cormack, Mike, "The cultural politics of minority language media", 1 *International Journal of Media and Cultural Politics* (No. 1, 2005), pp. 107–122.

Cormack, Mike, "Minority Language Media in Western Europe: Preliminary Considerations", 13 *European Journal of Communication* (No. 1, 1998), pp. 33–52.

Cram, Ian, "Hate speech, the First Amendment and cross burning in the United States", 8 *Communications Law* (No. 6, 2003), pp. 389–395.

Craufurd Smith, Rachael, "From heritage conservation to European identity: Article 151 EC and the multi-faceted nature of Community cultural policy", 32 E.L. Rev. (February 2007), pp. 48–69.

Craufurd Smith, Rachael, "The UNESCO Convention on the Protection and Promotion of the Diversity of Cultural Expressions: Building a New World Information and Communication Order?", 1 *International Journal of Communication* (2007), pp. 24–55.

Craufurd Smith, Rachael, "Rethinking European Union competence in the field of media ownership: the internal market, fundamental rights and European citizenship" 29 E.L.Rev. (2004), pp. 652–672.

Craufurd Smith, R. & Böttcher, B., "Football and Fundamental Rights: Regulating Access to Major Sporting Events on Television", 8 *European Public Law* (No. 1, 2002), pp. 107–133.

Crump, David, "Camouflaged Incitement: Freedom of Speech, Communicative Torts, and the Borderland of the Brandenburg Test", 29 Ga. L. Rev. 1–80 (Fall 1994).

Cucereanu, Dragos, "Cyberlibel Cases before the European Court of Human Rights: Estimating Possible Outcomes", 19 *Netherlands Quarterly of Human Rights* (No. 1, 2001), pp. 5–20.

Dacko, Scott G. & Hart, Martin, "Critically Examining Theory and Practice: Implications for Coregulation and Coregulating Broadcast Advertising in the United Kingdom", 7 *The International Journal on Media Management* (2006, Nos. 1&2), pp. 2–15.

Dale, Alexander C., "Countering Hate Messages that Lead to Violence: The United Nations's Chapter VII Authority to Use Radio Jamming to Halt Incendiary Broadcasts", 11 Duke J. of Comp. & Int'l L. 109–131 (Fall-Winter 2001).

Davies, Gareth, "Banning the Jilbab: Reflections on Restricting Religious Clothing in the Light of the Court of Appeal in *SB v. Denbigh High School.* Decision of 2 March 2005.", 1 *European Constitutional Law Review* (No. 3, 2005), pp. 511–530.

Deets, Stephen, "Liberal Pluralism: Does the West Have Any to Export?, *JEMIE* (Issue 4/2002).

Delgado, Richard & Stefancic, Jean, "Four Observations about Hate Speech", 44 Wake Forest L. Rev. 353 (2009).

Delgado, Richard & Stefancic, Jean, "Hateful Speech, Loving Communities: Why Our Notion of "A Just Balance" Changes So Slowly", 82 *Cal. L. Rev.* 851 (July 1994) (pp. 851–869).

Delgado, Richard, "Words that Wound: A Tort Action for Racial Insults, Epithets, and Name-Calling", 17 *Harvard Civil Rights-Civil Liberties Law Review* (1982), pp. 133–181.

Derhemi, Eda, "Protecting Endangered Minority Languages: Sociolinguistic Perspectives – Thematic Introduction", 4 *International Journal on Multicultural Studies* (No. 2, 2002).

Desai, Anuj C., "Attacking *Brandenburg* with History: Does the Long-Term Harm of Biased Speech Justify a Criminal Statute Suppressing It?", 55 *Federal Communications Law Review* (No. 2, 2003), pp. 353–394.

De Cillia, Rudolf, Reisigl, Martin & Wodak, Ruth, "The discursive construction of national identities", 10 *Discourse & Society* (No. 2, 1999), pp.149–173.

Dolmans, Maurits, "Quotas without Content: The Questionable Legality of European Content Quotas under the Television without Frontiers Directive", 6 *Ent.L.R.* (No. 8, 1995), pp. 329–333.

Dommering, E.J., "De Deense beeldenstorm", 11 *Nederlands Juristen Blad* (17 March 2006) 634–638.

Dreyer, Emmanuel, "Government Banning of Foreign Publications in France", [1998] *ENT.L.R.* (Issue 4) 163–169.

Drijber, Berend Jan, "Jurisdictie in de Richtlijn audiovisuele mediadiensten", 20 *Mediaforum* (Themanummer Richtlijn Audiovisuele Mediadiensten, Nr. 2, februari 2008), pp. 62–27.

Drzemczewski, Andrew, "Monitoring by the Committee of Ministers of the Council of Europe: a useful 'human rights' mechanism?", 2 *Baltic Yearbook of International Law* (2002), pp. 83–103.

Drzemczewski, Andrew, "The European Human Rights Convention: Protocol No. 11 – Entry into Force and First Year of Application", 21 *Human Rights Law Journal* (No. 1-3, 2000), pp. 1–17.

Drzemczewski, Andrew, "La prévention des violations des droits de l'homme: les mécanismes de suivi du Conseil de l'Europe", 11 *Revue trimestrielle des droits de l'homme* (No. 43, 2000), pp. 385–428.

Dunbar, Robert, "Is There a Duty to Legislate for Linguistic Minorities?", 33 *Journal of Law and Society* (No. 1, March 2006), pp. 181–198.

Dunbar, Robert, "Minority Language Rights in International Law", 50 *ICLQ* (2001) 90–120.

Dworkin, Ronald, "Is the Press Losing the First Amendment?", 27 *New York Review of Books* (No. 19, 4 December 1980), pp. 49–57.

Eatwell, Roger, "Why are Fascism and Racism Reviving in Western Europe?", 65 *Political Quarterly* (No. 3, July/September 1994), pp. 313–325.

Eco, Umberto, "Tolerance and the Intolerable", 23 *Index on Censorship* (Nos. 1 & 2, 1995), 47–56.

Eide, Asbjorn, "The Oslo Recommendations Regarding the Linguistic Rights of National Minorities: An Overview", 6 *International Journal on Minority and Group Rights* p. 319 (Issue No. 3, 1999), pp. 319–328.

Eijk, Nico van, "Search Engines: Seek and Ye Shall Find? The Position of Search Engines in Law", *IRIS plus* (Supplement to *IRIS – Legal Observations of the European Audiovisual Observatory*), 2006–2.

Eijk, Nico van, "New European Rules for the Communications Sector", *IRIS plus* (Supplement to *IRIS – Legal Observations of the European Audiovisual Observatory*), 2003–2.

Ekeus, Rolf, "From the Copenhagen criteria to the Copenhagen Summit: Minority issues in an enlarging Europe", *Helsinki Monitor* (No. 1, 2003), pp. 38–41.

Ely, John Hart, "Flag Desecration: A Case Study in the Roles of Categorization and Balancing in First Amendment Analysis", 88 *Harv. L. Rev.* 1482 (May, 1975), 1482–1508.

Epstein, Michael M., "Broadcast Technology as Diversity Opportunity: Exchanging Market Power for Multiplexed Signal Set-Asides", 59 Fed. Comm. L.J. 1 (December 2006), pp. 1–45.

Errera, Roger, "La Cour européenne des droits de l'homme et les limites de la liberté d'expression: Réflexions sur de singulières variations", *Gazette du Palais*, 21–22/6/1995, pp. 37–42.

Esposito, Gianluca, "Racist and Xenophobic Content on the Internet – Problems and Solutions", *International Journal of Communications Law and Policy* (Issue 7, Winter 2002/2003).

Fabri, Hélène Ruiz, "Jeux dans la fragmentation: la Convention sur la promotion et la protection de la diversité des expressions culturelles", R.G.D.I.P. 2007–1, 43–87.

Farrior, Stephanie, "Molding the Matrix: The Historical and Theoretical Foundations of International Law Concerning Hate Speech", 14 *Berkeley J. Int'l L.* 1–98 (1996).

Farrior, Stephanie, "The Neglected Pillar: The "Teaching Tolerance" Provision of the International Convention on the Elimination of All Forms of Racial Discrimination", 5 *ILSA J. Int'l & Comp. L.* 291 (1999), pp. 291–299.

Favro, Karine, "L'Affaire Al Manar: suite et fin?", *Légipresse* No. 220, avril 2005, pp. 49–56.

Feagin, Joe R., Early, Kevin E. & McKinney, Karyn D., "The Many Costs of Discrimination: The Case of Middle-Class African Americans", 34 *Ind. L. Rev.* 1313 (2001) (pp. 1313–1360).

Feldman, David, "Human Dignity as a Legal Value – Part I", *Public Law* p. 682 (Winter 1999), 682–702.

Feldman, David, "Human Dignity as a Legal Value – Part II", *Public Law* p. 61 (Spring 2000), 61–76.

Fennema, Meindert & Maussen, Marcel, "Dealing with Extremists in Public Discussion: Front National and 'Republican Front' in France", 8 *The Journal of Political Philosophy* (No. 3, 2000), pp. 379–400.

Ferrari, Silvio, "The New Wine and the Old Cask. Tolerance, Religion and the Law in Contemporary Europe", 10 *Ratio Juris* (No. 1, March 1997), pp. 75–89.

Finch, George A., "[Editorial Comment] The Genocide Convention", 43 *The American Journal of International Law* (No. 4, October 1949), pp. 732–738.

Firester, Robert and Jones, Kendall T., "'Catchin' the heat of the beat': First Amendment Analysis of Music Claimed to Incite Violent Behavior", 20 *Loyola of Los Angeles Entertainment Law Review* p. 1 (No. 1, 2000), at pp. 1–31.

Fishman, Joshua A., "Endangered Minority Languages: Prospects for Sociolinguistic Research", 4 *International Journal on Multicultural Studies* (No. 2, 2002).

Fiss, Owen M., "Silence on the Street Corner", XXVI *Suffolk University Law Review* (No. 1, Spring 1992), pp. 1–20.

Fiss, Owen M., "Free Speech and Social Structure", 71 *Iowa Law Review* 1405 (1986).

Flanagan, Anne, "Blogging: A Journal Need Not A Journalist Make", 16 *Fordham Intell. Prop. Media & Ent. L.J.* 395–427 (Winter 2006).

Flanagan, Anne, "The blogger as journalist under UK law", 10 *Communications Law* (No. 4, 2005), pp. 125–129.

Follesdal, Andreas, "The Constitutional Treaty: the Answer to the European Union's Quest for a Consistent Human Rights Policy?", 13 *International Journal on Minority and Group Rights* (2006), pp. 209–222.

Fonblanque, John de, "Integrating minorities and migrants", *Helsinki Monitor* (No. 4, 2006), pp. 337–343.

Fox, Gregory, "The Right to Political Participation in International Law", 17 *Yale Journal of International Law* (1992) 539.

Fredman, Sandra, McCrudden, Christopher and Freedland, Mark, "An EU Charter of fundamental rights", *Public Law* (Summer 2000), pp. 178–186.

Furtado, Charles F., Jr., "Guess Who's Coming to Dinner? Protection for National Minorities in Eastern and Central Europe under the Council of Europe" 34 *Colum. Hum. Rts. L. Rev.* 333–411 (Spring 2003).

Gál, Kinga, "The Council of Europe Framework Convention for the Protection of National Minorities and its Impact on Central and Eastern Europe", *JEMIE* (Winter 2000).

Gál, Kinga, "The role of bilateral treaties in the protection of national minorities in Central and Eastern Europe", *Helsinki Monitor* (No. 3, 1999), pp. 73–88.

Galenkamp, Marlies, "Collective Rights", in *SIM Special* 16 (Utrecht, University of Utrecht, 1994), pp. 53–106.

Garnham, Nicholas, "From cultural to creative industries: An analysis of the implications of the 'creative industries' approach to arts and media policy making in the United Kingdom", 11 *International Journal of Cultural Policy* (No. 1, 2005), pp. 15–29.

Garton Ash, Timothy, "Stop this folly now. There is no need to sacrifice free speech in order to protect British Muslims", *The Guardian,* 17 February 2005.

Gaudreault-DesBiens, Jean-François, "From Sisyphus's Dilemma to Sisyphus's Duty? A Meditation on the Regulation of Hate Propaganda in Relation to Hate Crimes and Genocide", (2000) 46 McGill L.J. 121.

Gearty, Conor A., "Reflections on Civil Liberties in an Age of Counter-Terrorism", 41 *Osgoode Hall Law Journal* (2003), pp. 185–211.

Geller, Henry, "Public Interest Regulation in the Digital TV Era", 16 *Cardozo Arts & Entertainment Law Journal* p. 341 (Nos. 2–3, 1998), pp. 341–368.

Gellman, Susan, "Hate Crime Laws are Thought Crime Laws", *Annual Survey of American Law* p. 509 (1992/1993), pp. 509–531.

Georgiou, Myria, "Diasporic Media Across Europe: Multicultural Societies and the Universalism-Particularism Continuum", 31 *Journal of Ethnic and Migration Studies* (No. 3, May 2005), pp. 481–498.

Geradin, Damien, "Access to content by new media platforms: a review of the competition law problems", 30 *E.L.Rev.* (February 2005), pp. 68–94.

Gerstenberg, Oliver, "Germany: Freedom of conscience in public schools", 3 *Int'l. J. Con. Law*, (No. 1, 2005), pp. 94–106.

Ghanea, Nazila, "Expression and Hate Speech in the ICCPR: Compatible or Clashing?", 5 *Religion and Human Rights* (2010), pp. 171–190.

Ghanea, Nazila, "Minorities and Hatred: Protections and Implications", 17 *International Journal on Minority and Group Rights* (2010), 423–446.
Gibbons, Thomas, "Competition policy and regulatory style – issues for OFCOM", 7 *info* (No. 5, 2005), pp. 42–51.
Gibbons, Thomas, "Aspiring to Pluralism: The Constraints of Public Broadcasting Values on the De-Regulation of British Media Ownership", 16 *Cardozo Arts & Entertainment Law Journal* p. 475 (Nos. 2–3, 1998), pp. 475–500.
Gibbons, Thomas, "Freedom of the Press: Ownership and Editorial Values", *Public Law* p.279 (1992), pp. 279–299.
Gilbert, Geoff, "The Burgeoning Minority Rights Jurisprudence of the European Court of Human Rights", 24 *Human Rights Quarterly* (2002) 736–780.
Gilbert, Geoff, "Autonomy and Minority Groups: A Right in International Law?", 35 *Cornell International Law Journal* (No. 2, Fall 2002), 307–353.
Gilbert, Geoff, "Religio-nationalist minorities and the development of minority rights law", 25 *Review of International Studies* (1999), 389–410.
Gilbert, Geoff, "Religious Minorities and their Rights: A Problem of Approach" 5 *International Journal on Minority and Group Rights* (1997), pp. 97–134.
Gilbert, Geoff, "The Council of Europe and Minority Rights", 18 *Human Rights Quarterly* (1996), pp. 160–189.
Gilbert, Geoff, "The Legal Protection Accorded to Minority Groups in Europe", XXIII *Netherlands Yearbook of International Law* 1992, pp. 67–104.
Goldberg, David, "Europe Bans Terrorist Media: What Sort of Antidote to Poisonous Voices?", 17 Cardozo J. Int. & Comp. L. 445 (2009).
Gorini, Sabina, "The Protection of Cinematographic Heritage in Europe", *IRIS plus* (Supplement to *IRIS – Legal Observations of the European Audiovisual Observatory*), 2004–8.
Greenawalt, Kent, "Insults and Epithets: Are They Protected Speech?", 42 *Rutgers Law Review* p. 287 (No. 2, Winter 1990), pp. 287–307.
Grin, Francois, Moring, Tom *et al.*, "Support for Minority Languages in Europe", Study, European Bureau for Lesser Used Languages and European Centre for Minority Issues, 15 May 2002.
Grin, Francois, "Evaluating Policy Measures for Minority Languages in Europe: Towards Effective, Cost-Effective and Democratic Implementation", European Centre for Minority Issues Report #6, Flensburg, Germany, June 2000.
Grünwald, Andreas, "Towards a Review of the European Convention on Transfrontier Television: Regulatory Options and Policy Considerations", 6 *Multimedia und Recht* (No. 9, 2003), pp. 551–556.
Gunn, T. Jeremy, "Religious Freedom and Laïcité: A Comparison of the United States and France", 2004 B.Y.U.L. Rev. 419.
Gunn, T. Jeremy, "The Complexity of Religion and the Definition of 'Religion' in International Law", 16 *Harvard Human Rights Journal* (2003), pp. 189–215.
Gunn, T. Jeremy, "Majorities, minorities, and the rights of religion and belief", *Helsinki Monitor* (No. 3, 1998), pp. 38–44.

Gutmann, Amy, "The Challenge of Multiculturalism in Political Ethics", 22 *Philosophy and Public Affairs* (No. 3, Summer 1993), pp. 171–206.

Habermas, Jürgen, " Equal Treatment of Cultures and the Limits of Postmodern Liberalism", 13 *The Journal of Political Philosophy* (No. 1, 2005), pp. 1–28.

Habermas, Jürgen, "Intolerance and discrimination", 1 *I.CON* (No. 1, 2003), pp. 2–12.

Habermas, Jürgen, "Constitutional Democracy: A Paradoxical Union of Contradictory Principles?", 29 *Political Theory* (No. 6, December 2001), pp. 766–781.

Harel, Alon & Parchomovsky, Gideon, "On Hate and Equality", 109 *Yale L.J.* 507 (1999–2000) (507–539).

Harrison, Jackie, "Interactive Digital Television (iDTV) and the expansion of the public service tradition: A new public service communications template for the digital age", 8 *Communications Law* (No. 6, 2003), pp. 401–412.

Harrison, Jackie & Wessels, Bridgette, "A new public service communication environment? Public service broadcasting values in the reconfiguring media", 7 *New Media & Society* (No. 6, 2005), pp. 834–853.

Harrison, Jackie & Woods, Lorna, "Television Quotas: Protecting European Culture?", 12 *Entertainment Law Review* (No. 1, 2001), pp. 5–14.

Harrison, Jackie & Lorna M. Woods, "Defining European Public Service Broadcasting", 16 *European Journal of Communication* (No. 4, 2001), pp. 477–504.

Hazewinkel, Harm J., "Religious freedom in the CSCE/OSCE process", *Helsinki Monitor* (No. 3, 1998) pp. 9–16.

Heintze, Hans-Joachim, "Minority Issues in Western Europe and the OSCE High Commissioner on National Minorities", 7 *International Journal on Minority and Group Rights* (2000), pp. 381–392.

Heintze, Hans-Joachim and Frederick, Howard H., "International legal prohibitions against media content advocating war, racism and genocide: indisputable principles, varying enforcement", *Media Law & Practice* (September 1990), pp. 91–97.

Helberger, Natali, "The 'Right to Information' and Digital Broadcasting: About Monsters, Invisible Men and the Future of European Broadcasting Regulation", Ent.L.R. (No. 2, 2006), pp. 70–80.

Helberger, Natali, "Access to Technical Bottleneck Facilities: The New European Approach", 46 *Communications & Strategies* (2nd quarter 2002), pp. 33–74.

Hellman, Heikki, "Diversity – An End in Itself?: Developing a Multi-Measure Methodology of Television Programme Variety Studies", 16 *European Journal of Communication* (No. 2, 2001), pp. 181–208.

Henrard, Kristin, "Charting the gradual emergence of a more robust level of minority protection: minority specific instruments and the European Union", 22 *Netherlands Quarterly of Human Rights* (Issue No. 4, 2004), 559–584.

Hervik, Peter, "The predictable responses to the Danish cartoons", 2 *Global Media and Communication* (No. 2, 2006), pp. 225–230.

Heyman, Steven J., "Righting the Balance: An Inquiry into the Foundations and Limits of Freedom of Expression", 78 *B.U.L.Rev.*1275 (December, 1998) (1275–1392).

Hiller, Harry H. & Franz, Tara M., "New ties, old ties and lost ties: the use of the internet in diaspora", 6 *New Media & Society* (No. 6, 2004), pp. 731–752.

Hillgenberg, Hartmut, "A Fresh Look at Soft Law", 10 *EJIL* (No. 3, 1999), pp. 499–515.

Hins, Wouter & Voorhoof, Dirk, "Access to State-Held Information as a Fundamental Right under the European Convention of Human Rights", *EuConst* 3 (2007), pp. 114–126.

Hofmann, Rainer, "Protecting the Rights of National Minorities in Europe. First Experiences with the Council of Europe Framework Convention for the Protection of National Minorities", 44 *German Yearbook of International Law/Jahrbuch für Internationales Recht* (2001), pp. 237–269.

Hogan, Gerard, "The Belfast Agreement and the Future Incorporation of the European Convention of Human Rights in the Republic of Ireland", 4 *The Bar Review* pp. 205–211 (No. 4, 1999).

Holt, Sally & Packer, John, "OSCE Developments and Linguistic Minorities", 3 *MOST Journal on Multicultural Societies* (No. 2, 2001).

Honig, David, "What Kind of Future for Television?", 32 *Intermedia* (No. 4, November 2004), pp. 10–15.

Horowitz, Paul, "*Citizenship and Speech. A Review of Owen M. Fiss,* The Irony of Free Speech *and* Liberalism Divided", 43 *McGill Law Journal* (1998), pp. 445–479.

Hourigan, Niamh, "New Social Movement Theory and Minority Language Television Campaigns", 16 *European Journal of Communication* (No.1, 2001), pp. 77–100.

Hughes, James & Sasse, Gwendolyn, "Monitoring the Monitors: EU Enlargement Conditionality and Minority Protection in the CEECs", *Journal on Ethnopolitics and Minority Issues in Europe (JEMIE)* (No. 1, 2003).

Humphrey, John P., "The United Nations Sub-Commission on the Prevention of Discrimination and the Protection of Minorities", 62 *The American Journal of International Law* (No. 4, October 1968), pp. 869–888.

Humphreys, Peter, "The Goal of Pluralism and the Ownership Rules for Private Broadcasting in Germany: Re-Regulation or De-Regulation?", 16 *Cardozo Arts & Entertainment Law Journal* (Nos. 2–3, 1998), pp. 527–556.

Husband, Charles, "Minority Ethnic Media As Communities Of Practice: Professionalism and Identity Politics in Interaction", 31 *Journal of Ethnic and Migration Studies* (No. 3, May 2005), pp. 461–479.

Ibán, Iván C., "Religious Tolerance and Freedom in Continental Europe", 10 *Ratio Juris* (No. 1, March 1997), pp. 90–107.

Imbert, Jean, "Toleration and Law: Historical Aspects", 10 *Ratio Juris* (No. 1, March 1997), pp. 13–24.

Iosifidis, Petros, "Digital Switchover in Europe", 68 *International Communication Gazette* (No. 3, 2006), pp. 249–168.

Jakubowicz, Karol, "Community media: 'Flavour of the decade' worldwide. A keynote address at the AMARC Europe Conference", 27 *Telematics and Informatics* (2010), pp. 119–121.

Jakubowicz, Karol, "Persons Belonging to National Minorities and the Media", 10 *International Journal on Minority and Group Rights* (2004), pp. 291–314.

Jakubowicz, Karol, "Ideas in our Heads: Introduction of PSB as Part of Media System Change in Central and Eastern Europe", *European Journal of Communication* 19(1), pp. 53–74.

Jimenez, Nuria Reguero & Scifo, Salvatore, "Community media in the context of European media policies", 27 *Telematics and Informatics* (2010), pp. 131–140.

Johnson, Howard, "Television without frontiers: timely change or premature extension?", 10 *Communications Law* (No. 6, 2005), pp. 197–204.

Jones, George (Series Editor), Holt, Sally & Packer, John (Guest Editors), *Mercator Media Forum 8* (Cardiff, University of Wales Press, 2005).

Jones, Peter, "Human Rights, Group Rights, and Peoples' Rights", 21 *Human Rights Quarterly* (1999), pp. 81–107.

Jones, Peter, "Group Rights and Group Oppression", 7 *The Journal of Political Philosophy* (No. 4, 1999), pp. 353–377.

Jovanovic, Miodrag, A., "Recognizing Minority Identities Through Collective Rights", 27 *Human Rights Quarterly* (2005), pp. 625–651.

Jovanovic, Miodrag A., "Territorial Autonomy in Eastern Europe – Legacies of the Past", *JEMIE* (Issue 4/2002).

Karppinen, Kari, "Media Diversity and the Politics of Criteria", 27 *Nordicom Review* (No. 2, 2006), pp. 53–68.

Katsirea, Irini, "The circumvention principle: an effective defence of national broadcasting systems against abuse?", 10 *Communications Law* (No. 4, 2005), pp. 130–134.

Katsirea, Irini, "Why the European broadcasting quota should be abolished", 28 *European Law Review* (No. 2, 2003), pp. 190–209.

Keane, David, "Cartoon Violence and Freedom of Expression", 30 *Human Rights Quarterly* (No. 4, November 2008), pp. 845–875.

Keane, David, "Attacking hate speech under Article 17 of the European Convention on Human Rights", 25 *Netherlands Quarterly of Human Rights* (No. 4, 2007), pp. 641–663.

Kearney, Michael, "The Prohibition of Propaganda for War in the International Covenant on Civil and Political Rights", 23 *Netherlands Quarterly of Human Rights* (No. 4, 2005), pp. 551–570.

Kelly, Erin & McPherson, Lionel, "On Tolerating the Unreasonable", 9 *The Journal of Political Philosophy* (No. 1, 2001), pp. 38–55.

Kemp, Walter, "Applying the Nationality Principle: Handle with Care", *JEMIE* (No. 4, 2002).

Kennedy, David, "The International Human Rights Movement: Part of the Problem?", 15 *Harvard Human Rights Journal* (Spring 2002), 101–126.

Kentridge, Syndney, "Freedom of Speech: is it the primary right?", Vol. 45 *International and Comparative Law Quarterly* (April 1996), pp. 253–270.

Klabbers, Jan, "International Legal Histories: The Declining Importance of *Travaux Préparatoires* in Treaty Interpretation?", *Netherlands International Law Review* (2003), pp. 267–288.

Klabbers, Jan, "The Redundancy of Soft Law", 65 *Nordic Journal of International Law* (1996), pp. 167–182.

Klabbers, Jan, "The Undesirability of Soft Law", 67 *Nordic Journal of International Law* (1998), pp. 381–391.

Klabbers, Jan & Leino, Päivi, "Death by Constitution? The Draft Treaty Establishing a Constitution for Europe", 4 *German Law Journal* (No. 12, 2003), pp. 1293–1305.

Klebes, Heinrich, "The Council of Europe's Framework Convention for the Protection of National Minorities", 16 *Human Rights Law Journal* (No. 1–3, 1995), pp. 92–98.

Kleijssen, Jan, "Council of Europe Standard-setting in the Human Rights Field", in J.P. Loof & R.A. Lawson, Eds., *60 jaar Europees Verdrag voor de Rechten van de Mens – Een lichtend voorbeeld?* – Special Issue of *Nederlands Tijdschrift voor de Mensenrechten*, Vol. 35 [2010], No. 7, pp. 897–904.

Kochenov, Dimitry, "A Summary of Contradictions: An Outline of the EU's Main Internal and External Approaches to Ethnic Minority Protection", 31 *Boston College International & Comparative Law Review* (No. 1, 2008), pp. 1–51.

Komorek, Ewa, "Is Media Pluralism a Human Right? The European Court of Human Rights, the Council of Europe and the Issue of Media Pluralism", [2009] E.H.R.L.R. (No. 3), 395–414.

König, Matthias & Varennes, Fernand de, "Editorial: Lesser Used Languages and the Law in Europe", 3 *MOST Journal on Multicultural Societies* (No. 1, 2001).

Kontra, Miklós, "Some Reflections on the Nature of Language and its Regulation", 6 *International Journal on Minority and Group Rights* (Issue No. 3, 1999), pp. 281–288.

Koskenniemi, Martti, "'The Lady Doth Protest Too Much': Kosovo, and the Turn to Ethics in International Law", 65 *The Modern Law Review* (No. 2, March 2002), pp. 159–175.

Kretzmer, David, "Freedom of Speech and Racism", 8 Cardozo L. Rev. 445–513 (February 1987).

Kronenthal, Melissa, "From Rhetoric to Reality? A Critical Assessment of EU Minority Language Policy and Practice", Mercator Working Paper 13 (2003).

Kübler, Friedrich, "How Much Freedom for Racist Speech?: Transnational Aspects of a Conflict of Human Rights", 27 *Hofstra Law Review* (1998), pp. 335–376.

Kuhn, Arthur K., "The Genocide Convention and State Rights", 43 *The American Journal of International Law* (No. 3, July 1949), pp. 498–501.

Künnemann, Rolf, "A Coherent Approach to Human Rights", 17 *Human Rights Quarterly* (No. 2, 1995), pp. 323–342.

Kunz, Josef L,. "The United Nations Convention on Genocide", 43 *The American Journal of International Law* (No. 4, October 1949), pp. 738–746.

Kusý, Miroslav, "Innate Dignity, Cultural Identity and Minority Language Rights", 6 *International Journal on Minority and Group Rights* (Issue No. 3, 1999), pp. 299–306.

Kymlicka, Will, "The internationalization of minority rights", 6 *I.CON* (No. 1, 2008), pp. 1–32.

Kymlicka, Will, "Multiculturalism and Minority Rights: West and East", *JEMIE* (Issue 4/2002).

Laborde, Cécile, "Secular Philosophy and Muslim Headscarves in Schools", 13 *The Journal of Political Philosophy* (No. 3, 2005), pp. 305–329.

Ladeur, Karl-Heinze, "Guaranteeing the Programming Mandate of Public Broadcasters and Restraints on Private Broadcasters' Programmes in Multimedia Conditions", 5 *German Law Journal* (No. 8, 2004), pp. 907–933.

Langenfeld, Christine & Mohsen, Sarah, "Germany: The teacher head scarf case", 3 Int'l. J. Con. Law, (No. 1, 2005), pp. 86–94.

Langlaude, Sylvie, "Indoctrination, Secularism, Religious Liberty, and the ECHR", 55 *ICLQ* (October 2006), pp. 929–944.

Langton, Rae, "Speech Acts and Unspeakable Acts", 22 *Philosophy & Public Affairs* 293–330 (No. 4, Autumn 1993).

Lasson, Kenneth, "Group Libel Versus Free Speech: When Big Brother *Should* Butt In", 23 *Duquesne Law Review* (1984), pp. 77–130.

Lawson, Rick, "Human Rights: The Best is Yet to Come", 1 *European Constitutional Law Review* (2005), pp. 27–37.

Leader, Sheldon, "Toleration without Liberal Foundations", 10 Ratio Juris (No. 2, June 1997), pp. 139–164.

Lennox, Corinne, "Reviewing Durban: Examining the Outputs and Review of the 2001 World Conference against Racism", 27 *Netherlands Quarterly of Human Rights* (No. 2, 2009), pp. 191–235.

Lerner, Natan, "Freedom of Expression and Advocacy of Group Hatred: Incitement to Hate Crimes and Religious Hatred", 5 *Religion and Human Rights* (2010), pp. 137–145.

Lerner, Natan, "The Nature and Minimum Standards of Freedom of Religion and Belief", 2000 B.Y.U.L. Rev. 905.

Lerner, Natan, "Proselytism, Change of Religion, and International Human Rights", 12 *Emory Int'l L. Rev.* 477 (Winter, 1998), 477–561.

Lord Lester of Herne Hill, Q.C., "The European Convention on Human Rights in the New Architecture of Europe: General Report", 38 *Yearbook of the European Convention on Human Rights* (1995), pp. 223–236.

Letschert, Rianne, "Successful integration while respecting diversity; 'Old' minorities versus 'New' minorities", *Helsinki Monitor: Security and Human Rights* (No. 1, 2007), 46–56.

Letschert, Rianne, "Towards a UN Special Representative on Minority Issues – drawing upon the experiences of the OSCE High Commissioner on National Minorities", *Helsinki Monitor* (No. 4, 2002), pp. 326–337.

Lewis, Anthony, "Law and the Press: A Deadly Embrace?", 33 *The Irish Jurist* (1998), pp. 34–46.

Liddy, Jane, "Procedures before the European Commission of Human Rights", 2 *Irish Journal of European Law* (1993), pp. 266–276.

Liebich, Andre, "Canadian, Eh?", *JEMIE* (Issue 4/2002).

Liebich, André, "Janus at Strasbourg: The Council of Europe between East and West", 10 *Helsinki Monitor* (No. 1, 1999), pp. 7–17.

Livingstone, Stephen, "Article 14 and the Prevention of Discrimination in the European Convention on Human Rights", *E.H.R.L.R.* (No. 1, 1997), pp. 25–34.

Loon, Ad van, "The end of the broadcasting era What constitutes broadcasting and why does it need to be regulated?", 9 *Communications Law* (No. 5, 2004), pp. 172–186.

Lord, Karen S., "The European retreat from religious liberty", *Helsinki Monitor* (No. 3, 1998), pp. 45–51.

Lukes, Steven, "Toleration and Recognition", 10 *Ratio Juris* (No. 2, June 1997), pp. 213–222.

MacKinnon, Catharine A., "Prosecutor v. Nahimana, Barayagwiza, & Ngeze. Case No. ICTR 99–52-T", 98 *The American Journal of International Law* (No. 2, April 2004), pp. 325–330.

Macklem, Patrick, "Minority rights in international law", 6 I.CON (Nos. 3 & 4, 2008), pp. 531–552.

Macklem, Patrick, "The Wrong Vocabulary of Right: Minority Rights and the Boundaries of Political Community", University of Toronto Legal Studies Series, Research Paper No. XX-05, December 2005.

Mahalic, Drew & Mahalic, Joan Gambee, "The Limitation Provisions of the International Convention on the Elimination of All Forms of Racial Discrimination", 9 *Human Rights Quarterly* (No. 1, February 1987), pp. 74–101.

Mahlmann, Matthias, "Religious Tolerance, Pluralist Society and the Neutrality of the State: The Federal Constitutional Court's Decision in the *Headscarf* Case", 4 *German Law Journal* (No. 11, 2003), pp. 1099–1116.

Mahoney, Kathleen E., "Hate Speech: Affirmation or Contradiction of Freedom of Expression?", 1996 *U. Ill. L. Rev.* 789–808.

Mahoney, Paul, "An Insider's View of the Reform Debate (How to Maintain the Effectiveness of the European Court of Human Rights)", 29 *NJCM-Bulletin* (No. 2, 2004), pp. 1170–175.

Mahoney, Paul, "The Charter of Fundamental Rights of the European Union and the European Convention on Human Rights from the Perspective of the European Convention", 23 *Human Rights Law Journal* (2002), pp. 300–303.

Malinverni, Giorgio, "Freedom of Information in the European Convention on Human Rights and in the International Covenant on Civil and Political Rights", 4 *Human Rights Law Journal* (No. 4, 1983), pp. 443–460.

Malinverni, Giorgio, "The draft Convention for the Protection of Minorities – The Proposal of the European Commission for Democracy through Law", 12 *Human Rights Law Journal* (No. 6–7, 1991) pp. 265–273.

Malloy, Tove H., "National Minority 'Regions' in the Enlarged European Union: Mobilizing for Third Level Politics?", ECMI Working Paper #24 (July 2005).

Marcus, Maria L., "Policing Speech on the Airwaves: Granting Rights, Preventing Wrongs", 15 Yale L. & Pol'y Rev. 447 (1997), pp. 447–501.

Marsden, Christopher T., "Co-Regulation in European Media and Internet Sectors", 8 *MultiMedia und Recht* (No. 1, 2005), pp. 3–7.

Marsden, Christopher T., "Co- and self-regulation in European media and Internet sectors: The results of Oxford University's study www.selfregulation.info", 9 *Communications Law* (No. 5, 2004), pp. 187–195.

Martinez-Torrón, Javier and Navarro-Valls, Rafael, "The protection of religious freedom in the system of the European Convention on Human Rights", *Helsinki Monitor* (No. 3, 1998), pp. 25–37.

Masmejan, Denis, "Le droit de réponse vingt ans après: une fausse bonne idée?", 10 *MediaLex* (No. 1, March 2005), pp. 27–33.

Massaro, Toni M., "The Hate Speech Dilemma", 32 *William and Mary Law Review* (1991), pp. 211–265.

Matsuda, Mari J., "Public Response to Racist Speech: Considering the Victim's Story", 87 *Michigan Law Review* (August 1989), pp. 2320–2381.

McGoldrick, Dominic, "Multiculturalism and its Discontents", 5 *Human Rights Law Review* (No. 1, 2005), pp. 27–56.

McGoldrick, Dominic & O'Donnell, Therese, "Hate-speech laws: consistency with national and international human rights law", Vol. 18 *Legal Studies* (December 1998), pp. 453–485.

McGonagle, Tarlach & De Beer, Kim, "*A brave new media world?* Een kritische blik op het nieuwe mediabeleid van de Raad van Europa", 22 *Mediaforum* 2010–5, pp. 146–156.

McGonagle, Tarlach, "Feature Case Note – The Islamic Headscarf Dilemma: *Leyla Şahin v. Turkey*", [2010] 1 *Irish Human Rights Law Review*, pp. 195–215.

McGonagle, Tarlach, "An Ode to Contextualisation: *İ.A. v. Turkey*", [2010] 1 *Irish Human Rights Law Review*, pp. 237–251.

McGonagle, Tarlach, "The Promotion of Cultural Diversity via New Media Technologies: An Introduction to the Challenges of Operationalisation", *IRIS plus* (Supplement to *IRIS – Legal Observations of the European Audiovisual Observatory*), 2008–6.

McGonagle, Tarlach, "European-level measures for promoting cultural diversity in broadcasting: quixotic tilting in a new technological era?", in Pia Letto-Vanamo, Ed., *Mikä Osa Yleisöllä? Yearbook of Communication Law 2007*, Institute of International Economic Law (KATTI), Faculty of Law, University of Helsinki, Finland (2008), pp. 119–136.

McGonagle, Tarlach, "Safeguarding Human Dignity in the European Audiovisual Sector", *IRIS plus* (Supplement to *IRIS – Legal Observations of the European Audiovisual Observatory*), 2007–6.

McGonagle, Tarlach, "Regulating minority-language use in broadcasting: international law and the Dutch national experience", 16 *Mediaforum* (No. 5, May 2004), pp. 155–160.

McGonagle, Tarlach & Richter, Andrei, "Regulation of Minority-Language Broadcasting", *IRIS plus* (Supplement to *IRIS – Legal Observations of the European Audiovisual Observatory*), 2004–2.

McGonagle, Tarlach, "The Potential for Practice of an Intangible Idea: Co-Regulation of the Media in Europe", *IRIS plus* (Supplement to *IRIS – Legal Observations of the European Audiovisual Observatory*), 2002–10.

McGonagle, Tarlach, "Wresting (Racial) Equality from Tolerance of Hate Speech", (2001) 23 *Dublin University Law Journal* (ns) 21, pp. 21–54.

McNamara, Luke, "The Impact of Legal Frameworks on the Resolution of Human Rights 'Clashes': the Case of Hate Speech Regulation, Socio-Legal Studies Association Annual Conference, Nottingham Law School, 14–16 April 2003.

McNamara, Luke, "The Merits of Racial Hatred Laws: Beyond Free Speech", 4 *Griffith Law Review* (1995), pp. 29–59.

McNamara, Luke, "Confronting the Reality of Hate Speech", 20 *Alternative Law Journal* (1995), pp. 231–234.

McNamara, Luke, "Criminalising Racial Hatred: Learning From the Canadian Experience"1 *Australian Journal of Human Rights* (1994), 198.

Meijer, Irene Costera, "Impact or Content? Ratings vs Quality in Public Broadcasting", 20 *European Journal of Communication* (No. 1, 2005), pp. 27–53.

Merle, Jean-Christophe, "Cultural Minority Rights and the Rights of the Majority in the Liberal State", 11 *Ratio Juris* (No. 2, September 1998), pp. 259–271.

Meron, Theodor, "The Meaning and Reach of the International Convention on the Elimination of All Forms of Racial Discrimination", 79 *The American Journal of International Law* (No. 2, April 1985), pp. 283–318.

Metzl, Jamie F., "Information Intervention: When Switching Channels Isn't Enough", 76 *Foreign Affairs* (No. 6, November/December 1997), pp. 15–20.

Metzl, Jamie F., "Rwandan Genocide and the International Law of Radio Jamming", 91 *The American Journal of International Law* (No. 4, October 1997), pp. 628–651.

Metzl, Jamie F., "Information Technology and Human Rights", 18 *Human Rights Quarterly* (No. 4, 1996), 705–746.

Michael, D.C., "Federal Agency Use of Audited Self-Regulation as a Regulatory Technique", 47 *Administrative Law Review* (Spring 1995), pp. 171–254.

Michelman, Frank, "Law's Republic", 97 *Yale Law Journal* 1493 (1988).

Minow, Newton N., "Television and the Public Interest", 55 *Federal Communications Law Journal* (No. 3, 2003), pp. 395–406.

Moon, Gay, "The Draft Discrimination Protocol to the European Convention on Human Rights: A Progress Report", E.H.R.L.R. (No. 1, 2000), 49–53.

Morawa, Alexander H. E., "The Concept of Non-Discrimination: An Introductory Comment", *JEMIE* (Issue 3/2002).

Moreno, Elda, "La Charte Europeenne des Langues Regionales ou Minoritaires: un instrument juridique au service du patrimoine linguistique europeen", 3 MOST *Journal on Multicultural Societies* (No. 1, 2001).

Moring, Tom, "New Media and the Implementation of Instruments in Support of Minority Rights Related to Media", 6 *European Yearbook of Minority Issues* (2006–7), pp. 19–50.

Morsink, Johannes, "Cultural Genocide, the Universal Declaration, and Minority Rights", 21 *Human Rights Quarterly* (No. 4, 1999), pp. 1009–1060.

Mowbray, Alastair, "An Examination of the European Court of Human Rights' Approach to Overruling its Previous Case Law", 9 *Human Rights Law Review* (No. 2, 2009), pp. 179–201.

Mowbray, Alastair, "The Creativity of the European Court of Human Rights", 5 *Human Rights Law Review* (No. 1, 2005), 57–79.

Mowbray, Alastair, "The Role of the European Court of Human Rights in the Promotion of Democracy", *Public Law* (Winter 1999), pp. 703–725.

Mufwene, Salikoko S., "Colonisation, Globalisation, and the Future of Languages in the Twenty-first Century", 4 *International Journal on Multicultural Studies* (No. 2, 2002).

Nagel, Thomas, "Personal Rights and Public Space", 24 *Philosophy and Public Affairs* (No. 2, Spring 1995), pp. 83–107.

Napoli, Philip M., "Deconstructing the Diversity Principle", *Journal of Communication* (Autumn 1999), pp. 7–34.

Neier, Aryeh, "Clear and present danger", 27(1) *Index on Censorship* 57–60 (1998).

Neuwirth, Rostam J., "'United in Divergency?': A Commentary on the UNESCO Convention on the Protection and Promotion of the Diversity of Cultural Expressions", ZaöRV 66 (2006), 819–862.

Nic Shuibhne, Niamh, "The European Union and Minority Language Rights", 3 *MOST Journal on Multicultural Societies* (No. 1, 2001).

Nic Shuibhne, Niamh, "Rethinking Irish Language Policy: A Legal Perspective", 3 *Contemporary Issues in Irish Law and Politics* (2000), pp. 36–53.

Nieuwenhuis, Aernout & Janssen, Esther, "De onduidelijke verhouding tussen vrijheid van meningsuiting en discriminatie: Een analyse van de groepsbelediging en het haatzaaien", *Mediaforum* 2011–4, pp. 94–104.

Nieuwenhuis, Aernout, "The Concept of Pluralism in the Case-Law of the European Court of Human Rights", *European Constitutional Law Review*, 2007–3, pp. 367–384.

Nieuwenhuis, Aernout, "State and Religion, Schools and Scarves, An Analysis of the Margin of Appreciation as Used in the Case of *Leyla Sahin v. Turkey*, Decision of 29 June 2004, Application Number 44774/98.", 1 *European Constitutional Law Review* (No. 3, 2005), pp. 495–510.

Nieuwenhuis, Aernout, "Freedom of Speech: USA vs Germany and Europe", 18 *Netherlands Quarterly for Human Rights* (No. 2, 2000), pp. 195–214.

Norby Bonde, Bent, "How 12 Cartoons of the Prophet Mohammed were Brought to Trigger an Interntaional Conflict", 28 *Nordicom Review* (No. 1, 2007), pp. 33–48.

Nowak, Manfred, "The Right of Self-Determination and Protection of Minorities in Central and Eastern Europe in light of the case-law of the Human Rights Committee", 1 *International Journal on Group Rights* (1993), pp. 7–16.

O'Connell, Donncha, "Beyond rights – towards interests", *Céide – A Review from the Margins* (January/February 1999), pp. 17–18.

Oestreich, Joel E., "Liberal Theory and Minority Group Rights", 21 *Human Rights Quarterly* (1999), pp. 108–132.

Oetheimer, Mario, "Protecting Freedom of Expression: The Challenge of Hate Speech in the European Court of Human Rights Case Law", 17 Cardozo J. Int'l & Comp. L. 427 (2009).

Oetheimer, Mario, "La Cour européenne des Droits de l'Homme face au discourse de haine", 69 Rev. trim. dr. h. (No. 1, 2007), pp. 63–80.

Olbourne, Ben, "Refah Partisi (The Welfare Party) v Turkey", *E.H.R.L.R.* 2003, 4, 437–444.
O'Neill, Onora, "Shoot the messenger", *The Guardian*, 1 May 2002.
Ó Riagain, Dónall, "The European Union and Lesser Used Languages", 3 *MOST Journal on Multicultural Societies* (No. 1, 2001).
Ó Riagáin, Dónall, "The Importance of Linguistic Rights for Speakers of Lesser Used Languages", 6 *International Journal on Minority and Group Rights* (Issue No. 3, 1999), pp. 289–298.
Ortner, Michael, "Serving a Different Master – the Decline of Diversity and the Public Interest in American Radio in the Wake of the Telecommunications Act of 1996", 22 Hamline J. Pub. L. & Pol'y 139 (Fall 2000), 139–173.
Owen, Ursula, "Hate Speech – The Speech That Kills", *27(1) Index on Censorship* 32–39 (1998).
Packer, John, "Confronting the contemporary challenges of Europe's minorities", *Helsinki Monitor* (No. 3, 2005), pp. 227–231.
Packer, John & Holt, Sally, "The use of minority languages in the broadcast media: Introducing new guidelines", *Helsinki Monitor* (2004, No. 2), pp. 103–126.
Packer, John, "The origin and nature of the Lund Recommendations on the Effective Participation of National Minorities in Public Life", *Helsinki Monitor* (No. 4, 2000), pp. 29–61.
Packer, John & Siemienski, Guillaume, "The Language of Equity: The Origin and Development of the Oslo Recommendations Regarding the Linguistic Rights of National Minorities", 6 *International Journal on Minority and Group Rights* (Issue No. 3, 1999), pp. 329–350.
Palzer, Carmen, "Co-Regulation of the Media in Europe: European Provisions for the Establishment of Co-regulation Frameworks", *IRIS plus* (Supplement to *IRIS – Legal Observations of the European Audiovisual Observatory*), 2002–6.
Pannick, David, "Religious Feelings and the European Court", *Public Law* (1995), pp. 7–10.
Pardo, Julian Rodriguez, "Les limites à la concentration des médias dans l'Union européenne", 26 *Légipresse* (No. 219, March 2005), pp. 21–27.
Parekh, Bhikhu, "Hate speech: Is there a case for banning?", 12 *Public Policy Research* (No. 4, December 2005-February 2006), pp. 213–223.
Parmar, Sejal, "The Challenge of 'Defamation of Religions' to Freedom of Expression and the International Human Rights System", [2009] E.H.R.L.R. (No. 3), 353–375.
Passmore, John, "Fanaticism, Toleration and Philosophy", 11 *The Journal of Political Philosophy* (No. 2, 2003), pp. 211–222.
Patten, Alan, "Liberal Neutrality and Language Policy", 31 *Philosophy & Public Affairs* (No. 4, 2003), pp. 356–386.
Patten, Alan, "Political Theory and Language Policy", 29 *Political Theory* (No. 5, October 2001), pp. 691–715.
Pentassuglia, Gaetano, "Minority Rights and the Role of Law: Reflections on Themes of Discourse in Kymlicka's Approach to Ethnocultural Identity", *JEMIE* (Issue 4/2002).
Pentassuglia, Gaetano, "Monitoring Minority Rights in Europe: The Implementation Machinery of the Framework Convention for the Protection of National Minorities –

With Special Reference to the Role of the Advisory Committee", 6 *International Journal on Minority and Group Rights* (1999), pp. 417–461.

Pentassuglia, Gaetano, "Minority Protection in International Law: From Standard-Setting to Implementation", 68 *Nordic Journal of International Law* (1999), pp. 131–160.

Petrova, Dimitrina, "'Smoke and Mirrors': The Durban Review Conference and Human Rights Politics at the United Nations", 10 *Human Rights Law Review* (No. 1, 2009), pp. 129–150.

Phillips, Alan, "The Framework Convention for the Protection of National Minorities: A Policy Analysis", Minority Rights Group International (September 2002).

Pinker, Robert, "Human Rights and self-regulation of the press", 4 *Tolley's Communications Law* (No. 2, 1999), pp. 51–54.

Pogány, István, "Refashioning Rights in Central and Eastern Europe: Some Implications for the Region's Roma", 10 *European Public Law* (No. 1, 2004), pp. 85–106.

Pogány, István, "Accommodating an Emergent National Identity: The Roma of Central and Eastern Europe", 6 *International Journal on Minority and Group Rights* (1999), pp. 149–167.

Post, Robert C., "Racist Speech, Democracy, and the First Amendment", 32 Wm. & Mary L. Rev. 267–327 (Winter 1991).

Post, Robert C., "The Social Foundations of Defamation Law: Reputation and the Constitution", 74 Cal. L. Rev. 691 (May, 1986).

Poulter, Sebastian, "The Rights of Ethnic, Religious and Linguistic Minorities", E.H.R.L.R. (No. 3, 1997), pp. 254–264.

Price, Monroe E. & Verhulst, Stefaan G., "Broadcasting Reform in India: A Case-Study in the Uses of Comparative Media Law", 5 *Cardozo J. Int'l & Comp. L.* 423 (Fall, 1997) (423–444).

Ramaga, Philip Vuciri, "The Bases of Minority Identity", 14 *Human Rights Quarterly* (1992), 409–428.

Raz, Joseph, "Multiculturalism", 11 *Ratio Juris* (No. 2, September 1998), pp. 193–205.

Raz, Joseph, "Free Expression and Personal Identification", 11 *Oxford Journal of Legal Studies* (No. 3, 1991), pp. 303–324.

Rehman, Javaid, "Accommodating Religious Identities in an Islamic State: International Law, Freedom of Religion and the Rights of Religious Minorities", 7 *International Journal on Minority and Group Rights* (2000), pp. 139–166.

Reidenberg, Joel R., "States and Internet Enforcement", 1 *University of Ottawa Law & Technology Journal* (2003–2004, Nos. 1 & 2), pp. 213–230.

Reidenberg, Joel R., "Yahoo and Democracy on the Internet", 42 *Jurimetrics* (Spring 2002), pp. 261–280.

Reidenberg, Joel R., "The Yahoo! Case and the International Democratization of the Internet", Fordham University School of Law Research Paper 11, April 2001.

Ringelheim, Julie, "Minority Rights in a Time of Multiculturalism – The Evolving Scope of the Framework Convention on the Protection of National Minorities", 10 *Human Rights Law Review* (No. 1, 2010), pp. 99–128.

Rodley, Nigel S., "Conceptual Problems in the Protection of Minorities: International Legal Developments", 17 *Human Rights Quarterly* (1995), pp. 48–71.

Romaine, Suzanne, "The Impact of Language Policy on Endangered Languages", 4 *International Journal on Multicultural Studies* (No. 2, 2002).

Rorive, Isabelle, "Strategies to Tackle Racism and Xenophobia on the Internet – Where are we in Europe?", *International Journal of Communications Law and Policy* (Issue 7, Winter 2002/2003).

Rosen, Mark D., "Exporting the Constitution", 53 *Emory L.J.* 171–232 (Winter 2004).

Rosenfeld, Michel, "Hate Speech in Constitutional Jurisprudence: A Comparative Analysis", 24 *Cardozo L. Rev.* 1523–1567 (2003).

Saban, Ilan, "Offensiveness Analyzed: Lessons for Comparative Analysis of Free Speech Doctrine", 2 *The Journal of International and Comparative Law at Chicago-Kent* (2002), pp. 62–83.

Sadurski, Wojciech, "Does the Subject Matter? Viewpoint Neutrality and Freedom of Speech" 15 *Cardozo Arts and Entertainment Law Journal* (No. 2, 1997), pp. 315–369.

Sadurski, Wojciech, "On 'Seeing Speech Through an Equality Lens': A Critique of Egalitarian Arguments for Suppression of Hate Speech and Pornography", 16 *Oxford Journal of Legal Studies* (No. 4, Winter 1996), pp. 713–723.

Sadurski, Wojciech, "Offending with Impunity: Racial Vilification and Freedom of Speech", 14 *SydLR* 163 (June 1992), pp. 163–195.

Sahin, Haluk & Aksoy, Asu, " Global Media and Cultural Identity in Turkey", 43 *Journal of Communication* (No. 2, Spring 1993), pp. 31–41.

Scanlon, Thomas, "A Theory of Freedom of Expression", Vol. 1 *Philosophy and Public Affairs* (1972), pp. 204–226.

Schabas, William A., "Hate Speech in Rwanda: The Road to Genocide", (2000) 46 *McGill L.J.* 141.

Schauer, Frederick, "The Wily Agitator and the American Free Speech Tradition", 57 *Stan. L. Rev.* 2157 (May, 2005).

Schauer, Frederick, "The Boundaries of the First Amendment: A Preliminary Exploration of Constitutional Salience", 117 *Harv. L. Rev.* 1765 (April, 2004).

Schauer, Frederick, "The Political Incidence of the Free Speech Principle", Vol. 64 *University of Colorado Law Review* (1993), pp. 935–957.

Schauer, Frederick, "The Sociology of the Hate Speech Debate", 37 *Vill. L. Rev.* 805–819 (1992).

Schauer, Frederick, "Internet Privacy and the Public-Private Distinction" 38 *Jurimetrics* (No. 4, Summer 1998), pp. 555–564.

Schauer, Frederick, "Commercial Speech and the Architecture of the First Amendment", 56 *University of Cincinnati Law Review* (1988), pp. 1181–1203.

Schauer, Frederick, "Public Figures", 25 *William and Mary Law Review* 905 (1984).

Scheffel, Evan, "Yahoo!, Inc. V. La Ligue Contra Le Racisme et L'Antisemitism: Court Refuses to Enforce French Court Order Attempting to Regulate Speech Occurring Simultaneously in the U.S. and in France", 19 *Computer & High Technology Law Journal* (2003), 549–558.

Schlesinger, Philip, "From cultural defence to political culture: media, politics and collective identity in the European Union", 19 *Media, Culture & Society* (1997), pp. 369–391.
Schlesinger, Philip, "Wishful Thinking: Cultural Politics, Media, and Collective Identities in Europe", 43 *Journal of Communication* (No. 2, Spring 1993), pp. 6–17.
Schlesinger, Philip, "On national identity: some conceptions and misconceptions criticized", 26 *Social Science Information* (No. 2, 1987), pp. 219–264.
Schulz, Wolfgang, Held, Thorsten & Laudien, Arne, "Search Engines as Gatekeepers of Public Communication: Analysis of the German framework applicable to internet search engines including media law and anti trust law", 6 *German Law Journal* (No. 10, 2005), pp. 1419–1433.
Schwarz, Ivo, "Broadcasting and the EEC Treaty", 11 *European Law Review* (1986), pp. 7–60.
Schwelb, Egon, "The International Convention on the Elimination of All Forms of Racial Discrimination", 15 *International and Comparative Law Quarterly* (October 1966), pp. 996–1068.
Schwellnus, Guido, "'Much ado about nothing?' Minority Protection and the EU Charter of Fundamental Rights", Constitutionalism Web-Papers, ConWEB No. 5/2001.
Scolnicov, Anat, "A dedicate follower of (religious) fashion?", 64 *The Cambridge Law Journal* (No. 3, 2005), pp. 527–529.
Segesvary, Victor, "Group rights: The definition of group rights in the contemporary legal debate based on socio-cultural analysis", 3 *International Journal on Group Rights* (1995), pp. 89–107.
Selznick, Philip, "The Idea of a Communitarian Morality", 75 *Cal. L. Rev.* 445–463 (January 1987).
Sen, Amartya, "Elements of a Theory of Human Rights", 32 *Philosophy & Public Affairs* (No. 4, 2004), pp. 315–356.
Serratore, Nicole, "How Do You Say 'Big Media' in Spanish? Spanish-Language Media Regulation and the Implications of the Univision-Hispanic Broadcasting Merger on the Public Interest", 15 *Fordham Intell. Prop. Media & Ent. L.J.* 203–271 (2004).
Servaes, Jan, "'Europe 1992': The audiovisual challenge", 49 *Gazette* (1992), pp. 75–97.
Shattuck, John, "Religion, Rights, and Terrorism", 16 *Harvard Human Rights Journal* (2003), pp. 183–188.
Shiffrin, Steven H., "Racist Speech, Outsider Jurisprudence, and the Meaning of America", 80 *Cornell Law Review* (1994), pp. 43–103.
Siapera, Eugenia, "Minority Activism on the Web: Between Deliberativve Democracy and Multiculturalism", 31 *Journal of Ethnic and Migration Studies* (No. 3, May 2005), pp. 499–519.
Siemienski, Guillaume, "Report on the Vienna Seminar on the Linguistic Rights of National Minorities, 27–28 February 1998", 6 *International Journal on Minority and Group Rights* (Issue No. 3, 1999), pp. 351–358.
Siemienski, Guillaume & Packer, John, "Integration through Education: The Origin and Development of The Hague Recommendations", 4 *International Journal on Minority and Group Rights* (1997), 187–198.

Silverstone, Roger & Georgiou, Myria, "Editorial Introduction: Media and Minorities in Multicultural Europe", 31 *Journal of Ethnic and Migration Studies* (No. 3, May 2005), pp. 433–441.

Singh, Anita Inder, "Minorities, Justice and Security in Post-Communist Europe: Continuing the Debate with Will Kymlicka", *JEMIE* (Issue 4/2002).

Smolla, Rodney A., "Rethinking First Amendment Assumptions about Racist and Sexist Speech", 47 *Washington and Lee Law Review* (1990), pp. 171–211.

Spiliopoulou Akermark, Sia, "The Limits of Pluralism – Recent Jurisprudence of the European Court of Human Rights with Regard to Minorities: Does the Prohibition of Discrimination Add Anything?", *Journal on Ethnopolitics and Minority Issues in Europe* (No. 3, 2002).

Spini, Giorgio, "Secularization and Tolerance", 10 *Ratio Juris* (No. 1, March 1997), pp. 9–12.

Sreberny, Annabelle, "'Not Only, But Also': Mixedness and Media", 31 *Journal of Ethnic and Migration Studies* (No. 3, May 2005), pp. 443–459.

Stefancic, Jean & Delgado, Richard, "A Shifting Balance: Freedom of Expression and Hate-Speech Restriction", 78 *Iowa Law Review* (1993), pp. 737–750.

Stein, Eric, "History Against Free Speech: The New German Law Against The 'Auschwitz' – And Other – 'Lies'", 85 *Mich. L. Rev.* 277–324 (November 1986).

Steiner, Henry, "Political Participation as a Human Right", 1 *Harvard Human Rights Yearbook* (Spring 1988), pp. 77–134.

Steketee, Frank, "The Framework Convention: A Piece of Art or a Tool for Action?", 8 *International Journal on Minority and Group Rights* (2001), pp. 1–15.

Stone, Geoffrey R., "Democracy and Distrust", 64 *Colorado Law Review* 1171 (1993).

Stone, Geoffrey, R., "Content Regulation and the First Amendment", 25 *Wm. & Mary L. Rev.* 189 (Winter 1983), 189–252.

Strauss, David A., "Persuasion, Autonomy, and Freedom of Expression", 91 *Colum. L. Rev.* 334–371 (March 1991).

Strossen, Nadine, "Incitement to Hatred: Should there be a Limit?", 25 *S.Ill.U.L.J.* 243–280 (Winter 2001).

Sunstein, Cass R., "Free Speech Now", Vol. 59 *The University of Chicago Law Review* (1992), pp. 255–316.

Swaine, Lucas A., "How Ought Liberal Democracies to Treat Theocratic Communities?", 111 *Ethics* (January 2001), 302–343.

Tabory, Mala, "Language Rights as Human Rights", 10 *Israel Yearbook on Human Rights* (1980), pp. 167–223.

Tahzib-Lie, Bahia, "The European definition of freedom of religion or belief", *Helsinki Monitor* (No. 3, 1998), pp. 17–24.

Tambini, Damian, "Universal Internet Access: A Realistic View" (London, Institute for Public Policy Research/Citizens Online, 2000).

Tebble, Adam James, "What is the Politics of Difference?", 30 *Political Theory* (No.2, April 2002), pp. 259–281.

Temperman, Jeroen, "Blasphemy, Defamation of Religions and Human Rights Law", 26 *Netherlands Quarterly of Human Rights* (No. 4, 2008), pp. 517–545.

Thio, Li-ann, "Battling Balkanization: Regional Approaches Toward Minority Protection Beyond Europe", 43 *Harvard International Law Journal* (No. 2, Summer 2002), pp. 409–468.

Thorgeirsdóttir, Herdís, "Self-Censorship among Journalists: A (Moral) Wrong or a Violation of ECHR law?", [2004] E.H.R.L.R. (No. 4), pp. 383–399.

Thornberry, Patrick, "Forms of Hate Speech and the Convention on the Elimination of all Forms of Racial Discrimination", 5 *Religion and Human Rights* (2010), pp. 97–117.

Thornberry, Patrick, "Confronting Racial Discrimination: A CERD Perspective", 5 *Human Rights Law Review* (No. 2, 2005), pp. 239–269.

Thornberry, Patrick, "The UN Declaration on the Rights of Persons Belonging to National or Ethnic, Religious and Linguistic Minorities: Background, Analysis and Observations", Minority Rights Group Occasional Paper (June 1993).

Thornberry, Patrick & Gibbons, Dianne, "Education and Minority Rights: A Short Survey of International Standards", 4 *International Journal on Minority and Group Rights* (1997), pp. 115–152.

Tierney, Stephen, "Press Freedom and Public Interest: The Developing Jurisprudence of the European Court of Human Rights", 4 *European Human Rights Law Review* (1998), pp. 419–429.

Trifunovska, Snezana, "Factors Affecting the Applicability and Efficiency of International Norms Protecting Linguistic Rights of Minorities", 9 *International Journal on Minority and Group Rights* (2002), pp. 235–263.

Troebst, Stefan, "The Council of Europe's Framework Convention for the Protection of National Minorities Revisited", Vol. XIV *Speaking About Rights* (Canadian Human Rights Foundation Newsletter) (No. 2, 1999).

Troebst, Stefan, "From paper to practice: The Council of Europe's Framework Convention for the protection of national minorities", 10 *Helsinki Monitor* (No. 1, 1999), pp. 19–26.

Tsesis, Alexander, "The Boundaries of Free Speech" 8 *Harvard Latino L. Rev.* 141 (Spring 2005).

Tsesis, Alexander, "Hate in Cyberspace: Regulating Hate Speech on the Internet", 38 San Diego L. Rev. 817 (Summer 2001).

Tsesis, Alexander, "The Empirical Shortcomings of First Amendment Jurisprudence: A Historical Perspective on the Power of Hate Speech", 40 Santa Clara L. Rev. 729 (2000).

Tsesis, Alexander, "Regulating Intimidating Speech", 41 Harv. J. on Legis. 389 (2004).

Tsilevich, Boris, "Development of the Language Legislation in the Baltic States", 3 *MOST Journal on Multicultural Societies* (No. 2, 2001).

Ungerer, Herbert, "Competition in the media sector – how long can the future be delayed?", 7 *info* (No. 5, 2005), pp. 52–60.

Valcke, Peggy, Picard, Robert, Sukosd, Miklos, Klimkiewicz, Beata, Petkovic, Brankica, Dal Zotto, Cinzia and Kerremans, Robin, "The European Media Pluralism Monitor:

Bridging Law, Economics and Media Studies as a First Step towards Risk-Based Regulation in Media Markets", 2 *Journal of Media Law* (No. 1, 2010), pp. 85–113.

Valdés, Ernesto Garzón, "Some Remarks on the Concept of Toleration", 10 *Ratio Juris* (No. 2, June 1997), pp. 127–138.

Varennes, Fernand de, "Language Rights as an Integral Part of Human Rights", 3 *MOST Journal on Multicultural Societies* (No. 1, 2001).

Varennes, Fernand de & Murray, Claire, "Thematic Introduction: The Human Rights of Linguistic Minorities and Language Policies", 3 *MOST Journal on Multicultural Societies* (No. 2, 2001).

Varennes, Fernand de, "Equality and Non-Discrimination: Fundamental Principles of Minority Language Rights", 6 *International Journal on Minority and Group Rights* (Issue No. 3, 1999), pp. 307–318.

Varennes, Fernand de, "Ethnic Conflicts and Language in Eastern European and Central Asian States: Can Human Rights Help Prevent Them?", 5 *International Journal on Minority and Group Rights* (1997), pp. 135–174.

Varennes, Fernand de, "To speak or not to speak: The Rights of Persons Belonging to Linguistic Minorities", Working Paper prepared for the UN Sub-Committee on the rights of minorities, 21 March 1997.

Varney, Mike, "Must-carry Obligations in the New European Regulatory Framework for Communications: A True Guardian of Pluralism and Diversity?", 14 *Utilities Law Review* (2004/2005), p. 68.

Varney, Mike, "European Controls on Member State Promotion and Regulation of Public Service Broadcasting and Broadcasting Standards", 10 *European Public Law* (No. 3, 2004), pp. 503–530.

Vermeule, Adrian, "Submajority Rules: Forcing Accountability upon Majorities", 13 *The Journal of Political Philosophy* (No. 1, 2005), pp. 74–98.

Vieytez, Eduardo Javier Ruiz, "The Protection of Linguistic Minorities: A Historical Approach", 3 *MOST Journal on Multicultural Societies* (No. 1, 2001).

Vieytez, Eduardo Ruiz, "The History of Legal Protection of Minorities in Europe (XVIIth – XXth Centuries)", University of Derby, Working Papers in International Law and Relations, No. 1, 1999.

Voorhoof, Dirk, "Freedom of Expression under the European Human Rights System. From Sunday Times (n° 1) v. U.K. (1979) to Hachette Filipacchi Associés ("Ici Paris") v. France (2009)", *Inter-American and European Human Rights Journal / Revista Interamericana y Europa de Derechos Humanos* (Nos. 1–2, 2009), pp. 3–49.

Voorhoof, Dirk, "Politieke propaganda in de klas is verboden, maar wat is politieke propaganda?", *Auteurs & Media* 2004/1, pp. 25–28.

Voorhoof, Dirk, Series of articles entitled 'Het Europese 'First Amendment'', published in *Mediaforum*: 1994/11, 116–124; 1995/11–12, 128–137; 1999/10, 264–271; 1999/11–12, 304–313; 2004/4, 106–116; 2004/6, 198–211; 2010/4, 106–116; 2010/6, 186–201.

Wal, Jessica Ter, d'Haenens, Leen & Koeman, Joyce, "(Re)presentation of ethnicity in EU and Dutch domestic news: a quantitative analysis", 27 *Media, Culture & Society* (No. 6, 2005), pp. 937–950.

Waldron, Jeremy, "Nozick and Locke: Filling the Space of Rights", 2005 *Social Philosophy & Policy Foundation*, pp. 81–110.
Waldron, Jeremy, "Judicial Review and the Conditions of Democracy", 6 *The Journal of Political Philosophy* (No. 4, 1998), pp. 335–355.
Waldron, Jeremy, "Rights in Conflict", 99 *Ethics* (No. 3, April 1989), pp. 503–519.
Walzer, Michael, "The Politics of Difference: Statehood and Toleration in a Multicultural World", 10 *Ratio Juris* (No. 2, June 1997), pp. 165–176.
Wang, Lu-in, "The Complexities of 'Hate'", 60 Ohio St. L. J. 799 (1999) (pp. 799–900).
Warbrick, Colin, "The European Response to Terrorism in an Age of Human Rights", 15 *EJIL* (2004), 989–1018.
Westphal, Dietrich, "Media Pluralism and European Regulation" [2002] EBLR 459–487.
Wheatley, Steven, "Minorities under the ECHR and the Construction of a 'Democratic Society'", [2007] *Public Law*, pp. 770–792.
Wheatley, Steve, "Deliberative Democracy and Minorities", 14 *EJIL* (No. 3, 2003), 507–527.
Wheatley, Steven, "Non-Discrimination and Equality in the Right of Political Participation for Minorities", *JEMIE* (No. 3, 2002).
Wheeler, Mark, "Supranational Regulation: Television and the European Union", 19 *European Journal of Communication* (No. 3, 2004), pp. 349–369.
White, Robin C.A. & Boussiakou, Iris, "Separate opinions in the European Court of Human Rights", 9 *Human Rights Law Review* (No. 1, 2009), pp. 37–60.
White, Robin C.A. & Boussiakou, Iris, "Voices from the European Court of Human Rights", 27 *Netherlands Quarterly of Human Rights* (No. 2, 2009), pp. 167–189.
Wiener, Antje & Schwellnus, Guido, "Contested Norms in the Process of EU Enlargement: Non-Discrimination and Minority Rights", Constitutionalism Web-Papers, ConWEB No. 2/2004.
Wildhaber, Luzius, "The European Convention on Human Rights and International Law", 56 *ICLQ* (April 2007), pp. 217–232.
Wildhaber, Luzius, "The right to offend, shock or disturb? – aspects of freedom of expression under the European Convention on Human Rights", 36 *Irish Jurist* (2001), 17–31.
Wilkinson, Kenton T., "Language Difference and Communication Policy in the Information Age", 20 *The Information Society* (2004), pp. 217–229.
Winfield, Richard N., "An Editorial Controversy Metastasizing: Denmark's Hate Speech Laws", 24 *Communications Lawyer* (Spring 2006), pp. 35–37.
Wintemute, Robert, "'Within the Ambit': How Big is the 'Gap' in Article 14 European Convention of Human Rights? Part 1", E.H.R.L.R. 2004, 4, 366–382.
Wintemute, Robert, "Filling the Article 14 'Gap': Government Ratification and Judicial Control of Protocol No. 12 ECHR: Part 2", E.H.R.L.R. 2004, 5, 484–499.
Witte, Bruno De, "Politics Versus Law in the EU's Approach to Ethnic Minorities", EUI Working Paper RSC No. 2000/4.
Wolff, Stefan, "Beyond Ethnic Politics in Central and Eastern Europe" *JEMIE* (Issue 4/2002).

Wolfson, Nicholas, "Free Speech Theory and Hateful Words", 60 *Cincinnati Law Review* (No. 1, 1991), 1–42.

Woods, Lorna, "Broadcasting, universal service and the communications package", 7 *info* (No. 5, 2005), pp. 29–41.

Wright, Sue, "Language and Power: Background to the Debate on Linguistic Rights", 3 *MOST Journal on Multicultural Societies* (No. 1, 2001).

Wright, Jane, "Minority Groups, Autonomy, and Self-Determination", 19:4 *Oxford Journal of Legal Studies* 1999, pp. 605–629.

Wright, Jane, "The Protection of Minority Rights in Europe: From Conference to Implementation", 2 *The International Journal of Human Rights* (No. 1, Spring 1998), pp. 1–31.

Wright, Jane, "The OSCE and the Protection of Minority Rights", 18 *Human Rights Quarterly* (1996), pp. 190–205.

Wurff, Richard van der, "Supplying and Viewing Diversity: The Role of Competition and Viewer Choice in Dutch Broadcasting", 19 *European Journal of Communication* (No. 2, 2004), pp. 215–237.

Young, Iris Marion, "Responsibility and Global Justice: A Social Connection Model", 2006 *Social Philosophy & Policy Foundation*, pp. 102–130.

Young, Iris Marion, "Reply to Tebble", 30 *Political Theory* (No.2, April 2002), pp. 282–288.

Young, Iris Marion, "Activist Challenges to Deliberative Democracy", 29 *Political Theory* (No. 5, October 2001), pp. 670–690.

Young, Iris Marion, "Equality of Whom? Social Groups and Judgments of Injustice", 9 *The Journal of Political Philosophy* (No. 1, 2001), pp. 1–18.

Zatz, Noah D., "Sidewalks in Cyberspace: Making Space for Public Forums in the Electronic Environment", 12 *Harv. J.L. & Tech.* 149 (1998).

Zittrain, Jonathan, "A History of Online Gatekeeping", 19 *Harvard Journal of Law & Technology* (No. 2, Spring 2006), pp. 253–298.

Zoonen, Liesbeth van, "Imagining the Fan Democracy", 19 *European Journal of Communication* (No. 1, 2004), pp. 39–52.

International instruments

I. United Nations

Treaties

Charter of the United Nations (as amended), 26 June 1945 (entry into force: 24 October 1945).

Draft Convention on Freedom of Information, United Nations Conference on Freedom of Information: Final Act (Lake Success, New York, United Nations Publishing, 1948).

Convention on the Prevention and Punishment of the Crime of Genocide Approved and proposed for signature and ratification or accession by General Assembly Resolution 260 A (III) of 9 December 1948 (entry into force 12 January 1951).

Convention on the International Right of Correction, United Nations General Assembly Resolution 630 (VII), 16 December 1952 (entry into force: 24 August 1962).

International Convention on the Elimination of All Forms of Racial Discrimination, United Nations General Assembly Resolution 2106 (XX), 21 December 1965 (entry into force: 4 January 1969).

International Covenant on Civil and Political Rights, United Nations General Assembly Resolution 2200A (XXI), 16 December 1966 (entry into force: 23 March 1976).

International Covenant on Economic, Social and Cultural Rights, United Nations General Assembly Resolution 2200A (XXI), 16 December 1966 (entry into force: 3 January 1976).

Vienna Convention on the Law of Treaties, 23 May 1969 (entry into force: 27 January 1980).

Indigenous and Tribal Peoples Convention, No. 169, International Labour Organisation, 27 June 1989 (entry into force: 5 September 1991).

Convention on the Rights of the Child, United Nations General Assembly Resolution 44/25, 20 November 1989 (entry into force: 2 September 1990).

UNESCO Convention on the Protection and Promotion of the Diversity of Cultural Expressions, 20 October 2005 (entry into force: 18 March 2007).

Statutes

Statute of the International Criminal Tribunal for the Prosecution of Persons Responsible for Genocide and Other Serious Violations of International Humanitarian Law Committed in the Territory of Rwanda and Rwandan Citizens Responsible for Genocide and Other Such Violations Committed in the Territory of Neighbouring

States, between 1 January 1994 and 31 December 1994, adopted by [UN] Security Council Resolution 955 (1994) of 8 November 1994, and amended by [UN] Security Council Resolutions 1165 (1998) of 30 April 1998, 1329 (2000) of 30 November 2000, 1411 (2002) of 17 May 2002 and 1431 (2002) of 14 August 2002.

Statute of the International Tribunal for the Prosecution of Persons Responsible for Serious Violations of International Humanitarian Law Committed in the Territory of the Former Yugoslavia since 1991 (International Tribunal for the Former Yugoslavia), adopted by [UN] Security Council Resolution 827 (1993) of 25 May 1993, and amended by [UN] Security Council Resolutions 1166 (1998) of 13 May 1998, 1329 (2000) of 30 November 2000, 1411 (2002) of 17 May 2002 and1431 (2002) of 14 August 2002.

Rome Statute of the International Criminal Court, United Nations Diplomatic Conference of Plenipotentiaries on the Establishment of an International Criminal Court, 17 July 1998 (entry into force: 1 July 2002).

Declarations

Universal Declaration of Human Rights, United Nations General Assembly Resolution 217A (III), 10 December 1948.

UN Declaration on the Elimination of All Forms of Intolerance and of Discrimination Based on Religion or Belief, United Nations General Assembly Resolution 36/55, 25 November 1981.

UN Declaration on the Rights of Persons Belonging to National or Ethnic, Religious and Linguistic Minorities, United Nations General Assembly Resolution 47/135, 18 December 1992.

UN Declaration on the Rights of Indigenous Peoples, United Nations General Assembly Resolution 61/295, 7 October 2007.

UNESCO

UNESCO Declaration on Race and Racial Prejudice, 27 November 1978.

UNESCO Declaration of Principles on Tolerance, 16 November 1995.

UNESCO Declaration on Cultural Diversity, 2 November 2001.

World Conference against Racism, Racial Discrimination, Xenophobia and Related Intolerance

Declaration and Programme of Action, Report of the World Conference against Racism, Racial Discrimination, Xenophobia and Related Intolerance, Durban, 31 August – 8 September 2001, Doc. No. A/CONF.189/12.

Outcome document of the Durban Review Conference, 24 April 2009.

World Conference on Human Rights

Vienna Declaration and Programme of Action, adopted by the World Conference on Human Rights in Vienna, 25 June 1993.

World Summit on the Information Society (WSIS)

"Building the Information Society: a global challenge in the new Millennium", Declaration of Principles, World Summit on the Information Society, Geneva, Doc. No. WSIS-03/GENEVA/DOC/4-E, 12 December 2003.

Tunis Commitment, World Summit on the Information Society, Tunis, Doc. No. WSIS-05/TUNIS/DOC/7-E, 18 November 2005.

UN Human Rights Council Resolutions

Human Rights Council Resolution 4/9, "Combating defamation of religions", 30 March 2007.

Human Rights Council Resolution 7/19, "Combating defamation of religions", 27 March 2008.

Human Rights Council Resolution 10/22, "Combating defamation of religions", 26 March 2009.

Human Rights Council Resolution 13/16, "Combating defamation of religions", 25 March 2010.

Human Rights Council Resolution 16/18, "Combating intolerance, negative stereotyping and stigmatization of, and discrimination, incitement to violence and violence against, persons based on religion or belief", 24 March 2011.

UN General Assembly Resolutions

UNGA Resolution 217 A (III), "International Bill of Human Rights", 10 December 1948.

UNGA Resolution 217 C (III), "Fate of Minorities", 10 December 1948.

UNGA Resolution 60/251, "Human Rights Council", 15 March 2006.

UNGA Resolution 60/150, "Combating defamation of religions", 16 December 2005.

UNGA Resolution 61/164, "Combating defamation of religions", 19 December 2006.

UNGA Resolution 62/154, "Combating defamation of religions", 18 December 2007.

UNGA Resolution 63/171, "Combating defamation of religions", 18 December 2008.

UNGA Resolution 64/156, "Combating defamation of religions", 18 December 2009.

UNGA Resolution 65/224, "Combating defamation of religions", 21 December 2010.

II. Council of Europe

Treaties

Statute of the Council of Europe, ETS No. 1 (as amended), 5 May 1949 (entry into force: 3 August 1949).

Convention on the Protection of Human Rights and Fundamental Freedoms (ECHR), ETS No. 5, 4 November 1950 (entry into force: 3 September 1953).

European Cultural Convention, ETS No. 18, 19 December 1954 (entry into force: 5 May 1955)

European Convention on Transfrontier Television, ETS No. 132, 5 May 1989 (entry into force: 1 May 1993), as amended by its Amending Protocol, ETS No. 171, 1 October 1998 (entry into force: 1 March 2002).

European Charter for Regional or Minority Languages, ETS No. 148, 5 November 1992 (entry into force: 1 March 1998).

Framework Convention for the Protection of National Minorities, ETS No. 157, 1 February 1995 (entry into force: 1 February 1998).

European Convention for the Protection of the Audiovisual Heritage, ETS No. 183, 8 November 2001 (entry into force: 1 January 2008).

Convention on Cybercrime, ETS No. 185, 23 November 2001 (entry into force: 1 July 2004).

Additional Protocol to the Convention on cybercrime concerning the criminalisation of acts of a racist and xenophobic nature committed through computer systems, ETS No. 189, 28 January 2003 (entry into force: 1 March 2006).

Council of Europe Framework Convention on the Value of Cultural Heritage for Society, CETS No. 199, 27 October 2005 (entry into force: 1 June 2011).

Recommendations and Declarations

Committee of Ministers

Declaration on the Freedom of Expression and Information, 29 April 1982.

Recommendation No. R (96) 10 on the guarantee of the independence of public service broadcasting, 11 September 1996.

Recommendation No. R (97) 19 on the portrayal of violence in the electronic media, 30 October 1997.

Recommendation No. R (97) 20 on "hate speech", 30 October 1997.

Recommendation No. R (97) 21 on the media and the promotion of a culture of tolerance, 30 October 1997.

Recommendation No. R (99) 1 on measures to promote media pluralism, 19 January 1999.

Recommendation No. R (99) 14 on universal community service concerning new communication and information services, 9 September 1999.

Recommendation Rec (2001) 8 on self-regulation concerning cyber content (self-regulation and user protection against illegal or harmful content on new communications and information services), 5 September 2001.

Recommendation Rec (2003) 9 on measures to promote the democratic and social contribution of digital broadcasting, 28 May 2003.

Declaration on freedom of communication on the Internet, 28 May 2003.

Declaration on freedom of political debate in the media, 12 February 2004.

Recommendation Rec (2004) 16 on the right of reply in the new media environment, 15 December 2004.
Declaration on freedom of expression and information in the media in the context of the fight against terrorism, 2 March 2005.
Declaration on human rights and the rule of law in the Information Society, 13 May 2005.
Recommendation Rec(2006)3 on the UNESCO Convention on the protection and promotion of the diversity of cultural expressions, 1 February 2006.
Declaration on the guarantee of the independence of public service broadcasting in the member states, 27 September 2006.
Declaration on protecting the role of the media in democracy in the context of media concentration, 31 January 2007.
Recommendation CM/Rec(2007)2 on media pluralism and diversity of media content, 31 January 2007.
Recommendation CM/Rec(2007)3 on the remit of public service media in the information society, 31 January 2007.
Recommendation CM/Rec(2007)11 on promoting freedom of expression and information in the new information and communications environment, 26 September 2007.
Recommendation CM/Rec(2007)15 on measures concerning media coverage of election campaigns, 7 November 2007.
Recommendation CM/Rec(2007)16 on measures to promote the public service value of the Internet, 7 November 2007.
Declaration on the allocation and management of the digital dividend and the public interest, 20 February 2008.
Declaration on the role of community media in promoting social cohesion and intercultural dialogue, 11 February 2009.
Declaration on measures to promote the respect of Article 10 of the European Convention on Human Rights, 13 January 2010.
Recommendation CM/Rec(2010)5 on measures to combat discrimination on grounds of sexual orientation or gender identity, 31 March 2010.

Parliamentary Assembly

Recommendation 213 (1959), Position of national minorities in Europe, 17 September 1959.
Recommendation 285 (1961), Rights of national minorities, 28 April 1961.
Recommendation 1134 (1990), Rights of minorities, 1 October 1990.
Recommendation 1177 (1992), Rights of minorities, 5 February 1992.
Recommendation 1201 (1993), Additional protocol on the rights of minorities to the European Convention on Human Rights, 1 February 1993.
Recommendation 1231 (1994), Follow-up to the Council of Europe Vienna Summit, 26 January 1994.
Recommendation 1255 (1995), Protection of rights of national minorities, 31 January 1995.
Recommendation 1276 (1995) on the power of the visual image, 30 June 1995.
Recommendation 1277 (1995) on migrants, ethnic minorities and media, 30 June 1995.

Recommendation 1285 (1996), Rights of national minorities, 23 January 1996.
Recommendation 1300 (1996), Protection of rights of minorities, 25 June 1996.
Resolution 1120 (1997) on the impact of the new communication and information technologies on democracy, 22 April 1997.
Recommendation 1345 (1997), Protection of national minorities, 24 September 1997.
Recommendation 1492 (2001), Rights of national minorities, 23 January 2001.
Recommendation 1623 (2003), Rights of national minorities, 29 September 2003.
Recommendation 1641 (2004), Public service broadcasting, 27 January 2004.
Resolution 1387 (2004), Monopolisation of the electronic media and possible abuse of power in Italy, 24 June 2004.
Resolution 1495 (2006), Combating the resurgence of Nazi ideology, 12 April 2006.
Resolution 1510 (2006), Freedom of expression and respect for religious beliefs, 28 June 2006.
Recommendation 1768 (2006), The image of asylum-seekers, migrants and refugees in the media, 5 October 2006.
Recommendation 1773 (2006), The 2003 guidelines on the use of minority languages in the broadcast media and the Council of Europe standards: need to enhance cooperation and synergy with the OSCE, 17 November 2006.
Resolution 1563 (2007), Combating anti-Semitism in Europe, 27 June 2007.
Recommendation 1804 (2007), State, religion, secularity and human rights, 29 June 2007.
Recommendation 1805 (2007), Blasphemy, religious insults and hate speech against persons on grounds of their religion, 29 June 2007.
Resolution 1577 (2007), Towards decriminalisation of defamation, 4 October 2007.
Recommendation 1814 (2007), Towards decriminalisation of defamation, 4 October 2007.
Resolution 1605 (2008), European Muslim communities confronted with extremism, 15 April 2008.
Recommendation 1831 (2008), European Muslim communities confronted with extremism, 15 April 2008.
Resolution 1636 (2008), Indicators for media in a democracy, 3 October 2008.
Recommendation 1848 (2008), Indicators for media in a democracy, 3 October 2008.
Recommendation 1855 (2009), The regulation of audio-visual media services, 27 January 2009.
Recommendation 1878 (2009), Funding of public service broadcasting, 25 June 2009.
Recommendation 1897 (2010), Respect for media freedom, 27 January 2010.
Resolution 1728 (2010), Discrimination on the basis of sexual orientation and gender identity, 29 April 2010.
Recommendation 1904 (2010), Minority protection in Europe: best practices and deficiencies in implementation of common standards, 12 March 2010.
Recommendation 1915 (2010), Discrimination on the basis of sexual orientation and gender identity, 29 April 2010.

III. European Union

Treaties

Treaty on European Union, as amended by the Treaty of Lisbon.

Treaty on the Functioning of the European Union, as amended by the Treaty of Lisbon.

Protocol to the Treaty of Amsterdam amending the Treaty on European Union, the Treaties establishing the European Communities and certain related acts, signed at Amsterdam, 2 October 1997, OJ C 340/109 of 10 November 1997.

Charter of Fundamental Rights of the European Union, Nice, 7 December 2000, as published in the *Official Journal of the European Communities* of 18 December 2000, C 364/1, as revised, OJ C 303/01 of 14 December 2007.

Treaty of Lisbon amending the Treaty on European Union and the Treaty establishing the European Community, signed at Lisbon, 13 December 2007, OJ 2007/C 306/01 of 17 December 2007 (entry into force: 1 December 2009).

Diverse regulatory instruments

Council Directive 89/552/EEC of 3 October 1989 on the coordination of certain provisions laid down by law, regulation or administrative action in Member States concerning the pursuit of television broadcasting activities, OJ L 298/23, 17 October 1989, and amended by Directive 97/36/EC of the European Parliament and of the Council of 30 June 1997, OJ L 202/60, 30 July 1997.

Directive 95/46/EC of the European Parliament and of the Council of 24 October 1995 on the protection of individuals with regard to the processing of personal data and on the free movement of such data, OJ L 281, 23 November 1995, p. 31.

Directive 2000/31/EC of the European Parliament and of the Council of 8 June 2000 on certain legal aspects of information society services, in particular electronic commerce, in the Internal Market (Directive on electronic commerce), OJ L 178, 17 July 2000, p. 1.

Decision No. 676/2002/EC of the European Parliament and of the Council of 7 March 2002 on a regulatory framework for radio spectrum policy in the European Community (Radio Spectrum Decision), OJ L 108/1, 24 April 2002.

Directive 2002/21/EC of the European Parliament and of the Council of 7 March 2002 on a common regulatory framework for electronic communications networks and services (Framework Directive), OJ L 108/33, 24 April 2002.

Directive 2002/22/EC of the European Parliament and of the Council of 7 March 2002 on universal service and users' rights relating to electronic communications networks and services (Universal Services Directive).

Council Regulation (EC) No 139/2004 of 20 January 2004 on the control of concentrations between undertakings (the EC Merger Regulation), OJ L 24/1, 29 January 2004.

Recommendation of the European Parliament and of the Council of 20 December 2006 on the protection of minors and human dignity and on the right of reply in relation to the competitiveness of the European audiovisual and on-line information services industry (2006/952/EC), *Official Journal of the European Communities*, L378/72 of 27 December 2006.
Directive 2007/65/EC of the European Parliament and of the Council of 11 December 2007 amending Council Directive 89/552/EEC on the coordination of certain provisions laid down by law, regulation or administrative action in Member States concerning the pursuit of television broadcasting activities, OJ L 332/27 of 18 December 2007.
Council of the European Union Framework Decision 2008/913/JHA of 28 November 2008 on combating certain forms and expressions of racism and xenophobia by means of criminal law, OJ L 328/55 of 6 December 2008.
Directive 2010/13/EU of the European Parliament and of the Council of 10 March 2010 on the coordination of certain provisions laid down by law, regulation or administrative action in member states concerning the provision of audiovisual media services (codified version), OJ L 95/2 of 15 April 2010.

European Commission

Communication from the Commission on the application of State aid rules to public service broadcasting (2001/C 320/04).
Communication from the Commission, "The Future of a European Regulatory Audiovisual Policy", COM(2003) 784 final, 15 December 2003.
Communication from the Commission concerning the State aid assessment criteria of the
Commission communication on certain legal aspects relating to cinematographic and other audiovisual works (Cinema Communication) of 26 September 2001 (2009/C 31/01).
Communication from the Commission on the application of State aid rules to public service broadcasting of 2 July 2009 (2009/C 257/01).

European Parliament

Resolution on the risks of violation, in the EU and especially in Italy, of freedom of expression and information (Article 11(2) of the Charter of Fundamental Rights) (2003/2237/(INI)), 22 April 2004.
Resolution on the protection of minorities and anti-discrimination policies in an enlarged Europe (2005/2008(INI)), 8 June 2005, OJ C 124 E/405 of 25 May 2006.
Resolution of 25 September 2008 on Community Media in Europe (2008/2011(INI)).
Resolution of 25 September 2008 on concentration and pluralism in the media in the European Union (2007/2253(INI)).

IV. OSCE

Final Act of the Helsinki Conference on Security and Co-operation in Europe, 1975.
Concluding Document of the Vienna Follow-up Meeting of the Conference on Security and Co-operation in Europe, 1986.
Document of the Copenhagen Meeting of the Conference on the Human Dimension of the Conference on Security and Co-operation in Europe, 1990.
Concluding Document of the Helsinki Meeting of the Conference on Security and Co-operation in Europe, "The Challenges of Change", 1992.
Budapest Summit, "Towards a Genuine Partnership in a New Era", 1994.

V. Miscellaneous

Joint Declarations and Statements by the IGO Special Mandates on Freedom of Expression/the Media

Joint Statement on Racism and the Media by the UN Special Rapporteur on Freedom of Opinion and Expression, the OSCE Representative on Freedom of the Media and the OAS Special Rapporteur on Freedom of Expression, 27 February 2001.
Joint Declaration by the UN Special Rapporteur on Freedom of Opinion and Expression, the OSCE Representative on Freedom of the Media and the OAS Special Rapporteur on Freedom of Expression, 21 December 2005.
Joint Declaration on Diversity in Broadcasting, adopted by the UN Special Rapporteur on Freedom of Opinion and Expression, the OSCE RFOM, the OAS Special Rapporteur on Freedom of Expression and the ACHPR Special Rapporteur on Freedom of Expression and Access to Information, 12 December 2007.
Joint Declaration on Defamation of Religions, and anti-terrorism and anti-extremism legislation, adopted by the UN Special Rapporteur on Freedom of Opinion and Expression, the OSCE RFOM, the OAS Special Rapporteur on Freedom of Expression and the ACHPR Special Rapporteur on Freedom of Expression and Access to Information, 9 December 2008.
Tenth Anniversary Joint Declaration: Ten New Challenges to Freedom of Expression in the Next Decade, adopted by the UN Special Rapporteur on Freedom of Opinion and Expression, the OSCE RFOM, the OAS Special Rapporteur on Freedom of Expression and the ACHPR Special Rapporteur on Freedom of Expression and Access to Information, 2 February 2010.

General and thematic comments and recommendations

United Nations

ICCPR

Draft General Comment No. 34 (Upon completion of the first reading by the Human Rights Committee), Doc. No. CCPR/C/GC/34/CRP.6, 3 May 2011.[1]

General Comment No. 31 – The Nature of the General Legal Obligation Imposed on States Parties to the Covenant, 29 March 2004.

General Comment No. 23 – The rights of minorities (Article 27), Doc. No. CCPR/C/21/Rev.1/Add.5, 8 April 1994.

General Comment No. 22 – The right to freedom of thought, conscience and religion (Article 18), 30 July 1993.

General Comment No. 18 – Non-discrimination, 10 November 1989.

General Comment No. 12 – The right to self-determination of peoples (Article 1), 13 March 1984.

General Comment No. 11 – Prohibition of propaganda for war and inciting national, racial or religious hatred (Article 20), 29 July 1983.

General Comment No. 10 – Freedom of expression (Article 19), 29 July 1983.

ICESCR

General Comment No. 3 – The nature of States parties obligations (Art. 2, para. 1 of the Covenant), 14 December 1990.

ICERD

General Recommendation XXXI on the prevention of racial discrimination in the administration and functioning of the criminal justice system, August 2005.

General Recommendation XXX – Discrimination Against Non Citizens, 1 October 2004.

General Recommendation XXVII – Discrimination against Roma, 16 August 2000.

General Recommendation XX – Non-discriminatory implementation of rights and freedoms (Art. 5), 15 March 1996.

General Recommendation XV – Organized violence based on ethnic origin (Art. 4), 23 March 1993.

General Recommendation VII – Legislation to eradicate racial discrimination (Art. 4), 23 August 1985.

---

1 As of this writing, only the first 22 paragraphs of the draft General Comment had been adopted by the UN Human Rights Committee.

Council of Europe

FCNM

Advisory Committee on the Framework Convention for the Protection of National Minorities, Commentary on Education under the Framework Convention for the Protection of National Minorities, Doc. No. ACFC/25DOC(2006)002, 2 March 2006.

Advisory Committee on the Framework Convention for the Protection of National Minorities, Commentary on the Effective Participation of Persons Belonging to National Minorities in Cultural, Social and Economic Life and in Public Affairs, Doc. No. ACFC/31DOC(2008)001, 5 May 2008.

ECRI

General Policy Recommendations

1. Combating racism, xenophobia, antisemitism and intolerance (1996).
2. Specialised bodies to combat racism, xenophobia, antisemitism and intolerance at national level (1997).
3. Combating racism and intolerance against Roma/Gypsies (1998).
4. National surveys on the experience and perception of discrimination and racism from the point of view of potential victims (1998).
5. Combating intolerance and discrimination against Muslims (2000).
6. Combating the dissemination of racist, xenophobic and antisemitic material via the Internet (2000).
7. On national legislation to combat racism and racial discrimination (2002).
8. On combating racism while fighting terrorism (2004).
9. On the fight against antisemitism (2004).
10. On combating racism and racial discrimination in and through school education (2006).
11. On combating racism and racial discrimination in policing (2007).
12. On combating racism and racial discrimination in the field of sport (2008).

OSCE

HCNM

Bolzano/Bozen Recommendations on National Minorities in Inter-State Relations (June 2008).

Recommendations on Policing in Multi-Ethnic Societies (February 2006).

Guidelines on the use of Minority Languages in the Broadcast Media (October 2003).

Lund Recommendations on the Effective Participation of National Minorities in Public Life (September 1999).

Oslo Recommendations Regarding the Linguistic Rights of National Minorities (February 1998).

The Hague Recommendations on the Education Rights of National Minorities (October 1996).

European Union

EU Network of Independent Experts on Fundamental Rights'
Thematic Comment No. 3, The Protection of Minorities in the European Union, 25 April 2005.

Table of cases

Judgments and decisions of the European Court of Human Rights (cited)

Abdullah Aydin v. Turkey (No. 2), no. 63739/00 (Sect. 3), 10 November 2005.
Agga v. Greece (No. 2), nos. 50776/99 & 52912/99 (Sect. 1), 17 October 2002.
Airey v. Ireland, Series A, no. 32, 9 October 1979.
Albert-Engelmann-Gesellschaft mbH v. Austria, no. 46389/99 (Sect. 1), 19 January 2006.
Alinak v. Turkey, no. 40287/98 (Sect. 2), 29 March 2005.
Anguelova v. Bulgaria, no. 38361/97, ECHR 2002-IV, 13 June 2002.
Appleby and Others v. the United Kingdom, no. 44306/98 (Sect. 4), ECHR 2003-VI, 6 May 2003.
Arslan v. Turkey [GC], no. 23462/94, 8 July 1999.
Autronic AG v. Switzerland, Series A, no. 178, 22 May 1990.
Aydin Tatlav v. Turkey, no. 50692/99 (Sect. 2), 2 May 2006.
"Belgian Linguistic" Case, Series A, vol. 6, 23 July 1968.
Bergens Tidende & Others v. Norway, no. 26132/95 (Sect. 3), ECHR 2000-IV, 2 May 2000.
Bladet Tromso & Stensaas v. Norway [GC], no. 21980/93, ECHR 1999-III, 20 May 1999.
Brook v. the United Kingdom, no. 38218/97 (Sect. 3), 11 July 2000.
Buckley v. the United Kingdom, Rep. 1996-IV, 26 August 1996.
Campbell & Cosans v. the United Kingdom, Series A, No. 48, 25 February 1982.
Canea Catholic Church v. Greece, Rep. 1997-VIII, 16 December 1997.
Ceylan v. Turkey [GC], no. 23556/94, Rep. 1999-IV, 8 July 1999.
Cha'are Ve Tsedek v. France [GC], no. 27417/95, ECHR 2000-VII, 27 June 2000.
Chapman v. the United Kingdom [GC], no. 27238/95, 18 January 2001.
Chassagnou & Others v. France [GC], nos. 25088/94, 28331/95 & 28443/95, ECHR 1999-III, 29 April 1999.
Chauvy & Others v. France, no. 64915/01 (Sect. 2), ECHR 2004-VI, 29 June 2004.
Christine Goodwin v. the United Kingdom [GC], no. 28957/95, ECHR 2002-VI, 11 July 2002.
Connors v. the United Kingdom, no. 66746/01 (Sect. 1), 27 May 2004.
De Haes & Gijsels v. Belgium, Rep. 1997-I, 24 February 1997.
D.H. and Others v. the Czech Republic [GC], no. 57325/00, 13 November 2007.
Erdogdu & Ince v. Turkey [GC], nos. 25067/94 and 25068/94, ECHR 1999-IV, 8 July 1999.
Féret v. Belgium, no. 15615/07 (Sect. 2), 16 July 2009.
Fressoz & Roire v. France [GC], no. 29183/95, ECHR 1999-I, 21 January 1999.
Fuentes Bobo v. Spain, no. 39293/98 (Sect. 4), 29 February 2000.
Garaudy v France (dec.), no. 65831/01, ECHR 2003-IX, 24 June 2003.

Giniewski v. France, no. 64016/00, ECHR 2006-I, 31 January 2006.
Goodwin v. the United Kingdom, Rep. 1996-II, 27 March 1996.
Gorzelik and others v. Poland [GC], no. 44158/98, ECHR 2004-I, 17 February 2004.
Groppera Radio AG & others v. Switzerland, Series A, no. 173, 28 March 1990.
Gündüz v. Turkey, no. 35071/97 (Sect. 1), ECHR 2003-XI, 4 December 2003.
Handyside v. the United Kingdom, Series A, no. 24, 7 December 1976.
Hasan & Chaush v. Bulgaria [GC], no. 30985/96, ECHR 2000-XI, 26 October 2000.
Hugh Jordan v. the United Kingdom, no. 24746/94 (Sect. 3), 4 May 2001.
İ.A. v. Turkey, no. 42571/98 (Sect. 2), ECHR 2005-VIII, 13 September 2005.
Informationsverein Lentia & Others v. Austria, Series A, no. 276, 24 November 1993.
Inze v. Austria, Series A, no. 126, 28 October 1987.
Jersild v. Denmark, Series A, no. 298, 23 September 1994.
Kenedi v. Hungary, no. 31475/05 (Sect. 2), 26 May 2009.
Khurshid Mustafa & Tarzibachi v. Sweden, no. 23883/06 (Sect. 3),16 December 2008.
Kjeldsen, Busk Madsen & Pedersen v. Denmark, Series A, no. 23, 7 December 1976.
Klein v. Slovakia, no. 72208/01 (Sect. 4), 31 October 2006.
Kokkinakis v. Greece, Series A, no. 260-A, 25 May 1993.
Kutlular v. Turkey, no. 73715/01 (Sect. 4), 29 April 2008.
Lehideux & Isorni v. France, Rep. 1998-VII, 23 September 1998.
Leroy v. France, no. 36109/03 (Sect. 5), 2 October 2008.
Liberty & Others v. the United Kingdom, no. 58243/00 (Sect. 4), 1 July 2008.
Lindon & Others v. France [GC], nos. 21279/02 & 36448/02, 23 October 2007.
Lingens v. Austria, Series A, no. 103, 8 July 1986.
Loizidou v. Turkey (preliminary objections), Series A, no. 310, 23 March 1995.
Manole & Others v. Moldova, no. 13936/02 (Sect. 4), 17 September 2009.
Manoussakis v. Greece, Rep. 1996-IV, 29 August 1996.
Marckx v. Belgium, Series A, no. 31, 13 June 1979.
Matthews v. the United Kingdom [GC], no. 24833/94, ECHR 1999-I, 18 February 1999.
Mehmet Cevher Ilhan v. Turkey, no. 15719/03 (Sect. 2), 13 January 2009.
Melnychuk v. Ukraine (dec.), no. 28743/03, ECHR 2005-IX, 5 July 2005.
Metropolitan Church of Bessarabia and others v. Moldova, no. 45701/99 (Sect. 1), ECHR 2001-XII, 13 December 2001.
Müller & Others v. Switzerland, Series A, no. 133, 24 May 1988.
Murphy v. Ireland, no. 44179/98 (Sect. 3), ECHR 2003-IX, 10 July 2003.
Nachova and Others v. Bulgaria [GC], nos. 43577/98 & 43579/98, ECHR 2005-VII, 6 July 2005.
Noack & Others v. Germany (dec.), no. 46346/99, ECHR 2000-VI, 25 May 2000.
Norwood v the United Kingdom (dec.), no. 23131/03, ECHR 2004-XI, 16 November 2004.
Nur Radyo Ve Televizyon Yayinciligi A.Ş v. Turkey, no. 6587/03 (Sect. 2), 27 November 2007.
Oberschlick v Austria (No. 1), Series A, no. 204, 23 May 1991.
Observer & Guardian v. the United Kingdom, Series A, no. 216, 26 November 1991.
Odabasi & Kocak v. Turkey, no. 50959/99 (Sect. 4), 21 February 2006.

Otto-Preminger-Institut v. Austria, Series A, no. 295-A, 20 September 1994.
Özgür Gündem v. Turkey, no. 23144/93, ECHR 2000-III, 16 March 2000.
Paturel v. France, no. 54968/00 (Sect. 1), 22 December 2005.
Pavel Ivanov v. Russia (dec.), no. 35222/04 (Sect. 1), 20 February 2007.
Plattform "Ärzte für das Leben", Series A, no. 139, 21 June 1988.
Prager & Oberschlick v. Austria, Series A, No. 313, 26 April 1995.
Pretty v. the United Kingdom, no. 2346/02 (Sect. 4), ECHR 2002-III, 29 April 2002.
Radio France v. France, no. 53984/00 (Sect. 2), ECHR 2004-II, 30 March 2004.
Refah Partisi (the Welfare Party) & Others v. Turkey [GC], nos. 41340/98, 41342/98, 41343/98 & 41344/98, ECHR 2003-II, 13 February 2003.
Sampanis & others v. Greece, no. 32526/05 (Sect. 1), 5 June 2008.
Schimanek v. Austria (dec.), no. 32307/96, 1 February 2000.
Serif v. Greece, no. 38178/9 (Sect. 2), ECHR 1999-IX, 14 December 1999.
Seurot v France (dec.), no. 57383/00, 18 May 2004.
Sidiropoulos & Others v. Greece, Rep. 1998-IV, 10 July 1998.
Sîrbu and others v. Moldova, nos. 73562/01, etc. (Sect. 4), 15 June 2004.
Soulas & Others v. France, no.15948/03 (Sect. 5), 10 July 2008.
Stafford v. the United Kingdom [GC], no. 46295/99, ECHR 2002-IV, 28 May 2002.
Stankov and the United Macedonian Organisation Ilinden v. Bulgaria, nos. 29225/95 and 29221/95 (Sect. 1), ECHR 2001-IX, 2 October 2001.
Steel & Morris v. the United Kingdom, no. 68416/01 (Sect. 4), ECHR 2005-II, 15 February 2005.
The Sunday Times (No. 1) v. the United Kingdom, Series A, no. 30, 26 April 1979.
Supreme Holy Council of the Muslim Community v. Bulgaria, no. 39023/97 (Sect. 1), 16 December 2004.
Sürek v. Turkey (No. 1) [GC], no. 26682/95, ECHR 1999-IV, 8 July 1999.
Sürek v. Turkey (No. 4) [GC], no. 24762/94, 8 July 1999.
Sürek & Özdemir v. Turkey [GC], nos. 23927/95 and 24277/99, 8 July 1999.
Társaság a Szabadságjogokért v. Hungary, no. 37374/05 (Sect. 2), 14 April 2009.
Thlimmenos v. Greece [GC], no. 34369/97, ECHR 2000-IV, 6 April 2000.
Thorgeirson v Iceland, Series A, no. 239, 25 June 1992.
Timishev v. Russia, nos. 55762/00 and 55974/00 (Sect. 2), ECHR 2005-XII, 13 December 2005.
Tyrer v. the United Kingdom, Series A, no. 26, 25 April 1978.
Unabhängige Initiative Informationsvielfalt v. Austria, no. 28525/95 (Sect. 3), ECHR 2002-I, 26 February 2002.
United Christian Broadcasters Ltd. v. the United Kingdom (dec.), no. 44802/98, 7 November 2000.
United Communist Party v. Turkey, Rep. 1998-I, 30 January 1998.
Vajnai v. Hungary, no. 33629/06 (Sect. 2), 8 July 2008.
Velikova v. Bulgaria, no. 41488/98 (Sect. 4), ECHR 2000-VI, 18 May 2000.
VgT Verein gegen Tierfabriken v. Switzerland, no. 24699/94 (Sect. 2), ECHR 2001-VI, 28 June 2001.

Wingrove v. United Kingdom, Rep. 1996-V, 25 November 1996.
Witzsch v. Germany (dec.), no. 41448/98, 20 April 1999.
Young, James & Webster v. United Kingdom, Series A, no. 44, 13 August 1981.

European Commission of Human Rights

Inadmissibility decisions (cited)

Ben El Mahi & others v. Denmark, no. 5853/06, 11 December 2006.
Choudhury v. the United Kingdom, no. 17439/90, 5 March 1991.
D.I. v. Germany, no. 26551/95, 26 June 1996.
Dubowska & Skup v. Poland, nos. 33490/96 and 34055/96, 18 April 1997.
Ediciones Tempo S.A. v. Spain, no. 13010/87, 18 June 1987.
E.F.A. Remer v. Germany, no. 25096/94, 82-A DR 117.
G. & E. v. Norway, nos. 9278/81 & 9415/81, 3 October 1983.
H., W., P. and K. v. Austria, no. 12774/87, 62 DR (1989) 216.
Haider v. Austria, no. 25060/94, 18 October 1995.
Hins & Hugenholtz v. the Netherlands, no. 25987/94, 7 March 1996.
Honsik v. Austria, no. 25062/94, 83-B DR 77 (1995).
Konkama & 38 other Saami villages v. Sweden, no. 27033/95, 25 November 1996.
Kühnen v. FRG, no. 12194/86, 56 DR 205 (1988).
Marais v. France, no. 31159/96, 86-A DR 184 (1996).
Nachtmann v. Austria, no. 36773/97, 9 September 1998.
Nationaldemokratische Partei Deutschlands Bezirksverband Munchen-Oberbayern v Germany, no. 25992/94, 84-A DR 149 (1996).
Ochensberger v. Austria, no. 21318/93, 18 EHRR-CD, pp. 170–172.
Purcell et al. v. Ireland, no. 15404/89, 16 April 1991.
Rebhandl v. Austria, no. 24398/94, 16 January 1996.
S. v. Switzerland, Report, no. 17116/90, 14 January 1993.
Sdružení Jihočeské Matky v. Czech Republic, no. 19101/03, 10 July 2006.
Walendy v. Germany, no. 21128/92, 80-A DR 94.
X. v. Austria, no. 8142/78, 18 DR 88 (1979).
X. v. FRG, no. 9235/81, 29 DR 194 (1982).
X. Ltd. & Y. v. the United Kingdom, no. 8710/79, 7 May 1982, 28 D.R. 77 (November 1982) (also referred to as *Gay News Ltd. & Lemon v. the United Kingdom*).

Views and Decisions of the UN Human Rights Committee (cited)

Ballantyne, Davidson & McIntyre v. Canada, Communication Nos. 359/1989 & 385/1989, 31 March 1993.
C.L.D. v. France, Communication No. 439/1990, 8 November 1991.
Faurisson v. France, Communication No. 550/1993, 8 November 1996.
J.R.T. and the W.G. Party v. Canada, Communication No. 104/1981, 6 April 1983.
Mavlonov & Sa'di v. Uzbekistan, Communication No. 1334/2004, 19 March 2009.

Ominayak and the Lubicon Lake Band v. Canada, Communication No. 167/1984, 10 May 1990.

Ross v. Canada, Communication No. 736/1997, 26 October 2000.

T.K. v. France, Communication No. 220/1987, 8 November 1989.

Opinions of the UN Committee on the Elimination of Racial Discrimination (cited)

The Jewish Community of Oslo & others v. Norway, Communication No. 30/2003, 22 August 2005.

UN International Criminal Tribunal for Rwanda

The Prosecutor v. Jean-Paul Akayesu, Case No. ICTR-96–4-T, ICTR (Chamber I) Judgment of 2 September 1998.

The Prosecutor v. Ferdinand Nahimana, Jean-Bosco Barayagwiza & Hassan Ngeze (the Media case), Case No. ICTR-99–52-T, ICTR (Trial Chamber I), Judgment of 3 December 2003

Ferdinand Nahimana, Jean-Bosco Barayagwiza & Hassan Ngeze v. The Prosecutor, Case No. ICTR-99–52-A, ICTR (Appeals Chamber), Judgment of 28 November 2007.

Case-law of the Court of Justice of the European Communities (cited)

Case 4/73, *Nold v. Commission* [1974], Judgment of 14 May 1974, ECR 491.

Case 352/85, *Bond van Adverteerders & others v. The Netherlands,* Judgment of 26 April 1988, ECR 1988, p. 2085.

Case C-260/89, *Ellinki Radiophonia Tiléorassi AE and Panellinia Omospondia Syllogon Prossopikou v. Dimotiki Etairia Pliroforissis and Sotirios Kouvelas and Nicolaos Avdellas and others* [1991], Judgment of 18 June 1991, ECR I-2925.

Case C-288/89, *Stichting Collectieve Antennevoorziening Gouda and others v. Commissariaat voor de media* [1991], Judgment of 25 July 1991, ECR I-4007.

Case C-353/89, *Commission of the European Communities v. Kingdom of the Netherlands* [1991], Judgment of 25 July 1991, ECR I-4069.

Case C-148/91, *Veronica Omroep Organisatie v. Commissariaat voor de Media* [1993], Judgment of 3 February 1993, ECR I-487.

Case C-23/93, *TV10 SA v. Commissariaat voor de media* [1994], Judgment of 5 October 1994, ECR I-4795.

Case C-11/95, *Commission of the European Communities v. Belgium* [1996], Judgment of 10 September 1996, ECR I-4115.

Case C-368/95, *Vereinigte Familiapress Zeitungsverlags- und vertriebs GmbH v. Heinrich Bauer Verlag* [1997], Judgment of 26 June 1997, ECR I-3689.

Case C-280/00, *Altmark Trans GmbH, Regierungspräsidium Magdeburg v. Nahverkehrsgesellschaft Altmark GmbH*, Judgment of 24 July 2003, Rec. 2003, p. I-7747.

Case C-89/04, *Mediakabel BV v. Commissariaat voor de Media*, Judgment of 2 June 2005, ECR I-4891.

Case C-250/06, *United Pan-Europe Communications Belgium SA v. Belgium,* Judgment of 13 December 2007.

Permanent Court of International Justice

Advisory Opinion No. 17, *Greco-Bulgarian "Communities"* case, 31 July 1930, Series B, No. 17, pp. 4 – 46.
Advisory Opinion No. 64, *Minority Schools in Albania*, 6 April 1935, Series A/B, No. 64, pp. 4–36.

United States case-law (cited)

Supreme Court

Abrams v US, 250 US 616 (1919).
Adarand Constructors, Inc. v. Pena, 515 US 200 (1995).
Associated Press v. United States, 326 US 1 (1945).
Brandenburg v. Ohio, 395 US 444 (1969).
Cantwell v. Connecticut, 310 US 296 (1940).
Chaplinsky v. New Hampshire, 315 US 568 (1942).
Gitlow v. New York, 268 US 652 (1925).
Jacobellis v. Ohio, 378 US 184 (1964).
Kunz v. New York 340 U.S. 290 (1951).
Marsh v. Chambers, 463 US 783 (1983).
Metro Broadcasting, Inc., v. Federal Communications Commission, et al., 497 US 547 (1990).
New York Times Co. v. Sullivan, 376 US 254 (1964).
Red Lion Broadcasting Co., Inc. v. Federal Communications Commission, 395 US 367 (1969).
Roth v. US, 354 US 476 (1957).
West Virginia State Board of Education v. Barnette, 319 US 624 (1943).

District Courts

ACLU v. Reno, 929 F. Supp. 824 (11 June 1996).

Index

A

B

C

J

K

L

M

P

Q

R

School of Human Rights Research Series

The School of Human Rights Research is a joint effort by human rights researchers in the Netherlands. Its central research theme is the nature and meaning of international standards in the field of human rights, their application and promotion in the national legal order, their interplay with national standards, and the international supervision of such application. The School of Human Rights Research Series only includes English titles that contribute to a better understanding of the different aspects of human rights.

Published titles within the Series:

1 Brigit C.A. Toebes, *The Right to Health as a Human Right in International Law*
ISBN 90–5095–057–4

2 Ineke Boerefijn, *The Reporting Procedure under the Covenant on Civil and Political Rights. Practice and Procedures of the Human Rights Committee*
ISBN 90–5095–074–4

3 Kitty Arambulo, *Strengthening the Supervision of the International Covenant on Economic, Social and Cultural Rights. Theoretical and Procedural Aspects*
ISBN 90–5095–058–2

4 Marlies Glasius, *Foreign Policy on Human Rights. Its Influence on Indonesia under Soeharto*
ISBN 90–5095–089–2

5 Cornelis D. de Jong, *The Freedom of Thought, Conscience and Religion or Belief in the United Nations (1946–1992)*
ISBN 90–5095–137–6

6 Heleen Bosma, *Freedom of Expression in England and under the ECHR: in Search of a Common Ground. A Foundation for the Application of the Human Rights Act 1998 in English Law*
ISBN 90–5095–136–8

7 Mielle Bulterman, *Human Rights in the External Relations of the European Union*
ISBN 90–5095–164–3

8 Esther M. van den Berg, *The Influence of Domestic NGOs on Dutch Human Rights Policy. Case Studies on South Africa,Namibia, Indonesia and East Timor*
ISBN 90–5095–159–7

9 Ian Seiderman, *Hierarchy in International Law: the Human Rights Dimension*
ISBN 90–5095–165–1

10 Anna Meijknecht, *Towards International Personality: the Position of Minorities and Indigenous Peoples in International Law*
ISBN 90–5095–166-X

11 Mohamed Eltayeb, *A Human Rights Approach to Combating Religious Persecution. Cases from Pakistan, Saudi Arabia and Sudan*
ISBN 90–5095–170–8

12 Machteld Boot, *Genocide, Crimes Against Humanity, War Crimes: Nullum Crimen Sine Lege and the Subject Matter Jurisdiction of the International Criminal Court*
ISBN 90–5095–216-X

13 Corinne Packer, *Using Human Rights to Change Tradition. Traditional Practices Harmful to Women's Reproductive Health in sub-Saharan Africa*
ISBN 90–5095–226–7

14 Theo R.G. van Banning, *The Human Right to Property*
ISBN 90–5095–203–8

15 Yvonne M. Donders, *Towards a Right to Cultural Identity?*
ISBN 90–5095–238–0

16 Göran K. Sluiter, *International Criminal Adjudication and the Collection of Evidence: Obligations of States*
ISBN 90–5095–227–5

17 Nicola Jägers, *Corporate Human Rights Obligations: in Search of Accountability*
ISBN 90–5095–240–2

18 Magdalena Sepúlveda, *The Nature of the Obligations under the International Covenant on Economic, Social and Cultural Rights*
ISBN 90–5095–260–7

19 Mitsue Inazumi, *Universal Jurisdiction in Modern International Law: Expansion of National Jurisdiction for Prosecuting Serious Crimes under International Law*
ISBN 90–5095–366–2

20 Anne-Marie L.M. de Brouwer, *Supranational Criminal Prosecution of Sexual Violence: The ICC and the Practice of the ICTY and the ICTR*
ISBN 90–5095–533–9

21 Jeroen Gutter, *Thematic Procedures of the United Nations Commission on Human Rights and International Law: in Search of a Sense of Community*
ISBN 90–5095–557–6

22 Hilde Reiding, *The Netherlands and the Development of International Human Rights Instruments*
ISBN 978–90–5095–654–3

23 Ingrid Westendorp, *Women and Housing: Gender Makes a Difference*
ISBN 978–90–5095–669–7

24 Quirine A.M. Eijkman, *We Are Here to Serve You! Public Security, Police Reform and Human Rights Implementation in Costa Rica*
ISBN 978–90–5095–704–5

25 Antoine Ch. Buyse, *Post-conflict Housing Restitution. The European Human Rights Perspective with a case study on Bosnia and Herzegovina*
ISBN 978–90–5095–770–0

26 Gentian Zyberi, *The Humanitarian Face of the International Court of Justice. Its Contribution to Interpreting and Developing International Human Rights and Humanitarian Law Rules and Principles*
ISBN 978–90–5095–792–2

27 Dragoş Cucereanu, *Aspects of Regulating Freedom of Expression on the Internet*
ISBN 978–90–5095–842–4

28 Ton Liefaard, *Deprivation of Liberty of Children in Light of International Human Rights Law and Standards*
ISBN 978–90–5095–838–7

29 Laura van Waas, *Nationality Matters. Statelessness under International Law*
ISBN 978–90–5095–854–7

30 Jeroen Denkers, *The World Trade Organization and Import Bans in Response to Violations of Fundamental Labour Rights*
ISBN 978–90–5095–855–4

31 Irene Hadiprayitno, *Hazard or Right? The Dialectics of Development Practice and the Internationally Declared Right to Development, with Special Reference to Indonesia*
ISBN 978–90–5095–932–2

32 Michał Gondek, *The Reach of Human Rights in a Globalising World: Extraterritorial Application of Human Rights Treaties*
ISBN 978–90–5095–817–2

33 Jeff Handmaker, *Advocating for Accountability: Civic-State Interactions to Protect Refugees in South Africa*
ISBN 978–90–5095–910–0

34 Anna Oehmichen, *Terrorism and Anti-Terror Legislation: The Terrorised Legislator? A Comparison of Counter-Terror Legislation and Its Implications on Human Rights in the Legal Systems of the United Kingdom, Spain, Germany and France*
ISBN 978–90–5095–956–8

35 Simon Walker, *The Future of Human Rights Impact Assessments of Trade Agreements*
ISBN 978–90–5095–986–5

36 Fleur van Leeuwen, *Women's Rights Are Human Rights: The Practice of the United Nations Human Rights Committee and the Committee on Economic, Social and Cultural Rights*
ISBN 978–90–5095–980–3

37 Eva Rieter, *Preventing Irreparable Harm. Provisional Measures in International Human Rights Adjudication*
ISBN 978–90–5095–931–5

38 Desislava Stoitchkova, *Towards Corporate Liability in International Criminal Law*
ISBN 978–94–000–0024–7

39 Paulien Muller, *Scattered Families. Transnational Family Life of Afghan Refugees in the Netherlands in the Light of the Human Rights-Based Protection of the Family*
ISBN 978–94–000–0021–6

40 Bibi van Ginkel, *The Practice of the United Nations in Combating Terrorism from 1946 to 2008. Questions of Legality and Legitimacy*
ISBN 978–94–000–0076–6

41 Christophe Paulussen, *Male captus bene detentus? Surrendering suspects to the International Criminal Court*
ISBN 978–94–000–0100–8

42 Brianne McGonigle Leyh, *Procedural Justice? Victim Participation in International Criminal Proceedings*
ISBN 978-1-78068-020-0

43 Maria Ventegodt Liisberg, *Disability and Employment. A Contemporary Disability Human Rights Approach Applied to Danish, Swedish and EU Law and Policy*
ISBN 978-1-78068-028-6